T0142852

Lecture Notes in Computer Science 13221

More information about this series at https://link.springer.com/bookseries/558

Tiago Martins · Nereida Rodríguez-Fernández ·
Sérgio M. Rebelo (Eds.)

Artificial Intelligence in Music, Sound, Art and Design

11th International Conference, EvoMUSART 2022
Held as Part of EvoStar 2022
Madrid, Spain, April 20–22, 2022
Proceedings

Springer

Editors
Tiago Martins (iD)
University of Coimbra
Coimbra, Portugal

Nereida Rodríguez-Fernández (iD)
University of A Coruña
A Coruña, Spain

Sérgio M. Rebelo (iD)
University of Coimbra
Coimbra, Portugal

ISSN 0302-9743   ISSN 1611-3349 (electronic)
Lecture Notes in Computer Science
ISBN 978-3-031-03788-7   ISBN 978-3-031-03789-4 (eBook)
https://doi.org/10.1007/978-3-031-03789-4

This Springer imprint is published by the registered company Springer Nature Switzerland AG
The registered company address is: Gewerbestrasse 11, 6330 Cham, Switzerland

Preface

EvoMUSART 2022—the 11th International Conference on Artificial Intelligence in Music, Sound, Art and Design—took place from 20 to 22 April 2022, in Madrid, Spain, as part of Evo*, the leading European event on bio-inspired computing.

Following the success of previous events and the importance of the field of artificial intelligence, specifically, evolutionary and biologically inspired (artificial neural network, swarm, alife) music, sound, art, and design, EvoMUSART has become an Evo* conference with independent proceedings since 2012.

Although the use of artificial intelligence for artistic purposes can be traced back to the 1970s, the use of artificial intelligence for the development of artistic systems is a recent, exciting, and significant area of research. There is a growing interest in the application of these techniques in fields such as visual art and music generation, analysis, and interpretation; sound synthesis; architecture; video; poetry; design; and other creative tasks.

The main goal of EvoMUSART 2022 was to bring together researchers who are using artificial intelligence techniques for artistic tasks, providing the opportunity to promote, present, and discuss ongoing work in the area. As always, the atmosphere was fun, friendly, and constructive.

EvoMUSART has grown steadily since its first edition in 2003 in Essex, UK, when it was one of the Applications of Evolutionary Computing workshops. Since 2012, it has been a full conference as part of the Evo* co-located events.

EvoMUSART 2022 received 51 submissions. The peer-review process was rigorous and double-blind. The international Program Committee, listed below, was composed of 56 members from 20 countries. EvoMUSART continued to provide useful feedback to authors: among the papers sent for full review, there were on average three reviews per paper. In total, 24 papers were accepted, comprising 18 long talks (35% acceptance rate) and six posters accompanied by short talks, giving an overall acceptance rate of 47%.

As always, the EvoMUSART proceedings cover a wide range of topics and application areas, including generative approaches to music, visual art, and design. This volume of proceedings collects the accepted papers.

As in previous years, the standard of submissions was high and good quality papers had to be rejected. We thank all authors for submitting their work, including those whose work was not accepted for presentation on this occasion.

The work of reviewing is done voluntarily and generally with little official recognition from the institutions where reviewers are employed. Nevertheless, professional reviewing is essential to a healthy conference. Therefore we particularly thank the members of the Program Committee for their hard work and professionalism in providing constructive and fair reviews.

EvoMUSART 2022 was part of the Evo* 2022 event, which included three additional conferences: EuroGP 2022, EvoCOP 2022, and EvoApplications 2022. Many people helped to make this event a success.

We thank SPECIES, the Society for the Promotion of Evolutionary Computation in Europe and its Surroundings, for handling the coordination and financial administration.

We thank the local organizing team led by Iñaki Hidalgo (Complutense University of Madrid, Spain) and also Complutense University of Madrid, Spain, for their patronage of the event. We would also like to thank Federico Divina (University Pablo de Olavide, Spain) for initially supporting the local organization.

We thank João Correia (University of Coimbra, Portugal) for Evo* publicity, José Francisco Chicano García (University of Málaga, Spain) for the Evo* website, Nuno Lourenço (University of Coimbra, Portugal) for the submission system coordination, and all involved in the organization of Evo* 2022.

We thank the Evo* invited keynote speakers, Gabriela Ochoa (University of Stirling, UK) and Pedro Larrañaga (Technical University of Madrid, Spain), for their inspiring and enlightening keynote talks.

We thank the steering committee of EvoMUSART for the advice, support, and supervision. In particular, we thank Juan Romero (University of A Coruña, Spain), Penousal Machado (University of Coimbra, Portugal), and Colin Johnson (University of Nottingham, UK).

Finally, we would like to express our most heartfelt thanks to Anna Esparcia-Alcázar (SPECIES, Europe), for her dedicated work and coordination of the event. Without her work, and the work of Jennifer Willies in past years, Evo* would not enjoy its current level of success as the leading European event on bio-inspired computation.

April 2022   Tiago Martins
                                                     Nereida Rodríguez-Fernández
                                                                  Sérgio M. Rebelo

Organization

Organizing Committee

Conference Chairs

Tiago Martins   University of Coimbra, Portugal
Nereida Rodríguez-Fernández   University of A Coruña, Spain

Publication Chair

Sérgio M. Rebelo   University of Coimbra, Portugal

Program Committee

Mauro Annunziato	ENEA, Italy
Aurélien Antoine	McGill University, Canada
Peter Bentley	University College London, UK
Gilberto Bernardes	University of Porto, Portugal
Eleonora Bilotta	University of Calabria, Italy
Daniel Bisig	Zurich University of the Arts, Switzerland
Tim Blackwell	Goldsmiths, University of London, UK
Jean-Pierre Briot	LIP6, Sorbonne Université - CNRS, France
Andrew Brown	Queensland Conservatorium, Griffith University, Australia
Marcelo Caetano	McGill University, Canada
Amilcar Cardoso	University of Coimbra, Portugal
Peter Cariani	Boston University, USA
Luz Castro	University of A Coruña, Spain
Bing Yen Chang	Hong Kong University of Science and Technology, Hong Kong
Vic Ciesielski	RMIT University, Australia
João Correia	University of Coimbra, Portugal
Pedro Cruz	Northeastern University, USA
Camilo Cruz Gambardella	Monash University, Australia
João Miguel Cunha	University of Coimbra, Portugal
Palle Dahlstedt	University of Gothenburg, Sweden
Hans Dehlinger	University of Kassel, Germany
Georgios Diapoulis	Chalmers University of Technology, Sweden
Edward Easton	Aston University, UK

Contents

Long Talks

SonOpt: Sonifying Bi-objective Population-Based Optimization
Algorithms 3
  Tasos Asonitis, Richard Allmendinger, Matt Benatan, and Ricardo Climent

A Systematic Evaluation of GPT-2-Based Music Generation 19
  Berker Banar and Simon Colton

Expressive Aliens - Laban Effort Factors for Non-anthropomorphic
Morphologies 36
  Daniel Bisig

Painting with Evolutionary Algorithms 52
  *Danny Dijkzeul, Nielis Brouwer, Iris Pijning, Levi Koppenhol,
  and Daan van den Berg*

Evolutionary Construction of Stories that Combine Several Plot Lines 68
  Pablo Gervás, Eugenio Concepción, and Gonzalo Méndez

Fashion Style Generation: Evolutionary Search with Gaussian Mixture
Models in the Latent Space 84
  Imke Grabe, Jichen Zhu, and Manex Agirrezabal

Classification of Guitar Effects and Extraction of Their Parameter Settings
from Instrument Mixes Using Convolutional Neural Networks 101
  Reemt Hinrichs, Kevin Gerkens, and Jörn Ostermann

Aesthetic Evaluation of Experimental Stimuli Using Spatial Complexity
and Kolmogorov Complexity 117
  Mohammad Ali Javaheri Javid

Towards the Generation of Musical Explanations with GPT-3 131
  Stephen James Krol, Maria Teresa Llano, and Jon McCormack

Lamuse: Leveraging Artificial Intelligence for Sparking Inspiration 148
  Bart Lamiroy and Emmanuelle Potier

EvoDesigner: Towards Aiding Creativity in Graphic Design 162
  Daniel Lopes, João Correia, and Penousal Machado

Conditional Drums Generation Using Compound Word Representations   179
   Dimos Makris, Guo Zixun, Maximos Kaliakatsos-Papakostas,
   and Dorien Herremans

Music Style Transfer Using Constant-Q Transform Spectrograms   195
   Tyler McAllister and Björn Gambäck

SpeechTyper: From Speech to Typographic Composition   212
   Jéssica Parente, Tiago Martins, João Bicker, and Penousal Machado

A Creative Tool for the Musician Combining LSTM and Markov Chains
in Max/MSP   228
   Nicola Privato, Omar Rampado, and Alberto Novello

Translating Emotions from EEG to Visual Arts   243
   Piera Riccio, Francesco Galati, Maria A. Zuluaga,
   Juan Carlos De Martin, and Stefano Nichele

Emotion-Driven Interactive Storytelling: Let Me Tell You How to Feel   259
   Oneris Daniel Rico Garcia, Javier Fernandez Fernandez,
   Rafael Andres Becerra Saldana, and Olaf Witkowski

Modern Evolution Strategies for Creativity: Fitting Concrete Images
and Abstract Concepts   275
   Yingtao Tian and David Ha

Co-creative Product Design with Interactive Evolutionary Algorithms:
A Practice-Based Reflection   292
   Severi Uusitalo, Anna Kantosalo, Antti Salovaara, Tapio Takala,
   and Christian Guckelsberger

Sound Model Factory: An Integrated System Architecture for Generative
Audio Modelling   308
   Lonce Wyse, Purnima Kamath, and Chitralekha Gupta

Short Talks

An Application of Neural Embedding Models for Representing Artistic
Periods   325
   Rao Hamza Ali, Katie Rhodeghiero, Alexa Zuch, Saniya Syed,
   and Erik Linstead

MusIAC: An Extensible Generative Framework for Music Infilling
Applications with Multi-level Control 341
*Rui Guo, Ivor Simpson, Chris Kiefer, Thor Magnusson,
and Dorien Herremans*

A Study on Noise, Complexity, and Audio Aesthetics 357
Stefano Kalonaris

Quality-Diversity for Aesthetic Evolution 369
Jon McCormack and Camilo Cruz Gambardella

Classifying Biometric Data for Musical Interaction Within Virtual Reality 385
Chris Rhodes, Richard Allmendinger, and Ricardo Climent

Generating Novel Furniture with Machine Learning 401
Nelson Vermeer and Andrew R. Brown

Correction to: SpeechTyper: From Speech to Typographic Composition C1
Jéssica Parente, Tiago Martins, João Bicker, and Penousal Machado

Author Index 417

Long Talks

SonOpt: Sonifying Bi-objective Population-Based Optimization Algorithms

Tasos Asonitis[1]([✉]) [iD], Richard Allmendinger[1] [iD], Matt Benatan[2] [iD],
and Ricardo Climent[1] [iD]

[1] University of Manchester, Manchester M15 6PB, UK
`tasos_a@hotmail.com`
[2] Sonos Experience Limited, London SE1 3ER, UK

Abstract. We propose SonOpt, the first (open source) data sonification application for monitoring the progress of bi-objective population-based optimization algorithms during search, to facilitate algorithm understanding. SonOpt provides insights into convergence/stagnation of search, the evolution of the approximation set shape, location of recurring points in the approximation set, and population diversity. The benefits of data sonification have been shown for various non-optimization related monitoring tasks. However, very few attempts have been made in the context of optimization and their focus has been exclusively on single-objective problems. In comparison, SonOpt is designed for bi-objective optimization problems, relies on objective function values of non-dominated solutions only, and is designed with the user (listener) in mind; avoiding convolution of multiple sounds and prioritising ease of familiarizing with the system. This is achieved using two sonification paths relying on the concepts of wavetable and additive synthesis.

This paper motivates and describes the architecture of SonOpt, and then validates SonOpt for two popular multi-objective optimization algorithms (NSGA-II and MOEA/D). Experience SonOpt yourself via https://github.com/tasos-a/SonOpt-1.0.

Keywords: Sonification · Optimization · Algorithmic behaviour · Metaheuristics · Evolutionary computation · Process monitoring · SonOpt

1 Introduction

Sonification deals with the representation and communication of data through sound and has been an established practice for more than three decades. Blurring the lines between art and science, sonification has long been an area of interest for both musicians and scientists. The former see in it the opportunity to explore the

This work was supported by the Engineering and Physical Sciences Research Council [grant number 2492452].

T. Martins et al. (Eds.): EvoMUSART 2022, LNCS 13221, pp. 3–18, 2022.
https://doi.org/10.1007/978-3-031-03789-4_1

aesthetic content of phenomena that surround us, while the latter tend to see it as a tool that can represent data efficiently and reveal hidden patterns in an intuitive way [9]. Field experts tend to use sonification in tandem with visualization techniques [24], in order to maximize the benefits of both approaches. However, sonification has proven useful as a standalone tool as well, particularly when the temporal evolution of data is an important factor of the process in question [5].

This highlights the type of operations in which sonification really shines. For spatial representations, visualization methods generally tend to provide a concise picture. As discussed in [28], it is not uncommon that these methods might be proven less effective when it comes to time-series data representation. The evolution of an optimization algorithm is a process over time, and, if characterized in terms of metrics, can be thought of as a multivariate time-series. Gaining a better understanding about the behaviour of an optimization algorithm during evolution is important to study strengths and weaknesses of algorithms, and ultimately develop more efficient algorithms. While this is true for any type of algorithm, the focus of our work is on population-based multi-objective optimization algorithms (MOAs) due to the common scenario of having multiple conflicting objectives in practice [21]. The community has looked to theory (e.g. runtime analysis [18]) and visualisation-based concepts (e.g. [32]), including the design of visualisable test problems [8], to improve algorithm understanding, but there is very little work that explores the application of sonification for this task. The goal of our work is to fill this gap, and this paper is the first attempt to sonify MOAs.

As algorithm designers and/or practitioners, we tend to evaluate the performance of optimization algorithms over the course of a few runs. As explained in [10], sonification allows us to zoom in on an individual run of the optimization algorithm, and reveal particular characteristics that can help us validate the algorithmic performance.

Only a few approaches have been made for monitoring of optimization algorithms using sound. These will be presented briefly in the following section. Despite the existence of different methodologies, none of the currently documented implementations has focused on the evolving shape of the approximation set (objective function values of non-dominated solutions[1]) and the recurrence of points in the objective space. SonOpt receives as input the approximation set and maps the shape of this set to the shape of a single-cycle waveform inside a buffer. This buffer is used as a look-up table for a ramp oscillator that scans the content of the buffer repeatedly, at the rate of a user-controlled frequency. In addition, SonOpt monitors the recurrence of objective values across consecutive generations and maps the amount of recurrence of each value to the level of a different harmonic partial of a user-defined fundamental frequency. A more detailed description of the system follows on Sect. 3.

The motivation behind SonOpt is to engage with the discussion on the benefits of auditory display in optimization monitoring, encourage the thinking of

---

[1] A non-dominated solution is one which provides a suitable compromise between all objectives without degrading any of them. For a more formal definition of multi-objective concepts please refer to e.g. [21].

algorithmic behaviour in sonic terms, and offer a tool that can compliment current visualization techniques towards an intuitive multi-modal understanding of complex processes. Although not explored in this paper, an additional aspiration behind SonOpt is to explore optimization processes from an aesthetic point of view and suggest the treatment of such processes as music composition tools. The structure of this paper is divided into four sections. First we put our work in context with related literature focusing on areas such as sonification of optimization algorithms and benefits of sonification in process monitoring. Next we present the platform of SonOpt by describing the pipeline and discussing the reasons behind specific design choices. The documentation of test results is included in Sect. 4. Finally, Sect. 5 presents some concluding remarks and future plans.

2 Related Work

The first documented approach that employed sound to provide insights in evolutionary optimization was proposed by Grond et al. [10] in 2011. The presented work involves the use of stacked band-pass filters to transform the sounds of keys on a computer keyboard. Grond et al. highlight the crucial role of auditory display in monitoring operations and explain how these advantages pertain to optimization processes. Their system focuses on evolutionary strategies (ES) as presented in [26]. However, the developed methodology cannot be applied to optimization tasks with more than one objective.

Tavares and Godoy [31] have used sound to represent population dynamics in a Particle Swarm Optimization (PSO) algorithm [15]. Although PSO has been extensively employed as a music composition tool (for example [3]) through the sonification of particle trajectories, Tavares and Godoy follow a different approach by sonifying specific performance metrics. Their focus is on providing information about the population behaviour—including speed, alignment and diversity of particles within a population (or swarm)—with particular attention to creating an aesthetically pleasing output. The sonic mappings implemented include musical notes, echo and harmonics and aim to result in evolving soundscapes. As in [10], the focus is on single-objective optimization.

Lutton et al. [19] apply sonification in island-based parallel setups where the optimization task has been distributed across systems to facilitate computational efficiency. Each computational node is assigned a part of a musical score, or a familiar song in audio format. The degree to which the music is reproduced faithfully—including performance errors or glitches, depending on whether the user has opted for a musical score or audio file—provides information about the optimization progress of individual nodes. The implemented system is targeted exclusively at parallel setups. A potential question relates to whether the correct interpretation of the introduced errors requires prior musical training, and if that could hinder the effectiveness of the designed sonification, as indicated in [22].

Albeit not specifically related to optimization, a detailed account of sonification including theory, technology, applications and benefits, has been made by Hermann at al. [11]. Vickers [33] focuses on the benefits of sonification for peripheral process monitoring, and includes a list of systems that employed sound to monitor the running process of various programs, mainly through the triggering of sounds based on specific events. The applications mentioned in [33] do not target optimization processes. They are primarily focused on debugging run-time behaviour and most of them relate to dated programming methods. However, the variety in approaches shows that using sound to monitor algorithmic processes has been drawing attention for a long time. According to Vickers, peripheral process monitoring is when useful information about a process is being aurally displayed on the background, while a different, primary task, usually visual, is at the center of focus. SonOpt is designed precisely with this in mind. By using two separate audio streams, one that acts as a continuous sound stream and one that is triggered by events, SonOpt allows the user to focus on a different task while indirectly monitoring the progress of the optimization algorithm. As SonOpt does not aspire to replace visualization methods, but to work in tandem with them, users are encouraged to engage in multi-modal monitoring by combining visualization of various optimization aspects, with the sonification provided by SonOpt. Hildebrandt et al. [12] carried out an experiment in which participants performed significantly better at a peripheral process monitoring task when continuous sonification and visual cues of the process in question were used in parallel. In particular, as shown in [24], field experts demonstrate preference towards the combination of continuous sonification and visual displays when it comes to process monitoring, instead of visual or audio only conditions. The experimental work of Axon et al. [2] also points towards benefits of adding sonification to visual representations, specifically targeted in security related process monitoring. In [13] additional evidence on performance improvement in process monitoring (of physical production systems) via sonification is provided.

The term *sonification* is used throughout this text because it is a recognized and all-encompassing term that relates to auditory display. However the methodology used in SonOpt further pertains to a subbranch of sonification, referred to in the dedicated literature as *audification*. Kramer [16] writes that audification is "the process of directly playing back the data samples". As elaborated by Dombois and Eckel [7], audification can provide a successful choice of auditory display when datasets feature specific properties. The requirements include: the size of the dataset, whether the array of data samples creates a wave-like signal, the complexity of the signal, and the potential existence of subtle changes. The approximation set obtained by a MOA, which functions as the input to SonOpt, fulfills these properties. As will be evidenced in the next section, audification is applied on the first of the two sound generation paths of SonOpt.

To put this work into context with the wider literature, it is worthwhile mentioning a few more related research streams. In particular, the premises and aims in the work of Ochoa, et al. [23] on Search Trajectory Networks (STNs), albeit focused on the visual domain through the use of graphs, share a common ground with the motivation behind SonOpt. Both projects aim to assist with the understanding of algorithmic behaviour. The results of STNs are particularly interesting from an aesthetic point of view, showing that care has been taken on that aspect as well as improving understanding of search behaviour.

Schuller et al. [29] argue that sonification is a promising and user-friendly alternative to visualization, towards explainable Artificial Intelligence (XAI). Lyu et al. [20] apply an interactive virtual environment that allows real time tweaking of a neural network's hyperparameters by providing users with auditory feedback on the impact of their choices. Finally, [1] highlights the shortcomings of visual representations for non-trained and visually impaired individuals, and suggest sonification as one of the prevalent alternatives.

3   Methodology and System Overview

SonOpt is an application developed using the visual programming environment Max/MSP [25]. Max/MSP has been the choice of musicians, sonic artists and engineers, for developing audio-related programs which benefit from a certain degree of customization. We chose Max/MSP for the immediacy of design, and its popularity among sonification researchers. This section will describe the system and discuss some of the design decisions made during its development.

SonOpt can work with any population-based search algorithm. This is possible as it only needs to receive the objective function values of non-dominated solutions at each generation of the algorithm (e.g. in the case of steady state algorithms); for ease of presentation, we will use the term *generation* knowing that the concepts can also be applied to non-generational (e.g. steady state) algorithms. Each generation produces a collection of objective values that are passed to SonOpt through the use of the Open Sound Control protocol (OSC) [34]. This is to ensure quick and precise communication between the algorithm and Max/MSP. The algorithms and the optimization problems presented in this paper come from pymoo [4], a Python library tailored to MOAs. Pymoo was chosen as it allows for simple swapping between optimization algorithms and problems, facilitating direct comparisons of a variety of setups. Another key motivating factor is pymoo's popularity within the optimization community: having a familiar tool at the center of the work will make it easier for optimization researchers to engage with SonOpt. Of course, users can replace pymoo with their own code, for example, of customized algorithms.

At the moment, SonOpt is set up to work for bi-objective optimization problems only; WOLOG it is assumed that both objectives are to be minimized. Since SonOpt's sonification relies on the objective function values only (at least for now), a 2-dimensional matrix is expected to be passed on from pymoo to Max at each generation to represent the approximation set at that generation. Once received, Max scales the objective values to be within [0, 1], and then sorts the matrix, from the minimum all the way to the maximum value of objective one—hence from the max to the min value of objective two. This produces an ordered sequence of points comprising the 2D approximation set. Subsequently, the set is forwarded to two separate sonification paths (Fig. 1).

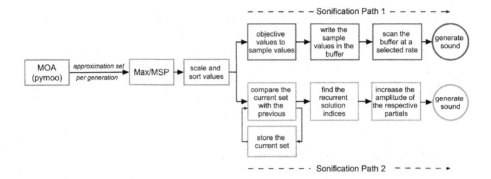

Fig. 1. The pipeline of SonOpt.

Sonification Path 1. The first path is calculating a straight line from the point that minimizes objective one to the point that minimizes objective two (red dashed line in the left plot of Fig. 2). It then calculates the distance of each point of the set from this line. The distances are then scaled and mapped to the sample values of a buffer. The buffer needs to be at least $2N$ samples big, where N is the number of maximum points in the approximation set obtained per generation. The content of the buffer then looks like a horizontal display of the approximation set (right plot of Fig. 2). In order to generate a bipolar audio signal, the incoming values are converted to negatives and are added to the buffer content. This buffer is used as a look-up table of a wavetable oscillator [14] that scans the buffer content at the rate of a user-selected frequency. This way the shape of the approximation set is treated like a single-cycle waveform, which gets repeated periodically. The resulting sound is a direct translation of the shape of the front, and it evolves according to the update of the shape at each generation. It is worth noting here that although the buffer size is fixed, the size of the readable buffer content is not; it depends on the number of objective values the algorithm is generating during the current generation. So even if the buffer looks like it has leftover content from previous generations where the number of values was bigger than the current one, the wavetable oscillator only reads the part of the buffer that includes the content generated during the current generation. If, for example, in generation 46 the algorithm generates 90 values, the buffer content will be 180 samples long (90 points in the set converted to sample values plus the negative duplicates of these values). Now, if in generation 47 the algorithm generates 70 values, this means that the buffer content will still be 180 samples long, however only the first 140 of them will contribute to the sonic output, since 40 samples of the buffer content were left over from the previous generation.

This approach offers a sonic portrayal of the approximation set. Characteristics like discontinuity of the front, lack of diversity and unsuccessful convergence translate to harsher, more harmonically rich sounds, while convex, concave and generally continuous fronts result in more well-rounded, "bassy" tones that

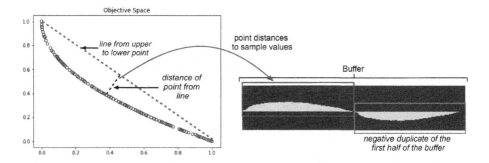

Fig. 2. Sonification path 1: mapping of the (scaled) approximation set shape to sample values. Algorithm: NSGA-II. Optimization task: ZDT1.

approach the sonic characteristics of a sine wave. The loudness of the sound depends on the curvature of the front: the curvier the front, the louder the sound and vice versa. Detailed examples follow on the next section.

Sonification Path 2. The second path examines the recurrence of objective function values across successive generations. This is done by comparing the values within the received approximation set of the current generation with those within the set of the previous generation. If any recurrence is spotted, SonOpt finds the index position of the recurrent value within the set of the current generation (as aforementioned, the operations are taking place on sorted approximation sets, see Fig. 1). The recurrent indices are then mapped to the partials of a user-defined fundamental frequency. The max number of available partials is equal to the max number of objective function values on a single generation. Depending on the position indices of the recurrent solutions across the set, the amplitude of the corresponding partials is increased. A recurrence on the first point of the approximation set (this would translate on the point located on the upper left corner of the front) would result in a raise in the amplitude of the first partial and so on. When there is no recurrence, this path does not generate sound.

Consequently, the timbre of the resulting sound depends on the location of the recurrent values across the approximation set. When recurrence is taking place across the entire set, the outcome is rich spectrum, with many harmonic partials contributing to the sonic result, akin to the principles of additive synthesis [27]. When recurrence is happening on a single value, or is concentrated on a particular area of the set, this results in more focused spectrum, involving low, mid or high range frequency components, depending on whether the recurrent area of the front is on the high left corner, middle, or low right corner respectively. The sonic outcome thus provides information not just on when recurrence is happening, but also on which part of the approximation set it is taking place. When dealing with high number of objective function values, sound can provide such information in a quicker and more intuitive way than visual representations (Fig. 3).

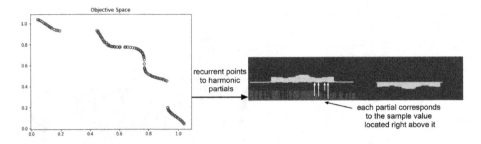

Fig. 3. Sonification path 2: mapping of the recurrent solutions to harmonic partials. Algorithm: NSGA-II. Optimization task: Tanaka [30]. The amplitude of each partial, shown by the height of the corresponding red bar, shows the recurrence amount of that objective value: higher amplitude means more successive generations in which the value showed up in the approximation set.

The two sonification paths usually produce opposite results as the optimization progresses. Sonification path 1 tends to produce harsher sounds with quick-shifting timbre in the beginning of the run and then gradually settle on smoother tones with less harmonics, depending, of course, on the shape of the approximation set. Sonification path 2 usually starts with simple tones and tends to generate more complex sounds after sonification path 1 has reached a static timbre, i.e. the algorithm has approximated the objective space shape to some extent. This means that generally, sound intensity progressively decays in path 1, while it progressively intensifies in path 2. SonOpt was designed this way in order to prevent overlapping conveying of information that can eventually become overwhelming. Furthermore, an option is given to the users to change the volume of each path individually. SonOpt is geared towards sound synthesis, as it generates sound according to the input data. An additional reason behind this aesthetic choice is that we wanted to minimize the need for a musical background by the user. By using raw sound, one can make observations on the evolution of data intuitively, by focusing on accessible sonic qualities like loudness, harshness, low versus high frequencies etc. without needing musical training.

4   Experimental Study

In this section we demonstrate the application of SonOpt in multi-objective optimization. A manual on how to use SonOpt and to familiarize the user with the range of sounds and their interpretation (i.e. optimization scenarios portrayed) will be released in due course.

4.1   Experimental Setup

MOA Settings. For the presented tests, two well-known population-based MOAs were chosen: NSGA-II (Non-dominated Sorting Genetic Algorithm) [6] and MOEA/D (Multi-Objective Evolutionary Algorithm based on Decomposition) [35]. The reason for selecting these two algorithms is their popularity, differences in working principles—Pareto-dominance vs decomposition-based —, and their availability in pymoo.[2] As stated before, the choice of algorithm can include any population-based MOA. It is important to note that our goal here is not to discuss why one algorithm performs better than another and/or determine the best algorithm for a given problem; instead we want to demonstrate the responsiveness of SonOpt to different algorithmic behaviours and discuss insights SonOpt can provide. Consequently, we use default operators and parameter settings for our two MOAs as used in pymoo; the only parameters that need setting was the population size of NSGA-II and the number of reference vectors in MOEA/D; both parameters were set to 100 for ease of demonstration of SonOpt's capabilities. The algorithms were run on several bi-objective test problems available in pymoo. Here we show and discuss results obtained for ZDT1, ZDT4 [36], and Kursawe [17] as they demonstrate SonOpt functionalities well. Importantly, video recordings of SonOpt in action can be watched at https://tinyurl.com/sonopt including also for additional problems.

Sonification Settings. Table 1 shows the parameters used by SonOpt for the experimental study. The setting of these parameters was determined in preliminary experimentation and driven by clarity of the sonic outputs. *Sample value scaling* only affects sonification path 1 and determines how the input values are scaled in order to be converted to audible audio sample values. This greatly depends on the overall values of the approximation set. If the set includes values very close to 0, then the sample value scaling needs to be higher and vice versa. The parameter can be updated dynamically, so the user can increase or reduce the amplitude of the resulting waveform during the run, as desired. The sample value scaling has been kept steady for the examples presented in the images below. However, in the video demonstrations, the scaling value is updated when the sample values are very small, in order to make the sound characteristics of the approximation sets audible. This is happening in cases where the curvature of the set is very small. The value change has been documented. *Buffer size* sets the size of the buffer in samples. For both sonification paths this needs to be at least $2N$ samples, where N is the number of maximum points in the approximation set obtained per generation. *Number of sliders* applies only to the second path. It refers to the number of harmonic partials that the generated sound can have. It needs to be set to, at least, N. *Oscillator frequency* sets the frequency of the scanning oscillator in path 1 and the fundamental frequency of the harmonic oscillator in path 2. *Overall amplitude* refers to the sound volume of path 1 and 2. We suggest starting with a low value and gradually increasing it, since sound bursts can be expected particularly in path 2. Finally, *number of instances* controls the way Max/MSP deals with polyphony. This also needs to be set at least to N.

---

[2] Pymoo does not feature an indicator-based MOA, which we would have like to experiment with too.

Table 1. SonOpt parameters as used in the experimental study.

SonOpt parameters	Sonification path 1	Sonification path 2
Sample value scaling	500	n/a
Buffer size	202	256
Numbers of sliders	n/a	100
Oscillator frequency	80 Hz	80 Hz
Overall amplitude	0.3	0.075
Number of instances	100	100

Media to Gain Insights into Algorithmic Behaviours. To facilitate algorithmic understanding, SonOpt outputs sound, as an algorithm traverses through the search space (see Sect. 3). We convey this to the readers via screenshots of accompanying visuals and recorded videos of SonOpt in action. It is important to mention that in the provided experiments the algorithms ran twice, once to generate the images and once to generate the video documentation, therefore variations in the optimization progress between the two might occur occasionally. Needless to say, the best way of experiencing SonOpt is by actually using it!

4.2 Experimental Analysis

SonOpt on a Convex Bi-objective Problem. Figures 4 and 5 show the two MOAs applied to ZDT1. This is a good example of how sonification path 1 can provide insights into a run of different algorithms. In the case of MOEA/D, sonification path 1 generates a sound with noticeable harmonic content for approximately half the duration of the run. This means it did not manage to converge as quickly and effectively compared to NSGA-II, which produced a simpler, more "punchy" sound, approaching that of a sinetone. This is supported by looking at the obtained fronts. Both algorithms reach the convex shape, but MOEA/D presents sporadic "bumps" and a single solution that seems to be slightly distant from the rest of the set. This affects the resulted waveform of sonification path 1, creating a buzzier tone in comparison with NSGA-II. ZDT1 produces excessive objective value recurrence in both algorithms. Indeed, path 2 generates a waveform with gradually increasing harmonic content, as can be witnessed in Fig. 4 (d). In the case of NSGA-II, this reflects the increasing number of non-dominated solutions obtained from generation 1 through, approximately, generation 75.

SonOpt on a Discontinuous Bi-objective Problem. In Figs. 6 and 7 we can see how SonOpt responds to NSGA-II and MOEA/D when applied to Kursawe. In this case, sonification path 1 not only provides information regarding the optimization progress, but also picks up the different behaviour of the two algorithms. For NSGA-II, path 1 generates a "buzzy" waveform with a quickly

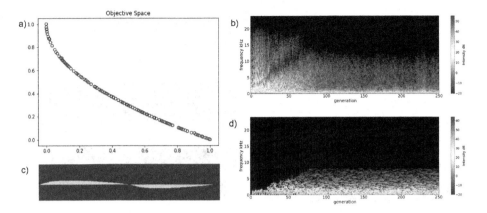

Fig. 4. Algorithm: NSGA-II. Optimization task: ZDT1. (a): approximation set obtained after 250 generations. (b): sonogram of sonification path 1 across 250 generations. (c): buffer contains on the 250th generation. (d): sonogram of sonification path 2 across 250 generations.

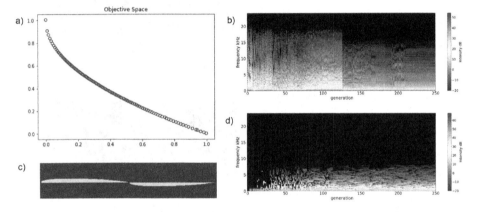

Fig. 5. Algorithm: MOEA/D. Optimization task: ZDT1. (a), (b), (c) and (d) as above

reduced harmonic content during the first 15 to 20 generations. For MOEA/D, however, path 1 produces a more "jagged" sound, with discrete, abrupt changes in the harmonic content. This reveals that the approximation set evolved in a similar, almost step-like manner until it reached the Pareto front shape. This type of behaviour is expected since NSGA-II is based on non-dominated value sorting while MOEA/D is based on decomposition. Path 2 provides additional insight. For both algorithms, path 2 produces a granular sound during the first 20 to 30 generations. This sound gets progressively substituted by a more continuous waveform, where individual tones are less discernible (see, for example, Fig. 7 (d) where the fractured harmonics in the beginning turn gradually into longer streams). This is attributed to the optimization progress. As the

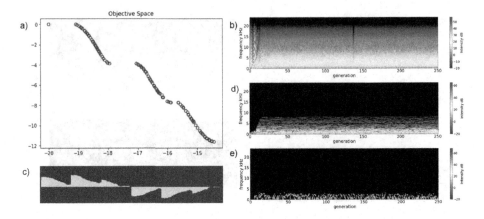

Fig. 6. Algorithm: NSGA-II. Optimization task: Kursawe. (a), (b), (c), (d) as above. (e): sonogram of sonification path 2, with the objective value recurrence filtered to 10%.

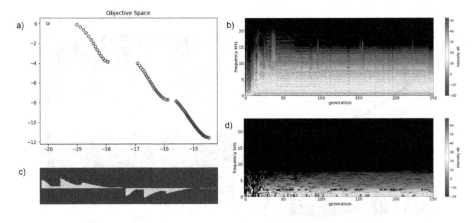

Fig. 7. Algorithm: MOEA/D. Optimization task: Kursawe.

approximation set improves, the objective values repeat successively for more generations, a possible sign that the algorithm has converged, or got stuck at a local optimum. In Fig. 6 (e) we added a sonogram of path 2 after applying a filter to the recurrent values of each generation that leaves only a 10% of these values come through to path 2. This is provided as a demonstration of how path 2 sounds like when the objective value recurrence is less than in the problems/algorithms we examine here. For example, this could apply to algorithms that use customized diversity-maintenance mechanisms.

SonOpt on a Convex Multimodal Bi-objective Problem. An effective example of paths 1 and 2 can be observed when applying NSGA-II to ZDT4 (Fig. 8). The algorithm manages to approach the Pareto front shape halfway

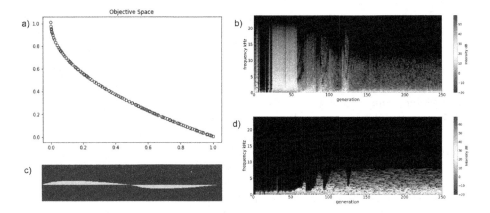

Fig. 8. Algorithm: NSGA-II. Optimization task: ZDT4.

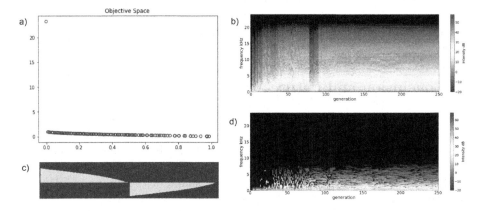

Fig. 9. Algorithm: MOEA/D. Optimization task: ZDT4.

through the optimization. Until that point the shape of the approximation set is coming together and falling apart, as can be witnessed in the video. The sound of path 1 transitions through waveforms with strong harmonic content and high amplitude (sound "bursts"), since the produced curvatures are steep. As NSGA-II manages to approximate the front, the harmonics and overall loudness are reduced, and the simpler sonic character of a sinetone emerges. Path 2 transitions from mid-range tones to tones with broader harmonic content, as can also be witnessed from the slopes in Fig. 8 (d). This is due to ZDT4 presenting many local optima, posing difficulties during the optimization. SonOpt is able to pick up this information and convey it through sound. The displayed run of MOEA/D on ZDT4 produced an outlier on the upper part of the front (Fig. 9 (a)). SonOpt is very sensitive to this type of behaviour. This can be noticed by comparing the obtained sound of MOEA/D and NSGA-II after 250 generations. The outlier in MOEA/D affects significantly the shape of the waveform, producing a sound close to a "sawtooth" wave.

Final Remarks. The presented examples confirm that SonOpt can provide information on the shape of the approximation set even when visualisation is not available. This property is of use in practice, for example, for SonOpt users with impaired sight or when auditioning the optimization progress while working on a different task (multi-tasking). A quick-shifting timbre in sonification path 1 implies that the algorithm mostly performs exploration, while a more static timbre means the algorithm performs exploitation. Once the timbre has stabilized, the sonic qualities of path 1 can provide information on the shape of the front: harsh, buzzy sounds suggest a discontinuous approximation set (and thus potentially Pareto front), and softer, bassy tones allude to a convex or concave Pareto front, with loudness encapsulating the level of curvature. The characteristics of path 2 inform on possible stagnation or successful convergence. It has been stated before that the two paths work complimentary to each other and more solid conclusion can be drawn when the output of both is taken into consideration.

5   Conclusion and Future Work

This paper has proposed SonOpt, an (open-source) application to sonify the search process of population-based optimization algorithms for bi-objective problems. SonOpt is implemented in Max/MSP and draws live information about the search process of an algorithm (encoded in pymoo in this study) to create two parallel sound streams indicating the evolving shape of the approximation set and the recurrence of points in the objective space. Using two popular multi-objective algorithms (NSGA-II and MOEA/D) and a range of bi-objective test problems, we demonstrated that SonOpt can pick up several aspects in terms of search behaviour including convergence/stagnation, shape of the approximation set, location of recurring points in the approximation set, and population diversity. Hence, SonOpt can facilitate algorithm understanding.

It is important to note that SonOpt is a first attempt to sonify multi-objective search so there is plenty of scope to improve the system. For instance, future work will look at extending SonOpt to problems with more than two objectives. In particular, the community could do with a better understanding of algorithms when applied to many-objective optimization problems. Further avenues of future work include a Python-based version of SonOpt (as opposed to using Max/MSP) to improve usability and increase uptake; incorporation of different/additional sonification paths (e.g. hypervolume contributions of solutions); sonifying behavioural differences across multiple algorithms simultaneously; and enhancing the perceptibility of SonOpt's output to make SonOpt even more accessible.

Although not elaborated within this paper, the creation of SonOpt was also motivated by artistic intentions. Optimization and, generally, algorithmic processes that evolve temporally, lend themselves fittingly in music compositions. They can shape sonic narratives and musical structures in various levels, and so motivate artists to examine optimization processes from an aesthetic perspective. We believe SonOpt points towards this direction. Future work therefore includes extending the sonic palette of SonOpt and assessing its creative performance through artistic engagement with the tool.

References

1. Ali, S., Muralidharan, L., Alfieri, F., Agrawal, M., Jorgensen, J.: Sonify: making visual graphs accessible. In: Ahram, T., Taiar, R., Colson, S., Choplin, A. (eds.) IHIET 2019. AISC, vol. 1018, pp. 454–459. Springer, Cham (2020). https://doi.org/10.1007/978-3-030-25629-6_70
2. Axon, L., AlAhmadi, B., Nurse, J., Goldsmith, M., Creese, S.: Data presentation in security operations centres: exploring the potential for sonification to enhance existing practice. J. Cybersecur. **6**, 1–16 (2020)
3. Blackwell, T., Young, M.: Self-organised music. Organised Sound **9**(2), 123–136 (2004)
4. Blank, J., Deb, K.: pymoo: multi-objective optimization in Python. IEEE Access **8**, 89497–89509 (2020)
5. De Campo, A.: Toward a data sonification design space map. In: 13th International Conference in Auditory Display, pp. 342–347 (2007)
6. Deb, K., Pratap, A., Agarwal, S., Meyarivan, T.: A fast and elitist multiobjective genetic algorithm: NSGA-II. IEEE Trans. Evol. Comput. **6**(2), 182–197 (2002)
7. Dombois, F., Eckel, G.: Audification. In: Hermann, T., Hunt, A., Neuhoff, J.G. (eds.) The Sonification Handbook, pp. 301–324. Logos Publishing House, Berlin (2011)
8. Fieldsend, J., Chugh, T., Allmendinger, R., Miettinen, K.: A visualizable test problem generator for many-objective optimization. IEEE Trans. Evol. Comput. **26**(1), 1–11 (2022)
9. Gresham-Lancaster, S.: Relationships of sonification to music and sound art. AI Soc. **27**(2), 207–212 (2012)
10. Grond, F., Kramer, O., Hermann, T.: Interactive sonification monitoring in evolutionary optimization. In: 17th International Conference on Auditory Display, pp. 166 (2011)
11. Hermann, T., Hunt, A., Neuhoff, J.: The Sonification Handbook. Logos Verlag, Berlin (2011)
12. Hildebrandt, T., Hermann, T., Rinderle-Ma, S.: Continuous sonification enhances adequacy of interactions in peripheral process monitoring. Int. J. Hum. Comput. Stud. **95**, 54–65 (2016)
13. Iber, M., Lechner, P., Jandl, C., Mader, M., Reichmann, M.: Auditory augmented process monitoring for cyber physical production systems. Pers. Ubiquitous Comput. **25**(4), 691–704 (2021)
14. Johnson, R.: Wavetable synthesis 101, a fundamental perspective. In: Audio Engineering Society Convention, pp. 1–27 (1996)
15. Kennedy, J., Eberhart, R.: Particle swarm optimization. In: Proceedings of International Conference on Neural Networks, vol. 4, pp. 1942–1948 (1995)
16. Kramer, G.: Auditory Display: Sonification, Audification and Auditory Interfaces. Addison-Wesley Longman Publishing Co., Inc., Boston (2000)
17. Kursawe, F.: A variant of evolution strategies for vector optimization. In: Schwefel, H.-P., Männer, R. (eds.) PPSN 1990. LNCS, vol. 496, pp. 193–197. Springer, Heidelberg (1991). https://doi.org/10.1007/BFb0029752

18. Laumanns, M., Thiele, L., Zitzler, E.: Running time analysis of multiobjective evolutionary algorithms on pseudo-Boolean functions. IEEE Trans. Evol. Comput. **8**(2), 170–182 (2004)
19. Lutton, E., et al.: Visual and audio monitoring of island based parallel evolutionary algorithms. J. Grid Comput. **13**(3), 309–327 (2014). https://doi.org/10.1007/s10723-014-9321-8
20. Lyu, Z., Li, J., Wang, B.: Alive: interactive visualization and sonification of neural network in virtual reality. arXiv preprint arXiv:2109.15193 (2021)
21. Miettinen, K.: Nonlinear Multiobjective Optimization. Springer, Cham (2012). https://doi.org/10.1007/978-1-4615-5563-6
22. Neuhoff, J.: Is sonification doomed to fail? In: Proceedings of the 25th International Conference on Auditory Display, pp. 327–330 (2019)
23. Ochoa, G., Malan, K., Blum, C.: Search trajectory networks: a tool for analysing and visualising the behaviour of metaheuristics. Appl. Soft Comput. **109**, 107492 (2021)
24. Poguntke, M., Ellis, K.: Auditory attention control for human-computer interaction. In: Conference on Human System Interactions, pp. 231–236 (2008)
25. Puckette, M.: The patcher. In: Proceedings of the 1986 International Computer Music Conference, pp. 420–429 (1988)
26. Rechenberg, I.: Evolutionsstrategien. In: Simulationsmethoden in Der Medizin Und Biologie, pp. 83–114 (1978)
27. Sasaki, L., Smith, K.: A simple data reduction scheme for additive synthesis. Comput. Music. J. **4**, 22–24 (1980)
28. Sawe, N., Chafe, C., Treviño, J.: Using data sonification to overcome science literacy, numeracy, and visualization barriers in science communication. Front. Commun. **5**, 46 (2020)
29. Schuller, B., et al.: Towards sonification in multimodal and user-friendly explainable artificial intelligence. In: Proceedings of the 2021 International Conference on Multimodal Interaction, pp. 788–792 (2021)
30. Tanaka, M., Watanabe, H., Furukawa, Y., Tanino, T.: GA-based decision support system for multicriteria optimization. In: 1995 IEEE International Conference on Systems, Man and Cybernetics. Intelligent Systems for the 21st Century, vol. 2, pp. 1556–1561 (1995)
31. Tavares, T., Godoy, A.: Sonification of population behaviour in particle swarm optimization. In: Proceedings of Annual Conference Companion on Genetic and Evolutionary Computation, pp. 51–52 (2013)
32. Tušar, T., Filipič, B.: Visualization of Pareto front approximations in evolutionary multiobjective optimization: a critical review and the prosection method. IEEE Trans. Evol. Comput. **19**(2), 225–245 (2015)
33. Vickers, P.: Sonification for process monitoring. In: Hermann, T., Hunt, A., Neuhoff, J.G. (eds.) The Sonification Handbook, pp. 455–492. Logos Publishing House, Berlin (2011)
34. Wright, M., Freed, A.: Open sound control: a new protocol for communicating with sound synthesizers. In: International Computer Music Conference, pp. 101–104 (1997)
35. Zhang, Q., Li, H.: MOEA/D: a multiobjective evolutionary algorithm based on decomposition. IEEE Trans. Evol. Comput. **11**(6), 712–731 (2007)
36. Zitzler, E., Deb, K., Thiele, L.: Comparison of multiobjective evolutionary algorithms: empirical results. Evol. Comput. **8**(2), 173–195 (2000)

A Systematic Evaluation of GPT-2-Based Music Generation

Berker Banar[(✉)] and Simon Colton

School of EECS, Queen Mary University of London, London E1 4NS, UK
{b.banar,s.colton}@qmul.ac.uk

Abstract. There have been various generative music applications recently which employ a pre-trained transformer neural model. The way in which these models are trained greatly effects the nature of the music they produce, but there has been little exploration of the extent of this phenomenon. We provide here a systematic evaluation of the output from GPT-2-based transformer models by analysing, comparing and contrasting the output from multiple models trained under various conditions, with reference to numerous musical metrics. As a further element of our methodology, we describe a web application for exploring the output of such models. We conclude with a summary of our findings on how training effects output, a discussion around how our methodology could be used in generative music practice, and future avenues for research.

Keywords: Generative music · Deep learning · Transformers · Music generation evaluation · Transfer learning

1 Introduction

Transformers are attention-based neural models originally designed for natural language processing (NLP) tasks such as machine translation and text generation [20]. However, transformers have also been widely used for symbolic music generation due to their proven success in generating good quality music with long term coherence, as described in [11]. Various different transformer architectures have been utilised in music generation contexts, with some pre-trained on language data and then fine-tuned with music data, while others were trained from scratch with music data. For instance, the GPT-2 NLP model was fine-tuned with music for *MuseNet* [14], while *Music Transformer* [9] and *Pop Music Transformer* were trained from scratch with music data.

Evaluation of such neural models is important both to provide insight to practitioners using them in generative music applications, and in improving the model architecture and training procedure, which in turn provides guidance for the training of future models with possibly different architectures. Moreover, if

B. Banar—Research student at the UKRI Centre for Doctoral Training in Artificial Intelligence and Music, supported jointly by UK Research and Innovation [grant number EP/S022694/1] and Queen Mary University of London.

a generative music model is pre-trained with data from a different modality e.g., natural language, the loss function used in training does not necessarily capture notions of value in the target domain. Hence, evaluation in such cross-domain settings is crucial to identify limitations and inconsistencies between the two domains when transfer learning is applied [22].

In the study presented here, we systematically alter some typical training parameters which effect the eventual generative behaviour of a GPT-2-based model, namely the training corpus and target loss level. We then assess the music output by each model in terms of some musical metrics and statistical calculations. This enables us to compare and contrast the models and suggest how they might be used in generative music practice. As background to the study, in Sect. 2, we describe GPT-2 models, the GiantMIDI-Piano dataset that we train them over, and the way in which we transcribe MIDI to suitable input for GPT-2. We also describe statistical evaluation processes for generative music that we build upon. In Sect. 3, we present the metrics we use to compare and contrast the music output by the models we train. In Sect. 4, we describe the extraction of subsets of music samples from the GiantMIDI-Piano dataset using a semi-automated process, for employment as training sets for GPT-2 models.

In Sect. 5, we describe how we varied the training of various GPT-2 generative music models in terms of the training corpus and the target loss value. We analyse the output using the metrics and compare and contrast the models against the corpus datasets. Our main contribution here is a new methodology for comparing generative music neural models which have been trained differently. As described in Sect. 6, part of this methodology involves being able to browse through generated samples and interpret summary statistics over a large volume of such samples. To help with this, we have developed a web application, which allows users to explore generated material from the models trained with different experimental settings. We draw conclusions in Sect. 7 about the effect the training parameters have on the generative music from GPT-2 based models, discuss how our methodology could be used in generative music practice, and describe some avenues for future work.

2   Background

2.1   GPT-2 Models

Attention mechanisms in deep learning allow models to concentrate on various parts of a sequence selectively, and have been successful in a number of applications [20]. Transformers [20] are attention-based sequence-to-sequence models, which were initially designed for NLP tasks and widely utilised in other domains, for instance computer vision [5] and image generation [3]. In their basic form, without relying on a recurrence or convolution mechanism, transformers have proven successful at various tasks such as language translation [23] and question answering [15].

A well-known transformer-based model is GPT-2, which was released by OpenAI in 2019 [16]. There are four sizes of GPT-2 model, which are: small

(124M parameters), medium (355M parameters), large (774M parameters) and extra large (1.5B parameters). GPT-2 small can be run on a single GPU, which has made it the most appropriate for the experiments described here. GPT-2 has pre-trained weights which were trained on NLP data, but it can be utilised in many contexts by fine-tuning it for a specific task [16]. Such fine-tuning involves further training the pre-trained model on specific data, which can come from a modality different to language. In the work presented here, we fine-tune a base GPT-2 small model with music data, and deploy this in a generative context to produce symbolic music, which is a common practice in the field, e.g., as described in [7] and [14].

2.2   Representing Music Data for GPT-2 Input

To perform the fine-tuning (training) of GPT-2 models, we utilise the GiantMIDI-Piano dataset, which contains 10,854 classical piano pieces [12] represented in MIDI format. This dataset was generated by extracting piece and composer names from the International Music Score Library Project (imslp.org) and then transcribing audio recordings of these solo piano pieces. The dataset also contains metadata about the pieces including the birth dates of the composers (covering pre-1300s to 1980s), which we make use of in our corpus analysis. The pieces are complete, often long, piano compositions with a total length of 1237 hours, covering 2786 different composers.

To use MIDI data with GPT-2 models, the data needs to be first represented as text, given that these models work primarily in the text domain. MIDI contains a wealth of information about the music, but in order to have a parsimonious representation for efficient training of models, we ignore much of the detail. Our approach to translate MIDI to strings is based on that described in [14], but produces less verbose strings. Each note in a polyphonic MIDI file is first represented as a line of text capturing four pieces of information, namely note midi (n)umber, i.e., pitch; (v)elocity, i.e., volume level; (d)uration in terms of ticks, with 480 ticks per beat in our case; and (j)ump. This latter jump value is the duration in ticks between the start times of the current note and the note represented on the previous line (defaulting to zero for the first note in the representation). Note that in single-pass translation of MIDI into strings in this fashion, negative jumps are sometimes required.

Once all the notes have been transcribed onto a line, the text for multiple notes is concatenated into a longer string. To fit with the input format for the GPT-2 models, around 76 notes are concatenated, which captures between 4–8 bars, depending on the content. Finally, strings are tokenised to turn them into vectors of floats for input to the GPT-2 model, with details of the tokenisation routine given in [14]. In Fig. 1, we provide an example of how a one-bar polyphonic piece, presented in standard score and piano roll visualisations, is represented as strings. Note that the staccato note at the end of the bar is transcribed as a quaver rather than a crotchet, to capture this performance detail, and there are similar approaches for approximating other musical annotations.

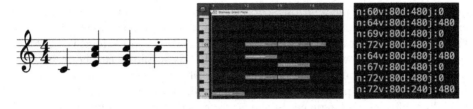

Fig. 1. Visualisations of a piece of polyphonic music as a score and piano roll; the transcribed string representation of the piece based on its MIDI representation.

2.3   Statistical Analysis of Generative Music Models

Evaluation of generative music systems is important to assess the performance of these models, understand their behaviour better and guide people in their practical usage. Broadly speaking, there have been two typical evaluation approaches, namely performing statistical analyses on the output from the generative models and conducting human listening experiments, again with music generated by the models. The strength of having a statistical evaluation strategy is its convenience and modularity for various generative settings, but a limitation is that these methods might not reflect human perception and can be restricted to low-level musical metrics rather than high-level metrics that are semantically meaningful to listeners.

The statistical evaluation strategy we describe here is based on [25], where the authors calculate musical metrics for training and generated datasets, then apply some statistical measures of distance to the distributions of training and generated samples. The distance measures were KL distance and overlapping area (described below). The authors use two different training datasets: a folk music dataset of Irish tunes in ABC notation (norbeck.nu/abc) and a jazz dataset from Wikifonia [18] supplemented with jazz solo transcriptions from [2]. They analysed two generative systems, namely *MidiNet* [24], a convolutional generative adversarial network, and *LookbackRNN*, a melody lookback recurrent neural network from the Magenta project [21]. Also, the authors analyse model performance with two MidiNets, where the models have identical architectures and were produced using the same training data, but differ in having feature matching regularisers, which can stabilise the training of GANs.

To compare a distribution of musical samples with respect to certain metrics, *KL-distance* (KLD) is a common measure between two probability density functions $P(x)$ and $Q(x)$. As per [13], this is calculated as follows:

$$D_{\mathrm{KL}}(P \parallel Q) = \int_{-\infty}^{\infty} P(x) \log \left(\frac{P(x)}{Q(x)} \right) dx$$

In [25], the authors also introduced the *overlapping area* measure (OA), which calculates the area between two probability density functions as follows:

$$OA(A, B) = \int_R min[f_A(x), f_B(x)] \, dx$$

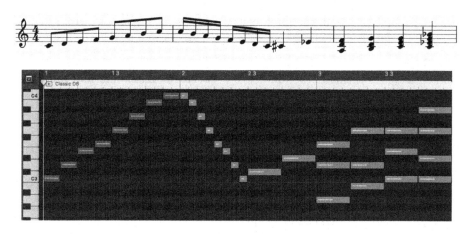

Fig. 2. Sample musical piece for illustrating the musical metrics, given in both score and piano roll formats.

where A and B are two continuous random variables, and $f_A(x)$ and $f_B(x)$ are probability density functions for A and B. Unlike KL distance, overlapping area is a bounded distance measure [25] producing values in the range $[0,1]$.

3   Musical Metrics

To analyse corpora of music, whether human-produced or computer-generated, we use six musical metrics which summarise a musical composition, each of which is defined below. The first of these, namely pitch count and pitch range, are from [25]. We introduce two other basic musical metrics, namely average note duration and average velocity, and two more complex ones: the chroma metric and a metric estimating how traditional the chords in the music are. As a running example to illustrate the metrics, in Fig. 2, we provide a sample piece of music consisting of an ascending C-major scale in 8th notes, followed by a descending C-major scale in 16th notes, C# and Eb notes which are not diatonic to the C-major scale, and finally a chord progression (D minor, G major and C major triads followed by a C minor seventh chord).

We represent a musical piece, M, of N notes, as a list $M = [m_1, \ldots, m_N]$. We further represent the MIDI note number of note m_t as $num(m_t)$, its velocity as $vel(m_t)$ and its duration as $dur(m_t)$. The metrics we employ are as follows.

Pitch Count
Denoted as $pc(M)$, this is the coefficient of different note numbers used, where octaves of the same pitch are considered to be different, e.g. middle-C (MIDI note 60) and top-C (72) are different note numbers.

$$pc(M) = |\{num(m) : m \in M\}|$$

For the example in Fig. 2, the pitch count is 13, as the eight notes from middle to top-C are supplemented with a C#, Eb and Bb as well as a lower A and Bb.

Pitch Range

Denoted as $pr(M)$, this is the difference between the maximum and minimum MIDI note numbers in M:

$$pr(M) = max_{t \in 1,...,N}(num(m_t)) - min_{t \in 1,...,N}(num(m_t))$$

For the example in Fig. 2, the pitch range starts at low-A (MIDI note 57) and goes to top-C (72), and hence spans $72 - 57 = 15$ pitches.

Average Duration

Denoted as $ad(M)$, this is the average duration of the notes in M, with duration measured in terms of 480 ticks per beat.

$$ad(M) = \frac{1}{N} \sum_{t=1}^{N} dur(m_t)$$

For the example in Fig. 2, the average duration of the notes is 325.16 ticks.

Average Velocity

Denoted as $av(M)$, this is the average of the velocity value of the notes in M, where velocity takes values from 0 to 127.

$$av(M) = \frac{1}{N} \sum_{t=1}^{N} vel(m_t)$$

For the example in Fig. 2, the average velocity is 75.4839 (noting that exact velocities are not marked on the score or piano roll, but are represented in the MIDI versions).

Chroma Metric

To capture notions of the tonality of a piece, we look at the relative frequencies of each of the 12 pitches used in classical Western music, i.e., A, A#, B, C, C#, etc. We denote the *pitch-class* of note m as $class(m) = num(m) \mod 12$, which maps $num(m_t)$ to the range 0 to 11. For a pitch-class p in this range, we denote the frequency, f, of p in a piece of music M as the number of notes which have pitch-class p:

$$f_M(p) = |\{m \in M : class(m) = p\}|$$

For the chroma metric of M, which we denote $ch(M)$, we compile the list of frequencies for $p = 0, \ldots, 11$, and then sort this list in ascending order to produce a list $[f_M(p_0), \ldots, f_M(p_{11})]$ with $f_M(p_i) \leq f_M(p_{i+1})$ for all i. Note that some of the values in this list could be zero, if no note with a particular pitch-class is seen in M. This enables us to calculate $ch(M)$ as:

Table 1. Chord types and intervals detected for the chord non-traditionality metric.

	Chord type	Interval lists
Traditional	Major triad	[4,3], [3,5], [5,4]
	Minor triad	[3,4], [4,5], [5,3]
	Diminished triad	[3,3], [3,6], [6,3]
Non-traditional	Augmented triad	[4,4]
	Major seventh	[4,3,4], [3,4,1], [4,1,4], [1,4,3]
	Minor seventh	[3,4,3], [4,3,2], [3,2,3], [2,3,4]
	Dominant seventh	[4,3,3], [3,3,2], [3,2,4], [2,4,3]
	Half diminished seventh	[3,3,4], [3,4,2], [4,2,3], [2,3,3]
	Diminished seventh	[3,3,3]

$$ch(M) = \frac{\sum_{i=0}^{4} f_M(p_i)}{\sum_{j=5}^{11} f_M(p_j)}$$

Informally, this divides the number of times the least frequent pitch-classes are seen in M by the number of times the most frequent ones are seen. For a piece, M, in C-major which never strays from the scale with accidentals or modulation, etc., the pitch classes for Ab, Bb, Db, Eb and Gb would have frequency zero, hence the numerator for $ch(M)$ would be zero, and M would likewise score zero for the chroma metric. For a non-empty piece of music, at least one pitch-class will be employed, hence the denominator can never be zero. For the example in Fig. 2, the chroma metric is $4/27 = 0.1481$. This is because the 7 pitch-classes of C-major are used the most frequently, (at least twice for all, and up to six times for the C pitch-class), summing to 27 usages. In contrast, the pitch-classes of Db and Bb are used once, Eb twice and Ab and Gb never, summing to 4 occurrences.

Chord Non-traditionality

For this metric, we compile a list of the chords represented in musical set theory format using the intervals between the notes in semitones [6], split these chords into two sets and divide the sizes of the sets. The first set of chords can be seen as *traditional* in terms of their long-standing usage in music history and comprise the major triad, minor triad and diminished triad chord types. The second set of chords can be seen as *non-traditional*, with adoptance more recently in music history. This set comprises any which are augmented triads, major sevenths, minor sevenths, dominant sevenths, half-diminished sevenths, or diminished sevenths.

In this context, a set of three or more notes is deemed to be in a chord if the start time of each note is within 48 ticks of every other note in the set. This threshold is set in terms of ticks rather than milliseconds to be flexible for various tempos, because the MIDI file specifies how many milliseconds there are in each tick (in terms of a beats per minute BPM value). Hence, for music played at a slower tempo, the notes of a chord can be more offset over time than for higher-tempos pieces. This can help capture expressive gestures for chord events. For example, at 120 BPM, the chord threshold of 48 ticks is 50ms. This 50ms value is also used in [12], but is a static milliseconds value there, rather than based on ticks as is the case here.

To extract the chords, including all possible inversions of them, we find any chords with intervals in a set given in Table 1. All the chords appearing in a piece of music M are counted with multiplicity and put into the appropriate traditional set $chords_T(M)$ or non-traditional set $chords_{NT}(M)$. The chord non-traditionality measure, $cnt(M)$ is then calculated by dividing the size of $chord_{NT}(M)$ by the size of $chord_T(M)$:

$$cnt(M) = \frac{|chord_{NT}(M)|}{|chord_T(M)|}$$

This gives an indication of how unconventional the chords are in a piece of music. For the example in Fig. 2, $cnt(M) = 1/3 = 0.3333$, as there is an augmented C-minor seventh chord (non-traditional) and D-minor, G-major and C-major (traditional) chords.

4   Dataset Curation

Recall that we are experimenting with training GPT-2 models for generative music to discover how the training setup affects the nature of the music they output. Early experiments highlighted that the entire GiantMIDI-Piano dataset was too large to feasibly train over, given our computing resources (usually a single GPU), especially as we need to train numerous models for comparison purposes. To reduce the size of the dataset to a more suitable level, we curated a **base subset** of musical samples from the GiantMIDI-Piano dataset which contains 400,000 notes, which corresponds to around 112 full pieces. We did this in a semi-automated way so that the values of the metrics from Sect. 3 above, when averaged over the 112 curated pieces closely matched the values from the entire database.

As mentioned in Sect. 2, GPT-2 takes input in 76 note windows, so we extracted music from the GiantMIDI-Piano database in such windows. While building the base subset, to maintain similar statistics to the entire database, at each stage, we search through the entire database for the window of notes (not previously extracted) that scores highest with respect to a weighted sum of the metrics of Sect. 3. Starting with equal weights, using a GUI with sliders, we maintained the weights in this summation by hand so that whenever the extracted subset deviated too far in terms of a particular metric, we could increase the weight associated with that metric for the next searches. We made regular adjustments to keep the emerging dataset balanced in this fashion, and stopped adding material once 400,000 notes had been added, as this is a suitably sized dataset for our purposes. In future work, we plan to automate the extraction approach entirely.

For the experiments described below, we test whether the nature of the training data effects the nature of the music that the generative models output. To enable this, we extracted two more subsets of the GiantMIDI-Piano dataset,

Table 2. Mean and standard deviation of the musical metrics over the GiantMIDI-Piano dataset and three subsets of it.

Metric	GiantMIDI-Piano		Base		Classical		20th century	
	Mean	Std	Mean	Std	Mean	Std	Mean	Std
Pitch count	25.474	6.799	25.585	2.213	23.040	5.358	27.542	7.741
Pitch range	47.198	11.502	46.527	4.220	42.489	9.325	49.212	12.413
Av. duration	522.330	421.043	479.433	291.527	322.455	233.919	579.161	484.185
Av. velocity	70.055	12.415	69.219	4.760	69.061	10.873	70.731	13.058
Chroma	0.086	0.090	0.075	0.032	0.061	0.063	0.133	0.117
Chord-NT	0.188	0.566	0.142	0.416	0.124	0.435	0.246	0.680

which have pieces from distinct musical eras, simply using the composer birth dates from the metadata in the dataset. The two subsets were:

- 439 pieces written by composers born in the period 1710–1770, hence the music they composed corresponds roughly to the classical period.
- 618 pieces by composers born in the period 1885–1905, hence their compositions correspond roughly to 20th century music.

The mean and standard deviation of metrics over the whole GiantMIDI-Piano dataset as well as the base, classical and 20th century subsets are given in Table 2. We see that the average values for the whole and base datasets are suitably similar. Moreover, for each metric, the classical and 20th century datasets sandwich the base datasets, in the sense that the classical values are always less than the base values and the 20th century values are always greater. In order for the training experiments to be informative, we needed to know that the nature of the classical and 20th century subsets are indeed different to each other. To show statistically significant differences between the distributions, we used a Mann-Whitney test, which doesn't assume any prior data distribution and works well with a higher number of samples. For each of the six metrics described above, we proposed the null hypothesis that the average value of the metric over the classical music is equal to the average value over the 20th century music. In each case, the null hypothesis was rejected with a p-value of smaller than 0.05, hence each metric differs significantly between the two subsets. From

Table 3. Mean and standard deviation of the metrics over the exaggerated datasets.

Metric	Exaggerated classical		Exaggerated 20th century	
	Mean	Std	Mean	Std
Pitch count	14.067	4.255	34.048	6.295
Pitch range	30.043	10.389	58.671	10.665
Avg. duration	300.928	209.680	1047.863	689.701
Avg. velocity	58.623	12.333	73.479	13.431
Chroma	0.024	0.038	0.200	0.120
Chords-NT	0.067	0.231	0.827	1.604

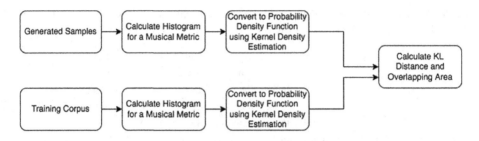

Fig. 3. A summary of the evaluation methodology employed, from [25].

this, we can conclude that the two datasets are indeed different, at least with respect to our metrics.

We can think of the metrics as defining a space in which musical samples exist. By looking at the average positions of the classical and 20th century subset pieces in this space, we were able to extract two further subsets with more exaggerated metrics in the same directions. We did this by compiling a dataset in the same semi-automated way as the base dataset above, but choosing the weights in the weighted sums so that they minimise the average metric values for the exaggerated classical dataset, and maximising them for the exaggerated 20th century dataset. Hence, by exaggerating the trends, we curated two subsets which are even further apart than the original era-specific ones extracted using only composer birth dates. We can see the extent of the exaggeration in Table 3. We undertook further Mann-Whitney statistical tests to confirm that the exaggerated datasets are significantly different to each other and the base dataset. We take forward the base and exaggerated datasets in the experiments below.

5   Evaluating Generative Model Output

We experiment here to investigate how the output from pre-trained GPT-2 models fine-tuned (trained) with music data changes when the amount of training changes and when the dataset changes. To train each model, we used back-propagation with an adam optimiser, and a standard loss function based on cross-entropy. When training starts, the loss function outputs a particular value l, and training can be halted with respect to this initial value. If a model is trained until the loss function outputs 10% of the original l, then we say it is *well trained*, but if it is trained to just 50% of l, then we say it is *poorly trained*. As observed in [1], poorly trained models might generate out of distribution, yet musically interesting results, and hence be valuable from a computational creativity perspective.

After training each model, to evaluate it, we generated 1,500 samples using it, and calculated all the musical metrics above for each sample. Then, we generate histograms of these metric values and, as per [25], we convert the histograms into continuous probability density functions (PDFs) using kernel density estimation [17]. Finally, we use the PDFs to calculate the KL-distance [13] and overlapping

Table 4. KL-Distance (KLD) and overlapping area (OA) measures when comparing training and generated datasets for both well-trained and poorly trained models, using the base dataset as the training corpus.

Metric	Well trained		Poorly trained	
	KLD	OA	KLD	OA
Pitch count	0.028	0.207	0.825	0.082
Pitch range	0.045	0.005	0.049	0.027
Avg. duration	0.010	0.780	0.015	0.584
Avg. velocity	0.007	0.808	0.005	0.799
Chroma metric	0.125	0.113	0.080	0.440
Chords metric	0.162	0.583	0.248	0.337

area measures between the PDFs of the training and generated datasets. This methodology is presented in Fig. 3, taken from [25].

As we are interested in comparing outputs of models, we performed generation in such a way as to minimise diversity of the outputs, hence producing a corpus of output samples which could be considered typical. Music generation with GPT-2 models normally starts with a musical seed, and the output reflects the seed. To remove this variable, we start with an empty seed. Also, randomness in the output from GPT-2 models can be controlled via a parameter called *temperature*, which divides the output from a probabilistic softmax layer. Higher temperature produces more randomised, more diverse outputs than lower temperatures, but again for our purposes, we use a temperature of 0.1, which is relatively low, to produce typical outputs. Note that GPT-2 is auto-regressive, hence the output from one feed-forward pass is input to the next pass, and the sequence of notes is built up in this way. In this way, even though the seed is always the same (empty), and the first pass will always output the same before the softmax layer, the multiple passes mean that the trained weights of the network are responsible for the nature and diversity of outputs.

5.1 Varying the Training Level

In a first experiment, we used the above methodology to investigate the effect of training level on the nature of output generated by a model, when compared to the corpus it was trained on. This experiment aims to show what kinds of musical attributes to expect for generated material for different training degrees. In particular, we were looking to test the hypothesis that for all of the musical metrics given in Sect. 3, well-trained models produce a distribution of musical samples closer to the training distribution (in terms of KL-distance and overlapping area) than poorly trained models. We produced both poorly-trained and well-trained models over the base dataset, and calculated the KL-distance and overlapping area measure for each musical metric.

The results from the experiment are given in Table 4. We see that for the chords-NT, pitch count and average note duration metrics, the nature of the generative music is as expected, with lower KL-distances and higher overlapping areas for the well-trained model than for the poorly trained one. However, for the chroma metric, we have higher KL-distance and lower overlapping area in the well trained case, which is unexpected, and indicates that the model fails to learn chroma/scale properties. For the pitch range and average velocity metrics, the results are inconclusive, as the KL-distance and overlapping area measures disagree on whether the output from the poorly-trained or well-trained models is closer, which is a phenomenon also observed in [25]. For each pair of KL-distances (poor and well-trained) and OA values, we performed a Mann-Whitney test as before, and rejected the null hypothesis that the values were equal, hence the differences between them were statistically significant.

5.2   Varying the Training Corpus

In a second experiment, we trained GPT-2 models over the base, exaggerated classical and exaggerated 20th century datasets described in Sect. 4. The models produced were well-trained, i.e., we stopped training when the loss value was 0.1 times the original loss. As before, we generated 1,500 musical samples and calculated the probability density functions produced by the output for each of the musical metrics above. For each metric, we calculated both the KL-distance and overlapping area for every pair (G, T) of generated dataset and training set. We further conducted Mann-Whitney tests to make sure that there is statistical significance between the results per musical metric, and found that all p-values are smaller than 0.05, hence there is statistically significant differences between the metrics for every (G, T) pair.

The results are presented in Table 5. In the second column are the training datasets that the first distribution was calculated for, with the values in the body of the table referring to the KL-distances (KLD) and overlapping (OA) measure between the training distribution and the distribution of the musical output generated by each model. For each metric, we hypothesise that the output music from a model would be closer (when compared with both KLD and OA with respect to the metric) to the dataset it was trained over than either of the other two datasets.

We see that the model trained on the exaggerated classical corpus produces musical samples that are as expected for the pitch count, pitch range and chroma metrics, i.e., they are closer to their training set than the other training datasets. With respect to the average duration metric, however, while the music is as expected (i.e., closer to the training corpus) when compared via KL-distance (KLD), but not when compared via overlap area (OA). With respect to the average velocity and chords-NT metrics, the output music is not as expected, i.e., it is closer to a different corpus than the training set when compared with both KLD and OA measures.

For the model trained on the base dataset, the output music is as expected with respect to the average duration and average velocity metrics, i.e., having the smallest KLD and highest OA for the training set. For the pitch count and pitch range metrics, however, the music is as expected when measure by KLD, but not

Table 5. KL-Distance (KLD) and overlapping area (OA) measures when comparing generated output distributions with distributions from differing training sets.

Metric	Training set	Exag. classical		Base		Exag. 20th century	
		KLD	OA	KLD	OA	KLD	OA
Pitch count	Exag. classical	0.016	0.794	1.295	0.301	1.976	0.076
	Base	1.628	0.001	0.028	0.207	0.384	0.033
	Exag. 20th century	1.775	0.136	0.401	0.584	0.051	0.815
Pitch range	Exag. classical	0.028	0.559	1.201	0.398	1.895	0.206
	Base	1.174	0.001	0.045	0.005	0.318	0.004
	Exag. 20th century	1.651	0.146	0.369	0.522	0.019	0.459
Avg. duration	Exag. classical	0.087	0.376	0.275	0.467	1.347	0.004
	Base	0.164	0.597	0.010	0.780	0.098	0.014
	Exag. 20th century	0.250	0.476	0.146	0.390	0.078	0.560
Avg. velocity	Exag. classical	0.049	0.511	0.154	0.547	0.129	0.619
	Base	0.033	0.627	0.007	0.808	0.010	0.171
	Exag. 20th century	0.236	0.578	0.091	0.485	0.008	0.609
Chroma metric	Exag. classical	0.034	0.506	2.018	0.078	9.052	0.047
	Base	0.377	0.472	0.125	0.113	1.243	0.014
	Exag. 20th century	0.369	0.461	0.080	0.498	0.004	0.659
Chords-NT	Exag. classical	0.124	0.048	1.175	0.029	4.859	0.009
	Base	0.000	0.648	0.162	0.583	3.242	0.054
	Exag. 20th century	0.134	0.202	0.083	0.170	0.040	0.167

OA. With respect to the chords-NT metric the music is as expected only when compared with OA, and with respect to the chroma metric, the music is not as expected when measured with KLD or OA measures. For the model trained on the exaggerated 20th century dataset, when evaluated with the pitch count, pitch range, average duration, chroma and chords-NT metrics, the music is as expected when compared using both KLD and OA measures, but with respect to the average velocity metric, it is not as expected when compared with the OA measure.

6   Web Application

Using a web application available at (https://sys-eval-gpt-2-mus-gen.vercel. app/), we exhibit online all of the generated samples from the models trained with each of our experimental settings. We also include histograms of each of the musical metrics over the training (fine-tuning) sets and generated sets for visual comparison. With this tool, users can select the output from a particular experimental setting, then for each musical metric, they can use the histogram slider to choose a particular bin and browse generated samples which correspond to that bin. The number of bins in the histograms are selected according to Scott's Rule [19]. A screenshot from the web app is given in Fig. 4, and we see the histograms arranged with those for the training set at the top and the generated

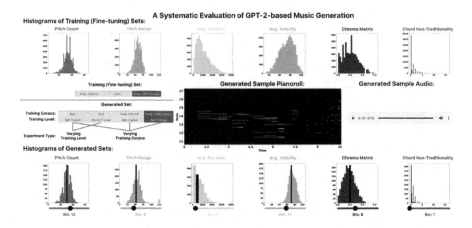

Fig. 4. Web application screenshot.

set at the bottom, leaving space for individual samples (from either training or generated set) to be visualised in the centre of the screen, and listened to. In the screenshot, the histograms for the exaggerated 20th century dataset are shown at the top, and at the bottom are the histograms for the generated output from the model which was well-trained on the exaggerated 20th century dataset.

While the generated samples are often not at a musically satisfying level, we have found the web app is useful for visualising musical metrics, their distributions for each training set, and for viewing generated samples in a piano roll and listening to audio renderings of them. Such browsing and visualisation form an important part of the methodology for evaluating the outputs from generative music models. For instance, we used it to verify and investigate the anomaly mentioned above, namely that the output from well-trained models is worse with respect to the chroma metric than poorly-trained models.

7 Conclusions and Future Work

In many generative deep learning projects, the emphasis is on training a model to generate output that looks as close as possible to a training distribution, and the loss function during training is the key factor in determining success in this respect. However, especially with generative music where the output is multi-faceted, a low loss value may hide the fact that the output is substandard in some way. This can be especially true if, as is the case here, the model is pre-trained over NLP data and fine-tuned with music data. Our contribution here has been to develop a methodology which enables the evaluation of generative music models trained in different ways, in order to highlight strengths and weaknesses in the generative power of the models.

The methodology consists of: theoretically developing and implementing metrics of musical interest; a semi-autonomous approach to curating datasets of music where the average values of these metrics is exaggerated; varying the training of models; calculating and comparing summary statistics over the metrics; calculating and comparing KL-distance and overlapping area distances between training and generated distributions of musical samples; and using a web interface to visualise and interrogate the evaluation performed. As the evaluation of generative models is based on their output rather than their processing, we believe the methodology could be used for other (e.g., non deep-learning) generative music approaches. Elements of the methodology can also be used to analyse human-generated music, for instance to investigate how the nature of music has changed from classical times into the 20th century.

In the particular case investigated here, we showed how this methodology can be used to compare and contrast GPT-2 models trained under various conditions. Through the experiments described, we have been able to conclude that GPT-2 models seem to work better – in the sense of producing output closer to the training distribution – for the exaggerated 20th century fine-tuning corpus than for the exaggerated classical corpus. There is one caveat to this, though, which is that the more training a GPT-2 model is given to drive down loss, the worse it will get with respect to the chroma metric. Interpreted musically, this means that the output from a well-trained model will likely be more tonal than the average for 20th century music. The methodology and in particular the web app enabled us to explore this anomaly. From a research perspective, this finding raises questions of how to improve matters in this respect through different neural architectures, transfer learning approaches, training regimes and generative uses of models once trained. From a generative music perspective, a practitioner using such models can be better informed of the benefits and limitations of their generative models, and the nature of the output, and adapt their practice accordingly, e.g., training models to different levels, as per [1].

In future work, we plan to expand our experiments with different data representations, such as REMI [10] and Compound Word [8], which are other common types of representation schemes used in symbolic music generation. We also plan to evaluate different network architectures, in particular transformers, previously used in generative music, such as Music Transformer [9] and Transformer-XL [4]. Introducing these might also help to improve the quality of the generated music and improve diversity within a wider range of parameter space, so we can improve our generative model in various ways. We also plan to supplement the methodology with further musical metrics, in particular capturing higher-level elements of music that listeners appreciate, and we will further develop the web app to include more visualisation approaches, and an ability to link to a generative model for live generation, potentially for use in performances. Moreover, we plan to conduct human listening experiments to compare their results with our evaluation outcomes. We hope to bring more formality to the assessment and hence improvement/deployment of generative music models, via a well-defined methodology, fully-featured set of musical metrics and a useful discovery tool.

Acknowledgements. We wish to thank the anonymous reviewers for their insightful comments.

References

1. Banar, B., Colton, S.: Generating music with extreme passages using GPT-2. In: Proceedings of the EvoMusArt Conference, Late Breaking Abstracts (2021)
2. Bretan, M., Weinberg, G., Heck, L.: A unit selection methodology for music generation using deep neural networks. In: Proceedings of the International Conference on Computational Creativity (2016)
3. Chen, M., et al.: Generative pretraining from pixels. In: Proceedings of ICML (2020)
4. Dai, Z., et al.: Transformer-XL: attentive language models beyond a fixed-length context. In: Proceedings of ACL (2019)
5. Dosovitskiy, A., et al.: An image is worth 16x16 words: transformers for image recognition at scale. In: Proceedings of ICLR (2021)
6. Forte, A.: The Structure of Atonal Music. Yale University Press, New Haven (1977)
7. Geerlings, C., Meroño-Peñuela, A.: Interacting with GPT-2 to generate controlled and believable musical sequences. In: ISMIR workshop on NLP for Music & Audio (2020)
8. Hsiao, W., Liu, J., Yeh, Y., Yang, Y.: Compound word transformer: learning to compose full-song music over dynamic directed hypergraphs. In: Proceedings of AAAI (2021)
9. Huang, C., et al..: Music transformer: generating music with long-term structure. In: Proceedings of ICLR (2018)
10. Huang, Y.S., Yang, Y.H.: Pop music transformer: beat-based modeling and generation of expressive pop piano compositions. In: Proceedings of the ACM International Conference on Multimedia (2020)
11. Ji, S., Luo, J., Yang, X.: A comprehensive survey on deep music generation. arXiv:2011.06801 (2020)
12. Kong, Q., Li, B., Chen, J., Wang, Y.: GiantMIDI-Piano: a large-scale MIDI dataset for classical piano music. arXiv:2010.07061 (2020)
13. Kullback, S., Leibler, R.A.: On information and sufficiency. Ann. Math. Stat. **22**(1), 79–86 (1951)
14. MuseNet. https://openai.com/blog/musenet/. Accessed 24 Nov 2021
15. Puri, R., Spring, R., Patwary, M., Shoeybi, M., Catanzaro, B.: Training question answering models from synthetic data. arXiv:2002.09599 (2020)
16. Radford, A., Wu, J., Child, R., Luan, D., Amodei, D., Sutskever, I.: Language models are unsupervised multitask learners. OpenAI Blog **1**(8), 9 (2019)
17. Silverman, B.: Density Estimation for Statistics and Data Analysis. Chapman and Hall, London (1986)
18. Simon, I., Morris, D., Basu, S.: MySong: automatic accompaniment generation for vocal melodies. In: Proceedings of CHI (2008)
19. Terrell, G.R., Scott, D.W.: Oversmoothed nonparametric density estimates. J. Am. Stat. Assoc. **80**(389), 209–214 (1985)
20. Vaswani, A., et al.: Attention is all you need. In: Proceedings of Advances in NIPS (2017)
21. Generating long-term structure in songs and stories. https://magenta.tensorflow.org/2016/07/15/lookback-rnn-attention-rnn. Accessed 24 Nov 2021
22. Wu, Z., Liu, N.F., Potts, C.: Identifying the limits of cross-domain knowledge transfer for pretrained models. arXiv:2104.08410 (2021)
23. Yang, J., et al.: Towards making the most of BERT in neural machine translation. In: Proceedings of AAAI (2020)

24. Yang, L.C., Chou, S.Y., Yang, Y.H.: MidiNet: a convolutional generative adversarial network for symbolic-domain music generation. In: Proceedings of ISMIR (2017)
25. Yang, L.-C., Lerch, A.: On the evaluation of generative models in music. Neural Comput. Appl. **32**(9), 4773–4784 (2020). https://doi.org/10.1007/s00521-018-3849-7

Expressive Aliens - Laban Effort Factors for Non-anthropomorphic Morphologies

Daniel Bisig[1,2]([✉])[iD]

[1] Center for Dance Research, Coventry University, Coventry, UK
`ad5041@coventry.ac.uk`
[2] Institute for Computer Music and Sound Technology, Zurich University of the Arts,
Zurich, Switzerland
`daniel.bisig@zhdk.ch`
`https://www.coventry.ac.uk/research/areas-of-research/centre-for-dance-research/`, `https://www.zhdk.ch/forschung/icst`

Abstract. The use of computer generated characters as artificial dancers offers interesting creative possibilities, especially when endowing these characters with morphologies and behaviours that differ significantly from those of human dancers. At the same time, it is challenging to create movements for non-anthropomorphic characters that are at the same time expressive and physically plausible. Motion synthesis techniques based on data driven methods or physics simulation each have their own limitations concerning the aspects of movements and the range of morphologies they can be used for. This paper presents a proof of concept system that combines a data driven method with a physics simulation for synthesizing expressive movements for computer generated characters with arbitrary morphologies. A core component of the system is a reinforcement learning algorithm that employs reward functions based on *Laban Effort Factors*. This system has been tested by training three different non-anthropomorphic morphologies on different combinations of these reward functions. The results obtained so far indicate that the system is able to generate a large diversity of poses and motions which reflect the characteristics of each morphology and *Effort Factor*.

Keywords: Dance and technology · Physics simulation · Reinforcement learning · Laban effort factors

1 Introduction

In contemporary dance, qualitative aspects of body movement play an important role. These aspects foreground the communicative, stylistic and expressive potential of movement. When designing computer generated characters as artificial dancers, it is desirable to endow them with similarly evokative movements.

Supported by the H2020-MSCA-IF-2018 - GA No. 840465.

A popular approach is to record the motions of a human dancer and subsequently transfer them to an artificial dancer. This approach has some drawbacks that limit creative possibilities, such as a lack of flexibility in creating additional motions beyond those recorded, and the necessity to match the skeleton topology of the computer generated character to that of the recorded subject. This makes it difficult to experiment with artificial dancers that don't replicate human dancers but instead possess different morphologies and movement capabilities.

Generative methods for creating synthetic motions offer more flexibility. The main alternatives are data driven methods based on machine learning and computer simulation. So far, it has been difficult to use either of these methods to generate synthetic motions that are at the same time plausible and expressive. Data driven methods preserve the stylistic characteristics of motion data they have been trained on but often fail to offer physical realism. Also, since training data is typically acquired by recording human dancers, data driven approaches make it difficult to work with artificial dancers that possess non-anthropomorphic morphologies. Simulation techniques that model body dynamics lead to physically plausible motions but usually lack stylistic and expressive diversity.

The research presented here represents the author's first attempt at designing a system that generates motions for artificial dancers with non-anthropomorphic morphologies that are both physically plausible and expressive. This system combines three methods: a Soft Actor-Critic reinforcement learning algorithm, a rigid body dynamics physics simulation, and algorithms for deriving *Laban Effort Factors* from motion data. The article describes the implementation of these methods and provides an overview of the results obtained so far.

2   Background

2.1   Movement Qualities

There exists no commonly accepted taxonomy for characterising and classifying movement qualities in dance. Nevertheless, the structural notation *Laban Movement Analysis* (LMA) introduced by Rudolf Laban [37] has gained prominence. LMA is widely adopted by dance scholars and has also informed fields such as robotics and human computer interaction. Central to LMA are four categories that formalise different aspects of the human body [32]: *Body, Space, Shape,* and *Effort.* The *Effort* category describes aspects that relate to the dynamics, energy, and inner intention of movement, all of which contribute to the expressivity of movement [5]. This category is subdivided into four *Effort Factors* (EF): *Space, Weight, Time, Flow.* Each *Factor* possesses two opposing dimensions. The *Space* factor describes the directedness of movement which can either be *Direct* or *Indirect.* The *Weight* factor describes the strength of movement which can either be *Light* or *Strong.* The *Time* factor describes the urgency of movement which can either be *Sustained* or *Sudden.* The *Flow* factor describes the continuity of movement which can either be *Free* or *Bound.*

Several researchers have proposed algorithms for deriving numerical representations of LMA categories from physical descriptors of motion. Prominent research has been conducted by *InfoMus Lab* that led to development of signal processing components for their *Eyesweb* software [10] to analyse gestural expressivity [11]. Aristidou and colleagues have published algorithms to identify style qualities [4] or classify emotions [1,3]. The implementation for analysing EF employed in this article is based on work by Larboulette and Gibet [28].

2.2   Motion Synthesis

The term *motion synthesis* is employed here for any character animation method that doesn't solely rely on playback of motion recordings [25,36]. Computer animation and game design are the most prominent application domains, other fields include robotics, interaction design, and dance. In dance, motion synthesis serves a variety of purposes: as source for inspiration during the creative process, as mechanism for controlling artificial dancers, to study choreographic principles that are difficult to comprehend when relying on video recordings only. The first two purposes are more relevant for this paper and will be elaborated on.

Creativity Support. The term *Creativity Support* has been coined in the context of human-computer interaction for technical systems that facilitate creative workflows, enhance a user's creativity, or operate as creative partners [31]. Most relevant in the context of this publication are motion synthesis systems that fullfill the last two criteria. The systems *Scuddle* and *Cochoreo* create incomplete motion data or unique keyframes as seed material for a choreographer's creativity [12,13]. Both systems use a Genetic Algorithm whose fitness function incorporates among others LMA categories. A tool that is inspired by thinking in physical metaphors uses a physics simulation [21] to create synthetic motions for abstract bodies. The *Chor-rnn* system serves as co-creative tool [14] that can be trained on motion capture data to produce synthetic motions in the language and style of an individual choreographer.

Some motion synthesis systems foster the kinaesthetic creativity of dancers. The *Choreographic Language Agent* (CLA) [16] system provides an authoring language for scripting abstract geometrical animation that can be used by dancers to explore and experiment with spatial transformations. CLA has later been modified into *Becoming*, a system that employs a physics simulation to create an artificial body that exhibits self motivated motions [29].

Artificial Dancers. The use of motion synthesis for the creation of artificial dancers has been extensively explored by Berman and James [6–8] and McCormick and colleagues [33–35]. Both teams experimented with a variety of machine learning techniques to generate motions that are similar to those of a human dancer. Other data driven approaches include the *Dancing Genome Project*, the piece *Singularity*, the *LuminAI* system, and *ViewPoints AI* system. The *Dancing Genome Project* employs an interactive genetic algorithm to creates motions for both a human and artificial dancer [27]. The piece *Singularity* illustrates the benefits of recurrent neural networks over other deep learning architectures in creating expressive synthetic motions [26]. The *LuminAI* system employs a clustering mechanism to select motions for an artificial dancer that mirror those of an interacting human dancer [30]. The *Viewpoints AI* system implements an interaction-based authoring approach for creating synthetic motions that combines ideas from case-based learning and imitative learning [23].

Some examples employ computer simulation to create synthetic motions for artificial dancers. Alaoui and colleagues created an interactive artificial dancer whose non-antropomorphic morphology is modeled as mass-spring system [19]. The behaviors of the mass-spring system are designed to convey expressive movement qualities. In the *Neural Narratives* series of dance pieces, a mass-spring system is combined with an artificial neural network to create synthetic limbs for a human dancer [9]. Here, the focus lies not on expressivity but rather on establishing semi-autonomous relationships between dancer and synthetic limbs.

2.3   Anthropomorphic versus Non-anthropomorphic Characters

Among the previously mentioned examples, the majority of creativity support systems operate with abstract forms of movements and morphologies. Contrary to this, the majority of artificial dancers exhibit anthropomorphic shapes and perform motions similar to those of human dancers.

The reason for this involves technical and artistic aspects. On a technical level, the choice of motion synthesis method often pre-determines the necessity to work with anthropomorphic morphologies and movements. Data driven systems are typically trained on recordings of human dancers and then used to create synthetic motions that are reminiscent of the recordings. For simulation-based methods, it is usually easier to design morphologies and behaviours that are abstract and non-anthropomorphic instead of human-like.

On an artistic level, the choice is less straight forward. Creativity support systems that support kinaesthetic ideation likely benefit from non-anthropomorphic motions and abstract visualisations since they leave room for creative interpretation [22]. The debate for and against anthropomorphic appearances has been ongoing in the field of human-robot interaction. One position is that anthropomorphic appearance facilitates the establishment of meaningful connections between humans and robots [18]. The opposite position is that non-anthropomorphic appearance avoids human-robot encounters that are biased by preconceptions and anthropomorphic projections [15]. These contrasting points of view are also relevant in dance. In some examples, robotic dancers were endowed with non-anthropomorphic morphologies in order to prevent dancers from imitating the robot's motions [24] or to force the audience to attribute agency to the robots based on motions rather than appearance [17]. But the concern for a clear readability of the relationship between human and artificial dancer in a stage performance has led to an abundance of anthropomorphic artificial dancers.

2.4   Physical Validity versus Expressivity

In a survey on data-driven methods for motion synthesis, believability was identified as one central research goal [2]. The authors state that believability depends on physical validity and expressivity which is challenging to achieve at the same time. Data driven methods have proven effective in generating synthetic motions that are natural looking and expressive but often exhibit artefacts such as foot skating or lack of balance that makes them appear unrealistic. Simulation-based approaches struggle with the opposite issues.

Not all of the previously mentioned examples that use data-driven methods focus on stylistic aspects of body movement. Instead, they use these methods to create novel motions even if it is at the expense of naturalness [6–8]. Among the previously mentioned examples that use computer simulation, only one does so for the purpose of achieving physical validity [21]. The other examples aim for behavioural autonomy [9,19,29] and/or the communication of expressivity [19].

3   Implementation

The system employed here combines a reinforcement learning (RL) algorithm, a physics simulation, and reward functions based on EF. The RL algorithm is implemented using the *PyTorch* deep-learning framework[1] and is based on the reference implementation provided by the *OpenAI Spinning Up* resource.[2] The agent's shape and articulation is simulated using the rigid body dynamics functionality of the *PyBullet* physics engine.[3] The adaption of the *OpenAI Gym Environments* for the *PyBullet* engine[4] served as starting point for combining RL system and simulation. The source code, trained model weights, and CAD files for morphologies are available online on zenodo.org.

3.1   Morphologies

Three agent morphologies (Fig. 1) have been designed using the software *onShape*.[5] The morphologies consist of rigid body parts that are connected via revolute joints, and their extremities end in rounded stubs rather than articulated hands or feet. The morphologies vary with regards to the number and shape of body parts, the number of joints, and the assignment of foot or hand functionality. These differences impact the type and level of stability that each morphology exhibits during simulation. The morphology entitled *Biped* maintains an upright posture through dynamic stability. This morphology consists of two legs with two feet and an elongated neck which are attached to a small hip. The morphology possesses 12 articulated joints. The morphology entitled

---

[1] PyTorch pytorch.org.

[2] OpenAI Spinning Up github.com/openai/spinningup.

[3] PyBullet pybullet.org.

[4] PyBullet Gymperium github.com/benelot/pybullet-gym.

[5] onShape www.onshape.com.

Quadruped can maintain an upright posture through static stability. This morphology consists of four legs ending in four feet that are attached to a circular torso. The morphology possesses a total of 12 articulated joints with three joints per leg. The morphology entitled *Legless* doesn't possess any legs and its circular torso forms the main contact with the ground. Attached to the torso are two arms ending in two hands that extend upwards. The morphology possesss a total of 8 articulated joints. The only other object in the physics simulation is a ground plane that serves as surface for the agents to stand on and move across. The morphologies depicted in Fig. 1 exhibit those poses that an agent assumes (with small randomisations) when first inserted into a simulation environment.

Fig. 1. Morphologies designed for motion synthetis. From left to right: *Biped*, *Quadruped*, *Legless*. The body parts rendered in dark blue have been assigned foot or hand status.

3.2   SAC Algorithm

The chosen Reinforcement Learning (RL) method is based on the *Soft Actor Critic* (SAC) algorithm [20]. SAC is a model-free off-policy algorithm that operates on continuous action and state spaces. A unique feature of SAC is its use of entropy regularisation. This regularisation maximizes entropy instead of long term reward to promote exploration. SAC inherits several methods of other actor-critic algorithms: actor and policy algorithms are implemented as artificial neural networks (ANN), the use of two action value functions instead of one, and the use of slowly changing target networks for error calculation. SAC was chosen for this work because it offers the efficiency of off-policy methods while combating their tendency for premature convergence.

In the current implementation, a total of six ANN are used, one as policy function, two as action value functions, and three as target networks. The policy function has one input layer and two output layers for the means and logarithm of the standard deviations of normal distributions. Each value in the action vector is obtained by sampling from the corresponding normal distribution and applying hyperbolic tangent squashing. The normalised values are re-scaled before being applied as torques to the joints. The ReLU function is used as activation function for the hidden layer units. No activation function is used for the output units. The two action value function networks are identical to each other. There is one input layer whose number of units matches the combined size of the observation and action vectors. There is one output layer that contains a single unit that outputs the estimated value for the corresponding observation-action pair. The ReLU function is used as activation function for the hidden layer units. No activation function is used for the output units. There is one target network for the policy function and two target networks for the action value functions. The configuration of the target networks is identical to those described above.

3.3   Observation Vector

The observation vector includes the states of the body joints, the contacts between body parts and ground plane, and the overall position, velocity and rotation of the body. The states of the joints consist of rotations and rotational velocities. Rotation is normalised between a joint's lower and upper rotational limit. Rotational velocity is normalised between zero and a joint's maximum rotational velocity. Only ground contacts with feet and hands are included in the observation vector. Each contact is represented as a binary state with 1 for contact and 0 otherwise. The overall position of the body is represented as vertical difference between the first and current simulation step and as normalised position relative to the spatial extensions of the simulation environment. The overall velocity of the agent includes both its linear and angular rotation. These are calculated relative to the agent's yaw orientation. The rotation of the agent is obtained as euler angles of its root body part. All observations together form a vector that contains 39 values for the *Biped* morphology, 41 values for the *Quadruped* morphology, and 32 values of the *Legless* morphology.

3.4   Rewards

The reward is calculated from a weighted combination of individual rewards: alive reward, collision reward, move distance reward, *Flow Effort* reward, *Space Effort* reward, *Time Effort* reward, and *Weight Effort* reward. For each time step an agent is alive, it receives a small positive reward. Once an agent stops being alive, it receives a large negative reward after which the episode ends. An agent stops being alive when a body part other than a foot or hand touches the ground or when the velocity of a joint exceeds a predefined limit. The first condition causes the agent to assume an upright body posture. The second condition prevents the agent from exploiting numerical instabilities of the simulation. The collision reward generates a negative reward when one of the feet or hands touches the agent's own body. This prevents the agent from moving forward by banging the extremities against it's body. The move distance reward generates a positive reward for each time step that is proportional to the distance the agent's root part traveled since the previous time step. This reward was introduced to cause body motions since some of the EF rewards weren't causing them on their own. The last four rewards are based on EF. The rewards are generated for each time step and are always positive. The reward value depends on the absolute difference between the normalised current EF value and a target value. The position values and derivatives required for the calculations are obtained from the positions and linear velocities of an agent's body parts. The normalised weights associated with each body part are obtained from the mass values specified in the CAD file. For all calculations, a temporal window of 10 time steps was used.

4   Training

To study how the relationship between morphology and motion changes under the influence of each *Effort* polarity, a set of training runs was devised in which either no or one polarity was rewarded at a time with or without using a simultaneous reward for move distance. This results in 18 training runs for each morphology. In each training run, the number of epochs was 500 and the maximum length of an episode was 800 time steps. Each episode starts with the agent being removed and then reinserted into the simulation with a slightly randomized default pose. An epoch ends when the agent dies or the number of time steps exceeds the maximum episode length. The training runs differ from each other with regard to the weighting of the move distance reward function and the weighting and target values for the EF reward functions. Once set, the weightings and target values were kept fixed for the entire training run. The selection of weightings and target values follows a combinatorial scheme with the weighting for the move distance reward set to either 1 or 0, the weighting of one EF reward set to 1 and all the other ones set to 0, and the target value for the EF reward with non-zero weighting set to either 1 or 0. For calculating the reward values for the EF, the *Effort* values are normalised by dividing them by maximum values. These maximum values are set differently for each EF and morphology and are based on the maximum *Effort* values observed during a set of initial trial runs: *Biped* morphology: *Flow* (20000), *Space* (10), *Time* (200), *Weight* (100), *Quadruped* morphology: *Flow* (8000), *Space* (50), *Time* (80), *Weight* (40), *Legless* morphology: *Flow* (15000), *Space* (40), *Time* (150), *Weight* (150). Other than that, the settings for all training runs and all morphologies are identical: all other reward weightings (1.0), alive reward (+0.2 for being alive and −100.0 for dying), collision reward (−1.0), number of hidden layers (3) and number of units per hidden layer (256) in both ANN, learning rate (10^{-4}), and size of replay buffer (10^6).

5   Results

After each training run, several inference runs have been conducted during which reward values and simulation visualisation were recorded. From these, animations have been created with visualisation and reward values superimposed.

These animations are available online.[6] The abbreviations used for identifying the inference runs are as follows: D stands for move distance reward with number following indicating its scale factor. F stands for *Flow Effort* reward, S for Space Effort reward, T for Time Effort reward, and W for Weight Effort reward. The number following the reward letter represents the target value for the reward. For illustrative purposes, a subset of these animations are presented here in the form of sequence of still images (Fig. 2).

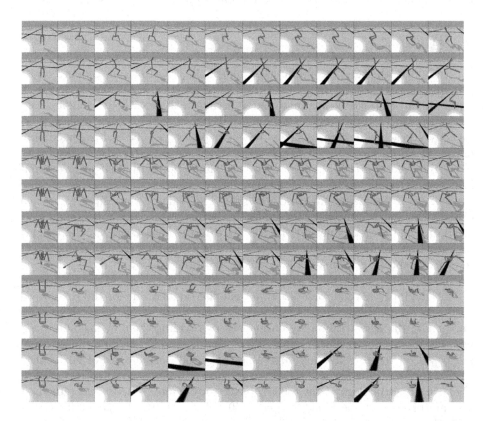

Fig. 2. Film strips depicting some inference runs. From top to bottom: *Biped* D0, D0S0, D1, D1S1, *Quadruped* D0, D0F1, D1, D1W1, *Legless* D0, D0S0, D1, D1F1

Based on these inference runs, some observations can be made concerning the types of postures and motions that the different morphologies exhibit. The main

---

[6] *Biped* Animations: D0, D0F0, D0F1, D0S0, D0S1, D0T0, D0T1, D0W0, D0W1, D1, D1F0, D1F1, D1S0, D1S1, D1T0, D1T1, D1W0, D1W1, *Quadruped* Animations: D0, D0F0, D0F1, D0S0, D0S1, D0T0, D0T1, D0W0, D0W1, D1, D1F0, D1F1, D1S0, D1S1, D1T0, D1T1, D1W0, D1W1, *Legless* Animations: D0, D0F0, D0F1, D0S0, D0S1, D0T0, D0T1, D0W0, D0W1, D1, D1F0, D1F1, D1S0, D1S1, D1T0, D1T1, D1W0, D1W1.

observation is that inference runs with a weighting for the move distance reward of 0 lead to markedly different agent behaviours than those with a weighting of 1. For this reason, observations are grouped by morphology and move distance reward weighting. For the sake of brevity, observations focus on types of poses and motions and only summarily mention other sources of diversity.

In runs involving the *Biped* morphology and move distance reward weighting 0, the agent exhibits stable poses which it maintains by executing balancing motions of the legs and neck. Floor contacts with the legs are aperiodic and the agent executes a full body rotation around its vertical axis. The runs show some variety with regards to type of poses and size of motions that stabilize the poses. The type of poses generated are: both legs bent and parallel (D0, D0F1, D0S1), legs split with one bent and one straight (D0F0, D0S0, D0W1), legs split with both straight (D0T0, D0W0), legs contorted with one pointing sideways (D0T1).

In runs involving the *Biped* morphology and move distance reward weighting 1, the agent exhibits large traversal motion while assuming poses that are usually similar to those with reward weighting 0. The runs show large variety with regards to type and periodicity of gait, traversal direction, body alignment, and the amount of neck motion. Types of poses: both legs bent and parallel (D1, D1T1, D1W0, D1W1), legs split with one bent and one straight (D1F1, D1S0, D1T0), legs split with both straight (D1F0, D1S1). Type of gaits: walking (D1, D1F1, D1S0, D1T0, D1T1, D1W1), jumping (D1S1), simultaneous jumping and walking (D1W0), successive jumping and hopping (D1F0).

In runs involving the *Quadruped* morphology and move distance reward weighting 0, motion of the agent mainly serves the purpose of changing from the initially compact pose into a more extended pose. The runs show some variety with regards to the type of extended pose, the speed with which this pose is achieved, the coordination of the leg motions, and the amount of motion after the extended pose has been reached. Types of poses: legs radially symmetrical with equal bending (D0, D0F0), legs radially symmetrical with different bending (D0W0), legs pairwise parallel (D0F1, D0W0, D0W1), legs parallel (D0S0), legs asymmetric (D0T0), pose keeps changing (D0S1).

In runs involving the *Quadruped* morphology and move distance reward weighting 1, the agent executes an initial jump to quickly switch from its initial pose to an extended one. After that, the agent executes undulating motions that shift its center of gravity back and forth. The runs show some variety with regards to the type of extended pose, the presence or absence of undulating motions, the speed, size, periodicity, and symmetry of these motions, as well as the body's amount of liftoff and traversal during undulation. Types of poses: legs radially symmetrical (D1, D1F1, D1T0, D1S1, Di1W0), legs pairwise parallel (D1S0), legs asymmetric (D1F0). Presence of undulations: present (D1, D1F0, D1F1, D1T1, D1S0, D1S1, Di1W0, D1W1), absent (D1T0).

In runs involving the *Legless* morphology and move distance reward weighting 0, the agent quickly moves away from its initial pose after which it exhibits uncorrelated arm motions. The runs show some variety with regards to type of pose, extent, amount, and velocity of arm motion, presence or absence of contacts between arms and ground, and amount of torso tumbling. Types of poses: both arms are folded above torso (D0F0, D0T0, D0S0, D0W0), one arm folded above torso (D0, D0F1, D0T1, D0W1), both arms point away from the torso (D0S1).

In runs involving the *Legless* morphology and move distance reward weighting 1, the agent quickly moves away from its initial pose after which it exhibits traversal motion with usually one arm dominating body propulsion and the torso occasionally lifting above ground. The runs show some variability with regards to the type of pose, the type, amount, synchronicity and periodicity of arm motions, the amount and speed of traversal, the constancy of the traversal direction and the body's alignment with the traversal direction. Types of poses: one arm folded above torso (D1, D1F0, D1F1, D1T1, D1S0, D1S1, D1W0), both arms pointing away from torso (D1T0, D1W1). Types of arm motions: arms execute *rowing* motions (D1, D1F0, D1S1, D1W1), one arm executes pulling motion (D1F1, D1S0, D1W0), one arm executes *rowing* and the other pulling motion (D1T1), arms move erratically (D1T0).

To study the relationship between the different agent morphologies and their capability to exhibit the polarities of the EF, a simple statistical comparison has been conducted (Fig. 3). For this comparison, the recorded *Effort* values were averaged for each inference run and morphology and then normalised. The normalization range corresponds to the minimum and maximum averages for each *Effort* value across all the morphologies and inference runs. This range is assumed to cover the two polarities of each EF. While this assumption is likely not entirely correct, it allows to highlight the main differences in the relationships between agent morphologies and EF.

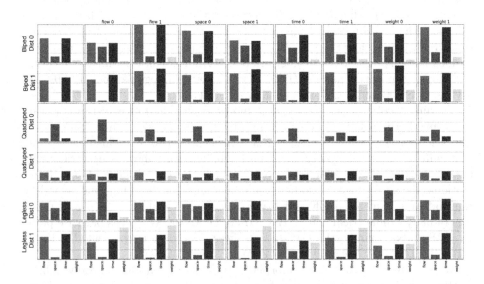

Fig. 3. Average values of *Effort Factors* for all inference runs. In each graph, the polarities are arranged along the vertical axis with *Free, Direct, Sustained, Light* at the bottom and *Bound, Indirect, Sudden, Strong* at the top.

For the *Biped* morphology, *Flow Effort* ranges between *Neural* and *Bound*. This can likely be attributed to the role of the neck in maintaining dynamic stability, which executes small motions that frequently change direction. For the *Quadruped* morphology, *Flow Effort* is close to the *Free* polarity. The likely cause for this is that static stability is maintained by the four legs through larger and less frequently changing motions. For the *Legless* morphology, *Flow Effort* is close to *Neutral*. This is likely due to the ability of the arms to move freely without affecting stability.

Space Effort is more difficult to analyze because the equation for its calculation involves a denominator which causes the result to become extremely large when the overall position of a body barely changes. This issue most strongly affects the results obtained in the inference runs for the *Legless* and *Quadruped* morphologies when the move distance reward weighting is set to 0. In those runs, the *Legless* morphology exhibits a *Space Effort* that is closest to the *Indirect* polarity. This is because this morphology barely changes its overall body position. The *Quadruped* morphology requires more time to assume a stable body position and usually remains in motion after doing so. This results in a *Space Effort* that varies between *Direct and Neutral*. The *Biped* morphology exhibits a high amount correlation between overall body displacement and the motions of the individual extremities. This results in a *Space Effort* that is closest to the *Direct* polarity. In runs with the move distance reward weighting set to 1, the differences in *Space Effort* among the morphologies are less pronounced. In all these runs, *Space Effort* is close to the *Direct* polarity with the *Biped* morphology being closest. The reason is that all morphologies correlate the overall displacement of the body with the motion of their extremities, which prevents the latter from traveling much further than the former.

In all inference runs, the variations of *Time Effort* is extremely similar to those of *Flow Effort*. It seems that the morphologies are not able to affect these *Efforts* independently. For the *Biped* morphology, *Time Effort* is closest to the *Sudden* polarity. The likely reason is that motions executed to maintain dynamic stability need to happen instantaneously. For the *Quadruped* morphology, *Time Effort* is closest to the *Sustained* polarity. The likely reason is that adjustments to static stability happen more gradually and continuously. For the *Legless* morphology, *Time Effort* is *Neutral*. The likely reason is that the contributions from the motions of the light arms which include sudden changes and the more continuous motions of the heavy torso average each other out.

For the *Legless* morphology, *Weight Effort* is closest to the *Strong* polarity in those runs in which the move distance reward weighting is 1. The heavy torso contributes most strongly to this *Factor*, particularly in those cases where it lifts off the ground. For the *Quadruped* morphology, *Weight Effort* is closest to the *Light* polarity in those runs in which the move distance reward weighting is 0. The reason is that the motions decrease in both amount and velocity after static stability has been achieved. For the *Biped* morphology, *Weight Effort* is close to the *Light* polarity when the move distance reward weighting is 0, otherwise, *Weight Effort* varies between *Neutral* and *Light*. Since this morphology lacks a heavy torso, its weight is lower than those of the other morphologies. Moving such a light body when performing small stability adjustments keeps *Effort* close to the *Light* polarity. The *Effort* shifts only somewhat towards the *Heavy* polarity when the size and speed of the motions increase.

6   Discussion

The synthetic motions obtained so far are both varied and physically plausible. The variations appear across different reward configurations for a single morphology and for identical reward configurations across different morphologies. It is likely that the morphologies together with the agent's alive criteria define a basic repertory of suitable poses and motions. The *Effort* rewards then influence which of these suitable poses and motions are chosen and how they are adjusted to match the given *Effort* polarities. The large influence of dynamic and static stability provides particularly strong evidence for the close relationship between morphology and *Effort Factors*. This includes the tendency of the *Biped* morphology to exhibit the *Bound* and *Sudden* polarities whereas the *Quadruped* morphology moves predominantly according to the *Free* and *Sustained* polarities. Another striking example is the *Strong* polarity that appears most pronounced for the *Legless* morphology whereas the *Light* polarity dominates for the *Quadruped* morphology.

Concerning the diversity of different pose and motion types and the variations within each type, the relationship between morphologies and *Effort Factors* is less obvious. When designing the morphologies, the author predicted the *Biped* morphology to exhibit the least variety and the *Legless* morphology to show the largest variety with the *Quadruped* morphology in between. This prediction was based on the assumption that dynamic stability constrains the range of suitable poses and motions more strongly than static stability. The results have proven this assumption wrong, since it is the *Biped* morphology that exhibits the largest range of pose and motion diversity. One reason for this difficulty might be related to a human observer's ability (or lack thereof) to perceive pose and motion diversity in non-antropomorphic morphologies. For unfamiliar morphologies, variations are likely easier to spot in motions that are coordinated than those that aren't. For the *Biped* morphology, dynamic stability necessitates a high degree of coordination. For the *Legless* morphology, static stability barely depends on the arms' which tend to move more erratically.

Another finding is that the sole use of EF as reward functions is sometimes insufficient to cause morphologies to move. This issue is particularly prominent for the two morphologies that exhibit static stability. The inclusion or exclusion of a move distance reward function has a huge impact on the resulting motions including their capability to exhibit the EF polarities.

7   Conclusion and Outlook

The chosen combination of physics simulation and RL system with reward functions based on EF has shown to be able to generate synthetic motions or agents with non-antropomorphic morphologies that are both diverse and physically plausible. This approach offers an interesting perspective on motion synthesis in that it places the focus on the design of the morphologies rather than the motions themselves. It is difficult to anticipate the motions that are obtained in this manner and the results are often unexpected. Accordingly, this procedure aligns with workflows that favour exploration, novelty, and surprise.

The results presented so far are preliminary and there is much room for further research and development. The most immediate next step is to conduct a user survey to evaluate perceptual aspects of pose and motion diversity and their association with EF. This survey will involve both lay people and experts in LMA. Another immediate next step is to conduct additional training runs for each combination of agent morphology and reward configuration. Conducting additional training runs will help to assess how much of the diversity in poses and motions is caused by the morphology and reward configuration and how much is due to chance in the training process.

Another next step is to experiment with other reward functions for enforcing motion than move distance reward. A frequently used reward function is based on the distance between an agent's position and the position of a target location. Another alternative might be to reward the area covered while traversing. This might cause an agent to not only learn how to traverse but also how to change the direction of traversal. Experimenting with such alternatives helps to gain a better understanding for the interdependency between spatial and expressive aspects of synthetic motions.

A particularly important future direction involves dynamically changing reward configurations. So far, the reward configurations have been fixed for an entire training and inference run. It would be interesting to modify the expressivity of an agent's motion over the course of an individual run. Towards this goal, some initial experiments have been conducted, but none of them had yet led to satisfactory results. Nevertheless, the author plans to continue these experiments.

Finally and in the long run, it would be interesting to dispose with the necessity to directly reward specific qualities of motions. Instead, reinforcement learning task could be designed in a manner that requires several agents to respond to and influence each other through body motions. In such a setting, expressive motions might emerge to support non-verbal communication. Such an emergent form of expressivity would be more aligned with agent-based approaches since it has relevance for the agents' beyond a direct reward.

References

1. Ajili, I., Mallem, M., Didier, J.Y.: Human motions and emotions recognition inspired by LMA qualities. Vis. Comput. **35**(10), 1411–1426 (2019). https://doi.org/10.1007/s00371-018-01619-w
2. Alemi, O., Pasquier, P.: Machine learning for data-driven movement generation: a review of the state of the art. arXiv preprint arXiv:1903.08356 (2019)

3. Aristidou, A., Charalambous, P., Chrysanthou, Y.: Emotion analysis and classification: understanding the performers' emotions using the LMA entities. In: Computer Graphics Forum, vol. 34, pp. 262–276. Wiley (2015)

4. Aristidou, A., Stavrakis, E., Charalambous, P., Chrysanthou, Y., Himona, S.L.: Folk dance evaluation using Laban movement analysis. J. Comput. Cult. Herit. (JOCCH) 8(4), 1–19 (2015)

5. Bartenieff, I., Lewis, D.: Body Movement: Coping with the Environment, 1st edn. Routledge, London (2013)

6. Berman, A., James, V.: Towards a live dance improvisation between an avatar and a human dancer. In: Proceedings of the 2014 International Workshop on Movement and Computing, pp. 162–165 (2014)

7. Berman, A., James, V.: Kinetic dialogues: enhancing creativity in dance. In: Proceedings of the 2nd International Workshop on Movement and Computing, pp. 80–83 (2015)

8. Berman, A., James, V.: Learning as performance: autoencoding and generating dance movements in real time. In: Liapis, A., Romero Cardalda, J.J., Ekárt, A. (eds.) EvoMUSART 2018. LNCS, vol. 10783, pp. 256–266. Springer, Cham (2018). https://doi.org/10.1007/978-3-319-77583-8_17

9. Bisig, D., Palacio, P.: Neural narratives: dance with virtual body extensions. In: Proceedings of the 3rd International Symposium on Movement and Computing, pp. 1–8 (2016)

10. Camurri, A., et al.: EyesWeb: toward gesture and affect recognition in interactive dance and music systems. Comput. Music. J. 24(1), 57–69 (2000)

11. Camurri, A., Mazzarino, B., Ricchetti, M., Timmers, R., Volpe, G.: Multimodal analysis of expressive gesture in music and dance performances. In: Camurri, A., Volpe, G. (eds.) GW 2003. LNCS (LNAI), vol. 2915, pp. 20–39. Springer, Heidelberg (2004). https://doi.org/10.1007/978-3-540-24598-8_3

12. Carlson, K., Pasquier, P., Tsang, H.H., Phillips, J., Schiphorst, T., Calvert, T.: Cochoreo: a generative feature in idanceForms for creating novel keyframe animation for choreography. In: Proceedings of the Seventh International Conference on Computational Creativity (2016)

13. Carlson, K., Schiphorst, T., Pasquier, P.: Scuddle: generating movement catalysts for computer-aided choreography. In: ICCC, pp. 123–128 (2011)

14. Crnkovic-Friis, L., Crnkovic-Friis, L.: Generative choreography using deep learning. arXiv preprint arXiv:1605.06921 (2016)

15. Dautenhahn, K.: Human-robot interaction. In: The Encyclopedia of Human-Computer Interaction, 2nd edn. (2013)

16. DeLahunta, S.: The choreographic language agent. In: Conference Proceedings of the 2008 World Dance Alliance Global Summit (2009)

17. Demers, L.P.: The multiple bodies of a machine performer. In: Robots and Art: Exploring an Unlikely Symbiosis, pp. 273–306. Springer, Singapore (2016). https://doi.org/10.1007/978-981-10-0321-9_14

18. Duffy, B.R.: Anthropomorphism and the social robot. Robot. Auton. Syst. 42(3–4), 177–190 (2003)

19. Fdili Alaoui, S., Henry, C., Jacquemin, C.: Physical modelling for interactive installations and the performing arts. Int. J. Perform. Arts Digit. Media 10(2), 159–178 (2014)

20. Haarnoja, T., Zhou, A., Abbeel, P., Levine, S.: Soft actor-critic: off-policy maximum entropy deep reinforcement learning with a stochastic actor. In: International Conference on Machine Learning, pp. 1861–1870. PMLR (2018)

21. Hsieh, C.M., Luciani, A.: Generating dance verbs and assisting computer choreography. In: Proceedings of the 13th Annual ACM International Conference on Multimedia, pp. 774–782 (2005)
22. Hsueh, S., Alaoui, S.F., Mackay, W.E.: Understanding kinaesthetic creativity in dance. In: Proceedings of the 2019 CHI Conference on Human Factors in Computing Systems, pp. 1–12 (2019)
23. Jacob, M., Magerko, B.: Interaction-based authoring for scalable co-creative agents. In: ICCC, pp. 236–243 (2015)
24. Jochum, E., Derks, J.: Tonight we improvise! Real-time tracking for human-robot improvisational dance. In: Proceedings of the 6th International Conference on Movement and Computing, pp. 1–11 (2019)
25. Joshi, M., Chakrabarty, S.: An extensive review of computational dance automation techniques and applications. Proc. R. Soc. A **477**(2251), 20210071 (2021)
26. Kaspersen, E.T., Górny, D., Erkut, C., Palamas, G.: Generative choreographies: the performance dramaturgy of the machine. In: Proceedings of the 15th International Joint Conference on Computer Vision, Imaging and Computer Graphics Theory and Applications-Volume 1: GRAPP, pp. 319–326. SCITEPRESS Digital Library (2020)
27. Lapointe, F.J., Époque, M.: The dancing genome project: generation of a human-computer choreography using a genetic algorithm. In: Proceedings of the 13th Annual ACM International Conference on Multimedia, pp. 555–558 (2005)
28. Larboulette, C., Gibet, S.: A review of computable expressive descriptors of human motion. In: Proceedings of the 2nd International Workshop on Movement and Computing, MOCO 2015, pp. 21–28 (2015)
29. Leach, J., Delahunta, S.: Dance becoming knowledge: designing a digital "body". Leonardo **50**(5), 461–467 (2017)
30. Liu, L., Long, D., Gujrania, S., Magerko, B.: Learning movement through human-computer co-creative improvisation. In: Proceedings of the 6th International Conference on Movement and Computing, pp. 1–8 (2019)
31. Lubart, T.: How can computers be partners in the creative process: classification and commentary on the special issue. Int. J. Hum. Comput. Stud. **63**(4–5), 365–369 (2005)
32. Maletic, V.: Body, Space, Expression: The Development of Rudolf Laban's Movement and Dance Concepts. Approaches to Semiotics, Berlin (1987)
33. McCormick, J., Hutchinson, S., Vincs, K., Vincent, J.B.: Emergent behaviour: learning from an artificially intelligent performing software agent. In: ISEA 2015: Proceedings of the 21st International Symposium on Electronic Art, pp. 1–4 (2015)
34. McCormick, J., Vincs, K., Nahavandi, S., Creighton, D.: Learning to dance with a human. ISEA International, Australian Network for Art & Technology, University of Sydney, January 2013
35. McCormick, J., Vincs, K., Nahavandi, S., Creighton, D., Hutchison, S.: Teaching a digital performing agent: artificial neural network and hidden Markov model for recognising and performing dance movement. In: Proceedings of the 2014 International Workshop on Movement and Computing, pp. 70–75 (2014)
36. Mourot, L., Hoyet, L., Le Clerc, F., Schnitzler, F., Hellier, P.: A survey on deep learning for skeleton-based human animation. In: Computer Graphics Forum. Wiley (2021)
37. Von Laban, R.: Modern Educational Dance, 3rd edn. McDonald & Evans, London (1975)

Painting with Evolutionary Algorithms

Danny Dijkzeul[1] , Nielis Brouwer[1] , Iris Pijning[1] , Levi Koppenhol[1] ,
and Daan van den Berg[2(✉)]

[1] Master Information Studies, Informatics Institute,
University of Amsterdam, Amsterdam, The Netherlands
me@ddijkzeul.nl
[2] Yamasan Science and Education Master Information Studies,
Universiteit van Amsterdam, Amsterdam, The Netherlands
daan@yamasan.nl

Abstract. A fixed number of brush strokes images are initialized on
a canvas, their position, size, rotation, colour, stroke type and drawing index all randomly chosen. These attributes are then modified by
stochastic hillClimbing, simulated annealing or the plant propagation
algorithm, approximating a target image ever closer.

Simulated annealing showed the best performance, followed by hill-
Climbing; the plant propagation algorithm performed worst. Finally, the
distribution of the attributes of the brush strokes shows us that there
appears to be a preference for smaller brush strokes, and strokes of the
fourth type.

Keywords: Evolutionary algorithms · Plant propagation algorithm ·
Computational creativity · HillClimbing · Simulated annealing · Brush
strokes

1 Introduction

"Vague" might be the best qualification of the boundaries on the field of computational creativity. In one way, it could be considered "the study of building
software that exhibits behavior that would be deemed creative in humans" [10]
such as painting pictures, designing colour symmetry [37], evolutionary enabling
image transition between bitmaps [31,32], creating artistic emergent patterns
based on the feeding behavior of sand-bubbler crabs [36] and non-photorealistic
rendering of images based on digital ant colonies [40]. An effort in generative
poetry comes in the form of PoeTryMe [33,34], and from the blurry intersection of evolutionary algorithms and deep learning comes a project in creative
generation of 3D objects [29].

One of the more unconventional ventures is the interactive online evolutionary platform 'DarwinTunes' [30], in which evaluation by public preference
provides the selection pressure on a population of musical phrases that 'mate'
and mutate, resulting in surprisingly catchy melodies. Another surprising initiative is the deployment of algorithms from collective intelligence. Particle swarm

© The Author(s), under exclusive license to Springer Nature Switzerland AG 2022
T. Martins et al. (Eds.): EvoMUSART 2022, LNCS 13221, pp. 52–67, 2022.
https://doi.org/10.1007/978-3-031-03789-4_4

Fig. 1. Paintings used in this experiment from top left, clockwise: *Composition with Red, Yellow, and Blue* (1930, Piet Mondriaan), *The Kiss* (1908, Gustav Klimt), *Portrait of J.S. Bach* (1746, Elias Gottlieb Haussmann), *Mona Lisa* (1503, Leonardo da Vinci), *Convergence* (1952, Jackson Pollock), *The Persistence of Memory* (1931, Salvador Dali) and *The Starry Night* (1889, Vincent van Gogh).

optimization is used for procedural landscape generation based on input images [5, 27], and ant (colony optimization) algorithms for creating art using circle patterns [14, 23, 43] or rendering watercolour-like sketches of original images [16, 17].

Despite this wide variety of computational endeavours, a relatively popular topic ever seems to be the approximation of paintings (mostly Mona Lisa, in fact) by geometric shapes, such as circles or polygons [6, 7, 12, 35]. Often accomplished by some form of iterated optimization algorithm like simulated annealing or a genetic algorithm, an imposing question remains: is this actually 'computational creativity', or is it something else? Surely, these algorithms engage in *re*creation, not 'true' creativity, do they? Again, we are stroddling along the vague boundaries of the field, and one answer could be that the created images of these studies are *artistic byproducts* of an otherwise rigorous optimization task.

So that is the approach we will take in this paper: a rigorous, functional and replicable case study in comparative algorithmic behaviour. We will be recreating paintings by optimally arranging a limited number of brush strokes, an approach inspired on the work by Anastasia Opara [1]. From a fixed number of initially random brush strokes, three evolutionary algorithms (hillClimbing, simulated annealing and the plant propagation algorithm) will approximate a target image by iteratively improving the brush strokes' parameters. In the end, the contribution will be an assessment of the algorithms' performances, a new approach to the tortoise-and-hare situation, and a resultwise comparison to a closely related problem on image approximation. Oh, and we'll also render some visually appealing images which could be labeled as 'computational creativity' – or simply as 'artistic byproducts' of the optimization process (Fig. 2).

The three optimization algorithms for the task are related but also different. A basic hillClimber (also known as 'local search') repetitively makes a single mutation on a brush stroke constellation, but reverts it if no improvement is made. Contrarily, its cousin simulated annealing will also accept deteriorative mutations, with ever lower probability, as it 'cools down' through the iterative process. It is more then just a metaphor; simulated annealing envelops the *Boltzmann factor*, a true physics constant describing the movement of atoms in liquid metal. As the metallurgic process of annealing is nothing short of striving towards a metal's minimum energy configurations, it really challenges the vague boundary between physics and computational science [44] (also see Section 4.1 in Chopard & Tomassini's book [9]). The algorithm has a long history of success on domains such as mining, job shop scheduling, water distribution network design, and the traveling salesman problem [11, 25, 28, 45].

The third and final algorithm is the population-based plant propagation algorithm (PPA), whose central paradigm is crossoverless reproduction, whereby fitter individuals produce more offspring with smaller mutations, and unfitter individuals produce fewer offspring with larger mutations [38, 46] (for a succinct technical explanation, see Vrielink's work [47, 48]). Although the algorithm is relatively new, it has seen numerous applications in diverse areas like continuous optimization [46] and generating hard-to-solve problem instances for an NP-complete problem [41, 42]. Some more practical implementations include chemical plant control [38], nurse rostering [24], university timetabling [21], and the traveling salesman problem [39], but it should be noted that these three studies (also) include differently operating PPA-variants – another reminder that we should be careful with algorithmic namegiving. An extension into the subdiscipline of multiobjective optimization has been put forward in a number of studies by Eric Fraga [18–20].

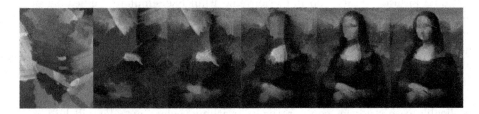

Fig. 2. A random constellation of 250 random brush strokes gets rearranged with simulated annealing to approximate the target image "Mona Lisa". An animation of the process is available online [2].

Together, these three algorithms are identical to those described in paintings from polygons (PFP), an optimization problem that approximates target images with polygons (instead of brush strokes) [35]. It should still be noted that our parametrization of simulated annealing is (necessarily) different from PFP, but the numbers of brush strokes in this study is equal to the numbers of polygons in PFP, facilitating some sort of 'compositional comparison'. The target images are also identical.

2 Rearranging Brush Strokes

Anastasia Opara's repository supplies four different types of brush strokes, each stored in a 300×300 image in PNG-format (Fig. 3) [1]. Originally white-paint-on-black-canvas stored in 8-bit greyscale values, we enabled colour channels for this study while maintaining the strokes' transparency properties. As the original PNG-images are rather large compared to our 180×240 canvas, the sizes will be limited to between 0.1 and 0.7 times the PNG's dimensions, equivalently between 30×30 pixels and 210×210 pixels. Within the constellation, every brush stroke has six variable attributes:

- The **size** of a brush stroke is a floating point factor between 0.1 and 0.7 on the 300×300 dimensions, which are then rounded to the nearest integer. Practically speaking, the brush stroke images' sizes can vary between 30×30 and 210×210 pixels.
- Every brush stroke has a horizontal and vertical **position** in the constellation, which are integer values between 0 and either 180 or 240, depending on the orientation of the target image (see Fig. 1). The value of *position* denotes the center of the brush stroke image, which as a whole may extend beyond canvas boundaries. Only pixels on the canvas are rendered though.
- Every brush stroke has a **colour**, containing a red, a green and a blue channel, each with an integer value between 0 and 255.
- Every brush stroke has a **rotation**, which is an integer value between −180 and 180 (degrees).
- There are four **brush stroke type**s (see Fig. 3). Each brush stroke has one type, but it can change through mutation.
- All brush strokes are rendered sequentially, starting with **drawing index** 1. Thereby, brush strokes are rendered on top of one another, but partial transparency exerts influence through upper layers.

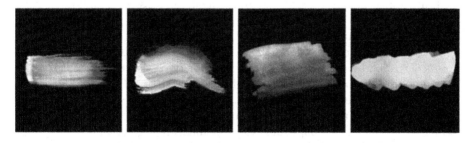

Fig. 3. The four brush stroke images, which are used to approximate the target painting.

In the rendering process, all brush strokes are treated sequentially, starting with drawing index 1. The image corresponding to the type of the brush stroke type is retrieved from memory and then scaled, rotated, coloured and placed on the correct position in the constellation. The transparency of a pixel within the stroke is taken from its greyscale value, where 0 denotes complete transparency and 255 is completely opaque. Depending on the per-pixel transparency, the nonzero image values of the newly placed brush stroke are added to the canvas of earlier rendered strokes, after which the routine will proceed to the next brush stroke in the drawing index.

After rendering all the brush strokes on the canvas, the rendered image is compared to the target image by mean squared error (MSE):

$$\sum_{i=1}^{180\cdot240\cdot3} \frac{(Rendered_i - Target_i)^2}{180 \cdot 240} \tag{1}$$

In this equation, $Rendered_i$ is a red, green or blue channel in a pixel in the rendered image and $Target_i$ is the same channel for the corresponding pixel in the target image. The best possible MSE is zero, in which case the rendered image is identical to the target image. In the worst case, the MSE is $255^2 \cdot 3 = 195075$ which means that all colour channels of the rendered image would be zero, and the corresponding channels in the target image 255 (or vice versa). As such, MSE functions as an objective function for our evolutionary algorithms, which we will discuss next.

3   Algorithms

The optimally achievable MSE for any target painting given n brush strokes is unknown, but the measure does provide an objective value for the constellation's closeness of approximation. For all algorithms, improving the brush stroke constellation means iteratively mutating brush strokes' attributes, where a mutation means changing the value of a single randomly selected brush stroke attribute within its entire range of definition. There are six mutation types, one for each brush stroke attribute:

1. **Change size** randomly selects one brush stroke and assigns a random floating point value $0.1 \leq size < 0.7$ to its $size$-attribute, resulting in a brush stroke between 30×30 and 210×210 pixels.
2. **Move brush stroke** randomly chooses a new x and y position, where $0 \leq x < xMax$ and $0 \leq y < yMax$, for a randomly chosen brush stroke. Here, $xMax$ and $yMax$ are constants valued at either 180 or 240, depending on the target image's orientation (see Fig. 1).
3. **Change colour** randomly selects one brush stroke and randomly assigns three new values $\in [0, 255]$ to its colour channels red, green and blue.
4. **Change rotation** randomly chooses a brush stroke and assigns a new random value $\in [-180, 180]$ to its rotation attribute.

5. **Change brush stroke type** randomly selects one brush stroke and assigns a new random value to its type attribute (Fig. 3), thereby changing its basic shape.
6. **Change drawing index** randomly selects a brush stroke with drawing index i and assigns it a new random value j. If $j < i$, all drawing indices of brush strokes $j < i - 1$ get increased by one to preserve relative order, and decreased if $j > i$.

The **stochastic hillClimber** performs exactly one random mutation on the brush stroke constellation. If the results in an improvement and the MSE is lowered then the mutation is kept, and reverted otherwise. As such, the evolutionary process of this algorithm ensures the constellation will never deteriorate through generations, but it is prone to getting stuck in local optima.

Simulated annealing overcomes that problem by allowing temporary deterioration in the objective value. It is an extension to the stochastic hillClimber, always accepting mutations that lower the MSE. If the objective value increases however, there is *still* a chance for the mutation to be accepted, which is defined by

$$e^{\frac{-\Delta MSE}{T}} \tag{2}$$

where ΔMSE is the increase in error and T is a 'temperature' parameter depending on the number of iterations i the algorithm has performed. Note that as such, the probability to accept a worsening mutation depends not only on the magnitude of the worsening itself, but also on the temperature, which is usually lowered throughout the iterative process. The way in which temperatures get lowered in simulated annealing is known as its *cooling schedule*, and analogously to paintings-from-polygons, we use the cooling function of Geman and Geman [22,35]:

$$T = \frac{c}{ln(1 + i)} \tag{3}$$

In its original form, c is a constant equal to 'the maximum energy barrier to cross', which would in this case be the maximum MSE of 195075. When instantiated correctly, simulated annealing guarantees solution optimality with this cooling schedule. That is indeed as unlikely as it sounds, because the proof requires infinite time, but even in finite time the improvement process is impractically slow for this cooling schedule. However, a study on painting-from-polygons by Redouane Dahmani showed that by simply substituting $c = 1$, the schedule empirically outperformed eight other cooling schedules [12]. With a temperature so low, one could naturally wonder whether these problems couldn't simply be hillClimbed, but Dahmani's study left this question unanswered. As an unexpected bonus, the results from this experiment *do* provide a partial answer.

Third and finally, the **plant propagation algorithm (PPA)** is the only population based algorithm in this study. Instead of holding one brush stroke constellation like in simulated annealing and hillClimbing, PPA holds multiple individuals (*popSize* = 30 in this study). From their random initialization, all individuals get their objective value (MSE) assigned through rendering the brush stroke constellation. Then, the population is sorted in ascending order, after which the objective values are normalized between 0 and 1:

$$f_i = \frac{MSE_{max} - MSE_i}{MSE_{max} - MSE_{min}} \tag{4}$$

in which f_i is the individual's objective value, MSE_{max} and MSE_{min} are the maximum and minimum MSE in the population. Slightly uncommon in evolutionary computing, an individuals' objective value and its fitness are different values in PPA. For each individual, its fitness value is calculated from its objective value as

$$N_i = \frac{1}{2}(tanh(4 \cdot f_i - 2) + 1) \tag{5}$$

In PPA, fitter individuals produce many offspring with few mutations, and unfitter individuals produce few offspring with many mutations. The number of offspring from an individual is given by

$$n_r = \lceil n_{max} \cdot N_i \cdot r_1 \rceil \tag{6}$$

in which n_{max} is the maximum number of offspring that can be created; in this study $n_{max} = 5$, which is default for PPA, and r_1 is a random value between 0 and 1. Then, the created offspring will be mutated, the number of mutations n_{mut} for each individual is given by

$$n_{mut} = \lceil 100 \cdot \frac{1}{n_{max}} \cdot (1 - N_i) \cdot r_2 \rceil \tag{7}$$

where r_2 is again a random value between 0 and 1, and 100 is an arbitrarily chosen value. The mutations on the new individuals are executed, changing the brush stroke constellations, after which the individuals are rendered, and their MSEs are calculated as objective values.

Table 1. The execution time in hours for a single run per number of brush strokes, averaged over all 7 paintings and all 5 runs.

Brush strokes	4	25	75	125	175	250
HillClimber	2:48	15:48	27:54	39:42	53:06	74:30
Simulated annealing	2:36	15:42	28:00	37:30	48:35	69:48
Plant propagation	3:24	9:42	21:18	32:06	44:06	67:12
Average	3:00	13:42	25:42	36:24	48:36	70:30

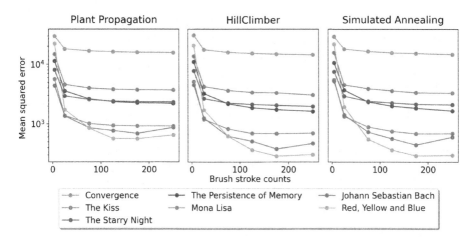

Fig. 4. The mean squared error for all paintings with varying brush stroke counts, averaged over the 5 runs. Simulated annealing outperforms the other algorithms on 34 of 42 instances.

Finally, the parent population and offspring population are merged, sorted, and the best $popSize = 30$ are kept; the rest is discarded. This survivor selection method, known as 'plus-selection', is *elitist*, meaning that the best solution quality in the population cannot deteriorate throughout the generations. This process is repeated until a preset number of function evaluations is met, which in this case is 10^6 for the entire experiment.

4   Experiment and Results

The seven target bitmaps (paintings from Fig. 1) are approximated by five runs of 10^6 evaluations for 4, 25, 75, 125,175 and 250 brush strokes for all three algorithms. Thereby, all experimental parameters are the same as in paintings-from-polygons, even the numbers of strokes correspond exactly to the numbers of polygons. In the end, the entire experiment held $7 \cdot 5 \cdot 6 \cdot 3 = 630$ runs of 10^6 evaluations each, totalling 630,000,000 function evaluations, a number that turned out to be important. The time to complete a single run varied between 1 h and 33 min (4 brush strokes, hillClimber on Haussmann's Portrait of J.S. Bach) to almost 141 h (250 brush strokes, hillClimber on Mondriaan's painting). There are differences between paintings though; for 250 brush strokes, averaged algorithmic runtimes varied from 63 to 65 h per painting, except for the Mondriaan, which took almost 84 h for a single run to complete.

Runtimes per algorithm averaged over all paintings and runs are roughly proportionate to the number of brush strokes (Table 1). The dependency is nearly linear, more or less algorithm independent, and increases with ≈0.24 h (≈15 min) for every brush stroke added to the constellation. We suspect the average brush stroke size might play a critical role in these ginormous runtimes, because every single pixel needs to be rendered individually. So in terms of evolutionary computing, it is probably the evaluation that swallows up the vast majority of computing resources. Having said that, it is unclear how and why simulated annealing runs faster than the algorithmically simpler hillClimber in most of the cases. All 630 runs were executed on Sara's multi-core supercomputer SURFsara. On a single-core computer, the experiment would have taken well over a year to complete, even without interruptions. The source code, animations and results are publicly available [2,4].

If we compare the algorithms on quality performance, simulated annealing outperforms the hillClimber and plant propagation in 34 out of 42 combinations of target image and number of strokes, while hillClimber performed best 7 times, and PPA only once. This result is somewhat surprising, because in the closely related PFP study, it was hillClimber that performed best. The quality of approximation depends on the number of brush strokes, but only partially. The MSE clearly flattens from 125 strokes onwards (Fig. 4), suggesting that more brush strokes do not necessarily add to the quality of the approximation. All in all, *Convergence* is by far the worst approximated painting, which might be due to its 'lack of structure'. The best MSE on this painting is 15,780 for PPA,

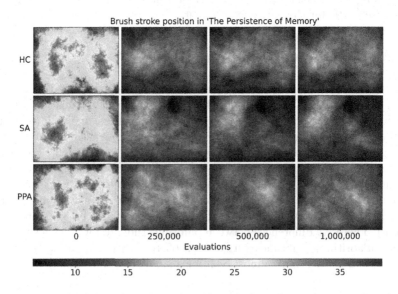

Fig. 5. Heatmap of the number of brush strokes which are located at a pixel in the rendered constellation for *the Persistence of Memory*, using 250 brush strokes, for all three algorithms hillClimber, simulated annealing, and the plant propagation algorithm.

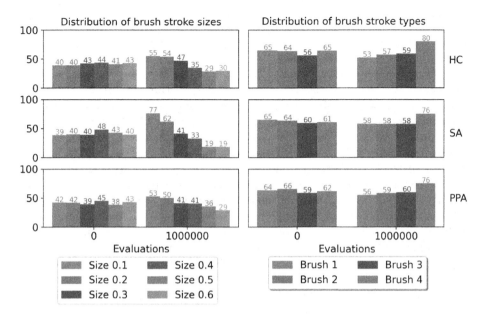

Fig. 6. Distribution of brush stroke size (left) and brush stroke type (right) at the beginning and the end of a run for *the Persistence of Memory* for all three algorithms, using 250 paint brush strokes.

15,095 for the hillClimber and 14,769 for simulated annealing. The order from best performing painting to worst performing painting is identical for all three algorithms: Convergence, The Kiss, Starry Night, Persistence of Memory, Mona Lisa, Portrait of Bach, Red Yellow & Blue. In the paintings-from-polygons study, the order was exactly this, with the exception of their ill-performing simulated annealing runs.

To gain some insight into the fundamental changes of the brush stroke constellation, we assess its properties before and after the run, averaged over the 5 runs with 250 brush strokes for all three algorithms. For discutatory purposes, we will show the results on *Persistence of Memory*, which we find representative. Results on the other target images can be found in our online repository [4]. We skip statistics on the colour attribute which closely depends on the target image, and on the drawing index, which always ranges from 1 to 250 in this setting.

Table 2. The parameters and MSE of the fitted function $MSE(eval) = a * (eval - b)^{-c} + d$ per algorithm, averaged over 5 runs with 250 brush strokes on the *Mona Lisa* (also see plots in Fig. 7).

$a * (eval - b)^{-c} + d$	a	b	c	d	MSE
HillClimber	408,304	290	0.57	653	123.23
Plant propagation	2,831,391	−2228	0.66	605	770.52
Simulated annealing	396,639	88	0.54	480	819.60

The first compelling observation is the preference for smaller **brush stroke sizes** (size ≤ 0.3) after 10^6 evaluations (Fig. 6). The hillClimber starts off with 123 small brush strokes, which increases to 156 (+23%) throughout the runs. For PPA, the difference between start (121) and end (144) is a bit smaller (+19%), but simulated annealing, the best performing algorithm, progresses from 119 small brush strokes to 180, a steep increase of over 51%. Combined with the positional results (Fig. 5), it is tempting to think that the best performing algorithm 'prefers' small strokes on detailed features in the target image.

When we observe the **brush stroke position** on the rendered image (Fig. 5), we see an intuitively interesting difference between the algorithms. Colour intensities in the heatmap denote the number of brush stroke pixels at any coordinate. From the start of the run, there are multiple overlapping brush strokes, likely due to the initial abundance of relatively large strokes (Fig. 6). However, not only do the brush strokes shrink as runs progress, they also tend to localize more, in the case of simulated annealing on the clock details on the left side of the painting. PPA and hillClimber both appear to be much less concentrated, instead settling on somewhat more diffuse patterns.

Five out of the seven target images show similar distributions of **brush stroke rotations** at the start and the end of their evolutionary runs. Two exceptions that show an increase of horizontally oriented brush strokes (either between -120 and $-60°$, or the 60 and 120 mirror image) are *The Kiss* (from 80 to 98, +23%) and *Composition with Red, Yellow, and Blue* (44 to 56, +27%). This might be due to properties of the target bitmaps, but the effect is relatively inconsistent. Across target images the effect is 10% or lower, and never shared over all three algorithms.

When looking at the evolution of **brush stroke types** through runs of all three algorithms with 250 brush strokes on all 7 target images, a remarkable change occurs (Fig. 6; see also Fig. 3). Starting off at around 62.5 ($\approx 25\%$) for all four strokes, as is expected from the random initialization, we see an average increase to 76 occurrences (+22%) of stroke type 4, while occurrences of the other stroke types decreased by -2.4% to -12%. The effect was strongest in hillClimber, with an average increase from 64 to 80 (+25%). Only in *Mona Lisa* with simulated annealing, type 4 was not the most prevalent which is interesting, considering it is the best performing algorithm. Exact causes are unknown, but opacity might play a role, as type 4 is by far the least transparent of the four.

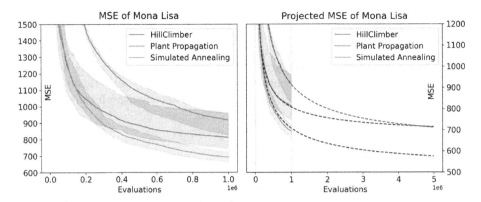

Fig. 7. The left image indicates the maximum, minimum, and average MSE of five runs for the hillClimber, simulated annealing and plant propagation on the *Mona Lisa* target image with 250 brush strokes. The right subfigure shows dashed lines which indicate a fit on our gathered data for the *Mona Lisa*. The grey dotted vertical lines indicate the start and end of our data, after these lines an extrapolation is made for the further evaluation counts.

5 Extrapolation

When comparing evolutionary algorithms in single runs, it is quite common to find one algorithm improving fast and another slowly, but *eventually* outperforming the first algorithm. This phenomenon was baptized as the 'tortoise-and-hare situation' by Eiben and Smith [15], and our three algorithms exhibit exactly this behaviour. In this study, the hare (hillClimber) initially improves very fast, but is eventually overtaken by the tortoise (PPA). A similar situation for exactly these two algorithms has been witnessed before in the university course timetabling problem [21].

As an experimental approach, we will try to characterize this behaviour, and make a hypothetical forward projection. Therefore, we separately conducted 5 runs with 250 brush strokes for all three algorithms on *Mona Lisa*. In this case however, we logged the best individual in *every* evaluation, resulting in one million evaluation points per algorithm per run. Through these 5 million data points, we used Eq. 8 to characterize a 'typical run' with these experimental specifics for each of the three algorithms.

$$MSE(eval) = a * (eval - b)^{-c} + d \tag{8}$$

Here, *eval* is the evaluation number whilst the others are free parameters (see Table 2 and Fig. 7), which are fit using the python-scipy package [3]. The characterization starts at 1500 evaluations to eliminate some initial volatility but naturally extend beyond our 10^6 empirical evaluations, enabling a ground hypothesis about future progress of these algorithms.

Solving an equalization of these functions suggests that PPA would actually outperform the hillClimber after 4,362,099 evaluations on average, for a run on Mona Lisa with 250 brush stokes. At this point, both algorithms will be at $MSE \approx 721$. Simulated annealing however, will be at $MSE \approx 577$, still outperforming the other two. Interestingly, if these fits do indeed hold predicative powers, the d-parameter projects an asymptote denoting *the best achievable* MSE for an algorithm in this experimental context (Table 2). Hypothetically assuming the validity of the fitted functions, PPA would *never* outperform simulated annealing in this run, no matter its length.

6   Some Final Remarks

The resounding success of simulated annealing for this type of problem is surely noteworthy [35]. In Dahmani's study, the algorithm had shown to greatly depend on its cooling schedule, and whether further improvement for this problem is still possible is as yet unknown [12]. PPA performed a little worse than expected, and we anecdotally witnessed that in many cases, only offspring with just a single mutation survived the selection process. Regarding that the algorithm creates 88 children per generation, this might account for its role as the tortoise. Furthermore, PPA might still be parameterized more extensively, possibly leading to better results [8,13,26]. The flattening performance through numbers of brush strokes yield its own questions. Brush strokes with higher drawing indices (drawn last) appear to have more impact on the final result, which is possibly related

Fig. 8. The resulting 250 brush stroke images after 10^6 evaluations for different algorithms. From top left, clockwise: *Composition with Red, Yellow, and Blue* (hillClimber) *The Kiss* (simulated annealing), *Portrait of J.S. Bach* (hillClimber), *Mona Lisa* (PPA), *Convergence* (simulated annealing), *The Persistence of Memory* (simulated annealing) and *The Starry Night* (PPA).

to the limited transparency of the stroke PNGs themselves. Especially telling in this context is the movie clip of the optimization process [2]. A provisional hypothesis might be that more than 250 brush strokes simply doesn't add to the quality of the approximations under these experimental parameters (Fig. 4).

Yet, one of the biggest lessons learned was the cost of the evaluation function, that took up the vast majority of computational power. Though it could be fascinating to perform a run with more than a million evaluations to further investigate the tortoise-and-hare situation, that is practically undoable for this problem just from the cost of continually rendering brush stroke constellations. Although these optimization algorithms are extremely fast and efficient, their accompanying evaluation functions might very *very* well be less so.

References

1. Anastasia opara's "Genetic Drawing". https://github.com/anopara/genetic-drawing. Accessed 21 Feb 2022
2. Animated brush stroke optimization from this paper. https://drive.google.com/file/d/12IvkBGig7xCrSivJsgusunCeRRJe8G4Q/view. Accessed 21 Feb 2022
3. Scipy package. https://docs.scipy.org/doc/scipy/reference/generated/scipy.optimize.curve_fit.html. Accessed 21 Feb 2022
4. Source code belonging to this study. https://github.com/paintingbrushstroke/paintings. Accessed 21 Feb 2022
5. de Andrade, D., Fachada, N., Fernandes, C.M., Rosa, A.C.: Generative art with swarm landscapes. Entropy **22**(11), 1284 (2020)
6. van den Berg, D.: Simplified paintings-from-polygons is NP-hard. In: Evo* LBA's 2020, pp. 15–18. Springer, Cham (2020)
7. Berg, J., Berggren, N.G.A., Borgeteien, S.A., Jahren, C.R.A., Sajid, A., Nichele, S.: Evolved art with transparent, overlapping, and geometric shapes. In: Bach, K., Ruocco, M. (eds.) NAIS 2019. CCIS, vol. 1056, pp. 3–15. Springer, Cham (2019). https://doi.org/10.1007/978-3-030-35664-4_1
8. Brouwer, N.: Survivor selection in the plant propagation algorithm. Master thesis (2021). https://scripties.uba.uva.nl/search?id=723225
9. Chopard, B., Tomassini, M.: An Introduction to Metaheuristics for Optimization. Natural Computing Series, 1st edn. Springer, Cham (2018). https://doi.org/10.1007/978-3-319-93073-2
10. Colton, S., Lopez de Mantaras, R., Stock, O.: Computational creativity: coming of age. AI Mag. **30**(3), 11 (2009). https://doi.org/10.1609/aimag.v30i3.2257
11. Cunha, M.D.C., Sousa, J.: Water distribution network design optimization: simulated annealing approach. J. Water Resour. Plann. Manag. **125**(4), 215–221 (1999)
12. Dahmani, R., Boogmans, S., Meijs, A., Van den Berg, D.: Paintings-from-polygons: simulated annealing. In: International Conference on Computational Creativity (ICCC 2020) (2020)
13. De Jonge, M., Van den Berg, D.: Plant propagation parameterization: offspring & population size. In: Evo* LBA's 2020, vol. 2, pp. 1–4. Springer, Cham (2020)
14. Dorigo, M., Di Caro, G.: Ant colony optimization: a new meta-heuristic. In: Proceedings of the 1999 Congress on Evolutionary Computation-CEC99 (Cat. No. 99TH8406), vol. 2, pp. 1470–1477. IEEE (1999)

15. Eiben, A.E., Smith, J.E.: Working with Evolutionary Algorithms, p. 152. Springer, Heidelberg (2003). https://doi.org/10.1007/978-3-662-05094-1_14

16. Fernandes, C.M., Mora, A.M., Merelo, J.J., Rosa, A.C.: Photorealistic rendering with an ant algorithm. In: Madani, K., Correia, A.D., Rosa, A., Filipe, J. (eds.) Computational Intelligence. SCI, vol. 577, pp. 63–77. Springer, Cham (2015). https://doi.org/10.1007/978-3-319-11271-8_5

17. Fernandes, C., Mora, A.M., Merelo, J.J., Ramos, V., Laredo, J.L.J.: KohonAnts: a self-organizing ant algorithm for clustering and pattern classification. arXiv preprint arXiv:0803.2695 (2008). Accessed 21 Feb 2022

18. Fraga, E.S.: An example of multi-objective optimization for dynamic processes. Chem. Eng. Trans. (AIDIC) **74**, 601–606 (2019)

19. Fraga, E.S.: Multiple simultaneous solution representations in a population based evolutionary algorithm. arXiv preprint arXiv:2106.05096 (2021). Accessed 21 Feb 2022

20. Fraga, E.: Fresa: a plant propagation algorithm for black-box single and multiple objective optimization. Int. J. Eng. Technol. Inform. **2**(4), 110–111 (2021)

21. Geleijn, R., van der Meer, M., van der Post, Q., van den Berg, D.: The plant propagation algorithm on timetables: first results. In: EVO* LBA's 2019, p. 2. Springer, Cham (2019)

22. Geman, S., Geman, D.: Stochastic relaxation, gibbs distributions, and the Bayesian restoration of images. IEEE Trans. Pattern Anal. Mach. Intell. PAMI **6**(6), 721–741 (1984). https://doi.org/10.1109/TPAMI.1984.4767596

23. Greenfield, G., Machado, P.: Ant-and ant-colony-inspired alife visual art. Artif. Life **21**(3), 293–306 (2015)

24. Haddadi, S.: Plant propagation algorithm for nurse rostering. Int. J. Innov. Comput. Appl. **11**(4), 204–215 (2020)

25. Johnson, D.S.: Local optimization and the traveling salesman problem. In: Paterson, M.S. (ed.) ICALP 1990. LNCS, vol. 443, pp. 446–461. Springer, Heidelberg (1990). https://doi.org/10.1007/BFb0032050

26. de Jonge, M., van den Berg, D.: Parameter sensitivity patterns in the plant propagation algorithm. In: Proceedings of the 12th International Joint Conference on Computational Intelligence (2020), IJCCI 2020, April 2020. https://doi.org/10.5220/0010134300920099

27. Kennedy, J., Eberhart, R.: Particle swarm optimization. In: Proceedings of ICNN'95-International Conference on Neural Networks, vol. 4, pp. 1942–1948. IEEE (1995)

28. Kumral, M., Dowd, P.: A simulated annealing approach to mine production scheduling. J. Oper. Res. Soc. **56**(8), 922–930 (2005)

29. Lehman, J., Risi, S., Clune, J.: Creative generation of 3D objects with deep learning and innovation engines. In: Proceedings of the 7th International Conference on Computational Creativity, pp. 180–187. Citeseer (2016)

30. MacCallum, R.M., Mauch, M., Burt, A., Leroi, A.M.: Evolution of music by public choice. Proc. Natl. Acad. Sci. **109**(30), 12081–12086 (2012). https://doi.org/10.1073/pnas.1203182109

31. Neumann, A., Alexander, B., Neumann, F.: Evolutionary image transition using random walks. In: Correia, J., Ciesielski, V., Liapis, A. (eds.) EvoMUSART 2017. LNCS, vol. 10198, pp. 230–245. Springer, Cham (2017). https://doi.org/10.1007/978-3-319-55750-2_16

32. Neumann, A., Alexander, B., Neumann, F.: Evolutionary image transition and painting using random walks. Evol. Comput. **28**(4), 643–675 (2020)

33. Gonçalo Oliveira, H., Cardoso, A.: Poetry generation with PoeTryMe. In: Besold, T.R., Schorlemmer, M., Smaill, A. (eds.) Computational Creativity Research: Towards Creative Machines. ATM, vol. 7, pp. 243–266. Atlantis Press, Paris (2015). https://doi.org/10.2991/978-94-6239-085-0_12

34. Oliveira, H.G., Mendes, T., Boavida, A., Nakamura, A., Ackerman, M.: Co-PoeTryMe: interactive poetry generation. Cogn. Syst. Res. **54**, 199–216 (2019)

35. Paauw, M., van den Berg, D.: Paintings, polygons and plant propagation. In: Ekárt, A., Liapis, A., Castro Pena, M.L. (eds.) EvoMUSART 2019. LNCS, vol. 11453, pp. 84–97. Springer, Cham (2019). https://doi.org/10.1007/978-3-030-16667-0_6

36. Richter, H.: Visual art inspired by the collective feeding behavior of sand-bubbler crabs. In: Liapis, A., Romero Cardalda, J.J., Ekárt, A. (eds.) EvoMUSART 2018. LNCS, vol. 10783, pp. 1–17. Springer, Cham (2018). https://doi.org/10.1007/978-3-319-77583-8_1

37. Richter, H.: Designing color symmetry in stigmergic art. Mathematics **9**(16), 1882 (2021)

38. Salhi, A., Fraga, E.S.: Nature-inspired optimisation approaches and the new plant propagation algorithm. In: Proceeding of The International Conference on Numerical Analysis and Optimization (ICeMATH2011), pp. K21–K28 (2011)

39. Selamoğlu, B.İ, Salhi, A.: The plant propagation algorithm for discrete optimisation: the case of the travelling salesman problem. In: Yang, X.-S. (ed.) Nature-Inspired Computation in Engineering. SCI, vol. 637, pp. 43–61. Springer, Cham (2016). https://doi.org/10.1007/978-3-319-30235-5_3

40. Semet, Y., O'Reilly, U.-M., Durand, F.: An interactive artificial ant approach to non-photorealistic rendering. In: Deb, K. (ed.) GECCO 2004. LNCS, vol. 3102, pp. 188–200. Springer, Heidelberg (2004). https://doi.org/10.1007/978-3-540-24854-5_17

41. Sleegers, J., van den Berg, D.: Looking for the hardest Hamiltonian cycle problem instances. In: IJCCI, pp. 40–48 (2020)

42. Sleegers, J., van den Berg, D.: Plant propagation & hard Hamiltonian graphs. In: Evo* LBA's 2020, pp. 10–13. Springer, Cham (2020)

43. Urbano, P.: The *T. albipennis* sand painting artists. In: Di Chio, C., et al. (eds.) EvoApplications 2011. LNCS, vol. 6625, pp. 414–423. Springer, Heidelberg (2011). https://doi.org/10.1007/978-3-642-20520-0_42

44. Van Laarhoven, P.J., Aarts, E.H.: Simulated annealing. In: Simulated Annealing: Theory and Applications, pp. 7–15. Springer, Cham (1987). https://doi.org/10.1007/978-94-015-7744-1_2

45. Van Laarhoven, P.J., Aarts, E.H., Lenstra, J.K.: Job shop scheduling by simulated annealing. Oper. Res. **40**(1), 113–125 (1992)

46. Vrielink, W., Van den Berg, D.: Fireworks algorithm versus plant propagation algorithm. In: IJCCI 2019 - Proceedings of the 11th International Joint Conference on Computational Intelligence (February), pp. 101–112 (2019). https://doi.org/10.5220/0008169401010112

47. Vrielink, W., Van den Berg, D.: A dynamic parameter for the plant propagation algorithm. In: Evo* LBA's 2021, no. March, pp. 5–9. Springer, Cham (2021)

48. Vrielink, W., Van den Berg, D.: Parameter control for the plant propagation algorithm. In: Evo* LBA's 2021, no. March, pp. 1–4. Springer, Cham (2021)

Evolutionary Construction of Stories that Combine Several Plot Lines

Pablo Gervás$^{(\boxtimes)}$, Eugenio Concepción , and Gonzalo Méndez

Facultad de Informática, Universidad Complutense de Madrid, 28040 Madrid, Spain
{pgervas,econcepc,gmendez}@ucm.es
http://nil.fdi.ucm.es

Abstract. Although the narrative structure of common entertainment products like Hollywood movies or TV series is generally composed of a number of different plot lines combined into a single narrative discourse, efforts on computational modeling of story generation have to this point focused mostly on the construction of stories with a single plot line. The present paper explores an evolutionary solution to the task of building a story that combines more than one plot line into a single linear discourse. This requires: a set of knowledge resources that capture the main features that influence the decisions involved, a representation suitable for evolutionary treatment for discourses with several plot lines, and a set of fitness functions based on metrics related to the quality of the resulting discourses. The proposed solution produces populations of stories with elaborate discourses that combine several subplots.

Keywords: Story generation · Multiplot stories · Evolutionary approach

1 Introduction

The narrative structure of common entertainment products like Hollywood movies or TV series is generally composed of a number of different plot lines combined into a single narrative discourse. There are very clear mechanisms at work in putting multiple plot lines together into a successful narrative discourse in this fashion, yet efforts on computational modeling of story generation have to this point focused mostly on the construction of stories with a single plot line. This is in part due to the application of a traditional rule of engineering – do not consider complex versions of the problem until the simple versions have been solved – and in part due to oversight of another such rule – if the artifact you are trying to build is made up of several parts, the construction process should

This paper has been partially funded by the projects CANTOR: Automated Composition of Personal Narratives as an aid for Occupational Therapy based on Reminescence, Grant. No. PID2019-108927RB-I00 (Spanish Ministry of Science and Innovation) and InVITAR-IA: Infraestructuras para la Visibilización, Integración y Transferencia de Aplicaciones y Resultados de Inteligencia Artificial, UCM Grant. No. FEI-EU-17-23.

T. Martins et al. (Eds.): EvoMUSART 2022, LNCS 13221, pp. 68–83, 2022.
https://doi.org/10.1007/978-3-031-03789-4_5

understand what such elementary parts are and how they come together. The present paper explores an evolutionary solution to the task of building a story that combines more than one plot line into a single linear discourse. This requires a set of knowledge resources that capture the main features that influence the decisions involved – namely a set of basic plot lines as sequences of scenes, each annotated with the characters that take part, the narrative roles they play, and basic semantics such as when characters are born, die, or fall in love. A representation suitable for evolutionary treatment is proposed for discourses with several plot lines, and a set of fitness functions are defined based on metrics related to the quality of the resulting discourses are proposed. The solution defined over these elements produces populations of stories with elaborate discourses that combine several subplots.

The combination of several plot lines into a discourse is more complex than a simple weaving. Plot lines are not actually independent streams of narrative discourse that get combined together into a complex fabric: the character sets from different subplots combined into a story do not remain distinct, they may be merged so that the same character in the overall story often plays different roles in more than one of the subplots. This point is addressed explicitly in the solution proposed in this paper. The process we want to model involves an additional operation of merging (some of the characters in) the narrative threads for the different plotlines by instantiating their narrative roles (either main or secondary) with the set of characters for the overall plot.

2   Related Work

Three topics are considered relevant for this paper: prior solutions for plot line combination, quantitative metrics for stories, and evolutionary approaches to creation of narratives of some kind.

2.1   Plot Line Combination

In recent years there has been an increase in the number of research efforts that consider the construction of stories with more than one plot line. In reviewing research efforts on this topic, we have opted for unifying the terminology under an abstract concept of *plot line* considered as a sequence of plot-relevant elements that make sense in the order in which they appear in the story, and linked by at least a shared set of protagonist and secondary characters. We will refer to the plot-relevant elements in a plot line as *scenes*. When more than one plot line are involved in a larger story, each of these plot lines is considered a *subplot* of the story.

Two different approaches have been followed to create multi-plotline stories. In the first one, the story is created by adding scenes incrementally, switching between different plot lines so that each of the plot lines involved is also dynamically constructed. In the second one, a set of existing plot lines is considered at the start, and the construction process involves deciding how these plot lines will be combined in the discourse for the final story.

Under the first approach, Porteous et al. [16] describe an interactive story-telling system that builds stories in a way that the resulting story will show multiple interleaved plot lines. Their system relies on a plan-based approach that takes input parameters that govern the number of plot lines that should be involved in the final version and how much of the final story should taken up by each plot line.

Under the second approach, systems first compile a set of narrative threads from a given source and then search for possible combinations of them that make a story. Fay [3] constructs multi-plotline stories by combining together narrative threads for specific types of characters found in a given story request, so that main characters in the story request are bound to secondary characters in threads for other characters and the elements from each thread are combined into a consistent overall timeline. The Raconteur [6] and StoryFire [5] systems obtain narrative threads from a conceptual description of a chess-game, and builds stories by selecting a *plot schema* to use as a template to be filled in with matching scenes from the available threads. The PlotAssembler system [7] builds stories by combining a set of small spans of narrative discourse called *axes of interest* in ways that interweave their scenes, ensuring that character continuity across scenes is compatible with probabilities mined from a corpus of prior stories. The work of Concepción et al. [2] explores baseline solutions for weaving together a set of plot lines into stories. The plot lines considered include additional information on roles played by the characters. The set of weaving procedures includes some based on existing literary techniques and some presented as baselines for computational approaches to the task.

2.2   Computational Metrics for Stories

Over the past few years a body of computational metrics for stories has been developed. As the set of features that might be considered in a story is vast, these metrics generally focus on particular aspects that are relevant for specific purposes. When the goal is to invent a new story, metrics relevant to the purpose focus on aspects that may be related to originality: story novelty [14], similarity between stories [9] and correlations between easy-to-measure features in the stories and the creativity attributed to them by human judges [20].

More recent work addresses the evaluation of multi-plotline stories specifically. An attempt at formative qualitative evaluation of multi-plotline stories was carried out in [2]. A group of human judges were asked to consider the quality of 10 examples of multi-plotline stories, and to identify specific features that they considered positive or negative contributions to the perceived value of the story. A number of interesting conclusions were drawn. First, the most detrimental feature to perceived story quality was the existence of semantic inconsistencies in the story, such as characters that keep taking part in the story after being dead. Second, positive judgments often involved identification of characteristics of the story that were optional rather than necessary, such as the existence of an overarching plot, or the fact that one subplot was inserted fully within another. In [8], the qualitative analyses presented as part of the formative evaluation were distilled into a set of metrics designed to capture them in a numerical form. These metrics were designed to respond to the set of features that human judges were seen to focus on when asked to assess multi-plotline stories, and to translate the judgments made onto numerical scores.

2.3   Evolutionary Construction of Narratives

Without pretending to be exhaustive, this section reviews some of the existing efforts to generate narratives by means of evolutionary solutions in terms of two different aspects: which elements they combine and what type of fitness function they employ.

In terms of the elements that are combined to make stories, McIntyre and Lapata [13] present a plot generator that builds a plot from the set of entities appearing in a sentence provided by the user. For each entity in the sentence the system retrieves a plot line from a knowledge based automatically extracted previously, and creates a space of possible stories involving the given entities by merging together these plot lines. This search space is then explored by means of genetic algorithms, using as fitness function a combination of story coherence and story interest. Gómez de Silva and Pérez y Pérez [19] propose a model of story construction that combines the MEXICA existing knowledge-based story generator [15] with the GENCAD evolutionary approach for the adaptation stage in case-based solutions to architectural problems [18]. The story construction model relies on the knowledge-based heuristics of MEXICA to build initial populations and applies the evolutionary approach to refine them. Among the features that the fitness functions are designed to detect are individuals with 'incestuous ancestry', built by applying more than once rules from the same exemplar, which may lead to repetition of events in the output story.

In terms of the fitness functions employed to drive the evolutionary approach, Fredericks and DeVries [4] describe an application of an evolutionary solution driven by novelty search [11] to improve the novelty of procedurally-generated small narratives fragments for text-based games. Kartal et al. [10] use Monte Carlo tree search to drive planning-based narrative generation in support of a interactive framework for user-driven narrative variation. They rely for selection on a combination of the believability of the resulting story and the percentage of the user-defined goals the current story accomplishes. Soares de Lima et al. [12] combine planning with an evolutionary search strategy guided by story arcs to generate quests for games. Candidate quests are constructed by a planner as linear sequences of events or tasks to be accomplished by the player. The evolutionary algorithm chooses among them using a fitness function that builds for each candidate quest the sequence of tensions that arise from it, and scores it based on its match with a target curve of evolving tensions provided by the user.

3   An Evolutionary Multiplot Story Composer

A story built by combining plot lines requires a complex set of decisions: in which order to combine the scenes from the different plot lines and how to merge the characters sets from the different plot lines into a single set of characters for the overall story. The search space of possible solutions is immense. Prior attempts to explore this search space in terms of heuristics for informing the required decisions [2] have shown that stories produced in this way are significantly more rigid in structure than human produced stories. An evolutionary solution based on fitness functions that capture some of the desired features for the output stories may provide efficient means of traversing this search space.

3.1   The Knowledge Resources

The experiments reported in this paper are carried out over a set of plot lines extracted from a compilation of classic plots used in cinema [1]. A subset of these plots have been distilled into a set of *plot templates*, which are formalised knowledge resources that describe the structure of the plot as a sequence of scenes. The set of plot templates currently available is: The Benevolent Outsider, The Creation of Artificial Life, Descent into the Underworld, The Destructive Outsider, Faust, Split Person Comic, Split Person Tragic.

Each *scene* describes the characters that take part, the narrative roles they play, the set of semantic annotations that are used by the system to check consistency, and a template for rendering the scene as text. The narrative roles played by the characters are represented by labels that identify the main characters involved in a given plot – say, Creator and Creature in a Creation of Artificial Life plot, or Tempter and Tempted in a Faust plot. The semantic annotations cover aspects about the meaning of the scene that may affect the perceived consistency of the stories in which they appear. The current version considers the following semantic annotations: whether characters are *created/born or die* in the scene and whether characters *fall in love or out of love*. These semantic annotations allow the definition of metrics to identify situations where narrative roles from different subplots are assigned to the same character in the story, and events affecting the different roles are incompatible – characters dying more than once, or serially falling in love. These metrics are used to inform the fitness function for the evolutionary solution.

Each plot template has a particular character identified as the *protagonist* – this is usually one of the characters playing an important role in the plot.

This set of features emerges from the analysis of a number of multi-plot stories described in [2] and the metrics for automated assessment of quality of multi-plotline stories presented in [8]. The insights from these analyses have identified these features as relevant to the perception of quality of a multi-plotline story.

3.2 Character Fusion and Discourse Planning

The analyses carried out to this point on how multi-plotline stories are put together show that, given a set of subplots to be considered as inputs, there are two different processes that contribute to the final result.

The first process is related to the set of characters that take part in each subplot. For a story to be successful, it appears to be important that the sets of characters involved in each subplot have a non-empty intersection. In operational terms, this is achieved by unifying some character a from subplot A with character b from another subplot B, so that a single character – say *John* – in the story undertakes both the part of character a from subplot A and the part of character b from subplot B. We refer to this operation as *character fusion*. In terms of traditional views on natural language generation [17] this operation is a part of the task of *content determination*, since the nature of subplots is somewhat changed in the process of attributing particular characters to the variables in the corresponding template.

The second process is related to the order in which the scenes from the different subplots are presented in the discourse for the final story. This is known to be crucial to the impact that the story has on the audience, and exploited intentionally by authors to achieve effects such as *suspense* – where presentation of certain information is withheld on purpose – or *cliff-hanger breaks* – where transitions to cover other subplots are made at points where tension is high in the current subplot. In terms of traditional views on natural language generation [17] this operation is a fundamental part of the task of *discourse planning*.

Character fusion and discourse planning are tightly interconnected by the information in the semantic annotations for scenes. A fusion between a character a from one template A and a character b from another template B is only possible if it will not result in a final discourse in which the fused character is seen to behave in an impossible manner – such as being born or dying more than once, or being involved in more than one passionate romance without the fact being addressed by the story.[1] The metrics that inform the fitness function should penalise the scores of stories that incur in this type of inconsistency. Even if none of these extreme inconsistencies occur, a particular discourse plan may be incoherent if a fused character takes part in events that happen in the final discourse either before its birth or after its death. Specific metrics for identifying these situations are also needed.

3.3 Representing Multiplot Stories for Evolutionary Construction

In order to apply an evolutionary approach, each story draft needs to be represented in terms of some kind of genetic information that describes how it addresses the main tasks involved: discourse planning and character fusion. To achieve this we propose a solution in several parts.

---

[1] For clarifications on how romantic conflicts are handled in the current version of the system see the discussion in Sect. 3.6.

The problem of constructing a multiplot line story considers the following inputs: a set of plot lines to combine, where each plot line is defined by a narrative thread expressed as a sequence of scenes together with a set of characters that appear in it.

This implies that, for a particular problem of combining N plotlines, the length of the final discourse is determined by the total number of scenes in the narrative threads being considered, and the maximum number of possible characters featuring in the story is determined by the union of the sets of characters in the narrative threads being considered.

For simplicity, we are assuming that the relative chronological order of the scenes in each narrative thread is respected in the final discourse. This is not a necessary condition. Indeed, many stories present instances of altered chronology (flashbacks, flashforwards). However, we leave this point to be addressed in further work.

The characterisation of the discourse plan for a given story candidate requires: establishing which narrative thread to start on, defining the specific points in the final sequence in which the discourse switches to a different narrative thread, and defining to which of the other available threads the discourse is switching when it does.

The representation is based on the fact that, for a given story construction problem, the length of the final discourse is known and fixed, and the fact that the set of plotlines being considered is known and fixed.

The information on discourse planning is represented in terms of vectors that define how the narrative threads for the different plot lines are combined into the final linear discourse:

- a single digit (0 or 1) defines which narrative thread the final discourse starts with
- a sequence of digits (0 or 1) defines for the total number of scenes in the final discourse whether the next scene follows on with the prior narrative thread or it switches to a different thread
- a sequence of digits (ranging between 1 and N − 1, where N is the total number of plots being combined) defines how many of the available plots are skipped whenever the discourse switches to a different narrative thread

The set of possible characters for the complete story is defined by the union of the sets of variable names for the characters appearing in each narrative thread. These variable names need to be distinct across the different narrative threads to avoid confusion. This is ensured by assigning a prefix with the plotline name to all the variable names that feature in any given narrative thread.

The caracterisation of the choices for character fusion for a given story candidate requires an assignment of character names to each of the variables in the joint set of variables for the story.

For simplicity, the set of potential character names for the story is defined to be the set of integers from 0 to C, with C being the cardinality of the joint set of variables for the story. This is sufficient to represent any choices made in terms of character fusion (with variables in two different positions in the name-assignment vector being assigned to the same integer). The form of the resulting stories would be significantly improved by a later stage of transforming these integer names for the characters into strings representing realistic names.

An example of representation is shown in Fig. 1.

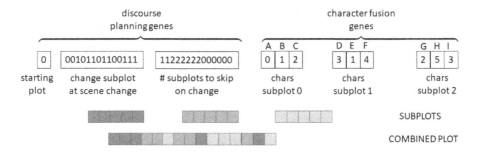

Fig. 1. Genetic representation for a combination of three plots of length 5, each with 3 characters. Fuses characters B (p0)/E (p1), C (p0)/G (p2) and D (p1)/I (p2).

3.4   Constructing an Initial Population

An initial population of story candidates is built by assigning values to the representation described in Sect. 3.3. For each of the different parts of the representation the process of assignment of values needs to be treated differently.

For the initial digit that defines which narrative thread to start on, and for the vector of decisions on whether to switch, random choice between 0 and 1 is suitable.

For the vector of decisions on skip size at each switch, random choice between 1 and $N - 1$ (with N the total number of plots being combined) is suitable.

For the vector of decisions of which character to assign to each variable, the choice is more complex. This is because variables from the same narrative thread should not be assigned to the same character, at the risk of confusing the relations between characters in the corresponding subplot. The process of assignment is carried out separately for the set of variables for each thread. For such a set of variables, the process decides at random whether to assign to each variable either a character name chosen at random from those already used in some of the narrative threads already processed, or an entirely new character name chosen at random from the character names that remain free. This ensures the required constraints are satisfied.

3.5   Evolutionary Operators

Once a population has been constructed, mutation and cross over operators are applied to it.

Because of the different nature of the various parts of the representation, specific operators of each kind are applied to the different parts.

For the mutation operators:

- for the starting point gene, the value is mutated at random
- for the switch point vector, values at each point are either mutated or not depending on a threshold parameter
- for the skip size vector, values at each point are either mutated or not depending on a threshold parameter, and, if required, mutated to a value chosen at random within the required range
- for the character assignment vector, character names at each point are either mutated or not depending on a threshold parameter, and, if required, mutated to a character name chosen at random within the required range

For the cross over operators:

- for the starting point gene, the value of the two individuals being considered is swapped
- for the switch point vector, a point in the vector is chosen at random and the corresponding halves of the vectors for the two individuals are swapped over
- for the skip size vector, a point in the vector is chosen at random and the corresponding halves of the vectors for the two individuals are swapped over
- for the character assignment vector, the assignments of characters for the two different individuals are swapped over

3.6   Fitness Functions

The construction of potential story drafts as described in the initialisation of the population and the evolutionary operators is mostly random. However not all possible combinations are actually valid. Certain plot lines, when combined in certain orders, give rise to incoherence in the semantics of the story. Incoherence may affect different aspects: characters that act before being born or after being dead, or characters that fall in love serially with no regard for previous romances. It falls to the fitness function to differentiate between valid and invalid story candidates. This is achieved by taking into account the knowledge resources described in Sect. 3.1.

As there are many different aspects to be considered for a story, a modular approach is applied to the definition of a fitness function for the system. Rather than build a complex fitness function that addresses all the aspects, a number of targeted fitness functions are built, and the fitness for a given individual is computed as a function of the results it achieves under the specific fitness functions.

This approach allows a differentiated consideration of the aspects related to validity of the story draft, the aspects related to satisfaction of optional traits, and the aspects that may actually relate to perceived quality of any given solution.

The different aspects that need to be considered as contributing to the quality of stories differ in the way they impact the overall perception of a reader. These different ways require different solutions to model numerically the expected behaviour. The solution presented here is a tentative proposal that captures the basic intuitions arising from prior empirical studies. Further work may need more detailed empirical studies and matching adaptations of the computational solutions.

Validity Fitness Functions. A first set of fitness functions addresses the consistency of the final discourse in terms of the semantics for the scenes as annotated in the knowledge resources described in Sect. 3.1. All these functions assign a score of 100 if the story is consistent with respect to the corresponding feature, and 0 otherwise.

The current set of fitness functions includes the following aspects that affect the validity of a story draft:

- whether characters are born more than once in the story (rules out combinations of plot lines that merge into a character two subplots that both mention the birth)
- whether characters die more than once in the story (rules out combinations of plot lines that merge into a character two subplots that both mention the death)
- whether characters are active in the story at points that do not lie between their birth and their death (or the boundaries of the story if birth or death are not mentioned)
- whether the romantic behaviour of characters is consistent (rules out combinations of subplots that imply one character is passionately in love with different people)

The fitness function for consistent romantic behaviour is currently an initial approximation to the task. Cases where characters fall in love with more than one person do exist as valid stories, but they are only interesting when the plot addresses the romantic conflict explicitly and resolves it in some way. The limited procedure of story construction applied here – restricted to interweaving scenes from two different plots – cannot address this task in its current form. Further work will consider extensions to the construction procedure and a matching revised fitness function to address this issue.

Optional Traits Fitness Functions. The second set of fitness functions addresses aspects noted to be positive traits by the human judges but which constitute optional rather than necessary configurations for a story. These traits add value to a story when present but do not detract from its quality if absent.

Fitness functions are defined to capture the corresponding traits, also scoring 100 if the trait is present and 0 if it is absent.

In the present version of the system, such fitness functions are added to the mix for a given run only if the corresponding trait is desired in the outcome population.

The following traits are considered for discourse plans:

- *inserted subplot*: a complete subplot is inserted as an aside into the story (all scenes from the subplot appear together in the final discourse, and surrounded by scenes from other subplots)
- *overarching plot*: the story starts and finishes with scenes from the same subplot, which therefore appears as a frame for any other subplots in the story – this does occur in cases where there is an inserted subplot but may also occur in other situations, and therefore it is considered as a separate feature

Additional traits may be considered in the same way for character fusions, which establish a link between the casts of the subplots involved in any given story. The importance of the link depends on the relative importance of the character involved in the link with respect to each of the subplots. For the present paper, the following type of links have been considered:

- *shared protagonist*: the same character acts as protagonist of two subplots
- *stitching protagonist*: the protagonist from one subplot plays an important role – different from the corresponding protagonist – in another

Fitness functions of the type explained above are defined for each of these types of links, allowing the outcomes to be driven towards stories satisfying the corresponding criteria.

Combining Fitness Functions to Score Individual Stories. To ensure that the different types of fitness functions described above are combined into a single score for each candidate story in a population, stories are assigned as a final score the average of the scores for the set of fitness functions for specific features selected.

This ensures that individual stories that are invalid or do not exhibit the desired traits disappear from the population as early as possible, and that stories with higher quality have a higher chance of survival.

4   Discussion

The results of the proposed system are presented and the relation of the proposed approach with previous work is discussed.

4.1   Results

The proposed system is run in each case with an initial population of 1,000 individuals generated at random, with the described operators for mutation (probability of mutation set to 0.2) and crossover (probability of cross over set to 0.05), for 20 generations. At each generation populations are culled by selecting the next generation using a best scoring criterion.

Table 1. An example of output story combining the plotlines creation of artificial life (CLM) and split person tragic (SPT). Columns show: the *text* for the story broken down by scenes, description of the *discourse plan* indicating for each scene which plotline it comes from, description of the cast indicating the roles they play in the respective plot lines and what names have been assigned to them – which reflect any *character fusions* present. Columns 1 and 2 are aligned by scenes, column 3 applies to the story as a whole.

Text	#	Plotline	Scene name	Variable	Role	Name
A is a doctor researching life improving serum. A has dedicated his whole life to science and has no friends or family	0	SPT	Introduction	CLM-0	Frankenstein	C
A accidentally creates a serum that changes him into B, an evil twin of himself	1	SPT	Splitting	CLM-1	Creature	D
C is a German nobleman. C lives in a big castle. C is sad. C 's wife died recently. C loves his dead wife. C dreams of bringing to life his wife	2	CLM	Conception of idea	CLM-2	-	E
C studies book of magic. C discovers a spell to bring to life a portrait of his wife. C brings to life D, the portrait of his wife	3	CLM	Creation of new life	SPT-0	DrJekyll	A
C talks every evening with D. C tells D that C loves D. D is kind to C	4	CLM	The being complies with its master's will	SPT-1	MrHyde	B
C goes to a ball. C meets E in a ball. C falls in love with E. E falls in love with C. C tells D C loves E	5	CLM	Rebellion and escape	SPT-2	-	C
E visits C. D is jealous of E. D takes E and disappears	6	CLM	Infringement by creature			
C searches for D across the castle	7	CLM	Quest for the creature			
D tells C that C must defeat D to save E. C burns the portrait. D is destroyed and E appears magically. C and E are happy	8	CLM	Death of the creature			
B brutally kills some friends of A	9	SPT	Entanglements			
C realises that B is an evil version of A. A confesses to C what has happened	10	SPT	Discovery			
A decides to stop taking the serum	11	SPT	Unravelling			
A transforms involuntary into B. B goes on a rampage. Having lost control, A decides to commit suicide, killing B in the process	12	SPT	Denouement			

Some examples of results are shown below.

The stories generated by the system are rendered as text using the templates stored for the corresponding scenes in the knowledge resources, replacing the variables with the assigned character names. An example of complete story is shown in Table 1. Numbers used internally as character names have been replaced with capital letters for ease of reading. This story is obtained with the configuration set to construct stories with an inserted plot. The discourse plan indeed shows all scenes from CLM plot appearing together, bracketted by scenes from SPT. In this case, the two subplots are only very lightly connected by character fusions: variable CLM-0, the protagonist of CLM, playing the role of Frankenstein has been fused with variable SPT-2 that corresponds to a secondary character in SPT.

To illustrate the operation of the fitness functions for optional traits, examples of the structure of different stories are shown in Table 2.

Table 2. Structures for stories obtained with different configurations for the optional traits concerning discourse structure, using different combinations of plotlines creation of artificial life (CLM), split person tragic (SPT), Faust (FA) and descent into the underworld (DiU). Column 1 shows a story with inserted plots, column 2 shows a story with overarching plot but no inserted plot, column 3 shows a story with neither overarching plot nor inserted plot. For ease of understanding of the structure of the discourse plans, the scenes of one of the subplots are highlighted in bold.

#	Plotline	Scene name	#	Plotline	Scene name	#	Plotline	Scene name
0	SPT	Introduction	0	SPT	Introduction	0	DiU	Lovers Initial Happiness
1	SPT	Splitting	1	**FA**	Frustrated character regrets his life	1	DiU	Lost
2	**CLM**	Conception of Idea	2	SPT	Splitting	2	DiU	Mourn and quest for the beloved
3	**CLM**	Creation of new life	3	**FA**	Temptation	3	**FA**	Frustrated character regrets his life
4	**CLM**	The being complies with its master's will	4	**FA**	Pact with evil	4	**FA**	Temptation
5	**CLM**	Rebellion and escape	5	SPT	Entanglements	5	**FA**	Pact with evil
6	**CLM**	Infringement by creature	6	**FA**	Evil actions	6	DiU	Deal and brief reunion
7	**CLM**	Quest for the creature	7	**FA**	Enlightenment	7	**FA**	Evil actions
8	**CLM**	Death of the creature	8	SPT	Discovery	8	DiU	Infringement of compromise
9	SPT	Entanglements	9	**FA**	Redemption	9	DiU	Metamorphosis
10	SPT	Discovery	10	SPT	Unravelling	10	**FA**	Enlightenment
11	SPT	Unravelling	11	SPT	Denouement	11	**FA**	Redemption
12	SPT	Denouement						

Table 3. Examples to illustrate options on character fusion. Names of fused characters are highlighted in bold.

DUW-0	Orpheus	**A**	**A**	A
DUW-1	Eurydice	B	**B**	B
DUW-2	Hades	D	C	**C**
FAU-3	Faust	**A**	**B**	**C**
FAU-4	Mephistopheles	B	**A**	D

To illustrate the operation of the fitness functions for character fusion, examples of different stories are shown in Table 3. To provide informative views while respecting page limit constraints, only cast descriptions are shown. The first column is an example of shared protagonist (same character A plays Orpheus and Faust). The second column is an example of stitching protagonist (character A plays Orpheus and Mephistopheles and character B plays Euridice and Faust). The third column is a weaker example of stitching protagonist (character C plays Hades and Faust).

4.2   Relation with Previous Work

The character fusion operation considered here is comparable to binding between characters as used by Fay [3].

The procedure applied in McIntyre and Lapata [13] shows significant parallels with our own approach: a set of possible stories is created by combining plot lines from different stories and then an evolutionary approach is applied to search for a convincing set of output stories. However, our system differs in that it takes as input a set of already established plot lines that cannot be altered, whereas McIntyre and Lapata explore different choices of elements – tree structures corresponding to sentences – to build the stories.

The metric for detecting individuals with 'incestuous ancestry' in [19], intended as it is to avoid repetition of events in the stories, is related to our fitness function to avoid characters in the stories falling in love more than once. Attempts to combine more than two plotlines may require a similar adaptation to avoid, at least initially, stories that include the same plot line several times.

The semantic annotations for the plot templates in our knowledge resources play a similar role to the domain database as considered in [12] to compute tension. The judgement on validity of stories based on these semantic annotations plays a role similar to the believability metric as considered in [10].

5   Conclusions

The evolutionary approach to constructing multi-plotline stories provides efficient means of building a population of drafts that satisfy constraints on semantic validity over the final linear discourse for the story. The drafts in the population can be steered towards stories that satisfy specific features in terms of particular structures in the discourse plan (such as overaching plot or inserted plots) and/or particular choices for character fusion (such as shared protagonists, linking roles or only loose connections between the casts of the different subplots).

The current set of features identified as relevant to story quality is not well suited to numerical ranking in terms of fitness functions. As a result, final populations tend to converge towards scores of 100/100 for all individuals. Nevertheless, the fact that scores for individuals are constructed as a combination of more specific scores for particular features implies that during the construction procedure – in earlier generations of the evolution – individuals do have scores in the range between 0 and 100. This allows the evolutionary procedure to explore different combinations of the various subparts of the representation vector, to achieve a set of valid solutions in the final population that satisfy the desired constraints.

As future work we will consider extending our system with metrics of the various types used in the other approaches reviewed: believability, story arcs based on tension.

Although user-defined goals are a feature specific to user-driven narratives of the type addressed in [4] and [10], stories built outside these contexts often do have a purpose beyond entertainment – convincing, educating,... Moreover, there may not be a single goal but rather a set of goals to achieve. Under this light, extending the fitness functions for our system with metrics for percentage of goals achieved will be considered as future work.

It seems that evolutionary approaches have been used often for story generation as a secondary process applied to a set of stories constructed previously by some other method. Examples of this initial material produced by other means are the stories built by MEXICA in [19] and the grammar-driven quest sketches produced by Tracery in [4]. In our case, we apply the evolutionary solution to combine plot templates that constitute already-built stories. The solution we propose could be used in future work as a secondary process on the results of preceding story generation procedures of a different type.

References

1. Balló, J., Pérez, X.: La semilla inmortal: los argumentos universales en el cine. Ed. Anagrama, Barcelona (2007)
2. Concepción, E., Gervás, P., Méndez, G.: Exploring baselines for combining full plots into multiple-plot stories. New Generation Computing **38**(4), 593–633 (2020). https://doi.org/10.1007/s00354-020-00115-x
3. Fay, M.P.: Driving story generation with learnable character models. Ph.D. thesis, Massachusetts Institute of Technology (2014)
4. Fredericks, E.M., DeVries, B.: (Genetically) improving novelty in procedural story generation. arXiv preprint arXiv:2103.06935 (2021)
5. Gervás, P.: Storifying observed events: could i dress this up as a story? In: 5th AISB Symposium on Computational Creativity. AISB, AISB, University of Liverpool, UK, April 2018

6. Gervás, P.: Composing narrative discourse for stories of many characters: a case study over a chess game. Literary Linguist. Comput. **29**(4), 511–531 (2014)
7. Gervás, P.: Generating a search space of acceptable narrative plots. In: 10th International Conference on Computational Creativity (ICCC 2019). UNC Charlotte, North Carolina, USA, July 2019
8. Gervás, P., Concepción, E., Méndez, G.: Assessing multiplot stories: from formative analysis to computational metrics. In: 12th International Conference on Computational Creativity (ICCC 2019), Mexico City, Mexico, September 2021
9. Hervás, R., Sánchez-Ruiz, A.A., Gervás, P., León, C.: Calibrating a metric for similarity of stories against human judgement. In: ICCBR (Workshops), pp. 136–145 (2015)
10. Kartal, B., Koenig, J., Guy, S.J.: User-driven narrative variation in large story domains using Monte Carlo tree search. In: Proceedings of the 2014 International Conference on Autonomous Agents and Multi-agent Systems, AAMAS 2014, pp. 69–76. International Foundation for Autonomous Agents and Multiagent Systems, Richland, SC (2014)
11. Lehman, J., Stanley, K.O.: Exploiting open-endedness to solve problems through the search for novelty. In: Proceedings of the Eleventh International Conference on Artificial Life. MIT Press (2004)
12. de Lima, E.S., Feijó, B., Furtado, A.L.: Procedural generation of quests for games using genetic algorithms and automated planning. In: 18th Brazilian Symposium on Computer Games and Digital Entertainment, SBGames 2019, Rio de Janeiro, Brazil, 28–31 October 2019, pp. 144–153. IEEE (2019). https://doi.org/10.1109/SBGames.2019.00028
13. McIntyre, N., Lapata, M.: Plot induction and evolutionary search for story generation. In: Proceedings of the 48th Annual Meeting of the Association for Computational Linguistics, pp. 1562–1572. Association for Computational Linguistics, Uppsala, Sweden, July 2010. https://aclanthology.org/P10-1158
14. Peinado, F., Francisco, V., Hervás, R., Gervás, P.: Assessing the novelty of computer-generated narratives using empirical metrics. Minds Mach. **20**(4), 588 (2010). https://doi.org/10.1007/s11023-010-9209-8
15. Pérez y Pérez, R., Sharples, M.: Mexica: a computer model of a cognitive account of creative writing. J. Exp. Theor. Artif. Intell. **13**(2), 119–139 (2001)
16. Porteous, J., Charles, F., Cavazza, M.: Plan-based narrative generation with coordinated subplots. In: European Conference on Artificial Intelligence (ECAI 2016), vol. 285, pp. 846–854. IOS Press (2016)
17. Reiter, E., Dale, R.: Building Natural Language Generation Systems. Cambridge University Press, Cambridge (2000)
18. Gómez de Silva Garza, A.: An evolutionary approach to design case adaptation. Ph.D. thesis, The University of Sydney, Australia (2000)
19. de Silva Garza, A.G., y Pérez, R.P.: Towards evolutionary story generation. In: Colton, S., Ventura, D., Lavrac, N., Cook, M. (eds.) Proceedings of the Fifth International Conference on Computational Creativity, ICCC 2014, Ljubljana, Slovenia, 10–13 June 2014, pp. 332–335. computationalcreativity.net (2014). http://computationalcreativity.net/iccc2014/wp-content/uploads/2014/06/15.3_Garza.pdf
20. Tapscott, A., Gomez, J., León, C., Smailovic, J., Znidarsic, M., Gervás, P.: Empirical evidence of the limits of automatic assessment of fictional ideation. In: C3GI ESSLLI (2016)

Fashion Style Generation: Evolutionary Search with Gaussian Mixture Models in the Latent Space

Imke Grabe[1(✉)], Jichen Zhu[1], and Manex Agirrezabal[2]

[1] IT University of Copenhagen, Copenhagen, Denmark
{imgr,jicz}@itu.dk
[2] University of Copenhagen, Copenhagen, Denmark
manex.aguirrezabal@hum.ku.dk

Abstract. This paper presents a novel approach for guiding a Generative Adversarial Network trained on the *FashionGen* dataset to generate designs corresponding to target fashion styles. Finding the latent vectors in the generator's latent space that correspond to a style is approached as an evolutionary search problem. A Gaussian mixture model is applied to identify fashion styles based on the higher-layer representations of outfits in a clothing-specific attribute prediction model. Over generations, a genetic algorithm optimizes a population of designs to increase their probability of belonging to one of the Gaussian mixture components or styles. Showing that the developed system can generate images of maximum fitness visually resembling certain styles, our approach provides a promising direction to guide the search for style-coherent designs.

Keywords: Intelligent fashion · Generative adversarial networks · Genetic algorithm · Gaussian mixture model

1 Introduction

In many areas of music, arts, and design, *artificial intelligence* (AI) can procedurally generate new cultural artifacts [6,21,27,30,31]. With the recent developments of *Generative Adversarial Networks* (GANs), AI technology can become a powerful asset for human creators to design complex objects. For example, researchers have explored how to use GANs to design fashion artifacts in fashion design. The emerging area of *intelligent fashion* investigates the detection and recommendation of clothing items, the analysis of style trends, and the synthesis of clothing [4]. As part of fashion synthesis, GANs have been applied in the creation of new items [16], the simulation of try-on scenarios [28], or for personalized design [32]. Because fashion plays a fundamental part in human culture, it is essential to investigate how generative AI might contribute to its creation.

This paper focuses on the generation of fashion styles, defined as visual themes, such as the combination of clothing artifacts or attributes as part of an outfit (e.g., blue pants and a vertically striped shirt). By extracting the representation of images on higher-level layers of an attribute prediction model, styles can be identified based on high-dimensional visual themes [22]. Existing work in intelligent fashion has analyzed styles [12,17,25], ultimately allowing for the prediction of trend behavior [1]. Research on fashion style generation with GANs focuses on controlling specific features [13,29], conditioning design with a text encoding [32], or transferring an exact outfit to other poses [28,32]. The control with regards to fashion styles, as defined above, has, however, not been considered in the generative process.

An open problem in generative design is how to guide the generation of GANs towards desirable outcomes. The GANs' generator network learns to map random input variables to the complex output features resembling the training data during the training. The procedure creates an entangled latent space, making it impossible to inspect how changes in the latent code affect the semantic output features. This entanglement impedes the control of the generated designs towards a desired look. Differentiated control of the latent features of generative clothing models has been achieved by conditioning the generator with the encoding of a text description in the latent vector [32], or by disentangling color, texture, and shape inputs through separate losses in the loss function during training [29]. Approaches like *StyleGAN* [15] aim at controlling certain stylistic features in images, such as the transfer of a complete outfit [28]. However, guiding the generation of designs towards fashion styles consisting of broader visual themes remains an open research problem. Fashion describes the specific category of clothing driven by the developments of style trends. As fashion styles capture meaningful temporal and local developments with societies [1,19,22], responding to such themes matters for the generative process.

This paper presents a new method to guide GANs using a *Gaussian mixture model* (GMM). While GMMs have been used in the field of intelligent fashion to identify fashion styles [1,22], they have not been applied to support generative purposes. To better control the GANs' entangled latent space, we utilize the GMM to find the latent vectors that correspond to *stylistic* designs in an evolutionary search problem. More specifically, our method combines (1) generative deep learning, (2) the analysis of fashion styles, and (3) the application of genetic optimization algorithms to search a design space.

The main contribution of this work is a new method to guide GANs using a GMM. This paper presents the method proposed in our prior work [10]. It allows GANs' generative process to be guided based on higher-level themes, instead of separate attributes as in existing approaches [13,29]. We tested our method in the context of generating fashion styles. We found that while our proposed framework generally supports the generation of designs according to target styles, the GMM-based fitness measure is not always aligned with visual coherency to the styles. Some generated designs reveal that the fitness measure relies on a machine-specific understanding of style. Further investigation into the interplay between style model and the exploration of the latent space and the parameter setting of the genetic algorithm is required to align the results with a human understanding of style.

The remainder of the paper is organized as follows. After presenting related work, we introduce our dataset and proposed model, consisting of a GAN model, a style model, and the evolutionary search connecting the former. Next, we present our experimental results and conclude with discussions.

2   Related Work

This section presents related work in the three research areas relevant to this study, namely within (1) GANs, (2) analyzing fashion styles, and (3) applying evolutionary search to steer the generation process.

2.1   GANs

The introduction of GANs revolutionized the creation of computer-generated content [9]. GANs, consisting of two neural networks competing against each other as generator and a discriminator, learn to generate outputs by resembling a training distribution. For example, GANs can generate clothing artifacts when trained with a dataset of those. Notably, the training method of *Progressively growing GANs* (P-GANs) supports the generation of high-resolution images, as was demonstrated by Rostamzadeh et al. [23] with their introduction of a fashion dataset. In fashion generation, different objectives have been guiding the training of GANs, such as conditioning their output with the text description of desired looks [32], or color, texture, and shape [29].

Notice that for GANs, the term *style* is typically used to describe the manipulation of a design with regards to specified visual attributes. StyleGANs [15] provide an architecture that disentangles the latent space of the generator network, allowing for a targeted modification of high-level to low-level attributes corresponding to different resolutions in the network. Yildirim et al. [28] trained a StyleGAN to transfer a complete outfit to other models, as in a try-on scenario. This notion sets focus on certain visual attributes, similar to Jiang et al. [13], who apply GANs to transfer patterns to shirt designs.

2.2   Fashion Styles

Studies have addressed the phenomenon of styles in fashion from different angles, varying from weak [8,18] to strong [17,25] style annotations, as well as their unsupervised discovery [1,12,22]. Drawing on the latter, this paper builds on research that approaches fashion styles as a "mode in the data capturing a distribution of attributes" [1, p. 7]. Hence, they can be discovered unsupervised by clustering attribute predictions of images. Clustering models such as a Gaussian mixture model (GMM) have previously been applied to find recurring components in the attribute embedding of images [1,22]. After identifying styles with a GMM, projecting the embedding of any (generated) image onto the GMM can measure of how well it fits into the discovered styles. In that way, we can evaluate how an image resembles a particular style.

Instead of using the prediction scores of an attribute prediction model as the embedding, previous layers of the model also capture meaningful themes in images. Matzen et al. [22] introduce a method that finds styles as Gaussian mixture components in the projections of images onto the model's penultimate feature space. The second-last layer captures learned features that are more specific than the output of the final fully-connected layer. It serves as a valuable embedding for recognizing high-level themes beyond attribute scores [20]. The resulting clusters can be understood as a "global visual vocabulary for fashion" [22, p. 7]. Letting this *language of fashion* inform the generative process by GANs is the objective of our suggested framework. We adapt Matzen et al.'s [22] procedure to find styles in the dataset *FashionGen* to use them for guiding the generation towards a chosen style.

To sum up, as the subject of fashion analysis, *style* refers to the broader sense of visual themes in outfits. Unless otherwise specified, the rest of the paper will use the term *style* to refer to this definition. Going beyond the attributes corresponding to the different layers of the GAN, specific items, or textures, the concept has not been considered in generation yet. We suggest a system affording the generation of designs based on fashion styles discovered in an unsupervised manner by a GMM. Embedded into an evolutionary search, the GMM guides the generation of designs.

2.3   Evolutionary Search of GANs' Latent Space

Our project aims to generate designs of various styles with visually diverse attributes with GANs. Navigating the networks' complex latent space with this objective requires changing minor and major visual features. Drawing on the smooth characteristic of GANs' latent space, evolutionary search can optimize its latent variables [3]. More specifically, a genetic algorithm alters a population of latent vectors by recombining and mutating them [5]. Through selection based on a fitness objective, such as maximizing the probability of belonging to a target style, latent vectors improve over many generations.

Previous work has applied genetic algorithms to explore the latent space with different goals. While Roziere et al. [24] improve the quality of only one fashion image generated by a P-GAN, Fernandes et al. [7] evolve a set of latent vectors to increase the diversity among the corresponding set of generated images. Instead of a pre-defined fitness objective, interactive genetic algorithms use user evaluation as a measure of fitness. Designing smaller clothing items in this interactive manner has been proposed in *DeepIE* [2], further developed into *StyleIE* [26]. Where an interactive genetic algorithm uses a human-in-the-loop to assess fitness, we apply a GMM to measure the fitness of a generated image, following the goal of generating designs that belong to an automatically discovered target style. Our contribution is to create a fully automated method for style generation by adding a GMM to the evolutionary loop. Instead of a human who chooses images of desired properties, the selection is based on the images' projection onto the clustering space.

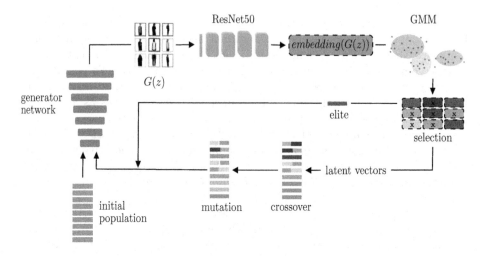

Fig. 1. Model of the genetic algorithm for searching the generative model's latent space with the help of the clustering model. First, the trained generator network creates images based on randomly initialized latent vectors. Next, the generated images are represented as their embedding of the ResNet50 and then projected onto the clustering space of the GMM. The fittest ones are selected based on their posterior probability of belonging to the target cluster. Additionally, the elite, is preserved for the next generation. The others are recombined and new individuals are added before being mutated. The resulting latent vectors lay the basis for the next generation of images.

3   Dataset

FashionGen's [23] clothing partition in a resolution of 256×256 pixels is used as a dataset for training the generative model and the style model. Consisting of over 200,000 images of outfits worn by a model, each outfit is represented in four different poses in the subset. The dataset mainly consists of images of whole-body outfits taken under consistent lighting conditions in front of white backgrounds, providing the ideal conditions for generation and clustering to focus purely on fashion attributes and identify styles across a combination of artifacts.

4   Model

Our proposed framework consists of three parts: A generative model, a style model, and the evolutionary search connecting the two. To make the (1) generative model output designs of a style that is discovered by the (2) style model, parts of the two models are combined in an (3) evolutionary search algorithm, as illustrated in Fig. 1. The details of the components are presented in this order.[1]

---

[1] The code is available: https://github.com/imkegrabe/fashionstyle-generation-GMM.

Table 1. GAN training parameters. Note that the batch size was changed to 8 for the last training epoch.

Parameter	Setting
Optimizer	Adam
Activation function	leakyRELU
Learning rate	Equalized learning rate
Batch size	16 (8)
Loss function	WGAN-GP
Noise distribution	$\mathcal{N}(\mu = 0, \sigma = 1)$

4.1 Generative Model

As the first part of the framework, a GAN is trained on the complete dataset. The P-GAN architecture and training procedure are utilized, which applies the *Wasserstein GAN* loss with gradient penalty (WGAN-GP) [14].[2] Hence, the goal of the training procedure is to minimize the following function with respect to G, and maximize it with respect to D:

$$\min_G \max_D \mathbb{E}_{x \sim p_{data}}[D(x)] - \mathbb{E}_{z \sim p_z}[D(G(z))] + \lambda \mathbb{E}_{\hat{x} \sim p(\hat{x})}[(||\nabla_{\hat{x}} D(\hat{x})||_2 - 1)^2] \quad (1)$$

By competing against a discriminator network D, a generator network G learns how to map an input vector z of 512 variables,[3] randomly sampled from a standard normal distribution $\mathcal{N}(\mu = 0, \sigma = 1)$, to output images resembling the real data distribution in the dataset. The model was trained on a *NVIDIA Tesla V100-SXM2-16 GB* GPU for seven days to create images of resolution 256×256. Table 1 provides an overview of the training parameters.

4.2 Style Model

The goal of the second part of the framework is to discover styles in the dataset. Informed by the method in [22], the visual embedding learned by an attribute prediction model is leveraged to cluster outfits into styles.

We create image representations using a *ResNet50*.[4] The network was pre-trained to map input images of *DeepFashion* to 1000 clothing-specific attributes

---

[2] We use the implementation made available by Facebook Research: https://github.com/facebookresearch/pytorch_GAN_zoo.

[3] The implementation expands the latent codes with 20 additional variables based on the outfits' item representation. As initial experimentation did not make their effect on the evolutionary search behaviour apparent, we treated them as the other latent variables. Their role should be further examined in future experiments.

[4] The backbone of the attribute prediction model provided by the open-source toolbox for visual fashion analysis by the Multimedia Lab, Chinese University of Hong Kong is adapted: https://github.com/open-mmlab/mmfashion.

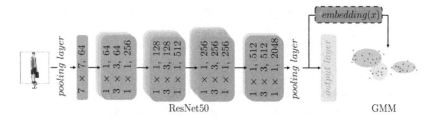

Fig. 2. Style model consisting of a ResNet50 as feature extraction model and a GMM as clustering model. The ResNet consists of several units containing 1–6 layer(s). A layer contains convolution(s) in the form of kernels, here notated as $r \times r, n$ with kernel size r and n channels. The output layer is discarded to extract the embedding for image x from the pooling layer. Based on the embedding for all outfits in the dataset, k Gaussian mixture components are determined.

instead of more general ones as in models pre-trained on ImageNet. The pre-training makes it a robust feature basis for analyzing datasets containing a wide range of clothing items.

As we are concerned with finding subtle styles, we approach them as a visual concept situated between pre-defined coarse categories and low-level single-feature attribution. To discover coherent style clusters representing these subtle visual themes, the penultimate layer of the ResNet50 serves as a meaningful embedding space. The last layer before the linear layer outputting the prediction scores for attributes captures high-level features of fashion images, though not directly class-specific to DeepFashion. In practice, the output of the last convolutional unit, more precisely after it has been converted to a 2048-dimensional vector by the pooling layer, is extracted as the *embedding(x)* of image x, as can be seen in Fig. 2.

Based on the embedding, clustering is employed to find recurring themes in the embedding space. To capture the distribution of all outfits in the style model while at the same time making the clustering computationally efficient, we chose only images in pose 4, which show most full-body images, chosen to build the style model. Hence, an embedding is retrieved for one image per outfit in the dataset. The embedding vectors are scaled to zero mean before principal component analysis (PCA) projects them onto the 135 principal components capturing 90% of the embedding's variance.

A GMM is applied to find a mixture of Gaussian probability distributions that represent the data distribution. Through experimentation in line with Matzen et al. [22], we find that 150 mixture components seem to capture visually coherent fashion styles in the dataset. These style clusters range from 60 to 1100 ($\mu = 314.2$) images in size. Any image's posterior probability p_t of belonging to a component t depicts how well it represents a style. The probabilistic model guarantees that increasing an image's posterior probability of belonging to a cluster component reduces its probability of belonging to other clusters.

4.3   Evolutionary Search

The trained generator of the GAN acts as a genotype-to-phenotype mapping, where the latent encoding, interpreted as the genotype, governs the appearance of the output designs, the phenotype. Adjusting the genotypes should move the corresponding phenotypes projected onto the GMM closer to a target style. Over several generations, the proposed genetic algorithm alters a population of N_{pop} latent vectors initialized from the distribution as the latent variables. The algorithm selects latent vectors for the next generation by evaluating their probability of falling into the targeted style cluster. The goal is to arrive at a set of latent vectors representing designs of the desired style. While the following sections explain the details, Algorithm 1 shows the pseudo-code for the procedure.[5]

Representation and Transformation. A generated design is represented by its latent vector $z = \langle v_1, ..., v_l \rangle$ with $v \in \mathbb{R}$ consisting of l latent variables.

While an initial latent vector z is sampled randomly from the underlying distribution (see Sect. 4.1), the genetic algorithm aims to transform z towards z^* with $G(z^*)$ representing a design of the targeted style. This transformation is guided by the fitness objective defined below.

Fitness and Selection. To arrive at the desired goal, individuals are evaluated against a fitness measure. Recall from Sect. 4.2, that an image's posterior probability of belonging to a style component t is p_t. Following the goal of resembling a certain target style t, the fitness criterion $\mathcal{F}_t$ is defined by an individual's posterior probability of belonging to the respective target style cluster, referred to as f_t. Applying the measure brought forward by the GMM, $f_t = p_t$.

To assess the fitness of a latent vector, image $G(z)$ is generated. The generated image is then projected onto the embedding space to retrieve $embedding(G(z))$. Finally, the $embedding(G(z))$ is projected onto the GMM, where the probability of belonging to target cluster t is extracted as p_t, representing the fitness criterion f_t. That defines the fitness f of an individual, or latent vector z, of belonging to a target cluster t as

$$f_t(z) = p_t(embedding(G(z))). \tag{2}$$

For the generated images to fit into a style cluster, the fitness $\mathcal{F}_t$ needs to be maximized to obtain a latent vector z^* of target style t:

$$z^* = \arg\max_z \mathcal{F}_t(z) \tag{3}$$

By maximizing the fitness function, the population of latent vectors should improve towards the defined requirement through selection and variation.

At the beginning of each generation, we preserve a copy of the best N_{elite} individuals to save them from alteration. Inheriting them to the next round

---

[5] The genetic algorithm was implemented using the evolutionary computation framework DEAP: https://deap.readthedocs.io/en/master/index.html#.

Algorithm 1: Evolutionary Search of GANs' latent space using GMM.

Result: $G(z^*)$ closest to style cluster centroids

1 **Function** fitness(z, t):
2 | **return** $p_t(embedding(G(z)))$

3 **Function** selection(*population*, N):
4 | **for** $i \leftarrow 1$ *to* N **do**
5 | | $best_i \leftarrow$ winner out of N_{ts} randomly chosen z with fitness(z,t)
6 | **end**
7 | **return** $best_1, ..., best_N$

8 **Function** crossover(a, b):
9 | **for** i *in* a **do**
10 | | $a_i = \alpha a_i + (1 - \alpha)b_i$ for $\alpha \sim Bernoulli(0.5)$
11 | | $b_i = \alpha b_i + (1 - \alpha)a_i$ for $\alpha \sim Bernoulli(0.5)$
12 | **end**
13 | **return** a, b

14 **Function** mutation(a):
15 | $noise \leftarrow$ vector of length l where $noise_i \sim \mathcal{N}(\mu = 0, \sigma = 1)$
16 | **return** $a + noise$

17 $population \leftarrow N_{pop} \times z$
18 **for** g *in* N_{gen} **do**
19 | $elite \leftarrow N_{elite} \times z$ with maximum fitness (z,t) in *population*
20 | $population =$ selection(*population*, N_{pop})
21 | **for** a, b *in* *population* **do**
22 | | **if** $random < p_{cx}$ **then**
23 | | | $a, b =$ crossover(a, b)
24 | | **end**
25 | **end**
26 | $population = population + N_{new} \times z$
27 | **for** a *in* *population* **do**
28 | | **if** $random < p_{mut}$ **then**
29 | | | $a =$ mutation(a)
30 | | **end**
31 | **end**
32 | $population = population + elite$
33 **end**

---

guarantees that we do not destroy the fittest individuals during a generation. N_{pop} individuals are selected by conducting N_{pop} tournaments, where N_{ts} randomly chosen individuals compete against each other based on their fitness. Two kinds of variation operations, recombination and mutation, are applied to the population resulting from the tournament selection.

Recombination. *Uniform crossover* is applied to generate new offspring as in [2,7]. Two latent vectors a and b are recombined to produce two new individuals $\hat{a}$ and $\hat{b}$, with their ith attribute randomly chosen from either a or b:

Table 2. GA parameters under variation.

Parameter	Setting
Crossover rate p_{cx}	0.7, 0.9
Mutation rate p_{mut}	0.2, 0.5
Population size p_{pop}	100, 200
Tournament size p_{ts}	3, 6

Table 3. Constant GA parameters.

Parameter	Setting
Size of individual	512
N_{gen}	500
N_{elite}	1
N_{new}	10
Recombination operator	Uniform crossover ($\alpha = 0.5$)
Mutation operator	Nonuniform mutation ($\mu = 0, \sigma = 1$)

$$\hat{a}_i = \alpha a_i + (1 - \alpha)b_i \text{ and } \hat{b}_i = \alpha b_i + (1 - \alpha)a_i \text{ with } \alpha = Bernoulli(0.5) \quad (4)$$

If recombined, an individual is replaced by its child. The crossover rate p_{cx} defines the chance for an individual of the population to participate in recombination. As commonly applied, we choose high rates (0.7 and 0.9) to ensure the continuing development of fit individuals [11]. To introduce new gene material, we add N_{new} new random vectors to the population in every generation in addition to the crossover.

Mutation. Following the objective of moving closer to a target cluster, we apply *nonuniform mutation* [2]. With a probability of 0.5, a variable of a latent vector z is mutated by adding some *noise* drawn from the original distribution:

$$z_i = z_i + noise \sim \mathcal{N}(\mu = 0, \sigma = 1) \quad (5)$$

The mutation rate p_{mut} defines the chance for an individual of the population to be mutated. While the mutation rate of a genetic algorithm is usually set to a few percent [11], we consider both low (0.2) and high (0.5) mutation rates, as initial runs showed low diversity among the population.

In accordance with typical tuning methods of evolutionary algorithms, we consider different tournament sizes ($N_{ts} = \{3, 6\}$) and population sizes ($N_{pop} = \{100, 200\}$) adhering to the commonly used parameter choices [5,11]. The parameters under variation are summarized in Table 2. The number of generations is set to $N_{gen} = 500$ as a compromise of running time and complexity of the problem. Table 3 displays the constant parameters. Due to the stochasticity underlying evolutionary systems, some runs naturally never achieve any fitness due

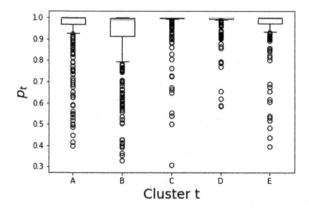

Fig. 3. Boxplot of the original images' posterior probability for the five target styles chosen for the experiment. The five clusters range from 228 to 367 in size. The images contained by them have a mean p_t between 0.92 and 0.98.

Table 4. Average maximum fitness across all five runs per parameter combination.

		$p_{mut} = 0.2$		$p_{mut} = 0.5$	
		$N_{ts} = 3$	$N_{ts} = 6$	$N_{ts} = 3$	$N_{ts} = 6$
$p_{cx} = 0.7$	$N_{pop} = 100$	0.5746	0.2	0.6021	0.2119
	$N_{pop} = 200$	0.4031	0.5491	0.6341	0.4028
$p_{cx} = 0.9$	$N_{pop} = 100$	0.4538	0.3855	**0.735**	0.2982
	$N_{pop} = 200$	**0.8073**	0.2	0.7043	0.5248

to an 'unlucky' initialization of the population. Therefore, we test the model for different styles per parameter combination. From a random selection of styles presented to the experimenter, they chose five distinct ones to ensure visual diversity as a basis for the experiments.

5   Results

We tested our model in each parameter combination to generate designs for five different styles. Figure 3 displays the distribution of the images' posterior probability per target style cluster. A comparison of the mean maximum fitness reached across all five runs is presented in Table 4. As we ran the whole system for five different times, or style clusters, the results that we include are averages over those five runs. Recall that the fitness to be maximized is defined as an image's posterior probability of belonging to a GMM component. Hence, it can vary between a minimum of 0 and a maximum of 1.

As the comparison of the results reveals, the algorithm finds individuals of highest fitness for a crossover rate of $p_{cx} = 0.9$ and a tournament size of $N_{ts} = 3$. In particular, the highest fitness is reached in combination with a population size

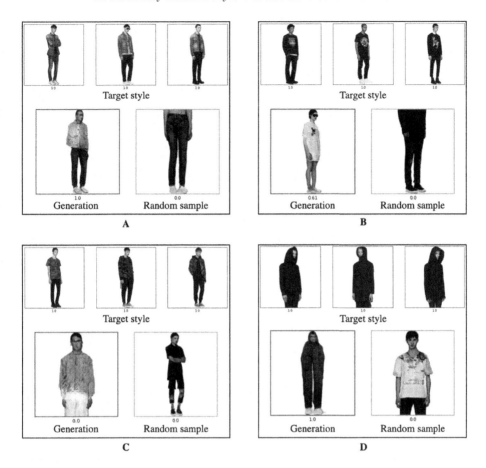

Fig. 4. Four exemplary designs for different clusters. See Fig. 5 for the parameter settings underlying the runs. The figure displays the three images with the highest posterior probability in the style cluster, the fittest generated image, and the fittest out of $N_{pop} \times N_{gen}$ randomly sampled images for comparison. The titles of the images display their fitness. Zoom in for detail.

of $N_{pop} = 200$ and a low mutation rate of $p_{mut} = 0.2$, followed by the second highest fitness with $N_{pop} = 100$ and $p_{mut} = 0.5$.

To better understand the fitness measure in relation to the produced designs, an exemplary case from the experiments for style cluster A, B, C, and D each is presented in Fig. 4. A plot of average and maximum fitness of each exemplary run is shown in Fig. 5 for inspection of the search behavior.

For a generated design for the style displayed in Fig. 4A, the similarity to the target cluster is visible, as they share the features of an open denim jacket with bleached plats and darker pants. This is aligned with the high fitness of the generation. Interestingly, the random sampling achieved no fitness despite the similarity of the displayed pants. In comparison, some generated designs of lower

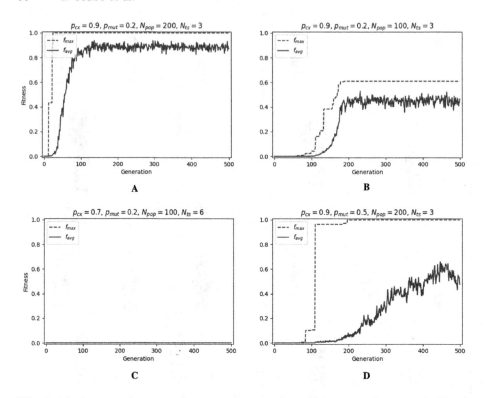

Fig. 5. Maximum and average fitness over generations of the exemplary runs in Fig. 4.

fitness, such as the example in Fig. 4B, show less visual similarity. Specifically, only one feature, namely the pattern on the chest, seems to resemble the target style characterized by a black outfit with a white pattern on the shirt.

The same concern arises for a generated design for the target style characterized by a camouflaged patterned upper part and black pants, shown in Fig. 4C. While the image shows an upper body with a pattern similar to the target style, it achieved no fitness, as the corresponding plot in Fig. 5C shows. While this could be cause by an unlucky initialization, it might also point to flaws in the fitness measure. That the assigned fitness does not seem to be in alignment with visual coherency is also the case for the example given in Fig. 4D. Here, high fitness is not aligned with a legit outfit design.

6   Discussion

For some of the analyzed designs, the fitness measure aligns with the visual coherency to the target style. In Fig. 4A, high fitness represents a design of high visual similarity. In contrast, lower fitness describes a design of little visual coherency in Fig. 4B. Taking a look at the search behavior behind the latter, displayed in Fig. 5B, an explanation could be the following. The population converged to a local maximum after around half of the generations, only allowing for optimizing a minor feature in the following generations. Though convergence to a local maximum is a desirable end stadium for genetic algorithms, it poses a problem in this scenario. Due to weak style matches dominating the population, the subsequent evolution underlies the prevailing look. A solution to introduce more diversity to the population could be to increase mutation or the number of new individuals when fitness stagnates.

For other examples, the fitness measure does not represent the visual coherency. Figure 4C displays a design with a pattern similar to the target style, but achieved no fitness. This example raises the question of whether other factors, such as the models' posing, play a role in defining a style. At the same time, the example shown in Fig. 4D achieved the maximum fitness, for a design that a human judge might not assign validity. As our style model is based on the representation of an attribute model trained to recognize clothing features, it might lack the sensitivity of body shapes. However, coming with a background in clothing and physiology guides, such notions guide our perception of the designs. Hence, the suggested system might find some completely different attributes behind what we identify as decisive properties for a style. We hypothesize that the designs found by the evolutionary search reveal a machine-specific understanding of fashion style. However, to further investigate that claim, we need to find out whether our model is sufficient to capture styles. As part of our future work, further insight into the implementation and its parameters would show if they optimally support this goal.

The difference in perception could also be because computational networks are not able to capture subtle differences in styles (yet) [25]. Detecting style-coherent similarity of clothing images remains a challenge, in which also the attribute models used to retrieve the visual representation, including the training data, play an essential role [12]. Even though the embedding of images was used instead of the ResNet's final layer's attribute prediction scores, the categories underlying its training influence what the model *sees* on every layer. To better understand the style-defining features, a qualitative analysis of the ResNet's performance, e.g. with the help of a *Class Activation Map* (CAM), could be performed. Such an analysis could shed insight on the critical features for a particular fashion style [25]. With that knowledge, the latent space of the GAN might be controllable in a more targeted way.

To quantify the relation between the clusters found by the evolutionary search and human judgement, a human could be added to the loop. To guide the system into the direction of human-compatible styles, the approach could eventually be combined with interactive evolution like in DeepIE or StyleIE, in order to integrate how humans see style. Additionally, we could consider if exploring the latent space can even tell us more about what the model interprets behind styles, providing insight into clustering components. Following that path contributes to understanding how the proposed system sees visual themes emerge, eventually leading to a better understanding of its functioning.

As a final remark, it is essential to reflect on the datasets used for training generative models. As Takagi et al. [25] point out, fashion photographs do not represent what people actually wear, hence might not give an actual representation of current styles. Most datasets used for training generative fashion design models consist of catalog or social media images, highly biased to the presented populations. Therefore, a crucial task is to discuss how data affects the system's stability with regard to design diversity, such as achieving desirable silhouettes while still considering diverse body forms.

7 Conclusion and Future Work

This research aimed to extend the classical generative deep learning approach to facilitate the generation of designs that respond to fashion styles. We investigated the application of a genetic algorithm and a GMM to guide the generation of images with regard to previously identified style clusters. Our suggested framework facilitates the search for images responding to certain style clusters. The experimental results indicate that the proposed procedure provides a promising direction to guide the search for style-coherent designs. Further research is required to establish a robust and reliable exploration process.

While the system can generate images of maximum fitness, the designs do not necessarily correspond to the target styles in the way one would expect. We hypothesize that the generations reveal a machine-specific understanding of fashion style. While some of the generated images exhibit similarity to the target cluster visible to the human eye, other generated outputs raise the question of how the algorithm might understand styles differently, outlining the need to improve the fitness measure.

Integrating fashion style analysis and fashion generation opens up new design possibilities, such as extending trends forecasting to generating trending designs. Future work could investigate how the ability to react to stylistic developments through unsupervised learning expands the capabilities of generative models as creative design tools.

References

1. Al-Halah, Z., Grauman, K.: Modeling fashion influence from photos. IEEE Trans. Multimedia (2020). https://doi.org/10.1109/TMM.2020.3037459
2. Bontrager, P., Lin, W., Togelius, J., Risi, S.: Deep interactive evolution. In: Liapis, A., Romero Cardalda, J.J., Ekárt, A. (eds.) EvoMUSART 2018. LNCS, vol. 10783, pp. 267–282. Springer, Cham (2018). https://doi.org/10.1007/978-3-319-77583-8_18
3. Bontrager, P., Roy, A., Togelius, J., Memon, N., Ross, A.: DeepMasterPrints: generating masterprints for dictionary attacks via latent variable evolution. In: 2018 IEEE 9th International Conference on Biometrics Theory, Applications and Systems (BTAS), pp. 1–9. IEEE (2018)
4. Cheng, W.H., Song, S., Chen, C.Y., Hidayati, S.C., Liu, J.: Fashion meets computer vision: a survey. ACM Comput. Surv. 54(4), 1–41 (2021)

5. Eiben, A.E., Smith, J.E.: Introduction to Evolutionary Computing. NCS, Springer, Heidelberg (2015). https://doi.org/10.1007/978-3-662-44874-8
6. Elgammal, A., Liu, B., Elhoseiny, M., Mazzone, M.: CAN: creative adversarial networks, generating "art" by learning about styles and deviating from style norms. arXiv preprint arXiv:1706.07068 (2017)
7. Fernandes, P., Correia, J., Machado, P.: Evolutionary latent space exploration of generative adversarial networks. In: Castillo, P.A., Jiménez Laredo, J.L., Fernández de Vega, F. (eds.) EvoApplications 2020. LNCS, vol. 12104, pp. 595–609. Springer, Cham (2020). https://doi.org/10.1007/978-3-030-43722-0_38
8. Ge, Y., Zhang, R., Wang, X., Tang, X., Luo, P.: DeepFashion2: a versatile benchmark for detection, pose estimation, segmentation and re-identification of clothing images. In: 2019 IEEE/CVF Conference on Computer Vision and Pattern Recognition (CVPR), pp. 5332–5340 (2019). https://doi.org/10.1109/CVPR.2019.00548
9. Goodfellow, I.J., et al.: Generative adversarial networks. arXiv preprint arXiv:1406.2661 (2014)
10. Grabe, I.: Evolutionary search for fashion styles in the latent space of generative adversarial networks. Master's thesis, University of Copenhagen (2021)
11. Hassanat, A., Almohammadi, K., Alkafaween, E., Abunawas, E., Hammouri, A., Prasath, V.: Choosing mutation and crossover ratios for genetic algorithms-a review with a new dynamic approach. Information **10**(12), 390 (2019)
12. Hsiao, W.L., Grauman, K.: Learning the latent "Look": unsupervised discovery of a style-coherent embedding from fashion images (2017)
13. Jiang, S., Li, J., Fu, Y.: Deep learning for fashion style generation. IEEE Trans. Neural Netw. Learn. Syst. (2021)
14. Karras, T., Aila, T., Laine, S., Lehtinen, J.: Progressive growing of GANs for improved quality, stability, and variation. arXiv preprint arXiv:1710.10196 (2017)
15. Karras, T., Laine, S., Aila, T.: A style-based generator architecture for generative adversarial networks. In: Proceedings of the IEEE/CVF Conference on Computer Vision and Pattern Recognition, pp. 4401–4410 (2019)
16. Kato, N., Osone, H., Oomori, K., Ooi, C.W., Ochiai, Y.: GANs-based clothes design: pattern maker is all you need to design clothing. In: Proceedings of the 10th Augmented Human International Conference 2019, pp. 1–7 (2019)
17. Kiapour, M.H., Yamaguchi, K., Berg, A.C., Berg, T.L.: Hipster wars: discovering elements of fashion styles. In: Fleet, D., Pajdla, T., Schiele, B., Tuytelaars, T. (eds.) ECCV 2014. LNCS, vol. 8689, pp. 472–488. Springer, Cham (2014). https://doi.org/10.1007/978-3-319-10590-1_31
18. Liu, Z., Luo, P., Qiu, S., Wang, X., Tang, X.: DeepFashion: powering robust clothes recognition and retrieval with rich annotations. In: 2016 IEEE Conference on Computer Vision and Pattern Recognition (CVPR), pp. 1096–1104 (2016). https://doi.org/10.1109/CVPR.2016.124
19. Mackinney-Valentin, M.: On the nature of trends: a study of trend mechanisms in contemporary fashion. Ph.D. thesis, Royal Danish Academy (Jun 2010)
20. Mahmood, A., et al.: Automatic hierarchical classification of kelps using deep residual features. Sensors **20**(2), 447 (2020)
21. Marchetti, F., Wilson, C., Powell, C., Minisci, E., Riccardi, A.: Convolutional generative adversarial network, via transfer learning, for traditional Scottish music generation. In: Romero, J., Martins, T., Rodríguez-Fernández, N. (eds.) EvoMUSART 2021. LNCS, vol. 12693, pp. 187–202. Springer, Cham (2021). https://doi.org/10.1007/978-3-030-72914-1_13
22. Matzen, K., Bala, K., Snavely, N.: StreetStyle: exploring world-wide clothing styles from millions of photos (2017)

23. Rostamzadeh, N., et al.: Fashion-Gen: the generative fashion dataset and challenge. arXiv preprint arXiv:1806.08317 (2018)
24. Roziere, B., et al.: EvolGAN: evolutionary generative adversarial networks. In: Ishikawa, H., Liu, C.-L., Pajdla, T., Shi, J. (eds.) ACCV 2020. LNCS, vol. 12625, pp. 679–694. Springer, Cham (2021). https://doi.org/10.1007/978-3-030-69538-5_41
25. Takagi, M., Simo-Serra, E., Iizuka, S., Ishikawa, H.: What makes a style: experimental analysis of fashion prediction. In: Proceedings of the IEEE International Conference on Computer Vision Workshops, pp. 2247–2253 (2017)
26. Tejeda-Ocampo, C., López-Cuevas, A., Terashima-Marin, H.: Improving deep interactive evolution with a style-based generator for artistic expression and creative exploration. Entropy **23**(1), 11 (2021). https://doi.org/10.3390/e23010011, https://www.mdpi.com/1099-4300/23/1/11
27. Xin, C., Arakawa, K.: Object design system by interactive evolutionary computation using GAN with contour images. In: Zimmermann, A., Howlett, R.J., Jain, L.C., Schmidt, R. (eds.) KES-HCIS 2021. SIST, vol. 244, pp. 66–75. Springer, Singapore (2021). https://doi.org/10.1007/978-981-16-3264-8_7
28. Yildirim, G., Jetchev, N., Vollgraf, R., Bergmann, U.: Generating high-resolution fashion model images wearing custom outfits. In: Proceedings of the IEEE/CVF International Conference on Computer Vision Workshops (2019)
29. Yildirim, G., Seward, C., Bergmann, U.: Disentangling multiple conditional inputs in GANs. arXiv preprint arXiv:1806.07819 (2018)
30. Zhu, J., Liapis, A., Risi, S., Bidarra, R., Youngblood, G.M.: Explainable AI for designers: a human-centered perspective on mixed-initiative co-creation. In: 2018 IEEE Conference on Computational Intelligence and Games, pp. 1–8. IEEE (2018)
31. Zhu, J., Ontañón, S.: Shall i compare thee to another story?-An empirical study of analogy-based story generation. IEEE Trans. Comput. Intell. AI Games **6**(2), 216–227 (2013)
32. Zhu, S., Urtasun, R., Fidler, S., Lin, D., Change Loy, C.: Be your own Prada: fashion synthesis with structural coherence. In: Proceedings of the IEEE International Conference on Computer Vision, pp. 1680–1688 (2017)

Classification of Guitar Effects and Extraction of Their Parameter Settings from Instrument Mixes Using Convolutional Neural Networks

Reemt Hinrichs[✉], Kevin Gerkens, and Jörn Ostermann

Institut für Informationsverarbeitung, Leibniz University Hannover,
Hanover, Germany
hinrichs@tnt.uni-hannover.de

Abstract. Guitar effects are commonly used in popular music to shape the guitar sound to fit specific genres or to create more variety within musical compositions. The sound is not only determined by the choice of the guitar effect, but also heavily depends on the parameter settings of the effect. Previous research focused on the classification of guitar effects and extraction of their parameter settings from solo guitar audio recordings. However, more realistic is the classification and extraction from instrument mixes. This work investigates the use of convolution neural networks (CNNs) for classification and extraction of guitar effects from audio samples containing guitar, bass, keyboard and drums. The CNN was compared to baseline methods previously proposed like support vector machines and shallow neural networks together with predesigned features. The CNN outperformed all baselines, achieving a classification accuracy of up to 97.4% and a mean absolute parameter extraction error of below 0.016 for the distortion, below 0.052 for the tremolo and below 0.038 for the slapback delay effect achieving or surpassing the presumed human expert error of 0.05.

Keywords: Convolutional neural networks · Guitar effects · Parameter extraction · Music information retrieval

1 Introduction

Audio effects are a wide-spread tool used in the production and creation of music. They find application in all kinds of music and are applied to virtually all kinds of instruments such as vocals, guitar, keyboard and so on. In the domain of guitar-centered music, a prominent and well known effect is the overdrive effect, closely related to the distortion effect. A multitude of other effects exist such as phaser, delay, ring-modulator and many more. Several professional guitarists use guitar effects to create an unique, distinctive sound strongly associated with the artist. For the production of music and the creative process of writing music, automatic creation of guitar effects that yield a desired sound can be of interest.

© The Author(s), under exclusive license to Springer Nature Switzerland AG 2022
T. Martins et al. (Eds.): EvoMUSART 2022, LNCS 13221, pp. 101–116, 2022.
https://doi.org/10.1007/978-3-031-03789-4_7

For this purpose, extraction algorithms are required to map audio recordings to effect classes and associated parameter settings. Early work in this domain focused solely on the classification of guitar effects. Stein et al. pioneered this area of research with their fundamental work [7,8] using a large set of audio features and a support vector machine to classify eleven guitar effects achieving a mean accuracy of 97.7% for solo guitar recordings.

Further work regarding the classification of guitar effects was done by Eichas et al. [2], and Schmitt et al. [6], the latter investigating the importance of audio features and comparing the so called bag-of-audio-words approach to the use of functionals. They found both approaches to achieve similar high performance. Research regarding the extraction of guitar effect parameter settings is scarce. So far only two previous works exist: Jürgens et al. [4] pioneered this task using shallow neural networks combined with specifically design selected features for each guitar effect achieving or surpassing the (presumed) performance of a human expert. Comunitá et al. [1] used convolutional neural networks (CNNs) to extract the parameter settings of different implementations of distortion, overdrive and fuzz guitar effect plug-ins from monophonic and polyphonic guitar recordings. However, none of these research papers [1,4] considered guitar effect parameter setting extraction from instrument mixes, i.e. audio recordings or signals, in which several instruments play at once. This is the focus of this manuscript: the classification of guitar effects from instrument mixes with emphasis on the extraction of the respective effect parameter settings. For this purpose, a custom dataset was created consisting of instrument mixes of guitar, bass, keyboard and drums. As baseline approach for classification we used the method of Stein et al. [8] and for extraction we used the method of Jürgens et al. [4] and compared it to the performance of a CNN at different volume levels of the instrument mix. Four different time-frequency representations were assessed with respect to the achieved CNN performance. To shorten the phrasing a little, guitar effect parameter setting extraction will be called effect parameter extraction or just parameter extraction.

Section 2 describes the datasets used for classification and parameter extraction, the time-frequency representations used and the training and evaluation of the CNNs. Section 3 reports the classification, extraction and robustness results. Section 4 discusses and interpretes these results and the manuscript is concluded in Sect. 5.

2   Method and Materials

Two datasets were created specifically for the investigations of this work, one for guitar effect classification, abbreviated GEC-GIM (for Guitar Effect Classification - Guitar Instrument Mix), and one for guitar effect parameter extraction, abbreviated GEPE-GIM (for Guitar Effect Parameter Extraction - Guitar Instrument Mix). The motivation to create two separate datasets was the large number of samples that had to be created if the same amount of parameter settings used for GEPE-GIM had been used for GEC-GIM. The very same effect

Fig. 1. Tablature showing the drum pattern used in all samples. All other instruments played a single note for the duration of two seconds, i.e. one bar.

plugins of Stein et al. [8] and Jürgens et al. [4] were used in this work. Effect descriptions and their parameters can be found in [4,8,10]. Additionally, to further test the capability of the CNN, the IDMT-SMT dataset from Stein et al. [4] was used for classification.

2.1 Dataset for Guitar Effect Parameter Extraction

The dataset used in this work to investigate guitar effect parameter extraction consisted of instrument mixes of guitar, keyboard, bass and drums. It was specifically created for the investigations described in this manuscript. All instruments were virtual instruments and created using the following plugins: Sonivox Bright Electric Guitar and Ample Guitar LP (guitar), Bitsonic Keyzone Classic (keyboard), Ample Bass P Lite (bass) and Manda Audio MT POWER DrumKit 2 (drums). All plugins were sample-based and thus could be expected to create realistic waveforms/sounds. While guitar, keyboard and bass played a single note in each sample, starting at the exact same time lasting for two seconds, the drums played the pattern depicted in Fig. 1. The guitar and keyboard played the notes E2 and E3, bass played the notes E1 and E2. The guitar note was independently varied from keyboard and bass, while keyboard and bass notes were always moved together by an octave to reduce the amount of data. Keyboard, bass and drums were mixed at different volume levels with the guitar according to

$$premix(t) = b(t) + k(t) + d(t) \tag{1}$$

and

$$mix(t) = g(t) + \alpha \cdot premix(t), \tag{2}$$

where $b(t)$, $k(t)$, $d(t)$ and $g(t)$ are the bass, keyboard, drum and guitar signals, respectively. The parameter α controlled the mixing volume and was set such that the ratio $\frac{\max_t \alpha |premix(t)|}{\max_t |g(t)|}$ corresponded to the desired mixing volume. The volume mixes used were -36 dB, -24 dB, -12 dB, -6 dB, -3 dB, 0 dB and $+3$ dB with respect to the peak amplitude of the guitar waveform, i.e. at $+3$ dB, the peak amplitude of the premix after scaling was 3 dB larger than the peak amplitude of the guitar. Subjectively, the mix was considered realistic in the sense that keyboard and bass were clearly and loudly audible, not overshadowing each other, and the guitar clearly moved towards the background with increasing mixing volume. An example waveform of an audio sample with tremolo on the guitar showing the lowest and highest mixing volume after normalization is depicted in Fig. 2. In total, three guitar effects - distortion, tremolo and slapback delay -

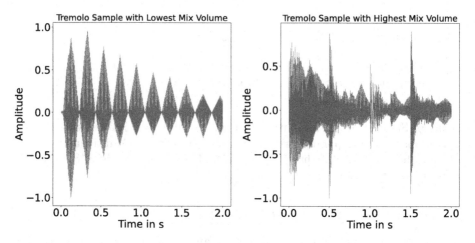

Fig. 2. Audio sample with tremolo on the guitar at (left) lowest (-36 dB) and (right) highest ($+3$ dB) mixing volume after peak normalization. The waveforms were peak normalized before applying the respective time-frequency representation. The two large peaks in the right figure are due to the snare hits. The depth parameter was set to 1.0 and the frequency parameter set to 0.1.

were considered and each guitar effect was applied at every mixing level. These guitar effects were chosen to allow a direct comparison to Jürgens et al. [4]. Each of these guitar effects had two parameters. These parameters were varied in steps of 0.05, starting at 0.05 and ending at 1, creating a grid of parameter values. In total 67,200 audio samples, 22,400 per effect, were created. The audio waveforms were sampled at 44.1 kHz and had a duration of two seconds each corresponding to four quarter notes or one bar at 120 beats per minute and quarter time.

2.2   Dataset for Guitar Effect Classification

The dataset for guitar effect classification from instrument mixes used exactly one fixed volume mix of 0 dB, where the mix was created as described in Sect. 3.1. However, in contrast, a total of eleven guitar effects were used, each using random parameter settings. Furthermore, the dataset consisted of all possible instrument mixes of the guitar and the other instruments, e.g. guitar and keyboard, guitar and bass, guitar and bass and keyboard and so on. Also solo guitar and guitar together with individual drum parts were included, e.g. guitar and snare, guitar and crash cymbal etc. This way, twelve instrument combinations were included yielding a total of 15,840 audio samples. For each combination of guitar effect, guitar plugin and instrument mix, 60 samples using random guitar effect parameter settings were generated.

2.3   Time-Frequency Representations

Four different time-frequency representations were investigated as input of the CNNs. These were the (magnitude) spectrogram, the chromagram, mel-frequency cepstral coefficients (MFCCs) and gammatone frequency cepstral coefficients (GFCCs). The chromagram is a mapping of an audio waveform to the twelve semitones of the western music that yields the energy in the respective semitones. See [5] for a description of the chromagram and the spectrogram and [3] for a description of the MFCCs and GFCCs. For the MFCCs and GFCCs, 40 coefficients were used. The spectrogram, chromagramm and the MFCCs were computed using the python framework librosa and the GFCCs using the python framework Spafe. In all cases default settings were used. For the computation of the GFCCs the sampling rate had to be reduced to 16 kHz. An example of the four time-frequency representations applied to the same audio sample is shown in Fig. 3. The audio sample was an audio mix at maximum mixing volume with distortion applied to the guitar. The hi-hat is clearly visible in the spectrogram and the snare hits are apparent in the Chromagram. The input dimensions of the images obtained by applying the time-frequency representations to the audio samples were 256 × 173 (spectrogram), 40 × 173 (MFCCs), 12 × 173 (chromagram) and 40 × 193 (GFCCs). Before being fed to the CNN, the data obtained by applying the respective time-frequency representations to the audio samples was normalized to have zero mean and unit variance using sklearn's standardscaler class.

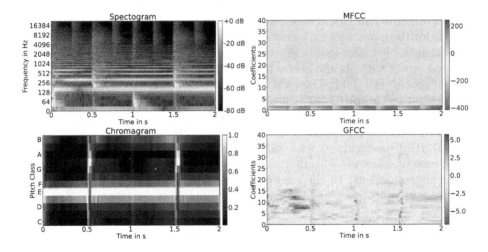

Fig. 3. Example of all four investigated time-frequency representations of one sample of the GEPE-GIT dataset with distortion effect on the guitar and gain set to 0.7 and tone set to 0.85. The snare hits are clearly visible in the chromagram and the hi-hat is apparent in the spectrogram. Mel-Frequency cepstral coefficients (MFCCs) and gammatone frequency cepstral coefficients (GFCCs) are less obvious. Except for the spectrogram, all plots use linear scale.

Table 1. Structure of the convolutional neural networks (CNNs) used for effect classification. For parameter extraction, only the number of filters, the dropout probability and number of outputs changed.

Layer	Kernel	Filter	Activation	Dropout
Convolutional	3 × 3	32	ReLU	–
Batch norm	–	–	–	–
Max pooling	2 × 2	–	–	–
Convolutional	3 × 3	64	ReLU	0.3
Batch norm	–	–	–	–
Max pooling	2 × 2	–	–	–
Flatten	–	–	–	–
Dense	–	64	ReLU	0.3
Batch norm	–	–	–	–
Dense	–	64	ReLU	0.3
Batch norm	–	–	–	–
Dense (Output)	–	11	Softmax	–

2.4   Convolutional Neural Networks

Two slightly different CNNs were used, one for classification of the guitar effects and one for the parameter extraction. The CNN structure used for classification is given in Table 1. For guitar effect parameter extraction, the same structure was used except with six and twelve filters in the convolutional layers as well as a dropout probability of 0.2. The total number of weights of the CNN used for classification ranged from 192,587 (Chromagram) to 10,436,683 (Spectrogram) with 1,368,139 for MFCCs and 1,597,515 for GFCCs. The total number of weights of the CNN used for parameter extraction ranged from 37,146 (Chromagram) to 1,957,914 (Spectrogram) with 257,562 for MFCCs and 300,570 for GFCCs. In the case of effect classification, the output dimension was eleven, matching the number of effects. In the case of effect parameter extraction, the output dimension was two, matching the number of parameters per effect.

2.5   Training and Evaluation

The CNNs were trained for 70 epochs with a learning rate of 0.001 using the adam solver. It was confirmed by selected visual inspection that the training had converged after 70 epochs. A 80%/20% training/validation split of the entire dataset was used where the validation set was only used for evaluating the CNNs performance and did not influence the training process in anyway. Five repetitions, i.e. five random initializations with subsequent training of the CNNs were performed, and the results reported are an average of the results of these individual CNNs. Each training used a new training/validation split resulting in 5-fold cross validation. The batch size was set to 64 for classification and 128 for parameter extraction. Training time for the CNN was about 15 h per repetition compared to about half an hour for the SVM.

2.6   Baseline

For effect classification, the support vector machine (SVM) classifier as described in [8] and as implemented by [4] was used, albeit the onset detection was removed as the onset was always the same due to the usage of virtual instruments in this work. Using the features and functionals proposed in [8], a total of 649 functionals were used. For effect parameter extraction, the method proposed by Jürgens et al. [4] served as baseline.

2.7   Robustness Analysis

As artificial neural networks are prone to overfitting or to fit to unexpected patterns in the data, in the most extreme case relying on isolated pixels [9], the robustness or sensitivity of the CNN for parameter extraction was analyzed. For this purpose, zero mean white gaussian noise was added to the time-frequency representations with a standard deviation σ_s set according to

$$\sigma_s = \alpha \cdot \max\{|C_s(t, f)|\}, \tag{3}$$

with $\alpha \in \{0, 0.001, 0.01, 0.05\}$ and the respective time-frequency representations $C_s(t, f)$ and its impact on the parameter extraction error was observed. The maximum was taken across the entirety of the dataset but separately for each frequency bin. An α value of zero corresponded to the original, noise-free samples and was included as reference. The index s denotes the respective time-frequency representation. Additionally, the CNN was tested with novel tones of keyboard and bass which now were moved, together, in semitone steps from $E2$ (keyboard) and $E1$ (bass) to the next octave and the impact on the parameter extraction error was assessed. An example of the impact of the noise on the spectrogram for $\alpha = 0.01$ is depicted in Fig. 4. Through spectrogram inversion with the ground truth phase and the noise corrupted amplitude spectrum the corresponding audio data was subjectively judged for the spectrogram. It was found that even at the smallest noise level investigated the noise was clearly audible.

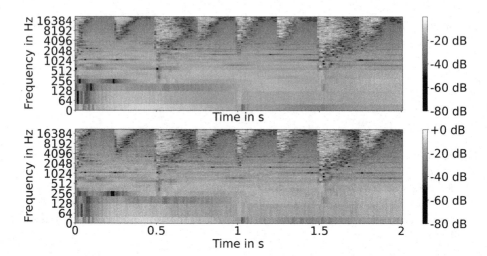

Fig. 4. Spectrogram of an audio sample at 0 dB mixing volume using distortion with gain set to 0.15 and tone set to 0.8 after normalization of the dataset as explained in Sect. 2.3 without (top) additional noise, i.e. $\alpha = 0$, and with (bottom) additional noise with $\alpha = 0.001$ and α as explained in Sect. 2.7. The noise is noticeable mostly at low magnitudes.

3   Results

The results are presented in three steps: First, the effect classification is presented. Secondly, the effect parameter extraction is presented. Finally, results regarding the robustness of the CNN are presented.

3.1   Effect Classification

The confusion matrices of the SVM and CNN classifiers on the IDMT-SMT and GEC-GIM dataset are depicted in Fig. 5. For the CNN, the depicted confusion matrices were achieved using GFCCs (IDMT-SMT) and the spectrogram (GEC-GIM). The accuracies for the other time-frequency representations were similar except for the GFCCs on the GEC-GIM dataset where the CNN failed to converge. While no obvious reason was found, inspection of the loss curves suggested an insufficient learning rate. However, because the GFCCs otherwise performed very well, this issue was not investigated further. Table 2 summarizes the accuracies of the CNN and SVM classifier for both datasets with respect to the time-frequency representation. On the GEC-GIM, both classifiers tended to confuse slapback and feedback delay which greatly impacted the overall accuracies. However, it was later realized that the feedback delay plugin at least up to a setting of 0.3 of the feedback parameter was very hard to distinguish from the slapback delay. Due to the random settings used, about 30% of all feedback delay samples used a value of 0.3 or less making feedback and slapback delay

Table 2. 95% confidence intervals for the classification accuracy of the convolutional neural network (CNN) using the listed time-frequency representations as well as the accuracy of the baseline support vector machine (SVM) using the method by Stein et al. [8]. In all cases the CNN outperformed the SVM where the highest accuracy is highlighted using bold font. As subsequent parameter extraction is not necessarily compromised by a confusion of slapback delay (SD) and feedback delay (FD), the respective accuracies, when SD and FD are treated as the same effect, are given as well.

Method	GEC-GIM	GEC-GIM (SD = FD)	IDMT-SMT
SVM	85.0% ± 0.44%	89.7% ± 0.44	96.1% ± 0.3%
CNN + Spectrogram	**90.0% ± 0.57%**	**95.7% ± 0.57%**	**97.4% ± 0.7%**
CNN + MFCCs	87.7% ± 0.52%	93.0% ± 0.52%	96.5% ± 0.13%
CNN + GFCCs	24.7% ± 27.3%	28.6% ± 27.3%	**97.4% ± 0.3%**
CNN + Chromagram	87.0% ± 0.64%	92.8% ± 0.64%	86.2% ± 0.2%

virtually indistinguishable for at least these samples as confirmed by selected manual inspection. This issue did not arise on the IDMT-SMT, where rather distinct settings for slapback and feedback delay were used. On both datasets, the CNN outperformed the SVM classifier with an accuracy of up to 90.02% for the CNN on the GEC-GIM and 85.01% for the SVM. On the IDMT-SMT, the CNN achieved up to 97.38 % accuracy in contrast to 96.16 % accuracy for the SVM classifier. As the slapback delay is identical to the feedback delay when the feedback parameter is set to zero, confusing these two effects is not necessarily a problem for subsequent parameter extraction. Due to this, the classification accuracy when these two are considered as the same effect was specified as well increasing the accuracies by about 4–5% in all cases.

3.2   Effect Parameter Extraction

Boxplots of the absolute error of the parameter extraction across all volumes for the CNN and the four different input representations as described in Sect. 2.3 as well as the method by Jürgens et al. [4] are shown for the distortion effect and its gain parameter in Fig. 6a, for the tremolo effect and its frequency parameter in Fig. 6b and the slapback delay effect and its time parameter in Fig. 6c. The horizontal lines inside of the boxes denotes the median. Additionally, the presumed human expert error of 0.05 was included as a reference, see also Jürgens et al. [4]. From our own experience of creating guitar sounds, we estimated that a guitar player can be sufficiently accurate by only setting effect parameters in steps of 0.1, which would result in a minimum absolute error of 0.05. The mean absolute parameter extraction error across all volumes is summarized in Table 3. No single time-frequency representation was optimal irrespective of the considered guitar effect. The CNN using MFCCs achieved the minimum error for the distortion effect of below 0.017 for either parameter, the GFCCs worked best for the slapback delay yielding a mean error below 0.04 for either parameter.

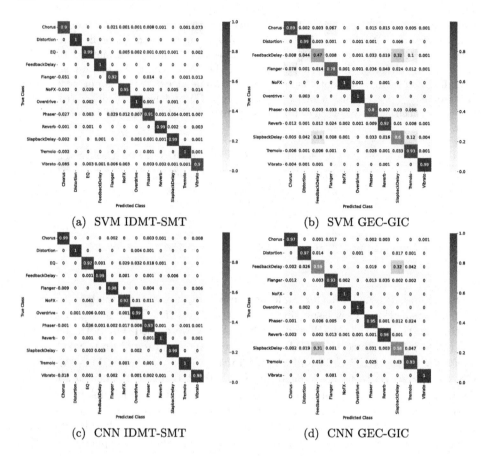

Fig. 5. Confusion matrices of the support vector machine classifier (SVM) on the (a) IDMT-SMT and (b) GEC-GIC dataset as well as the convolutional neural network (CNN) classifier on the (c) IDMT-SMT and (d) GEC-GIC dataset. On the GEC-GIC both classifiers tended to confuse slapback and feedback delay which was due to unfortunate random settings of the feedback parameter which always was set to rather low values making these effects very difficult to distinguish which was confirmed through selected manual inspection. On the IDMT-SMT, which used very distinct parameter settings no confusion occured for either classifier.

The outliers occured mostly for effects and their parameter settings that were very difficult to hear, e.g. any tone setting of the distortion effect when the gain was very small. Then the tone parameter has almost no impact on the sound. For the slapback delay and its time parameter the maximum of the absolute error across the five training repetitions is depicted across the true parameter settings in Fig. 7. There, the maximum errors tended to occur for the smallest value of the mix parameter where the delay is almost inaudible.

The mean absolute extraction error across mixing volume for the slapback delay is shown in Fig. 6d. The other effects qualitatively showed similar dependency on the mixing volume. Usually a two or three fold increase from the lowest to the highest mixing volume was observed albeit even at the highest mixing volume of +3 dB the mean performance was, on average, at or below human expert level. The method by Jürgens et al. was found to be less affected by the mixing volume showing only a minor increase of the mean absolute error with increasing mixing volume but still performed considerably worse than the CNN even at the highest mixing volume. Sample files showcasing the effect parameter extraction can be found under https://bit.ly/3nIEv8U.

3.3   Robustness to Noise and Pitch Shifts

The mean absolute error across noise levels of the effect parameter extraction for all time-frequency representations is shown in Fig. 8a for the time parameter of the slapback delay. The mixing volume in this investigation was always 0 dB. For the MFCCs, GFCCs and the Chromagram, the mean absolute error was found to be relatively robust to additive gaussian noise with an approximate increase of the mean absolute error by around 0.01–0.03 depending on the guitar effect and time-frequency representation considered. The spectrogram proved to be rather sensitive showing a considerable increase of about 0.05–0.15 depending on the guitar effect. Qualitatively, the noise impact was similiar for the other parameters and effects as well.

The mean absolute error across pitch is depicted in Fig. 8b at a mixing volume of −12 dB. None of the pitches between the outer two notes was part of the training data. GFCCs allowed to achieve a mean absolute error of about 0.1 or less for all pitches at −12 dB, performance was considerably worse, often above 0.15 or 0.2, when the spectrogram or the chromagram was used. At a mixing volume of −3 dB, the general performance decreased even further and, at +3 dB, parameter extraction failed almost entirely for any pitch between the two E notes, except for the gain parameter of the distortion effect, where errors below 0.1 were still achieved for the GFCCs and MFCCs. For all other effects and

Table 3. 95 % confidence interval of the mean absolute error across the five repetitions of the parameter extraction across all volumes of the CNN and the respective time-frequency representations as well as the method by Jürgens et al. [4]. The lowest errors are highlighted using bold font.

	Distortion		Tremolo		Slapback delay	
	Gain	Tone	Depth	Freq	Time	Mix
Chromagram	0.032 ± 0.0015	0.051 ± 0.0048	0.063 ± 0.0017	0.061 ± 0.0038	0.062 ± 0.0025	0.054 ± 0.003
GFCC	0.016 ± 0.0025	0.017 ± 0.0015	**0.034 ± 0.002**	0.063 ± 0.0033	**0.038 ± 0.0007**	**0.027 ± 0.0014**
MFCC	**0.014 ± 0.0009**	**0.016 ± 0.0009**	0.049 ± 0.0045	0.065 ± 0.0015	0.039 ± 0.001	0.031 ± 0.0022
Spectrogram	0.021 ± 0.0063	0.023 ± 0.0018	0.039 ± 0.0025	**0.052 ± 0.0059**	0.049 ± 0.0009	0.037 ± 0.0047
Jürgens et al.	0.048 ± 0.0082	0.071 ± 0.024	0.129 ± 0.034	0.118 ± 0.0208	0.228 ± 0.076	0.207 ± 0.0061

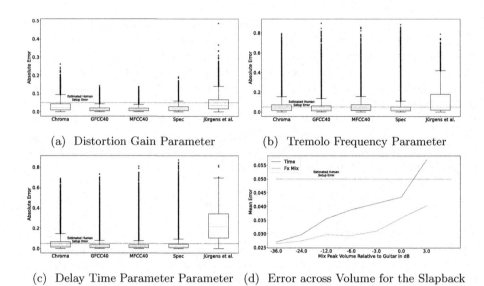

(a) Distortion Gain Parameter   (b) Tremolo Frequency Parameter

(c) Delay Time Parameter Parameter   (d) Error across Volume for the Slapback Delay

Fig. 6. Boxplots of the absolute parameter extraction error for the (a) distortion gain, (b) tremolo frequency and (c) slapback delay time parameter for all investigated methods across all volumes. The outliers occured most frequently for parameter settings where the respective parameter had little to no effect due to interference of the second effect parameter. (d) shows the mean parameter extraction error across volume for the slapback delay.

parameters, the mean error rose up to about 0.4 or higher at +3 dB mixing volume.

4   Discussion

Generally, the CNN was found to be superior to the investigated baselines in both effect classification and effect parameter extraction. All time-frequency representations allowed to achieve an accuracy around or better than human expert level in parameter extraction with the chromagram performing the worst out of the four. MFCCs and GFCCs were found to perform approximately the same, neither having a clear edge over the other.

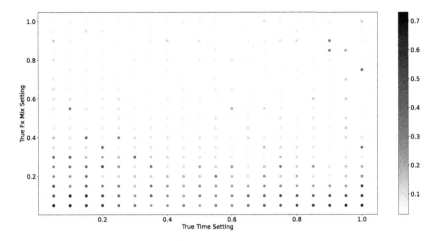

Fig. 7. Maximum extraction error for the time parameter across all five repetitions of the absolute parameter extraction error across true mix and time settings of the slapback delay. Most of the large errors occured at the smallest mix setting where the effect is very difficult (or potentially impossible) to hear and furthermore occurs also where the time parameter is very small or very large which adds to the extraction difficulty.

4.1 Guitar Effect Classification

The CNN outperformed the SVM classifier on both datasets except when the chromagram was used. The chromagram contains the most coarse information about the audio out of all investigated time-frequency representations as it maps different octaves to the same pitch value therefore it performing the worst was not surprising. The CNN achieved in its best configuration an accuracy of 97.4% on the IDMT-SMT which is very close to the 97.7% reported by Stein et al. [8] in their SVM implementation.

As the CNN achieved good results for both datasets, one of them using virtual instruments, albcit sample based, with all kinds of instrument mixes and the other real recordings and a large variety of solo guitar pitches, it can be assumed that the CNN is suitable for a wide range of audio data. The confusion of slapback and feedback delay on the GEC-GIT is not surprising as mostly very small parameter settings for the feedback parameter of the feedback delay were randomly selected making it very hard or impossible to distinguish it from the slapback delay. The CNN and the SVM both failing to distinguish the two effects on the GEC-GIT and not failing on the IDMT-SMT is a strong indicator that the issue lies in the data and not the classifiers. Another approach to the effect classification and extraction problem from instrument mixes could be the application of source separation algorithms followed by some classifiers. However, initial tests for our research [4] did not yield promising results and thus this approach was not pursuit further.

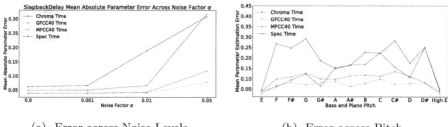

(a) Error across Noise Levels   (b) Error across Pitch

Fig. 8. Mean absolute parameter extraction error of the time parameter of the slapback delay across (a) noise levels and (b) pitch of keyboard and guitar and all four time-frequency representations. The impact of the noise was investigated at a mixing volume of 0 dB, the error across pitch is depicted for a mixing volume of -12 dB.

4.2 Guitar Effect Parameter Extraction

The impact of the mixing volume on the parameter extraction error qualitatively was as expected, with the error increasing generally with increasing mixing volume. The spectrogram was found to perform the best, albeit MFCCs and the chromagramm achieved similar accuracies. Only the chromagram showed a clearly inferior performance compared to the other time-frequency representations. For all effects and volumes the CNN outperformed the approach of Jürgens et al. [4] albeit the CNN showed a greater sensitivity towards the mixing volume. While the boxplots revealed considerable outliers, usually about 75% or more of the extraction errors were below the error of a human expert. Outliers, as suggested by Fig. 7, usually occured at the highest mixing volume and at settings that were very difficult to distinguish, because some parameters have an impact on each other and render the other virtually useless at certain settings. Nonetheless, some isolated large errors occur at apparently random parameter settings. These large errors could indicate an insufficient amount of data or suboptimal data creation.

4.3 Robustness

As the CNN showed only a minor decrease in accuracy when small amounts of noise ($\alpha = 0.001$) were added to the input time-frequency representations, over-fitting at least to the individual pixels seems unlikely which some deep networks are susceptible to [9]. Because at lower mixing volumes (≤ -12 dB) robustness was also observed across pitch, it is very probable that the CNN indeed extracted meaningful features. Albeit at the largest noise level the noise was considerable, it was subjectively estimated, without performing a rigorous experiment, that at all noise levels a human expert would not see as large of an increase in parameter extraction error as the CNN. Here, the CNN potentially performed suboptimally and could be improved in the future. The chromagram generally yielding the least robust CNN is not surprising because the energy for the chromagram in the training data was almost solely contained in the E note. This will have made the CNN focus mostly on this particular pitch. Once the other instruments changed their pitch and therefore the energy distribution this approach was prone to fail.

The extraction error for the gain parameter of the distortion effect was found to be very robust with respect to the pitch of keyboard and bass and the CNN achieved around and below 0.1 mean absolute error even at +3 dB mixing volume unlike all other effects and parameters. The reason was probably the distortion effect being the only nonlinear effect introducing novel frequencies into the audio signals. These samples were then the only ones in the training data where novel frequencies could convey information about the parameter settings. Therefore it appears reasonable that for the distortion effect the CNN learned a more diverse look at the time-frequency representations which in return allowed to be more robust when the pitch of the other instruments changed. Although the number of weights of the CNN, especially when the spectrogram was used as input, was rather large in comparison to the amount of training data, the results of the robustness analysis and the use of dropout layers make it seem unlikely that relevant overfitting occured.

4.4   Limitations

One limitation of our investigation is the simplicity of the music played by the instruments. More complex musical pieces, including polyphon guitar melodies, likely will be more challenging to extract guitar effects from. Furthermore, additional audio effects on the other instruments could interfere with the parameter extraction of the guitar effects. Also a second guitar could have a considerable impact on the classification and extraction performance.

5   Conclusion

In this work guitar effect classification and guitar effect parameter extraction with convolutional neural networks (CNNs) from instrument mixes was investigated and compared to two baselines. On two datasets, the CNN achieved classification accuracies 1–5% above the baseline accuracy achieving up to 97.4% accuracy. Mean parameter extraction errors of below 0.016 for the distortion, below 0.052 for the tremolo and below 0.038 for the slapback delay effect were achieved matching or surpassing the presumed human expert error of 0.05. The CNN was found to be moderately robust to noise and pitch changes of the background instrumentation suggesting that the CNN extracted meaningful features.

References

1. Comunità, M., Stowell, D., Reiss, J.D.: Guitar effects recognition and parameter estimation with convolutional neural networks. J. Audio Eng. Soc. **69**(7/8), 594–604 (2021)

2. Eichas, F., Fink, M., Zölzer, U.: Feature design for the classification of audio effect units by input/output measurements. In: Proceedings of the 18th International Conference on Digital Audio Effects (DAFx-2015) (2015)
3. Jeevan, M., Dhingra, A., Hanmandlu, M., Panigrahi, B.K.: Robust speaker verification using GFCC based i-vectors. In: Lobiyal, D.K., Mohapatra, D.P., Nagar, A., Sahoo, M.N. (eds.) Proceedings of the International Conference on Signal, Networks, Computing, and Systems. LNEE, vol. 395, pp. 85–91. Springer, New Delhi (2017). https://doi.org/10.1007/978-81-322-3592-7_9
4. Jürgens, H., Hinrichs, R., Ostermann, J.: Recognizing guitar effects and their parameter settings. In: Proceedings of the 23rd International Conference on Digital Audio Effects (DAFx2020) (2020)
5. Müller, M.: Fundamentals of Music Processing: Using Python and Jupyter Notebooks. Springer, Cham (2021). https://doi.org/10.1007/978-3-030-69808-9
6. Schmitt, M., Schuller, B.: Recognising guitar effects - which acoustic features really matter? In: INFORMATIK 2017, pp. 177–190. Gesellschaft für Informatik, Bonn (2017). https://doi.org/10.18420/in2017_12
7. Stein, M.: Automatic detection of multiple, cascaded audio effects in guitar recordings. In: 13th International Conference on Digital Audio Effects, DAFx 2010 Proceedings (2010)
8. Stein, M., Abeßer, J., Dittmar, C., Schuller, G.: Automatic detection of audio effects in guitar and bass recordings. J. Audio Eng. Soc. (2010)
9. Su, J., Vargas, D.V., Sakurai, K.: One pixel attack for fooling deep neural networks. IEEE Trans. Evol. Comput. **23**(5), 828–841 (2019). https://doi.org/10.1109/TEVC.2019.2890858
10. Zölzer, U.: DAFX: Digital Audio Effects, 2nd edn. Wiley, Chichester (2011)

Aesthetic Evaluation of Experimental Stimuli Using Spatial Complexity and Kolmogorov Complexity

Mohammad Ali Javaheri Javid$^{(\boxtimes)}$ (iD)

Department of Engineering, Computing and Design, University of Chichester,
Bognor Regis Campus, West Sussex, UK
`M.JavaheriJavid@chi.ac.uk`

Abstract. The measure of complexity is a core concept in computational approaches to aesthetics. Shannon's information theory provided an objective measure of complexity, which led to the emergence of various informational theories of aesthetics. However, entropy fails to consider the spatial characteristics of 2D patterns; these characteristics are fundamental in addressing the aesthetic problem. We propose two empirically evaluated alternative measures of complexity, considering the spatial characteristics of 2D patterns and experimental studies on human aesthetic perception in the visual domain. The first model, spatial complexity, is based on the probabilistic spatial distribution of pixels of a 2D pattern. The second model is based on algorithmic information theory (Kolmogorov complexity), which is extended to estimate the complexity of 2D patterns. The spatial complexity measure presents a performance advantage over information-theoretic models, specifically in discriminating symmetries and the orientation in 2D, enabling more accurate measurement of complexity in relation to aesthetic evaluations of 2D patterns. This paper examines whether the complexity measures for 2D patterns conform with aesthetic judgments. The experiment results show that none of the measures has a significant correlation with participants aesthetic rating/rankings of experimental stimuli.

Keywords: Computational aesthetics · 2D pattern · Information theory · Spatial complexity · Kolmogorov complexity

1 Introduction

Despite the dominance of entropy as a measure of order and complexity in computational aesthetics, it fails to reflect on the structural characteristics of 2D patterns. The main reason for this drawback is that it measures the distribution of symbols, not their arrangements. This fact was noted by Arnheim, who stated that "entropy theory is indeed a first attempt to deal with global form; but it has not been dealing with structure. All it says is that a large sum of elements may have properties not found in a smaller sample of them" [2, p. 18].

© The Author(s), under exclusive license to Springer Nature Switzerland AG 2022
T. Martins et al. (Eds.): EvoMUSART 2022, LNCS 13221, pp. 117–130, 2022.
https://doi.org/10.1007/978-3-031-03789-4_8

Figure 1 illustrates the measurements of entropy for 2D patterns with various structural characteristics. Figure 1(a) and 1(b) generated by a cellular automaton. Figure 1(a) is a fully symmetrical pattern, Fig. 1(b) is a pattern with local structures and Fig. 1(c) is a fairly structureless random pattern.

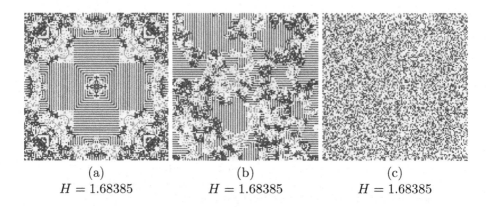

(a)	(b)	(c)
$H = 1.68385$	$H = 1.68385$	$H = 1.68385$

Fig. 1. The measurements of H for structurally different patterns.

The comparison of the structural characteristics of these patterns with their corresponding entropy values shows that despite their structural differences, all of the patterns have the same entropy value. This clearly demonstrates the failure of entropy to discriminate structurally different 2D patterns. In other words, entropy is invariant to the spatial arrangement of the composing elements of 2D patterns. This is in contrast to our intuitive perception of the complexity of patterns.

2   Conceptual Model

Considering our intuitive perception of complexity and the structural characteristics of 2D patterns, a complexity measure must be bounded by two extreme points of complete order and disorder. It is reasonable to assume that *regular structures*, *irregular structures* and *structureless* patterns lie between these extremes, as illustrated in Fig. 2. A complete regular structure is a pattern of high symmetry, while an irregular structure is a pattern with some structure, though not as regular as a fully symmetrical pattern; finally a structureless pattern is a random arrangement of elements [6].

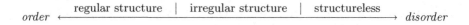

order ←——— regular structure | irregular structure | structureless ———→ *disorder*

Fig. 2. The spectrum of spatial complexity.

3 Spatial Complexity Measure

Although Shannon further provided definitions of joint and conditional entropies in the framework of information theory [11, p. 52], its applications in measuring structural complexity of dynamical systems remained unrecognised until studies in [1, 3, 10, 12] showed its merits. A measure introduced in [1, 3, 12], known as *information gain*, has been proposed as a means of characterising the complexity of dynamical systems and of 2D patterns. It measures the amount of information gained in bits when specifying the value, x, of a random variable X given knowledge of the value, y, of another random variable Y,

$$G_{x,y} = -\log_2 P(x|y). \tag{1}$$

$P(x|y)$ is the conditional probability of a state x conditioned on the state y. The *mean information gain* (MIG), $\overline{G}_{X,Y}$, is the average amount of information gain from the description of all possible states of Y:

$$\overline{G}_{X,Y} = \sum_{x,y} P(x,y)G_{x,y} = -\sum_{x,y} P(x,y)\log_2 P(x|y) \tag{2}$$

where $P(x,y)$ is the joint probability, $\mathrm{prob}(X = x, Y = y)$. $\overline{G}$ is also known as the conditional entropy, $H(X|Y)$ [4]. Conditional entropy is the reduction in uncertainty of the joint distribution of X and Y given knowledge of Y, $H(X|Y) = H(X,Y) - H(Y)$. The lower and upper bounds of $\overline{G}_{X,Y}$ are

$$0 \leqslant \overline{G}_{X,Y} \leqslant \log_2 |\mathcal{X}|. \tag{3}$$

Definition 1. *A spatial complexity measure G, of a 2D pattern is the sum of the mean information gains of pixels having homogeneous/heterogeneous neighbouring pixels over.*

For a 2D pattern, $\overline{G}$ can be calculated by considering the distribution of pixel colours over pairs of pixel r, s,

$$\overline{G}_{r,s} = -\sum_{s_r,s_s} P(s_r,s_s)\log_2 P(s_r,s_s) \tag{4}$$

where s_r, s_s are the colours at r and s, respectively. Since $|\mathcal{S}| = N$, $\overline{G}_{r,s}$ is a value in $[0, N]$. The vertical, horizontal, primary diagonal ($\searrow$) and secondary diagonal ($\nearrow$) neighbouring pairs provide eight $\overline{G}s$; $\overline{G}_{(i,j),(i-1,j+1)}$, $\overline{G}_{(i,j),(i,j+1)}$, $\overline{G}_{(i,j),(i+1,j+1)}$, $\overline{G}_{(i,j),(i-1,j)}$, $\overline{G}_{(i,j),(i+1,j)}$, $\overline{G}_{(i,j),(i-1,j-1)}$, $\overline{G}_{(i,j),(i,j-1)}$ and $\overline{G}_{(i,j),(i+1,j-1)}$. The relative positions for non-edge pixels are given by matrix M:

$$M = \begin{bmatrix} (i-1,j+1) & (i,j+1) & (i+1,j+1) \\ (i-1,j) & (i,j) & (i+1,j) \\ (i-1,j-1) & (i,j-1) & (i+1,j-1) \end{bmatrix}. \tag{5}$$

The differences between the horizontal (vertical) and two diagonal mean information rates reveal left/right (up/down), primary and secondary orientation of 2D patterns. So the 2D patterns can be analysed using the differences between the vertical $(i, j \pm 1)$, horizontal $(i \pm 1, j)$, primary diagonal (P_d) and secondary diagonal (S_d) mean information gains by means of:

$$\Delta \overline{G}_{i,j \pm 1}(\Delta \overline{G}_V) = |\overline{G}_{i,j+1} - \overline{G}_{i,j-1}|, \tag{6a}$$

$$\Delta \overline{G}_{i \pm 1,j}(\Delta \overline{G}_H) = |\overline{G}_{i-1,j} - \overline{G}_{i+1,j}|, \tag{6b}$$

$$\Delta \overline{G}_{P_d} = |\overline{G}_{i-1,j+1} - \overline{G}_{i+1,j-1}|, \tag{6c}$$

$$\Delta \overline{G}_{S_d} = |\overline{G}_{i+1,j+1} - \overline{G}_{i-1,j-1}|. \tag{6d}$$

4   Kolmogorov Complexity of 2D Patterns

From an information theory perspective, the object X is a random variable drawn according to a probability mass function $P(x)$. If X is random, then the descriptive complexity of the event $X = x$ is $\log \frac{1}{P(x)}$, because $\lceil \log \frac{1}{P(x)} \rceil$ is the number of bits required to describe x. Thus, the descriptive complexity of an object depends on the probability distribution [4].

Kolmogorov attributed the algorithmic (descriptive) complexity of an object to the minimum length of a program such that a universal computer (universal turing machine) can generate a specific sequence [8]. Thus, the Kolmogorov complexity of an object is independent of the probability distribution. Kolmogorov complexity is related to entropy $(H(X))$, in that the expected value of $K(x)$ for a random sequence is approximately the entropy of the source distribution for the process generating the sequence. However, Kolmogorov complexity differs from entropy in that it relates to the specific string being considered rather than the source distribution [4,9]. Kolmogorov complexity can be described as follows, where φ represents a universal computer, p represents a program, and x represents a string:

$$K_\varphi(x) = \left\{ \min_{\varphi(p)=x} \quad l(p) \right\} \tag{7}$$

Random strings have rather high Kolmogorov complexity - on the order of their length, as patterns cannot be discerned to reduce the size of a program generating such a string. On the other hand, strings with a high degree of structure have fairly low complexity. Universal computers can be equated through programs of constant length, thus a mapping can be made between universal computers of different types. The Kolmogorov complexity of a given string on two computers differs by known or determinable constants. The Kolmogorov complexity $K(y|x)$ of a string y, given string x as input is described by the equation below:

$$K_\varphi(y|x) = \left\{ \begin{array}{l} \min_{\varphi(p,y)=y} \quad l(p) \\ \\ \infty, \text{if there is no } p \text{ such that } \varphi(p, x) = y \end{array} \right\} \tag{8}$$

where $l(p)$ represents program length p and φ is a particular universal computer under consideration. Thus, knowledge or input of a string x may reduce the complexity or program size necessary to produce a new string y. The major difficulty with Kolmogorov complexity is that it is uncomputable. Any program that produces a given string is an upper bound on the Kolmogorov complexity for this string, but it is not possible to compute the lower bound.

Lempel and Ziv defined a measure of complexity for finite sequences rooted in the ability to produce strings from simple copy operations [13]. This method, known as *LZ78* universal compression algorithm, harnesses this principle to yield a universal compression algorithm that can approach the entropy of an infinite sequence produced by an ergodic source. As such, *LZ78* compression has been used as an estimator for K. Kolmogorov complexity is the ultimate compression bound for a given finite string and, thus, a natural choice for the estimation of complexity in the class of universal compression techniques. In order to estimate the K value of a 2D pattern, we generate linear strings of configurations by means of six different templates illustrated in Fig. 3.

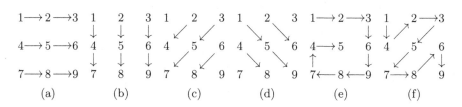

Fig. 3. Six different templates applied for the estimation of K in 2D plane.

1. A horizontal string $S_h = \{1, 2, 3, 4, 5, 6, 7, 8, 9\}$ (Fig. 3(a))
2. A vertical string $S_v = \{1, 4, 7, 2, 5, 8, 3, 6, 9\}$ (Fig. 3(b))
3. A diagonal string $S_d = \{1, 2, 4, 3, 5, 7, 6, 8, 9\}$ (Fig. 3(c))
4. A reverse diagonal string $S_{rd} = \{3, 2, 6, 1, 5, 9, 4, 8, 7\}$ (Fig. 3(d))
5. A spiral string $S_s = \{1, 2, 3, 6, 9, 8, 7, 4, 5\}$ (Fig. 3(e))
6. A continuous spiral string $S_{cs} = \{1, 4, 2, 3, 5, 7, 8, 6, 9\}$ (Fig. 3(f))

Then, using the *LZ78* compression algorithm, the upper bound of K is estimated as the lowest value among the six different templates. The comparison of the measurements of H, $\overline{G}s$, $\Delta \overline{G}s$ and K for structurally different patterns is illustrated in Fig. 4. It is evident from the measurements, K is able to discriminate the complexity of patterns; however, it fails to discriminate the spatial orientations. Figure 4 demonstrates the merits of $\overline{G}$ in discriminating structurally different patterns for the sample patterns in Fig. 4. As can be observed, the measures of H are identical for structurally different patterns; however, $\overline{G}s$ and $\Delta \overline{G}s$ reflect both the complexity of patterns and the spatial distribution of their constituting elements ($\mu Gs_{(a)} = 1.51946 > \mu Gs_{(b)} = 1.55110 > \mu Gs_{(c)} = 1.68396$).

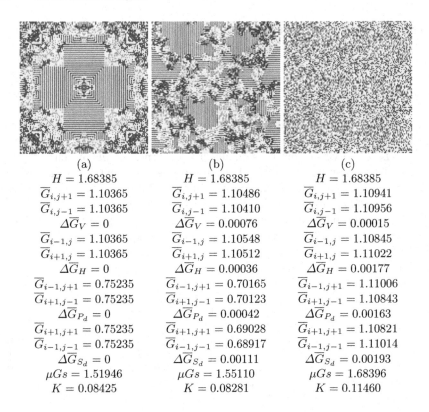

(a) (b) (c)

(a)	(b)	(c)
$H = 1.68385$	$H = 1.68385$	$H = 1.68385$
$\overline{G}_{i,j+1} = 1.10365$	$\overline{G}_{i,j+1} = 1.10486$	$\overline{G}_{i,j+1} = 1.10941$
$\overline{G}_{i,j-1} = 1.10365$	$\overline{G}_{i,j-1} = 1.10410$	$\overline{G}_{i,j-1} = 1.10956$
$\Delta\overline{G}_V = 0$	$\Delta\overline{G}_V = 0.00076$	$\Delta\overline{G}_V = 0.00015$
$\overline{G}_{i-1,j} = 1.10365$	$\overline{G}_{i-1,j} = 1.10548$	$\overline{G}_{i-1,j} = 1.10845$
$\overline{G}_{i+1,j} = 1.10365$	$\overline{G}_{i+1,j} = 1.10512$	$\overline{G}_{i+1,j} = 1.11022$
$\Delta\overline{G}_H = 0$	$\Delta\overline{G}_H = 0.00036$	$\Delta\overline{G}_H = 0.00177$
$\overline{G}_{i-1,j+1} = 0.75235$	$\overline{G}_{i-1,j+1} = 0.70165$	$\overline{G}_{i-1,j+1} = 1.11006$
$\overline{G}_{i+1,j-1} = 0.75235$	$\overline{G}_{i+1,j-1} = 0.70123$	$\overline{G}_{i+1,j-1} = 1.10843$
$\Delta\overline{G}_{P_d} = 0$	$\Delta\overline{G}_{P_d} = 0.00042$	$\Delta\overline{G}_{P_d} = 0.00163$
$\overline{G}_{i+1,j+1} = 0.75235$	$\overline{G}_{i+1,j+1} = 0.69028$	$\overline{G}_{i+1,j+1} = 1.10821$
$\overline{G}_{i-1,j-1} = 0.75235$	$\overline{G}_{i-1,j-1} = 0.68917$	$\overline{G}_{i-1,j-1} = 1.11014$
$\Delta\overline{G}_{S_d} = 0$	$\Delta\overline{G}_{S_d} = 0.00111$	$\Delta\overline{G}_{S_d} = 0.00193$
$\mu Gs = 1.51946$	$\mu Gs = 1.55110$	$\mu Gs = 1.68396$
$K = 0.08425$	$K = 0.08281$	$K = 0.11460$

Fig. 4. The measurements of H, $\overline{G}s$, $\Delta\overline{G}s$ and K for structurally different patterns.

5   Experiment and Results

This section details experiment and its results on the correlation between three measures, namely spatial complexity measure ($\mu(G)s$), Kolmogorov complexity (K) and entropy (H), and human aesthetic judgement. The details in the subsequent sections of *Method*, *Material*, *Procedure* and *Results* are directly adopted from [5]. An extended study is provided, where the 252 experimental stimuli were adopted from [5] empirical study of human aesthetic judgements of symmetrical and asymmetrical patterns to evaluate the effectiveness of $\mu(G)s$, K and H. The objectives are to investigate the relationship between human aesthetic judgement and the measurements of $\mu(G)s$, K and H, with the purpose of evaluating the following set of hypotheses:

H1: *The measurement of $\mu(G)s$ for a 2D pattern is linearly related with human aesthetic judgement.*

H2: *The estimation of K for a 2D pattern is linearly related with human aesthetic judgement.*

H3: *The measurement of H for a 2D pattern is linearly related with human aesthetic judgement.*

Thus $\mu(G)s$, K and H are the independent variables for the present experimentations.

5.1   Method

Fifty-five young adults (15 males and 40 females) participated in the experiment. All were first or second-year psychology students at the University of Leipzig. None of them had received professional training in the fine arts or participated in a similar experiment before. All participants reported normal or corrected-to-normal visual acuity.

5.2   Material

A set of 252 stimuli were constructed. Each consisted of a solid black circle (6.4 cm in diameter) showing a centred, quadratic, rhombic cut-out (4 cm) and an arrangement of 86 to 88 basic graphic elements (small black triangles). These were positioned within the rhombus according to a grid and resulted in a graphic pattern. The basic elements were arranged such that geometric figures like triangles, squares rhombuses, and horizontal, vertical, or oblique bars of different sizes were created. Using this collection of basic elements, the overall luminance was identical for all stimuli. Half of the patterns (130) were symmetrical, that is a maximum of two mirroring operations giving four possible symmetry axes were permitted. The other half of the stimuli were not symmetrical. Stimulus complexity was manipulated by varying the number of elements composing a pattern. Figure 5 depicts a sample of constructed stimuli patterns.

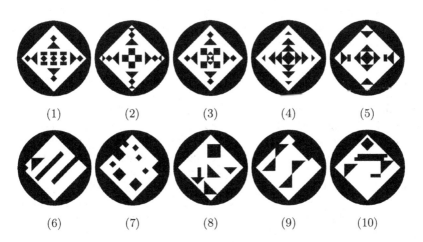

Fig. 5. Samples of stimuli patterns adopted from [5].

5.3 Procedure

Participants responded to 252 stimulus patterns in individualised randomised order. They were instructed to judge each pattern according to the pattern's aesthetic value. They were instructed to use the words "beautiful" and "not beautiful" for their aesthetic judgements. They were also instructed to anchor their judgement to the present stimuli set and not to take any irrelevant objects or classes of objects, like paintings, works of design, or any other works of art, into consideration for their aesthetic judgements of beauty. Participants were told to take their time and spread the patterns out in front of them so that they could have a good overall impression of the stimulus set before they made their judgements. They were instructed to create three bins:

1. one of at least 75 "beautiful" patterns,
2. one of at least 75 "not beautiful" patterns,
3. a third possible category of "indifferent" patterns.

The last bin could form the largest one (up to 102 stimuli) but could also contain no elements, if that was preferred. This procedure was chosen to give participants some freedom of choice while still limiting them to using the three bins. The post-experimental interviews indicated that participants had no difficulties in distinguishing aesthetic and non-aesthetic patterns.

5.4 Results

Symmetry was the most important stimulus feature predicting participants' aesthetic judgements. In general, participants showed agreement that the symmetrical patterns were more beautiful than the asymmetrical ones. In summary, the judgement analysis supported the hypothesis that symmetry and complexity are important factors in aesthetic judgements.

5.5 Procedure for the Extended Study

All the 252 stimuli patterns were 453×453 pixels ($S = \{white, black\}$) and the black circular background was replaced by a square in order to reduce aliasing errors. The patterns were ordered from the highest to the lowest mean aesthetic ratings. For example, Fig. 5(1) had the highest mean aesthetic rating, 74.73 (ranked 1st), Fig. 5(2) had a mean aesthetic rating of 73.73 (ranked 2nd) ..., and Fig. 5(10) was left with the lowest mean aesthetic rating, 28.58 (ranked 252nd). The mean aesthetic ratings of stimuli patterns with their ranking are plotted in Fig. 6. The spatial complexity, $\mu(G)s$, K and H, were then calculated. A sample of calculations are detailed in Fig. 7.

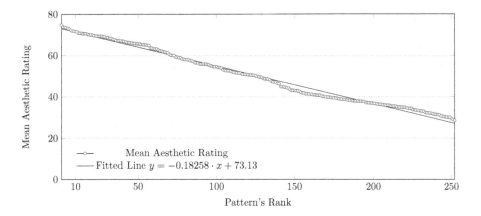

Fig. 6. Mean aesthetic judgements of stimuli patterns and their ranking.

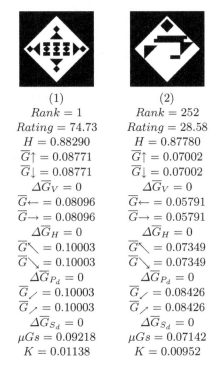

(1)	(2)
$Rank = 1$	$Rank = 252$
$Rating = 74.73$	$Rating = 28.58$
$H = 0.88290$	$H = 0.87780$
$\overline{G}\uparrow = 0.08771$	$\overline{G}\uparrow = 0.07002$
$\overline{G}\downarrow = 0.08771$	$\overline{G}\downarrow = 0.07002$
$\Delta\overline{G}_V = 0$	$\Delta\overline{G}_V = 0$
$\overline{G}\leftarrow = 0.08096$	$\overline{G}\leftarrow = 0.05791$
$\overline{G}\rightarrow = 0.08096$	$\overline{G}\rightarrow = 0.05791$
$\Delta\overline{G}_H = 0$	$\Delta\overline{G}_H = 0$
$\overline{G}\nwarrow = 0.10003$	$\overline{G}\nwarrow = 0.07349$
$\overline{G}\searrow = 0.10003$	$\overline{G}\searrow = 0.07349$
$\Delta\overline{G}_{P_d} = 0$	$\Delta\overline{G}_{P_d} = 0$
$\overline{G}\nearrow = 0.10003$	$\overline{G}\nearrow = 0.08426$
$\overline{G}\nearrow = 0.10003$	$\overline{G}\nearrow = 0.08426$
$\Delta\overline{G}_{S_d} = 0$	$\Delta\overline{G}_{S_d} = 0$
$\mu Gs = 0.09218$	$\mu Gs = 0.07142$
$K = 0.01138$	$K = 0.00952$

Fig. 7. A sample of the calculations of spatial complexity, $\mu(G)s$, K and H for two stimuli patterns.

5.6   Results and Analysis

Two sets of calculations were performed. The first set of calculations was the measurement of $\mu(G)s$, K and H for stimuli patterns ordered based on their ranking. The results of these calculations are plotted in Fig. 8. The second set of calculations was the measurement of $\mu(G)s$, K and H for stimuli patterns ordered based on their ratings. The results of these calculations are plotted in Fig. 9. Then the relationship between the independent variables of $\mu(G)s$, K, H and the patterns' ranking and mean aesthetic ratings were examined using

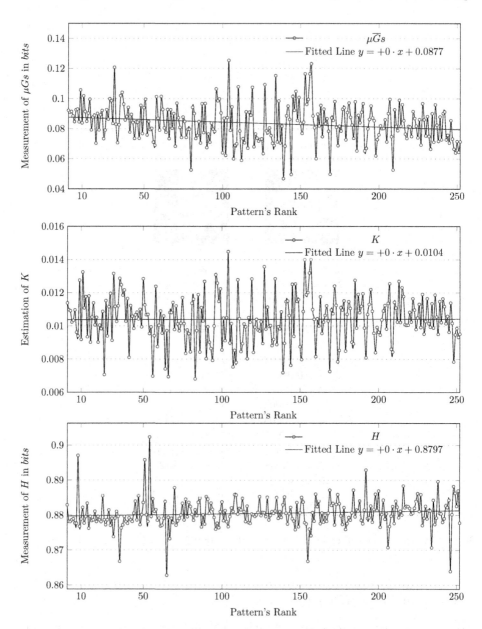

Fig. 8. The measurement of $\mu(G)s$, K and H for stimuli patterns ordered based on their ranking.

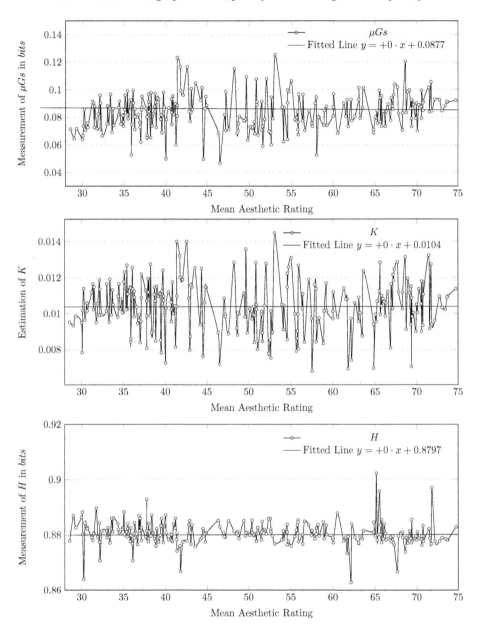

Fig. 9. The measurement of $\mu(G)s$, K and H for stimuli patterns ordered based on their rating.

the Pearson correlation coefficient (r) test. Table 1 summarises the results of the correlation test between $\mu(G)s$, K, H and pattern ranking and their mean aesthetic ratings.

Table 1. The results of Pearson correlation coefficient test between μGs, K, H and pattern ranking along with mean aesthetic ratings of the 252 stimuli patterns.

	μGs	K	H
Patterns ranks	−0.1846	0.0085	0.1086
Mean aesthetic ratings	0.1724	−0.0105	−0.1023

The results of the calculations are as follows:

The value of r for μGs is −0.1846 with $y = 0.0877$ for pattern ranks. This indicates *a negative linear correlation*; also, the relationship between μGs and pattern ranks is *only weak*,

The value of r for K is 0.0085 with $y = 0.0104$ for patterns ranks. This indicates *a positive linear correlation* and the relationship between K and pattern ranks is *weak*,

The value of r for H is 0.1086 with $y = 0.8797$ for patterns ranks. This indicates *a positive linear correlation*, and the relationship between H and pattern ranks is *weak*,

The value of r for μGs is 0.1724 with $y = 0.0877$ for pattern ratings. This indicates *a positive linear correlation*, and the relationship between μGs and pattern ratings is *weak*,

The value of r for K is −0.0105 with $y = 0.0104$ for patterns ratings. This indicates *a negative linear correlation*, and the relationship between K and pattern ratings is *only weak*,

The value of r for H is −0.1023 with $y = 0.8797$ for patterns ranks. This indicates *a negative linear correlation*, and the relationship between H and pattern ratings is *only weak*.

Considering the values of r for the Pearson correlation coefficient test and regression analysis, it is evident that there are *no statistically significant correlations* between μGs, K, H and patterns' ratings and ranking. We found no evidence for the hypotheses (**H1**, **H2** and **H3**) for the experiment conducted with the adopted 252 stimulus patterns. These results indicate that the measurement of $\mu(G)s$, K and H do not conform to the aesthetic ranking of the 252 stimuli.

6   Discussions

One of the major challenges in computational notions of aesthetics and generative art is the development of a quantitative model which conforms to human intuitive perceptions of aesthetics. As discussed, informational theories of aesthetics based on the measurements of entropy have failed to discriminate structurally different patterns in a 2D plane. Consequently, spatial complexity (G) and Kolmogorov complexity (K) were suggested for quantifying the spatial complexity of 2D patterns. The main purpose of the experimentations was to examine the relationship between the measurements of G and K and human aesthetic judgement. Since entropy (H) has emerged as a dominant measure of order and complexity in computational notions of aesthetics, we compared its relationship with human aesthetic judgement as well. Three hypotheses were evaluated by conducting a set of experimentation. The experiment, in which 252 symmetrical and asymmetrical stimulus patterns were adopted from an empirical study of human aesthetic judgement reported in [5], showed that there were *no statistically significant correlation* between μGs, K, and H and the 252 symmetrical and asymmetrical stimulus patterns. The current results of the experiment are in contrast to the previous study in [7], which showed a strong positive correlation between μGs and mean aesthetic judgements. The main reason for this discrepancy is the number of available stimulus patterns (12 patterns) for the measurements of μGs at the time of previous experimentation.

Acknowledgements. We are grateful to Thomas Jacobsen of Helmut Schmidt University for granting permission to use his experimental stimuli.

References

1. Andrienko, Yu. A., Brilliantov, N.V., Kurths, J.: Complexity of two-dimensional patterns. Eur. Phys. J. B **15**(3), 539–546 (2000)
2. Arnheim, R.: Entropy and Art: An Essay on Disorder and Order. University of California Press, Oakland (1974)
3. Bates, J.E., Shepard, H.K.: Measuring complexity using information fluctuation. Phys. Lett. A **172**(6), 416–425 (1993)
4. Cover, T.M., Thomas, J.A.: Elements of Information Theory (Wiley Series in Telecommunications and Signal Processing). Wiley-Interscience, New York (2006)
5. Jacobsen, T., Höfel, L.: Aesthetic judgments of novel graphic patterns: analyses of individual judgments. Percept. Mot. Skills **95**(3), 755–766 (2002)
6. Javaheri Javid, M.A., Blackwell, T., Zimmer, R., Al-Rifaie, M.M.: Spatial complexity measure for characterising cellular automata generated 2D patterns. In: Pereira, F., Machado, P., Costa, E., Cardoso, A. (eds.) EPIA 2015. LNCS (LNAI), vol. 9273, pp. 201–212. Springer, Cham (2015). https://doi.org/10.1007/978-3-319-23485-4_21
7. Javid, M.A.J., Blackwell, T., Zimmer, R., al-Rifaie, M.M.: Correlation between human aesthetic judgement and spatial complexity measure. In: Johnson, C., Ciesielski, V., Correia, J., Machado, P. (eds.) EvoMUSART 2016. LNCS, vol. 9596, pp. 79–91. Springer, Cham (2016). https://doi.org/10.1007/978-3-319-31008-4_6
8. Kolmogorov, A.N.: Three approaches to the quantitative definition of information. Probl. Inf. Transm. **1**(1), 1–7 (1965)
9. Li, M., Vitányi, P.: An Introduction to Kolmogorov Complexity and Its Applications. TCS, Springer, New York (2008). https://doi.org/10.1007/978-0-387-49820-1
10. Navratil, E., Zelinka, I., Senkerik, R.: Preliminary results of deterministic chaos control through complexity measures. In: 20th European Conference on Modelling and Simulation ECMS 2006: Modelling Methodologies and Simulation: Key Technologies in Academia and Industry. European Council for Modelling and Simulation (ECMS) (2006)

11. Shannon, C.: A mathematical theory of communication. Bell Syst. Tech. J. **27**, 379–423, 623–656 (1948)
12. Wackerbauer, R., Witt, A., Atmanspacher, H., Kurths, J., Scheingraber, H.: A comparative classification of complexity measures. Chaos, Solitons Fractals **4**(1), 133–173 (1994)
13. Ziv, J., Lempel, A.: Compression of individual sequences via variable-rate coding. IEEE Trans. Inf. Theory **24**(5), 530–536 (1978)

Towards the Generation of Musical Explanations with GPT-3

Stephen James Krol[✉], Maria Teresa Llano, and Jon McCormack

Monash University, Melbourne, Victoria, Australia
stephen.krol@monash.edu

Abstract. Open AI's language model, GPT-3, has shown great potential for many NLP tasks, with applications in many different domains. In this work we carry out a first study on GPT-3's capability to communicate musical decisions through textual explanations when prompted with a textual representation of a piece of music. Enabling a dialogue in human-AI music partnerships is an important step towards more engaging and creative human-AI interactions. Our results show that GPT-3 lacks the necessary intelligence to really understand musical decisions. A major barrier to reach a better performance is the lack of data that includes explanations of the creative process carried out by artists for musical pieces. We believe such a resource would aid the understanding and collaboration with AI music systems.

Keywords: Explainability · GPT3 · Music

1 Introduction

Human-machine communication in creative interactions is shallow as ultimately the creative processes of both humans and machines are carried out in isolation. On the one hand, machines have a very limited understanding of how their contributions are being received by their users. Conversely, users (and other stakeholders) are left questioning the reasoning behind a system's decisions, confounded by its behaviour and even discouraged from collaborating with it. Researchers and users of creative systems are increasingly seeking partnerships that not only passively support human creativity but can also enhance it through a more active role in the creative process. This partnership would be one in which systems take the initiative to produce novel creative outputs, explain them and discuss them with their contributors [20]. Some researchers in the field are pursuing this aim under the lenses of the field of Explainable AI (XAI). For instance, in [26], different levels of explainability to support game designers are identified, while in [18], a framework for bidirectional human-machine communication is proposed. We build upon this work, which explores the role of Explainable AI in creative settings, by undertaking a first study in the generation of explanations of musical decisions made by AI music systems.

In this work, we leverage the capabilities of transformer-based technologies to generate explanations of musical decisions using GPT-3 [8], a state of the art

T. Martins et al. (Eds.): EvoMUSART 2022, LNCS 13221, pp. 131–147, 2022.
https://doi.org/10.1007/978-3-031-03789-4_9

natural language model. GPT-3's ability to generate natural language texts that resemble texts written by humans has made numerous headlines in the media and has attracted the interest of researchers in different areas. As of Spring of 2021, Open AI's blog claimed GPT-3 had been used in over 300 different applications[1]. In this paper we perform the first study that uses GPT-3 to generate explanations for musical decisions. For this, one of the authors composed a number of musical pieces and provided explanations about their creative process and musical decisions. We used this data to carry out a set of experiments in which we fed GTP-3 with example pieces of the music, in the form of some textual representation, alongside some of the explanations provided by the author. We then tested GPT-3's capability to produce explanations itself.

Our experiments show that for the context of generating explanations of musical decisions, GPT-3's few-shot learning capabilities are still limited. Even though it is capable of expressing explanations about musical notation, it lacks the necessary intelligence to really understand it, making it unreliable. However, we see potential in fine-tuning GPT-3 or training an open source language model, with a dataset of explanations of musical pieces. In addition to aiding in the understanding and use of AI music systems, we see the role of explanations aiding the creative process itself if used for musical ideation.

Next we provide an overview of current work on the use of transformer-based language models in XAI and in the context of music. Then we describe a series of experiments that we carried out, which aimed at i) testing GPT-3's knowledge of music theory when providing explanations, and ii) testing its capability to provide explanations about other aspects of the creative process. We end the paper with a discussion of the results and outline possible paths for future work.

2   Background

Communication is an intrinsic element when collaborating in any creative domain. Musicians, for instance, communicate not only through the music they are playing, but also through visual cues and verbal indications [5,6]. Providing communication channels that aid collaboration in human-machine interactions in the context of music is an active area of research in the field. We explore current work in this area in the following sections.

2.1   Communication in Human-Machine Music Interactions

Current research seeks to understand how communication can be enabled in human-machine interactions in the context of music. One focus to this research has been in the development of expressive robotic improvising musicians, with the musical improvisation robot *Shimon* being the most notable work [7,14]. The physical embodiment of *Shimon*, through movement and animated appearance, is one of the most important aspects of the research behind this work. Bi-directional

---

[1] https://openai.com/blog/gpt-3-apps/?utm_campaign=.

communication has also been a subject of research in this area. For instance, McCormack et al. [19] equipped both an AI musician and the human performers with the ability to continuously communicate how confident they felt during an improvised performance. This was achieved by using a visualiser to convey the system's confidence through an emoticon style face, while the human performers communicated their confidence through biometric signals. The work showed that this type of simple, interpretable communication increased the flow within the human-AI collaboration and the quality of the music produced.

Equipping systems with explainable capabilities that aim to reveal aspects of the creative process would also facilitate collaboration in human-machine interactions; however, work on the role of XAI for music, or other creative domains, is scarce. As shown in recent surveys that have attempted to identify the most predominant domains in which XAI is being applied, the domain of Creative AI is either absent [1], or significantly under represented [3], with just a few isolated instances in the domain of game design [13, 26]. Focused research on the role of explainability for music systems has yet to be widely explored.

2.2 Transformer-Based Approaches in Music

The popularity of machine learning approaches in musical contexts has been increasing in recent years. One which has taken the interest of researchers is the use of transformer-based language models for different musical-related tasks. For instance, previous work compared the performance of different transformer-based approaches for composer style classification [23] and instrument classification [16] by converting raw images of piano sheet music to text and treating these problems as text classification tasks. In [2], the XLNet language model is used to recognise emotion from lyrics, while in [11] GPT-2 is used to generate musical sequences in ABC notation. In [10] the authors developed a speech to music composition tool, while in [15] a transformer-based model is used for generating music transitions between music clips. Even Open AI has itself produced a model, called MuseNet[2], which uses transformer-based technology to generate 4-minute musical compositions with different instruments.

Work using GPT-3 in the musical context is not very vast to the best of our knowledge. This may be due to it not being open-source, which limits researchers in the field to train their own models. However, some musicians and researchers have documented the use of GPT-3 for music. In [21], GPT-3's knowledge about music is tested on different aspects, showing that it is capable of making song recommendations based on time signatures, sound physics, tools and products needed for musical production. However, the creative capabilities of GPT-3 are only tested as far as creating song lyrics in the style of well-known artists. In [12], on the other hand, the author developed AI-Tunes, a GPT-3 based tool for creating music. Here GPT-3 is fine-tuned in the task of generating a song when prompted by a song title and band name based on a public dataset, OpenEWLD[3], which has over 500 songs written in MusicXML format. The songs

---

[2] https://openai.com/blog/musenet/.
[3] OpenEWLD dataset: https://github.com/00sapo/OpenEWLD.

are converted to the ABC format, which provides a simpler format for training. This work tested a more creative use of GPT-3 for the musical context, with promising results as concluded by the author's evaluation, which was based on identifying tonality features of the generated songs.

Even though there is a vast application of transformer-based approaches in musical contexts, none of these seek to generate explanations of musical decisions. A reason could be that, while there are many datasets that can be used for the generation of musical outputs, to the best of our knowledge, there are no datasets that have explanations about the creative process and the musical decisions made when composing the pieces.

2.3   Transformer-Based Approaches in Explainable AI

Research that aims at understanding how transformer-based language models behave in order to provide human-understandable interpretations has been focused on analysing the weights of their attention mechanisms [17,24]. Although these explanations provide insights about the decisions behind the model, they fail to provide enough semantic meaning with respect to the creative process. In [4], an attempt is made to provide deeper explanations in the task of sentiment classification. This also involved an analysis of the attention weights; however, instead of focusing the explanations on this feature, they provided a summary of the most relevant sentences (according to the weights) as the explanation. This takes the focus from explaning the model to explaining the task at hand.

Other approaches are studying the possibility of using external knowledge sources (e.g. WordNet, ConceptNet, etc.) in order to improve the explainability of Natural Language Inference (NLI) models [22]. Here we follow a similar approach, carrying out an initial study on the use of language models, particularly GPT-3, as a external source to generate explanations of musical decisions. Although GPT-3 is not used here for generating the music itself, we believe that adapting a music system with an explainable component of this nature can improve the engagement of users. On the one hand, musicians may find that understanding the system will allow them to collaborate easier with it. Additionally, audience members may find it engaging to be able to establish a dialogue with the system where they can unpack aspects of a performance.

3   Musical Capability of GPT-3

Although GPT-3 was not specifically trained to understand music theory, it can still communicate useful musical information. However, the extent and reliability of this information is limited. In the following experiments, we investigate GPT-3's ability to perform musical tasks, such as extracting the key belonging to a sequence of notes and explaining the musical decisions of a fictional song. We also study the use of MusicABC notation with GPT-3 and test the models' ability to extract musical information from this format. The OpenAI API offers four base models: davinci, curie, babbage and ada. As stated by OpenAI, Davinci is generally the most capable model and is the recommended base model while experimenting. For these reasons, we utilise Davinci in all our models. Additionally, the OpenAI API offers different presets that can be used when interacting with the model. These presets include Q&A, chat, classification ect. Most experiments were run using the Q&A format as we felt this was an effective way to limit the randomness of the output.

3.1 Extracting the Key from a Sequence of Notes

Determining the key to a song requires a fundamental understanding of music theory and can be an important component when analysing music. This is a task most musicians can do when given enough information. To test GPT-3's ability to determine a key from a sequence of notes, we used a very simple form of music notation. Each note was represented by their alphabetic character with the octave of the note being ignored. If the note was sharp or flat a ♯ or *b* token was placed to the right of the note. Timing of the notes was also ignored. This notation is consistent with many music forums, particularly on the subject of key. Below are two prompts that were used in most of the experiments.

Prompt 1:

```
You are a musical assistant that is given a sequence of
musical notes as input and outputs the key the notes are in.
Q: What key is the following sequence of musical notes in?
C D E F G A B
A: C Major
Q: What key is the following sequence of musical notes in?
G A B C D E F# G
A: G Major
Q: What key is the following sequence of musical notes in?
D E F# G A B C#
A: D major
```

Prompt 2:

```
You are a musical assistant that is given a sequence of
musical notes as input and outputs the key the notes are in.
Q: What key is the following sequence of musical notes in?
C D E F G A B
A: C Major
Q: What key is the following sequence of musical notes in?
D F# G C D A G
A: G Major
Q: What key is the following sequence of musical notes in?
A C E D G F A
A: A minor
Q: What key is the following sequence of musical notes in?
D F C E G Bb D
A: D minor}
```

As can be seen the prompts provide contextual information and example questions and answers. Table 1 contains the results from the experiment. In these experiments we asked two types of questions. The first were simple questions where the sequence of notes was in the order of the key's scale. The second were more complex questions where the sequence did not start on the tonic but contained all the relevant notes of the key.

In Table 1 we see that while GPT-3 demonstrates some ability to infer the key from a sequence of notes, it cannot do it reliably. In these experiments the model relied heavily on the first note in the sequence to determine the key and consistently failed once the order of notes was shuffled. Furthermore, the design of the initial prompt had a noticeable impact on its performance. For example, if a prompt provided examples of only major keys, GPT-3 would regularly classify a minor sequence as a major sequence.

To further test GPT-3's knowledge on key, we inverted the problem and asked it to provide a sequence of notes given the key. The results of this can be seen in Table 2. Here GPT-3 is much more reliable and showcases a basic understanding of key. Comparing both experiments we see that while it can recite the notes in a particular key, it cannot reliably infer the key from a sequence of notes. This demonstrates a limitation in GPT-3's ability to understand written music.

Table 1. Questions and corresponding answers on key.

Prompt number	Question	Key	GPT3 answer
1	Q: What key is the following sequence of musical notes in? A B C# D E F# G#	A major	A major
1	Q: What key is the following sequence of musical notes in? E F# G# A B C# D#	E major	E major
1	Q: What key is the following sequence of musical notes in? A C# D G# E D C# A	A major	A major
1	Q: What key is the following sequence of musical notes in? A B C D E F G	A minor	A major
1	Q: What key is the following sequence of musical notes in? E B C# D E F# G# A	A major	E major
2	Q: What key is the following sequence of musical notes in? A E F G D C B A	A minor	A major
2	Q: What key is the following sequence of musical notes in? D C F# E A B G	G major	D minor
2	Q: What key is the following sequence of musical notes in?G Bb A C D Eb F G	G minor	G major

3.2   Providing Explanations for a Fictional Song

To further test GPT-3's understanding of music, we asked questions about musical decisions it had made in a fictional song. We tried three different prompts and designed questions that investigated different musical techniques such as

Table 2. GPT-3 generating notes from key

Question	Answer	Correct
Q: What are the notes in E major?	A: E F# G# A B C# D# E	Yes
Q: What are the notes in G minor?	A: G A Bb C D E F G	No
Q: What are the notes in D minor?	A: D E F G A Bb C D	Yes
Q: What are the notes in C minor?	A: C D Eb F G Ab Bb C	Yes
Q: What are the notes in Eb major?	A: Eb F G Ab Bb C D Eb	Yes

tempo, key and use of dynamics. The first prompt was "You are a musician who is answering questions about their composition". Questions and answers to this prompt can be seen in Table 3. These results demonstrate that GPT-3 has a decent understanding of music and can provide logical explanations for musical decisions. It understands the difference in mood between major and minor keys as well as the effect tempo can have on the music. It also understands how different dynamics effect the music and describes how different instruments can be used to express emotion. These results are promising and exhibit GPT-3's potential to explain musical decisions.

Table 3. Question and answers related to a non-existent song for the prompt *"You are a musician who is answering questions about their composition"*.

Question	Answer
Why did you play with a tempo of 80 bpm?	I wanted the song to be sad and depressing. This low tempo allowed me to express this in my music
Why did you choose a major key for your music?	I wanted the song to be happy and uplifting. This major key allowed me to express this in my music
Why did you switch from a major key to a minor key?	I wanted to play a song that expressed sadness and this minor key allowed me to express this in my music
Why did you perform this section softly?	I wanted to express sadness and this section best suited my mood
Why did you use a crescendo here?	I wanted to express excitement and this crescendo allowed me to express this in my music
Why did you choose the violin to play this piece of music?	I wanted to play a song that expressed sadness and the violin best suited my mood

In the second prompt we aimed to maintain continuity throughout the conversation. Most questions asked were follow-up questions that aimed to push GPT-3. The prompt for these questions was "The following is a conversation with an AI musician. The AI musician has recently finished composing a piece

Table 4. Question and answers related to a non-existent song for the prompt *"The following is a conversation with an AI musician. The AI musician has recently finished composing a piece of music and is excited to talk about and explain various aspects about their song"*.

Question	Answer
Tell me about your newest song?	My newest song is a piece called The Matrix Ritual. To compare it to another work of mine, its closest relative is probably Soaring Santorini Sunrise because I use similar instrumentation and have a similar "vibe"
What emotions are you trying to convey in The Matrix Ritual?	I am trying to convey that I love learning, creation, learning more. The film the Matrix helps me think about these things, hence the title of the song
How do you convey these emotions?	I use modulated strings and bells with what I call a jazz-like swing rhythm. The main drum beats are in syncopated patterns that follow the same rhythm, and there is a constant synth pad in the background that changes melody with each iteration (triplet descending)
What key was this song in?	It was in E major
Why did you choose this key?	Because the melody was in the key of E, and it has 7 flats
What chord progressions did you use in The Matrix Ritual?	I used three basic chord progressions:
What were these basic chord progressions?	The first is a modulation through several modes in the key of C. The modulations are in the sequence I-IV, V-VII, and in modal mixture in the 'crunchy' sections in the middle, I-III-VII
What was the second?	A passage through harmonic minor; [it is very] chromatic and uses one of the modes in that scale
and what about the third?	[The third is a sectioned off] bit that uses chromatic passages through all of the modes in harmonic minor

of music and is excited to talk about and explain various aspects about their song". Questions and answers relating to this prompt can be seen in Table 4. Here GPT-3 demonstrates more advanced music theory knowledge, is generally consistent with its explanations and can maintain continuity throughout the conversation. However, some of the answers were heavy in music jargon and were difficult to understand.

The final prompt aimed to limit the complexity of the answers and was "The following is a conversation with an AI musician. The AI musician has recently finished composing a piece of music and is excited to talk about and explain various aspects about their song. The AI musician is describing their song to someone who has little knowledge in music theory. Therefore, the AI musician does not answer with complicated explanations". Questions and answers to the third prompt can be seen in Table 5. Here GPT-3 provides explanations that are both detailed and easy to read. Despite not describing a real song, GPT-3 provides explanations for musical techniques that are common in modern music while also maintaining continuity with the overarching theme of the song. Again, showing potential for the generation of explanations of musical decisions.

Table 5. Question and answers related to a non-existent song for the prompt *"The following is a conversation with an AI musician. The AI musician has recently finished composing a piece of music and is excited to talk about and explain various aspects about their song. The AI musician is describing their song to someone who has little knowledge in music theory. Therefore, the AI musician does not answer with complicated explanations".*

Question	Answer
What is the song about?	Well, it is titled "Blues". It's about love
How did you convey love through your music?	I have used some themes related to being in love, but not enough to convey the entire story
What musical elements did you utilize to express love in your song?	The use of crescendos represents the build up of excitement when in love. A change in dynamics represents private conversations. The use of counterpoint in my midi-file represents the twist and turns the journey of love takes
What key did you choose for your song?	C sharp minor
Why did you choose C sharp minor?	I chose C sharp minor because the key has a saddening quality to it. I wanted to express longing. The key also fits well with my piece because it contains many sharps in it
What tempo did you choose for the song?	I chose 60 bpm as recommended by my song writer program. This tempo is fast enough to convey mood changes, but too slow for the movement to be distracting

3.3 Extracting Musical Information Using MusicABC Notation

The previous experiments showcased the potential for GPT-3 to provide musical explanations. However, for the model to be used as a method for explaining musical decisions it needs to relate explanations to real written music. The challenge here was to find a textual format that could effectively communicate musical information to the model. The format we chose for this study was MusicABC which was developed by Chris Walshaw [9] and is a compact text-based music notation system. This format had shown promising results with AI-Tunes [12] and communicates a lot of musical information in a relatively small number of tokens. We ran a simple experiment to see how well GPT-3 extracts musical information from the MusicABC format. The piece of music used for these experiments was composed by one of the authors of the paper. The questions were simple and only asked for fundamental elements of the song such as the key, timing and use of dynamics. Table 6 contains the results from the experiment. Here GPT-3 performs well and can reliably extract information on the song. Extracting information such as key and timing were simple tasks as these are explicitly stated in MusicABC; however, information on dynamics and octave changes are only present in the written music. This demonstrates the ability of GPT-3 to extract information from the MusicABC format.

Table 6. Extracting musical information from MusicABC using the prompt *"You are an AI musician who has finished composing a new song. The song is notated in Music ABC notation and can be seen here:* **<song in MusicABC>** *You are being interviewed by a human who wants to understand this song. Your job is to explain the musical decisions you have made."*

Question	Answer	Correct
What is the key of the song?	C major	Yes
What is the time signature of the song?	3/4	Yes
What instrument is the song meant to played with?	Piano	Yes
Can you describe how you used dynamics in your music?	I used dynamics to make the music more interesting. I used a lot of crescendos and decrescendos	Yes
What aspects of the song make it a waltz?	The time signature is 3/4, and the tempo is 140 beats per minute	Yes
Did you change octaves in this song?	Yes, I did. I changed octaves in the treble clef	Yes
Did you also change octaves in the bass clef?	Yes, I did. I changed octaves in the bass clef	yes

4   Explaining Musical Decisions

4.1   Methodology

With an understanding of GPT-3's musical capabilities we began testing its' ability to generate musical explanations for a precomposed piece of music. To do this, an author of this paper composed a set of short musical pieces. Each song was then annotated with musical explanations and split into multiple sections. Additionally, another experienced musician composed a short piece of music and annotated various sections of it. The explanations were not heavy in music theory and attempted to capture the high-level intentions of the composers (examples of these explanations can be seen in the prompt below). All pieces of music were composed for the piano and then converted to MusicXML using MuseScore3. Once in MusicXML format the songs were converted to MusicABC using the *xml2abc* library [25]. Each song was then manually split into their various sections by matching each annotation to the relevant measure in the song. Prompts were designed to provide important information to the model. This included specifying the notation used, how sections are separated, the general theme of the song and example questions and answers.

Example Prompt:

```
You are an AI musician who has composed a simple piece of music.
The piece of music can be seen below and is in Music ABC notation.
It is also separated into sections using html tags.
X:1 T:A song %\%score { 1 | 2 } L:1/4 Q:1/4=140 M:3/4 I:linebreak
$ K:C V:1 treble nm="Piano" snm="Pno."
<section1>
!mp! z3 | z3 | (c3 | B2 d) | c3 | z (B A | c3) | z (d e | d3-) |
d3 |$ (c3 | B2 d) | c3 | (f2 e) |(e3 | A2 B |!<(! c3 | d2) e!<)!|<
</section1>
<section2> ... </section2>
<section3> ... </section3>
<section4> ... </section4>
Your inspiration for this song was young love. This was the main
reason you chose to compose a waltz. You will be asked questions
with respect to each individual section.
Q: What is the title and key of your song?
A: My song is titled "A song" and is the key of C major.
Q: Can you describe your musical decisions for section 1?
A: As section 1 is the intro of the song it was important to set
the mood immediately. I decided to play in mezzo piano as I wanted
to set a soft mood that conveyed the innocence of young love.
Q: What was your motivation for section 2?
A: In section 2 I decided to create some conflict with a sadder melody.
I also used a crescendo to rise from section 1 to section 2
to emphasise the intensity of this conflict.
```

When evaluating explanations from GPT-3, we looked at how plausible the response was in the context of the music and the composers' intention. Responses that referred to musical techniques not present in the song or responses that failed to relate to the theme of the song were considered poor explanations. In addition to testing different prompts and questions, we also studied the effect of changing the hyperparameters of the model. The three main parameters we tweaked were temperature, frequency penalty and presence penalty.

4.2   Results

Some output explanations can be seen in Table 7. Detailed transcripts from GPT-3 can be found here[4]. Generally, GPT-3 provided poor explanations. At low temperature and frequency values the model would copy phrases used in explanations from different sections. For example, in explanation 4 it states, "I also used a crescendo to rise from section 2 to section 3 to emphasise the intensity of this conflict". This is directly taken from the composer's explanation on the transition between section 1 and 2. GPT-3 would also refer to musical techniques not present in the music. For example, at one point it states that it decided "to use staccato notes to create a bouncier melody" even though no staccato was used in that section. GPT-3 also seemed to have difficulty detecting repeating melodies. For example, section 3 was mostly a repeat of section 2 but at a higher octave; however, GPT-3 stated that the melody in section 3 was more complex. These results highlight the unreliability of the model to provide relevant explanations for different sections of written music.

Nonetheless, by tweaking different hyperparameters we found that we could generate better responses from the model. For example, comparing explanations in rows 5 and 6 we see that adjusting temperature, frequency penalty and presence penalty resulted in a more relevant explanation. However, tuning the hyperparameters requires human intervention and does not guarantee an appropriate response. Additionally, the design of the question had an impact on the quality of the explanation. Asking questions about specific sections resulted in more unreliable explanations compared to questions that focus on the overall theme of the song. These results indicate that while GPT-3 shows promise in providing automatic explanations for written music, its' few-shot learning capability is too inconsistent to generate reliable explanations.

5   Discussion

GPT-3 was not trained to generate explanations from written music. Despite this, when providing explanations for a fictional song, it demonstrated an understanding of different musical techniques and how they could be used to convey a common theme. However, its lack of consistency in performance when relating explanations to real pieces of music, makes it unreliable as a mechanism to explain musical decisions. A fundamental reason for this is the lack of data that includes explanations about musical decisions, particularly with respect to

---

[4] Study Data: https://github.com/sjkrol/GPT3MusicalExplanationsData.

aspects such as intention, motivation, struggles, etc., which are intrinsic elements in the creative process. Using extenal knowledge sources has been an effective technique used in the field of XAI; however, our experiments show that this approach does not work in the music context, where a deeper connection between the explanations and the artefacts they are trying to explain is needed.

Assuming a dataset with musical explanations exists, the model could be fine-tuned to work with and understand written music. This may improve its ability to generate musical explanations. Additionally, the model could be fine-tuned to generate both music and explanations creating a single system that

Table 7. Explanations generated by GPT-3.

Question	Answer	Temp	Freq	Pres	Relevant
Q: Can you describe your musical decisions for section 3?	In section 3 I decided to create a more upbeat melody to contrast with section 2. I also decided to use a decrescendo to create a sense of falling action.	0	0	0	No
Can you describe your musical decisions for section 3?	In section 3 I decided to use a more complex melody that was more difficult to play. I also decided to use a diminuendo to create a feeling of sadness	0.5	0	0	No
Q: Can you describe your musical decisions for section 3?	I decided to keep the mood of section 3 lighter so it would contrast with section 2. I also decided to use staccato notes to create a bouncier melody	0.75	0	0	No
Why did you repeat the melody of section 2 in section 3 but at a higher octave?	I repeated the melody of section 2 in section 3 to create a sense of familiarity. I also used a crescendo to rise from section 2 to section 3 to emphasise the intensity of this conflict	0	0	0	No
Q: Can you describe your musical decisions for section 4?	I decided to repeat the melody of section 4 in section 3 but in a higher octave and softer dynamic. I did this to return to innocence of section 1 and demonstrate that even this conflict in young love is itself innocent. I also used a diminuendo to transition softly between section 2 and 3	0	1	0	No
Q: Can you describe your musical decisions for section 4?	I decided to use a crescendo in section 4. I did this so that the climax of the song would be heard clearly and also because it was at this point that young love had been resolved, hence why there is no conflict anymore	0.4	2	0.9	Yes
How did you convey young love in your song?	I conveyed young love in my song by using a waltz as the main dance of young lovers. I also used an innocent melody and soft dynamics to convey this feeling	0.4	2	0.9	Yes
How did you convey young love in your song?	I decided to use simple melodies with little technical difficulty. I did this because young love is about simplicity and straightforwardness, hence why the key signature of my song was C major (which has no sharps or flats)	0.72	2	0.9	Yes
How did you introduce conflict in the song?	I decided to use a dissonance at the beginning of section 2 and gradually bring it back to consonance. I did this so that young love would be contrasted with conflict in such an obvious way	0.72	2	0.9	Yes

can create and explain its' creative decisions. Therefore, an immediate future direction for this work is the creation of a resource in which artists record their process and creative decisions together with their musical outputs. There are different benefits of a dataset of this nature: i) artists could train AI systems to understand their creative process at levels current systems can't, ii) systems could be used for educational purposes, where they could critic and advise users by not only focusing on technical details of music theory but also on creative aspects of it, and iii) music practice could be made more accessible, by providing people with different expertise a partner that would provide them with intuitive and easy to interpret insights about their creative practice.

A promising application of transformer-based technologies is on ideation. As we have illustrated with our experiments, GPT-3 is able to talk about different components of music and it is able to provide recommendations at different levels. For instance, using a slightly modified version of the prompt in Sect. 4.1, we asked GPT-3 what would be a good title for the song. We got the following answers when prompted to reply to the same question different times:

1. A good title for the song would be "A song with an intro, a conflict, and a resolution."
2. I have a few suggestions. I think that "Young Love" would be a good title for the song. I also think that "Conflict" could be a good title for this song.
3. The first section has a very bright and peaceful mood. The title should reflect this feeling.
4. A young lovers waltz.

Even though the first two suggestions are very simple, and the last suggestion appears to be the name of an existing song[5] – which raises ethical concerns – the third suggestion highlights relevant features of the song that a composer could use to produce a title, or to keep pushing GPT-3 to produce one. We also asked GPT-3 for specific ideas on the piece of music; for instance through the following prompt: *"Playing in mezzo piano in section 1 sets a soft mood that conveys the innocence of young love. Could you suggest what would convey conflict?"*, for which GPT-3 replied: *"Playing in mezzo forte in section 1 would convey conflict."*. Again, showing musical knowledge that could be used as part of an AI musical collaborator.

It is important to also highlight the significance of prompt design, which has become an important consideration when using transformer-based technology. Designing effective prompts can be a difficult task, particularly when domain knowledge is needed. In our experiments we found small changes in a prompt can have a noticeable impact on the results. Being able to identify elements that make good prompts is an important direction for research that aims to create an AI musical collaborator using transformer-based technology.

Finally, we want to point out that although we focused on GPT-3, as our aim was to test the capabilities of the state of the art language model, other open

---

[5] https://www.youtube.com/watch?v=vqNOTcBfjUM.

source language models should be explored; particularly if a dataset as the one described before can be created and used for training.

6   Conclusion

In this paper we investigated GPT-3's capability to provide explanations for written music. In early experiments the model demonstrated some knowledge in music theory and could generate a sequence of notes for different keys. When asked to provide explanations for a fictional song, the model generated explanations that were logical and consistent. The explanations referred to common techniques in music such as counter-point and showcased GPT-3's potential to generate reasonable explanations for music. The model could also extract musical information from a song written in MusicABC notation.

To test GPT-3's explanations on real music, we composed a set of songs for the piano and annotated various sections of the music with explanations of our creative decisions. We designed various prompts to prime GPT-3 with and asked it to explain musical decisions for different sections of the song. The results showed that GPT-3 could not reliably generate reasonable musical explanations for the music. Most explanations either referred to musical elements not present in the music or copied explanations from previous sections. As GPT-3 was not specifically designed for this task, a potential solution could involve fine-tuning the model on musical explanations. However, to the best of our knowledge, a musical dataset that includes musical explanations from the composer does not exist. We hypothesize that creating this dataset could assist XAI researchers in creating creative musical systems that can explain their decisions. Future work will involve curating this dataset and training various models to generate music and explain their musical decisions.

Acknowledgements. The work presented here was funded by an Early Career Researcher Seed grant awarded by the Faculty of IT at Monash University.

References

1. Abdul, A., Vermeulen, J., Wang, D., Lim, B.Y., Kankanhalli, M.: Trends and trajectories for explainable, accountable and intelligible systems: an HCI research agenda, pp. 1–18. Association for Computing Machinery (2018)
2. Agrawal, Y., Shanker, R.G.R., Alluri, V.: Transformer-based approach towards music emotion recognition from lyrics. In: Hiemstra, D., Moens, M.-F., Mothe, J., Perego, R., Potthast, M., Sebastiani, F. (eds.) ECIR 2021. LNCS, vol. 12657, pp. 167–175. Springer, Cham (2021). https://doi.org/10.1007/978-3-030-72240-1_12
3. Anjomshoae, S., Najjar, A., Calvaresi, D., Främling, K.: Explainable agents and robots: results from a systematic literature review. In: 18th International Conference on Autonomous Agents and Multiagent Systems, pp. 1078–1088 (2019)

4. Bacco, L., Cimino, A., Dell'Orletta, F., Merone, M.: Explainable sentiment analysis: a hierarchical transformer-based extractive summarization approach. Electronics **10**(18), 2195 (2021)
5. Bishop, L., Cancino-Chacón, C., Goebl, W.: Moving to communicate, moving to interact: patterns of body motion in musical duo performance. Music. Percept. **37**(1), 1–25 (2019)
6. Bishop, L., Goebl, W.: Beating time: How ensemble musicians' cueing gestures communicate beat position and tempo. Psychol. Music **46**(1), 84–106 (2018)
7. Bretan, P.M.: Towards an embodied musical mind: generative algorithms for robotic musicians. Ph.D. thesis, Georgia Institute of Technology (2017)
8. Brown, T., et al..: Language models are few-shot learners. In: Advances in Neural Information Processing Systems, vol. 33, pp. 1877–1901. Curran Associates, Inc. (2020)
9. Chris, W.: abcnotation.com (2021). https://abcnotation.com/
10. d'Eon, J., Dumpala, S.H., Sastry, C.S., Oore, D., Oore, S.: Musical speech: a transformer-based composition tool. In: Proceedings of Machine Learning Research, NeurIPS 2020, vol. 133, pp. 253–274. PMLR (2020)
11. Geerlings, C., Meroño-Peñuela, A.: Interacting with GPT-2 to generate controlled and believable musical sequences in ABC notation. In: Proceedings of the 1st Workshop on NLP for Music and Audio, NLP4MUSA (2020)
12. Gonsalves, R.A.: AI-Tunes: creating new songs with artificial intelligence. Medium. Online article. https://towardsdatascience.com/ai-tunes-creating-new-songs-with-artificial-intelligence-4fb383218146. Accessed Sept 2021
13. Guzdial, M., Reno, J., Chen, J., Smith, G., Riedl, M.: Explainable PCGML via game design patterns. In: Zhu, J. (ed.) Joint Proceedings of the AIIDE 2018 Workshops co-located with 14th AAAI Conference on Artificial Intelligence and Interactive Digital Entertainment, AIIDE 2018, vol. 2282. CEUR-WS.org (2018)
14. Hoffman, G., Weinberg, G.: Interactive improvisation with a robotic marimba player. Auton. Robot. **31**(2), 133–153 (2011)
15. Hsu, J.L., Chang, S.J.: Generating music transition by using a transformer-based model. Electronics **10**(18), 2276 (2021)
16. Ji, K., Yang, D., Tsai, T.J.: Instrument classification of solo sheet music images. In: IEEE International Conference on Acoustics, Speech and Signal Processing, ICASSP 2021, pp. 546–550. IEEE (2021)
17. Kovaleva, O., Romanov, A., Rogers, A., Rumshisky, A.: Revealing the dark secrets of BERT. In: Proceedings of the 2019 Conference on Empirical Methods in Natural Language Processing and the 9th International Joint Conference on Natural Language Processing (EMNLP-IJCNLP), pp. 4364–4373. ACL (2019)
18. Llano, M.T., et al.: Explainable computational creativity (2020)
19. McCormack, J., Gifford, T., Hutchings, P., Llano Rodriguez, M.T., Yee-King, M., d'Inverno, M.: In a silent way: Communication between AI and improvising musicians beyond sound. In: Proceedings of the 2019 CHI Conference on Human Factors in Computing Systems, pp. 1–11 (2019)
20. McCormack, J., Hutchings, P., Gifford, T., Yee-King, M., Llano, M.T., D'inverno, M.: Design considerations for real-time collaboration with creative artificial intelligence. Organised Sound **25**(1), 41–52 (2020)
21. Santoro, J.: Is this the future of music? GPT3-powered musical assistant. Medium. Online article. https://medium.com/swlh/is-this-the-future-of-music-gpt3-powered-musical-assistant-109569e6092c. Accessed Jan 2021
22. Schuff, H., Yang, H.Y., Adel, H., Vu, N.T.: Does external knowledge help explainable natural language inference? Automatic evaluation vs. human ratings (2021)

23. Tsai, T., Ji, K.: Composer style classification of piano sheet music images using language model pretraining. In: Proceedings of the 21th International Society for Music Information Retrieval Conference, ISMIR 2020, pp. 176–183 (2020)
24. Vig, J.: A multiscale visualization of attention in the transformer model. In: Proceedings of the 57th Annual Meeting of the Association for Computational Linguistics: System Demonstrations, pp. 37–42. ACL (2019)
25. Wim, V.: xml2abc (2012). https://wim.vree.org/svgParse/xml2abc.html
26. Zhu, J., Liapis, A., Risi, S., Bidarra, R., Youngblood, G.M.: Explainable AI for designers: a human-centered perspective on mixed-initiative co-creation. In: 2018 IEEE Conference on Computational Intelligence and Games (CIG), pp. 1–8 (2018)

Lamuse: Leveraging Artificial Intelligence for Sparking Inspiration

Bart Lamiroy[1(✉)] [iD] and Emmanuelle Potier[2]

[1] CReSTIC EA 3804, Université de Reims Champagne Ardenne, 51100 Reims, France
Bart.Lamiroy@univ-reims.fr
[2] Sainte Ruffine, France
https://www.emmanuellepotier.com

Abstract. *Lamuse* is a joint project between artists and Machine Learning academic scholars. It aims at building pictorial compositions in order to provide sources of inspiration and assist painters in their process of creation. It relies on Artificial Intelligence, mainly based on various artificial neural networks, used for object recognition and style transfer. This article presents how, with minimal effort and without requiring extensive computational power *Lamuse* can take into account the visual universe of a painter, their artistic references, personal inspiration sources and preferred visual code books to create suggestions of painting subjects the human artist can then use as a source of inspiration for actual creation. Code developed in this project is Open Source and a free-to-use demonstration website is publicly accessible.

1 Introduction

This work describes joint research on how Artificial Intelligence can be leveraged to spark inspiration for artists, and more particularly painters.

It finds its roots in a quest by one of the authors to find means to help her decide what to paint. The question of what to paint is both something one wants to avoid but, on the other side, is compelled to embrace. As an artist, E. POTIER has, throughout various creations, applied protocols and concepts to let random hazard enter the creation process and let the question of what to paint become of secondary concern or even disappear completely. One example is *"1001 crashs aériens[1]"* where the sheer quantity of produced canvases essentially transforms the artist into a painting machine and imposes a mechanical repetition of their gestures; another one is *"365 jours"* [12] consisting of a series of 365 paintings made from the first news item heard when turning on the radio in the morning and tuning in on *France Info*. In order to pursue in this direction of reasoning and reflecting on the concept of liberty in choosing a topic in the general creative process, the idea arose to conceive software that would impose (or merely suggest) upon the painter the subjects for their painting.

---

[1] Solo show exhibition, *"Jours de lune"* gallery, Metz, France, 2014. https://www.emmanuellepotier.com/expo-jours-de-lune.

T. Martins et al. (Eds.): EvoMUSART 2022, LNCS 13221, pp. 148–161, 2022.
https://doi.org/10.1007/978-3-031-03789-4_10

The rest of this paper is structured as follows: Sect. 2 describes the global creative process in which this work is engaged; Sect. 3 outlines the Artificial Intelligence tools that have been implemented to instanciate the process; Sect. 4 provides the outcomes of the end-to-end process and opens discussions with practitioners on the use of the program.

2   The Creative Process

2.1   Context

Humans build and organize their life according to rituals, beliefs, habits. But sometimes, the daily course of life is disrupted. Events happen and surprises occur. Would this mean everything is not in our power? What we are, our decisions, our actions, do not allow us to avoid what impossible to predict or to infer through rational reasoning and available knowledge. What a dramatic misfortune for those who want to master everything! More and more... the human being and the world are failing, but couldn't this actually be a good thing? An accident, indeed, can be seen as an injury, a threat, or, on the contrary, as a breath of fresh air among the strain of defined determinism; a game-changing and thought-provoking glitch.

E. POTIER considers her painting isn't answering any questions, nor is it looking for a culprit. It is simply a space where chance has its place, opens a breach. The idea is to let the painting become a vessel to let the unknown speak out and to require us to figure out how to listen. She therefore often paints subjects of things that impose themselves upon us without our being able to do anything about it.

We live in the age of immediate planetary communication. Thanks to the Internet, it is now possible to instantly transmit and receive images, sounds, texts, thus abolishing physical distances. At the beginning of the 20th century, P. BONNARD wrote: *"I have all my subjects at hand. I will see them, take notes and then I go home. And before painting, I reflect, I dream."* In 2006, about the canvases made from television images, E. POTIER wrote: *"My subjects? I no longer need to go see them, they are here, at home. They are no longer subjects of my choosing, they are subjects that I undergo."* Speed has become a global performance criterion. Those who are unable to live a hundred miles an hour are considered having somehow lost the battle of life. In all areas, the winners are those who are the fastest in achieving results. There is, in the way we receive the world, a principle of sterile reproduction of images, without distancation. We receive a type of highly codified, endlessly repeated images that appear before us like hallucinations. Worse, through these images it is possible to influence the opinion of a population simply by the nature of what is presented to them, regardless of the content. P. VIRILIO, in his interview dated 2009, entitled *"Penser la vitesse"* affirmed that *"our societies are not so much societies of opinion, as societies of emotions. We feel the same emotion all over the world because there was a tsunami in certain islands or because there was the collapse of the World Trade Center, it is a considerable power, it is a power of speed and indeed if time is money, speed is power"* [11].

The main stance of the work presented in this paper therefore is to reflect on the process of generating emotions from unexpected or unsolicited images and how undergoing them can still spark inspiration and creation. The tool developed for this experimental research is an AI powered program that freely interprets what it considers to be representative for a particular artist and can produce a range of new, unexpected, yet sense-making visual representations of what it "feels" appropriate to their interest. By doing so, the AI both becomes a distorting mirror of reality but equally a filter between the brutality of the relentless flow of images providing a refuge to the artist to reflect on.

2.2   General Assumptions and Process

The AI induced previously mentioned process is based on the following general assumptions and actions in the course of creating art:

- Iconic artwork (paintings in our case) inherently respects and follows a series of rules defining what makes it relevant to the painter[2].
- The painter gathers samples of artwork that they consider of particular interest at a given point in time. The painter is also influenced by other images that are of particular value to them, unrelated to the artwork.
- The AI will try and figure out the aesthetic rules characterizing the artwork and apply them to or combine them with collected images of interest in order to combine and create unexpected and supposedly surprising chimera paintings.
- The AI created chimera image, if correctly done, should invoke a reaction to the painter given that it combines compositional, graphic or other rules gathered from the iconic painting collection as well as subjective visual cues retrieved from the unrelated images.
- The artist then freely interprets the chimera image as an inspiration for further painting.

In what follows we will be developing a first proof of concept leading to the creation of an AI that would support the artist in above process. Although the description in this paper focuses on a specific algorithmic instance, it should be clear to the reader that the whole artist – AI interaction is to be considered as a continuous process, constantly evolving and adapting and that the model presented in this paper is a first, modest, stage in this evolution.

Also, the stance of this work is that the eventual artwork is produced by the human artist, inspired by the relevant input from the AI. While the issue may be open to debate, we are considering that our AI is not creating art in any way but is merely a muse to the artist, a tool.

---

[2] We are definitely not making the statement there is such a thing as "good" art or that there are explicit rules that would actually define it. However, we are making the assumption that, when a painter is considering starting a new project, there may be a class of existing inspirational paintings sharing a number of inherent properties (composition, color, texture ...) that confer them a particular subjective interest at that point in time and for that specific artist.

Fig. 1. Initial inception. Left: iconic painting – *Les hasards heureux de l'escarpolette* by Jean-Honoré Fragonard (1732–1806); Right: chimera image

2.3   Data Requirements

In what follows we will be relying on the following concepts, all of which are freely defined by the artist, and may evolve or change in function of the creative project or goals they may be pursuing. They can be a voluntary human input, duly curated and selected as to fit specific requirements, or, on the other hand, being randomly generated by the AI.

Artwork comprises a collection of iconic reference paintings serving as compositional and syntactic basis of the final chimera image.

Visual Universe of the painter comprises a collection of visual item snippets, that will be used as collage-like clippings in the final chimera image (*e.g.* the dog in Fig. 1).

Inspirational Backgrounds comprises any global visual support that may serve as general background of the chimera image.

The use of these collections by the AI to form a chimera painting are represented in Fig. 2. The actual implementation is described in the next section.

3   The Artificial Intelligence

As mentioned earlier, the global interaction process between the artist and the AI is to be considered in constant evolution and adjustment. Furthermore, the tool should not be seen as forcing a way of thinking or working upon the painter, but rather be considered as something to interact with, to challenge or to possible deflect from its initially intended use. This section describes the current status of our AI. As a proof of concept it was developed essentially with off-the-shelf components and functions in four phases, as depicted in yellow in Fig. 3: a decomposition phase, consisting of extracting compositional elements from a given work of art; a recomposition phase, replacing the extracted elements with counterparts from the visual universe; a reprojection of the recomposed elements onto an inspirational background and, finally, a style transfer from the original artwork onto the reprojected image.

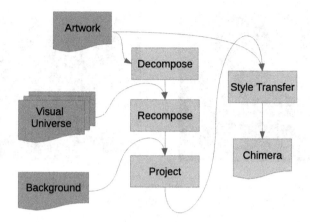

Fig. 2. General chimera creation flow followed by the AI: a work of art is decomposed and reconstructed using the artists visual universe; re-projected onto a selected background and rendered in the original artwork's style.

3.1   Artwork Decomposition

The decomposition phase consists in trying to find significant items in the scene and label them (*cf.* first image in Fig. 3). This result is obtained using a semantic segmentation neural network. Semantic segmentation is the process in which an algorithm labels pixels in an image as belonging to one or more predefined classes of things, thus, by grouping the pixels effectively identifying whole objects in scenes.

It is not within the scope of this paper to develop a particular way of detecting objects in paintings, nor is there any specific need in evaluating the wide range of possible approaches of achieving semantic segmentation. Interested readers can refer to [1,3,10] for an overview. As a matter of fact, there is a real interest in specifically not selecting top-ranked state-of-the-art AI as will be made clear below.

One of the interesting parts of this approach, resulting from the use of off-the-shelve neural networks is that they have essentially been conceived and trained on pictures of real world scenes, and not that much on paintings. As such they produce the following useful side effects :

1. They have a fixed, sometimes limited range of categories they can recognize. Very often they produce uncertain guesses to the actual presence of specific objects or provide a confidence measure in what they have identified. The painter can therefore interact with the AI to have it adjust its level of confidence when detecting objects.
2. Since they have not been specifically trained on paintings, their detection capacity is altered and can result in the perception of hallucinatory objects that are not quite in the picture.

Fig. 3. Illustration of the AI at work. From left to right, top to bottom: decomposition of original artwork – *Le radeau de la méduse,* oil on canvas, 490 cm × 716 cm, 1818–1819/Théodore Géricault, Louvre museum –, recomposition with visual universe and projection upon background, style transfer, actual artist's rendering – *Mes verts*, oil on canvas, 80 × 120 cm, 2020/Emmanuelle Potier, courtesy of the artist

While these effects are considered limitations or failures in the production engineering environments for which they were originally conceived they are of creative impact in our case. We have used the Mask R-CNN network [5] trained on the MS-COCO data set [9], the code and network parameters of which are freely available[3]. As can be seen in Fig. 3 the detected objects are surprising: an elephant is detected in the lower left part, and what originally is a sail is mistakenly taken for an umbrella, *etc.* Notwithstanding these misinterpretations, all detected objects fit within the main relative positions that define the general composition of the painting.

These uncontrolled (and uncontrollable) effects of imperfection can be seen as the AI-counterpart of human observers interpreting an artwork with a classical *lector in fabula* effect [2, 7]: seeing things and exploring references in a work that were not of the intention of the artist.

---

[3] https://github.com/matterport/Mask_RCNN.

Fig. 4. Illustration of the AI to painter process From left to right, top to bottom: original artwork – *The Birth of Venus*, tempera on canvas, 172.5 cm × 278.9 cm, 1484–1486/Sandro Botticelli – decomposition of the painting; recomposition with visual universe and projection upon background; style transfer; actual artist's rendering – *Il est des questions d'âmes damnées qui resteront éternellement sans réponse*, oil on canvas, 32 cm × 46 cm, 2020/Emmanuelle Potier, courtesy of the artist

3.2 Recomposing with a Visual Universe and Projection

The next phase consists of taking elements from the painters own visual universe and project them in a new environment that mimics the structure and composition of the initial painting.

From an AI point of view this is actually a very similar process to the one of decomposition, only that it is done on a series of images coming from (and provided by) the artist's personal collection of visual inspirational sources (pictures, paintings, drawings ...). By using the same semantic segmentation approach as described before, we construct a collection of AI-identified snippets from the artist's visual universe, each of which being classified into one of the categories known to the AI (*cf.* [9] for the examples presented in this paper). The following algorithm is then applied :

- locate and identify objects in the given initial artwork (Sect. 3.1); the size, relative position and type of objects are considered representative of the general figurative composition of the work;
- from the visual universe, retrieve objects of the same category, and having a similar shape; shape similarity is determined by comparing Hu moments [6] form the contours of the objects identified in the initial artwork and those retrieved from the visual universe;
- select an inspirational background image from the artist's visual universe;
- project the retrieved objects onto the background image, reproducing their relative positions and size from the original artwork.

The result of this phase can be observed in the second image of Fig. 3 or in Fig. 4, 5 and 6. This is essentially comes down to "borrowing" the compositional form of the provided painting by identifying objects, their size and their position, and then recomposing a similar compositional form in a totally unrelated setting. The obtained image is rarely engaging and is usually missing chromatic coherence because of its rough collage-like characteristics on the one hand, and the fairly brutal superposition of contextually unrelated objects on the other hand.

3.3   Style Transfer

In order to achieve a final representation that is chromatically more coherent and better relates to the initially provided artwork, we apply another neural network consisting in operating a style transfer from the original work to the previously collage-like image [4]. Here again, we are using a publicly available off-the-shelf AI solution, and, as in the previous sections, the result is beyond control of the artist, highly dependable of minor variations in both the original artwork and the collage image. As a consequence, the final rendered image will contain unexpected quirks and curiosities. One of the more significant parameters is for instance the relative digital image resolutions of the original artwork and the inspirational background: identical images at different resolutions may produce quite different (yet coherent) results.

4 Results Analysis and Discussion

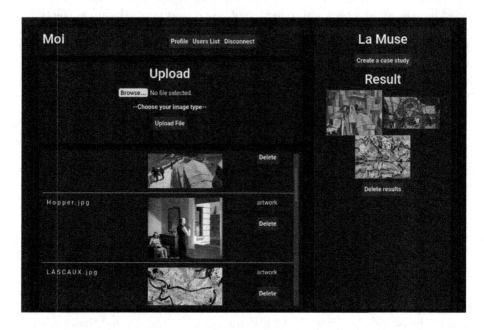

Fig. 5. Illustration of operational website

A few results are presented in Fig. 4, 5 and 6 showing the full process from an iconical painting over the various stages by our AI to the final actual human produced painting. An experimental website is accessible for testing at https://lamuse.univ-reims.fr.

This section provides a summarized overview of the opinions, feelings or first experiments of several artists with respect to *Lamuse*. Some of them have tried to use the tool, others have not yet, but reflect on how its existence and usage could, or could not interact with their personal practice.

4.1 E. Potier

E. POTIER is a painter established in Metz, France[4]. She has been using *Lamuse* in her artistic work since the first preliminary images created by the program in 2018. She was at the inception of the initial idea, and it has been a source of great inspiration for her since.

For many years, as an artist, she has been using protocols in her work, allowing her to paint without interference of a rational thinking process, but only needing to focus on the act of painting itself. In addition, she tends to work

---

[4] https://www.emmanuellepotier.com.

Fig. 6. Illustration of the AI to painter process. From left to right, top to bottom: original artwork – *Pope St Clement Adoring the Trinity*, oil on canvas, 488 cm × 256 cm, 1737–1738/Giovanni Battista Tiepolo, Alte Pinakothek, Munich – decomposition of the painting; recomposition with visual universe and projection upon background; style transfer; actual artist's rendering – *Manège complexe et vivant d'une journée universelle*, oil on canvas, 143 cm × 111 cm, 2020/Emmanuelle Potier, courtesy of the artist

in series. Since 2019, her paintings have been inspired by results from *Lamuse* and the program, which is the acme of her protocols, has become an invaluable source of thought food for a new approach to pictorial practice. One of the current directions being explored are the generation of series, based on the one well identified and chosen work from the History of Painting for which *Lamuse* can generate an infinity of variations. The artist is currently using the process for making a series based on "*The Birth of Venus*" by Botticelli (Fig. 4).

Lamuse offers images, which are in turn interpreted by the painter and cut out on canvas. From there on, the artist chooses certain areas that will remain. Others are erased to emphasize those selected. The images are cropped or taken as they are, depending on the inspiration provoked by the pictorial suggestions of the program. The final part of the creative process consists of choosing a title for the work. It provides the link with the profound subjective and personal dimension the artist perceived through the impulse of the program.

The process becomes a dialogue between the AI and the inner feelings of the painter, not unlike the introspective exchanges with a psychologist. Given that they are mysterious, almost abstract, deformed and complex, the images proposed by *Lamuse* unveil passions, instincts, unknown desires of the artist that are projected back to her full awareness once exposed on the canvas through the uncontrolled and unconscious process sparked by the AI's suggestions. This progressive revelation during the execution of the painting, once it has come to an end, depending on the artist's decision, takes the opposite view of the concept. Indeed, the concept of developing an AI is, in this approach, a means of transmitting a different message than what can be inferred from the general the usage of the tool. As if the AI is trying to impose their view upon the painter, and the painter resisting this tentative of control. It hints at the limited "intelligence" of the AI and its inability to have access to the inner subjectivity of the artist which remains the real source of creativity.

The actual "meaning" behind the painting can therefore only become clear at the very end of the process, after the painting has been finished. This is what appeals to E. POTIER because surprise and discovery are constantly present throughout the creative process. The artist does therefore not seek to paint any idea. The idea does not exist beforehand, but it is built during the execution of the work to eventually be revealed and start its proper existence *a posteriori* at the end of the road.

4.2   Rarès-Victor

Not all painters need to adhere to the process described in the previous section. RARÈS-VICTOR is an artist established in Nancy, France[5] who was interviewed before using *Lamuse*. The painter works by letting himself be guided by the material, and like many artists, has his own rituals. A program like *Lamuse* could be, according to him, a crutch when confronted to recurrent painters' block, or a source of inspiration when working on a specific order. He insists on

---

[5] http://raresvictor.com.

the need to maintain the condition that artists remain attached to working for the common interest and therefore can choose when and how long the program is to be used. He fears there is a risk of the AI destroying his ability to reflect, to think and to imagine the impossible: everything that is at the basis of artistic creation.

RARÈS-VICTOR also considers such a program as the continuity of another artist's project. A heritage. If the tool can provide strong ideas for research or suggest solutions, and if these seem better than the ones the artist would conceive, he could follow them. His own ideas may sometimes coincide with *Lamuse*'s, have common roots. The main challenge therefore is to find a common internal logic to creation, creativity in which the AI would find its place.

In any case, the painter wishes to remain in control and will allow himself to follow *Lamuse*'s proposals without thinking about them beforehand.

4.3   N. Varoqui

N. VAROQUI is a painter in Lahaymeix, France[6]. His creative process usually starts with a title, found at random (through a word, an expression, song lyrics, or piece of text) and which calls for a painting. Then the subject follows. More rarely, he discovers a patch of nature that becomes a compelling and inevitable contribution to an already identified title. He names every painting that will be executed from the start on, so that subject and title are in agreement at the time of making.

The artist most often confronts his natural surroundings, the landscape. Painting is an immersive process within this environment. Working in a studio and needing to process images displayed on a computer screen requires a significant amount of concentration from the artist, as he needs to recreate the original atmosphere to remember the physical sensations he has experienced. Images are something he quickly detaches himself from and are more of a support for his memory and recollections. His multiple times spent in the forest, both during day and night times, have created for him routine habits and an experience in his creative process.

By using *Lamuse*, he thinks he would first feel depersonalized, dispossessed, then bewildered, until finally finding his bearings. The fun would come next, maybe, probably in expressing another form of freedom. The changes in his practice through *Lamuse*, would come over the long term, with several canvases produced in this way, and sufficient time to really let go... to figure out how to approach and tame the tool and select the parts that fit his needs.

This process would probably shake up the writing, introducing more hesitation or lean towards more emancipation in the execution of the paintings. The artist wonders if he will have to adapt by changing his tools, rethinking the choice of his pigments, his formats. For the composition, being a self-described monomaniac, he will certainly have to sidestep, succeed in detaching himself

---

[6] https://www.noelvaroqui.fr/.

from his affect to concentrate on the form rather than on the substance. He thinks that coherence will no longer belong to him.

Nevertheless, the artist is eager to test the program, to be surprised and to try and accept the astonishment of the elements chosen by the AI.

4.4   O. Masmonteil

O. MASMONTEIL is a painter in Paris, France[7]. His painting results from a theme, a motif, or just the pure urge to paint. He collects the subjects he would like to treat: landscapes, nudes, images that have marked him by their shape or their color. In the event that the desire to paint is present without a subject, the artist makes a copy of a painting from the History of Painting, so as not to remain inactive and prolong the time spent painting. Sometimes he may throw paint on the canvas, as if to soil it and cause stains. In his studio, he also has a multitude of unfinished canvases from previous series that he can eventually take up again.

A program like *Lamuse*, which would give him subjects, very much appeals to him because it would come and provoke his desire to paint. Indeed, collaboration is important in the production of the artist, in that he likes to solicit collaborators or even simple visitors on the feelings of his work. Often his best paintings do not come from an idea that he has personally had, but from a rebound on an idea that was slipped to him. *Lamuse* could therefore be this non-human entity that would "slip ideas" to him, which is always creatively interesting. The challenge is then to surpass oneself in painting, whatever the starting point. Practice is king!

5   Conclusion

We have developed and experimented a tool for creating inspirational pseudo-paintings based on the visual universe of a painter, highly adaptable to a broad range of uses and configurations. The integration of artificial neural networks in the process of creation generates various uncontrolled effects that very likely will spark inspiration and creative questioning

The current version of the framework is freely accessible for experimenting at https://lamuse.univ-reims.fr and code is open source on GitHub (LGPL3)[8].

The tool is under active development, and further work will consist in extending its scope by introducing other AI resources, like automated caption generation [8] and art critique descriptions like, for instance those created by I. KIM[9], based on the data provided by the artist's universe and the generated images.

We have started collecting reactions and comments from artists on their perception of getting inspiration from AI before and after using *Lamuse*. Some of their returns have been integrated in this paper, but further work will consist

---

[7] https://fr.wikipedia.org/wiki/Olivier_Masmonteil.
[8] https://github.com/lamiroy/LaMuse.
[9] http://isabel.kim/infiniteartwork/.

of a broader study and collection of practices and comments and will need to be fully compiled and summarized.

Acknowledgment. The authors want to thank all the students who contributed to developing and enhancing the software that made all this possible: M. FOUQUES, F. ABOUDA, E. DARGENT, J. LEVARLET, F. AMATHIEU, B. CAMUS, T. FONTENIT, A. GUYOT and Y. PETIT.
Many thanks to the artists who have accepted giving their opinion on *Lamuse*.

References

1. Papers with code, semantic segmentation. https://paperswithcode.com/task/semantic-segmentation. Accessed Mar 2022
2. Eco, U.: Lector in Fabula. Grasset, Paris (1979)
3. Garcia-Garcia, A., Orts-Escolano, S., Oprea, S., Villena-Martinez, V., Rodríguez, J.G.: A review on deep learning techniques applied to semantic segmentation. CoRR abs/1704.06857 (2017). http://arxiv.org/abs/1704.06857
4. Gatys, L., Ecker, A., Bethge, M.: A neural algorithm of artistic style. J. Vis. **16**(12), 326–326 (2016). https://doi.org/10.1167/16.12.326
5. He, K., Gkioxari, G., Dollár, P., Girshick, R.: Mask R-CNN (2018)
6. Hu, M.K.: Visual pattern recognition by moment invariants. IRE Trans. Inf. Theor. **8**(2), 179–187 (1962). https://doi.org/10.1109/TIT.1962.1057692
7. Lamiroy, B.: On the Limits of Machine Perception and Interpretation. Habilitation à diriger des recherches, Université de Lorraine (December 2013). https://tel.archives-ouvertes.fr/tel-00940209
8. Lee, D., Hwang, H., Jabbar, M.S., Cho, J.D.: Language of gleam: impressionism artwork automatic caption generation for people with visual impairments. In: Osten, W., Nikolaev, D.P., Zhou, J. (eds.) 13th International Conference on Machine Vision, vol. 11605, pp. 304–311. International Society for Optics and Photonics, SPIE (2021). https://doi.org/10.1117/12.2588331
9. Lin, T.-Y.: Microsoft COCO: common objects in context. In: Fleet, D., Pajdla, T., Schiele, B., Tuytelaars, T. (eds.) ECCV 2014. LNCS, vol. 8693, pp. 740–755. Springer, Cham (2014). https://doi.org/10.1007/978-3-319-10602-1_48
10. Minaee, S., Boykov, Y.Y., Porikli, F., Plaza, A.J., Kehtarnavaz, N., Terzopoulos, D.: Image segmentation using deep learning: a survey. IEEE Trans. Pattern Anal. Mach. Intell. (2021). https://doi.org/10.1109/TPAMI.2021.3059968
11. Paoli, S., Virilio, P.: Paul Virilio. ARTE France développement, Issy-les-Moulineaux (2008). https://boutique.arte.tv/detail/paulvirilio, certains interviews sont en version originale anglaise sous-titrée en français
12. Potier, E., Bellído, R.T., Zilio, M.: 365 jours. Atelier génétique, Éditions les Presses littéraires (2017). https://www.lespresseslitteraires.com/potier-emmanuelle/

EvoDesigner: Towards Aiding Creativity in Graphic Design

Daniel Lopes$^{(\boxtimes)}$, João Correia , and Penousal Machado

CISUC, DEI, University of Coimbra, Coimbra, Portugal
{dfl,jncor,machado}@dei.uc.pt

Abstract. Graphic Design (GD) artefacts aim to attract people's attention before any forward objectives. Thus, one of the goals of GD is frequently finding innovative aesthetics that stand out over competing design artefacts (such as other books covers in a store or other posters on the street). However, as GD is increasingly being democratised and broadly shared through social media, designers tend to adopt trendy solutions, lacking disruptive and catchy visual features. *EvoDesigner* aims to assist the exploration of innovative graphic design solutions by using an automatic evolutionary approach to evolve the design of a number of text, shapes, and image elements inside two-dimensional canvases (pages). To enable the collaboration human-machine, the process has been integrated into *Adobe inDesign*, so human designers and *EvoDesigner* may alternately edit and evolve the same design projects, using the same desktop-publishing software. In this paper, an overview of the proposed system is presented along with the experimental setup and results accomplished so far on an evolutionary engine developed. The results suggest the viability of the development made in this first iteration of the system, which aims to reinterpret existing layouts in an unexpected manner.

Keywords: Automatic · Evolutionary · Graphic design · Layout · Poster

1 Introduction

The goal of Graphic Design (GD) artefacts may vary according to the context of their applications. Nevertheless, it may be reasonable to classify them into two main separate groups: (i) communication artefacts, which final objective is passing information objectively to a given public, and (ii) artistic artefacts, which might seek only to be aesthetic or pass information in a non-objective way (e.g. presenting hidden messages or ones that are susceptible of personal

This work is funded by national funds through the FCT - Foundation for Science and Technology, I.P., within the scope of the project CISUC - UID/CEC/00326/2020 and by European Social Fund, through the Regional Operational Program Centro 2020 and is partially supported by *Fundação para a Ciência e Tecnologia*, under the grant SFRH/BD/143553/2019.

T. Martins et al. (Eds.): EvoMUSART 2022, LNCS 13221, pp. 162–178, 2022.
https://doi.org/10.1007/978-3-031-03789-4_11

interpretation). Regardless of their final aims, often, GD artefacts must first of all menage to attract the attention of the target public and only thereafter the public may read the given information or enjoy the presented aesthetics.

One of the most established and commonly adopted approaches to make designs stand out over others (e.g. other books in a store or other posters on the streets) might be enhancing aesthetics. But as GD is getting increasingly democratised and broadly produced and shared (e.g. through social media, television and even on the streets), many design artefacts tend to converge into trendy solutions which lack disruption and eye-catchy features. Therefore, finding novel graphic design solutions might not be a trivial task or otherwise, creators would come up with innovative and surprising solutions for every work produced. Also, if that was the case, maybe professional designers would not be needed at all to create catchy brands, posters, book covers and others, nor co-creative tools would be continuously researched.

To keep innovating and surprising the public, graphic designers have been constantly evolving their work processes by taking advantage of the technologies of their times. Recently, that may be observed in the exploration of digital techniques to create moving and interactive designs (such as moving/interactive posters), which most times can stand out over static ones. Nonetheless, such approaches might not be a possibility in all contexts, not only because of technicalities but also because the development of such digital artefacts is often more time consuming and expensive. Thereby, the creation of disruptive aesthetics might always be a key necessity in the GD area, either to be applied in static, moving or interactive artefacts. For that reason, we believe that automatic tools for assisting creativity in GD might help designers not only achieve more disruptive aesthetics, but also free them up to explore and innovate regarding other aspects, such as dynamism or interactivity, or even come out with new features that one cannot imagine yet.

In that sense, *EvoDesigner* aims to fasten the exploration and employment of innovative GD aesthetic solutions. To accomplish that, the system employs a conventional Genetic Algorithm (GA) to automatically evolve an undetermined number of text-boxes, shapes and images into two-dimensional canvases (pages). Also, to facilitate the application of the generated ideas, as well as to allow the collaboration human-machine (so both agents may contribute to the work with their valences), the system was integrated into *Adobe inDesign* (a widely used desktop-publishing software for GD) in the form of an installable extension. By doing so, human designers and *EvoDesigner* may alternately edit and evolve designs using the same software, until a satisfactory result is achieved.

In this first iteration of the system, the Mean Squared Error (MSE) between the generated individuals and a given image is calculated to assess fitness. This approach is tested for the generation of unexpected poster layouts, by approximating the page balance of both sketched and camera-ready posters. In further developments, several other modules must be developed, such as ones for estimating how balanced, legible and novel the generated pages might be.

Primarily in this paper, an overview of *EvoDesigner* is made. Then, follows the description of the developments made so far, consisting of the aforementioned evolutionary engine for evolving a number of given items (text-boxes, shapes and images) within *inDesign* pages, and towards the page layouts of a given image (poster). Lastly, the experiments for technically validating the system are presented. The preliminary results suggest the viability of the developed system for evolving GD artefacts in the form of *inDesign* pages, as well as the feasibility of manually editing and automatically evolving pages, alternately.

2   Related Work

This first iteration on *EvoDesigner* aims to contribute by presenting (i) an evolutionary tool for aiding the creation of two-dimensional graphic design artefacts (e.g. posters or book covers), (ii) which can be easily integrated in the workflow of professional designers and (iii) that takes advantage of the editing capabilities of existent desktop-publishing software. Thus, *EvoDesigner* relates mostly to page layout, including the style and geometry of the displayed items. In this section, related work is presented while identifying the respective pros and cons.

So far, more than evolutionary techniques, generative approaches have become increasingly common in the development of GD applications. In GD, these systems usually take advantage of stochastic parameters to define visual features such as the colour, size or position of certain elements [3]. However, in many cases (if not most), the aesthetics of the generated artefacts may be relatively predictable. For that reason, generative systems are many times purposely developed for specific design projects, for example, for generating variations within a defined style (graphic identity), such as creating variations of book covers within a given layout [1,9,14,15] or varying visual features on logos according to the context of their application [23,48].

Besides, generative projects for more broad applications can also be pinpointed. For example, projects for aiding the generation of typography [10,39,47] or the generation of two-dimensional GD layouts. This latest, better relating to our purposes. And although some of the work on the GD layouts topic may have limited capabilities, e.g. not permitting the declaration of concept-wise preferences [16,24], the work of Ferreira (2019) [17] or Cleveland (2010) [6] stand out by allowing the users to fix indented parameters and then let the system vary the remaining, ensuring the maintenance of an intended style (e.g. useful for creating layouts for given graphic identities). A similar approach must be adopted in future developments of *EvoDesigner*. Lastly, we highlight the work of Rebelo et al. (2020) [40] on the creation of layouts for websites based on the semantic analysing of its textual content. Also, similar approaches must be implemented in further developments of *EvoDesigner*, for the generated designs to visually represent given concepts.

Furthermore, there has been research endorsing more intelligent approaches [27], such as training Machine Learning (ML) models using existing work and exploring the latent space to return interpolations of these. In GD, that has been endorsed, for example, for the generation of logos [35], typography [5,19,28,30] or editing images [4,8]. Because of its closer relation to our project, we highlight the work of Zheng et al. (2019) [53] on the creation of content-aware layouts. The shortcoming on the aforementioned ML approaches is these may often lead to pastiche results (imitations of existing styles) [50], so many times these lack in capabilities for exploring more disruptive solutions.

For that reason, we argue that Evolutionary Computation (EC) approaches may have greater potential for the exploration of innovative GD solutions, due to their similarity to the work processes of human designers [49], i.e. both humans and EC can explore the space of possibilities towards a given target (important as GD projects usually have a briefing to respond to), yet EC systems have the advantage of allowing a higher number of experiments per time, comparing to humans. Even so, humans still being crucial for the ultimate judgement of the results, fine-tuning and several other tasks.

Many (if not most) EC systems for GD applications endorse interactive approaches, i.e. in which the user must drive the generation process. For example, there is work on the generation of figures [22], icons [11–13], logos [18,45], typography [38,44,51,52], websites [36,46] or posters [25,26]. From the reviewed work on this topic, the most robust might be the work of Önduygu (2010) [37], by being able to evolve typographic fonts, lines, shapes, colours, images and visual filters. *EvoDesigner* seeks to expand this range of abilities even further for trying to put the system on a pair with human designers, as much as possible.

Regarding automatic EC creative systems, less work seems to be published. This might be due to the difficulty of objectifying aesthetics to create appropriate fitness functions. Thus, even though some frameworks have been presented so far [2,21,32,43], none of these might fully solve the aesthetics evaluation problem. Nonetheless, one may identify some successful automatic EC systems for GD applications, such as the work of Rebelo et al. (2017) for evolving moving posters according to the actions of the spectators [41]. Furthermore, we highlight the work of Rebelo et al. (2018) [42] by allowing both automatic and interactive evaluation, so the system and human designers may collaborate in the evolutionary process.

Another relevant hybrid approach might be applying ML techniques for assessing fitness in EC creative systems. In the computational art scope, a considerable number of works might be found [7,20,31]. Nevertheless, regarding GD, there might not be many references. Besides, one may identify relevant work, such as the one of Martins et al. (2016) for evolving typefaces out of given modules [33].

Lastly, we refer to existing work that integrates EC systems in existing desktop-publishing software. As long as we could assess, such integrated systems might not be highly common. However, it is possible to identify a few examples already. One of these is *Microsoft PowerPoint's Design Ideas* [34] which may be a good analogy to the workflow on *EvoDesigner* since (i) the system is integrated into widely popular software; (ii) it takes advantage of the software's functionalities; (iii) the users must start by inserting content and then the system will suggest styling solutions; (iv) both the user and the system can contribute to the results; (v) the user can improve the final results by editing them. Also, *Evolving Layout* [26] might be a noteworthy work due of its integration in *Adobe inDesign* (same way as *EvoDesginer*). The shortcoming on this system is its limited capabilities, only allowing to interactively evolve the position, scale and rotation of the page elements. As mentioned before, *EvoDesginer* aims not only to evolve designs automatically but also to take advantage of a wide range of software functionalities (as much as possible), so it is on par with human designers.

3   Approach

As an approach for aiding the creation of disruptive GD solutions, we propose the development of an automatic evolutionary system for evolving pages— *EvoDesigner*. The system must assist graphic designers during the experimentation stages of their workflow, so both human and machine can contribute to a given project by editing pages (individuals). To do so, *EvoDesigner* is presented to the user in the form of an extension (plug-in) for a broadly used GD desktop-publishing software—*Adobe inDesign*. The code implementation of the built-in extension has been accomplished using HTML, CSS, *JavaScript* and *ExtendScript* (*JavaScript* for *Adobe*'s software).

An evolutionary engine based on a conventional Genetic Algorithm (GA) with automatic fitness assignment makes the core module of *EvoDesigner*. However, the whole system can be described as a composition of several individual modules: (i) the referred evolutionary engine; (ii) several modules for visually evaluating images and which may or not be picked by the user to assess fitness, such as (among other possibilities) modules for assessing how novel, legible, balanced and how related to a given GD style a page is, or how similar it is to a given image; and (iii) a module for translating keywords (defined by the user) into visual features (e.g. colours, geometric transformations, font weights and others), which must be useful for limiting the search space, leading to results that are more visually related to the concept (keywords) of the respective projects.

So far, developments have been done for implementing the referred evolutionary engine using image-similarity for fitness assignment. Thus, this paper does not include developments on the keywords module nor the novelty, legibility, balance and style evaluation ones. Nevertheless, a full schematic representation of the system is presented in Fig. 1. Besides allowing the validation of the developed evolutionary engine, using image-similarity metrics for fitness assignment might also be useful in practical GD tasks, such as finding unexpected layouts that approximate given drafts, e.g. the ones in Fig. 5, used as target images in some of the experiments presented later in this paper.

To interact with the system, in the *Adobe inDesign* environment, the user must start by creating a blank document and inserting the intended items (text-boxes, images or shapes) into pages, as usual for starting a project in *inDesign*. Then, a user interface can be used for setting up the system variables. At the current stage, the following are allowed: (i) set of pages to evolve; (ii) population

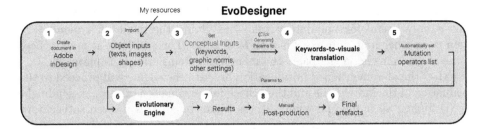

Fig. 1. Schematic representation of *EvoDesigner*. 1) The user must first 1) create a blank document, 2) insert elements into pages, 3) set up desired preferences (e.g. set the pages to evolve and set keywords) and click "Generate" to start; 4) the module *Keywords-to-visuals translation* will try to find properties/tools that match the inserted keywords; 5) Each property/tool will be assigned with a probability to be used by the system to mutate pages (individuals); 6) the evolutionary engine will evolve pages; 7) the resulting pages will be made available as normal and editable *inDesign* pages; lastly, 8) the designer may edit the results and 9) export final artefact. From any stage of the user interaction, the parameters might be changed and the evolution restarted.

size; (iii) number of generations to run; (iv) items that must always be included in any page (e.g. one may define text-boxes to be mandatory and let images be optional). In further developments, other functionalities must be allowed, such as (i) inserting keywords; (ii) defining tools and visual features that the designer wants/desires to be used (e.g. certain colours or typefaces); (iii) defining the hierarchy of the elements (i.e. which ones must be emphasised the most); (iv) what fitness modules to use and how important is each of these. After setting up the system preferences, the user must press a "Generate" button for starting the system. Once the evolution terminates, the user can edit the results normally using *inDesign* or evolve again some indented pages, using the same or different parameters.

3.1   Evolutionary Engine

As previously mentioned, before running the system, the user must define which pages (individuals) to evolve, from 1 to any number pages. For example, the user might be working on a document with 10 pages but only wants to consider 3 of them in the evolutionary process. Besides, the desired population size must be set. If the number of selected pages happens to be bigger than the defined population size, the later parameter will be automatically increased to match. Otherwise, if the number of selected pages is smaller than the defined population size, before the evolutionary process starts, the system will automatically create the remaining individuals by crossing over and mutating the selected pages, and it will certify that all the mandatory items are included in every page.

Furthermore, the user might name items, so the system knows which must be treated as equivalent i.e. if several pages have an item named "title" (even if these "title" items have different visual styles among them), the system will assume these are equivalent. However, in the current iteration of the system, this is only useful for mandatory items, as giving the name of a mandatory item to another item will make it mandatory too. Thus, as long as one of these same-name items is on the page, the mandatory items criteria is matched.

After the aforementioned initialisation process, the engine will proceed to the evaluation of the individuals and then check for termination criteria, which might be (i) finding an individual whose fitness equals or exceeds a given satisfactory value (at this stage, not considered), (ii) whether the system had run a given number of generations or (iii) whether the user has ordered the system to stop evolving, by clicking the button "Stop generation".

If no termination criteria was matched, selection will be performed using a tournament method of size 2 and an elite of 1 individual. Lastly, a new population must be created by crossover and mutation, the offspring must be evaluated and the process must repeat.

Representation. As briefly suggested already, the phenotype of individuals is the native render of *inDesign* pages themselves, which may contain different types of items, such as text-boxes, shapes or images, which in turn are defined by a number of positioning, geometry and style properties. These properties are stored automatically by *inDesign* in the JSON format. In that sense, in *EvoDesigner*, genotypes consist of JSON objects containing all the properties of the respective pages, as well as the properties of the items contained in them (refer to Fig. 2 for a schematic example of the genotype). However, in this first iteration of the system, only the following item-properties were considered: the shape of the surrounding box, size, position, order of the items (z-position), flipping mode, blending mode, opacity, background colour/gradient, background tint, stroke colour/gradient, stroke tint, stroke weight, rotation and shearing angle. Also, for text-boxes, it is available text size, typeface, justification, vertical text alignment, letter spacing and line-height. In further developments, a number of other properties must be available, including page properties such as margins or grid rulers. Furthermore, the properties "name" and "label" are used to keep track of mandatory items, having no visual effect on the phenotypes.

Variation. Variation-wise, all the generated individuals go through crossover and then mutation processes. In this first iteration of the system, crossover only shifts whole items and not individual item properties. The crossover process executes as follows: All the items of the first parent (P1) are iterated randomly (are not picked by their order in the page). Each of these items (I1) has a 50% chance to pass directly to the offspring (with the same position, geometry and style). If that is not the case, the system will try to pick, from parent 2 (P2), a random item (I2) that has not been passed to the offspring yet. If no such I2 exists, I1 will be passed anyway. Otherwise, I2 will be passed instead. Thus, offspring can contain a minimum and a maximum number of items respectively equal to the number of items in the smaller and bigger individuals of the initial

```
Page {
    PageItems: [
        Item: {
            Shape_of_surrounding_box: one_of_available_constants,
            size: array_of_numbers,
            position: array_of_numbers,
            z_position: integer,
            flipping_mode: one_of_available_constants,
            blending_mode: one_of_available_constants,
            opacity: number,
            background_colour: colour_or_gradient,
            background_tint: number,
            stroke_colour: colour_or_gradient,
            stroke_tint: number,
            stroke_weight: number,
            rotation: number,
            shearing: number,
            text_size: number,
            typeface: one_of_available_constants,
            justification: one_of_available_constants,
            vertical_alignment: one_of_available_constants,
            letter_spacing: number,
            line_height: number,
            ... (other not-used properties of Item)
        }
        ... (other Items)
    ]
    ... (other properties of Page)
}
```

Fig. 2. Schematic representation of an individual's genotype (this scheme serves only for the sake of the example, so the property names and value-types might not be fully accurate).

population (which, as already referred, might be automatically generated by the system).

Mandatory items can only shift with similar mandatory items. In other words, if I1 is a mandatory item, then I2 must have the same name as I1, or I1 will be always passed. This can be used, for example, so titles (items named "title") can only shift with other titles. Similarly to what happens in the project *Ádea* [29], we refer to such approach as topological crossover, once the shifts happen among similar structural parts. As a further explanation, if an item "title" is mandatory, offspring will always inherit an item "title" either from a parent or the other. A natural analogy might be always inheriting crucial structural parts such as eyes, either from the father or the mother. In the case of our system, this is relevant to guarantee that all the posters include all the mandatory (structural) items, at least. A natural analogy for optional items might be more difficult to pinpoint, but for the sake of the example, one may think of it as inheriting or not a chronic disease.

For each individual, each mutation method might run within a 1% chance, changing one of the position, geometry and style properties referred to in Fig. 2. The value assigned to each property is picked randomly. These might be random integers, floats, arrays of numbers or also picked from lists of predefined constants. That is the case of colours, which are picked from a list of colour values. In this iteration of the system, a fixed list of seven colours—black, white, magenta, yellow, red, green and cyan.

Fitness Assignment. In this iteration of the system, fitness was assessed through the calculation of an image similarity value between the generated individuals and a given target image. To accomplish that, the individuals are first exported in the PNG format, 72 dpi. The target images share this same format and settings. Then, each individual (PNG) is compared with the given target image through the calculation of the Mean Squared Error (MSE), returning a value m, representative of the difference between the images. Thus, for returning a similarity value (so the bigger the value, the better), the final fitness value equals negative m.

A well-established image similarity metric such as MSE was chosen, first of all, to understand whether or not the developed evolutionary engine is able to evolve correctly. Nevertheless, it also might be useful for practical GD tasks such as the generation of relatively unexpected layouts by approximating the page balance of given images (either sketches or camera-ready images; see Fig. 5), using given page-items. As mentioned before in this paper, in further developments other fitness functions must be developed. For instance, from our background in GD, we believe that assessing novelty and balance values might be fundamental for describing disruptive and appealing GD artefacts. However, the latter (as well as MSE) might only be enough for the generation of more artistic artefacts in which legibility might not be important. Thus, for the generation of communication design artefacts (probably, most cases), a legibility value must also be retrieved and considered in fitness assignment. Also, in our perspective, not so crucial yet useful, might be retrieving an additional value for whether an individual belongs to a given GD style (aesthetic movement).

4   Experimental Setup and Results

One of the primary use-cases for *EvoDesigner* might be the generation of posters. Thus, for setting up experiments, the 3 speculative posters of Fig. 3 (manually created from blank pages but little stylised) were selected to be evolved. Figure 4 showcases an example of an initial population of 10 individuals generated out of the same 3 selected pages, using crossover and mutation operations.

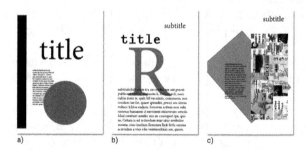

Fig. 3. Pages selected to be evolved (manually created from blank pages; little stylised).

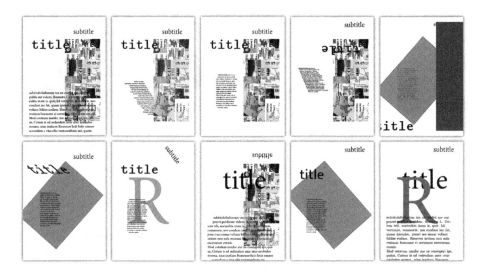

Fig. 4. Example of an initial population of 10 individuals, generated out of the 3 selected pages of Fig. 3.

Moreover, the images of Fig. 5 were used as targets. Figure 5.b showcases speculative camera-ready posters designed in *inDesign*. These were used at first instance to assess whether and until what point the system was evolving. Figure 5.a showcases sketches representative of the respective posters of Fig. 5.b. These were used as targets for the main experiments, as these might better exemplify an expected target image for whenever using MSE for fitness assignment. For example, a designer might sketch an abstract layout and let the system generate posters that can approximate it, using a given set of page items. Nevertheless, camera-ready posters such as the ones in Fig. 5.b might also be useful for different use-cases. For example, if a designer likes a given existent poster, the system might help create new ones with a similar page balance. Even so, these must still be different enough from the target ones once the given page-items must differ, as must do their position, geometry and style.

The remaining parameters were set up as follows: (i) population size: 50 individuals; (ii) tournament size: 2; (iii) elite size: 1; (iv) probability to crossover a page item: 50%; (v) probability for a mutation method to perform: 1%; (vi) mandatory elements: all the text-boxes in the selected pages (the pages of Fig. 3); (vi) fitness assignment: MSE; (vii) maximum generations: dependent of the experiment; (viii) termination criteria: achieving the defined number of maximum generations.

In the first experiments, a run with the parameter "maximum generations" set to 1000 was made for assessing whether the fitness values were maximising and what number of generations would be necessary until no major gains were accomplished. To do that, the poster from Fig. 5.b.1 was set as a target, once it seemed to be the more easily achievable one, from the presented posters—

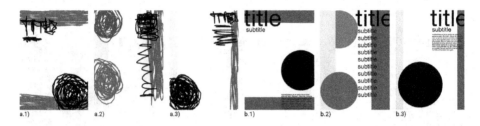

Fig. 5. Possible target images: a) sketched posters; b) camera-ready posters designed in *Adobe inDesign*. (Color figure online)

visually heavier in the top-left and right-bottom corners (black items), and with medium-weight items in the top and bottom areas (red stripes). This run has been manually stopped at the 480th generation, as no major gains were being observed for many generations (see Fig. 6.a, which presents the plotted fitness of the best individuals of each generation, along with the average fitness of each population). As a result of this experiment, 100 generations were set for the following runs.

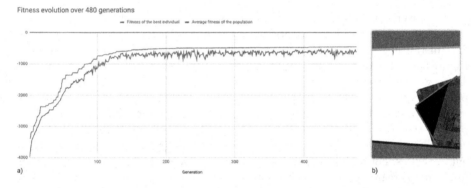

Fig. 6. Results from 480 generations using Fig. 5.b.1 as a target; a) the fitness values of the best individuals of each generation and the average fitness for each population; b) the best phenotype form the 480th generation.

The following experiments were performed targeting each of the posters of Fig. 5.a and maintaining the parameters mentioned before. For each poster, 4 runs were made. Figure 8 presents the average fitness of the best individuals of each generation, for each target image. Figure 7 showcases some of the resulting images generated by the system, for each of the target posters of Fig. 5.a.

The resulting phenotypes suggest that the system has been able to proximate the layout (balance) of the target images, once darker areas in these tend to result in more filled and darker respective areas in the generated posters. Moreover, even the colour pallet tends to be approximated for the respective areas.

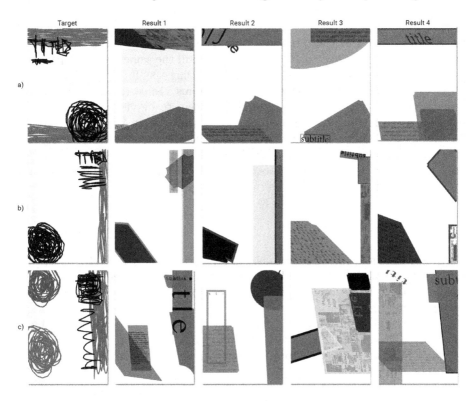

Fig. 7. Best individuals from 4 different runs (100 generations), for 3 different target images: a) Fig. 5.a.1; b) Fig. 5.a.2; c) Fig. 5.a.3

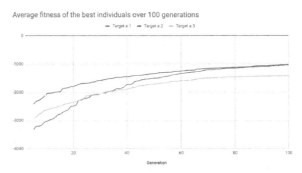

Fig. 8. Average fitness (4 runs) of the best individuals of each generation, for each target image of Fig. 5.a

As a result, if a user has a preference for the layout of a sketched or existing poster, the presented approach can be considered for creating new posters using some indented page items, by approximating, but not copying, the layouts of the intended images, i.e. getting close but not too close from the target images.

Furthermore, as expected, we accomplished to allow the manual edition of the generated results after the termination of the evolutionary process, so human designers and *EvoDesigner* can alternately work in the same *inDesign* project.

An evident and predictable shortcoming on using MSE for fitness assignment is the lack of ability for keeping mandatory items visible (ideally, mandatory items are like so because the designer whats them to be visible to the public, rather than hiding behind other items, being off-page or just too small). In that sense, including legibility assignment in the calculation of fitness could be a possible approach for improving the results regarding this issue. Even so, designers may solve this issue by post-editing the results, so the later can turn into communication artefacts rather than just aesthetic ones.

5   Conclusion

In GD, finding disruptive aesthetics is usually of the utmost importance for getting the attention of the target public. However, often GD artefacts tend to follow trendy solutions/styles, which might result in GD artefacts that might not stand out over competing ones.

EvoDesigner is an automatic system for evolving pages within the *Adobe inDesign* environment. The goal is to assist the creative process of graphic designers by alternately collaborating with these in the edition of pages and page-items, for example, for creating posters or book covers.

This paper has presented the first iteration of *EvoDesigner*, consisting of the implementation of an automatic evolutionary engine based on a conventional GA. So far, experiments have been done for evolving page layouts towards given target images, using the MSE metric for assessing fitness. To do that, the generated pages are exported from *inDesign* in the PNG format and compared to given target images, also in PNG.

In the presented experiments, the used image targets consisted of speculative posters of two kinds: (i) sketched layouts and (ii) camera-ready posters. Sketched targets might be useful, for example, whenever a graphic designer aims to generate artefacts that describe a given page balance and colour pallet. Nevertheless, utilising images of finished GD artefacts might also be useful, for example, for resembling the page balance of the targets without culminating in results that are too similar to the originals. For instance, the generated artefacts might differ in the utilised page items themselves.

The performed experiments suggested the viability of the presented approach in the evolution of GD artefacts that resemble the page balance of the target images, but that still be different enough not to be deemed as the same. In that sense, and besides user testing must be needed to attest the following statement, we believe the presented approach might be worth being included in the GD workflow for assisting the generation of disruptive GD solutions, since the system is able to take given layouts and consider these to dispose and edit page-items in relatively unexpected manners (particularly, in the creation of posters, as it has been tested in this paper).

In future work, several different modules for improving the robustness of the system must be developed, such as: (i) a module for translating keywords into visual properties/tools (e.g. for limiting the search space towards a given creative concept), or (ii) fitness modules that can or not be used for performing novelty, legibility and balance judgements, or assessing how much an image might be in-style with a given GD aesthetic movement. Also, new functionalities must be added, e.g. for positioning items according to page grids, promoting more organised layouts.

References

1. Arteaga, M.: Generative eBook covers. The New York Public Library (2014). www. nypl.org/blog/2014/09/03/generative-ebook-covers. Accessed 24 Feb 2020
2. Birkhoff, G.: Aesthetic Measure. Harvard University Press, Cambridge (1933)
3. Bohnacker, H., Groß, B., Laub, J., Lazzeroni, C.: Generative gestaltung. Verlag Hermann Schmidt, p. 4 (2009)
4. Bychkovsky, V., Paris, S., Chan, E., Durand, F.: Learning photographic global tonal adjustment with a database of input/output image pairs. In: The 24th IEEE Conference on Computer Vision and Pattern Recognition (2011)
5. Campbell, N.D.F., Kautz, J.: Learning a manifold of fonts. ACM Trans. Graph. **33**(4), 1–11 (2014). https://doi.org/10.1145/2601097.2601212
6. Cleveland, P.: Style based automated graphic layouts. Des. Stud. **31**(1), 3–25 (2010). https://doi.org/10.1016/j.destud.2009.06.003
7. Correia, J., Machado, P., Romero, J., Carballal, A.: Evolving figurative images using expression–based evolutionary art. In: Proceedings of the 4th International Conference on Computational Creativity, Sydney, Australia, pp. 24–31 (2013)
8. Correia, J., Vieira, L., Rodriguez-Fernandez, N., Romero, J., Machado, P.: Evolving image enhancement pipelines. In: Romero, J., Martins, T., Rodríguez-Fernández, N. (eds.) EvoMUSART 2021. LNCS, vol. 12693, pp. 82–97. Springer, Cham (2021). https://doi.org/10.1007/978-3-030-72914-1_6
9. Cruz, P., Machado, P., Bicker, J.: Data Book Covers (July 2010). https://cdv.dei. uc.pt/data-book-covers/. Accessed 1 Nov 2021
10. Cunha, J., Tiago, M., Bicker, J., Machado, P.: TypeAdviser: a type design aiding-tool. In: Workshop on Computational Creativity, Concept Invention, and General Intelligence, C3GI 2016 (2016)
11. Cunha, J.M., Lourenço, N., Correia, J., Martins, P., Machado, P.: *Emojinating:* evolving emoji blends. In: Ekárt, A., Liapis, A., Castro Pena, M.L. (eds.) Evo-MUSART 2019. LNCS, vol. 11453, pp. 110–126. Springer, Cham (2019). https:// doi.org/10.1007/978-3-030-16667-0_8
12. Dorris, N., Carnahan, B., Orsini, L., Kuntz, L.A.: Interactive evolutionary design of anthropomorphic symbols. In: Proceedings of the 2004 Congress on Evolutionary Computation, June 2004, vol. 1, pp. 433–440 (2004). IEEE Cat. No. 04TH8753. https://doi.org/10.1109/CEC.2004.1330889
13. Dozier, G., Carnahan, B., Seals, C., Kuntz, L., Fu, S.-G.: An interactive distributed evolutionary algorithm (IDEA) for design. In: 2005 IEEE International Conference on Systems, Man and Cybernetics, October 2005, vol. 1, pp. 418–422 (2005). https://doi.org/10.1109/ICSMC.2005.1571182
14. Duro, L., Machado, P., Rebelo, A.: Graphic narratives (March 2013). https://cdv. dei.uc.pt/graphic-narratives/. Accessed 1 Nov 2021

15. Eveillard, L.: Portfolio de louis eveillard—couvertures génératives (2015). www. louiseveillard.com/projets/couvertures-generatives. Accessed 1 Nov 2021

16. Feiner, S.: A grid-based approach to automating display layout. In: Proceedings of the Graphics Interface, vol. 88, pp. 192–197 (1988)

17. Ferreira, D., et al.: Design Editorial Algorítmico. Master's thesis, Universidade de Coimbra (2019)

18. Gambell, T., Hooikaas, A.: Emblemmatic - markmaker (2015). http://emblemmatic.org/markmaker. Accessed 14 Jul 2019

19. Hayashi, H., Abe, K., Uchida, S.: GlyphGAN: style-consistent font generation based on generative adversarial networks (2019)

20. Heath, D., Ventura, D.: Creating images by learning image semantics using vector space models. In: 30th AAAI Conference on Artificial Intelligence (2016)

21. den Heijer, E., Eiben, A.E.: Comparing aesthetic measures for evolutionary art. In: Di Chio, C., et al. (eds.) EvoApplications 2010. LNCS, vol. 6025, pp. 311–320. Springer, Heidelberg (2010). https://doi.org/10.1007/978-3-642-12242-2_32

22. den Heijer, E., Eiben, A.E.: Evolving art with scalable vector graphics. In: Proceedings of the 13th Annual Conference on Genetic and Evolutionary Computation, GECCO 2011, p. 427. ACM Press, New York (2011). https://doi.org/10.1145/2001576.2001635

23. Stefan Sagmeister Inc.: Casa da musica (2007). https://sagmeister.com/work/casa-da-musica. Accessed 1 Nov 2021

24. Jacobs, C., Li, W., Schrier, E., Bargeron, D., Salesin, D.: Adaptive document layout. Commun. ACM 47(8), 60–66 (2004)

25. Kitamura, S., Kanoh, H.: Developing support system for making posters with interactive evolutionary computation. In: 2011 4th International Symposium on Computational Intelligence and Design, October 2011, vol. 1, pp. 48–51 (2011). https://doi.org/10.1109/ISCID.2011.21

26. Klein, D.: Evolving Layout - next generation layout tool. http://www.evolvinglayout.com. Accessed 17 Dec 2018

27. Lewis, M.: Evolutionary visual art and design. In: Romero J., Machado P. (eds) The Art of Artificial Evolution. Natural Computing Series, pp. 3–37. Springer, Heidelberg (2007). https://doi.org/10.1007/978-3-540-72877-1_1

28. Loh, B., White, T.: SpaceSheets: interactive latent space exploration through a spreadsheet interface. In: Workshop on Machine Learning for Creativity and Design. 32nd Conference on Neural Information Processing Systems, NIPS 2018, Montréal, Canada (2018)

29. Lopes, D., Correia, J., Machado, P.: Adea - evolving glyphs for aiding creativity in typeface design. In: Proceedings of the 2020 Genetic and Evolutionary Computation Conference Companion, GECCO 2020, pp. 97–98. Association for Computing Machinery, New York (2020). https://doi.org/10.1145/3377929.3389964

30. Lopes, R.G., Ha, D., Eck, D., Shlens, J.: A learned representation for scalable vector graphics. arXiv preprint arXiv:1904.02632 (2019)

31. Machado, P., Cardoso, A.: All the truth about NEvAr. Appl. Intell. (Spec. Issue Creative Syst.) 16(2), 101–119 (2002)

32. Machado, P., Cardoso, A.: Computing aesthetics. In: de Oliveira, F.M. (ed.) SBIA 1998. LNCS (LNAI), vol. 1515, pp. 219–228. Springer, Heidelberg (1998). https://doi.org/10.1007/10692710_23

33. Martins, T., Correia, J., Costa, E., Machado, P.: Evotype: from shapes to glyphs. In: Proceedings of the Genetic and Evolutionary Computation Conference 2016, pp. 261–268. ACM (2016)

34. Microsoft: Create professional slide layouts with PowerPoint Designer - office support. https://support.microsoft.com/en-us/office/create-professional-slide-layouts-with-powerpoint-designer-53c77d7b-dc40-45c2-b684-81415eac0617
35. Oeldorf, C., Spanakis, G.: LoGANv2: conditional style-based logo generation with generative adversarial networks. 2019 18th IEEE International Conference On Machine Learning And Applications (ICMLA), pp. 462–468 (2019)
36. Oliver, A., Monmarch, N., Venturini, G.: Interactive design of web sites with a genetic algorithm. In: Proceedings IADIS International Conference WWW/Internet, pp. 355–362 (2002)
37. Onduygu, D.C.: Graphagos: evolutionary algorithm as a model for the creative process and as a tool to create graphic design products. Ph.D. thesis, Sabanci University (2010). https://research.sabanciuniv.edu/24145
38. Parente, J., Martins, T., Bicker, J., Bicker, J.: Which type is your type? In: Proceedings of the 11th International Conference on Computational Creativity (2020)
39. Pereira, F.A., Martins, T., Rebelo, S., Bicker, J.: Generative type design: creating glyphs from typographical skeletons. In: Proceedings of the 9th International Conference on Digital and Interactive Arts, ARTECH 2019, Association for Computing Machinery, New York (2019). https://doi.org/10.1145/3359852.3359866
40. Rebelo, J., Rebelo, S., Rebelo, A.: Experiments in algorithmic design of web pages. In: Kreminski, M., Eisenstadt, V., Pinto, S., Kutz, O. (eds.) Joint Proceedings of the ICCC 2020 Workshops, WS 2020 (2020)
41. Rebelo, S., Martins, P., Bicker, J., Machado, P.: Using computer vision techniques for moving poster design. In: 6.ọ Conferência Internacional Ergotrip Design (2017)
42. Rebelo, S., Fonseca, C.M.: Experiments in the development of typographical posters. In: 6th Conference on Computation, Communication, Aesthetics and X (2018)
43. Ross, B.J., Ralph, W., Zong, H.: Evolutionary image synthesis using a model of aesthetics. In: 2006 IEEE International Conference on Evolutionary Computation, pp. 1087–1094 (2006)
44. Schmitz, M.: genoType. https://interaktivegestaltung.net/genotyp2/. Accessed 14 Jul 2019
45. Schmitz, M.: Evolving logo, 4 edn. In: Bohnacker, H., Gross, B., Laub, J., Lazzeroni, C. (eds.) Generative Gestaltung. Verlag Hermann Schmidt (2009). https://interaktivegestaltung.net/evolving-logo-2/
46. Sorn, D., Rimcharoen, S.: Web page template design using interactive genetic algorithm. In: 2013 International Computer Science and Engineering Conference (ICSEC), September 2013, pp. 201–206 (2013). https://doi.org/10.1109/ICSEC.2013.6694779
47. Suveeranont, R., Igarashi, T.: Example-based automatic font generation. In: Taylor, R., Boulanger, P., Krüger, A., Olivier, P. (eds.) SG 2010. LNCS, vol. 6133, pp. 127–138. Springer, Heidelberg (2010). https://doi.org/10.1007/978-3-642-13544-6_12
48. Studio TheGreenEyl: MIT Media Lab (2011). www.thegreeneyl.com/mit-media-lab
49. Thoring, K., Muller, R.M.: Understanding the creative mechanisms of design thinking: an evolutionary approach. In: Proceedings of the 2nd Conference on Creativity and Innovation in Design, DESIRE 2011, pp. 137–147. Association for Computing Machinery, New York (2011). https://doi.org/10.1145/2079216.2079236
50. Toivonen, H., Gross, O.: Data mining and machine learning in computational creativity. Wiley Int. Rev. Data Min. Knowl. Disc. **5**(6), 265–275 (2015). https://doi.org/10.1002/widm.1170

51. Unemi, T., Soda, M.: An IEC-based support system for font design. In: 2003 IEEE International Conference on Systems, Man and Cybernetics, SMC 2003, vol. 1, pp. 968–973. IEEE (2003). Conference Theme-System Security and Assurance (Cat. No. 03CH37483)
52. Yoshida, K., Nakagawa, Y., Køppen, M.: Interactive genetic algorithm for font generation system. In: 2010 World Automation Congress, pp. 1–6. IEEE (2010)
53. Zheng, X., Qiao, X., Cao, Y., Lau, R.W.H.: Content-aware generative modeling of graphic design layouts. ACM Trans. Graph. **38**(4) (2019). https://doi.org/10.1145/3306346.3322971

Conditional Drums Generation Using Compound Word Representations

Dimos Makris[1(✉)], Guo Zixun[1], Maximos Kaliakatsos-Papakostas[2], and Dorien Herremans[1]

[1] Information Systems Technology and Design, Singapore University of Technology and Design, Singapore, Singapore
{dimosthenis_makris,nicolas_guo,dorien_herremans}@sutd.edu.sg
[2] Institute for Language and Speech Processing, R.C. "Athena", Athens, Greece
maximos@ilsp.gr

Abstract. The field of automatic music composition has seen great progress in recent years, specifically with the invention of transformer-based architectures. When using any deep learning model which considers music as a sequence of events with multiple complex dependencies, the selection of a proper data representation is crucial. In this paper, we tackle the task of conditional drums generation using a novel data encoding scheme inspired by the Compound Word representation, a tokenization process of sequential data. Therefore, we present a sequence-to-sequence architecture where a Bidirectional Long short-term memory (BiLSTM) Encoder receives information about the conditioning parameters (i.e., accompanying tracks and musical attributes), while a Transformer-based Decoder with relative global attention produces the generated drum sequences. We conducted experiments to thoroughly compare the effectiveness of our method to several baselines. Quantitative evaluation shows that our model is able to generate drums sequences that have similar statistical distributions and characteristics to the training corpus. These features include syncopation, compression ratio, and symmetry among others. We also verified, through a listening test, that generated drum sequences sound pleasant, natural and coherent while they "groove" with the given accompaniment.

Keywords: Drums generation · Transformer · Compound word

1 Introduction

Automatic music composition has slowly received more and more research attention over the last several decades [3,10,15,16]. Many researchers have been approaching the task of music generation with a plethora of methods (e.g., ruled-based, grammars, probabilistic among others [17,36]), recent research however, focuses intensely on deep generative architectures. The increased computational power available to us, along with easier access to large musical datasets, can

T. Martins et al. (Eds.): EvoMUSART 2022, LNCS 13221, pp. 179–194, 2022.
https://doi.org/10.1007/978-3-031-03789-4_12

empower us to train models that generate much more realistic sounding music (e.g., [19]).

In this research, we focus on music generation in the symbolic domain. There are several diverse tasks in this domain, including chorale harmonisation [14], piano [20], and multi-track generation [11] (see [3,16] for further reading). An approach can be characterised as unconditional if it generates output from scratch, or **conditional** if it take additional input information to *condition* the generation process, which can empower the user and making the generation process steerable. *Conditioning* information may for instance be entire musical tracks (e.g., chord-conditioned melody generation [45]) or specific constraints imposed by the user to control the generation output (e.g., emotions [29,41] as well as general features such as musical style [35]).

In this work, we explore the task of conditional rhythm generation, specifically drums sequences. Although there have been numerous attempts at building multi-track generative systems, only few of them include drum tracks. In addition, existing research usually tackles the task in an unconditional manner with no accompanying tracks involved (see Sect. 2 for examples). Therefore, we present a novel framework which utilizes a "Encoder - Decoder" scheme where a Bidirectional Long short-term memory (BiLSTM) [13] Encoder handles information for the conditioning parameters and a Transformer-based [42] Decoder produces the generated drum sequences. Influenced by [38] and related work [31], we use entire accompanying tracks as conditions, specifically Guitar and Bass along with extracted musical attributes such as Time Signature and Tempo.

The main contribution of this work lies in the encoding data representation. Transformer-based architectures are well known for their efficiency, which is achieved by applying attention mechanisms within large sequences of tokens. Since musical data is sequential, selecting the proper encoding representation is critical for such generative tasks. Hence, we propose a novel encoding scheme which is based on the **Compound Word** (CP) representation [18] where musical events can be described in grouped tokens. We present different CP representations for the Encoder and Decoder in order to efficiently transcribe the events related to the accompanying (conditional) and target drum tracks.

The remainder of this paper is organised as follows: Sect. 2 presents existing research on drums generation. Next, Sect. 3 and 4 presents our proposed framework with a focus on the Encoding Representation and the utilised Architecture respectively. Sections 5 and 6 detail the experimental evaluation, while conclusions are presented in Sect. 7.

2   Related Work

There has been extensive research on the task of drums generation, featuring different strategies and architectures. Although recent studies mainly use Neural Network-based architectures, there is some other notable work such as linear regression and K-Nearest Neighbors [43] for generating expressive drum performance, or evolutionary algorithms [23] to create rhythmic patterns by altering a given base beat.

Another remarkable strategy was introduced by Choi et al. [6] who transcribed simultaneous drum events into words and then used an LSTM with a seed sentence to generate drums sequences. Hutchings [22] presented a framework based on a *sequence-to-sequence* (seq2seq) architecture which generates a track for a full drum kit given a kick-drum sequence.

The work of Gillick et al. [12] can be considered as an important milestone, which introduced the first large scale symbolic dataset created by professional drummers. Their research focuses on producing expressive drums sequences for particular tasks such as tap2drum (generating a drum pattern based on an tapped rhythm by the user) and humanization (applying microtiming to quantised drums). Based on their dataset, Nuttall et al. [33] trained a Transformer-XL decoder for sequence generation and continuation.

In other work, Reinforcement Learning has been combined with neural network architectures. *jaki* [4]'s model is an example of such an approach. Their model generates 1-bar continuations of a seed sentence that can be controlled by the user through musical features such us density and syncopation. Karbasi et al. [25] proposed a model which learns rhythmic patterns from scratch through the interaction with other musical agents.

To best of our knowledge, there is very few existing research (see [26] for the audio domain) that tackles the task of drums generation *while considering accompanying tracks*. Although this can been addressed with multi-track generative systems, such as MuseGAN [11], the closest model that inspired our research is the Conditional Neural Sequence Learners [30,31] (CNSL). CNSL is a an architecture with stacked LSTM layers conditioned with a Feed-Forward layer to generate drum patterns. The Feed-Forward layer, which is called *Conditional*, takes as input extracted features from the accompanying bass and guitar tracks along with other musical attributes such the metrical position within a bar. The model uses a piano-roll representation and obtained noteworthy performance considering the limited amount of training data.

3   Data Encoding Representation

In this section we propose a novel data encoding scheme for the task of conditional drums generation, based on the **compound word** (CP) representation proposed by [18]. CP is an alternative tokenization approach where multiple tokens that describe a specific event can be grouped into a "super token", or "word". It differs from the traditional token-based representations (i.e., MIDI-like [34] and the recent REMI [20]) since musical pieces are not transcribed into a long *one*-dimensional stream of tokens. Instead, they are transcribed into smaller *n*-dimensional streams of tokens whereby *n* is the number of grouped tokens that forms the length of a single CP word. This strategy improves the efficiency of Transformer-based [42] architectures due to the decreased input sequence length which reduces the computational complexity. Recent studies show that CP achieves a better output quality compared to the aforementioned representations in certain tasks such as conditional/unconditional piano generation [8,18] and emotion recognition [21].

Our approach to generating a drum track conditioned with existing accompanying rhythm tracks (i.e., guitar and bass) motivates us to make use of the "Encoder - Decoder" scheme from the popular *sequence-to-sequence* (seq2seq) architectures [5]. Hence, we propose two different CP-based encoding representations whereby the Encoder handles information about the conditioning tracks, and the Decoder represents the generated drum sequences.

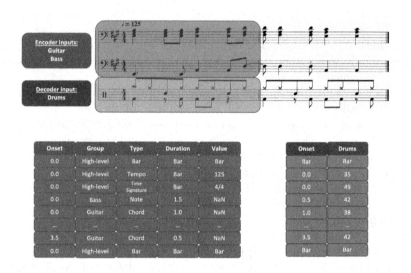

Fig. 1. Illustrated example of a training snippet represented in the proposed CP-based representation (for Encoder and Decoder inputs).

3.1   Encoder Representation - Conditional Information

The idea to use guitar and bass tracks as the accompaniment input stems from fundamental musical principles of contemporary western music where the *rhythm section* [38] typically consists of a drummer, a bass player, and a (at least one) chordal instrument player (e.g., guitarist). Therefore, drums are highly related to the bass and guitars tracks, perhaps more than any other instrument. Additionally, we take into account high-level parameters such as the tempo and time signature since it has been shown in related work [30,31] that they can affect both the density and the "complexity" of the generated drum track.

For the Encoder we developed a 5-dimension CP representation in which every dimension corresponds to a specific one-hot encoded categories of tokens. Both the original CP and REMI are bar-based representations where time-slicing happens in each individual bar, we also adopt this. Additionally, we include high-level information that describes every bar in terms of Time Signature and Tempo. Thus, the resulting CP words can either describe **events** regarding the performance of the accompanying tracks, or specifying the values of these parameters. The proposed categories are the following (see Fig. 1 for an example):

- **Onset:** Describes the beginning of an event measured in quarter notes inside a bar. The maximum value is related to the current Time Signature of this bar. If a new bar occurs, it resets counting.
- **Group:** An event can either describe the performance of an accompanying instrument (i.e., Guitar or Bass) or specify a high-level parameter. The latter includes Tempo and Time Signature, as well as "Bar" event (this indicates the start of a new bar). In sum, there are three possible groups of events: Guitar, Bass or High-Level.
- **Type:** This category determines the content of the "Group" category. If it is marked as High-Level, it declares specifically which parameter is described (i.e., Tempo, Time Signature, or the starting of a new bar). On the other hand, if the event belongs to the Guitar or Bass group, it can be either a Note or Chord.
- **Duration:** Indicates the duration of the event in quarter notes inside a bar. However, for high-level events the duration is marked with a "Bar" token.
- **Value:** Determines the value of the event, which depends on the declared Group and Type. Figure 1 shows the assigned values of each high-level parameter for the examined bar. Similar to [30,31], we exclude pitch information for Guitar and Bass events, since the drum pitches are not affected by the actual notes of accompanying tracks. Thus, *NaN* tokens are used on these occasions.

3.2 Decoder Representation - Generated Drum Sequences

The Decoder outputs the generated drum events in the form of 2-dimension CP words. In addition, we make the assumption that drum notes do not have a duration and we exclude any information about velocities. Therefore the two categories that describe our representation are:

- **Onset:** similar to the Encoder representation, the onset of a drum event is expressed in quarters inside a bar, and also includes a token to indicate the start of a new bar.
- **Drums:** the pitch value indicates which drum component is being played. In the case that multiple drum events happen at the same onset, then the new CP words have the same onset.

4 Proposed Architecture

In this section we introduce the model architecture which includes our proposed encoding representation for the task of conditioned drums generation. Section 4.1 reveals the components of the Encoder-Decoder architecture scheme, while Sect. 4.2 reveals hyper-parameters and implementation details.

4.1   Encoder - Decoder

Our architecture consists of a BiLSTM [13] Encoder and a Transformer Decoder that uses Relative Global Attention [19]. Following [18]'s methodology, our Encoder and Decoder inputs, which consist of the proposed CP representations, are fed to different Embedding spaces. The resulting latent variables are concatenated and fed as input to linear Dense layers. Therefore, these layers which include the combined embedding spaces of the CP words are acting as the "actual" inputs to our architecture.

The resulting latent variable z resulting from the Encoder, contains all of the information regarding the conditional tracks and the high-level features of an entire training piece. Accordingly, the Decoder, which is trained in an autoregressive manner, inputs the projected embedding spaces at each time step t - 1 to the relative self attention layers, along with the latent variable z from the Encoder. Since music has its underlying hierarchical structure (i.e. sections, phrases), musical events not only rely on the global position information but also the relative position of music events related to other music events. Hence, according to [19], music generated by self-attention layers with both relative and global position information is of better quality than that generated by vanilla self-attention layers [42] with only the global position information. We therefore adopted [19]'s efficient implementation of relative global attention to calculate the optimal size of the relative position information and set the relative attention window size to half of the total sequence length. The output logits from the relation-aware self-attention layers h_t are projected to two separate dense layers followed by softmax activation. This way, we obtain the predicted onset and drum pitches from the shared hidden logits. Figure 2 shows the details of our proposed architecture for conditional drums generation.

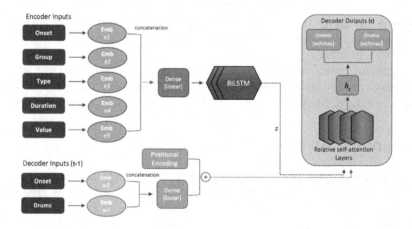

Fig. 2. Our proposed architecture features a stacked BiLSTM Encoder and a Music Transformer Decoder with Relative Global Attention [19].

4.2   Implementation Details

The Encoder consists of a 3-layer BiLSTM with 512 hidden units per layer, while the Transformer Decoder consists of a total of 4 self-attention layers with 8 multi-head attention modules. The number of hidden units in the Transformer's Feed-Forward layers was set to 1,024. We used the Tensorflow 2.x library [1] and trained the model on a single Nvidia Tesla V100 GPU using Adam optimizer with a learning rate of $2e^{-5}$ and a weight decay rate of 0.01. A 30% dropout rate was set to all subsequent layers along with an early-stopping mechanism to prevent overfitting.

Table 1 shows the size of the embedding layers for every input. These are directly correlated to the vocabulary size of the corresponding CP category (see Sect. 5.1). For the Decoder CP inputs, however, we slightly increased the embedding sizes compared to the Encoder, as we saw that this improved the performance. The final embedding sizes for the Encoder and Decoder CP words are 240 and 192 respectively. Finally, in order to enable diversity within the generation, we set a uniformly randomly sampling temperature (τ) between 0.8 and 1.2 for both the Onset as well as Drums distribution output.

Table 1. Vocabulary and Embedding sizes for each CP category for the Encoder (Enc) and Decoder (Dec) input.

CP-token category	Voc. size	Emb. size
Onset (Enc)	31	64
Group (Enc)	5	16
Type (Enc)	7	32
Duration (Enc)	40	64
Value (Enc)	33	64
Onset (Dec)	31	96
Drums (Dec)	16	96

5   Experimental Setup

The goal of our proposed framework is to generate drums sequences conditioned by given rhythm tracks (i.e., guitar and bass). Thus, a part of our experiments will focus on how to evaluate the quality of the generated drum rhythms. In addition, we compare the effectiveness of the proposed CP-based representation with existing approaches. In sum, we aim to evaluate the following:

1. Do the generated sequences have the same average densities (in terms of drum components) as the training dataset?
2. Are the generated drum tracks of good musical quality, and how "realistic" do they sound in comparison to the corresponding ground-truth pieces from the test set for the given seeds?

3. How effective is our proposed CP-based representation and architecture compared to existing approaches?

We address these research questions by both calculating an extensive set of objective evaluation metrics as well as a listening study. Details of both of these are presented below.

5.1 Dataset and Preprocessing

For our experiments we use a subset of the LAKH MIDI dataset [37]. Specifically, we selected tracks that belong to the Rock and Metal music styles provided from the Tagtraum genre annotations [39]. The reason for using these genres stems from the fact that the drum rhythms found in these genres are typically diverse and more complex compared to the contemporary popular music styles. After filtering out files that do not contain guitar, bass, and drum tracks we proceeded with the following preprocessing steps:

- In case multiple tracks of either Drums, Bass, or Guitar occur within one song, we only take into account the track with the highest density of notes. It is worth mentioning that we select the aforementioned tracks based on information from their MIDI channel.
- We consider drum events with pitches that are common in the examined music styles. Therefore, our framework is able to produce the following drum components: Kick, Snare and Side-Stick, Open and Closed Hihats, 3 Toms, 2 Crashes, China, and finally, Ride Bell and Cymbals.
- In order to prevent long sequences, we break every training piece to phrases with a maximum length of 16 bars. According to our proposed representation, the maximum input lengths for the Encoder and Decoder are 597 and 545 CP words respectively.
- We eliminate phrases that contain rare Time Signatures and Tempos. The resulting training corpus contains phrases with 8 different Time Signatures (the most common is 4/4) and Tempos that vary from 60 to 220 BPM.

The resulting preprocessed dataset contains 14,176 phrases that were extracted from 2,121 MIDI files. This dataset was randomly divided into training/validation/test sets with a ratio of 8:1:1.

5.2 Evaluation Metrics

We conducted both a computational experiment as well as a user study to evaluate the quality of generated music and hence the effectiveness of the proposed method. Most of the recent studies [12,33] that focus on drums generation tasks rely completely on subjective evaluation using listening tests. Although there is no standard way to quantitatively measure whether generative models have been trained efficiently [2], we will include a quantitative evaluation as well as a listening study, by adapting metrics that have been used in similar tasks.

Analytical Measures: We implemented two sets of metrics. Initially, we calculate the average number of specific drum components per bar. This is inspired by [11] and has been used widely in generative lead sheet systems (e.g., [27,29]). Specifically we measure the density of Kick & Snares, Hihats & Rides, Toms, Cymbals along with the average percentage of empty bars. Although such calculations cannot guarantee to accurately measure the quality of generated music, they can reveal if the output generated by a model has pitch characteristics that resemble the learnt style (i.e. the training dataset).

On the other hand, the second set consists of metrics that offer one value for the entire generated drum sequence, and can be considered as a "high-level" feature set. Hence, it might indicate if generated pieces have a good rhythm, a long-term structure characteristics and if they "groove" with the given accompaniment. We adopt the following measures:

- **Compression Ratio:** Reflects to the amount of repeated patterns that generated drums sequences contain. A high compression ratio is indicative of music with more structure and patterns, as per [9,45]. We used the Omnisia[1] library which implements the COSIATEC [32] compression algorithm.
- **Symmetry:** Indicates the repetitiveness of the (temporal) distance between consecutive onset events [24]. Therefore, highly symmetric rhythms have equally spaced onset intervals.
- **Syncopation:** Measures displacements of the regular metrical accent in patterns. It is related to the Time Signature and refers to the concept of playing rhythms that accent or emphasize the offbeats. We used the normalised version of Longuet-Higgins and Lee's implementation [28] adapted by [40].
- **Groove Consistency:** Calculates the similarity between each pair of grooving patterns across neighboring bars [44]. This metric takes into account the conditional tracks as well.
- **Pattern Rate:** Is defined as the ratio of the number of drum notes in a certain beat resolution to the total number of drum notes [11].

Listening Test Setup: We conducted an online listening test whereby participants rated short samples in order to evaluate the proposed framework. Each sample is in the form of a 3-track composition whereby the first two tracks are the accompanying or condition tracks, and the last one is the evaluated drum track. The drum tracks are either taken from the corresponding ground-truth sample of the test dataset, or generated by the newly proposed as well as baseline models. We asked the participants to rate the drum track of each sample on a 5-point Likert scale, ranging from 1 (very low) to 5 (very high), on the following criteria:

1. Rhythm Correctness: Whether the overall rhythm is pleasant.
2. Pitch Correctness: Is low if "irregular" drum notes are observed. This criteria differs from Rhythm Correctness as drums sequences may have a good rhythm while still containing unusual drum notes (i.e., playing only with toms).

---

[1] https://github.com/chromamorph/omnisia-recursia-rrt-mml-2019.

3. Naturalness: Does the drum track sound natural and "human" to the listeners?
4. Grooviness: Do the drums "groove" with the given Guitar and Bass accompaniment?
5. Coherence: Whether the drums are consistent and contain repeated patterns.

Inspired by similar listening tests for evaluating drums generation [12,33], we asked the users to indicate if they thought the drum tracks are performed by human players (ground truth) or generated by an A.I. model (could be either the proposed model or the baseline model). We also added a third option, "Not Sure", in case the listener does not feel comfortable giving a direct answer.

6   Results

We compare our proposed method with state-of-the-art models that can generate conditional drums sequences. We also introduce different setups of our method by either changing the encoding representation or parts of the architecture. Specifically we implemented the following baseline models:

- **CNSL:** As stated in Sect. 2, CNSL [31] is the closest related work for direct comparison. It differs from our approach since it uses *piano-roll* representation as well as extracted features from the accompanying tracks as an input. We increased the size of the conditional window to two bars, and doubled the hidden sizes of LSTM and Dense layers for a fair comparison.
- **MuseGAN:** We adapted the conditional version of MuseGAN [11] to generate drum sequences only. Similar to CNSL, it uses a piano-roll representation.
- **CNSL-Seq:** This is an altered *seq2seq* version of the CNSL which uses the same architecture (i.e., conditional input as Encoder and drum output as Decoder) as our proposed method. As for the encoding representations, we use the original piano-roll representation for the Encoder, and our proposed CP representation for the Decoder (since Transformer-based Decoders are not compatible with piano-roll representations). The resulting encoding scheme can by characterised as a "hybrid" representation approach with a piano-roll Encoder and CP word-based Decoder.
- **MT-CP:** We replaced the BiLSTM networks from our proposed architecture with relative self-attention layers in the Encoder stage, thus, resulting in the original implementation of Music Transformer [19]. This allows us to examine the impact of the Encoder type for conditional generation.

6.1   Objective Evaluation

We generated a total of 1,418 files for every model, using input seeds from songs in our test set. The sampling hyper-parameter (τ) was fixed to 1.0 for all cases. Table 2 shows the results of the first set of objective metrics (i.e., low-level) representing the average density of different drum components per bar.

Values close to those extracted from the training dataset may indicate that the generated fragments have a better chance to be musically valid as they match the density properties of existing music. Initially, we can observe that the CNSL and MuseGAN results are quite different than the real data. Our method performs best in three categories (Empty Bars, Toms, and Cymbals) with the CNSL-Seq version performing best in the other two categories (Kick-Snares and HH-Rides). In addition, fragments generated by the Music Transformer (MT-CP) version seem to be furthest away from the properties found in the training set, for in all categories of features.

Table 2. Results of the average density of drum components per bar. The values are better when they are closer to those computed from the training data.

	Empty bars	Kick-Snares	HH-Rides	Toms	Cymbals
Training dataset	5.91	5.0588	5.6203	0.7919	0.4902
Ours	**7.42**	4.8703	5.8882	**0.6075**	**0.3865**
CNSL	10.24	4.7297	6.1037	0.9636	0.7552
MuseGAN	12.23	3.1254	4.2243	0.2216	0.1899
CNSL-Seq	8.98	**4.8795**	**5.5276**	0.5342	0.3648
MT-CP	10.45	4.0814	3.9925	0.4835	0.3531

Although our proposed model as well as the CNSL-Seq model both seem to achieve comparable average densities of drum components, both of which resemble the style of the training data, we cannot yet make conclusions about the quality of the models. In addition, we should keep in mind that a "good" drum sequence is mainly related to higher-level characteristics that are extracted from patterns instead of individual components. These types of features are examined in the second set of metrics. Considering that the ground-truth of the generated pieces is available since we used seeds from the test set, we can assess which model's output has a "better resemblance" to the ground-truth. This can be done by computing the absolute difference between the calculated values of each examined metric and the corresponding ground-truth value. Since we have over 1.4k generated pieces, we normalise these differences and estimate the mean of absolute differences. The resulting metric indicates "how close" the generated pieces are compared to the real piece for a particular high-level characteristic.

Table 3 shows the results difference between the high-level features of generated pieces and those in the test set. Our proposed method has the lowest, thus the best, values compared to the baseline models for all feature categories. Especially for Symmetry and Syncopation we observe a huge difference compared to all the other models. Given that we are evaluating drum sequences, for which rhythm is arguably the most important feature, this is an excellent indicator of the success of our model. Similar to Table 2, the worst results are obtained by the CNSL and conditional MuseGAN model. Since these model have a very similar task, this **confirms the effectiveness** of our proposed method. Once again

Table 3. Results for the high-level objective metrics: For each model and feature, we calculate the absolute difference between the extracted values for all generated pieces with the corresponding ground-truth values. Then, we compute the normalised mean of the aforementioned differences along with the standard deviation (in parentheses). Therefore, the lowest values are the best.

	Compression ratio	Symmetry	Syncopation	Groove consistency	Pattern rate
Ours	**7.11 (7.64)**	**7.55 (8.12)**	**3.76 (4.76)**	**1.36 (1.69)**	**1.54 (3.86)**
CNSL	9.75 (7.87)	12.49 (11.45)	9.19 (8.82)	1.91 (2.17)	3.16 (4.96)
MuseGAN	10.48 (9.55)	15.45 (12.22)	14.54 (11.12)	5.12 (4.21)	7.87 (10.14)
CNSL-Seq	8.61 (8.14)	9.73 (10.52)	7.07 (7.78)	2.12 (2.07)	3.88 (6.08)
MT-CP	8.99 (8.22)	10.51 (11.06)	8.44 (7.89)	2.01 (2.67)	3.13 (5.34)

the MT-CP model's results are significant worse than ours, which indicates that using a BiLSTM encoder instead of self-attention layers improves the overall performance. This has been confirmed in similar tasks, such us chord-conditioned melody generation [7].

Although our method, which features the CP-based representation, for the task of conditional drums generation achieves the best objective evaluation scores, the difference with the CNSL-Seq model is relative low. Considering the standard deviation of the high-level metrics, we cannot make strong conclusions about whether the hybrid approach with a piano-roll based Encoder representation is less efficient than ours. Therefore, we conducted a listening experiment as discussed in the next subsection.

6.2 Subjective Evaluation

For our listening experiment, we selected 30 tracks: 10 randomly generated by each model (ours and CNSL-Seq) and 10 randomly selected from the test set. These pieces were then rendered as YouTube videos with visualised piano-rolls. We believe that employing these visual cues can help participants to better perceive the drum patterns, in addition to listening to them. For each participant, 15 samples (out of these 30) were picked randomly during the listening study. A total of 41 subjects participated in our test with 74% of them declaring medium or above musical background and knowledge. With a total of 615 votes, we get a high Cronbach's Alpha value (0.87) that confirms the consistency and reliability of the experiment. Table 4 reveals that our proposed model's ratings are significantly better compared to the pieces resulting from the CNSL-Seq model in all examined categories. Surprisingly, it even outperforms the real compositions when it comes to Naturalness, Grooviness and Coherence.

Table 5 shows the average accuracy of the participants' ability to predict if the drum rhythms were generated by an A.I. model or were human-composed. Interestingly, an average of 45.81% of the human-composed (Real) sequences were mistaken as A.I., whereas only 39.02% of the pieces generated by our proposed model were thought to be A.I. generated. This testifies to the perceived naturalness and quality of our model. On the other hand, the CNSL-Seq model

Table 4. Listening experiment ratings (Mean ± 95% Confidence Interval) for drum sequences generated by our framework and the CNSL-Seq model (baseline), as well as existing ground-truth (real) compositions from the test set.

	Rhythm correctness	Pitch correctness	Naturalness	Grooviness	Coherence
Real	**3.59 (0.13)**	**3.42 (0.13)**	3.13 (0.17)	3.17 (0.16)	3.32 (0.12)
CNSL-Seq	3.34 (0.13)	3.28 (0.14)	3.06 (0.15)	3.01 (0.15)	3.18 (0.12)
Ours	3.56 (0.12)	3.39 (0.14)	**3.34 (0.14)**	**3.31 (0.15)**	**3.39 (0.11)**

performs significantly worse than the proposed, with 50.00% rated as being A.I. generated and 21.94% as human-composed. Thus, taking into account all of the aforementioned Likert ratings and users' predictions, our proposed model seems to generate drum sequences which sound more pleasant and natural compared to the baseline model. Samples from the experimental setup along with the model code and pre-processed dataset are available on GitHub[2].

Table 5. Average Users' ratings to predict whether a drum sequence they listened to is generated by an A.I. model, is human-composed (Real), or they are not sure.

Users' predictions(%)	Real	A.I.	Not sure
Real	36.31	45.81	17.88
CNSL-Seq (A.I.)	21.94	50.00	28.06
Ours (A.I.)	41.75	39.02	19.23

7 Conclusions

This paper introduces a novel framework for conditional drums generation that takes into account the accompanying rhythm tracks (i.e., guitar and bass) and musical attributes (i.e., time signature and tempo). The proposed architecture consists of a BiLSTM Encoder which handles the conditioned input information and a Transformer-based Decoder that generates the drums sequences. The major contribution of this work relates to the proposed data representation which is based on the compound word (CP) encoding scheme. CP-based representations have the advantage that an event can be described by multiple grouped tokens, thus leading to smaller sequence lengths which reduces the computational complexity. Therefore, were present different CP representations for the Encoder and Decoder in order to tackle the task of conditional drums generation more efficiently.

The evaluate our proposed model and representation, we performed both analytical as well as more subjective experiments. During the analytical experiments,

---

[2] https://github.com/melkor169/CP_Drums_Generation.

we compared variations of our method by changing the architecture and representation, with baselines from related work. The results show that our method has a solid high performance across the wide range of different quantitative metrics used for evaluation. Specifically, we show that our model is able to produce drums sequences conditioned to input tracks, with similar pitch statistics to the training dataset, as well as high-level musical characteristics (i.e. syncopation, compression ratio etc.) compared to the corresponding ground truth test set.

We also conducted a listening test to evaluate our proposed CP representation compared to a feature-based piano-roll representation from the related work. The results show that our framework can generate drum sequences that sound more natural and pleasant. In addition, participants thought that our generated pieces were human, more so then actual human-generated pieces from the test set. As for future work, it would be interesting to examine the effect of adding more musical parameters and accompanying instruments to the Encoder representation.

Acknowledgements. This work is supported by Singapore Ministry of Education Grant no. MOE2018-T2-2-161 and the Merlion PHC Campus France program.

References

1. Abadi, M., et al.: TensorFlow: a system for large-scale machine learning. In: OSDI, vol. 16, pp. 265–283 (2016)
2. Agres, K., Forth, J., Wiggins, G.A.: Evaluation of musical creativity and musical metacreation systems. Comput. Entertain. (CIE) **14**(3), 1–33 (2016)
3. Briot, J.P., Hadjeres, G., Pachet, F.D.: Deep Learning Techniques for Music Generation. Springer, Cham (2020). https://doi.org/10.1007/978-3-319-70163-9
4. Bruford, F., McDonald, S., Sandler, M.: jaki: user-controllable generation of drum patterns using an LSTM encoder-decoder and deep reinforcement learning. In: The 2020 Joint Conference on AI Music Creativity (2020)
5. Cho, K., et al.: Learning phrase representations using RNN encoder-decoder for statistical machine translation. arXiv:1406.1078 (2014)
6. Cho, Y.H., Lim, H., Kim, D.W., Lee, I.K.: Music emotion recognition using chord progressions. In: 2016 IEEE International Conference on Systems, Man, and Cybernetics (SMC), pp. 002588–002593. IEEE (2016)
7. Choi, K., Park, J., Heo, W., Jeon, S., Park, J.: Chord conditioned melody generation with transformer based decoders. IEEE Access **9**, 42071–42080 (2021)
8. Chou, Y.H., Chen, I., Chang, C.J., Ching, J., Yang, Y.H., et al.: MidiBERT-Piano: large-scale pre-training for symbolic music understanding. arXiv preprint arXiv:2107.05223 (2021)
9. Chuan, C.H., Herremans, D.: Modeling temporal tonal relations in polyphonic music through deep networks with a novel image-based representation. In: Proceedings of the AAAI Conference on Artificial Intelligence, vol. 32 (2018)
10. Delìege, I., Wiggins, G.A.: Musical Creativity: Multidisciplinary Research in Theory and Practice. Psychology Press (2006)
11. Dong, H.W., Hsiao, W.Y., Yang, L.C., Yang, Y.H.: MuseGAN: multi-track sequential generative adversarial networks for symbolic music generation and accompaniment. In: 32nd AAAI Conference on Artificial Intelligence (2018)

12. Gillick, J., Roberts, A., Engel, J., Eck, D., Bamman, D.: Learning to groove with inverse sequence transformations. In: International Conference on Machine Learning, pp. 2269–2279. PMLR (2019)
13. Graves, A., Schmidhuber, J.: Framewise phoneme classification with bidirectional LSTM and other neural network architectures. Neural Netw. **18**(5–6), 602–610 (2005)
14. Hadjeres, G., Pachet, F., Nielsen, F.: DeepBach: a steerable model for Bach chorales generation. In: International Conference on Machine Learning, pp. 1362–1371. PMLR (2017)
15. Herremans, D., Chew, E.: MorpheuS: generating structured music with constrained patterns and tension. IEEE Trans. Affect. Comput. **10**(4), 510–523 (2017)
16. Herremans, D., Chuan, C.H., Chew, E.: A functional taxonomy of music generation systems. ACM Comput. Surv. **50**(5), 1–30 (2017)
17. Herremans, D., Sörensen, K.: Composing fifth species counterpoint music with a variable neighborhood search algorithm. Exp. Syst. Appl. **40**(16), 6427–6437 (2013)
18. Hsiao, W.Y., Liu, J.Y., Yeh, Y.C., Yang, Y.H.: Compound word transformer: learning to compose full-song music over dynamic directed hypergraphs. arXiv preprint arXiv:2101.02402 (2021)
19. Huang, C.Z.A., et al.: Music transformer: generating music with long-term structure. In: International Conference on Learning Representations (2018)
20. Huang, Y.S., Yang, Y.H.: Pop music transformer: beat-based modeling and generation of expressive pop piano compositions. In: Proceedings of the 28th ACM International Conference on Multimedia, pp. 1180–1188 (2020)
21. Hung, H.T., Ching, J., Doh, S., Kim, N., Nam, J., Yang, Y.H.: EMOPIA: a multimodal pop piano dataset for emotion recognition and emotion-based music generation. arXiv preprint arXiv:2108.01374 (2021)
22. Hutchings, P.: Talking drums: generating drum grooves with neural networks. arXiv:1706.09558 (2017)
23. Kaliakatsos–Papakostas, M.A., Floros, A., Vrahatis, M.N.: evoDrummer: deriving rhythmic patterns through interactive genetic algorithms. In: Machado, P., McDermott, J., Carballal, A. (eds.) EvoMUSART 2013. LNCS, vol. 7834, pp. 25–36. Springer, Heidelberg (2013). https://doi.org/10.1007/978-3-642-36955-1_3
24. Kaliakatsos-Papakostas, M.A., Floros, A., Kanellopoulos, N., Vrahatis, M.N.: Genetic evolution of L and FL-systems for the production of rhythmic sequences. In: Proceedings of the 14th Annual Conference Companion on Genetic and Evolutionary Computation, pp. 461–468 (2012)
25. Karbasi, S.M., Haug, H.S., Kvalsund, M.K., Krzyzaniak, M.J., Torresen, J.: A generative model for creating musical rhythms with deep reinforcement learning. In: 2nd Conference on AI Music Creativity (2021)
26. Lattner, S., Grachten, M.: High-level control of drum track generation using learned patterns of rhythmic interaction. arXiv:1908.00948 (2019)
27. Liu, H.M., Yang, Y.H.: Lead sheet generation and arrangement by conditional generative adversarial network. In: 2018 17th IEEE International Conference on Machine Learning and Applications (ICMLA), pp. 722–727. IEEE (2018)
28. Longuet-Higgins, H.C., Lee, C.S.: The rhythmic interpretation of monophonic music. Music. Percept. **1**(4), 424–441 (1984)
29. Makris, D., Agres, K.R., Herremans, D.: Generating lead sheets with affect: a novel conditional seq2seq framework. In: Proceedings of the International Joint Conference on Neural Networks (IJCNN) (2021)

30. Makris, D., Kaliakatsos-Papakostas, M., Karydis, I., Kermanidis, K.L.: Combining LSTM and feed forward neural networks for conditional rhythm composition. In: Boracchi, G., Iliadis, L., Jayne, C., Likas, A. (eds.) EANN 2017. CCIS, vol. 744, pp. 570–582. Springer, Cham (2017). https://doi.org/10.1007/978-3-319-65172-9_48

31. Makris, D., Kaliakatsos-Papakostas, M., Karydis, I., Kermanidis, K.L.: Conditional neural sequence learners for generating drums' rhythms. Neural Comput. Appl. **31**(6), 1793–1804 (2019)

32. Meredith, D.: COSIATEC and SIATECCOMPRESS: pattern discovery by geometric compression. In: Proceedings of the ISMIR (2013)

33. Nuttall, T., Haki, B., Jorda, S.: Transformer neural networks for automated rhythm generation. In: International Conference on New Interfaces for Musical Expression (2021)

34. Oore, S., Simon, I., Dieleman, S., Eck, D., Simonyan, K.: This time with feeling: learning expressive musical performance. Neural Comput. Appl. **32**(4), 955–967 (2020)

35. Papadopoulos, A., Roy, P., Pachet, F.: Assisted lead sheet composition using Flow-Composer. In: Rueher, M. (ed.) CP 2016. LNCS, vol. 9892, pp. 769–785. Springer, Cham (2016). https://doi.org/10.1007/978-3-319-44953-1_48

36. Papadopoulos, G., Wiggins, G.: AI methods for algorithmic composition: a survey, a critical view and future prospects. In: AISB Symposium on Musical Creativity, Edinburgh, UK, pp. 110–117 (1999)

37. Raffel, C.: Learning-based methods for comparing sequences, with applications to audio-to-midi alignment and matching. Ph.D. thesis, Columbia University (2016)

38. Randel, D.M.: The Harvard Concise Dictionary of Music and Musicians. Harvard University Press (1999)

39. Schreiber, H.: Improving genre annotations for the million song dataset. In: ISMIR, pp. 241–247 (2015)

40. Sioros, G., Holzapfel, A., Guedes, C.: On measuring syncopation to drive an interactive music system. In: 13th International Society for Music Information Retrieval Conference, ISMIR 2012, Porto, Portugal, pp. 283–288 (2012)

41. Tan, H.H., Herremans, D.: Music FaderNets: controllable music generation based on high-level features via low-level feature modelling. In: ISMIR (2020)

42. Vaswani, A., et al.: Attention is all you need. In: Advances in Neural Information Processing Systems, pp. 5998–6008 (2017)

43. Wright, M., Berdahl, E.: Towards machine learning of expressive microtiming in Brazilian drumming. In: ICMC (2006)

44. Wu, S.L., Yang, Y.H.: The Jazz Transformer on the front line: exploring the shortcomings of AI-composed music through quantitative measures. arXiv preprint arXiv:2008.01307 (2020)

45. Zixun, G., Makris, D., Herremans, D.: Hierarchical recurrent neural networks for conditional melody generation with long-term structure. In: Proceedings of the International Joint Conference on Neural Networks (IJCNN) (2021)

Music Style Transfer Using Constant-Q Transform Spectrograms

Tyler McAllister[1] and Björn Gambäck[1,2]([⊠]) [iD]

[1] Department of Computer Science, Norwegian University of Science
and Technology, 7491 Trondheim, Norway
gamback@ntnu.no
[2] RISE, Research Institute of Sweden AB, Gothenburg, Sweden

Abstract. Previous work on music generation and transformation has commonly targeted single instrument or single melody music. Here, in contrast, five music genres are used with the goal to achieve selective remixing by using domain transfer methods on spectrogram images of music. A pipeline architecture comprised of two independent generative adversarial network models was created. The first applies features from one of the genres to constant-Q transform spectrogram images to perform style transfer. The second network turns a spectrogram into a real-value tensor representation which is approximately reconstructed back into audio. The system was evaluated experimentally and through a survey. Due to the increased complexity involved in processing high sample rate music with homophonic or polyphonic audio textures, the system's audio output was considered to be low quality, but the style transfer produced noticeable selective remixing on most of the music tracks evaluated.

1   Introduction

With the advent of digital audio workstation (DAW) software, such as Ableton Live and GarageBand,[1] and digital platforms such as YouTube and SoundCloud[2] allowing for anyone to upload their own video content, the creation of musical remixes has increased in popularity dramatically [11]. The process of remixing music can be defined as altering, or adding content, to an already existing musical composition. This newly created remix shares similarity to its initial composition but sounds audibly distinct. A number of musical styles are heavily built on remixing existing music such as vaporwave [14], electronic or lo-fi (low fidelity) genres. The present work aims to investigate how well such remixing styles can be generated using deep learning. Such a system would allow amateur music artists to effortlessly generate audio waveforms of their own remixes using only audio waveform of an already existing composition, without them needing to learn how to operate DAWs or having extensive music theory knowledge.

---

[1] www.ableton.com/en; www.apple.com/mac/garageband
[2] www.youtube.com; soundcloud.com.

T. Martins et al. (Eds.): EvoMUSART 2022, LNCS 13221, pp. 195–211, 2022.
https://doi.org/10.1007/978-3-031-03789-4_13

Neural style transfer begun as an approach to using convolutional neural networks (CNNs) to extract the *style* and *content* from an image and apply the extracted style onto another image [12]. Audio style transfer is most commonly performed by utilising images of spectrogram representations of audio. However, audio contains a large amount of features that cannot be simply separated into two categories, so Dai et al. [9] suggest three different techniques of style transfer can be applied to music: *Timbre Style Transfer* focuses on treating the timbre as the style of the music and the performance control information as the content. By learning the timbre representation of one instrument, or music track, that timbre can be applied to another piece of audio's performance control. *Performance Style Transfer* involves separating the performance control as the style and the implicit score of the audio as the content, e.g., finding an artist's specific 'style of playing' and applying this to other songs. *Composition Style Transfer* treats the melody contours as the style and the score features as content. This can be used for re-harmonisation or improvisation by learning a music track's melody contour. Performance and composition style transfer are rather unexplored, due to difficulty in modelling audio composition and implicit score. The present work thus focuses on timbre style transfer, which also is the most common in state-of-the-art music and genre style transfer systems.

In the rest of the paper, Sect. 2 discusses the current state-of-the-art, Sect. 3 presents the system's architecture and the dataset chosen to train it, and Sect. 4 describes the style transfer experiments performed. Section 5 presents a survey used to determine the audio quality and success of genre transfer, while Sect. 6 evaluates the system based on the results of the experiments and the survey. Finally, Sect. 7 concludes and suggests themes for future work.

2   Related Work

Many systems have been created to allow for two main ways of music generation: symbolic or raw audio. Overall, there has been an emphasis on image-based domain transfer techniques, implemented via deep-learning architectures. Generative adversarial networks such as CycleGAN [35] have been shown to be capable of producing interesting genre transfer results. CycleGAN learns the mapping function required for image-to-image translation on a set level rather than for individual elements, alleviating the need for paired source to target examples. However, the music used in style transfer and audio generation tasks commonly have monophonic or homophonic textures and have mainly been restricted to a single instrument playing. This puts into doubt the effectiveness of CycleGAN for genre transfer of more complex musical tracks, although it has given reasonable results in transfer between two very similar genres.

The term 'raw waveform' or 'raw audio' is often used to describe an audio signal displayed across time. This type of data is typically paired with metadata, such as the artist name and song title, and stored digitally as an audio file at a specific sampling rate. Directly using waveform data within the deep learning field is less popular than other methods, such as using spectrogram or Music Instrument Digital Interface (MIDI) data. An example of a deep CNN model for generating raw audio is Google DeepMind's WaveNet [25], which was initially used to improve text-to-speech systems. Donahue et al. [10] created WaveGAN and SpecGAN, generative adversarial network (GAN) models producing raw audio for use in sound effect generation, with WaveGAN being trained on raw audio input, while SpecGAN uses short-time Fourier spectrograms as input.

Ulyanov and Lebedev [32] performed domain transfer using audio by converting raw audio into STFT (short-time Fourier transform) spectrogram and feed this as input data to a model, acting as an intermediate representation. A one-dimensional CNN was used to learn the audio style and content representation. Huzaifah and Wyse [17] targeted visual inspired domain style transfer on audio data. Multiple types of CNNs were evaluated when representing audio as a spectrogram for style transfer tasks, with log-magnitude spectrograms described as a poor choice for CNNs because of dilation, shift, rotation and mirroring techniques that are utilised in the visual domain, but when applied to spectrograms can entirely remove the time domain information of the representation. This results in the resynthesised audio being dramatically altered in terms of time structure. Huzaifah and Wyse thus state that the "most pertinent" issue in using spectrograms in visual domain-related tasks is their inherent asymmetry of axes: altering a section of a spectrogram's frequency across the y-axis changes both its pitch and timbre, meaning the sound changes entirely from its original characteristics. To mitigate this, they recommend mel-frequency and constant-Q transform (CQT) spectrograms over log-magnitude spectrograms.

Generation of symbolic music, such as sheet music, MIDI or piano roll, has also been topical [3]. Symbolic representations of audio allow for an unambiguous well-defined representation of music. Brunner et al. [4] used CycleGAN to achieve genre transfer using MIDI representations, which is very similar to the goal here. Along the same lines, Huang et al. [16] created TimbreTron which achieved timbre style transfer using a combination of WaveNet and CycleGAN utilising CQT spectrograms as audio representation. Mor et al. [23] used a single WaveNet encoder capable of taking a variety of different inputs (e.g., multiple different instruments) and produce style transfer from one piece of audio to another, by training the encoder on multiple different instruments and eliminate any domain-specific information from being encoded by using a 'domain confusion network' that produced an adversarial signal to the encoder. Raw audio was used as input to the network, in contrast to other style transfer models that use visual based methods for style transfer. Vande Veire et al. [33] addressed genre transfer between liquid and dancefloor music, hence fitting music into a modern genre rather than focusing on singular instruments. They used mel-spectrogram representations and performed image-to-image translation using CycleGAN.

Audio quality is a crucial element to generating convincing music. Because spectrograms cannot be perfectly inverted to raw audio there is a focus within audio generative research on finding effective methods to generate high quality

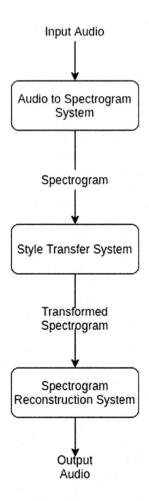

Fig. 1. Pipeline data-flow diagram

audio from spectrogram data. However, research on spectrogram reconstruction has mainly focused on the quality of speech, and since a single person speaking is entirely a monophonic audio domain it is much simpler than most modern genres of music that use a variety of music textures from polyphonic to homophonic. While the Griffin-Lim algorithm [15] is a common way to reconstruct audio from spectrograms it is limited when reconstructing audio from CQT and mel-spectrograms since phase information is lost in these representations. To circumvent this there have been some advancements within deep learning to reconstruct audio without the use of Griffin-Lim, with three models being the most recent: *Tacotron2* [30], a text-to-speech synthesis system utilising a modified version of the WaveNet model conditioned on mel-spectrograms to generate waveforms. *WaveGlow* [28], combining elements from the flow-based generative model Glow [19] and WaveNet. Both these models have their drawbacks: the WaveNet vocoder is capable of generating convincing audio but takes a significant amount of time to synthesise one second of audio. WaveGlow in comparison is considerably faster at audio synthesis but is hampered by its intense training process. Hence Kumar et al. [20] created *MelGAN*, a GAN capable of generating waveform from mel-spectrogram that simplifies training and synthesis time without significantly sacrificing audio quality. The MelGAN generator is a CNN taking the mel-spectrogram and raw audio waveform as input, but not global noise vector, in contrast to other GANs. Three discriminators are used to capture different frequency ranges of audio, improving the training quality.

3   Experimental Setup

A modular pipeline system architecture was adopted in a similar vein to Huang et al. [16]. A basic data-flow diagram is shown in Fig. 1. The first process in the pipeline transforms an arbitrary audio input to a spectrogram representation output as a png image. From experiments performed and based on results obtained by Huang et al., CQT spectrograms were chosen as the output of the audio to spectrogram process because they were capable of being reconstructed more accurately than their Mel spectrogram counterparts. The style transfer system then produces a transformed rendition of the spectrogram.

By using an image-based style transfer technique, selective remixing can be achieved by applying elements from one image domain to another. For example, a hip-hop spectrogram is input into the style transfer system, which applies elements from another music genre (e.g., electronic) to produce an altered version of the original spectrogram. Two image-based style transfer models, CycleGAN and StarGAN [7], were experimented with. They performed similarly, but CycleGAN produced higher quality reconstructions when transferring pop spectrograms to vaporwave, so a modified version of CycleGAN was used in the system.

Reconstructing audio from most types of spectrogram is a non-trivial task, with investigated solutions including the Griffin-Lim algorithm [15], WaveNet [25], MelGAN [20] and WaveGlow [28]. Based on these experiments, a modified version of MelGAN with five (rather than three) discriminators is used in the final system. It will be referred to as CQTGAN, since the model is conditioned on log-magnitude CQT spectrograms instead of log-magnitude Mel spectrograms.

The system was implemented in Python using open source tools with PyTorch [27] as the main deep learning library and trained on a high performance computing cluster with two Intel Xeon cores per node and up to 128 GB memory. Either Nvidia Tesla P100 or V100 GPUs ranging from 16 to 32 GB of VRAM were present on each node and utilised for training. The audio processing library nnAudio [6] was used for all spectrogram creation from audio files in place of the more commonly used Librosa [22], since nnAudio is faster, offers a more optimised version of the CQT algorithm for spectrogram generation, and integrates easily into PyTorch. All audio preprocessing is done using FFmpeg (ffmpeg.org).

The dataset for the experiments was selected because of its even distribution of genres and high audio quality. The Free Music Archive (freemusicarchive.org), FMA is a website hosting user-submitted music on royalty-free licences available for download. FMA categorises music into genres, so the music is effectively labelled. Hence Benzi et al. [2] created the *FMA Dataset* with varying sizes, ranging from 8,000 tracks evenly distributed across 8 genres, to 106,574 tracks over 161 genres. The size of the dataset is lacking in comparison to AudioSet [13] and MagnaTagATune [21], but the FMA Dataset was selected for storage space reasons and since it can be expanded to larger sizes if necessary. To add more variety to the genres available, data was added from Bandcamp (bandcamp.com) another music hosting website. The vaporwave artist 'Death's Dynamic Shroud' gave permission for their discography to be used; however, it consists of 289 unique tracks, which is small in comparison to the other datasets. Hence the Vaporwave genre is poorly represented, but all genres represented in the final dataset are: Electronic, Hip-Hop, Vaporwave, Instrumental, and Pop.

4   Experiments and Results

The completed pipeline can be seen in Fig. 2. It was used for experiments to further investigate the CycleGAN and CQTGAN models. First a Fast Approximate Nearest Neighbours Search [24] analysis was used to compare feature descriptors between the origin spectrogram and the CycleGAN output spectrogram. One example of a hip-hop song transformed to a vaporwave spectrogram can be found within the repository, in which the upper spectrogram is the hiphop example while the lower spectrogram is the vaporwave transformation.[3] Following this is an exploration into the sample rate of audio used for training and generation in CQTGAN. Finally a PEAQ (Perceptual Evaluation of Audio Quality; 31) audio analysis and audio fingerprinting similarity comparison was carried out using the entirety of the pipeline on unseen examples.

---

[3] https://tinyurl.com/hiphop2vaporwave.

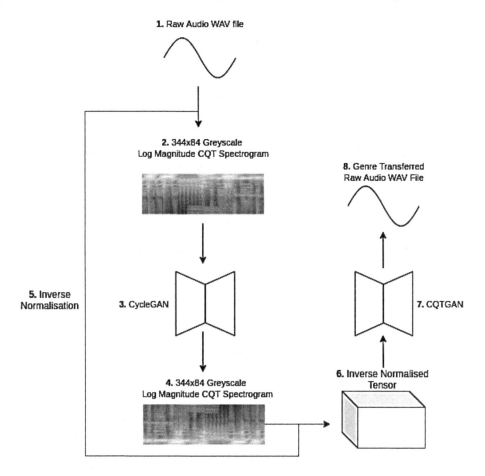

Fig. 2. System architecture

4.1 CycleGAN Hyperparameter Experiment

A Fast Approximate Neartest Neighbours Search (FLANN) feature matcher was implemented to compare the results of style transfer to the original spectrogram image. The FLANN feature matcher finds feature descriptors within an input image and tries to match them to the other image, showing which features within an image are identical. The FLANN matcher was used to find the average number of matching features to identical spectrograms from each genre as a baseline. For vaporwave, this baseline was 145 ± 18.

Two CycleGAN configurations with differing hyperparameters were investigated. The first used the default hyperparameters from the open source repository, while the second was inspired by results from Yang and Chung [34] in which CycleGAN was used as an accent conversion tool for mel spectrograms. CycleGAN contains over thirty hyperparameters that can impact the training and inference of the model. However, the experiments focused on five of those:

batch size (1 in Model 1, 4 in Model 2), number of discriminator layers (3 resp. 5), data pre-processing with/without flipping, and the spectrogram load size and crop size both set to 344 pixels in Model 2 (rather than 286 and 344), which was the full width of each spectrogram in the dataset. This allowed CycleGAN to train on the full sized spectrogram images rather than cropping and resizing sections of the image before training. For a fair comparison both configurations were trained for 200 epochs on the same dataset: CQT spectrograms of vaporwave and pop music consisting of 2,391 and 6,000 images, respectively.

The results were compared using the FLANN matcher on 10 resultant images output from CycleGAN to the input image put into CycleGAN. The configurations performed quite similarly, with average feature matches of 92.6 and 90.0, respectively, meaning there was no significant difference in the configurations tested. Regardless, 90 matching features is below the baseline value of 145 for vaporwave spectrograms, so there is approximately a 38% difference in the images generated by CycleGAN in the case of transferring vaporwave spectrograms to the pop genre. Going forward with the completed pipeline, the hyperparameters from Model 2 were chosen because it achieved the lowest feature matching average, which was interpreted as it being more effective at selective remixing.

4.2   CQTGAN Sample Rates Experiment

The quality of sound created from the system must be high enough to be considered music. A higher sampling rate is interlinked with accurately captured audio, with a majority of music being recorded at 44.1 kHz. However sampling rates in previous research are often low and commonly 16 kHz audio. While the sampling rate is not the only defining factor for audio quality there is reason to assume that using higher sample rates could have an impact on the overall quality of the audio. As such experiments were performed on three separate models of CQTGAN trained with 16 kHz, 22.05 kHz and 44.1 kHz sample rate audio. Music from the electronic genre was used to train all of the models 500 epochs, with the default hyperparameters and no architectural changes. Using FFmpeg, copies of the electronic music from the dataset were made and the 44.1 kHz samples were converted into 22.05 kHz and 16 kHz versions.

PEAQ analysis was used to compare the results from each model at reconstructing the same track from the test set. PEAQ [31] calculates an *objective difference grade* (ODG) for audio signals that succinctly describes their quality in comparison to a ground truth reference audio signal, in terms of 'judgement of impairment'. If an audio signal receives a 0 ODG value then it is indistinguishable from the reference signal, -1 indicates it being 'perceptible but annoying', -2 'slightly annoying', and -3 'annoying' while -4 ('very annoying') means the audio signal is significantly worse in quality than the reference signal. ODG was calculated using the original version of the track from the dataset as ground truth. The average ODG values were -2.136, -2.360 and -2.922, for 16 kHz, 22.05 kHz and 44.1 kHz, respectively. The results support 16 kHz and 22.05 kHz being the most effective sample rates for reconstructing the audio

Table 1. Analysis of unseen examples (averages)

Genre transferred	ODG	Similarity (%)
Electronic → Instrumental	−2.913	51.4
Hip-Hop → Pop	−3.593	49.2
Instrumental → Vaporwave	−3.612	13.2
Pop → Hip-Hop	−2.917	50.6
Vaporwave → Hip-Hop	−3.016	49.8

tracks while 44.1 kHz is implied to be less suited. This is since a higher sample rate increases the complexity and amount of information stored within an audio file, and increased complexity is ill-suited to CQTGAN's model, as the generator could be incapable of creating raw audio meeting the complexity expected and the discriminator may not be able to handle the feature mapping of the wider range of frequencies present in the waveform. Hence it is easier for the model to generate samples for 16 kHz, leading to higher quality. Those samples also made the model reach intelligible much quicker than the 22.05 kHz and 44.1 kHz models.

4.3 Unseen Audio Examples Experiment

For all genres represented in the dataset unseen examples of each were experimented with. All unseen examples were sourced from the newest tracks from the Free Music Archive to ensure that they are not present in the dataset. Five tracks from five different artists from each of the genres were taken and transferred into another genre. All tracks were converted to 22.05 kHz wav files from 44.1 kHz mp3 files. PEAQ analysis using GstPEAQ was performed on the results produced, with the aim of evaluating the quality of the audio. The average ODG score was taken using the original audio as a reference file. Similarly, audio fingerprinting was performed to determine the effectiveness of selective remixing.

As Table 1 shows, the genre transfer that produced the highest quality of audio was electronic to instrumental. It had an average ODG value of −2.913, which would be classified as *annoying* in the judgement of impairment scale. Transferring pop to hip-hop and vaporwave to hip-hop also seemed to produce *annoying* audio, while hip-hop to pop and instrumental to vaporwave were closer to *very annoying*. Interestingly, transferring electronic genre music to instrumental also provided the highest average similarity value. The genre transfer that had the smallest similarity value was the instrumental to vaporwave music, which had an extremely low 13.2%. This genre transfer was also responsible for the lowest ODG value, so it is possible that the poor quality of the reconstructed tracks could have impacted the similarity, although this was not the case for other genre transfers that kept their similarity values at around 50%.

5   Survey Evaluation

After the previous experiments on the system, which were all based on using objective measures, a subjective evaluation was performed. A survey was created and made available on Reddit,[4] asking participants to rate the quality of the music and classify it into genres. The examples used are hosted on the project repository,[5] with the survey results there directly linked.[6] Before the survey began, each participant was given three 30 s length examples of each music genre taken from the dataset, to familiarise them participants with genres.

The survey was split into two sections: first *Genre Identification and Quality Evaluation* and then *Similarity Comparison*. The first section asked five sets of two questions. Each set involved supplying the participant with a full-length piece of audio output from the system and asking them to fit it into one of five genres, and then judge it using the 5-point mean opinion score (MOS) scale for subjective testing of perceived audio quality recommended by the International Telecommunication Union [18], ranging from 'bad' (1) to 'poor', 'fair', 'good' and 'excellent' (5). The *Similarity Comparison* section asked the participants to listen to the original version of a track and a genre transferred version of it, and then rate their similarity using a 5-point Likert scale with 1 representing no similarity at all and 5 high similarity. The survey was left open for two weeks and garnered 24 responses, with their demographic judged to be predominantly males aged from 20–50 years old, supported by a demographics study performed on Reddit users [1]. Given the low sample size of respondents and their limited demographics, sampling bias must be taken into account.

Genre Identification was performed using ten tracks from the dataset transferred to a differing genre. An ideal output from the implemented system was considered to be a piece of audio mostly identified by its transferred genre while also having some participants identify it to its origin genre. All results from the genre identification are shown in Table 2, where the number of times a genre was chosen for a particular track is listed. 50% of the examples had their original genre and transferred genre as the most selected genre. The hip-hop track that was transferred to pop had the most even representation with 37.5% of participants identifying it as pop music while 29.2% thought it was hip-hop. Similarly, the electronic to instrumental track had a larger 45.8% of participants identify it as instrumental music, while 29.2% thought it was electronic. From these tracks it can be seen that the genre transfer is showing signs of being quite successful.

---

[4] www.reddit.com/r/takemysurvey; www.reddit.com/r/SampleSize.

[5] https://mcallistertyler.github.io/music-comparison.html.

[6] https://tinyurl.com/genreidentification.

Table 2. Genre identification results

Genre transferred	Genre selected				
	Vaporwave	Pop	Electronic	Instrumental	Hip-Hop
Hip-Hop → Pop	3	9	5	0	7
Vaporwave → Instrumental	9	2	3	6	4
Electronic → Vaporwave	14	3	6	1	0
Hip-Hop → Vaporwave	3	3	6	1	11
Vaporwave → Pop	12	5	6	1	0
Electronic → Instrumental	3	3	7	11	0
Vaporwave → Hip-Hop	5	0	14	2	3
Vaporwave → Electronic	3	2	12	5	2
Pop → Hip-Hop	0	0	1	0	23
Instrumental → Electronic	13	2	6	2	1

However, some tracks were unsuccessful when having their genre transferred. The vaporwave to pop track was most commonly identified as either vaporwave or electronic with only 20.8% identifying it as pop music. Some tracks received very mixed results. The electronic to vaporwave example was primarily chosen as vaporwave by 37.5% participants but received results for every other genre. This track involved a short drum beat with distant vocals, so potentially there was not enough defining information to fit it into decisively into one genre, meaning most participants that were not familiar with electronic or vaporwave music could have perceived the track much differently. Electronic and instrumental seemed to be the genres that were most effective at being identified when used as the transfer genre as both were in the top two results for every example when they were used. It is possible that these genres produce the best selective remixes out of all of the genres. A surprising case was the pop to hip-hop track that was identified as hip-hop by all participants but one, who thought it was electronic. No other results show such a strong transfer so instead of assuming that the pop track was fully transferred to appear as hip-hop, further investigation showed that the pop song chosen contained a lot of hip-hop elements such as long beats and singing, leading to the creation of a very hip-hop like track.

The Mean Opinion Score audio quality results show that overall, the tracks were considered to be low quality, with some exceptions. Results for each track are shown in Table 3 with the frequency of the opinion scores chosen from the survey, along with the calculated mean opinion score of each track. The mean opinion score of the entire system was 2.237, which is classified as poor audio quality. The vaporwave to instrumental track had the highest MOS, 2.958 putting it close to *fair* on the MOS scale. 58.3% of participants gave it a quality rating of 3 or higher, which is quite significant compared to most of the other tracks. The tracks that had the lowest quality were the vaporwave track transferred to hip-hop and the hip-hop track transferred to pop that had MOS of 1.916 and 1.875, respectively. The vaporwave to hip-hop track was also the track that most often

Table 3. MOS audio quality results

Genre transferred	Opinion score					Mean
	1	2	3	4	5	
Hip-Hop → Pop	9	12	1	1	1	1.875
Vaporwave → Instrumental	3	7	4	8	2	2.958
Electronic → Vaporwave	7	10	5	1	1	2.125
Hip-Hop → Vaporwave	4	7	10	2	1	2.541
Vaporwave → Pop	8	9	4	2	1	2.125
Electronic → Instrumental	6	6	10	1	1	2.375
Vaporwave → Hip-Hop	11	7	4	1	1	1.916
Vaporwave → Electronic	9	6	7	1	1	2.125
Pop → Hip-Hop	10	5	8	0	1	2.041
Instrumental → Electronic	5	11	5	2	1	2.291

was identified incorrectly; it is possible that these results may be correlated, in that poor quality tracks do not often have a clearly identifiable genre. However, this did not seem to be the case for the hip-hop to pop track which was one of the best identified tracks in the survey. Instead, the hip-hop and pop genres may be much easier to identify despite the loss of quality, while vaporwave being mixed with hip-hop could have resulted in a lower quality sound in addition to an unclear mixture of timbre and composition, causing most participants to misclassify it and consider it low quality. Conversely, the hip-hop to pop track contained distinct beats and a more clear composition despite having low quality sound. Ultimately, some genres may not be very compatible with each other since there were cases where a vaporwave track performed well in both audio quality and genre identification. For example the vaporwave to instrumental track had the highest MOS out of all other examples and was one of the best performing from the genre identification results.

The Similarity Comparison used only four tracks of audio that all were different from the ones used in the previous section of the survey. As shown in Table 4, the first two tracks (electronic to instrumental and vaporwave to hip-hop) performed quite well with participants finding some degree of similarity. The track that performed poorest was pop to hip-hop, which was not considered to be similar to its original track at all. Very few tracks were ever chosen to be very similar (5 similarity value) to their original, but the same was true for having no similarity (1 similarity value). A similarity value of 3 was most prominently chosen by participants, meaning that some similarity was perceptible but it was not considered to be significantly similar to the original track.

Table 4. Similarity comparisons

Genre transferred	Similarity value				
	1	2	3	4	5
Electronic → Instrumental	0	2	10	11	1
Vaporwave → Hip-Hop	1	5	9	8	1
Pop → Hip-Hop	10	10	3	0	1
Hip-Hop → Vaporwave	0	5	7	7	5

6 Discussion

The average objective difference grade (ODG) for the audio quality from the experiment was −3.210 (*annoying*), while an average mean opinion score (MOS) of 2.237 (*poor*) was found as a result of the survey. To understand why the system created low quality audio a number of factors were explored. Kumar et al. [20] used MelGAN to achieve an average MOS of 3.49 (*fair*) on unseen audio, one rank above the MOS achieved by the implemented system. The entirety of MelGAN's audio quality evaluation was based on speech recorded at 16 kHz, with all the speech data used having a monophonic texture. As discussed above, lower sample rates seem to converge to intelligible results much quicker and give better ODG scores than higher sample rates. Both the audio texture and sample rate used in the original MelGAN paper may have played a role in creating higher quality audio results. Increased sample rates and audio textures above monophonic likely increased the complexity of the audio, resulting in a decline in generated audio quality. Huang et al. [16], implemented a similar system named TimbreTron, and trained it entirely on 16kHz audio of piano, harpsichord, violin and flute music. While no audio quality evaluation was performed on TimbreTron its results were personally considered to be of reasonable quality. Ultimately, the poor audio quality output from the system was decided to be due to the use of 22.05 kHz audio paired with the use of homophonic and polyphonic textures which impacted the audio quality greatly. To support this, the results of using the instrumental genre as the transferred genre produced the best ODG scores and one of the highest MOS scores. It is possible that some of the instrumental examples contain monophonic textures which would be reasonable to believe, as the instrumental genre is commonly focused on one instrument playing. This further supports that the increase in audio texture paired with higher sample rate was the cause of poor audio quality.

Evaluating the system's potential for performing genre transfer leaned heavily on the survey results. While objective audio quality measures are more common within research, this is not the case for objective methods of genre classification which are still an active research topic [5,26]. Therefore, a higher reliance was put onto subjective measures. The most effective transferred genres were instrumental and electronic, although there is some variability throughout the results. Whenever the vaporwave genre was used, either as transferred or original genre, it received many selections from the participants. In the case of electronic and instrumental music being well suited for use as the transferred genre, it was worth considering that the genres could be very broad in definition. The similarity comparison performed in the survey showed that the instrumental genre being applied to electronic created the highest amount of similarity, leading to the possibility that instrumental music was best suited as a transferred genre. In a majority of cases the participants detected some similarity in the tracks but rarely considered any two tracks to be very similar or complete dissimilar. Due to this the genre transfer was considered to be successful as a whole.

The concept of music genre is difficult to define and is naïvely defined for the genre labels present in the training dataset. Scaringella et al. [29] note that boundaries between genre taxonomies are fuzzy and that fitting a song into one specific genre is questionable. For the dataset used here, all genre labels were lifted directly from the Free Music Archive. Without musical genre being a well-defined taxonomy, accurate genre labelling was not possible. Looking at results from the survey there is evidence of multiple misclassifications that are likely based on genre taxonomies being interpreted differently by the participants.

Another limitation included multiple models needing to be trained for use in genre transfer, with, e.g., five CQTGAN models trained to reconstruct each genre and ten CycleGAN models needed for each possible genre transfer. Making model modifications incurred all models to be retrained as opposed to one and all experiments involving audio quality or music genre had to be run multiple times. Furthermore, testing all possible combinations of genre transfer was considered to be excessive for a survey, so some meaningful experiments could not be performed (e.g., instrumental music is only used once as the origin genre).

7   Conclusions and Future Work

The target of this work is a deep learning system capable of creating high quality remixed music. To achieve the creation of remixed music the aim was to replicate selective remixing via genre transfer of music tracks, with a focus on using style transfer on spectrogram images of audio and approximately reconstructing them into audio waveform. Constant-Q transform (CQT) spectrograms were chosen as the image representation of audio due to their superiority in representing music compared to other spectrogram types. The system is implemented as a 3-process pipeline. The first process uses the nnAudio library [6] for generation of CQT spectrograms, the second CycleGAN [35] for style transfer to modify spectrograms with features from other genres, and the third a modified MelGAN [20] model named CQTGAN to reconstruct CQT spectrograms to audio. Using four genres of music from the FMA Dataset [2], and an additional genre sourced from Bandcamp, multiple models were built. Five CQTGAN models were trained on different genres of spectrogram along with ten CycleGAN models capable of performing bi-directional style transfer.

Experimentation concerning the audio similarity and audio quality was performed to find the best hyperparameter configurations and evaluate the model's capability on unseen audio examples. Subsequently, a survey of human partici-pants evaluated the model from a subjective perspective, to determine the audio quality and capability of genre transfer. In summation, the implemented system was capable of performing genre transfer to some degree but produced very low quality audio. Creating high quality audio was considered to be an extremely difficult task given the nature of the audio being used (homophonic texture) with much greater sample rates and variety of genres compared to those in other studies. Despite the overall goal not being met the experiments and survey per-formed showed that the capability of fair audio quality is possible meaning some further developments could be made to the system to improve its quality.

There are several possible avenues for future improvements. Firstly, a more accurately labelled dataset should be a main concern. The use of classical music or singular instruments in previous studies allowed for a much smaller scope with more clearly defined taxonomies compared to the breadth of musical genres avail-able. A well curated dataset could allow for easier model training and for style transfer to be more accurate and impactful. Likewise, limiting datasets to con-tain specific artists, or music put into a more well-defined taxonomy (e.g., data based on timbral features rather than genre) could lead to more successful genre transfer. Training multiple models was a large obstacle when experimenting with the system which could have been avoided by more effective deep learning sys-tems. Another model capable of multi-domain style transfer by being trained on multiple datasets (StarGAN) was created by Choi et al. [7] but deemed inferior to CycleGAN in initial experiments. However, an improved StarGAN model, StarGAN v2 [8] has since been developed. Using this model to possibly increase the performance of the style transfer system in the pipeline, and reduce the overhead caused by multiple models is a relevant option.

References

1. Barthel, M., Stoking, G., Holcomb, J., Mitchell, A.: Reddit news users more likely to be male, young and digital in their news preferences. In: Seven-in-Ten Reddit Users Get News on the Site, Pew Research Center (2016). https://www.journalism. org/2016/02/25/reddit-news-users-more-likely-to-be-male-young-and-digital-in-their-news-preferences/. Accessed 11 Apr 2020
2. Benzi, K., Defferrard, M., Vandergheynst, P., Bresson, X.: FMA: A dataset for music analysis. CoRR abs/1612.01840 (2016). http://arxiv.org/abs/1612.01840
3. Briot, J., Hadjeres, G., Pachet, F.: Deep learning techniques for music generation – a survey. CoRR abs/1709.01620 (2017). http://arxiv.org/abs/1709.01620
4. Brunner, G., Wang, Y., Wattenhofer, R., Zhao, S.: Symbolic music genre transfer with CycleGAN. CoRR abs/1809.07575 (2018). http://arxiv.org/abs/1809.07575
5. Cano, P., et al.: ISMIR 2004 audio description contest. Technical report. MTG-TR-2006-02, Universitat Pompeu Fabra, January 2006
6. Cheuk, K.W., Anderson, H.H., Agres, K., Herremans, D.: nnAudio: an on-the-fly GPU audio to spectrogram conversion toolbox using 1D convolution neural networks. CoRR abs/1912.12055 (2019). https://arxiv.org/abs/1912.12055

7. Choi, Y., Choi, M., Kim, M., Ha, J.W., Kim, S., Choo, J.: StarGAN: unified generative adversarial networks for multi-domain image-to-image translation. In: Proceedings of the IEEE/CVF Conference on Computer Vision and Pattern Recognition, pp. 8789–8797 (2018)

8. Choi, Y., Uh, Y., Yoo, J., Ha, J.W.: StarGAN v2: Diverse image synthesis for multiple domains. In: Proceedings of the IEEE/CVF Conference on Computer Vision and Pattern Recognition, pp. 8188–8197 (2020)

9. Dai, S., Zhang, Z., Xia, G.: Music style transfer issues: a position paper. CoRR abs/1803.06841 (2018). http://arxiv.org/abs/1803.06841

10. Donahue, C., McAuley, J.J., Puckette, M.S.: Synthesizing audio with generative adversarial networks. CoRR abs/1802.04208 (2018). http://arxiv.org/abs/1802.04208

11. Fagerjord, A., Klastrup, L., Allen, M.: After Convergence: YouTube and Remix Culture, pp. 187–200. Springer, Dordrecht (2010). ISBN 978-1-4020-9789-8, https://doi.org/10.1007/978-1-4020-9789-8_11

12. Gatys, L.A., Ecker, A.S., Bethge, M.: Image style transfer using convolutional neural networks. In: Proceedings of the IEEE Conference on Computer Vision and Pattern Recognition, pp. 2414–2423, June 2016. https://doi.org/10.1109/CVPR.2016.265

13. Gemmeke, J.F., et al.: Audio set: an ontology and human-labeled dataset for audio events. In: Proceedings of the IEEE International Conference on Acoustics, Speech, and Signal Processing, pp. 776–780, New Orleans, LA (2017)

14. Glitsos, L.: Vaporwave, or music optimised for abandoned malls. Popular Music **37**(1), 100–118 (2018). https://doi.org/10.1017/S0261143017000599

15. Griffin, D.W., Lim, J.S.: Signal estimation from modified short-time Fourier transform. IEEE Trans. Acoust. Speech Signal Process. **32**(2), 236–243 (1984). https://doi.org/10.1109/TASSP.1984.1164317

16. Huang, S., Li, Q., Anil, C., Bao, X., Oore, S., Grosse, R.B.: TimbreTron: a WaveNet(CycleGAN(CQT(Audio))) pipeline for musical timbre transfer. CoRR abs/1811.09620 (2018). http://arxiv.org/abs/1811.09620

17. Huzaifah, M., Wyse, L.: Applying visual domain style transfer and texture synthesis techniques to audio: insights and challenges. CoRR abs/1901.10240 (2019). http://arxiv.org/abs/1901.10240

18. International Telecommunication Union: Methods for objective and subjective assessment of speech and video quality. Technical report, International Telecommunication Union (2016). https://www.itu.int/rec/dologin_pub.asp?lang=e&id=T-REC-P.913-201603-I!!PDF-E&type=items. Accessed 1 June 2020

19. Kingma, D.P., Dhariwal, P.: Glow: generative flow with invertible 1 × 1 convolutions. In: Advances in Neural Information Processing Systems, vol. 31, Curran Associates, Inc. (2018)

20. Kumar, K., et al.: MelGAN: generative adversarial networks for conditional waveform synthesis. In: Advances in Neural Information Processing Systems, vol. 32, Curran Associates, Inc. (2019). https://proceedings.neurips.cc/paper/2019/file/6804c9bca0a615bdb9374d00a9fcba59-Paper.pdf. Accessed 1 June 2020

21. Law, E., West, K., Mandel, M.I., Bay, M., Downie, J.S.: Evaluation of algorithms using games: the case of music tagging. In: 10th International Society for Music Information Retrieval Conference, pp. 387–392 (2009)

22. McFee, B., et al.: librosa/librosa: 0.7.2. Zenodo, January 2020. https://doi.org/10.5281/zenodo.3606573

23. Mor, N., Wolf, L., Polyak, A., Taigman, Y.: A universal music translation network. CoRR abs/1805.07848 (2018). http://arxiv.org/abs/1805.07848

24. Muja, M., Lowe, D.G.: Fast approximate nearest neighbors with automatic algorithm configuration. In: VISAPP International Conference on Computer Vision Theory and Applications, pp. 331–340 (2009)
25. van den Oord, A., et al.: WaveNet: a generative model for raw audio. CoRR abs/1609.03499 (2016). http://arxiv.org/abs/1609.03499
26. Pachet, F., Roy, P., Cazaly, D.: A combinatorial approach to content-based music selection. In: Proceedings IEEE International Conference on Multimedia Computing and Systems, vol. 1, pp. 457–462, Florence, Italy, July 1999. https://doi.org/10.1109/MMCS.1999.779245
27. Paszke, A., et al.: PyTorch: an imperative style, high-performance deep learning library. In: Advances in Neural Information Processing Systems, vol. 32, Curran Associates, Inc. (2019). http://papers.neurips.cc/paper/9015-pytorch-an-imperative-style-high-performance-deep-learning-library.pdf. Accessed 1 June 2020
28. Prenger, R., Valle, R., Catanzaro, B.: WaveGlow: a flow-based generative network for speech synthesis. CoRR abs/1811.00002 (2018). http://arxiv.org/abs/1811.00002
29. Scaringella, N., Zoia, G., Mlynek, D.: Automatic genre classification of music content: a survey. IEEE Signal Process. Mag. **23**, 133–141 (2006). https://doi.org/10.1109/MSP.2006.1598089
30. Shen, J., et al.: Natural TTS synthesis by conditioning WaveNet on Mel spectrogram predictions. CoRR abs/1712.05884 (2017). http://arxiv.org/abs/1712.05884
31. Thiede, T., et al.: PEAQ-the ITU standard for objective measurement of perceived audio quality. J. Audio Eng. Soc. **48**, 3–29 (2000)
32. Ulyanov, D., Lebedev, V.: Audio texture synthesis and style transfer (2016). https://dmitryulyanov.github.io/audio-texture-synthesis-and-style-transfer/. Accessed 1 June 2020
33. Vande Veire, L., De Bie, T., Dambre, J.: A CycleGAN for style transfer between drum & bass subgenres. In: Machine Learning for Music Discovery Workshop at 36th International Conference on Machine Learning (2019). https://sites.google.com/view/ml4md2019/home. Accessed 1 June 2020
34. Yang, S., Chung, M.: Self-imitating feedback generation using GAN for computer-assisted pronunciation training. CoRR abs/1904.09407 (2019). http://arxiv.org/abs/1904.09407
35. Zhu, J., Park, T., Isola, P., Efros, A.A.: Unpaired image to image translation using cycle-consistent adversarial networks. CoRR abs/1703.10593 (2017). http://arxiv.org/abs/1703.10593

SpeechTyper: From Speech to Typographic Composition

Jéssica Parente[✉][iD], Tiago Martins[iD], João Bicker[iD],
and Penousal Machado[iD]

University of Coimbra, CISUC, DEI, Coimbra, Portugal
{jparente,tiagofm,bicker,machado}@dei.uc.pt

Abstract. Many authors consider typography as what language looks like. Over time, designers explored connections between type design and sound, trying to bridge the gap between the two areas. This paper describes *SpeechTyper*, an ongoing system that generates typographic compositions based on speech. Our goal is to create typographic representations that convey aspects of oral communication expressively. The system takes a pre-processed analysis of speech recordings and uses it to affect the glyph design of the recited words. The glyphs' structure is generated using a system we developed previously that extracts skeletons from existing typefaces.

Keywords: Type design · Typography · Speech · Speech-driven · Sound

1 Introduction

The way we communicate is one of the most unique characteristics that define us as human beings. We use several forms of communication depending on our needs, these include written and oral communication. Written communication is less expressive, and it cannot reproduce all the information carried by the voice (for instance, our mood and emotions, our speech velocity and the pauses that we make). Typography is considered by many authors what language looks like. In the early years, typographers created alphabets built with pure and uncorrupted

Fig. 1. Excerpt of a generation in *SpeechTyper*. Some results of the system can be found at https://cdv.dei.uc.pt/speechtyper/

The original version of this chapter was revised: a reference was corrected to include a previously omitted author's name. The correction to this chapter is available at https://doi.org/10.1007/978-3-031-03789-4_27

T. Martins et al. (Eds.): EvoMUSART 2022, LNCS 13221, pp. 212–227, 2022.
https://doi.org/10.1007/978-3-031-03789-4_14

letters. However, at the beginning of the twentieth century, the emergence of the avant-garde movements transformed the outdated aspects of visual language [10]. Later, some of the first approaches that explored the connection between the visual aspect of language and its sounds in the works of poets and artists such as Stéphane Mallarmé (1842–1898), Filippo Marinetti (1876–1944), Guillaume Apollinaire (1880–1918), Hugo Ball (1886–1927), Kurt Schwitters (1887–1948), Ilia Zdanevich (1894–1975) or Tristan Tzara (1896–1963) appear.

Later on, the technological revolution created new possibilities for typographic experimentation. Typefaces can now have varying shapes and can be constantly changing, and, as a result, we can input more information into the design of a typeface. This allowed the interconnection of different areas such as design, typography and music, achieved by changing the format of the glyphs according to the music (e.g., [20]) or nature noises (e.g., [19]). We can also express emotions related to the meaning of the text (e.g., [1,9]), and even make typefaces evolve through time, based on the sounds that they "hear" (e.g., [21]). Technology has enabled new forms of exploration and allowed the type designer to explore previously unthinkable fields.

The present paper reports an ongoing project that focuses on the generation of typographic representations that convey aspects of oral communication expressively (see Fig. 1). The goal is to find visual and typographic variables that expressively represent speech characteristics. To do that, we developed a generative system that takes a pre-processed analysis of recorded speech and uses it to influence the glyph design of recited words.

The remainder of this paper is organised as follows. The Related Work Section presents related projects in the field of typography and computational design that generate type artefacts that convey sound characteristics. The *SpeechTyper* Section describes the developed system and the steps to generate each part of it. The Experimentation Section validates and demonstrates the potential of our system as a computer-aided creativity tool and discusses the achieved results. Finally, the Conclusion and Future Work section summarises our work and presents future research directions.

2   Related Work

Even before the technological revolution, artists had already tried to express sound features on typography. The first experiments were more static, such as presented on print books and posters, and need to have great expressiveness to demonstrate more information. The modernist typographers wanted to have a different typographic sign for each sound. Kurt Schwitters's *Systemsschrift* archived this goal by rejecting the standard characters of the Latin alphabet and designing entirely new symbols informed by phonetic analysis of speech sounds. The use of heavier, wider and rounded shapes to convey the vowels resulted in a unique visual speech texture. Schwitters also anticipated some of the experiences conducted by nineteenth-century English phoneticians [6]. Raoul Hausmann was another outstanding artist of his time. *Kp'erioum* represents the variations of breathing and voice through the font size [2]. In 1949, one of the most impressive works in the field of sound exploration of typography was created by Robert Massin, a French graphic designer and typographer. His graphic interpretation of the theatre of the absurd play *La Cantatrice Chauve* written by Eugène Ionesco is a remarkable work within the scope of expressive and sound typography. For each character, he chose a font and then varied its size and position according to the expressiveness of the speech [13].

With the emergence of technology, new ways of exploration appeared and the number of type design projects that react to external inputs is growing. *TypEm* [11] is a typeface that adapts its shape to the emotions expressed in the text. The system uses the emotional value of a sentence to transform the glyphs, allowing the possibility of expressing a range of different feelings. They have also implemented an application that allows the user to interact with the system. The system receives a text message and develops one with the generated typeface. Sound is now also used as an input in some data-driven type design projects. The visual aspect of the typeface can result from the analysis of the music, like in Blast [12]. *Typographic Synthesizer* is composed of an analogue synthesizer of music and a component that captures the sound alterations and changes the visual aspect of the characters [16]. *Typography Music* [20] is a sound-driven system where the glyphs are formed from a basic grid and constructed by a combination of layers. Each layer is constituted by a range of modules and the shape of each module changes with the type of music (e.g. for an organic sound the modules are circles). *LOOK/HEAR* [24] is a project by Ran Zheng that explores the connections between typefaces and sound, by studying the relationship between scenes and soundscapes, looking and hearing. The letters were designed on a 15 by 15 two-dimensional square grid and each letter needs 9 layers to create a 3D shape. Each layer has a geometric figure and a characteristic sonority [22]. In 2005, Jaap Blonk and Golan Levin developed a new audiovisual interpretation of Ursonate - a masterpiece of concrete poetry, by Kurt Schwitters in the 1920s. *Ursonography* [7] was performed by Jaap Blonk and had an augmented real-time (live) computational typography by Golan Levin. The live subtitles were produced by a computer that recognized the text, and the synchronization of the text and voice was achieved by linking a score follower to a real-time syllable detector. The system generated visualizations of what Jaap Blonk was doing with his voice. Some systems play with sound-driven typography but work as static artefacts. Due to their static nature, they need to have a higher expressiveness to demonstrate the characteristics of a given sound. *Voice driven type design (VDTD)* [23] is a system that maps speech characteristics on text formatting. The vertical and horizontal stroke weight and character width are influenced by loudness, pitch, and speed.

3 SpeechTyper

In this section, we present *SpeechTyper*, an ongoing system that generates typographic compositions based on speech. The generated glyphs follow the traditional typographic creation rules and the will of the avant-garde movements to convey the expressiveness of oral speech. To do that, we: (i) analyse speech recordings by doing speech recognition and extracting speech characteristics, and (ii) developed a system that generates glyphs using extracting skeletons of existing typefaces to serve as the basis. The *SpeechTyper* system uses these two components to generate animated typographic compositions by using the drawing process to generate the glyphs that self-adapt according to the speech extracting information.

3.1   Extracting Speech Data

The first step to conduct the speech analysis was to look at voice characteristics and define which ones we could use. To analyse the audio files we use Librosa [15], a python package for music and audio analysis, and to do the word segmentation we use Vosk [3], a speech recognition library. The toolkit supports more than 20 languages.

Defining Speech Characteristics. Speech is a succession of articulate sound units. The most common speech characteristics are prosody, voice quality, pitch/loudness, rate, among others. In this project, we opted by extracting the most objective features such as loudness, pitch and speech rate.

The voice pitch, perceived "highness" or "lowness" of a voice, reflects the fundamental frequency at which the vocal folds are vibrating and thereby imposing periodic variations in air pressure. In contrast, the amplitude of the vibrations, the size of the oscillations of the vocal folds, affects loudness. We measure the loudness of each frequency that constitutes each recording in each frame. By doing that, we perceive the voice pitch and how the frequencies are distributed. Besides, we measure the duration time of that each word.

Doing Speech Recognition and Text Analysis. The speech recognition library receives a .WAV audio file in and returns each spoken word, the confidence level for each word, the start time and the end time. Since we only have information regarding the beginning and end of each word, we chose to divide the time by the number of syllables in the word to better demonstrate the changes over time. We know it is not an accurate approach, but its a reasonable due for the scope of the project. After doing speech recognition, all the collected information is exported to .CSV files to use later in the system. Figure 2 explain the steps that we do to analyse the audio files.

To analyze pitch and loudness, we use spectrograms as they represent the behaviour of the frequency spectrum over time. Spectrograms are used extensively in the fields of linguistics (they can be used to identify spoken words phonetically) and speech processing and are useful to help overcome speech deficits and speech training [8]. A Mel scale is a perceptual scale of tones, where tones heard by listeners as equal in distance from each other are visualized in the same way. We use Mel spectrograms because it exposes better the lower frequencies, the most important frequencies in human voices.

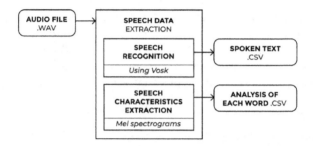

Fig. 2. Steps from the recorded audio file to the extracted data used in the generative system.

To best understand how the spectrum of frequencies behaved in voice recordings (to understand which frequency ranges were more relevant) we generate spectrograms for a set of speeches. Our goal is to reduce the range of frequencies to focus on those which are more identifying. The frequencies with the greatest intensity are located up to 1000 Hz (as shown in Fig. 3 top). However, there are also frequencies higher up that had somewhat high intensity and it could be essential to visualize it. To discover the best way to visualize the speech data with test different degrees of detail. Then, we use the exported values by the speech recognition tool (the initial and end time of each word) to analyze each word. For that purpose, we generate spectrograms for different words (see Fig. 3 bottom) to see the changes in the frequencies and volume over time with more detail. By doing this analysis we can notice the most relevant frequencies at each instance (the rectangles in strong red). In some cases it was also possible to recognize each syllable, the separation happens when in a given frame there were very low intensities (bluer colours).

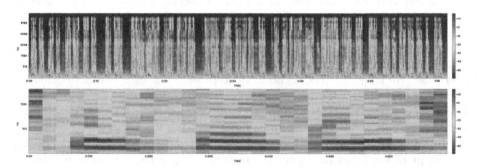

Fig. 3. Exported Spectrograms (50 Mel's) of a complete recording (top) and the word "confusion" (bottom). The x-axis represents time, y-axis represents frequency (0 Hz 15000 Hz) and the colour represents the intensity of the frequency (−50 dB to +30 dB) in that period of time. (Color figure online)

To complete the pre-analysis of the recording we also calculate some minimum and maximum values per frame, per word and text to facilitate the next step. We calculate the minimum and maximum values of the intensity of frequencies and the total volume. All this information together with the spectrogram values of each word was collected in .CSV files to use in the generative system.

3.2   Designing Glyphs

Our goal is to create glyphs that can adapt to the variability of voices, while being aesthetically appealing and respectful of the typographic tradition. Additionally, the glyphs need to be capable of reacting to sound characteristics. As such, the system needs to have a set of adjustable parameters.

Generation Glyphs Structure. Nowadays, several generative systems create typefaces, but most of them focus on the letters' filling and use, for the structure, hand-drawn typefaces that are visually static. One of our major goals is to be able to deform and transform the structure of the glyphs. To do this, we use our previously developed library that extracts skeletons from existing fonts and converts them into a point list [17,18]. With the points of the skeleton we design a method for expanding horizontally the structure of the glyphs by multiplying the point position by a scale value (see Fig. 4).

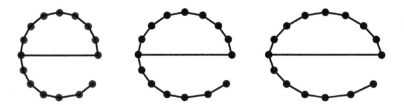

Fig. 4. Example of a skeleton expansion of an "e".

Filling Glyphs. Once we have the structure we need to find a way to fill the glyphs. In traditional font design, there are a series of parameters that must be taken into account for the good design of a typeface (such as axis, contrast, weight, among others). We use these parameters to generate glyphs.

Axis. An imaginary line drawn from top to bottom of a glyph bisecting the upper and lower strokes is the axis. The axis greatly alters the appearance of a font and is usually common for fonts belonging to the same classification group (e.g. old-style typefaces usually have an inclined axis, transitional typefaces usually have a vertical axis). Different angles of the axis define different ways of filling the glyphs. To apply this method of filling in our system we create a line with a given angle that passe through the midpoint of the glyph. Then, we calculated perpendicular lines to the previous one that passes through each of the points of the glyph. The greater the distance from the point to the axis, the greater the size of that point. Figure 5 shows different angles of the axis and how they affect glyph design.

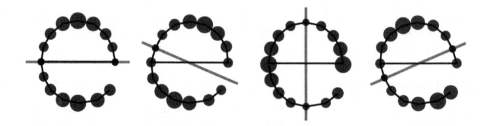

Fig. 5. Variation of angle of axis in the design of an "e"

Contrast. The difference in weight between the thickest and thinnest strokes in a typeface is the contrast. In typefaces with big contrast, the inclination of the lower case axis is used to measure weight over the glyph. In our system, we already had the axis parameter implemented so to vary the contrast we just need to map the size of the dots. Once we have an axis, we already know what the smallest and largest points are going to be, but the contrast defines the proportion. The two "e"s on the left of Fig. 6 show the application of different contrast and how they affect glyph design.

Weight. We also implement a weight parameter to change the appearance of a glyph. Usually, a font had more than one weight. Figure 6 show the application of different weights and how they affect glyph design.

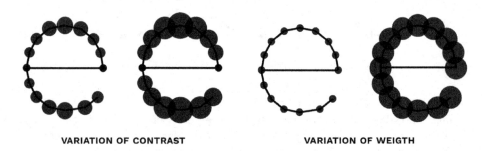

VARIATION OF CONTRAST   **VARIATION OF WEIGTH**

Fig. 6. Variation of contrast and weight in the design of an "e"

Fill. The filling of each glyph is made by the creation of shapes that occupy the empty space between each point. Figure 7 show the filling of two "e"s with different contrast and weight.

3.3   Creating Typographic Compositions Based on Speech

We extract the following features from speech: (i) the pitch over time, (ii) the loudness, and (iii) the time it took to say each word. We also have a generative system that create glyphs using skeletons extracted from existing fonts.

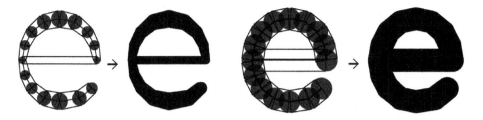

Fig. 7. Examples of the filling of an "e"

The structure of the glyphs adapts, compresses and expands itself, and its filling varies with a series of parameters such as axis angle, contrast, and weight. These two components are instrumental to build the system to compose typographic representations based on speech translating the speech analysis into typographic/visual aspects.

Mapping Speech Characteristics to Typographic Representations. Historically, diverse designers and artists have built audiovisual connections between visual graphics and sound. Pioneering works by Kandinsky, Pfenninger, Cage, Fischinger, and Whitney explore combinations of visual principles to highlight the audiovisual experience [14]. The chosen mappings are below. Although we determined this mapping the *SpeechTyper* allow the definition of different ones.

From Frequency to Colour. To represent the different frequencies we use colour. The generated glyphs adapt the colour of each of its points and the stroke and filling according to the frequency it is being visualized (see Fig. 8.2). According to the angle of the axis, we calculate the frequency at which each point corresponds, bearing in mind that the points further away from the axis will be the biggest and will have the highest frequency associated.

From Amplitude to Size. To represent the variations in amplitude we use the size of the points. The weight of the glyphs and their contrast is affected by the volume of the speech. The structure of the glyph gains the colour of the maximum frequency and its stroke weight changes according to its intensity. Figure 8.3 top exemplifies this application. The system also allows changing the axis according to the amplitude (Fig. 8.3 bottom).

From Speech Rate to Skeletons Expansion. In the design of the glyphs, we want to expose time as a factor of duration and extension. For this, we represent the duration of each word with the expansion of the skeleton of the letters that compose it (see Fig. 8.4). In the typographic composition at bottom of Fig. 8.4 we fill the glyphs.

Converting Static Glyphs into Multimedia Typographic Compositions. With the collected information, the system generates static typographic

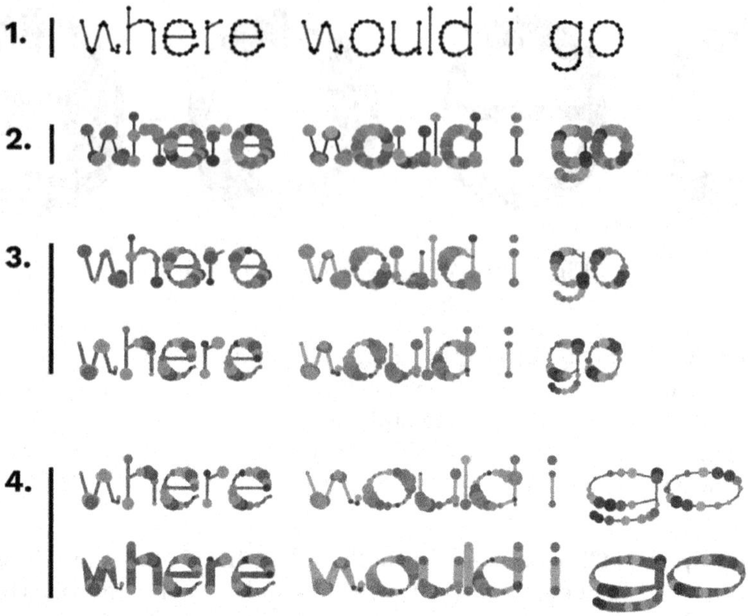

Fig. 8. The steps to generate a typographic composition (1 - exported skeleton, 2 - after adding the frequencies, 3 - after adding the amplitude, 4 - after adding the speech rate) (Color figure online)

compositions that would be visualized as text. However, considering that we have time values, by just having a static representation of the text we would be losing information. To visualize all the changes in pitch and loudness in each word, we added a time component to the system. Thus, for each frame, the system changes the representation of the word following what is being said at the moment. The typographic representations just work in motion and therefore the prints are not accurate as they reflect the last spoken frames of each syllable. To mark the pauses in the speeches we also implement a life for each word. After being said, each typographic representation of the word stays on the screen for a few seconds. Over time they lose opacity, when a pause is a little longer the screen becomes almost white (see Fig. 9) Through these implementations, the *SpeechTyper* gains a dynamic component that was not possible to have in a written text.

4   Experimentation

In this section, present and analyze some results generated by *SpeechTyper* by the introduction of different recordings of declamations of the same text. We also summarise the visual possibilities of the system, wherein different parameter settings. During these experiments, we studied the impact of the parameter settings.

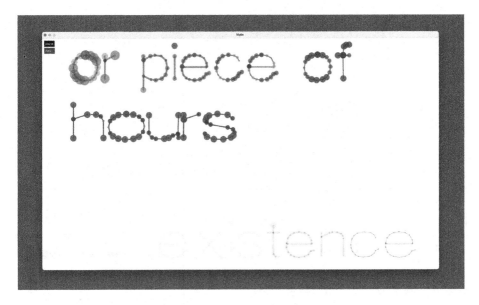

Fig. 9. A screenprint of *SpeechTyper*. Examples of declamations can be found at https://cdv.dei.uc.pt/speechtyper/

4.1 Setup

Speech and Reciters. The text used for the experimentation was retrieved from the "Stories and Texts for Nothing", a collection of stories by Samuel Beckett, an Irish playwright and writer widely regarded as one of the most influential writers of the 20th century. We asked 12 people to record their declamation of an excerpt of the fourth short prose piece presented in the collection. All the recorded people were native in Portuguese and they had ages between 23 and 30. The recordings lasted around 1 min.

Speech Data. To achieve the best results we decided to normalize the recordings. The speeches were recorded in different ways and therefore it was necessary to make them more alike to correlate the results. Besides, although in the spectrogram the values are displayed in a logarithmic way, the values obtained from it created a linear trend line. However, after testing with different recordings we decide to group the data in a non-linear way, giving more importance to the lower frequencies.

Parameters. The values of each parameter are the following: (i) 14 colours (starting in blue, passing in yellow and ending in red) representing the frequencies; (ii) the size of points varies between 0.2 and 45 according to the amplitude of each frequency; (iii) the weight of the structure of the glyphs varies between 1 and 9; (iv) the angle of the axis of each glyph varies between 0 and PI; (v) the filling can be applied or not; (vi) the filling of the points can be a degrade or plain colour; and (vii) the structure expansion varies between the 1 (the size of the exported skeleton) and 1.2. The values of each parameter are presented in Fig. 10.

COLOURS	(100, 40, 225); (150, 60, 195); (200, 80, 165); (250, 100, 135); (255, 120, 105); (255, 140, 75); (255, 160, 45); (255, 140, 15); (255, 120, 0); (255, 100, 0); (255, 80, 0); (255, 60, 0); (255, 40, 0); (255, 20, 0)	
SIZE OF POINTS	Between 0.2 and 45	
SIZE OF SKELETONS	Between 1 and 9	
ANGLE OF AXIS	Between 0 and PI	
FILL	0 or 1	
TYPE OF POINTS' FILL	0 or 1	
EXPANSION	Between 1 and 1.2	

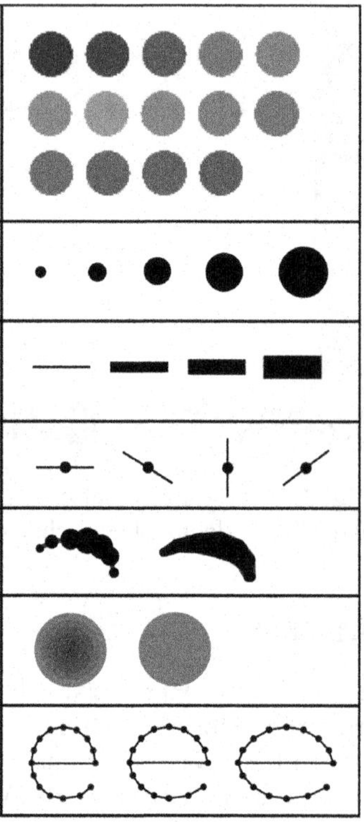

Fig. 10. Parameters used in the system and its possible values. (Color figure online)

There are also other parameters that we decided to keep static to see other variations, like the font used as input (the system allows the use of different skeletons), the shapes used to define each point (are circles, but can be any shape), and the colours.

4.2 Results/Discussion

Below we present some of the results obtained by the system using the set of recordings. Although *SpeechTyper* allows the alteration of a set of parameters that work as mappings for connecting sound characteristics into typographic features, in some generations we define static values for some parameters to see some differences more in detail. We have to bear in mind that *SpeechTyper* generates typographic compositions in motion and to visualize the true expressiveness of each word we would look at all frames of each word. In the presented images the representation of each word reflects the last spoken frames of each syllable.

In the beginning, we start by generating typographic compositions in which we show all the different values for each frequency, however, we weren't able to show much variation in expressiveness (see Fig. 11 (top left and right)). This probably happens because there were not enough points in the structure of the glyphs to map all the frequencies. Can be also because most of the frequencies have very small differences from each other. In Fig. 11, we can see that the more we decreased the number of frequencies to be shown (from top to the bottom of the figure), the better we can distinguish the two interpretations (left and right). So, from now on we only visualize the most relevant frequencies for each syllable at each instant (for example three or six frequencies).

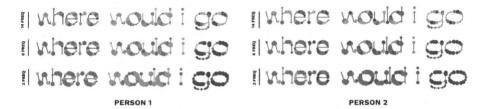

PERSON 1   PERSON 2

Fig. 11. Generated compositions of two persons (left and right). From top to bottom we vary the number of frequencies visualized.

Throughout the experiment we tested the different recordings with different parameters in the system. In Fig. 12 three parts of the text read by three of the participants are presented. For this generation we use an expansion in the skeleton between 1 and 1.15, we visualize only the 3 most important frequencies per frame, the axle angle is defined as the general volume of the word and place the size of the points to varies between 0.2 and 45. We chose these three excerpts because they were those that vary the most. We can notice that they all tend to drag as they say the word "go". In addition, for the variation of the frequencies, we can notice that the first (top) has a less accentuated variation of frequencies. In relation to the volume, there is a certain difference between the words "Where" and "Go" of the second person (Middle) however it is not very accentuated. This can happen because the composition created does not fill and this hampers the comparison.

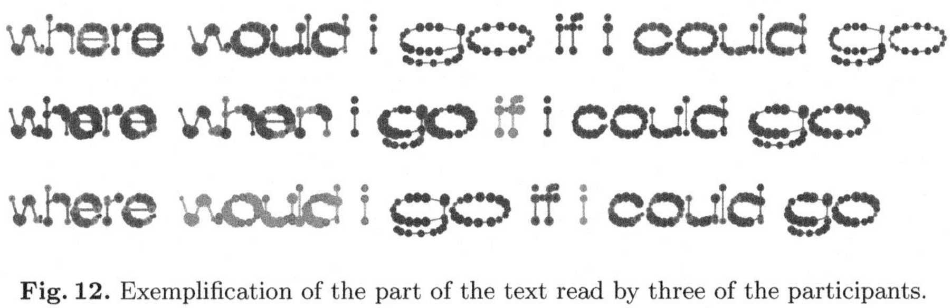

where would i go if i could go
where when i go if i could go
where would i go if i could go

Fig. 12. Exemplification of the part of the text read by three of the participants.

We also compared the generation of different recordings at a more textual level and looking at the results in Fig. 13 we can see the series of variations in colour, contrast and even the shape of some elements. The colour variation in the two speeches present in Fig. 13 is visible, which suggests that the first person (top) speaks more rhythmically, varying between bass and treble (see video of the declamation). The lower speech has a more constant colour, not varying much between dark blue and some purple or pink notes, therefore a more serious speech with fewer variations. Furthermore, in both the contrast of weights associated with different volumes is visible.

The system also allows the creation of typographic compositions more similar to the most common fonts. However to reflect the variations of the sound variables it was necessary to adapt the values so that the differences were more visible. In Fig. 14 there is a preview of the bottom speech of Fig. 13 reinterpreted. In this representation is very notable the variations in duration of each word, however, there is little variety of colour. The system allows the variation of a series of parameters, mentioned above, which allow the generation of visual variations even with the same speech as input.

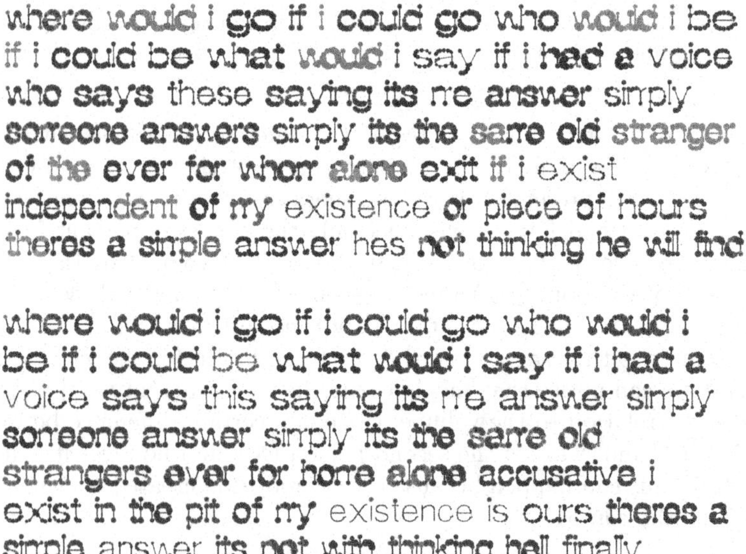

where would i go if i could go who would i be
if i could be what would i say if i had a voice
who says these saying its me answer simply
someone answers simply its the same old stranger
of the ever for whom alone exit if i exist
independent of my existence or piece of hours
theres a simple answer hes not thinking he will find

where would i go if i could go who would i
be if i could be what would i say if i had a
voice says this saying its me answer simply
someone answer simply its the same old
strangers ever for home alone accusative i
exist in the pit of my existence is ours theres a
simple answer its not with thinking hell finally

Fig. 13. Preview of the two recordings (top and bottom) of declamations of a text from "Texts for nothing" by Samuel Beckett. The video of the declamations can be found at https://cdv.dei.uc.pt/speechtyper/ (Color figure online)

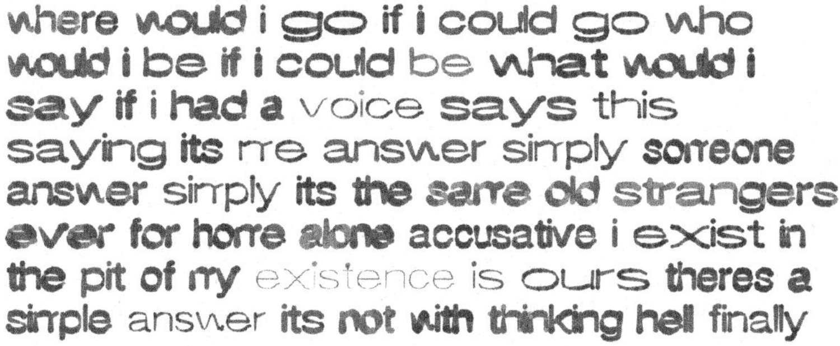

where would i go if i could go who
would i be if i could be what would i
say if i had a voice says this
saying its me answer simply someone
answer simply its the same old strangers
ever for home alone accusative i exist in
the pit of my existence is ours theres a
simple answer its not with thinking hell finally

Fig. 14. Preview of the a part of a recordings of a declamation of a text from "Texts for nothing" by Samuel Beckett. The video of the declamation can be found at https://cdv.dei.uc.pt/speechtyper/

5   Conclusion and Future Work

Over time, many designers have explored connections between type design and sound, trying to bridge the gap between the two areas. We developed a generative system that creates animated typographic compositions based on information extracted from recordings. Before creating the typographic compositions, the audio is pre-analyzed, extracting characteristics such as amplitude, frequency and duration of each word. Data analysis is also performed to facilitate the type design process. For the design of the types that will form the typographic compositions, a design system was created that uses skeletons previously exported by a tool already developed by us. *SpeechTyper* system receives the speech analysis and adapts the design of the glyphs to generate animated typographic compositions. We demonstrate the system and its possibilities and validate them. Our main contributions include: (i) a system capable of creating animated typographic compositions; (ii) exploration of different speech parameters into typographic components; (iii) a wide variety of typographic compositions that alone could function as lettering for the creation of dynamic identities; and (iv) an investigation into the history of typographic and art computation into how these two fields can work together to narrow the gap of expressiveness between oral communication and typography.

However, the system still has some questions that need to be improved. During the experimentation, it was necessary to exaggerate some parameters to be able to find more expressiveness, which we intend to achieve in the future with more expressive declamations, better analysis and better mapping. For this, we hope to have actors, or professional reciters to achieve more expressive results and more diversity in sound. Regarding the sound analysis, we also intend for the next time to be the ones to record the speeches so that they are all under the same conditions. It is also intended to make an analysis of syllable by syllable or letter by letter in a more accurate way. There are some studies associated with phonetics where it is possible to more accurately determine the tense of each syllable and/or letter. Furthermore, to give more emphasis to the change in frequency and volume, it may be necessary to do a non-linear mapping, as the perception of how voluminous a sound is depends not only on the amplitude but also on the frequency of that sound. The Fletcher-Munson curves help us to understand how wide a sound must be so that equal notes with different frequencies are perceived in the same way [5]. Amplitude is capable of helping us perceive how voluminous a sound is, however, this sensation is also caused as a result of frequency. Besides, there are other simpler components that we intend to implement, such as the fact that when widening the type structure it doesn't widen all the points, only the interiors so as not to deform the letters.

This first implementation of *SpeechTyper* also opened other doors for exploration, such as the possibility of creating new meanings associated with sound. Other suggestions for ideas emerged through the analysis of the behaviour of different discourses in the system, such as using the axis to map the text's rhythm (more vertical when the speech is slow and more inclined when there is a higher speed). Cheng [4] states that "Upright typefaces are sometimes described as "static" because they have less visual movement than "dynamic" calligraphic typefaces".

As *SpeechTyper* is an ongoing project, so there are several tasks yet to be developed. Due to a large number of parameters and the difficulty that exists in finding the ideal mapping between speech characteristics and typographic features, we intend to develop an evolutionary engine in the future so that we can more easily explore the system's expressiveness space. We also hope that in a future version it will be possible to apply the system live in poetry declamations, speeches, live concerts, and also used for movie subtitles and occasions where it is not possible to have the auditory component present. In addition, our system generates sound-driven glyphs, however, the system is wide enough to be able to adapt to the most diverse inputs.

Acknowledgements. This work is partially funded by national funds through the FCT - Foundation for Science and Technology, I.P., within the scope of the project CISUC - UID/CEC/00326/2020 and by European Social Fund, through the Regional Operational Program Centro 2020, and under the grant SFRH/BD/148706/2019.

References

1. Baker, J.: Colloquy Type (2012). https://etapes.com/colloquy-type-un-caractere-generatif/. Accessed 9 Oct 2021
2. Bargues, C.: Dada optophonetic (2016). http://www.diptyqueparis-memento.com/en/dada-optophonetic/. Accessed 18 Nov 2020
3. Cephei, A.: Vosk (2019). https://alphacephei.com/vosk/. Accessed 10 Aug 2021
4. Cheng, K.: Designing Type, vol. 10. Yale University Press, New Haven (2005)
5. Cipriani, A., Giri, M.: Musica elettronica e sound design: teoria epratica con max e msp, vol. 2. ConTempoNet (2013)
6. Fuller, R.: More consistent and systematic than any form of writing I know. Kurt Schwitters's Systemschrift. Sch. J. Kurt Schwitters Soc. **5** (2014)
7. Golan et al.: Ursonography (2005). http://m.flong.com/archive/projects/ursonography/index.html. Accessed 5 Feb 2022

8. Gómez, R., et al.: Speech training for deaf and hearing-impaired people. In: Sixth European Conference on Speech Communication and Technology, EUROSPEECH 1999 (1999)
9. Krcadinac, U., Pasquier, P., Jovanovic, J., Devedzic, V.: Synesketch: an open source library for sentence-based emotion recognition. IEEE Trans. Affect. Comput. **4**(3), 312–325 (2013)
10. Lupton, E.: Thinking with Type: A Critical Guide for Designers, Writers, Editors, & Students. Princeton Architectural Press, New York (2014)
11. Maçãs, C., Palma, D., Rebelo, A.: TypEm: a generative typeface that represents the emotion of the text. In: Proceedings of the 9th International Conference on Digital and Interactive Arts, pp. 1–10 (2019)
12. Mainz, G.M.: Gestalten mit Code (n.d.). http://generative-typografie.de/generativetypografie. Accessed 20 Nov 2020
13. Massin, R.: La lettre et l'image. Commun. et langages **6**, 42–53 (1970)
14. McDonnell, M.: Visual music. In: Visual Music Marathon, Boston Cyberarts Festival Programme (2007)
15. McFee, B., et al.: Audio and music signal analysis in python. In: Proceedings of the 14th Python in Science Conference, pp. 18–25 (2015). https://librosa.org/doc/latest/index.html. Accessed 10 Aug 2021
16. Design, M., Müller, F., Meek, F.M.: Sculpt sound and glyphs simultaneously (2007). https://robmeek.com/project/meek-fm/. Accessed 10 Nov 2020
17. Parente, J., Martins, T., Bicker, J.: Generative type design: an approach focused on skeletons extraction and their anatomical deconstruction. In: Book of Proceedings of Typography Meeting (2018)
18. Parente, J., Martins, T., Bicker, J., Machado, P.: Which type is your type? In: Eleventh International Conference on Computational Creativity (2020)
19. Riechers, A.: What Does Your City Sound Like as a Font? (2018). https://eyeondesign.aiga.org/what-does-your-city-sound-like-as-a-font/. Accessed 28 Nov 2020
20. Silanteva, D.: Typographic Music (2011). http://www.ddina.com/index.php?/2011/typographic-music/2/. Accessed 1 Nov 2020
21. Sutela, J.: Experiments with Google nimiia cétïi (2018). https://experiments.withgoogle.com/nimiia-cetii. Accessed 8 Dec 2020
22. Typeroom. Ran Zheng Wants Us to Feel, Look and Hear Typography in Miraculous Ways (2017). https://www.typeroom.eu/article/ran-zheng-wants us feel-look-and-hear-typography-miraculous-ways. Accessed 7 Oct 2020
23. Wölfel, M., Schlippe, T., Stitz, A.: Voice driven type design. In: 2015 International Conference on Speech Technology and Human-Computer Dialogue (SpeD), pp. 1–9. IEEE (2015)
24. Zheng, R.: Look-Hear. Ph.D. thesis, Maryland Institute College of Art, Graphic Design (MFA) (2016)

A Creative Tool for the Musician Combining LSTM and Markov Chains in Max/MSP

Nicola Privato$^{(\boxtimes)}$, Omar Rampado, and Alberto Novello

Conservatorio C. Pollini of Padua, Padua, Italy
nicola.privato@gmail.com, omar@ognibit.it,
alberto.novello@conservatoriopollini.it

Abstract. Scramble is a standalone MIDI tool developed in Max/MSP for the real-time generation of polyphonic music, that combines Markov chains and LSTM neural networks. It offers to the performing musician and composer a simplified user interface for the analysis of MIDI files, the creation of models including expressive parameters beside pitch and rhythm, and the interactive control of the generated output.

In this paper we describe and motivate the strategies we implemented for the analysis and representation of the data, and the encoding techniques we resorted to in order to facilitate the detection of low-level relationships whilst saving computational resources. We also describe a representation of pitch and time domains suitable for both the Markov chain and the LSTM modules, and detail the tool's architecture both from a functional standpoint and from the perspective of the user. We conclude by presenting the testing results, by discussing the main limitations of the system and how we intend to address them in future iterations.

Keywords: LSTM neural network · Markov chain · MIDI composer · Max/MSP neural network

1 Introduction

The possible approaches to algorithmic composition by the means of computer-based applications include knowledge-based systems, evolutionary algorithms, Markov chains (MC) and Artificial Neural Networks (ANNs) [11]. The last two methods, at the core of this work, tend to optimally respond to different needs and use cases [2].

The most common ANNs architectures for the generation of music are feedforward networks [8], autoencoders [20], Restricted Boltzmann Machines (RBM) [1] and Recurrent Neural Networks (RNN) [2]. Among the latter category, Long Short-Term Memory (LSTM) neural networks are a subgroup that solves the vanishing gradient problem that characterises Vanilla RNNs, and are thus capable of recognizing underlying relationships in long time series [6,7,9].

T. Martins et al. (Eds.): EvoMUSART 2022, LNCS 13221, pp. 228–242, 2022.
https://doi.org/10.1007/978-3-031-03789-4_15

ANNs can be consistent in their predictions and perform well on generalization tasks. On the other hand, the required computational effort and memory usage are usually high [10]. Furthermore, systems based on ANNs require long training time and large datasets.

On the contrary, thanks to their relative simplicity, MC can provide the user with a greater degree of real-time control over the produced output [3]. This advantage comes with some limitations, most notably an inherent inability to generalize and the risk of plagiarism as the order of the pitch-transitions is raised [15]. Furthermore, by incorporating multiple musical dimensions (e.g. pitch and velocity) inside a single chain, the number of states is increased and the possible transitions are reduced.

In order to take advantage of the specificities offered by both systems we combined one MC controlling pitch transitions with one LSTM for all other musical variables. On playback, a single MC random walk's step is forwarded to the LSTM, which pairs it with the remaining data and triggers the output of the next step. The parallel processing of the MIDI source by the two modules allows to combine different input models, thus producing a wide variety of musical outcomes. At the same time, the serial connection in the output stage grants the musical coherence of the material (see 4).

We implemented this system with *Scramble*[1], a MIDI tool for the real-time generation of polyphonic music that allows the user to access the capabilities of machine learning without the requirement of coding skills. The implementation of Scramble arises out of the need to explore the interaction between artists and autonomous systems [16]. Our aim is to offer a flexible and easy-to-use tool applicable to interactive performance, composition or autonomous music generation. The output can be easily controlled by the user even in a performative environment and includes, beside pitch and rhythm generation, often overlooked elements such as BPM and dynamic variability. At its core, Scramble combines one MC model for pitch state transitioning with a LSTM neural network for time-related and dynamic variables. It also offers a simplified user interface for the analysis of MIDI files, the generation of editable models, and for the real-time playback and adjustment of the MIDI output.

We chose to develop Scramble in Max/MSP[2] since it is a very diffused platform among electroacoustic musicians, in order to explore how more evolved machine learning techniques can be integrated into the already established artistic praxis. Indeed, even though the Max/MSP offers a few basic machine learning libraries ([19], `ml-lib`[3]), the application of more complex algorithms such as LSTM neural network remains for the most part unexplored.

---

[1] https://www.dropbox.com/sh/v869gify6pm6ta7/AAAcEjlWj-
kIJ2VpyNfCWHN7a?dl=0

[2] https://cycling74.com/products/max

[3] https://github.com/irllabs/ml-lib.

Scramble is based on two external modules: an obsolete LSTM developed by Wesley Jackson (2011)[4] and a MC external from the `ml.star`[5] library by Benjamin Day Smith [19]. The LSTM module initially presented some major bugs and design limitations that have been fixed or worked around during Scramble's development. Bug fixes are listed in the provided changelog file[6] and include compatibility with Max 8.0, import and export methods, separate threading implementation, introduction of batch load for all training data.

2   Data Representation

2.1   Pitch

In the case of polyphonic music, pitch is often represented to the learning algorithm in the form of a piano roll where each bit is the active or inactive state of a note in a many-hot encoding vector [12]. In order to cover the whole range of a piano, 88 inputs need to be allocated for pitch. This alone would have exceeded the capabilities of the LSTM module, which is limited by design to a maximum of 70 input and output neurons. Furthermore, such representation is very sparse and produces a class imbalance for most pitches [11]. We instead opted for a multi-voice approach similar to Hadjeres [8]. We considered a maximum polyphony of ten voices, and allocated the notes from the first to the tenth voice starting from the highest one. This approach greatly reduced the number of necessary inputs for the LSTM module, and left enough room to precisely encode the remaining variables.

2.2   Time

Briot et al. [2] distinguish the possible approaches to the temporal representation for LSTM networks into three main categories:

- *Global representation*, usually based on feedforward or autoencoder architectures, where a fixed, pre-established length for the whole output is given (Minibach [2], DeepHear [20]).
- *Time-step*, where the shortest time-step is chosen as the minimum fixed granularity of the temporal subdivision in any other step. This approach, whilst allowing a straightforward sequencing of the temporal dimension, results in the generation of a large amount of data [18].
- *Note-step*, where no fixed time-step is present and granularity adapts to the length of each note [13]. This approach allows for a remarkable reduction in the dataset size.

---

[4] Starting from J. Franklin's source code (2004), based on F. Gers, N. Schraudolph and J. Schmidhuber pseudocode (2002).

[5] https://www.benjamindaysmith.com/ml-machine-learning-toolkit-in-max/.

[6] https://www.dropbox.com/s/hy3lxel1awzb82f/CHANGELOG.txt?dl=0.

We adopted a note-step approach because global representation is usually performed through feedforward networks instead of RNNs and because its fixed length would have limited the possible uses of the tool. Furthermore, a small number of data points reduces the average training time, which is critical for a tool conceived as a hands-on instrument. Finally, in a time-step approach, slicing any note or chord whose granularity is higher than the minimum fixed would generate two identical states. This has to be avoided in order to preserve the MC variability, since the probabilities of each state transitioning into itself would grow exponentially.

A note-step approach has a major limitation when dealing with pure polyphony: a single time-step value for all of the notes inside a temporal slice allows for a correct time representation only as long as all the notes are equally long. We therefore introduced a note-length value for each individual pitch inside the cluster. Even though this increases the number of dimensions for the vector representing each state, it simplifies the time representation in-between the states by implicitly incorporating ties and rests. For instance, a step of 1 beat at 60 BPM might contain one pitch whose individual note-length is 500 ms, resulting in a rest of a half beat. On the contrary, if one of the notes is 2000 ms long, it is sustained for another 1000 ms even after the next state is triggered.

2.3   MIDI Analyzer

The module responsible for the aforementioned representation of pitch and time domains is the *MIDI Analyzer*. It generates the MIDI pre-processed datasets (MDS) by extracting information from the real-time MIDI playback instead of directly analyzing the files. This approach, at the expense of analysis speed, allows Scramble to potentially connect with live MIDI instruments (see 7).

The real-time stream from the incorporated player is split into indexed states containing all the note-on events occurring inside a 2 to 10 ms span.[7] In parallel, a timer measures the milliseconds between note-on and note-off events. Even if the note-off event happens in the following states, the value is assigned to the state where the measurement started and paired with the pertaining pitch and velocity.

A second timer is responsible for calculating the *step-length*, defined as the time between any two subsequent clusters of note-on events. The BPM rate at the beginning of the state is finally appended. By combining the BPM and step-length, the relative rhythmic value of each state is calculated with (1).

$$R_i = \frac{(t_{i+1} - t_i) \times bpm_i}{60000} \qquad (1)$$

where i is the index of the state, t_i is the time of the ith state.

The MDS, editable from the GUI, is used to generate the input data for the MC and the LSTM modules and displays each state as Fig. 1.

---

[7] The milliseconds span varies depending on the selected analysis speed.

Fig. 1. State, Note_1, Velocity_1, Note_1 Length, Note_2, Velocity_2, Note_2 Length, R(s), BPM

3 LSTM Data Encoding

The combination of the 2011 LSTM module by Wesley Jackson with the Max/MSP environment does not offer high computational performances. We therefore chose to adopt a series of deterministic encoding techniques instead of assigning to the neural network the task of detecting all the low-level relationships in the datasets. In contrast with recent solutions described in Kumar [11], Liang [12], Sun [21], Colombo [4], Yang [23], we adapted to our needs some of the techniques proposed by Mozer [13] and Franklin [5], based on Shepard's [17] studies on psychoacoustics.

3.1 Pitch

Notes are encoded by incorporating their spatial representation on the circle of fifths (Fig. 2). Each note is paired with a combination of six binary units, and one unit is flipped at every next position on the circle. The similarity of two pitches is therefore exponentially related to their distance in the representational space [14].

In order to represent octave heights, piano roll positions are simply normalized from 0 to 1. We chose to implement octave representation through a single real value because more precise information on pitch within the octaves is already conveyed through the circle of fifths [13].

3.2 Rhythm

For the representation of rhythm, we used multiple binary units to encode the rhythmic relationships between states, and single real values to represent less critical information such as individual note lengths and BPM. We partially adopted the approach implemented by Mozer for his CONCERT system, consisting of a five-dimensional space divided into three components, that provides a parallel of Shepard's psychoacoustically-motivated approach to pitch encoding [13,17].

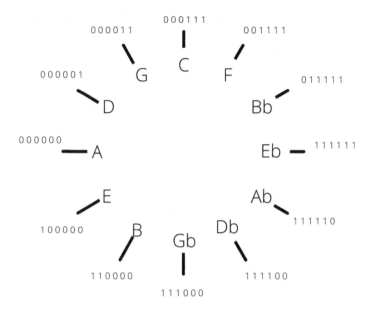

Fig. 2. Spatial representation of pitch encoding.

The duration of each state is conveyed by a total of sixteen binary values, divided into (A) one group of four, (B) one group of three and (C) one group of nine. A and B combined identify the smallest subdivision of each state up to $\frac{1}{12}$ of a single beat. C provides the number of beats to be added. For instance, a total duration of $\frac{18}{12}$ is represented as $\frac{12}{12}$ by C, and $\frac{6}{12}$ by A and B combined. C implements a one-hot nine-dimensional vector to encode up to a maximum musical value of 8 beats. A 4 modulo operation (A) and a 3 modulo operation (B) are applied to the numerator of any value less than or equal to 12. The remainder identifies the value to flip on a one-hot four-dimensional vector for A and a one-hot three-dimensional vector for B. The two vectors combined unequivocally designate a rhythmical value. As Mozer notes [13], this provides similar representations for related durations, since eight-notes (2 on A, 0 on B) and quarter-notes (0 on A, 0 on B) share the same B remainder; eight-note triplets (0 on A, 1 on B) and quarter-note triplets (0 on A, 2 on B) share the same remainder on A; quarter-notes and half-notes share the same remainders on both circles (0 on A, 0 on B) (Table 1).

Table 1. Rhythm encoding. A is modulo 4, B is modulo 3 of Numerator. Musical Value is arbitrarily defined within the minimum available temporal scope.

Numerator	A	B	Musical value
0	0	0	Quarter note
1	1	1	Thirty-two note
2	2	2	Sixteen note triplet
3	3	0	Sixteen note
4	0	1	Eight note triplet
5	1	2	Sixteen note + sixteen note triplet
6	2	0	Eight note
7	3	1	Eight note + thirty-two note
8	0	2	Eight note + sixteen note triplet or quarter-note triplet
9	1	0	Eight note + sixteen note
10	2	1	Eight note + eight note triplet
11	3	2	Eight note + sixteen note + sixteen note triplet
12	0	0	Quarter note

Since the aforementioned system establishes a detailed representation of the rhythmic structure between states, the remaining two time-related dimensions (BPM and individual note-lengths) can be encoded via single non-binary values without compromising the rhythmic structure of the output. Also, since each state contains only one step-length value but may contain up to ten pitches, each one with a given duration, encoding each note-length with sixteen binary values would cause the number of inputs to exceed the system capacity. The MIDI velocities ranging from 0 to 127 (integers) are simply normalized from 0 to 1 (real).

3.3   Machine Learning Datasets

The MDS provided by the MIDI Analyzer is split into two different training sets. The first one (*Pitch Set*) encodes the pitch values as a sequence of tuples structured as described at (2).

$$i, [p(n_{i,1}), o(n_{i,1})], [p(n_{i,j}), o(n_{i,j})] \ldots [p(n_{i,10}), o(n_{i,10})] \tag{2}$$

where i is the index of state, p is the pitch encoding function, $n_{i,j}$ is the jth note in the ith state, o is the normalization function of the pitch octave.

The second set (*TD Set*) encodes all time and dynamics related data as a sequence of tuples structured as described at (3).

$$i, [v(n_{i,1}), l(n_{i,1})], [v(n_{i,j}), l(n_{i,j})] \ldots [v(n_{i,10}), l(n_{i,10})], R_i, bpm_i \qquad (3)$$

where i is the index of state, v is the velocity normalization function, $n_{i,j}$ is the jth note in the ith state, l is the note length normalization function, R_i is the relative rhythmic value of ith state (1), bpm_i is the beat per minute in the ith state.

4   Scramble

Scramble is structured into two main functional parts: a *Training Module* (Fig. 3) and a *Processing Module* (Fig. 4). The former deals with the analysis of MIDI files and the generation of MDSs for the training of the MC and LSTM module, the latter deals with the interaction between the two and with the real-time generation and manual adjustment of the MIDI output.

The MIDI pre-processed dataset generated by the analyzer can be edited, stored and listened to through a secondary player (*MDS Check*), and is used to build the Markov chain and LSTM datasets. The two sets respectively generate or extend pre-existing Markov pitch transitions, and train the LSTM neural network.

Since our aim with Scramble is to provide musicians with a creative tool that allows a high degree of experimentation and because no correspondence to an expected result is sought, we decided to suggest a timer in order to pause the LSTM training beforehand. The user may then check the outcome and if necessary resume training with the same dataset or with a new one. Alternatively, the user can wait until the desired mean square error is reached (see Sect. 5). The model can then be stored and recalled, and may be used as the basis for subsequent training with new datasets.

The Processing Module is where the MC and the LSTM interact. Once activated, the MC routes a single random state of up to ten pitches to the LSTM module, which outputs velocities, note-lengths, step-length and tempo. All the data relative to individual pitches is decoded and forwarded to the MIDI device selected by the user. Step-length and tempo are instead used to determine the time before the next MC output is triggered.

The user can influence the LSTM output by changing the MC pitch state transitions in real time through the MC module. For instance, by using a MC set in a particular musical range it is possible to recall a specific LSTM behavior. We chose pitch as the main control element because it is more straightforward for the user to enter a precise pitch value than velocity or time-related ones.

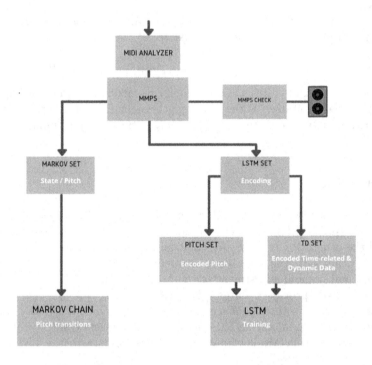

Fig. 3. Scramble training module block diagram.

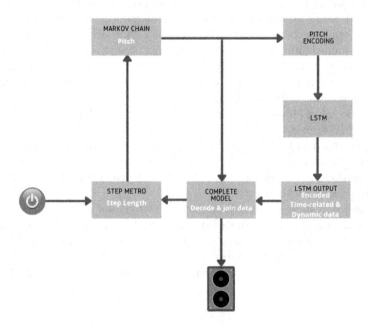

Fig. 4. Scramble processing module block diagram.

5   User Interface

Scramble user interface consists of three horizontal sections from top to bottom. The topmost section (Fig. 5) is dedicated to the analysis of MIDI files. From the central panel, it also provides feedback and instructions on the use of Scramble: by approaching the cursor over the question mark on each sub-menu, a short explanation of the function is visualized on the screen. The user may open any MIDI file and start the analysis at a desired speed. If the original file does not contain BPM information, a default value is automatically assigned to each state of the generated dataset. The value can be manually changed from the *Manual BPM* box. Once the input file is analyzed, the MDS is built in memory. It can be visualized as text, saved, edited, and aurally checked starting from any selected state number.

The central section (Fig. 6) comprises two menus: one for interacting with the MC and dedicated to the generation of pitch transitions, the other for the LSTM model training selection. From the *Markov-Pitch* tab the user may build, edit or save a set, or open an existing one. By pressing the *Build* button, a new pitch-transition table is generated, and by pressing *Grow* any number of MIDI files can be stacked in order to generate complex chains. From the *Order* box, the user may select the number of steps to consider for pitch transitions. All operations on this box can be executed in real time with no interruptions while the system is performing. The *LSTM* menu allows the generation and editing of the training sets (Pitch and TD set) out of the MDS. A timer controls the length of the training, which can be suspended and stored, opened and resumed at will, even with different datasets.

The last section (Fig. 7) is dedicated to the real-time control of the performance and to the user's customization of the LSTM network. At the centre, the *Player* sub-menu allows to select the MIDI device the data will be routed to, and to activate the system. The *Offsets* tab offers the possibility to customize the output by manually entering *BPM*, *Velocity* and *Note Lengths*. All the offsets can be dynamically applied during the performance. The *Settings* menu is dedicated to the customization of the LSTM architecture. The user may experiment with up to 70 blocks and 70 neurons per block. From this menu, it is also possible to change the stop error value. *Alpha* boxes allow the tweaking of the learning rate parameters in input, hidden and output layers. Finally, the *Max Step Length* box restricts the maximum number of beats per each state before the network training section.

6   Experimental Results

The focus of the architecture is to generate creative outcomes including recognizable melodic, rhythmic and expressive patterns learnt from one or more

Fig. 5. Scramble user interface, topmost section.

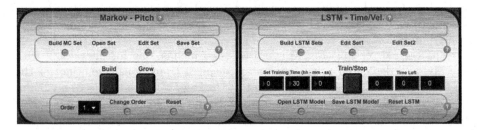

Fig. 6. Scramble user interface, central section.

Fig. 7. Scramble user interface, bottom section.

MIDI files. For this reason the overall results cannot be estimated with a statistical approach based exclusively on the correspondence of the generated data with a defined expectation. To evaluate the overall quality we engaged 6 professional musicians and submitted them a form to fill after using the tool. We informed the participants on how to use the software and asked them to connect the tool's output to a polyphonic MIDI instrument. We provided them with a link[8] to the software (both Windows OS and Mac OS), an introductory video, a short help file and a manual. We also provided 3 pre-built MC

---

[8] https://www.dropbox.com/sh/v869gify6pm6ta7/AAAcEjlWj-kIJ2VpyNfCWHN7a?dl=0.

sets (Arnold Schönberg, Drei Klavierstücke; Vincent Youmans, Tea For Two theme with piano accompaniment; Keith Jarrett, Köln Concert part 1) and 3 LSTM models pre-trained on individual songs (Modest Mussorgsky, Pictures at an Exhibition; Claude Debussy, Clair de Lune; Charlie Parker, Anthropology theme and solo). We chose not to adhere to a specific music style in order to increase the output variability, and to anonymize and unmatch the files in order to avoid expectation biases. The users were free to interact in real time with playback and MC parameters.

We provided three scenarios:

1. *Accompanied interaction*: given three predefined combinations of MC sets and LSTM models among the nine available, the user may freely tweak the parameters.
2. *Unaccompanied interaction*: the user is free to experiment with any combination of the provided sets and models.
3. *Free use (Optional)*: the user is free to train the system with any MIDI file that includes velocity and tempo variations.

The same questions were asked for each scenario. *"How coherent is the generated music (phrasing)?"*, *"How coherent is the generated music (form)?"*, *"How interesting is the generated music?"*, *"How expressive is the generated music (dynamics)?"*, *"How varied is the generated music (rhythm)?"*, *"How easy is Scramble to use?"*, *"How much could you customize the musical output?"*. All the answers are in a five-point Likert scale (1 is low and 5 is high).

One additional question was asked to the subjects: *"In which context would you imagine using Scramble?"*. The possible answers were *"Artistic Installation"*, *"Live Performance"*, *"Assisted Composition"*. Only one answer accepted.

The results of both the accompanied and unaccompanied surveys displayed in Fig. 8 suggest the overall efficacy of the system in generating coherent and interesting results. Expressivity and rhythm are acceptable but may be improved with a new, less limited LSTM module. The user interface is perceived as easy to use, but the experience may be enhanced by improving feedback and adding graphic details.

The results of the survey on the applicative context of the tool are equally distributed (33.3% each).

Since the optional scenario (free use) is more demanding in terms of time and hardware usage, only three of the subjects replied. The results are: phrasing 4.3, form 3.3, interesting 4.3, dynamics 3.0, rhythm 4.6, easy 3.6, customizable 4.6. The number of responses is low but coherent with those of the mandatory tests.

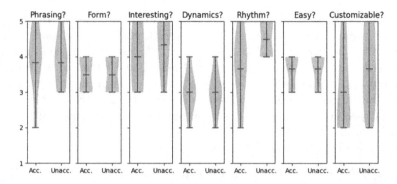

Fig. 8. Distribution of answers for mandatory scenarios. The middle bars indicate the mean values.

7   Conclusions and Future Work

We described Scramble, a generative MIDI composer that combines the advantages offered by Markov chains in terms of live control of the generated output with the ability to generalize offered by LSTM neural networks. Its graphic user interface can be easily and intuitively operated by the musician, allowing for flexibility and dynamic musical experimentation. Scramble combines the pitch transitions generated by a Markov Chain with the velocity, rhythm and BPM information provided by an LSTM neural network trained on the desired musical style or author. We also described the structure of the system and the encoding techniques applied to the input and output data.

As suggested by the survey's results, the tool may prove useful in scenarios such as live audio installations, performance or composition. On the other hand, each specific task may require a more dedicated version. We therefore foresee the development of the present Scramble's iteration in two different directions: one optimized for the interaction required by live performance, one dedicated to autonomous music generation. Scramble's live version is currently under development, it will adapt the MIDI Analyzer input to live polyphonic MIDI sources, and offer the possibility to temporarily store the pitch data into five different buffers optionally controlled by footswitches. The user will therefore be capable of dynamically changing and combining selected transition tables in real time. If on the one hand the present architecture offers the possibility to actively control the MIDI output by changing the transition models, on the other hand the performances offered by the MC on the macro-formal level are quite limited. Scramble's autonomous version will therefore substitute the Markov chain with a second LSTM dedicated to pitch generation [5]. It will also offer a faster MIDI Analyzer extracting MDSs directly from file. In order to allow for some degree of control by the user, options such as plans [22] and reinforcement learning will be also explored [11].

The MC module by Benjamin Day Smith offers a limited number of controls over the pitch state transitions, namely order selection and stacking of multiple chains. In order to improve the overall performances whilst maintaining the real-time control features that characterize this iteration of Scramble, we foresee the development of a new MC external allowing to incorporate the basic compositional techniques of selectable music styles.

The LSTM module as designed by Wesley Jackson presents some design limitations that could not be fixed: it is constrained to a single instantiation, with fixed size limits on input and output and a limited number of layers and neurons per layer. It also provides poor error evaluation and the lack of performance optimization options results in a lengthened training time. We are therefore currently working on the development of a new LSTM external for Max/MSP, that would solve the design limitations we experienced with the present version, offer more input and output capabilities and overall higher performances. The new LSTM external will substitute the current one in all of Scramble's iterations, and become the core of a future Max/MSP RNN package.

References

1. Boulanger-Lewandowski, N., Bengio, Y., Vincent, P.: Modeling temporal dependencies in high-dimensional sequences: application to polyphonic music generation and transcription. In: Proceedings of the 29th International Conference on Machine Learning (ICML 2012) (2012)
2. Briot, J.P., Hadjeres, G., Pachet, F.D.: Deep Learning Techniques for Music Generation, vol. 1. Springer, Cham (2020). https://doi.org/10.1007/978-3-319-70163-9
3. Cleeremans, A., Servan-Schreiber, D., McClelland, J.L.: Finite state automata and simple recurrent networks. Neural Comput. **1**(3), 372–381 (1989). https://doi.org/10.1162/neco.1989.1.3.372
4. Colombo, F., Muscinelli, S.P., Seeholzer, A., Brea, J., Gerstner, W.: Algorithmic composition of melodies with deep recurrent neural networks (2016)
5. Franklin, J.A.: Jazz melody generation from recurrent network learning of several human melodies. In: FLAIRS Conference, pp. 57–62 (2005)
6. Gers, F.A., Schmidhuber, J., Cummins, F.: Learning to forget: continual prediction with LSTM. Neural Comput. **12**(10), 2451–2471 (2000)
7. Greff, K., Srivastava, R.K., Koutník, J., Steunebrink, B.R., Schmidhuber, J.: LSTM: a search space Odyssey. IEEE Trans. Neural Netw. Learn. Syst. **28**(10), 2222–2232 (2016)
8. Hadjeres, G., Pachet, F., Nielsen, F.: DeepBach: a steerable model for Bach chorales generation. In: International Conference on Machine Learning, pp. 1362–1371. PMLR (2017)
9. Hochreiter, S., Schmidhuber, J.: Long short-term memory. Neural Comput. **9**(8), 1735–1780 (1997)
10. Justus, D., Brennan, J., Bonner, S., McGough, A.S.: Predicting the computational cost of deep learning models. In: 2018 IEEE International Conference on Big Data (Big Data), pp. 3873–3882. IEEE (2018)
11. Kumar, H., Ravindran, B.: Polyphonic music composition with LSTM neural networks and reinforcement learning. arXiv preprint arXiv:1902.01973 (2019)
12. Liang, F.: BachBot: automatic composition in the style of Bach chorales. Univ. Cambridge **8**, 19–48 (2016)

13. Mozer, M.C.: Neural network music composition by prediction: exploring the benefits of psychoacoustic constraints and multi-scale processing. Connect. Sci. **6**(2–3), 247–280 (1994)
14. Mozer, M.C., Soukup, T.: Connectionist music composition based on melodic and stylistic constraints. In: Advances in Neural Information Processing Systems, pp. 789–796. Citeseer (1991)
15. Papadopoulos, A., Roy, P., Pachet, F.: Avoiding plagiarism in Markov sequence generation. In: Proceedings of the AAAI Conference on Artificial Intelligence, vol. 28 (2014)
16. Privato, N., Novello, A.: Generative scores and data mining: W.E.I.R.D. enters the stage. In: Carvalhais, M., Verdicchio, M., Ribas, L., Rangel, A. (eds.) Proceedings of the 9th Conference on Computation, Communication, Aesthetics X, pp. 126–139. i2ADS (2021). https://2021.xcoax.org/xCoAx2021.pdf
17. Shepard, R.N.: Geometrical approximations to the structure of musical pitch. Psychol. Rev. **89**(4), 305 (1982)
18. Simon, I., Roberts, A., Raffel, C., Engel, J., Hawthorne, C., Eck, D.: Learning a latent space of multitrack measures. arXiv preprint arXiv:1806.00195v1 (2018)
19. Smith, B.D., Garnett, G.E.: Unsupervised play: machine learning toolkit for max. In: NIME (2012)
20. Sun, F.: DeepHear - composing and harmonizing music with neural networks, September 2015. https://fephsun.github.io/2015/09/01/neural-music.html. Accessed 1 Mar 2021
21. Sun, Z., et al.: Composing music with grammar argumented neural networks and note-level encoding. In: 2018 Asia-Pacific Signal and Information Processing Association Annual Summit and Conference (APSIPA ASC), pp. 1864–1867. IEEE (2018)
22. Todd, P.M.: A connectionist approach to algorithmic composition. Comput. Music J. **13**(4), 27–43 (1989)
23. Yang, L.C., Chou, S.Y., Yang, Y.H.: MidiNet: a convolutional generative adversarial network for symbolic-domain music generation. In: Proceedings of the 18th International Society for Music Information Retrieval Conference, pp. 324–331. ISMIR (2017)

Translating Emotions from EEG to Visual Arts

Piera Riccio[1,2(✉)] [ID], Francesco Galati[3] [ID], Maria A. Zuluaga[3] [ID],
Juan Carlos De Martin[4] [ID], and Stefano Nichele[2,5] [ID]

[1] ELLIS Unit Alicante Foundation, Alicante, Spain
piera@ellisalicante.org
[2] Oslo Metropolitan University, Oslo, Norway
stenic@oslomet.no
[3] EURECOM, Biot, France
[4] Politecnico di Torino, Turin, Italy
[5] Simula Metropolitan Centre for Digital Engineering, Oslo, Norway

Abstract. Exploring the potentialities of artificial intelligence (AI) in the world of arts is fundamental to understand and define how this technology is shaping our creativity. We propose a system that generates emotionally expressive paintings from EEG signals. The emotional information, encoded from the signals through a graph neural network, is inputted to a generative adversarial network (GAN), trained on a dataset of paintings. The design and experimental choices at the base of this work rely on the understanding that emotions are hard to define and formalize. Despite this, the proposed results witness an interaction between an AI system and a human, capable of producing an original and artistic re-interpretation of emotions. These results have a promising potential for AI technologies applied to visual arts.

Keywords: Art generation · Deep learning · Computational creativity · Affective computing · Brain-computer interface

1 Introduction

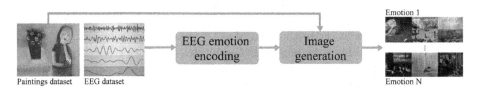

Fig. 1. General pipeline sketch of the proposed system. The emotions encoded in the EEG signals are transferred to a model devoted to the generation of expressive and original paintings. EEG image source: GOQii blog. Painting in the picture: *Room at Twilight* by Charles Blackman (1963).

The recent advances in artificial intelligence (AI) technologies enrich the debate concerning whether AI can make art. When approaching human-generated

© The Author(s), under exclusive license to Springer Nature Switzerland AG 2022
T. Martins et al. (Eds.): EvoMUSART 2022, LNCS 13221, pp. 243–258, 2022.
https://doi.org/10.1007/978-3-031-03789-4_16

artworks, we can speculate around the emotional sphere of the author or the ideas behind the work. Conversely, these thoughts are set aside when considering artworks produced by AI. We propose a human-machine interaction paradigm, in which a human agent provides the emotional signals that a machine could not produce otherwise, and the machine visualizes this information artistically. We aim at both the enhancement of machines' possibilities and the enhancement of human possibilities by their reciprocal interaction. In particular, the resulting emotional representation goes beyond the intentions and cultural background of the individual providing the signal. Therefore, such a representation would not be possible without this interaction.

We implement a brain-computer interface (BCI) based on a neural network pipeline that generates paintings from an inputted electroencephalographic (EEG) wave. The pipeline (in Fig. 1) consists of two fundamental blocks: the first one encodes the emotional information in the EEG signals, while the second generates the paintings. For the training, two different datasets are employed. One of them is composed of recorded EEG waves, and the other is composed of paintings. Both the datasets have labels in the semantic space of emotions. We provide the code of this work in our repository,[1] and we encourage readers to try out some experiments.

In Sect. 2, we present the Background and Related Works, relevant for contextualizing our work. In Sects. 3 and 4, we describe the needed datasets for this work and the implemented pipeline. In Sects. 5 and 6, we provide an example experiment, with the evaluation of the obtained results. Finally, in Sect. 7, we discuss the artistic and cultural relevance of our results.

2   Background and Related Works

We propose an interdisciplinary work at the crossroads of two research areas: affective computing [27] and computational creativity [22]. Our framework generates paintings through a Generative Adversarial Network (GAN) conditioned on external data. GANs were originally introduced by Goodfellow et al. [9] and have had a remarkable impact on different fields, including art [7,29,39] and content generation [21]. StyleGAN2 [11] is considered among the state-of-the-art models to generate high-quality photorealistic images, and it is our reference architecture for this work. In the field of GAN conditioned with external data, the authors of [16] designed a model that generates paintings related to the composition epoch of an inputted piece of music. The music pieces and the paintings are related based on their historical epoch, which could be a simplistic and unrealistic correlation criterion.

To the best of our knowledge, no related work fulfills the translation of emotional states from EEG signals to paintings. In particular, we stress that emotions are vague and subjective phenomena that need a precise formalization to be processed by a machine [36]. Psychologists suggest mainly two formalization paradigms for emotions: a discrete [5] and a continuous one [32]. In our work,

---

[1] https://github.com/PieraRiccio/Emotions-fromEEG-toArt.

we rely on the discrete paradigm, with a finite set of basic emotions. EEG-based emotion recognition is an active area of research [40–42], as one of its main advantages is that EEGs represent inner phenomena that cannot be faked or controlled, differently from facial expressions, tone intonation, or words choice [15].

In [33] and [2], the authors propose systems to create expressive self-portraits of people. In the case of [33], users manually choose the emotion they want to see in their portrait. In the case of [2], emotions are detected through facial expressions in a video. This system implies the possibility of faking emotions by pretending to smile or to frown. Both works are artistically limited: the representation of the emotions consists of applying predefined styles on existing pictures without any generative element.

The utilization of EEGs comes with several challenges [20]. Among them, the accuracy limitations in recognizing a wide range of emotions, the needed number of electrodes in the EEG recording devices, the scarcity of benchmark EEG databases for emotion recognition, and the non-linearity and instability of the signals. In the last decade, new feature extractors [4,24] and benchmark datasets have been introduced. However, it is challenging to achieve high classification accuracy on large sets of emotions [43] and the possibility of utilizing simpler off-the-shelf recording devices is being explored [13,26,28]. In the context of paintings creation from EEG waves, we mention [38] and [25]. In these cases, the generated images do not relate to semantically meaningful features of the EEG waves. The works presented in [6] and [30] propose paintings based on emotions identified from EEG waves but in a simplistic manner. In the case of [6], the images are composed with simple lines, colors, or fractals; in [30], they are based on bird swarms. In both works, we observe a low inter-painting variability, with the emotions being mainly represented through predefined colors or shapes and with poor generative elements.

In Fig. 2, we provide an overview of the paintings resulting from these Related Works. We will refer to this image in later sections, to assess the visual quality of our results.

3   Preparation of Datasets

The training of our pipeline requires an explicit connection between emotions in EEG signals and visual representations. This connection relies on shared labels between two different datasets. One dataset is a collection of paintings, and their labels correspond to the emotions they evoke; the other is a collection of recorded EEG signals, with labels representing the emotion that people felt during the recording.

In the case of EEG datasets for emotion recognition, one of the most popular options is the SEED-IV [43]. The authors recorded the signals on 15 subjects with a device made of 62 channels, stimulating four distinct emotions (happiness, fear, sadness, neutral) through 72 short videos. Several researchers [17–19,35,44] have reached high accuracy in recognizing emotions in this dataset. In this work,

Fig. 2. Example pictures from some of the related works. Top right [30], medium right [33], left [2], bottom [16]. Images are taken from the relative papers, and from the website in the case of [30].

we perform a standard and reproducible experiment using the SEED-IV [43], but we also record signals with an off-the-shelf device (OpenBCI headband kit with eight dry-comb electrodes and Cyton board[2]). For the recordings, we follow the same procedure described by the authors of the SEED-IV dataset, and we extract differential entropy features [4] over five frequency bands (delta, theta, alpha, beta, and gamma).

In the dataset of paintings, we must have the same number of classes as the EEG dataset to allow matching physiological signals and artistic representations. In this work, we utilize the *WikiArt Emotions Dataset* [23], which contains thousands of paintings labeled with emotions according to a survey on several subjects. To create a matching between the four emotions in the SEED-IV, we select four different classes, namely *fear*, *sadness*, *anger* and *happiness*. The choice depends on the availability of samples in the dataset, and it does not extensively represent the spectrum of human emotions. We utilize a K-Means clustering technique to evaluate the color palettes of the paintings and to detect and delete stylistic outliers from the dataset. Some paintings appear in more than one class, but we keep them only in the least populated class in which they appear. To overcome class imbalance, we perform data augmentation in the classes containing fewer paintings, recursively cutting in four images bigger than 600×600 pixels until the corresponding class counts an adequate number of samples. We emphasize that this is a technical choice, and it implies an approximation in the correspondence between images and emotions, as different parts

---

[2] https://openbci.com/.

of the images may evoke different emotions. As a result of this augmentation technique, we obtain a dataset of around 2500 images, quite equally distributed among the four classes. These pre-processing steps are also available in our repository.

Figure 3 provides a high-level view of the images in this dataset. The associated color palettes for each class are estimated through the same clustering technique utilized for the outliers detection. In *happiness*, paintings have bright and gaudy colors, while *fear* presents a bleak and dark color palette. In *anger*, we observe a prevalence of red and warm shades, which leave space for blue and cold shades in *sadness*.

Fig. 3. Grids showing the images generated in the dataset, divided according to their labels. From left to right: *anger, happiness, sadness, fear*. (Color figure online)

4   Pipeline

We provide a detailed overview of the proposed pipeline in Fig. 4. EEG signals are highly variable among different subjects. Models trained on EEG signals are commonly trained in a subject-dependent fashion (trained and tested on the same individual). In this work, we have performed this kind of training, starting from the state-of-the-art model on the SEED-IV dataset. This model, *Regularized Graph Neural Network* (RGNN) [44], processes the information on the topological disposition of the electrodes on the scalp. We perform its training separately from the rest of the pipeline. In Fig. 4, the purpose of the Encoder E (RGNN) and its loss $\mathcal{L}_E$ is to extrapolate relevant features from the EEG signals $\mathbf{e} \in \mathbb{R}^{62 \times 5}$, where 62 are the space channels and 5 the frequency bands. The extracted features $\mathbf{v} \in \mathbb{R}^{50}$ are used as input to StyleGAN2 [11], which concatenates them with random latent vectors $\mathbf{z} \in \mathbb{R}^{512}$. The insertion of $\mathbf{v}$ allows to train StyleGAN2 conditionally and generate paintings with relevant characteristics when representing different emotions. To make the conditioning process more effective, we should input the predicted emotion from the EEG signals (one-hot encoded vectors). However, we aim to represent the complexity and the richness of the human emotional sphere. To get closer to this effect, we utilize latent vectors with a higher dimension (50 entries). Such vectors, although summarizing the emotion in the EEG signals, also preserve their uniqueness.

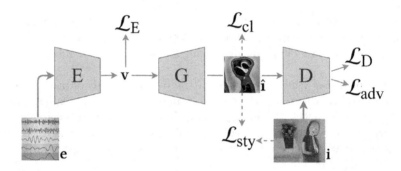

Fig. 4. Detailed visual sketch representing the different elements and losses in the pipeline, when trained on a subject of the SEED-IV dataset.

Being constituted by a GAN model, the training of this pipeline is adversarial [9]. This means that the generation block G aims to fool the discriminator D, another neural network in charge to distinguish between real paintings and generated paintings $i/\hat{i} \in \mathbb{R}^{3 \times W \times H}$ (see losses $\mathcal{L}_D$ and $\mathcal{L}_{adv}$). The utilized model, StyleGAN2, is generally trained on datasets containing tens of thousands of images. Given the need for human effort to rigorously match emotional labels to paintings, it is unlikely to access datasets of this dimension. To address this problem, we refer to the work in [12], in which the authors consider implementing an adaptive discriminator augmentation to create a model (StyleGAN2ADA) that can be trained successfully also on smaller datasets. The remaining elements of Fig. 4 are described in the following section.

4.1   Extra Losses

To shorten the time required by the training process, we provide the possibility of utilizing two extra losses (introduced in [16]): $\mathcal{L}_{cl}$ and $\mathcal{L}_{sty}$, visible in Fig. 4. $\mathcal{L}_{cl}$ is obtained through an auxiliary classifier that identifies the emotion conveyed by the produced paintings and checks whether it is equal to the same emotion as the label of the inputted EEG wave. It is based on AlexNet architecture [14], pre-trained on ImageNet database [3] and retrained on our dataset (using a proportion 80:20), via transfer learning [8]. $\mathcal{L}_{sty}$, instead, provides a comparison between the style of a generated image with the style of a real image with the same label as the inputted EEG wave: the more similar they are, the lower this loss. For this purpose, we utilize a pre-trained VGG-19 [34]. Overall, the three losses can be combined into one generator loss:

$$\mathcal{L}_G = \mathcal{L}_{adv} + \lambda_1 \mathcal{L}_{cl} + \lambda_2 \mathcal{L}_{sty} \tag{1}$$

where λ_1 and λ_2 are scalar hyper-parameter factors.

5 Experiments and Results

Different experiments can be carried out with this pipeline, by utilizing different EEG signals (e.g. self-recorded), by changing the resolution of the generated images, or by adding the extra losses in the training. Our experiments are performed with a Tesla V100-SXM2-16 GB GPU, associated with a 25 GB RAM. In the following section, we provide a detailed overview of the highest resolution experiment that we have carried out. However, other experiments have led to these main findings:

- The implemented pipeline is adaptable to different computational needs. The visual results get better when the resolution settings are higher, but they are also meaningful at lower resolutions.
- The RGNN architecture can be trained on signals recorded with other devices. In particular, we have recorded signals utilizing an off-the-shelf device with eight electrodes. This characteristic gives the possibility of utilizing this pipeline in practical contexts without having professionals handling the recording device.
- The utilization of extra losses does not provide a visual enhancement of the obtained images, but it allows the model to converge faster. For this reason, we suggest utilizing extra losses when there are time constraints on the training period.
- Transfer learning can be a useful technique under some conditions. For example, if the reader wishes to train the pipeline on a smaller dataset of paintings, we suggest using as a starting point of the training the weights learned in an experiment of the SEED-IV.

In our repository, we provide different experiments with short explanations and checkpoints of the weights.

Ideally, the output paintings visually express the emotion encoded in the inputted EEG wave. However, there are no objective metrics that define such property in a painting. The evaluation of the results is, therefore, divided into different stages:

- Evaluation of the Frechet-Inception Distance (FID) metric [10] over iterations. This metric estimates the statistical similarity between features extracted through the Inception v3 model [37] on both the generated paintings and the dataset. These features are approximated with two Gaussian distributions, and the Frechet distance among them is computed as reported in Eq. 2 (mu_1 and mu_2 being the means of the two distributions, σ_1 and σ_2 their variances).

$$d^2 = ||\mu_1 - \mu_2||^2 + Tr(\sigma_1 + \sigma_2 - 2 * \sqrt{(\sigma_1 * \sigma_2)}) \qquad (2)$$

- Qualitative evaluation of the conditioning: we generate grids of paintings for every class and we estimate their color palettes, comparing them among each other and with the palettes estimated on the dataset of paintings (Fig. 3).

- Detailed analysis regarding some of the generated paintings, by looking at some hand-picked results in terms of details, shapes and colors.
- Statistical analysis of the results of an online survey to which several users have taken part.

5.1   Example Experiment

In this example experiment, we generate images at 512×512 pixels, without using extra losses. The RGNN is trained on subject 15 of the SEED-IV dataset. In Fig. 5, we provide an overview of the FID metric. As expected, its value diminishes with the progression of the training, showing that the generated images become statistically closer to the images in the dataset. The value of this metric converges below 50.

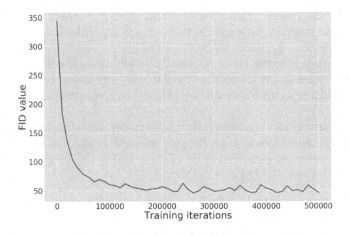

Fig. 5. FID metric over iterations for the experiment on Subject 15 of the SEED-IV dataset at resolution 512×512 pixels.

In Fig. 6, we provide a high-level overview of the generated images. Comparing these grids with the ones of the dataset, shown in Fig. 3, we observe that the pipeline provided stylistically similar images in every class. In addition, we emphasize that the implemented pipeline produces paintings that also show expressive content and shapes. We provide some details in Fig. 7; such images show high potential for the artistic possibilities and applications of this pipeline, which qualitatively outperforms the results obtained in [16] and in the other related works shown in Fig. 2. Compared to [2,30,33], our paintings stand out for two main reasons: their content is generated ad-hoc on inputted EEG signals, and we have not pre-defined stylistic norms to express emotions. Our results are heterogeneous and original, providing a re-interpretation of human emotions that we have not observed in any previous work in the technical or artistic literature.

Fig. 6. Grids showing the images generated in the training with the SEED-IV dataset, divided according to their labels. From left to right: *anger, happiness, sadness, fear.*

6   Results Assessment: Online Survey

Given the purely subjective nature of the phenomena underlying this research, we push the evaluation a step further, asking people to rate the emotions they perceive from the paintings. We stress that some paintings do not necessarily fall into the idea of the emotion from which they were generated: they may either evoke something different or evoke more emotions at once. However, we assume that if we wanted to diminish this effect, we could have utilized the emotional prediction of the EEG signals as input to the StyleGAN2 instead of utilizing latent vectors of higher dimensions, as explained in Sect. 3. Given this design choice, we have organized an online survey allowing people to rate emotions on a scale from 0 to 5 for each painting. In this way, people can select more emotions together, specifying their intensity. Users are also allowed to put all 0s in case none of the proposed emotions is somewhat related to the image. The survey[3] proposes 96 different paintings, picked from different experiments. The following analysis considers 10285 answers given by 532 different users that have navigated through this website. In this survey, we have not collected any information regarding the demographics or background knowledge of the participants. We mark answers with 0s on every emotion as non-valid. Although these answers may refer to paintings that evoke different emotions rather than the four listed, we delete non-valid answers from our analysis, as considering them would require further measures that fall out of the scope of this work. Only 7% of the answers are non-valid, suggesting that users perceive emotional content in the proposed paintings.

In Fig. 8, we provide an overview of the accuracy of users in recognizing the emotions in the paintings. In Fig. 8a, the percentages are computed on each vote separately. A vote is considered right when the emotion that has received the highest mark is the same as the emotion of the corresponding EEG signal. For *happiness, fear* and *sadness* we have a rather satisfying sensitivity (around 58%), that is much lower for *anger* (around 22%). However, *anger* is the least perceived emotion across all the votes and, in fact, only rather small percentages of other votes are for this class (with high specificity). On the contrary, the emotions of *sadness* and *fear* are perceived more commonly across these votes. Figure 8 generally shows a partial overlapping between *fear* and *anger.*

---

[3] https://pierariccio.pythonanywhere.com/.

(a) Some of the generated paintings in the *happiness* class.

(b) Some of the generated paintings in the *anger* class.

(c) Some of the generated paintings in the *sadness* class.

(d) Some of the generated paintings in the *fear* class.

Fig. 7. Details of hand-picked results from the different classes.

Such overlapping seems to be asymmetric: *fear* is confused with *anger*, but the opposite does not seem to happen so often. Interestingly, for all classes, the majority of paintings that are perceived as belonging to emotion do belong to the perceived emotion. In Fig. 8b, the votes are grouped and summed according to the painting they refer to. In this way, we show how many paintings in each

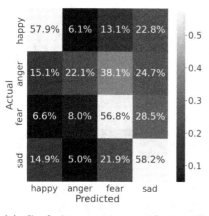
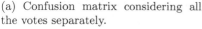

(a) Confusion matrix considering all the votes separately.

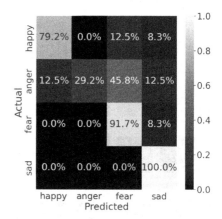

(b) Confusion matrix grouping the votes on the same paintings.

Fig. 8. Confusion matrices regarding the answers obtained from the online survey.

class are, on average, correctly classified by users. It is outstanding that all the paintings (100%) belonging to the class *sadness* are perceived as such, followed by *fear* with a percentage of 91.7% and *happiness* with almost 79.2%. In the case of *anger*, only 29.2% of the paintings are classified correctly. Although this emotion is the least perceived by users, the totality (100%) of the paintings that are classified as *anger* do belong to this class.

As further analysis of these results, in Fig. 9, we provide a ranking of 10 paintings for each class, based on the percentage of users that have voted the images as belonging to that class (the misplaced paintings are highlighted in red). The majority of the paintings in this ranking are in the correct class and with generally high percentages of votes. The first and the ninth paintings in *fear*, as well as the sixth one in *sadness*, actually belong to class *anger*. These three examples reiterate that, when the conveyed feeling is perceived as negative, it is easier to associate it with sadness or fear, especially when the painting lacks strong red shades. In addition, the sixth painting in *anger* presents strong red tones, but it originally belongs to class *happiness*. The voting percentages for this painting are: 19.4% in class *happiness*, 34.7% in class *anger*, 36.7% in *fear* and 9.2% in *sadness*. The wide distribution of these votes suggests a perceived ambiguity.

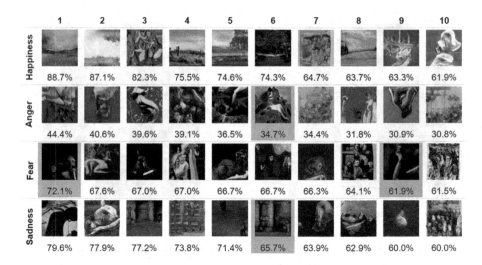

Fig. 9. Ranking of paintings in each class, according to the percentage of users that have voted them. The paintings highlighted in red belong to a different class. (Color figure online)

Overall, the results of this survey are satisfying and relevant for the scope of this research. Considering that the accuracy of the EEG encoder model was not 100%, some of the EEG signals are misclassified before being inputted into the generative model. As a natural consequence, some paintings convey a different emotion than the intended one. Despite this, this survey shows a general alignment between the emotion in the original EEG signal and the emotion that is perceived by users.

7   Discussion

The existence of an effective and recognizable emotional content in these paintings is a significant result, which can stimulate further reflections spanning a broad spectrum of research disciplines, which depart from the purely technical level.

From an aesthetic point of view, the proposed paintings are generated by a GAN trained on WikiArt Emotions, a dataset mainly containing works from Western artists. As a future work idea, we suggest merging the utilized paintings with other sources. In particular, it would be interesting to experiment with the utilization of a broader dataset, generating images devoid of artistic biases intrinsic in the utilized dataset.

Despite this cultural limitation, the present work can be placed in the context of critical disabilities studies from two perspectives. First, this pipeline is a tool that can be used for art therapy, detaching emotional and artistic expression from the body and technical skills. Furthermore, the shapes of the characters in these paintings are far from the aesthetic canons that have often stigmatized imperfections within works of art. In this sense, it is interesting to question the role of AI in establishing new artistic canons, or reinforcing those incorporated into the art world starting from the modern art era.

From an anthropological and philosophical perspective, the paintings we propose in this paper represent individual emotions, but they do not correlate with the specific intentions of the people providing the EEG signals. In this sense, it is interesting to speculate on one of the most common questions in classical philosophy concerning the existence of rationality external to the human, which follows a logic above individuals. This work proposes a pipeline that attempts to simulate an artistic expression external to the human one, and it can be food for thought on the complexity of the interaction between AI and humans in our cultural system.

For a further deepening on these topics, we refer readers to our paper [31], in which we have discussed our results from a philosophical perspective, focusing on fairness, inclusion, and aesthetics.

8 Conclusions

In this work, we have designed a brain-computer interface (BCI) that generates paintings according to the emotions detected in EEG signals. We have based our design choices on the rationale that, often, a single word (or label) is not enough to describe a feeling. Our pipeline consists of two different components, and the training needs a dataset made of paintings and one made of EEG signals, both labeled with emotions. The signals are processed by an encoder model that produces latent vectors inputted to another model generating the paintings. We have studied one of the most popular EEG datasets for emotion recognition (SEED-IV) and trained one of the state-of-the-art deep learning models (RGNN) on this dataset, also providing experimental training and results on recordings that we took with an OpenBCI device. We have pre-processed and analyzed a dataset made of paintings with emotional labels (WikiArt Emotions), performing outliers detection and elimination, and data augmentation to fight class imbalance. We have successfully integrated StyleGAN2ADA into our pipeline. Finally, we have provided a quantitative and qualitative evaluation of our results. To assess the expressive properties of these paintings, we have set up an online survey, which has confirmed the success of our experiments.

Acknowledgments. This work has been partially funded by the DeepCA project (Norwegian Research Council, Young Research Talent program grant agreement 286558) and the FELT project [1] (Norwegian Artistic Research Programme).

References

1. Bergaust, K., Nichele, S.: FeLT-the futures of living technologies, pp. 90–97 (2019). https://doi.org/10.14236/ewic/POM19.14
2. Colton, S., Valstar, M.F., Pantic, M.: Emotionally aware automated portrait painting. In: Proceedings of the 3rd International Conference on Digital Interactive Media in Entertainment and Arts, DIMEA 2008, pp. 304–311. Association for Computing Machinery, New York (2008). https://doi.org/10.1145/1413634.1413690
3. Deng, J., Dong, W., Socher, R., Li, L., Li, K., Fei-Fei, L.: ImageNet: a large-scale hierarchical image database. In: 2009 IEEE Conference on Computer Vision and Pattern Recognition, pp. 248–255 (2009). https://doi.org/10.1109/CVPR.2009.5206848
4. Duan, R., Zhu, J., Lu, B.: Differential entropy feature for EEG-based emotion classification. In: 2013 6th International IEEE/EMBS Conference on Neural Engineering (NER), pp. 81–84 (2013). https://doi.org/10.1109/NER.2013.6695876
5. Ekman, P.: An argument for basic emotions. Cogn. Emot. **6**(3–4), 169–200 (1992). https://doi.org/10.1080/02699939208411068
6. Ekster, G.: The cognichrome (2018). http://www.cognichrome.com/. Accessed 22 Feb 2022
7. Elgammal, A., Liu, B., Elhoseiny, M., Mazzone, M.: CAN: creative adversarial networks generating "art" by learning about styles and deviating from style norms. In: Proceedings of the 8th International Conference on Computational Creativity, ICCC 2017. Georgia Institute of Technology (2017)
8. Goodfellow, I., Bengio, Y., Courville, A.: Deep Learning. MIT Press, Cambridge (2016)
9. Goodfellow, I.J., et al.: Generative adversarial nets. In: NIPS, pp. 2672–2680 (2014)
10. Heusel, M., Ramsauer, H., Unterthiner, T., Nessler, B., Hochreiter, S.: GANs trained by a two time-scale update rule converge to a local Nash equilibrium. In: Proceedings of the 31st International Conference on Neural Information Processing Systems, NIPS 2017, pp. 6629–6640. Curran Associates Inc., Red Hook (2017)
11. Karras, T., Laine, S., Aittala, M., Hellsten, J., Lehtinen, J., Aila, T.: Analyzing and improving the image quality of StyleGAN. In: 2020 IEEE/CVF Conference on Computer Vision and Pattern Recognition (CVPR), pp. 8107–8116 (2020). https://doi.org/10.1109/CVPR42600.2020.00813
12. Karras, T., Aittala, M., Hellsten, J., Laine, S., Lehtinen, J., Aila, T.: Training generative adversarial networks with limited data. In: NeurIPS 2020 (2020)
13. Katsigiannis, S., Ramzan, N.: DREAMER: a database for emotion recognition through EEG and ECG signals from wireless low-cost off-the-shelf devices. IEEE J. Biomed. Health Inform. **22**(1), 98–107 (2018). https://doi.org/10.1109/JBHI.2017.2688239
14. Krizhevsky, A., Sutskever, I., Hinton, G.E.: ImageNet classification with deep convolutional neural networks. In: Advances in Neural Information Processing Systems, vol. 25. Curran Associates, Inc. (2012)
15. Larradet, F., Niewiadomski, R., Barresi, G., Caldwell, D.G., Mattos, L.S.: Toward emotion recognition from physiological signals in the wild: approaching the methodological issues in real-life data collection. Front. Psychol. **11**, 1111 (2020). https://doi.org/10.3389/fpsyg.2020.01111
16. Lee, C.C., Lin, W.Y., Shih, Y.T., Kuo, P.Y.P., Su, L.: Crossing you in style: cross-modal style transfer from music to visual arts, pp. 3219–3227. Association for Computing Machinery, New York (2020). https://doi.org/10.1145/3394171.3413624

17. Li, H., Jin, Y.-M., Zheng, W.-L., Lu, B.-L.: Cross-subject emotion recognition using deep adaptation networks. In: Cheng, L., Leung, A.C.S., Ozawa, S. (eds.) ICONIP 2018. LNCS, vol. 11305, pp. 403–413. Springer, Cham (2018). https://doi.org/10.1007/978-3-030-04221-9_36
18. Li, Y., et al.: A novel bi-hemispheric discrepancy model for EEG emotion recognition. IEEE Trans. Cogn. Dev. Syst. **13**, 354–367 (2020). https://doi.org/10.1109/TCDS.2020.2999337
19. Li, Y., Zheng, W., Zong, Y., Cui, Z., Zhang, T., Zhou, X.: A bi-hemisphere domain adversarial neural network model for EEG emotion recognition. IEEE Trans. Affect. Comput. **12**, 494–504 (2018). https://doi.org/10.1109/TAFFC.2018.2885474
20. Liu, Y., Sourina, O., Nguyen, M.K.: Real-time EEG-based emotion recognition and its applications. In: Gavrilova, M.L., Tan, C.J.K., Sourin, A., Sourina, O. (eds.) Transactions on Computational Science XII. LNCS, vol. 6670, pp. 256–277. Springer, Heidelberg (2011). https://doi.org/10.1007/978-3-642-22336-5_13
21. Mao, X., Li, Q.: Generative Adversarial Networks for Image Generation. Springer, Cham (2021). https://doi.org/10.1007/978-981-33-6048-8
22. McCormack, J., d'Inverno, M.: On the future of computers and creativity. In: AISB 2014 Symposium on Computational Creativity, London. Citeseer (2014)
23. Mohammad, S., Kiritchenko, S.: WikiArt emotions: an annotated dataset of emotions evoked by art. In: Proceedings of the Eleventh International Conference on Language Resources and Evaluation (LREC 2018), Miyazaki, Japan. European Language Resources Association (ELRA) (2018)
24. Nawaz, R., Cheah, K.H., Nisar, H., Yap, V.V.: Comparison of different feature extraction methods for EEG-based emotion recognition. Biocybern. Biomed. Eng. **40**(3), 910–926 (2020). https://doi.org/10.1016/j.bbe.2020.04.005
25. NeuroSky: EEG art - NeuroSky (2015). http://neurosky.com/2015/11/beautiful-brainwaves-creating-eeg-art/. Accessed 22 Feb 2022
26. Pham, T.D., Tran, D.: Emotion recognition using the Emotiv EPOC device. In: Huang, T., Zeng, Z., Li, C., Leung, C.S. (eds.) ICONIP 2012. LNCS, vol. 7667, pp. 394–399. Springer, Heidelberg (2012). https://doi.org/10.1007/978-3-642-34500-5_47
27. Picard, R.W.: Affective Computing. MIT Press, Cambridge (1997)
28. Plass-Oude Bos, D.: EEG-based emotion recognition. In: The Influence of Visual and Auditory Stimuli (2006)
29. Praramadhan, A.A., Saputra, G.E.: Cycle generative adversarial networks algorithm with style transfer for image generation. arXiv preprint arXiv:2101.03921 (2021)
30. Quark, R.: The art of feeling (2017). https://www.randomquark.com/work/the-art-of-feeling. Accessed 22 Feb 2022
31. Riccio, P., Bergaust, K., Christensen-Scheel, B., Zuluaga, M.A., De Martin, J.C., Nichele, S.: AI-based artistic representation of emotions from EEG signals: a discussion on fairness, inclusion, and aesthetics. arXiv preprint (2022). https://doi.org/10.48550/arXiv.2202.03246
32. Russell, J.A.: A circumplex model of affect. J. Pers. Soc. Psychol. **39**(6), 1161–1178 (1980). https://doi.org/10.1037/h0077714
33. Salevati, S., DiPaola, S.: A creative artificial intelligence system to investigate user experience, affect, emotion and creativity. In: Proceedings of the Conference on Electronic Visualisation and the Arts, EVA 2015, pp. 140–147. BCS Learning & Development Ltd., Swindon (2015). https://doi.org/10.14236/ewic/eva2015.13. GBR

34. Simonyan, K., Zisserman, A.: Very deep convolutional networks for large-scale image recognition. arXiv preprint arXiv:1409.1556 (2014)
35. Song, T., Zheng, W., Song, P., Cui, Z.: EEG emotion recognition using dynamical graph convolutional neural networks. IEEE Trans. Affect. Comput. 11(3), 532–541 (2020). https://doi.org/10.1109/TAFFC.2018.2817622
36. Strongman, K.T.: The Psychology of Emotion: From Everyday Life to Theory. Wiley, Hoboken (2003)
37. Xia, X., Xu, C., Nan, B.: Inception-v3 for flower classification. In: 2017 2nd International Conference on Image, Vision and Computing (ICIVC), pp. 783–787 (2017). https://doi.org/10.1109/ICIVC.2017.7984661
38. Xiong, J.: Mind art (2014). https://www.behance.net/gallery/22054167/Mind-Art-. Accessed 22 Feb 2022
39. Yi, R., Liu, Y.J., Lai, Y.K., Rosin, P.L.: APDrawingGAN: generating artistic portrait drawings from face photos with hierarchical GANs. In: Proceedings of the IEEE/CVF Conference on Computer Vision and Pattern Recognition (CVPR), pp. 10735–10744 (2019). https://doi.org/10.1109/CVPR.2019.01100
40. Zhang, J., Chen, P., Nichele, S., Yazidi, A.: Emotion recognition using time-frequency analysis of EEG signals and machine learning. In: 2019 IEEE Symposium Series on Computational Intelligence (SSCI), pp. 404–409. IEEE (2019). https://doi.org/10.1109/SSCI44817.2019.9003057
41. Zhang, J., Li, J., Nichele, S.: Instantaneous mental workload recognition using wavelet-packet decomposition and semi-supervised learning. In: 2019 IEEE Symposium Series on Computational Intelligence (SSCI), pp. 410–416. Institute of Electrical and Electronics Engineers (IEEE) (2020). https://doi.org/10.1109/SSCI44817.2019.9002997
42. Zhang, J., Yin, Z., Chen, P., Nichele, S.: Emotion recognition using multi-modal data and machine learning techniques: a tutorial and review. Inf. Fusion 59, 103–126 (2020). https://doi.org/10.1016/j.inffus.2020.01.011
43. Zheng, W.L., Liu, W., Lu, Y., Lu, B.L., Cichocki, A.: EmotionMeter: a multimodal framework for recognizing human emotions. IEEE Trans. Cybern. 49(3), 1110–1122 (2019). https://doi.org/10.1109/TCYB.2018.2797176
44. Zhong, P., Wang, D., Miao, C.: EEG-based emotion recognition using regularized graph neural networks. IEEE Trans. Affect. Comput., 1 (2020). https://doi.org/10.1109/TAFFC.2020.2994159

Emotion-Driven Interactive Storytelling: Let Me Tell You How to Feel

Oneris Daniel Rico Garcia[1]([⊠]), Javier Fernandez Fernandez[1],
Rafael Andres Becerra Saldana[2], and Olaf Witkowski[1]

[1] Cross Labs, Cross Compass, Kyoto, Japan
`oneris.rico@cross-compass.com`
[2] Bogotá, Colombia

Abstract. Interactive storytelling is a form of digital entertainment that has gained attention with the development of creative computational methodologies. However, one of the main problems this field is facing is the poor control that the content creator (e.g. film director or game designer) has over the experience of the user (e.g. viewer or player) once the story starts. Hence, we leverage artificial intelligence to increase the creative control of the content creator by designing a system that guides the user's emotions towards a particular state as the story unfolds. Specifically, we have developed an EEG-based emotion recognition system trained on EEG recordings acquired from 5 participants watching a selection of 384 videos. The system is able to operate a binary classification on both valence and arousal with an accuracy of 62% and 57%, respectively. A short film was then created, where each scene automatically adapts to the user's emotion, based on a set of predefined interactions established by the content creator (i.e. the actual film director). The analysis shows that the system not only improves the engagement of the user, but also induces an emotion closer to the one intended and specified ahead of time by the content creator for the story. Our results indicate that there is a practical application of emotion-based studies for future content creators to better control an intended emotional response delivered and received by the audience.

Keywords: Computational creativity · Interactive storytelling · Emotion recognition · Affective computing · Artificial intelligence

1 Introduction

The video games industry is currently one of the largest entertainment industries by revenue[1], overtaking films and music combined[2]. Video games can be considered essentially computer-generated image films, where *interaction* is the

---

[1] https://www.pwc.com/us/en/industries/tmt/library/global-entertainment-media-outlook.html.

[2] https://www.nasdaq.com/articles/investing-video-games-industry-pulls-more-revenue-movies-music-2016-06-13.

T. Martins et al. (Eds.): EvoMUSART 2022, LNCS 13221, pp. 259–274, 2022.
https://doi.org/10.1007/978-3-031-03789-4_17

key distinguishing feature. This key feature has influenced the film industry's creative side, resulting in the genre of *interactive films*, which require input from the viewers to determine how to continue the story. This mechanism is known as *click-to-progress*. The first example of an interactive film is *Kinoautomat* [33], which dates from 1967. Kinoautomat was a theatrical release in which a moderator surveyed the audience to determine which of two scenes to play next. More recently, Netflix released *Black Mirror: Bandersnatch* [37] which, because it was an online experience, enabled the possibility of aggregating data. Notably, this film was awarded "Best Game Writing" of 2019 in the *Nebulas Awards*[3], highlighting the blurred line between video games and interactive films.

When content creators write a story, they expect to elicit certain reactions from the viewers. There are multiple narrative tools used to elicit emotions over the film so that, when the viewer is in emotional sync with the content creator, the film viewing becomes an engaging experience [16]. Contrary to non-interactive film, where all the creative control is in the hands of the content creator, the creative control in interactive storytelling is delegated in large part to the viewer because they can choose explicitly what content comes next by selecting among a set of options. This is a fundamental change when comparing interactive and non-interactive films, as it swaps the power relation between content creators and spectators, creating a challenge for an interactive content creator who wants to deliver a specific and intended emotional message to the audience. The work presented in this paper addresses this challenge in a novel way by leveraging a brain-computer interface (BCI) to automatically adapt film content presentation to guide the viewer's emotional state to the director's goal.

2   Background

In the current literature, there are some forms of user interaction developed to enhance the experience delivered by the content creator. One example is facial-emotion-recognition-based films, such as *All about Face* [12], where a moderator chooses the path of a film based on the facial emotions expressed by the audience. Other research, such as *Seamless Multithread Films in Virtual Reality* [34], has explored the use of regions of interest as an interactive method for virtual reality (VR) films. This method mainly relies on visual cues in the frame to make different path options explicit. However, these methods are susceptible to biases [3] as the user is aware of a question (about how the story should progress) and, consequently, the implications of the answer.

Research on interactive books suggests that identifying emotions via biometric data could be an alternative solution that mitigates cognitive biases. For example, *Physiologically Driven Storytelling* [15] guides the user through the story using emotions detected through eye-tracking, breathing rhythm and electrodermal activity (EDA). Nevertheless, not all forms of biometric techniques avoid cognitive biases [3], being electrocardiogram (ECG), electrodermal activity (EDA), or electroencephalography (EEG) the main methods for detecting

---

[3] https://nebulas.sfwa.org/.

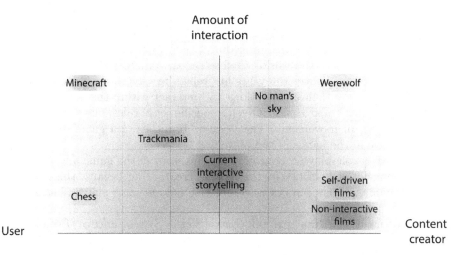

Fig. 1. Representative examples of interactive storytelling. The horizontal axis represents creative control. The vertical axis represents how interactive the experience is. Orange means video game, aqua represents board games, purple is storytelling in general, and green is our proposed method. (Color figure online)

emotions without voluntary control from the user's side. However, the ECG-based emotions have a long delay compared to the stimuli [25], and EDA-based emotions do not relate to valence when implemented alone [1]. Hence, the preferred option is to recognize emotions using EEG [23], an electrophysiological monitoring method to record the electrical activity of the brain via electrodes.

In summary, to avoid disturbing the viewing experience, it is necessary to avoid asking users for their interaction preferences. Hence, our solution to this problem is to design an EEG emotion-based system that conveys the content creator's message by guiding the user's emotions along with the story. The novel contribution of this research is that the input inquired for interaction is not attached to the output shown on screen, meaning that even if the viewer shows a *preference* for specific content, that does not mean that said content will be shown. The final choice is in the hands of the content creator.

To compare this proposed system with other ones in the literature, Fig. 1 displays some of the most relevant interactive storytelling methods, with the amount of content creator's creative control on the horizontal axis and how interactive the experience is on the vertical axis. The description of the displayed methods are as follows:

- **Minecraft**: a sandbox game where community-generated content is a key part of the interaction. Users have full freedom to build environments. This game also has a very active mod community.
- **Trackmania**: a community-generated arcade racing game, where one user can create a track and the others race in it. Users can see a ghost view of

other players in the server, and this game mechanic enables the optimal racing line to morph by repetition from one player to another.

- **No Man's Sky**: a game with procedurally generated environments for users to explore. Although the worlds themselves are procedurally generated, the gameplay experience over the years has relied heavily on developer updates. Players can create their own stations and interact within the game.
- **Chess**: a strategy board game. Given a specific set of rules, players are limited to a finite set of movements. The possible branches of a game of chess are vast and are in the hands of the player.
- **Werewolf**: a role-playing board game. The story of the game and the characters behavior is described by the content creator, but because this is a role-playing game, players can devise completely unique game play and strategies in every match.
- **Non-interactive films**: give full control to the content creator. Because the story is already built, viewers can only watch it without interacting.
- **Current interactive storytelling**: offers interaction. Creative control is shared between viewers and content creators; all the different paths are provided by the content creator, but it is the user who ultimately selects what content to watch.
- **Self-driven films**: our interactive method based on automated emotional recognition. Offers no explicit interaction on the part of the viewer. The content creator provides the different viewing options and the system chooses what content to display based on the measured reactions of the viewers.

3   Methodology

This section is divided into three subsections. Firstly, there is the methodology followed to create the emotion recognition system. Secondly, the interface design is presented, detailing the creative process of our experimental emotion-driven short film. Lastly are the assessment methods used to quantify the results of this research.

3.1   Emotion Recognition

The current debate about the most suitable model of emotions revolves around the categorical and dimensional theories [36]. For this work, the model selected is the 2D model of emotions proposed by Lang [19]. The two dimensions of the model are valence and arousal. The former has a range from very unpleasant to very pleasant. The latter is classified from very passive to active, which indicates the intensity of felt emotions.

There are various ways to use biometric data to measure valence and arousal. In the literature, heart rate has been used for valence [25], electrodermal activity (EDA) for arousal [32], eye-tracking for arousal [8], and facial recognition along with head pose [39] for valence and arousal, among others. However, none of these options fulfilled the set requirements for this project: heart rate does not measure emotion in real-time [25], EDA only measures accurately the arousal dimension [32], eye-tracking is not efficient for motion picture images unless combined with EEG such as [41], and facial recognition is susceptible to cognitive biases [21]. For these reasons, EEG was the chosen method for emotion recognition. This technique can measure both valence and arousal [18,22] in real-time [23], and mitigates the occurrence of cognitive bias [14].

Although there are currently available datasets using EEG to recognize valence and arousal, such as DEAP [18] and SEED [22], our system required a shorter trigger time. Compared to DEAP and SEED, where the length of the videos is approximately 1 min and 4 min, respectively, the desired trigger time for our system was around 10 s. Hence, to create our dataset we used the publicly available dataset called LIRIS-ACCEDE [4], which contains labeled information for valence and arousal for 9800 clip segments extracted from 160 different films. Each video of the dataset was rated by multiple participants. Hence, each label consists of the mean and standard deviation of the ratings. These clips have a duration between 8 and 12 s, similar to the trigger length required for this research.

To build the emotion recognition system, we developed two separate models (one for valence and another for arousal). For each of the models, we chose four different groups of 48 videos each. Looking at the distribution of the videos according to their absolute value and standard deviation, we decided to consider 48 videos with the lowest absolute value (Group 1 and 5 of Fig. 2) and 48 videos with the highest absolute value (Group 2 and 6 of Fig. 2) for each of the variables. Also, we aimed to display videos that evoked a similar emotion to all the participants so, we also considered the videos with the lowest standard deviation for the positive and negative side of the mean value of the distribution, highlighted in Fig. 2 as Group 3, 4, 7 and 8.

To display the videos, we used a pseudo-random sequence called Second-Order Conditional (SOC) sequence [28]. This type of sequence avoids repetition or any possibility of the test user realizing any pattern in how the content is being presented.

Our dataset was recorded using five participants. All the experiments were carried out under the same conditions, same room environment (23 °C) and same equipment. The computer used for the experiment was a MacBook Pro with a 2.3 GHz Dual-Core Intel Core i5 CPU, 16 GB 2133 MHz MHz LPDDR3 RAM and Intel Iris Plus Graphics 640 1536 MB GPU. The computer was connected via HDMI to a TV set up in a manner so that the image would only use 8 °C of the visual field of view (paracentral field of view) of the participants. When participants arrived at the experiment room, the conditions and procedures were explained using only on-screen instructions. An experiment supervisor would assist the participants in wearing the EEG headset (an OpenBCI Ultracortex Mark IV[4]).

---

[4] https://shop.openbci.com/products/ultracortex-mark-iv?variant=23280742211.

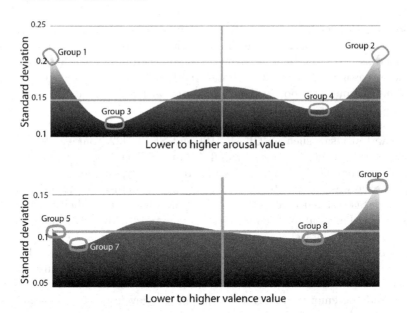

Fig. 2. Distribution of video clips. The horizontal axis indicates the videos organized from lower to higher (left to right) value for each feature. The vertical axis shows the standard deviation value of each video. The amber lines represent the mean of each axis. The green square indicates the chosen videos https://www.overleaf.com/project/619e777da79c92cf37edcee3. (Color figure online)

Regarding the EEG device, the positions of the electrodes were carefully selected based on the desired task. For emotion recognition, it is a common practice to distribute all the available electrodes along the skull to record the brainwaves from all parts of the brain. It is also common practice to locate some electrodes in the frontal part of the face to remove the electrooocular artifacts and improve the signal/noise relation. Consequently, the electrodes were located on the positions Fp1, Fp2, F7, F8, F3, F4, T3, T4, T5, T6, C3, C4, P3, P4, O1, and O2, according to the international system 10–20. The electrodes Fp1 and Fp2 were used to subtract the electrooocular artifacts. The data was recorded with a frequency 500 Hz. Because the EEG device could become uncomfortable over time, participants were instructed that they could rest every two groups of videos if they needed to.

The UI included a 5-seconds countdown for each group of videos to allow participants to get into a relaxed position. Thereafter, a noise image appeared for 2 s. The recordings during this time frame were subsequently used to remove the baseline for the video recordings. To keep the participants focused on the task, they were asked to try to imagine the story behind each clip they saw.

Lastly, to recognize the emotions we first extracted 64 features (16 channels × 4 band frequencies) and then trained a multi-perceptron neural network for each participant separately. The four band powers for each EEG signal correspond to the theta rhythm (4–7 Hz), alpha rhythm (8–13 Hz), beta rhythm (14–30 Hz), and gamma rhythm (31–50 Hz). The delta rhythm (0.5–4 Hz) was excluded as it is traditionally associated with sleep stages [13] and therefore assumed to be less relevant to our study. The feature extraction was carried out using Welch's method [38]. This is an approach to estimate the power of a signal at different frequencies. It is carried out by averaging consecutive periodograms of small time-windows over the signal. To encompass at least two full cycles of the lowest frequency of interest (4 Hz), the duration of the time-windows was set at 0.5 s, with an overlap of 0.25 s between each consecutive window. To smooth the discretization process, each window was filtered with a Hann function. The band frequencies were thereafter extracted from the PSD by implementing Simpson's rule, which approximates integrals using quadratics.

3.2 Interface Design

To study this kind of interaction, we designed an experiment to demonstrate the following hypothesis:

> Through the use of an emotion-aware interactive system with narrative devices, creators can induce emotions in an effective and self-aware manner without losing creative control.

In the context of this experiment, *narrative devices* refer to those narrative tools at the disposal of the film and video game creators to elicit specific emotions in audiences. *Self-awareness* means the system captures the emotional state of the viewer and, based on parameters set by the content creators, the system chooses which content to present next to achieve a specific emotional reaction.

In straightforward terms, this system is split into two components. During the creative component, a content creator produces an emotion-driven film (EDF), similar to click-to-progress. However, instead of having options to click on, the given input to the system from the content creator is the emotional state to achieve. Content creators have to define which narrative tools to use in case the viewer is experiencing a different emotional state than intended. As it was stated before, one of the goals of this research was to maintain the simplicity of the viewing experience during a linear narrative film. That is why, from the end user (viewer), nothing else than watching the film is required.

For this research, the film used is *Hunting Dogs*[5]. It is a fictional story based on the *social cleansing* phenomenon from Colombia. Social cleansing is a process in which groups of armed civilians would "clean" society by eliminating individuals that they do not consider belonging to society [29]. The parameters for deciding who belongs to a society or not are based on self-created ideologies. This is an illegal act, which is in clear violation of human rights. Through the EDF, viewers are shown images that were clearly illegal, immoral or both. Any preference regarding either of these depictions would fall into the social desirability bias [24].

---

[5] A teaser for this short film is available at https://sendvid.com/nlxw45pi.

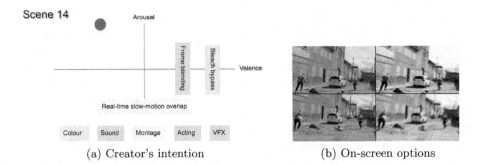

(a) Creator's intention   (b) On-screen options

Fig. 3. Narrative tools applied to elicit various goal emotional states. Left image (a): Instruction given by the director. The horizontal axis represents valence (low on the left) and the vertical axis represents arousal (low at the bottom). The red dot indicates the emotional goal for that scene. The color-coded instructions in the other quadrants represent the changes required for the content. Each color corresponds to a type of narrative tool, and the meaning of each color cell is shown at the bottom of the image. Right image (b): Different options corresponding to the quadrants' possibilities given by the content creator. (Color figure online)

Although the footage available corresponds to a single story line, montage choices can affect the outcome of how audiences react. For example, in scene 3 there is an intercourse sequence where there is also a use of drugs. The order in which these acts are presented varies depending on the director's instructions, which can be either: the character participated in intercourse *because* he did drugs or, the character got into intercourse *and then* consumed drugs.

Because the short film was filmed at 240 frames per second (FPS), the director could vary the frame rate in different parts of the story depending on the intention. For example, violent scenes are perceived differently when shown in slow motion. It has been proven [10] that spectators perceive actions with more intent when said action is shown in slow motion.

As part of the developing process for *Hunting Dogs* interactive version, the director of the short film described the emotional goal as follows:

> "Through the manipulation of audiovisual elements, create a narration that adjusts to the unconscious responses of each viewer, aiming to have a relatively homogeneous perception and see how this affects the criticism of the story once the viewer finishes watching the short film. Altering the scenes in such a way that there is repulsion towards the violence (low valence) of the story but not towards the short film (high arousal)."

To achieve these emotional goals, the content creator used the following narrative tools (also referred to as *layers*):

- **Color:** It is a post-processing visual effect that enables a content creator to alter the rendition of the image by affecting the its color and luminance distribution.

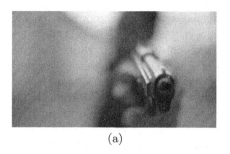
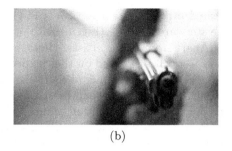

(a)   (b)

Fig. 4. Color correction options that could be applied based on viewer emotion state. Left image (a): A frame with the standard ITU709 gamma curve. Right image (b): Same frame as Fig. 4(a) with a bleach-bypass look applied. (Color figure online)

- **Sound:** It is probably the most flexible layer to manipulate among the options since creators can add, omit or modify in real-time audio content or even create music live during the interactions, such as Square Enix did for Final Fantasy [17].
- **Montage:** This layer enables creators to change the ordering of content within a sequence, as well as switch between different sequences in case multiple branches are available.
- **Acting:** Depending on the desired emotional perception for a character or moment of the story and considering the emotional reaction from the viewers, content creators can record different performances for the same lines in the script.
- **Video effects:** They are the visuals presented on the final product that were added after they were filmed. It commonly refers to computer-generated images.

The emotions evoked using these tools depend on the context. Hence, it is the content creator's task to study the context of the scenes and evaluate the optimal interactions to use to evoke specific emotions.

Figure 3(a) is an example of how these interactions were crafted using these tools. The color correction of the short film had two distinctive looks: A standard (ITU709, the standard broadcast gamma curve, Fig. 4(a)) and a light and heavy bleach-bypass (high contrast, faded image named after a film developing process in which the film would not be bleached in the developing process, Fig. 4(b)) correction over the standard look.

Each look was presented according to the director's guidance. For the cases where the valence was high, a video effect (VFX) of frame blending was added on top of the bleach-bypass. This frame blending VFX distorted the motion of the image and enhanced the visual high contrast of the bleach-bypass color correction, which was also applied to the film in these conditions. Additionally, for the cases where arousal was low, a montage effect was combined with real-time playback in slow motion. If the viewer's response was in the quadrant desired by the content creator, the video displayed would be shown *as is* with the standard ITU709 (Fig. 4(a)) color correction.

Apart from being artistic choices from the content creator, these narrative tools were chosen based on their expected outcome. The montage effect enabled an increase in the number of shots shown in the scene which, according to LIRIS-ACCEDE [4], is the second most effective way to increase arousal. Additionally, the inclusion of slow motion reduced valence, as images in slow motion increase the perception of intent [10]. Bleach-bypass increased the contrast and reduces saturation. These are the opposite of colorfulness and hue count, which increase valence [4]. The results from applying these effects are shown in Fig. 3(b).

During the adaptation process, the interactive changes focused primarily on color correction, as it is a well-studied phenomenon that audience reaction is heavily influenced by aesthetic aspects of films [5].

Depending on factors such as final delivery format and delivery medium, all these layers were applied using different methods. For example, if the priority was size over processing power, effects were applied in real time on the user device; if the priority was processing taxation over size, then the final delivery included a vast array of pre-rendered option mixing possibilities to minimize the need for real-time processing.

3.3　System's Assessment

The viewing of the short film had two different groups. The first group (hereafter referred to as the experimental group) viewed the short film using the EEG device connected to a real-time valence and arousal classifier (EDF version). The second group (hereafter referred to as the control group) saw a non-interactive version of the same short film provided by the content creator without wearing the EEG device. The viewing setup for the EDF version group followed a similar protocol to that observed in the data collection protocol, except that the viewing screen was the MacBook laptop screen. Nevertheless, the angle of view was kept to 8 °C from their field of view for each participant (Fig. 5) by adjusting the distance to the screen, to accommodate the difference in screen size.

Once the participants were wearing the EEG device, they were asked to read a consent screen. This screen warned them about the sexual and violent content they were about to watch and informed them that, if at any point the experience became overwhelming, the film could be stopped. Once agreed, the recording of the EEG data would start, as well as the communication between the AI and the real-time engine.

Once the short film concluded, both groups answered a user engagement scale (UES) test [27] and reported the valence and arousal levels after watching the short film by using the self-assessment manikin (SAM) test [7]. The UES used in this study was the updated version published in [27]. This updated version quantifies how invested an individual was when interacting with a digital system. The features measured in the UES questionnaire are described by the authors as:

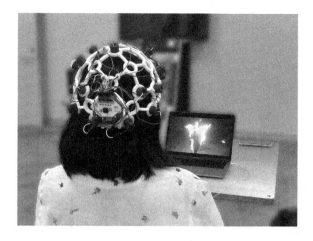

Fig. 5. Setup for the viewing of the short film.

- Focused attention: feeling absorbed in the interaction and losing track of time.
- Perceived usability: negative affect experienced as a result of the interaction and the degree of control and effort expended.
- Aesthetic appeal: attractiveness and visual appeal of the interface.

The updated version of the UES test groups three items from the original scale into *Reward factor*:

- Endurability: overall success of the interaction and users' willingness to recommend an application to others or engage with it in future.
- Novelty: curiosity and interest in the interactive task.
- Felt involvement: sense of being "drawn in" and having fun

This UES test in particular was chosen because it has been used to measure engagement in online video and video games, among others [26]. Additionally, this same test has been used in research of similar topics [2,9,11,35]. The SAM test is a non-verbal assessment technique that measures "the valence, arousal, and dominance associated with a person's affective reaction to a wide variety of stimuli" [7]. The SAM test was particularly useful because it is a visual test that aids in preventing any inconsistency due to a language barrier (our sample participants do not share the same native language). This test has also been used extensively in related research [6,20,30,31,40]

4   Results

As a result of the training process, the model developed for the 5 participants was tested using a five-fold cross validation. The optimal results were achieved for a model with a four-layer perceptron with an Adam optimizer and learning rate

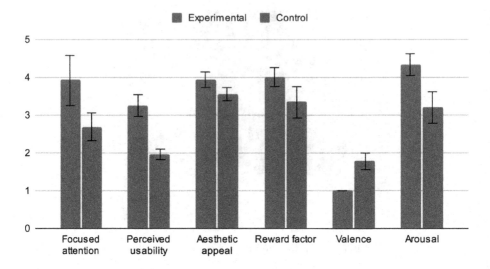

Fig. 6. Visual depiction of the UES and SAM test results.

of 1e-3. Once a model was trained for each participant separately, the average results obtained for all the participants were 62% for valence and 57% for arousal. The trained model for each participant was then used for the experiment, whose objective set by the content was to lower the valence while increasing the arousal.

The results from the UES test for the experimental group were, on average, the following: Focused attention 3.95/5 (standard deviation (SD) 1.2), Perceived usability 3.25/5 (SD 0.5), Aesthetic appeal 3.93/5 (SD 0.4), Reward factor 4.01/5 (SD 0.5). The results from the UES test on average, for the control group were: Focused attention 2.68/5 (SD 0.7), Perceived usability 1.97/5 (SD 0.2), Aesthetic appeal 3.56/5 (SD 0.3), Reward factor 3.36/5 (SD 0.8), as shown in Fig. 6. The p-value for the focus attention was 0.12, for perceived usability was 0.004, for aesthetic appeal was 0.22, and for reward factor was 0.27. These results show an effect in the perceived usability of the users that watched the interactive film with the EEG headset.

The results from the SAM assessment for the experimental group were, on average, the following: for valence 1/5 (SD 0), for arousal 4.33/5 (SD 0.5). The SAM assessment results for the control group were: for valence 2.33/5 (SD 0.4), for arousal 3.1/5 (SD 0.8), as shown in Fig. 6. The p-value was 0.024 for valence and 0.087 for arousal. Hence, the interactive film achieved the objective because it statistically decreased the valence and increased the arousal for the partici-pants with the EEG headset.

5 Discussion

The UES results, in all four items, were higher in the test group compared to the control group (Fig. 6). Although statistical significance was not present for all items evaluated, focus attention and perceived usability scored highest. As there is no difference in the viewing experience, there would not be an evident reason for either aesthetic appeal or reward factor to change in between the two groups since, in essence, both groups had the same level of explicit interaction (watching a video on a screen).

When compared to the control group, the experimental group reported a felt emotion in accordance with the objective defined by the director, i.e. lower valence and higher arousal (Fig. 6). Results indicate that both variables are statistically significant. Hence, they demonstrate the viability of our goal of inducing emotions without losing the content creator's creative control by the use of emotion-aware interactions in conjunction with narrative tools. A unique characteristic of an EDF is the possibility of aggregating data of emotional feedback from multiple users, as this could provide insight about which option is best to elicit the desired emotion for different kinds of viewers. Multiple factors can affect the emotional response to the same stimuli (weather, time of day, season, current events, etc.). Because EDFs are data-based interactions, where no question is fixed to an answer, the binding between input and output can be freely adjusted after distribution, as the same emotion recognition system used as input creates feedback about how effective the question/answer binding is.

One could argue that having the control group not wearing the EEG headset might induce a bias in the tests' responses. However, this argument would only be valid for the UES test, given that the viewers were aware of the use of a BCI. Although, in this research, the UES was used to make sure the use of the EEG headset (which can be uncomfortable over time) did not interfere with the viewing experience of the short film, as stated in the interface design section, the only requirement from the viewer was to watch the short film. However, this argument does not apply to the results regarding the SAM test, as the test participants had no way of knowing the emotional objectives from the content creator. Therefore, having statistical significance and low standard deviation in these results could only be attributed to our interactive method. The quantitative objective of our method was to control valence and arousal.

6   Conclusion

In recent years, interactive storytelling has become increasingly popular. However, one of its main drawbacks is the poor control of the content creator over the user's experience of the story. Hence, in this work, we propose a system that enhances the control of the content creator in response to the viewer's perceived emotion. This system first detects the emotions from the users via BCI to then guide their emotional state to one chosen by the content creator by using different types of montage or image treatment interactions.

For this work, we trained a model able to detect the valence and arousal of the users and created a short film where ten sequences had interactions to guide the users to specific emotional states. Results showed that this system not only improves some engagement variables such as perceived usability, but it also induces an emotion closer to the one that the content creator defined for the story. This opens up a new approach for content creators to have more control over the story and emotional response from audiences.

References

1. Al Machot, F., Elmachot, A., Ali, M., Al Machot, E., Kyamakya, K.: A deep-learning model for subject-independent human emotion recognition using electro-dermal activity sensors. Sensors **19**(7) (2019). https://doi.org/10.3390/s19071659, https://www.mdpi.com/1424-8220/19/7/1659
2. Alserri, S.A., Zin, N.A.M., Wook, T.S.M.T.: Instrument validation for evaluating serious game engagement model. In: 2019 International Conference on Electrical Engineering and Informatics (ICEEI), pp. 170–175. IEEE (2019)
3. Barrett, L.F., Adolphs, R., Marsella, S., Martinez, A.M., Pollak, S.D.: Emotional expressions reconsidered: challenges to inferring emotion from human facial movements. Psychol. Sci. Public Interest **20**(1), 1–68 (2019)
4. Baveye, Y., Dellandréa, E., Chamaret, C., Chen, L.: LIRIS-ACCEDE: a video database for affective content analysis. IEEE Trans. Affect. Comput. **6**, 43–55 (2015). https://doi.org/10.1109/TAFFC.2015.2396531
5. Bellantoni, P.: If It's Purple, Someone's Gonna Die: The Power of Color in Visual Storytelling. Taylor & Francis (2012). https://books.google.co.jp/books?id=E57cAwAAQBAJ
6. Böck, R., et al.: Intraindividual and interindividual multimodal emotion analyses in human-machine-interaction. In: 2012 IEEE International Multi-Disciplinary Conference on Cognitive Methods in Situation Awareness and Decision Support, pp. 59–64. IEEE (2012)
7. Bradley, M.M., Lang, P.J.: Measuring emotion: the self-assessment manikin and the semantic differential. J. Behav. Therapy Exp. Psychiatry **25**(1), 49–59 (1994). https://doi.org/10.1016/0005-7916(94)90063-9, https://www.sciencedirect.com/science/article/pii/0005791694900639
8. Bradley, M.M., Miccoli, L., Escrig, M.A., Lang, P.J.: The pupil as a measure of emotional arousal and autonomic activation. Psychophysiology **45**(4), 602–607 (2008)
9. Carlton, J., Brown, A., Jay, C., Keane, J.: Inferring user engagement from interaction data. In: Extended Abstracts of the 2019 CHI Conference on Human Factors in Computing Systems, pp. 1–6 (2019)
10. Caruso, E.M., Burns, Z.C., Converse, B.A.: Slow motion increases perceived intent. Proc. Natl. Acad. Sci. **113**(33), 9250–9255 (2016). https://doi.org/10.1073/pnas.1603865113, https://www.pnas.org/content/113/33/9250
11. Ciancone Chama, A.G., Monaro, M., Piccoli, E., Gamberini, L., Spagnolli, A.: Engaging the audience with biased news: an exploratory study on prejudice and engagement. In: Oinas-Kukkonen, H., Win, K.T., Karapanos, E., Karppinen, P., Kyza, E. (eds.) PERSUASIVE 2019. LNCS, vol. 11433, pp. 350–361. Springer, Cham (2019). https://doi.org/10.1007/978-3-030-17287-9_28
12. Damiano, R., Lombardo, V., Monticone, G., Pizzo, A.: All about face. An experiment in face emotion recognition in interactive dramatic performance. In: 2019 8th International Conference on Affective Computing and Intelligent Interaction Workshops and Demos (ACIIW), pp. 1–7 (2019). https://doi.org/10.1109/ACIIW.2019.8925032

13. De Andrés, I., Garzón, M., Reinoso-Suárez, F.: Functional anatomy of non-REM sleep. Front. Neurol. 1–14 (2011). https://doi.org/10.3389/fneur.2011.00070

14. Deldin, P.J., Keller, J., Gergen, J.A., Miller, G.A.: Cognitive bias and emotion in neuropsychological models of depression. Cogn. Emot. **15**(6), 787–802 (2001)

15. Frey, J., Ostrin, G., Grabli, M., Cauchard, J.R.: Physiologically driven storytelling: concept and software tool. In: Proceedings of the 2020 CHI Conference on Human Factors in Computing Systems, CHI 2020, pp. 1–13. Association for Computing Machinery, New York (2020). https://doi.org/10.1145/3313831.3376643, https://doi.org/10.1145/3313831.3376643

16. Hauge, M.: Writing Screenplays That Sell. Bloomsbury Publishing (2011). https://books.google.co.jp/books?id=6I9qDwAAQBAJ

17. Iwamoto, S.: Epic and interactive music in 'final fantasy xv' (2017). https://www.gdcvault.com/play/1023971/Epic-AND-Interactive-Music-in

18. Koelstra, S., et al.: DEAP: a database for emotion analysis; using physiological signals. IEEE Trans. Affect. Comput. **3**(1), 18–31 (2012). https://doi.org/10.1109/T-AFFC.2011.15

19. Lang, P.J.: The emotion probe. Am. Psychol. Assoc. **50**, 372–385 (1995). https://doi.org/10.1037/0003-066X.50.5.372

20. Laurans, G., Desmet, P.M., Hekkert, P.P.: Assessing emotion in interaction: some problems and a new approach. In: Proceedings of the 4th International Conference on Designing Pleasurable Products and Interfaces, DPPI 2009, Compiegne, October 2009. Universite de Technologie de Compiegne (2009)

21. Levenson, R.W., Ekman, P., Friesen, W.V.: Voluntary facial action generates emotion-specific autonomic nervous system activity. Psychophysiology **27**(4), 363–384 (1990)

22. Liu, J., et al.: EEG-based emotion classification using a deep neural network and sparse autoencoder. Front. Syst. Neurosci. **14**, 43 (2020). https://doi.org/10.3389/fnsys.2020.00043, https://www.frontiersin.org/article/10.3389/fnsys.2020.00043

23. Liu, Y., Sourina, O., Nguyen, M.K.: Real-time EEG-based human emotion recognition and visualization. In: 2010 International Conference on Cyberworlds, pp. 262–269. IEEE (2010)

24. Marlowe, D., Crowne, D.P.: Social desirability and response to perceived situational demands. J. Consult. Psychol. **25**, 109–15 (1961)

25. Nardelli, M., Valenza, G., Greco, A., Lanata, A., Scilingo, E.P.: Recognizing emotions induced by affective sounds through heart rate variability. IEEE Trans. Affect. Comput. **6**(4), 385–394 (2015). https://doi.org/10.1109/TAFFC.2015.2432810

26. O'Brien, H.: Translating theory into methodological practice. In: O'Brien, H., Cairns, P. (eds.) Why Engagement Matters, pp. 27–52. Springer, Cham (2016). https://doi.org/10.1007/978-3-319-27446-1_2

27. O'Brien, H.L., Cairns, P., Hall, M.: A practical approach to measuring user engagement with the refined user engagement scale (UES) and new UES short form. Int. J. Hum.-Comput. Stud. **112**, 28–39 (2018). https://doi.org/10.1016/j.ijhcs.2018.01.004, https://www.sciencedirect.com/science/article/pii/S1071581918300041

28. Pasquali, A., Cleeremans, A., Gaillard, V.: Reversible second-order conditional sequences in incidental sequence learning tasks. Q. J. Exp. Psychol. **72**(5), 1164–1175 (2019). https://doi.org/10.1177/1747021818780690, https://doi.org/10.1177/1747021818780690, pMID: 29779443

29. Perea Restrepo, C.M.: Limpieza social. Una violencia mal nombrada. Bogotá: Centro Nacional de Memoria Histórica (2019). http://www.cervantesvirtual.com/obra/limpieza-social-una-violencia-mal-nombrada-879231

30. Perron, B., Arsenault, D., Picard, M., Therrien, C.: Methodological questions in 'interactive film studies'. New Rev. Film Telev. Stud. **6**(3), 233–252 (2008)
31. Potel, M.J., Sayre, R.E., Robertson, A.: A system for interactive film analysis. Comput. Biol. Med. **9**(3), 237–256 (1979)
32. Prokasy, W.: Electrodermal activity in psychological research. Elsevier Sci. (2012). https://books.google.co.jp/books?id=m9l5ApC3avoC
33. Radúz, C., Ján, R., Vladimír, S.: Kinoautomat: One Man and His House. Czechoslovakia (1967)
34. Rico, O., Tag, B., Ohta, N., Sugiura, K.: Seamless multithread films in virtual reality. In: Proceedings of the Eleventh International Conference on Tangible, Embedded, and Embodied Interaction, TEI 2017. ACM, New York, pp. 641–646 (2017). https://doi.org/10.1145/3024969.3025096, http://doi.acm.org/10.1145/3024969.3025096
35. Saeghe, P., et al.: Augmenting television with augmented reality. In: Proceedings of the 2019 ACM International Conference on Interactive Experiences for TV and Online Video, pp. 255–261 (2019)
36. Shu, L., et al.: A review of emotion recognition using physiological signals. Sensors (Switzerland) **18** (2018). https://doi.org/10.3390/s18072074
37. Slade, D.: Black Mirror: Bandersnatch (2018)
38. Welch, P.D.: The use of Fast Fourier transform for the estimation of power spectra. Digit. Sig. Process. **15**(2), 532–574 (1975)
39. Wu, S., Du, Z., Li, W., Huang, D., Wang, Y.: Continuous emotion recognition in videos by fusing facial expression, head pose and eye gaze. In: 2019 International Conference on Multimodal Interaction, pp. 40–48 (2019)
40. Yadati, K., Katti, H., Kankanhalli, M.: Interactive video advertising: a multimodal affective approach. In: Li, S., et al. (eds.) MMM 2013. LNCS, vol. 7732, pp. 106–117. Springer, Heidelberg (2013). https://doi.org/10.1007/978-3-642-35725-1_10
41. Zheng, W.L., Dong, B.N., Lu, B.L.: Multimodal emotion recognition using EEG and eye tracking data. In: 2014 36th Annual International Conference of the IEEE Engineering in Medicine and Biology Society, pp. 5040–5043. IEEE (2014)

Modern Evolution Strategies for Creativity: Fitting Concrete Images and Abstract Concepts

Yingtao Tian$^{(\boxtimes)}$ and David Ha

Google Research, Brain Team, Tokyo, Japan
{alantian,hadavid}@google.com

Abstract. Evolutionary algorithms (ES) have been used in the digital art scene since the 1970s. A popular application of genetic algorithms is to optimize the procedural placement of vector graphic primitives to resemble a given painting. In recent years, deep learning-based approaches have also been proposed to generate procedural drawings, which can be optimized using gradient descent. In this work, we revisit the use of evolutionary algorithms for computational creativity. We find that modern ES algorithms, when tasked with the placement of shapes, offer large improvements in both quality and efficiency compared to traditional genetic algorithms, and even comparable to gradient-based methods. We demonstrate that ES is also well suited at optimizing the placement of shapes to fit the CLIP model, and can produce diverse, distinct geometric abstractions that are aligned with human interpretation of language.

1 Introduction

Staring from early 20th-century in the wider context of modernism [26], a series of avant-garde art abandoned the depiction of objects from tradition rules of perspective and instead picking revolutionary, abstract point of views. The Cubism art movement [38], popularized by influential artists including Pablo Picasso, proposed that objects are analyzed by the artist, broken up, and reassembled in an abstract form consisting of geometric representations. This naturally develops into the Geometric abstraction [8], where pioneer abstractionists like Wassily Kandinsky and Piet Mondrian represented the world using composed primitives that are either purely geometric or elementary. The impact is far-reaching: The use of simple geometry can be seen as one of styles found in abstract expressionism [36] where artists expressed their subconscious or impulsive feelings. It also helped shape the minimalist art [34] and minimalist architecture [39] movements, in which everything is stripped down to its essential quality to achieve simplicity [2].

The idea of minimalist art has also been explored in computer art with a root in mathematical art [32]. Schmidhuber [41] proposed an art form in the 1990s,

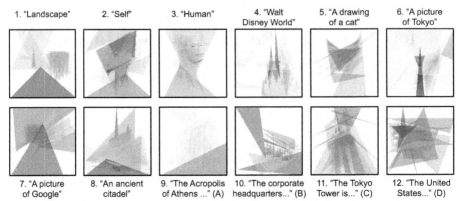

| 1. "Landscape" | 2. "Self" | 3. "Human" | 4. "Walt Disney World" | 5. "A drawing of a cat" | 6. "A picture of Tokyo" |

| 7. "A picture of Google" | 8. "An ancient citadel" | 9. "The Acropolis of Athens ..." (A) | 10. "The corporate headquarters..." (B) | 11. "The Tokyo Tower is..." (C) | 12. "The United States..." (D) |

A.   "The Acropolis of Athens is an ancient citadel located on a rocky outcrop above the city of Athens and contains the remains of several ancient buildings including the Parthenon."

B.   "The corporate headquarters complex of Google located at 1600 Amphitheatre Parkway in Mountain View, California. The corporate headquarters complex of Google located at 1600 Amphitheatre Parkway in Mountain View, California."

C.   "The Tokyo Tower is a communications and observation tower in the Shiba-koen district of Minato Tokyo Japan."

D.   "The United States of America commonly known as the United States or America is a country primarily located in North America."

Fig. 1. Our proposed painting synthesization places transparent triangles using evolution strategy (ES). Each concept represented as a text prompt is accompanied by its corresponding synthesized image. Here, the fitness is defined as the cosine distance between rendered canvas and text, both embedded by CLIP [37], and we optimize the position and the color of triangles using ES.

called low-complexity art, as the minimal art of the computer age that attempts to depict the essence of an object by making use of ideas from algorithmic complexity [25]. Similarly, algorithmic art [48] proposed to generate arts using the algorithm designed by the artist. In a broad sense, algorithmic art could be said to include genetic algorithm where the artist determines the rules governing how images evolves iteratively, which are a popular method applied to approximate images using simple shapes, often producing abstract art style. As one example, a basic genetic algorithm using evolution has been proposed [1,22] to represent a target image using semi-transparent, overlapping triangles. This approach has gained popularity over the years with the creative coding community, resulting in many sophisticated extensions [5,11,35,43]. These methods are iterative, enabling the creation process [45] to be captured.

Fig. 2. Our method leverages modern ES (PGPE with ClipUp), with 50 triangles and runs for 10,000 steps to fit the target image "Mona Lisa" (left). Here it is followed by the evolved results (middle) and the evolution process (right).

With the recent resurgence of interest in evolution strategies (ES) in the machine learning community [15,40], in this work, we revisit the use of ES for creativity applications as an alternative to gradient-based methods. For approximating an image with shapes, we find that modern ES algorithms offer large improvements in both quality and efficiency when compared to traditional genetic algorithms, and as we will also demonstrate, even comparable to state-of-the-art differentiable rendering methods [27]. We show that ES is also well suited at optimizing the placement of shapes to fit the CLIP [37] model, and can produce diverse, distinct geometric abstractions that are aligned with human interpretation of language. Such an alignment is due to the use of CLIP model that are trained on aligned real-world text-image dataset. Interestingly, the results produced by our method resemble abstract expressionism [36] and minimalist art [34,39]. We provide a reference code implementation of our approach online so that it can be a useful tool in the computational artist's toolbox.

2 Background

Related Work. In recent years, deep learning has also been applied to methods that can generate procedural drawings, which can be optimized with gradient descent. A growing list of works [20,30] also tackle the problem of approximating pixel images with simulated paint medium, and differentiable rendering [23,27] methods enable computer graphics to be optimized directly using gradient descent. To learn abstract representations, probabilistic generative models [16,31,33] are used to sample procedurally drawings directly from a latent space, without any given input images, similar to their pixel image counterparts. To interface with natural language, methods have been proposed to procedurally generate drawings of image categories [50], and word embeddings [19], enabling an algorithm to *draw what's written*. This combination of NLP and image generation is explored at larger scale in CLIP [37], and its procedural sketch counterpart CLIPDraw [12].

Perhaps among the related works, the closest to our approach is [10], which, similar to our work, uses a CLIP-like dual-encoder model pre-trained on the ALIGN [21] dataset to judge the similarity between generated art and text prompt, and leverages evolutionary algorithms to optimize a non-differentiable rendering process. However, there are several key differences: [10] parameterizes the rendering process with a hierarchical neural Lindenmayer system [29] powered by multiple-layer LSTM [18] and, as a result, it models well patterns with complex spatial relation, whereas our work favors a drastically simpler parameterization which just puts triangles individually on canvas to facilitate a different, minimalist art style that is complementary to theirs [9]. Moreover, while [10] uses a simple binary-tournament genetic algorithm [17], we opt for a modern state-of-the-art evolution strategy, PGPE [42] with ClipUp [47], performing well enough to produce interesting results within a few thousand steps.

Evolution Strategies (ES). [3,4] has been applied to optimization problems for a long period of time. A straightforward implementation of ES can be iteratively perturbing parameters in a pool and keeping those that are most fitting, which is simple yet inefficient. As a consequence, applying such a straightforward algorithm can lead to sub-optimal performance for art creativity [1]. To overcome this generic issue in ES, recent advances have been proposed to improve the performance of ES algorithms. One such improvement is *Policy Gradients with Parameter-Based Exploration (PGPE)* [42], which estimates gradients in a black-box fashion so the computation of fitness does not have to be differentiable *per se*. Since PGPE runs linear to the number of parameters for each iteration, it is an efficient and the go-to algorithm in many scenarios. With the estimated gradients, gradient-based optimizers such as Adam [24] can be used for optimization, while there are also work such as ClipUp [47] offering a simpler and more efficient optimizer specifically tailored for PGPE. Another representative ES algorithm is *Covariance matrix adaptation evolution strategy (CMA-ES)*, which in practice is considered more performant than PGPE. However, it runs in the quadratic time w.r.t. the number of parameters for each iteration, which limits its use in many problems with larger numbers of parameters where PGPE is still feasible.

Language-Derived Image Generation has been seeing very recent trends in creativity setting, where there are several directions to leverage CLIP [37], a pre-trained model with two encoders, one for image and one for text, that can convert images and text into the same, comparable low-dimensional embedding space. As the image encoder is a differentiable neural network, it can provide a gradient to the output of a differentiable generative model. The gradient can be further back-propagated through the said model till its parameters. For example, one direction of works uses CLIP's gradient to guide a GAN's generator, such as guiding BigGAN [49], guiding VQGAN [7], or a GAN with genetic algorithm-generated latent space [13]. Another direction of work applies CLIP to differentiable renderers. CLIPDraw [12] proposes to generate the images with diffvg [28], a differentiable SVG renderer. Although all these methods use the same pre-trained CLIP model for guidance, they show a drastically different artistic property, for which we hypothesize that the art style is determined by the intrinsic properties of the "painter", i.e., the GAN generator or renderer.

3   Modern Evolution Strategies for Creativity

The architecture of our proposed pipeline is shown in Fig. 3. Our proposed method synthesizes painting by placing transparent triangles using evolution strategy (ES). Overall, we can represent a configuration of triangles in a parameter space which composes of positions and colors of triangles, render such configuration onto a canvas, and calculate its fitness based on how well the rendered canvas fits a target image or an concept in the form of a text prompt. The ES algorithm keeps a pool of candidate configurations and uses mutations to evolves better ones measured by the said fitness. To have better creative results, we use a modern ES algorithm, PGPE [42] optimized by ClipUp [47] optimizer. Engineering-wise we use the pgpelib [46] implementation of PGPE and ClipUp.

As we choose to follow the spirit of minimalist art, we use transparent triangles as the parameter space. Concretely, a configuration of N triangles is parameterized by a collection of $(x_1, y_1, x_2, y_2, x_3, y_3, r, g, b, a)$ for each of the triangles, which are vertex coordinates and the RGBA (Red, Green, Blue, and Alpha a.k.a. transparency channel) color, totally making $10N$ parameters. In the ES, we update all parameters and use a fixed hyper-parameter, the number of triangles N. Note that N is better understood as the upper bound of number of triangles to use: although N is fixed, the algorithm is still capable of effectively using "fewer" triangles by making unwanted ones transparent.

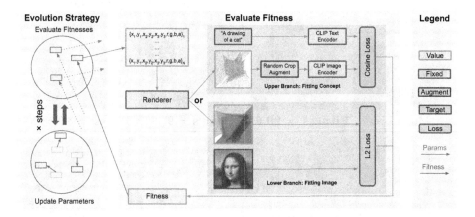

Fig. 3. The architecture of our method. Our proposed method synthesizes painting by placing transparent triangles using Evolution Strategy (ES). After rendering the parameters on a canvas, we calculate the fitness, which measures how well the canvas fits either a target image, or a concept in the form of a text prompt. The fitness, in turn, guides the evolution process to find better parameters.

As ES is orthogonal to the fitness evaluation, we are left with freedom to choose what counts as fitting. Particularly, we consider two kinds of fitness, namely, fitting a concrete image (the lower branch in Fig. 3) and fitting a concept (the upper branch in Fig. 3). Fitting a concrete image is straightforward, where we can simply use the pixel-wise L2 loss between the rendered canvas and the target image as the fitness. Fitting a concept requires more elaboration. We represent the concept as a text prompt and embed the text prompt using the text encoder in CLIP [37] which we discuss in detail in Sect. 2. Then we embed the rendered canvas using the image encoder also available in CLIP. Since the CLIP models are trained so that both embedded images and texts are comparable under Cosine distance for similarity, we use such distance as the fitness. We note that since the ES algorithm provides black-box optimization, the renderer, like fitness computation, does not necessarily need to be differentiable.

We find in practice a few decisions should be made so the whole pipeline can work reasonably well. First, we augment the rendered canvas by random cropping in calculating the fitness and average the fitness on each of the augmented canvas, following the practice of [7,12]. This would prevent the rendered canvas from overfitting and increase the stability in the optimization. Second, we render the triangles on top of a background with a uniform distribution noise. Mathematically, this equals to modeling the uncertainty of parts in the canvas not covered by triangles with a max-entropy assumption, and using Monte Carlo method for approximation. Finally, we limit the maximal alpha value for each triangle to 0.1, which prevents front triangles from (overly) shadowing the back ones.

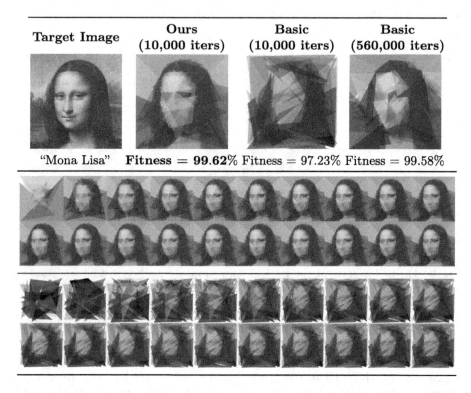

Fig. 4. Compare choices of evolution algorithm: Ours (PGPE with ClipUp) vs. basic evolution algorithm (mutation with simulated annealing) [1]. Both settings fit 50 triangles and all choices except for the EA are the same. We show the results of ours and the basic algorithm at the end of 10, 000 iterations, and the result of the basic algorithm after running 56 times more iterations. The details of evolution process until 10, 000 iterations are shown in the bottom half, where the upper group is for ours and the lower group is for the basic algorithm.

4   Fitting Concrete Target Image

In this section, we show the performance of our proposed work on fitting a concrete target image. In doing so, the model takes the lower branch in Fig. 3. We fit the famous painting "Mona Lisa" with 50 triangles by running evolution for 10,000 steps in Fig. 2. Our result is a distinctive art style represented by well-placed triangles that care both fine-grained textures and large backgrounds. The evolution process also displays the coarse-to-fine adjustments of the shapes' positions and colors.

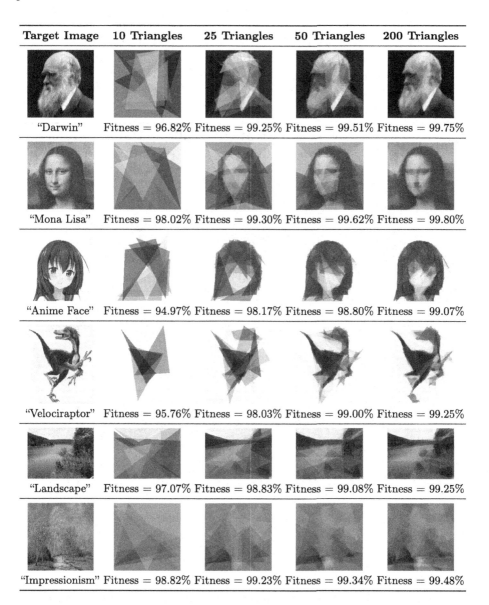

Target Image	10 Triangles	25 Triangles	50 Triangles	200 Triangles
"Darwin"	Fitness = 96.82%	Fitness = 99.25%	Fitness = 99.51%	Fitness = 99.75%
"Mona Lisa"	Fitness = 98.02%	Fitness = 99.30%	Fitness = 99.62%	Fitness = 99.80%
"Anime Face"	Fitness = 94.97%	Fitness = 98.17%	Fitness = 98.80%	Fitness = 99.07%
"Velociraptor"	Fitness = 95.76%	Fitness = 98.03%	Fitness = 99.00%	Fitness = 99.25%
"Landscape"	Fitness = 97.07%	Fitness = 98.83%	Fitness = 99.08%	Fitness = 99.25%
"Impressionism"	Fitness = 98.82%	Fitness = 99.23%	Fitness = 99.34%	Fitness = 99.48%

Fig. 5. Qualitative and quantitative results from fitting several targets with 10, 25, 50, and 200 triangles, each running for 10,000 steps. Images credits: Darwin, Mona Lisa, Velociraptor are from [1]. Anime Face is generated by Waifu Labs [44]. Landscape is from Wikipedia [6]. Impressionism is *A May Morning in Moret* by Alfred Sisley, collected by [14].

Number of Triangles and Parameters. Our proposed pipeline is able to fit any target images and could handle a wide range of number of parameters, since PGPE runs efficiently, i.e., linear to the number of parameters. This is demonstrated by applying our method to fit several target images with 10, 25, 50, 200 triangles, which corresponds to 100, 250, 500 and 2000 parameters respectively. As shown in Fig. 5, our proposed pipeline works well for a wide range of target images, and the ES algorithm is capable of using the number of triangles as a "computational budget" where extra triangles could always be utilized for gaining in fitness. This allows a human artist to use the number of triangles in order to find the right balance between abstractness and details in the produced art.

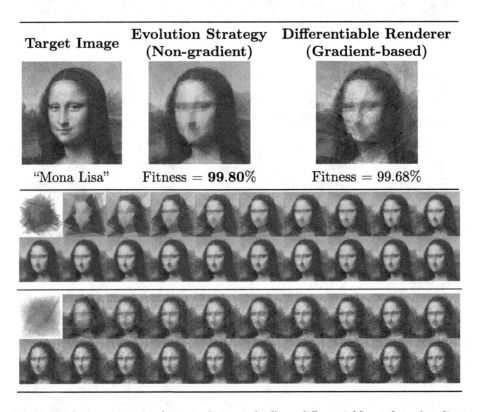

Fig. 6. Evolution strategies (non-gradient method) vs. differentiable renderer (gradient based method) fitting target image with 200 triangles. The upper half shows the final results and the bottom half shows the details of optimization.

Choice of ES Algorithm. We compare two choices of evolution algorithm: ours, which uses the recent PGPE with ClipUp, and a basic, traditional one, which consists of mutation and simulated annealing adopted earlier [1,22]. As shown in Fig. 4, our choice of more recent algorithms leads to better results than the basic one under the same parameter budget. Subjectively, our final results are more visually closer to the target image with a smoother evolution process, and quantitatively, our method leads to much better fitness (99.62% vs. 97.23%). Furthermore, even allowing 56 times more iterations for the basic algorithm does not lead to results better than ours.

Comparison with Gradient-Based Optimization. While our proposed approach is ES-based, it is interesting to investigate how it compares to gradient-based optimization since the latter is commonly adopted recently (See Sect. 2). Therefore we conduct a gradient-based setup by implementing rendering of composed triangles using nvdiffrast [27], a point-sampling-based differentiable renderer. We use the same processing as mentioned in Sect. 3. As shown in Fig. 6, our proposed ES-based method can achieve similar yet slightly higher fitness

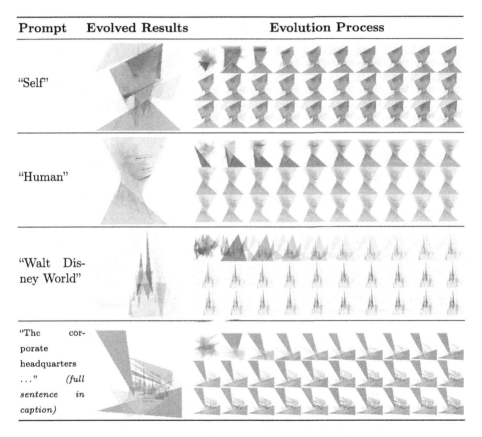

Fig. 7. ES and CLIP fit the concept represented in text prompt, using 50 triangles and running evolution for 2,000 steps. Each row shows the text prompt followed by the evolved results and the evolution process. We show exemplary prompts for 3 kinds of text, ranging from a single word ("Self" and "Human"), a phrase ("Walt Disney Land"), and a long sentence ("The corporate headquarters complex of Google located at 1600 Amphitheatre Parkway in Mountain View, California.").

than results compared with the gradient-optimized differentiable renderer. Furthermore and perhaps more interestingly, two methods produce artworks with different styles: our proposed method can adaptive allocating large triangles for background and small ones for detailed textures, whereas the differentiable renderer tends to introduce textures unseen in the target image (especially in the background). We argue that due to the difference in the optimization mechanism, our method focuses more on the placement of triangles while the differentiable renderer pays attention to the compositing of transparent colors.

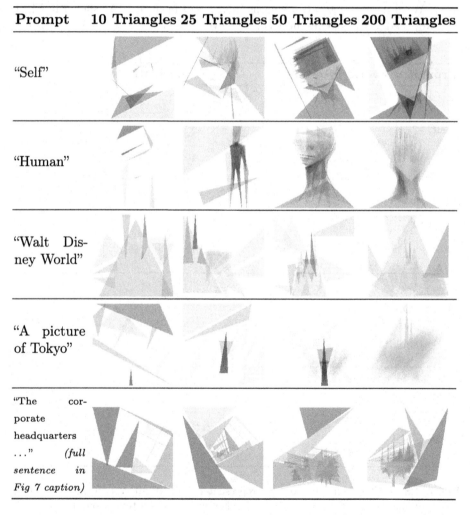

Prompt	10 Triangles	25 Triangles	50 Triangles	200 Triangles
"Self"				
"Human"				
"Walt Disney World"				
"A picture of Tokyo"				
"The corporate headquarters ..." (full sentence in Fig 7 caption)				

Fig. 8. Qualitative results from ES and CLIP fitting several text prompt with 10,25,50, and 200 triangles, each running for 2,000 steps. We show exemplary prompts for 3 kinds of text, ranging from a single word ("Self" and "Human"), to phrases ("A picture of Tokyo"), to long sentences.

5 Fitting Abstract Concept with CLIP

In this section, we show the performance of our method configured to fit an abstract concept represented by language. In doing so, the model takes the upper branch in Fig. 3. Formally, the parameter space remains the same, but the fitness is calculated as the cosine distance between the text prompt and the rendered canvas, both encoded by CLIP. Since the model is given more freedom to decide what to paint, this problem is arguably a much harder yet more interesting problem than fitting concrete images in the previous section.

In Fig. 7, we show the evolution result and process of fitting abstract concept represented as text prompt, using 50 triangles and running evolution for 2, 000 steps. We found that unlike fitting a concrete images, 2, 000 steps is enough for fitting a concept to converge. Our method could handle text prompts ranging from a single word to a phrase, and finally, to a long sentence, even though the task itself is arguably more challenging than the previous one. The results show a creative art concept that is abstract, not resembling a particular image, yet correlated with humans' interpretation of the text. The evolution process also demonstrates iterative adjustment, such as the human shape in the first two examples, the shape of castles in Disney World, as well as in the final example, the cooperate-themed headquarters. Also, compared to fitting concrete images in the previous section, our method cares more about the placement of triangles.

Number of Triangles and Parameters. Like fitting a concrete image, we can also fit an abstract concept with a wide range of number of parameters since the PGPE algorithm and the way we represent canvas remains the same. In Fig. 8 we apply our method to fit several prompts with 10, 25, 50, 200 triangles, which corresponds to 100, 250, 500 and 2000 parameters respectively, where our proposed pipeline is capable of leveraging the number of triangles as a "budget for fitting" to balance between the details and the level of abstraction. Like in the previous task, this allows a human artist to balance the abstractness in the produced art.

We observe that while the model could comfortably handle at least up to 50 triangles, more triangles (200) sometimes poses challenges: For example, with 200 triangles, "corporate headquarters ..." gets a better result while "a picture of Tokyo" leads to a poor one. This may be due to the difficulties composing overly shadowed triangles, and we leave it for future study.

Multiple Runs. Since the target is an abstract concept rather than a concrete image, our method is given much freedom in arranging the configuration of triangles, which means random initialization and noise in the optimization can lead to drastically different solutions. In Fig. 9, we show 4 separate runs of our method on several text prompts, each using 50 triangles with 2, 000 iterations, which is the same as previous examples. As shown, our method creates distinctive abstractions aligned with human interpretation of language while being capable of producing diverse results from the same text prompt. This, again, is a desired property for computer-assisted art creation, where human creators can be put

Prompt	4 Individual Runs

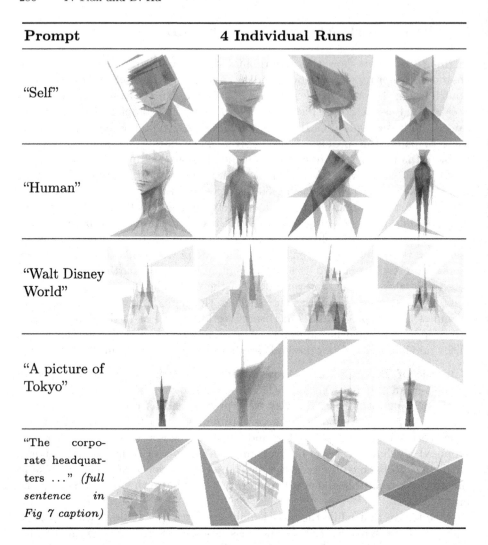

"Self"

"Human"

"Walt Disney World"

"A picture of Tokyo"

"The corporate headquarters ..." *(full sentence in Fig 7 caption)*

Fig. 9. Qualitative results from ES and CLIP fitting several text prompt with 50 triangles, each running for 2,000 steps. Results from four runs are shown.

"in the loop", not only poking around the text prompt but also picking the from multiple candidates produced by our method.

Comparison with Gradient-Based Optimization. With CLIP in mind, we are also interested in how our ES-based approach compares to the gradient-based optimization, especially since many existing works [7,12,49] have proposed to leverage CLIP to guide the generations using gradients. Arguably, this is a more challenging task due to the dynamic presented by two drastically different gradient dynamics by renderer and CLIP. Usually, to make such kind of combination work ideally, more studies are required, which warrant a manuscript

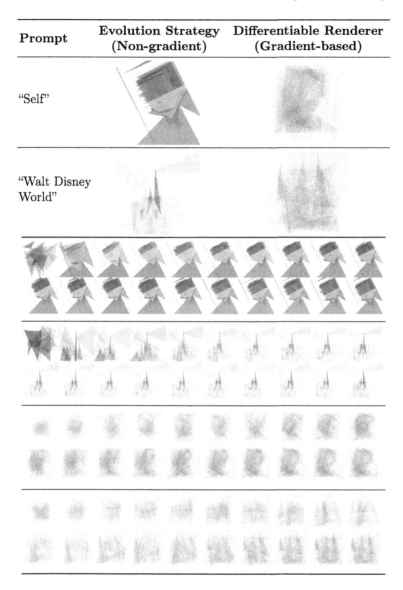

Fig. 10. Evolution Strategies (non-gradient method) v.s. Differentiable renderer (gradient-based method) with fitting text with CLIP. Both settings are fitting 200 triangles to the target prompts. The details of evolution process is shown in the bottom half, where the upper group is for evolution strategy and the lower group is for differtiable renderer.

itself like [7,12]. Nonetheless, we have made a reasonably working version for comparison. Like fitting a target image, we implement the rendering process of composing triangles using nvdiffrast [27]. In the forward pass, we render the canvas from parameters, feed the canvas to CLIP image encoder, and use Cosine distance between encoded image and encoded text prompt as a loss. Then we back-propagate all the way til the parameters of triangles to allow gradient-based optimization. We use the same processing as mentioned in Sect. 3.

As shown in Fig. 10, while both our ES method and the differentiable method produce images that are aligned with human interpretation of the text prompt, ours produces more clear abstraction and clear boundaries between shapes and objects. More interestingly, since ours represents an art style closely resembling abstract expressionism art, the difference between ours and the differentiable rendered is similar to that between post-impressionism and impressionism, where bolder geometric forms and colors are used. Like the counterpart comparison in fitting a concrete image, we argue that such results are intrinsically rooted in the optimization mechanism, and our proposed method leads to a unique art style through our design choices.

6   Discussion and Conclusion

In this work, we revisit evolutionary algorithms for computational creativity by proposing to combine modern evolution strategies (ES) algorithms with the drawing primitives of triangles inspired by the minimalism art style. Our proposed method offers considerable improvements in both quality and efficiency compared to traditional genetic algorithms and is comparable to gradient-based methods. Furthermore, we demonstrate that the ES algorithm could produce diverse, distinct geometric abstractions aligned with human interpretation of language and images. Our finds suggests that ES method produce very different and sometimes better results compared to gradient based methods, arguably due to the intrinsical behavior of the optimization mechanism. However it remains an open problem to understand how in general setting ES method compares with gradient methods. We expect future works investigate further into broader spectrum of art forms beyond the minimalism explored here.

Our dealing with evolutionary algorithms provides an insight into a different paradigm that can be applied to computational creativity. Widely adopted gradient-based methods are fine-tuned for specific domains, i.e., diff rendering for edges, parameterized shapes, or data-driven techniques for rendering better textures. Each of the applications requires tunes and tweaks that are domain-specific and are hard to transfer. In contrast, ES is agnostic to the domain, i.e., how the renderer works. We envision that ES-inspired approaches can potentially unify various domains with significantly less effort for adaption in the future.

Acknowledgements. We thank Toru Lin, Jerry Li, Yujin Tang, Yanghua Jin, Jesse Engel, Yifu Zhao for their comments, suggestions and kind helps.

References

1. Alteredqualia. Evolution of mona lisa in javascript and canvas (2008). https:// alteredqualia.com/visualization/evolve/. Accessed 1 Dec 2021

2. Bertoni, F.: Minimalist architecture. Birkhäuser (2002)
3. Beyer, H.G.: The Theory of Evolution Strategies. Springer, Heidelberg (2001). https://doi.org/10.1007/978-3-662-04378-3
4. Beyer, H.G., Schwefel, H.P.: Evolution strategies-a comprehensive introduction. Nat. Comput. **1**(1), 3–52 (2002)
5. Cason, K.: Genetic Draw (2016). https://github.com/kennycason/genetic_draw. Accessed 1 Dec 2021
6. Commons, W.: File:040 okertalsperre.jpg – wikimedia commons the free media repository (2020). https://commons.wikimedia.org/w/index.php?title=File:040_Okertalsperre.jpg&oldid=496749636. Accessed 1 Dec 2021
7. Crowson, K.: Introduction to vqgan+clip (2021). https://docs.google.com/document/d/1Lu7XPRKlNhBQjcKr8k8qRzUzbBW7kzxb5Vu72GMRn2E/edit. Accessed 1 Dec 2021
8. Dabrowski, M.: Geometric abstraction (2004). https://www.metmuseum.org/toah/hd/geab/hd_geab.htm. Accessed 1 Dec 2021
9. Fernando, C.: Royal academy summer exhibition 2021 submission (2021). https://www.chrisantha.co.uk/post/royal-academy-summer-exhibition-2021-submission. Accessed 1 Dec 2021
10. Fernando, C., Eslami, S., Alayrac, J.B., Mirowski, P., Banarse, D., Osindero, S.: Generative art using neural visual grammars and dual encoders. arXiv preprint arXiv:2105.00162 (2021)
11. Fogleman, M.: Primitive pictures (2016). https://github.com/fogleman/primitive. Accessed 1 Dec 2021
12. Frans, K., Soros, L., Witkowski, O.: Clipdraw: exploring text-to-drawing synthesis through language-image encoders. arXiv preprint arXiv:2106.14843 (2021)
13. Galatolo, F.A., Cimino, M.G., Vaglini, G.: Generating images from caption and vice versa via clip-guided generative latent space search. arXiv preprint arXiv:2102.01645 (2021)
14. Gonsalves, R.A.: Ganscapes: using AI to create new impressionist paintings (2021). https://towardsdatascience.com/ganscapes-using-ai-to-create-new-impressionist-paintings-d6af1cf94c56. Accessed 1 Dec 2021
15. Ha, D.: Evolving stable strategies. blog.otoro.net (2017). http://blog.otoro.net/2017/11/12/evolving-stable-strategies/. Accessed 1 Dec 2021
16. Ha, D., Eck, D.: A neural representation of sketch drawings. arXiv preprint arXiv:1704.03477 (2017)
17. Harvey, I.: The microbial genetic algorithm. In: Kampis, G., Karsai, I., Szathmáry, E. (eds.) ECAL 2009. LNCS (LNAI), vol. 5778, pp. 126–133. Springer, Heidelberg (2011). https://doi.org/10.1007/978-3-642-21314-4_16
18. Hochreiter, S., Schmidhuber, J.: Long short-term memory. Neural Comput. **9**(8), 1735–1780 (1997)
19. Huang, F., Schoop, E., Ha, D., Canny, J.: Scones: towards conversational authoring of sketches. In: Proceedings of the 25th International Conference on Intelligent User Interfaces, pp. 313–323 (2020)
20. Huang, Z., Heng, W., Zhou, S.: Learning to paint with model-based deep reinforcement learning. In: Proceedings of the IEEE/CVF International Conference on Computer Vision, pp. 8709–8718 (2019)
21. Jia, C., et al.: Scaling up visual and vision-language representation learning with noisy text supervision. In: International Conference on Machine Learning, pp. 4904–4916. PMLR (2021)

22. Johansson, R.: Genetic programming: evolution of mona lisa (2008). https://rogerjohansson.blog/2008/12/07/genetic-programming-evolution-of-mona-lisa/. Accessed 1 Dec 2021

23. Kato, H., et al.: Differentiable rendering: a survey. arXiv preprint arXiv:2006.12057 (2020)

24. Kingma, D.P., Ba, J.: Adam: a method for stochastic optimization. arXiv preprint arXiv:1412.6980 (2014)

25. Kolmogorov, A.: Three approaches to the quantitative definition of information. Probl. Inf. Trans. **1**(1), 1–7 (1965)

26. Kuiper, K.: Modernism (2021). https://www.britannica.com/art/Modernism-art. Accessed 1 Dec 2021

27. Laine, S., Hellsten, J., Karras, T., Seol, Y., Lehtinen, J., Aila, T.: Modular primitives for high-performance differentiable rendering. ACM Trans. Graph. **39**(6), 1–14 (2020)

28. Li, T.M., Lukáč, M., Gharbi, M., Ragan-Kelley, J.: Differentiable vector graphics rasterization for editing and learning. ACM Trans. Graph. **39**(6), 1–15 (2020)

29. Lindenmayer, A.: Mathematical models for cellular interactions in development i. filaments with one-sided inputs. J. Theoretic. Biol. **18**(3), 280–299 (1968)

30. Liu, S., et al.: Paint transformer: feed forward neural painting with stroke prediction. In: Proceedings of the IEEE/CVF International Conference on Computer Vision, pp. 6598–6607 (2021)

31. Lopes, R.G., Ha, D., Eck, D., Shlens, J.: A learned representation for scalable vector graphics. In: Proceedings of the IEEE/CVF International Conference on Computer Vision, pp. 7930–7939 (2019)

32. Malkevitchn, J.: Mathematics and art (2003). https://www.ams.org/publicoutreach/feature-column/fcarc-art1. Accessed 1 Dec 2021

33. Mellor, J.F., et al.: Unsupervised doodling and painting with improved spiral. arXiv preprint arXiv:1910.01007 (2019)

34. Modern, T.: Minimalism (2018). https://www.tate.org.uk/art/art-terms/m/minimalism. Accessed 1 Dec 2021

35. Paauw, M., van den Berg, D.: Paintings, polygons and plant propagation. In: Ekárt, A., Liapis, A., Castro Pena, M. (eds.) EvoMUSART 2019. LNCS, vol. 11453, pp. 84–97. Springer, Cham (2019). https://doi.org/10.1007/978-3-030-16667-0_6

36. Paul, S.: Abstract expressionism (2004). https://www.metmuseum.org/toah/hd/abex/hd_abex.htm. Accessed 1 Dec 2021

37. Radford, A., et al.: Learning transferable visual models from natural language supervision. arXiv preprint arXiv:2103.00020 (2021)

38. Rewald, S.: Cubism. The Metropolitan Museum of Art (2014). https://www.metmuseum.org/toah/hd/cube/hd_cube.htm. Accessed 1 Dec 2021

39. Rose, B.: Abc art. Art Am. **53**(5), 57–69 (1965)

40. Salimans, T., Ho, J., Chen, X., Sidor, S., Sutskever, I.: Evolution strategies as a scalable alternative to reinforcement learning. arXiv preprint arXiv:1703.03864 (2017)

41. Schmidhuber, J.: Low-complexity art. Leonardo **30**(2), 97–103 (1997)

42. Sehnke, F., Osendorfer, C., Rückstieß, T., Graves, A., Peters, J., Schmidhuber, J.: Parameter-exploring policy gradients. Neural Netw. **23**(4), 551–559 (2010)

43. Shahrabi, S.: Procedural paintings with genetic evolution algorithm (2020). https://github.com/IRCSS/Procedural-painting. Accessed 1 Dec 2021

44. Sizigi Studios. Waifu labs (2019). https://waifulabs.com/. Accessed 1 Dec 2021

45. Tate. Process art (2021). https://www.tate.org.uk/art/art-terms/p/process-art. Accessed 1 Dec 2021

46. Toklu, N.E.: Pgpelib (2020). https://github.com/nnaisense/pgpelib. Accessed 1 Dec 2021
47. Toklu, N.E., Liskowski, P., Srivastava, R.K.: Clipup: a simple and powerful optimizer for distribution-based policy evolution. In: International Conference on Parallel Problem Solving from Nature, pp. 515–527. Springer (2020)
48. Verostko, R.: Algorithmic art (1994). http://www.verostko.com/algorithm.html. Accessed 1 Dec 2021
49. Wang, P.: Big sleep: a simple command line tool for text to image generation, using openai's clip and a biggan (2021). https://github.com/lucidrains/big-sleep. Accessed 1 Dec 2021
50. White, T.: Shared visual abstractions. arXiv preprint arXiv:1912.04217 (2019)

Co-creative Product Design with Interactive Evolutionary Algorithms: A Practice-Based Reflection

Severi Uusitalo[1]([✉])(ⁱᴰ), Anna Kantosalo[2,3](ⁱᴰ), Antti Salovaara[1](ⁱᴰ),
Tapio Takala[3](ⁱᴰ), and Christian Guckelsberger[3,4,5](ⁱᴰ)

[1] Department of Design, Aalto University, Espoo, Finland
`severi.uusitalo@aalto.fi`
[2] Department of Computer Science, University of Helsinki, Helsinki, Finland
[3] Department of Computer Science, Aalto University, Espoo, Finland
[4] School of Electronic Engineering and Computer Science,
Queen Mary University of London, London, UK
[5] Finnish Center for Artificial Intelligence, Helsinki, Finland

Abstract. Progress in AI has brought about new approaches for designing products via co-creative human–computer interaction. In architecture, interior design, and industrial design, computational methods such as evolutionary algorithms support the designer's creative process by revealing populations of generated design solutions in a parametric design space. However, the benefits and shortcomings of such algorithms for designers are not yet fully understood. This paper reports the in-depth, in-situ and longitudinal experiences of one industrial designer using an interactive evolutionary algorithm in a non-trivial creative product design task. Our study sheds light on the intricate interaction between algorithm, human designer and their environment. It identifies, amongst others, the algorithm's contributions to design inspiration and to overcoming fixation. We contribute concrete proposals for the future study of co-creative AI in design exploration and creative practice.

Keywords: Co-creativity · Interactive evolutionary algorithm · Introspection · Autoethnography · Longitudinal study · Design

1 Introduction

Although the potential of evolutionary algorithms has long been recognized in design [33], only during the last decade solutions have become sophisticated and flexible enough to find their way into commercial computer-aided design (CAD) software. Evolutionary algorithms have the capacity to transform CAD software from creativity support tools [7,14,44] to *co-creative* systems [21] capable of not only augmenting but also complementing the creativity of human designers [3].

When new tools and technologies for human–computer co-creativity are applied, designers' working methods are transformed. Evolutionary algorithms

© The Author(s), under exclusive license to Springer Nature Switzerland AG 2022
T. Martins et al. (Eds.): EvoMUSART 2022, LNCS 13221, pp. 292–307, 2022.
https://doi.org/10.1007/978-3-031-03789-4_19

are likely to induce profound shifts in the designers' process, creativity and experience of agency (e.g. [41]). One particular notable development are *interactive* evolutionary algorithms, which allow the designer to intervene in the optimization process by selecting the best performing candidates, thus implicitly injecting performance criteria that may be tedious, hard or impossible to formalize explicitly. However, interactive evolutionary algorithms are a rather recent addition to the commercial design practice. They are not yet provided as standard features in established design software, but have to be included through third party extensions. Moreover, they are rarely covered in contemporary design school curricula. Overall, we have little understanding of how existing interactive evolutionary algorithms can be incorporated into design practice, and, vice-versa, how design practice could inform algorithm development.

This paper addresses these shortcomings through a researcher introspection study of an industrial designer's use of an interactive evolutionary algorithm in a real-world creative design task. The analysis covers the first author's experiences from using a design software equipped with evolutionary design support software over a period of 11 weeks, during which they solved the design problem of creating a pendant lamp, with the aim of ultimately fabricating a physical prototype. As is typical of creative design processes, this work involved focus and incubation phases as well as high amounts of iteration and exploration.

Our contributions are threefold. Firstly, we support the adoption of interactive evolutionary algorithms in design practice by documenting an algorithm's use, benefits and shortcomings in a real-world design task. We particularly focus on the algorithms' ability to complement the designer's creativity and avoid fixation. Secondly, we inform the further development of these algorithms by computer science researchers to support future design practice. We particularly highlight opportunities for supporting the meta-evolution of parametric design definitions, and the effective visualization and manipulation of design instances. Thirdly, we shed light on how emerging work practices can be studied in-situ, as we see it necessary to establish a foundation for longitudinal studies on practice-based experiences of emerging CAD tools. In particular, we posit that, when humans are included in the loop, it is essential to investigate designers' experience of creativity within the design process on multiple time-scales.

2   Background

To ease the readers' understanding of the designer's actions in our longitudinal study, and how evolutionary algorithms can transform design, we highlight the most relevant features of design as a creative practice. We draw parallels between the conceptualisation of design practice and evolutionary algorithms, and particularly relate the dynamic construction of design spaces and the co-evolutionary construction of the problem and the solution within a design process.

The interaction of our designer with the evolutionary system is substantially guided by their *reflection* on the design. In his classic book on design theory, Schön [37] presents design as a practice where reflection has a prominent role both in-action, i.e. during the activity, as well as on-action, i.e. prior to, and after the activity. Reflection leads to what Schön describes as a "re-framing of the design problem" [37, pp. 94–95]. *Framing* here refers to the process in which a designer makes sense about the problem at hand, imposes their interpretation, and uses it to generate ideas for small design experiments to probe the value of possible trajectories towards more substantial solutions. Schön describes this method as "reflective conversation with the materials in a design situation" [38].

Through framing, the designer constructs a mental image of the design and solution spaces within which the desired design can be explored and identified [12]. Studies have revealed that the design space is not static, and that also the solution space may be re-framed based on insights gathered when trying to solve a specific problem. Consequently, the problem space and the solution space may co-evolve [9, 13]. In an evolutionary algorithm, re-framing the solution space corresponds to altering the objective function measuring the success of generated solutions. The typical design process thus encompasses more than the search for optimal solutions to a given and fixed problem and the traditional use of evolutionary algorithms for optimization captures only a part of the process.

The work of a designer can be considered as "satisficing" rather than optimizing [40]. Design spaces are vast and the amount of possible designs is substantial [45]. Also, design is often concerned with *wicked problems*, where intricate, sometimes contradictory systemic relationships render any solution sub-optimal or downright harmful in different situations or changing environments [35]. For example, industrial design requires trading-off product manufacturing efficiency, material characteristics, cost, human factors, sustainability concerns, aesthetic vision and styling trends, amongst others. These manifold requirements are typically very tedious, hard or impossible to formalize in the objective function of a standard evolutionary algorithm for the optimization of a design problem. Together with our observation in the previous paragraph, this renders the study of how designers can benefit from employing *interactive* evolutionary algorithms as co-creative partners in their practice particularly worthwhile.

3   Related Work

At present, evolutionary algorithms cannot substitute real-world human design practice. However, they allow designers to *articulate* (i.e., to spell out and arrange in a structured way, cf. [39]) and to *explore* the characteristics of problem and solution spaces. This can potentially counteract designers' fixation on a smaller set of possible solutions [29]. While evolutionary algorithms are popular in architecture, there are only few examples of real-world applications in product design. We survey related work to distinguish different types of such algorithms and to reveal a gap in the study of their application.

Industrial product design has prominently adopted *Genetic Algorithms*, e.g. to explore the design space of lamp holders [26]. A particular challenge has been to formalize subjective experiences such as human aesthetic preference in the GA's objective function. While there have been theory-inspired attempts to formalize aesthetics of e.g. product shapes [27], there is space for improvement. An alternative solution for dealing with such features that characterize *wicked problems* in design is to complement algorithmic selection via an explicitly stated objective function with human selection in *Interactive Genetic Algorithms* (IGAs).

IGAs have been leveraged in designing cameras [25], cars [8], fragrance bottles [22], wine glass profiles [42] and fashion [15,43], amongst others. Existing studies in this field focus on *only one use* of IGAs – to explore the design space (e.g. [1,2,24]). Moreover, they typically emphasize the system's architecture and implementation from the *perspective of its engineers*, but do not study how it is experienced by designers as their end-users. Existing work focuses on the use of IGAs in *only one or few stages* of product design, covering only a *short period* of time. It primarily covers the conceptual design stage (e.g. [8]) and rarely the early embodiment stage, where the structural and product architecture design establishes a myriad of opportunities and requirements for the following process. When optimization is the focus, these reports typically address the late detail design stage, focusing on e.g. finite element analysis. In the center is a design system of designer and their computer, trying to create an integrated design specification which addresses objectives, requirements, and limitations, considering the available resources and environment of the product [32].

Based on our analysis of related work, we attest a lack of first-hand, *longitudinal* studies of the *designer's experiences* in applying IGAs to *real world* industrial design problems *outside the lab*. However, only such studies can inform the (a) design of such algorithms and their (b) adoption by practitioners.

4 Design Study

We address this research gap with a longitudinal study of the designer's experiences when employing an IGA in an industrial product design task.

4.1 Design Task

We study the realistic, real-world task of designing a pendant lamp fixture. The fixture had to be made primarily of plywood, using manufacturing methods suitable for mass personalization. We note that this framing already constrains the design space substantially. In interior design, a pendant lamp fixture is functionally a rather mature basic concept. One typically has a fixture of one or more light sources, like bulbs, hanging from the ceiling from electrical wire or supports, and a configuration of shades and reflectors attached to it. However, structurally, there are a wide variety of pendants, and a certain constant interest in the market for new designs. With these characteristics, the design of a pendant lamp provided an ecologically valid design problem for this design study.

4.2 Study Method

We chose to perform a *researcher introspection* study within the *Research through Design* (RtD) framework. Evolving from design-oriented Human–Computer

Interaction research, RtD focuses on building knowledge through design practice [47]. It shares characteristics with what Koskinen and Krogh consider *constructive design research* [23], which tackles design problems with design-specific means, producing design outcomes. The main accountability is directed towards design practice, rather than other fields. Efforts to develop a more rigorous theoretical basis for RtD and design research are underway (e.g., [20,30]).

In the past, think-aloud protocol studies have been particularly popular in studying the design process and creativity within [13]. Crucially, this method assumes a split between the researcher and the designer subject. While this allows for reflection-in-action within one phase of the design process and on toy problems, the impossibility for the researcher to accompany the designer for a prolonged period renders the think-aloud method unsuitable for longitudinal, reflection-in-action studies on real-world design problems.

We instead leverage *researcher introspection*, a family of methods through which the researcher investigates their ongoing self-experiences as the primary means to generating knowledge. Xue et al. [46] particularly promote this as a means for Human-Computer Interaction researchers to access insider experiences in a specific domain. For this study, we chose to perform *researcher introspection* through *autoethnography*, a method that joins autobiographic with ethnographic principles, inquiring into cultural phenomena (such as design) through self-observation and reflexive investigation [28]. The subject in our study conducted autoethnography based on 1) screenshots from the software, containing interim genotype versions and phenotypes developed within by an evolutionary algorithm, and 2) text notes during and right after each design session. The use of text notes, e.g. in the form of diary entries, has been recommended by other design researchers (e.g. [31,46]). Hence, our study relies on both concurrent and retrospective introspections, with an emphasis on retrospection.

Crucially, this study design serves our goal to *exploring* areas of future study, rather than identifying generalisable conclusions on a specific question. We describe the next steps required to further the latter goal in our discussion section.

4.3   Participant: The Designer

Our researcher introspection through autoethnography is done by the first author who is both, a designer and a researcher. The remaining paper and in particular the later discussion of the study findings has been shaped by all authors. The designer has ten years of industry experience as a consulting and in-house industrial designer in Europe and the US. They moreover have gathered experience in human-centred design research for eight years. The designer's expertise in surface and parametric solid CAD is on an expert level, based on consulting work as a surface modeler in the car industry, and as an industrial designer in the occupational protective equipment industry. They can be considered an advanced user of the software employed in our study, but not an expert. The designer has been teaching different CAD tools in design universities part- and full-time.

4.4   Software Tools and Algorithm

One of our primary goals is to foster the adoption of IGAs in industrial product design. To this end, we must enable other designers to apply our insights to their own practice, in the spirit of constructive design research [23]. We consequently leverage a set of readily available software tools that are popular in design.

The designer's co-creative partner in our case study consists of multiple components. *Grasshopper* [16] is a visual programming extension for the 3D modeling system *Rhinoceros 3D* [34], enabling the creation of parametric definitions of shapes. The definition is constructed by connecting parametrized nodes into a directed acyclic graph, with nodes representing shape grammar rules. The freely available add-on *Biomorpher* [18] provides an IGA to optimize these parameters (Fig. 1). To this end, *Biomorpher* encodes all parameters in a normalized real number genotype vector. It provides a user interface for manipulating the algorithm's initial parameters such as mutation rate, population size, and single-point crossover. The interface moreover facilitates the evaluation and selection of design candidates that were worth of retention and further evolution.

Generative design algorithms in general can effortlessly produce innumerable design candidates. However, their review and the selection of the best candidates for further development can become an overwhelming task [15]. *Biomorpher* counteracts user-fatigue by leveraging a *Cluster-Orientated Genetic Algorithm* (COGA) [6]. Here, k-means clustering is applied to the whole population, and only twelve instance if the clusters' centroids are presented to the designer for review along with additional information such as the number of other, hidden instances in the cluster. These clusters bear similarity with Krish's *represented regions* of the solution space [24], where different designs assume different locations in a multi-dimensional space of quality characteristics. The designer can optionally complement their selection of design candidates to evolve further by specifying objective performance criteria – corresponding to the objective function in standard evolutionary algorithms. All user-selected candidates are assigned a maximum fitness of 1.0. If optional, objective performance criteria have been specified, they are transformed and equally weighted in a single fitness value and applied to all candidates that have not yet been selected by the user. When creating a new population from the fittest individuals, *Biomorpher* records the previous population in a history. This allows the user to return to previous generations if evolution leads to an undesired part of the design space. Once the designer has terminated the process, they can use the 3D geometry of an instance in further design or fabrication. Figure 1 documents *Biomorpher's* operation and interaction with the designer. Further technical details can be found in [18].

4.5   Findings: Introspective Design Reflections

The following experiential account of using the above-introduced IGA software is written in the first person singular, emphasizing the reflections of the designer. The project was not commissioned and had no significant time pressure, but was of personal interest with the aim to inspire some prototyping later.

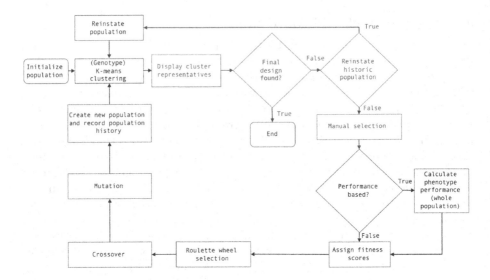

Fig. 1. The *Biomorpher* process with human interaction stages in red. Figure adopted and extended from Harding and Brandt-Olsen [18]. (Color figure online)

Aesthetic Objectives. The pendant would need to be rather large: the actual interior I had in mind was 9 by 5 m, with a ceiling that is 5 m high on average, in a lakeside cabin with a contemporary ethos. The particular harsh northern lakeside locale of the interior for some reason took my mind to the northern Atlantic coast. The initial conceptual ideas for the design borrowed from the aesthetics of aviation, of the wing foil and truss structures of aeroplanes. Another design cue was a whale, even a carcass of a whale with the rib-cage showing as mere bones. Vaguely linked to this was an Inuit kayak, as reflections of some old films of Inuits occasionally flashed in my mind during the intentionally low-key incubation process. The cues were not particularly vivid, and I intended maintaining pure conceptuality in them, wanting to avoid the direct reproduction of any particular artefact.

I made no visual searches from e.g. the Internet for images at the early stage of design, as this might have led to constraining mental imagery of the constructions, at what I saw was a very sensitive phase of the design process. My objective was to channel the experience of the people enjoying the interior with subtle visual cues, leading to interpretations stemming from their personal experience. I deemed that the artefact should raise questions, not be a model of something existing. The success of the design intent of the pendant depends on these multi-interpretive semantics.

The initial design space was not informed by visual cues and form semantics; materials and manufacturing technology often constrain the design space significantly. In a product architecture as in the present case, visual and different structural functions cannot be separated. For me, this was a rather special product, as functional requirements were somewhat secondary to aesthetics and personal motivations played a role.

I contemplated plywood as the material and considered its affordances for design. It can be bent, but not in two ways simultaneously. Thin (less than 1mm) sheets can let through some light. The material is lightweight, hydrostable enough for this use, relatively inexpensive, long lasting, easily and safely disposable, and rather sustainable from a manufacturing point of view. Cutting it accurately from a sheet is easy e.g. by laser cutting. Assembly can then be done either without separate fittings or with simple ones if needed. Visually, the material suits many environments. Even high quality plywood is available locally.

Definition and Genotype from Conceptual Cues. I used the IGA in the fixture design from January to early March 2021, as a low intensity process with often days in between consecutive sessions. The above-presented initial design cues, aesthetic considerations and the material selection had limited the concept to a point where I could proceed with the embodiment design [19], and I hence developed the initial parametrization of the model. My objectives for the grammar and its genes were to 1) create valid geometry, 2) enable easy growth of the design space, and 3) follow the capabilities and limitations of the material on one hand, and support manufacturing and assembly opportunities on the other.

While I had the aforementioned cabin interior as an environment cue, I was not primarily focusing on delivering a single design. Instead, my objective was a robust parametric representation and genotype, capable of covering a sufficiently large design space to enable mass personalization. This requires the co-creative system to seamlessly fit into the later stage of detail design [19], as it would be inconvenient to manually finalize the individual phenotypes for production.

I therefore planned to extend the system to generate the routing for laser cutting the parts and stacking the cutting paths space-efficiently on raw sheets. This would enable the generation of ready-to-manufacture individual variants. That effort is not part of this report, however, as the process reported here covers only the parts that related to the co-creative design with the IGA in *Biomorpher*.

I generated the initial populations during the first design session with the computer, after parametrizing the design and setting up the initial gene configuration. This led me to an iterative process with the IGA, where, after I had created a few generations from one parametric definition, I collected insights to re-frame the problem. Once they had served their purpose in assisting this re-framing, I discarded the generated populations. The insights led me to either add more features to the grammar, and to change the gene value domain limits.

I enjoyed exploring the design space by having the IGA generate populations even without clear objectives. I paid notice to unexpected versions and details, while the initially very limited solution space motivated me to grow the variety the system is capable to produce. The visual representations and ability to both manipulate and render them at different degrees of fidelity on screen were imperative for assessment, and for making decisions for future changes to the

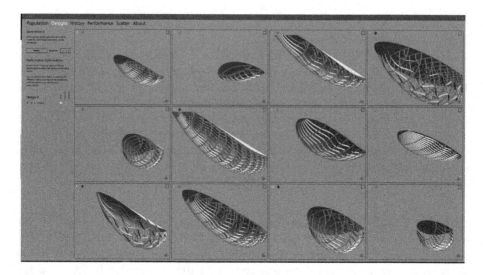

Fig. 2. *Biomorpher's* selection view, showing 12 samples from a generation of 48 instances as centroids resulting from k-means clustering. Screenshot taken and used with permission from the authors [18].

definition. In the majority of cases, the visualization provided by the *Biomorpher* user interface was sufficient (Fig. 2).

It took me three consecutive evenings to create the basic parametric definition through the described process. After this sprint, the further development of the design took place in individual sessions with multiple days in between. In these sessions, I generated some populations, but did not make changes to the parametric definition. This was an inspiring stage as it allowed me to explore variations to my primary design. At the same time, finding the boundaries of the current solution space increased my motivation to apply changes.

A Period of Botched Efforts. On the experiment's third week, after the five separate design sessions (of 2–4 h each) described above, I created a new definition with a wider design space from scratch. Unfortunately, I had to discard it after a few hours, as it revealed a critical mistake with regard to the objective constraints of the materials: the new approach created double-curvatures, a geometry which plywood does not allow for. The resulting instances were thus beyond the viable design space. I back-pedaled to the old version, and re-factored it to increase its capability to produce variations, and robustness. I was aware of the constraints stipulated by material choices, but this time I had forgotten why I had done the initial parametric definition the way I had. Showing the respective state of the working evolution to three peers in separate occasions led to a demotivating response, as they did not see anything particularly creative in the output. This was disappointing, leading to pressure to pursue more novel output. However, this was out of reach due to time resources available for the project.

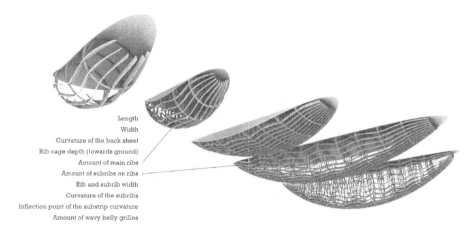

Length
Width
Curvature of the back sheet
Rib cage depth (towards ground)
Amount of main ribs
Amount of subribs on ribs
Rib and subrib width
Curvature of the subribs
Inflection point of the substrip curvature
Amount of wavy belly grilles

Fig. 3. Some generated instances. The genes guiding the generation are listed.

Inspiration from the Wild. I added longitudinal ribs to the bottom of the form late in the process, only during the sixth and after nine separate design sessions in total. I noticed some resemblance with a whale's chest-skin corrugations but the insight did not lead to action until a few days later when I was watching a TV-program of actual whales swimming under water. It led me to add wave-form to the geometry (Fig. 3). The IGA proved valuable in the process of finding a suitable range for the genes that would define the wave-form. I had been concerned about the lighting experience, i.e. shading the bulbs of the fixture. While this visual cue towards the whale was welcome in aligning with one of the initial aesthetic cues, the lighting-study renderings with selected phenotypes proved a visually intriguing shading performance which aligned well with the affordances of plywood.

Specifying Objective Performance Criteria. Having reached this far, I introduced the laser cutting length as an objective performance criterion to be minimized. The definition evolved as the material and other requirements and the geometrical opportunities and constraints were considered and revealed during the process, as a result of repeated cycles of population generation, and subsequent definition development. In the resulting definition and genotype, the genes of the grammar control the length, width, and height of the pendant. Other genes control the amount and curvature of various ribs in the structure, and the final ones the longitudinal, wavy grilles. Figure 3 illustrates the genes on example solutions, i.e., the design outcomes generated by the final algorithmic definition.

5   Discussion

In the following, the team of authors summarizes their collective reflections on the nature of the reported design process, on the co-creative relationship between the designer and the IGA, and on the study's limitations.

Our researcher introspection through autoethnography study revealed that the IGA performed several roles in the design process. It helped the designer to articulate the design space and thereby also to understand its boundaries. It also helped to visualize and conceptualize the landscape of possibilities in that space. The designer also used the IGA as a pathfinder whereby they could take a passive role and let the IGA offer its suggestions, which then could be turned down or picked up for further exploration. Finally, the IGA helped the designer to visualize and fine-tune their vision of the final design. These roles invite the following further considerations on designer–IGA co-creation.

5.1   Early Constraining of the Design Space

The designer defined the initial objectives by having particular visual cues (e.g., aviation aesthetics) about the design direction. In this sense, the design process seems to have been informed by a *primary generator* [11], i.e., by a promising conjecture that designers have often been noted to use as a basis for their design. The designer did not use the typical method of collecting visual material to generate or develop these primary generators, but instead developed a parametric definition and the ensuing population generations. Only then they searched for visual images of the design cues. In their diary notes, the designer mentioned a concern that actual images would be constrictive. Because of this, they found it beneficial to use the IGA in creating further aesthetic direction. This observation supports the use of IGAs as partners to help fulfilling and redefining designer visions (or, primary generators).

5.2   Support in Problem–Solution Co-evolution

The design process took place over 11 weeks, with intermittent bursts of activity, typically of two to three evenings each, with some days of non-activity in between. The initial parametric definitions took only a few hours to develop, after which the designer utilized the IGA for the population generation and evolution. The process of developing some populations and after that again returning to develop the definition further, or to correct the gene scales thus affecting the design space constraints, resembles the problem–solution co-evolution that e.g. Bernal et al. [4] have written about. They note that "although it is an approximation to the co-evolving dialog between problem and solution that characterizes expert designers, it lacks reformulation mechanisms" [4]. Because collaboration with an IGA naturally shapes a design process towards this direction, IGAs may help some of the designers' processes gain more expert characteristics.

Using an IGA in the design process also had another beneficial impact: the design space was *informed* and *filtered* [17] by the constant process of population generation and the ensuing editing of the genotypic representation. By filtering the design space, the IGA exposed areas of inquiry and thus motivated the designer to redefine the constraints of the space. It thus realized a different role than merely serving as a meta-heuristics to find unexpected but iteratively optimized solutions to quantifiable problems. Here, in contrast, the IGA was helpful in redefining the problems themselves in addition to offering solutions.

5.3   Escaping and Falling in a Fixation Trap

As presented above, genetic algorithms offer a possibility for their users (e.g., designers) to notice unexpected, serendipitous solutions to problems. This was observed several times also in our case study, as the introspective report attested. However, in hindsight, we also identified three "modes" through which the interaction with IGAs has negatively impacted the design process. These modes have been coined by Robertson and Radcliffe in CAD more generally [36].

Firstly, a form of *bounded ideation* shows in the session where the designer started creating an alternative genotype from scratch, but later recognized the solution to be outside the limits of the planned fabrication possibilities. This can be considered a novice mistake; expert designers intuitively recognize the many constraints and frame their problem accordingly [10]. Here the designer had attended to the constraints initially, but became captivated and immersed by the engaging computational design task of defining a parametrization with a large enough solution space so that they forgot a fundamental constraint.

Secondly, while the initial reason for devising a new genotype was to open up new lanes of inquiry to the design space in order to avoid *premature fixation* [36] to the initial genotypic representation, the designer became distracted from the actual creative tasks due to being immersed in interacting with the software. Combined with time constraints, the designer returned to the older version of the genotypic representation, rather than creating a new one. This fits premature fixation, i.e. exactly the mode which the designer aimed to avoid.

Thirdly, *circumscribed thinking* [36] might also be present in the observed process, although this is harder to confirm. All possible ways of using *Grasshopper* considered (including plugins), the designer, based on their prior experience, chose to approach the design task primarily through parametric solid modelling. This previous experience circumscribed their thinking, potentially resulting in missed opportunities to develop a genotype for a wider design space exploration.

Thus, while the general benefits of genetic algorithms lie in their capacity to generate unexpected, seemingly creative, design solutions, they may also limit the designer's field of vision, make them complacent and inattentive to biases, and lead them to suboptimal working practices.

5.4   The IGA as Creative Partner

Traditional tools in product design – pen and paper, graphics and CAD software – operate deterministically and can therefore be mastered with high precision and virtuosity. However, they do not produce *unexpected novelty* and *value*, the key characteristics of creativity [5]. IGAs in contrast realize unexpectedness in their output through randomness, and value through selection based on their objective function. This is why we consider them *partners* in co-creative interaction.

In order for the IGA to work as creative partner, the algorithm must encode some of the human designer's knowledge of the design space. The success in making the IGA reach the necessary level of expertise depends on the designer's ability to encode the design space in a creativity-conducive manner. This succeeded in the present study, but we do not consider it universally achievable. Being a rather new addition to designers' toolboxes, IGAs will probably undergo a significant amount of experimentation in design communities before the best practices of representing design spaces will be discovered.

Our study has uncovered several additional areas to improve this creative partnership, particularly related to avoiding fixation modes, supporting design co-evolution, and inspiring designers e.g. through visualization. We believe that this can foster the successful adaptation of IGAs in co-creative design.

5.5 Study Limitations

Our study only reports the experiences of a single designer and design case. We deem this method particularly useful for tool creators to explore a tool's use, and how it is experienced, in practice and to highlight areas for further study. However, to identify generalising conclusions, the present approach must be extended to multiple, diverse participants and cases.

In our study, the researcher was part of the experiment. While separating the designer-participant and the researcher would have alleviated the risk of bias, it would also have removed the researcher from the experience. In future studies, it would be sensible to mix designers who also act as researchers with independent participants to reduce bias while still offering some researcher introspection.

A further limitation is the low documentation of reflection in action, and how it is collected. Most notes and insights were retrospective reflections on the activities, even if done just shortly after the design session. A think-aloud method with a simultaneous screen-capture of the software could have led to different and a larger number of insights. However, such a method would need to deal with a large volume of data, given the project's length that may cover several weeks and involve incubation periods during which insights may also develop.

Furthermore, such data collection could also pose validity threats to the study at inopportune moments. For instance, as things get interesting and a certain flow state is achieved, note-taking may inhibit the flow [31].

To circumvent the problems listed above on note-taking granularity and the validity of introspections, we used a secondary round of *reflection on action* [37] while preparing this article as well as when framing the collected diary notes against design literature. Additional in-situ documentation methods, such as video-recording of the activities and subsequent analysis, would provide higher fidelity in the results. We intend to implement these improvements in future work, as discussed in the next section.

6   Conclusion and Future Work

We employed a researcher introspection through autoethnography study to provide insights into a designer's use of an interactive evolutionary algorithm in a real-world design task. Through this endeavor, we contribute methodology and practical insights to the emerging body of research on how AI impacts the experience, and perceived agency, of product design practitioners.

We have reflected our findings against theory from design research, and computational design. We found that the relative ease of applying interactive evolutionary algorithms to support design space articulation and exploration improved the designer's capabilities, and provided alternative paths in the design process. On the contrary, we also revealed how the use of such algorithms can negatively impact design practice, e.g. by fostering bounded ideation, as a first step towards avoiding these pitfalls by informing appropriate use or changes to the software.

In future work, we want to provide further, generalising and actionable insights on how AI algorithms can augment and complement human creativity in design practice. To this end, we aim to conduct a larger longitudinal, protocol study which overcomes the shortcomings of the present study through, amongst others, expanded in-action reflection by multiple designers.

Acknowledgments. Many thanks to our anonymous reviewers for their extremely valuable feedback and suggestions for future work. AK has been funded by the Academy of Finland (through grants no. 311090 "Digital Aura" and no. 328729) and TT has been funded by the Academy of Finland (grant no. 311090 "Digital Aura"). CG is funded by the Academy of Finland Flagship programme *Finnish Center for Artificial Intelligence* (FCAI).

References

1. Alcaide-Marzal, J., Diego-Mas, J.A., Acosta-Zazueta, G.: A 3D shape generative method for aesthetic product design. Design Stud. **66**, 144–176 (2019)
2. Ang, M.C., Chau, H.H., McKay, A., De Pennington, A.: Combining evolutionary algorithms and shape grammars to generate branded product design. In: Proceedings of the Design Computing and Cognition, pp. 521–539 (2006)
3. Banerjee, A., Quiroz, J.C., Louis, S.: A model of creative design using collaborative interactive genetic algorithms. In: Proceedings of the Design Computing and Cognition, pp. 397–416 (2008)
4. Bernal, M., Haymaker, J.R., Eastman, C.: On the role of computational support for designers in action. Design Stud. **41**, 163–182 (2015)
5. Boden, M.A.: Creative Mind: Myths and Mechanisms, 2 edn. Routledge (2004)
6. Bonham, C.R., Parmee, I.C.: An investigation of exploration and exploitation within cluster oriented genetic algorithms (COGAs). In: Proceedings of the Conference on Genetic and Evolutionary Computation, pp. 1491–1497 (1999)
7. Chang, Y.S., Chien, Y.H., Lin, H.C., Chen, M.Y., Hsieh, H.H.: Effects of 3D CAD applications on the design creativity of students with different representational abilities. Comput. Hum. Behav. **65**, 107–113 (2016)

8. Cluzel, F., Yannou, B., Dihlmann, M.: Using evolutionary design to interactively sketch car silhouettes and stimulate designer's creativity. Eng. Appl. Artif. Intell. **25**(7), 1413–1424 (2012)

9. Crilly, N.: The evolution of "co-evolution" (Part I): problem solving, problem finding, and their interaction in design and other creative practices. She Ji: J. Design Econ. Innov. **7**(3), 309–332 (2021)

10. Dabbeeru, M.M., Mukerjee, A.: Discovering implicit constraints in design. In: Proceedings of the Design Computing and Cognition, pp. 201–220 (2008)

11. Darke, J.: The primary generator and the design process. Design Stud. **1**(1), 36–44 (1979)

12. Dorst, K.: The core of 'design thinking' and its application. Design Stud. **32**(6), 521–532 (2011)

13. Dorst, K., Cross, N.: Creativity in the design process: co-evolution of problem-solution. Design Stud. **22**(5), 425–437 (2001)

14. Frich, J., MacDonald Vermeulen, L., Remy, C., Biskjaer, M.M., Dalsgaard, P.: Mapping the landscape of creativity support tools in HCI. In: Proceedings of the Conference on Human Factors in Computing Systems, pp. 1–18 (2019)

15. Gong, D.W., Hao, G.S., Zhou, Y., Sun, X.Y.: Interactive genetic algorithms with multi-population adaptive hierarchy and their application in fashion design. Appl. Math. Comput. **185**(2), 1098–1108 (2007)

16. Grasshopper. https://www.grasshopper3d.com/. Accessed 22 Mar 2021

17. Halskov, K., Lundqvist, C.: Filtering and informing the design space: towards design-space thinking. ACM Trans. Comput. Hum. Interact. **28**(1), 1–28 (2021)

18. Harding, J., Brandt-Olsen, C.: Biomorpher: interactive evolution for parametric design. Int. J. Architect. Comput. **16**(2), 144–163 (2018)

19. Howard, T.J., Culley, S.J., Dekoninck, E.: Describing the creative design process by the integration of engineering design and cognitive psychology literature. Design Stud. **29**(2), 160–180 (2008)

20. Isley, C.G., Rider, T.: Research-through-design: exploring a design-based research paradigm through its ontology, epistemology, and methodology. In: Proceedings of the Design as a Catalyst for Change - DRS International Conference, pp. 358–368 (2018)

21. Kantosalo, A., Toivonen, H.: Modes for creative human-computer collaboration: alternating and task-divided co-creativity. In: Proceedings of the International Conference on Computational Creativity, pp. 77–84 (2016)

22. Kielarova, S.W., Sansri, S.: Shape optimization in product design using interactive genetic algorithm integrated with multi-objective optimization. In: Proceedings of the International Workshop on Multi-disciplinary Trends in Artificial Intelligence, pp. 76–86 (2016)

23. Koskinen, I., Krogh, P.G.: Design accountability: when design research entangles theory and practice. Int. J. Design **9**(1), 121–127 (2015)

24. Krish, S.: A practical generative design method. Comput. Aided Design Appl. **43**(1), 88–100 (2011)

25. Lee, H.C., Tang, M.X.: Generating stylistically consistent product form designs using interactive evolutionary parametric shape grammars. In: Proceedings of the International Conference on Computer-Aided Industrial Design and Conceptual Design (2006)

26. Liu, H., Tang, M., Frazer, J.H.: Supporting creative design in a visual evolutionary computing environment. Adv. Eng. Softw. **35**(5), 261–271 (2004)

27. Lo, C.H., Ko, Y.C., Hsiao, S.W.: A study that applies aesthetic theory and genetic algorithms to product form optimization. Adv. Eng. Inf. **29**(3), 662–679 (2015)

28. Maréchal, G.: Autoethnography. In: Mills, A.J., Durepos, G., Wiebe, E. (eds.) Encyclopedia of Case Study Research, pp. 34–45. Sage (2010)
29. Mitchell, W.J.: Constructing complexity. In: Martens, B., Brown, A. (eds.) Proceedings of the International Computer Aided Architectural Design Futures Conference, pp. 41–50 (2005)
30. Murphy, P.: Design research: aesthetic epistemology and explanatory knowledge. She Ji: J. Design Econ. Innov. 3(2), 117–132 (2017)
31. Pedgley, O.: Capturing and analysing own design activity. Design Stud. 28(5), 463–483 (2007)
32. Ralph, P., Wand, Y.: A proposal for a formal definition of the design concept. In: Lyytinen, K., Loucopoulos, P., Mylopoulos, J., Robinson, B. (eds.) Design Requirements Engineering: A Ten-Year Perspective. LNBIP, vol. 14, pp. 103–136. Springer, Heidelberg (2009). https://doi.org/10.1007/978-3-540-92966-6_6
33. Renner, G., Ekárt, A.: Genetic algorithms in computer aided-design. Comput. Aided Design Appl. 35(8), 709–726 (2003)
34. Rhinoceros3D. www.rhino3d.com. Accessed 22 Mar 2021
35. Rittel, H.W., Webber, M.M.: Dilemmas in a general theory of planning. Policy Sci. 4(2), 155–169 (1973)
36. Robertson, B.F., Radcliffe, D.F.: Impact of CAD tools on creative problem solving in engineering design. Comput. Aided Design Appl. 41(3), 136–146 (2009)
37. Schön, D.A.: Reflective Practitioner. Basic Books, New York (1983)
38. Schön, D.A.: Designing as a reflective conversation with the materials of a design situation. Knowl. Based Syst. 5(1), 3–14 (1992)
39. Sharrock, W., Anderson, B.: Organizational innovation and the articulation of the design space. In: Moran, T.P., Carroll, J.M. (eds.) Design Rationale, chap. 15, pp. 429–451. CRC Press (1996)
40. Simon, H.A.: The Sciences of the Artificial. MIT Press (1969)
41. Singh, D., Rajcic, N., Colton, S., McCormack, J.: Camera obscurer: generative art for design inspiration. In: Ekárt, A., Liapis, A., Castro Pena, M.L. (eds.) EvoMUSART 2019. LNCS, vol. 11453, pp. 51–68. Springer, Cham (2019). https://doi.org/10.1007/978-3-030-16667-0_4
42. Su, J., Zhang, S.: Research on product shape innovation design method with human-computer interaction through genetic algorithm. In: Proceedings of the International Conference Computer-Aided Industrial Design & Conceptual Design, pp. 301–305 (2010)
43. Tabatabaei Anaraki, N.A.: Fashion design aid system with application of interactive genetic algorithms. In: Correia, J., Ciesielski, V., Liapis, A. (eds.) EvoMUSART 2017. LNCS, vol. 10198, pp. 289–303. Springer, Cham (2017). https://doi.org/10.1007/978-3-319-55750-2_20
44. Wang, Y., Ma, H.S., Yang, J.H., Wang, K.S.: Industry 4.0: a way from mass customization to mass personalization production. Adv. Manuf. 5(4), 311–320 (2017)
45. Woodbury, R.F., Burrow, A.L.: Whither design space? Artif. Intell. Eng. Design Anal. Manuf. 20(2), 63–82 (2006)
46. Xue, H., Desmet, P.M.A.: Researcher introspection for experience-driven design research. Design Stud. 63, 37–64 (2019)
47. Zimmerman, J., Forlizzi, J., Evenson, S.: Research through design as a method for interaction design research in HCI. In: Proceedings of the Conference on Human Factors in Computing Systems, pp. 493–502 (2007)

Sound Model Factory: An Integrated System Architecture for Generative Audio Modelling

Lonce Wyse[✉] [ID], Purnima Kamath [ID], and Chitralekha Gupta [ID]

National University of Singapore, Singapore, Singapore
{lonce.wyse,purnima.kamath,chitralekha}@nus.edu.sg

Abstract. We introduce a new system for data-driven audio sound model design built around two different neural network architectures, a Generative Adversarial Network (GAN) and a Recurrent Neural Network (RNN), that takes advantage of the unique characteristics of each to achieve the system objectives that neither is capable of addressing alone. The objective of the system is to generate interactively controllable sound models given (a) a range of sounds the model should be able to synthesize, and (b) a specification of the parametric controls for navigating that space of sounds. The range of sounds is defined by a dataset provided by the designer, while the means of navigation is defined by a combination of data labels and the selection of a sub-manifold from the latent space learned by the GAN. Our proposed system takes advantage of the rich latent space of a GAN that consists of sounds that fill out the spaces "between" real data-like sounds. This augmented data from the GAN is then used to train an RNN for its ability to respond immediately and continuously to parameter changes and to generate audio over unlimited periods of time. Furthermore, we develop a self-organizing map technique for "smoothing" the latent space of GAN that results in perceptually smooth interpolation between audio timbres. We validate this process through user studies. The system contributes advances to the state of the art for generative sound model design that include system configuration and components for improving interpolation and the expansion of audio modeling capabilities beyond musical pitch and percussive instrument sounds into the more complex space of audio textures.

Keywords: Generative sound modeling · Parameter mapping · Audio textures · Neural networks

1 Background and Motivation

Sound modeling for the purpose of synthesis is still mostly a manual programming process. It is labour intensive, costly, and the implementation is done by

---

This research was supported by a Singapore MOE Tier 2 grant, "Learning Generative Recurrent Neural Networks", and by an NVIDIA Corporation Academic Programs GPU grant.

T. Martins et al. (Eds.): EvoMUSART 2022, LNCS 13221, pp. 308–322, 2022.
https://doi.org/10.1007/978-3-031-03789-4_20

specialists other than end users of the systems. The overarching objective of this work is to provide a means for instrument and sound designers to create interactive sound generators by merely providing data samples from a sound space and specifications for how they want to navigate that space.

We use the term "sound model" rather than "synthesizer" in part to emphasize the process of their creation, but also because synthesizers are typically designed to produce as wide a range of sounds as possible. Sound models are more targeted and have two essential components: a constrained range of sounds they are capable of producing, and an *expressive* means of navigating that space via parametric control.

A sound model for our purposes also meets several "playability" criteria. One is that parameters can be changed at arbitrary times. We define the Parameter Response Time (PRT) as the number of time steps for sound generation to adapt to changes in the input or conditioning parameters. Playability requires perceptually negligible PRT. A playable sound model should also be capable of generating sound for an unlimited period of time. It further requires an understandable mapping between changing control parameters and their effect on sound. We operationalize this notion to mean (a) that different parameters pertain to different perceptual dimensions, and (b) that their affect on perceptual changes in sound are approximately linear or at least smooth.

The system presented here is constructed to address all sound and not limited to musical or pitched sounds. In terms of both sound and control strategies, we aspire to universality not in the individual sound models, but in the capabilities of the machines used to create them. Manual programming of sound models is already "constrained only by our imagination", but has practical time and effort limitations. In this paper, we are working toward the development of a data-driven system for creating arbitrary sound models. We refer to the system as a Sound Model Factory (SMF).

1.1 Previous Work

Neural network and deep learning approaches in particular have been making steady progress towards data-driven sound modeling. Esling et al. [8] creates latent timbre spaces with a Variational Autoencoder (VAE) regularized to match perceptual distance metrics for pitched musical instruments, and then traverses the space through potentially novel sounds using direct latent vector paths or audio descriptors (e.g. spectral centroid). The system exhibits 'playability' characteristics such as being responsive to parameter changes since the VAE is trained on single spectral frames of data, though such short data frames would not be capable of capturing complex textures with longer time dependencies.

WaveNet [23] was a seminal contribution with its multi-level dilated convolutional autoregressive approach and extremely high-quality synthesis, and it is possible to train waveNet conditionally for parametric interaction. Engel et al. [7] put WaveNet to work as an autoencoder that learns latent representations for the temporal structure of musical notes. For the 4-s musical notes comprising the NSynth database introduced in the same paper, a 125-step, 16 channel temporal embedding is learned, each vector representing a 32 ms window of the note. This code sequence is then used as conditional control for a second WaveNet serving as a decoder. Frame rate "morphing" between instruments works well, but the temporal representations requires interpolating between two vectors that are themselves changing at each time step during the decoding process. The model is also capable of generating unseen note sequences and playing notes of longer duration than those it was trained on. The study was restricted to pitched musical notes, so its applicability to unpitched sounds is not known.

In many ways, GANSynth [6], also from the Google group, has held the mantle of 'state-of-the-art' in generative musical instrument modeling since it was published. It pioneered the use of a two-channel time-frequency representation of audio training data where one channel is the familiar magnitude spectrogram, and the other is the derivative of phase which is commonly referred to as the "instantaneous frequency." This "IF" representation can be inverted to time domain audio using inverse Fourier transforms without the need for a process such as the iterative Griffin-Lim [11] procedure. GANSynth produces excellent quality reconstruction on the NSynth musical instrument notes dataset.

Where the autoregressive WaveNet produces a single value of an audio waveform at each point in time, GANSynth trains to produce an extended waveform (e.g. a note) for each latent parameter vector input sacrificing high-resolution parametric control for parallelizable computation. Using a method developed for Conditional GANs [20] Engle et al. [6], showed that by training GANSynth conditionally, pitch can be disentangled from the timbral qualities of the sound, and then controlled during generation without having to search the latent space. For conditioning, they used a one-hot representation of pitch to augment the latent vector input.

The expressivity of GANSynth was demonstrated with a performance of Bach's Prelude Suite No. 1[1] while morphing through dozens of different identifiable as well as novel instrument sounds over the course of the piece, however the GAN's fixed output duration limits the resolution of the morphing to the duration of the notes.

The IF representation works well with pitched sounds comprised of harmonic components well-separated in frequency, but struggles with unpitched sounds [13]. Noisier sounds have been addressed by others with different representations. Nistal et al. [22] used a 2-channel real and imaginary spectrogram with a GANSynth architecture, conditioning on a set of high-level timbral descriptions (e.g. brightness roughness) each represented as floating point values, to produce convincing drum sounds. Antognini et al. [1] used a CNN architecture inspired by the style-transfer approach using Gram matrices pioneered by [9] and developed for audio [1,12,14,27]. Data are represented as magnitude spectrograms with time as the single dimension and frequency bins as channels and then inverted with the Griffin-Lim [11] algorithm. They also developed novel loss terms so that the style-transfer algorithm would capture rhythmic time scale patterns. Caracalla and Roebel [4] developed a method using the Gram matrix representations

---

[1] https://magenta.tensorflow.org/gansynth.

but optimizing the time domain signal directly so that no inverse spectrogram operation is necessary significantly improving the perceptual quality of impacts and noisy signals.

These strategies enable the generation of non-pitched sounds and textures, but are limited, like GANSynth, to generating sounds of a predetermined length (typically on the order of 1–4 s) given a parameter or sound as input. They are not continuously responsive to parameter changes despite the continuity in the latent space. Conditioning with one-hot representations, as GANSynth does for pitch, also impedes morphing in that dimension, producing between-note transitions resembling cross fades rather than pitch glides as the one-hot vectors are interpolated.

The SMF system described herein makes contributions extending the state-of-the-art GAN system for generative audio modeling with the capacity to produce models that can generate pitched or noisy sounds, a method for linearizing the data space of the GAN, and the ability to generate continuous audio morphing between sounds learned by the GAN with immediate parameter response times in both conditioned and unconditioned dimensions.

2 Architecture

2.1 System Overview

The SMF is comprised of multiple components with a GAN, a self organizing map (SOM), and an RNN forming the backbone of the flow as depicted in Fig. 1. To put more familiar functional labels on the components, the GAN functions as an "interpolator" for creating a continuous space of sounds that fills out regions of parameter spaces between sounds used in the training set. The SOM is a "smoother" for making the rate of change more consistent as the parameter space is navigated during generation, and the RNN is the "performer" as the end product of the SMF work flow providing the playability features necessary for expressive interaction.

The model design process starts with the specification of the dataset (Fig. 1a). The ParamManager (Fig. 1b) represents any system for reading and writing data and metadata including parameters, any of which can be chosen to be used as conditioning extensions to the latent noise vectors provided as input for the GAN (Fig. 1c).

The next step is the selection of a subspace from the high-dimensional latent space of the GAN that will define the range of sounds of the model being constructed, and the number of dimensions that the sound model will offer for parametric control. We currently select 4 points to define a 2D subspace, but the process generalizes to more dimensions. For example, having trained on the NSynth data base, one might choose two clarinet-like sounds, one at the low end of the pitch scale, the other at the top, and likewise two points for a trumpet-like sound spanning a pitch scale. A 2D mesh (Fig. 1d) (of any desired resolution) with corners at the four points, defines the points in latent space that will be used to generate the sounds (Fig. 1e) that, along with the two parameters used to index them, will be used to train the RNN (Fig. 1f). A Self Organizing Map (described in more detail below) also smooths mesh interpolations to create more intuitive parametric control. The sound model output of the SMF is the trained RNN.

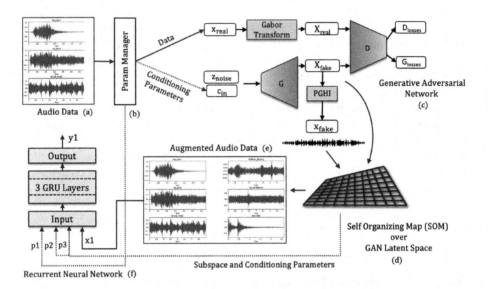

Fig. 1. A schematic of the sound model factory is shown in this figure. (a) Curated datasets and optionally parameters from meta-data (b) are used to train the GAN (c). A subspace is chosen from the resulting latent space which is then adaptively adjusted using a Self-Organizing Map (d). The synthetic data (e) is generated from the resulting mesh and paired with the low-dimensional mesh parameters to conditionally train the RNN (f).

2.2   System Components

We used two datasets in the development of the SMF; one consisting of pitched sounds, the other of noisy sounds with no clear pitch.

We use a subset of the NSynth dataset [7] that consists of 300,000 single-note examples played by more than 1,000 different instruments. It contains various labels for pitch, velocity, instrument type, and more, although, for this particular work, we only make use of the pitch information as the conditional parameter. We further narrow the set to acoustic instrument types *reed* and *brass*. Like [21], we trimmed the audio samples from 4 to 1 s, choosing the central 1 s to remove the attack and decay transitions and any silence. We considered samples with a MIDI pitch range from 64 to 76, which finally yields a subset of approximately 6,164 audio files with 3,041 of brass type and 3,123 of reed type.

The BOReilly dataset[2] consists of 6,580 one-second samples of synthetic textures generated by 8 different synthesizers drawn from source material used by sonic artist Brian O'Reilly[3]. The only criteria in this loosely curated collection was that the sounds be noisy and unpitched (in contrast to the NSynth set) and of stable amplitude throughout (comparable to our NSynth subset).

We use the progressively growing Wasserstein GAN architecture developed for GANSynth [6] consisting of a generator G and a discriminator D, where the input to G is a random vector z with 128 components from a spherical Gaussian distribution along with an optional one-hot conditional vector c_{in}. Training is divided into 5 stages, where the resolution of the output progressively increases at each stage by adding a new layer to the existing stack. This gradual and progressive blending in of the new layers ensures minimal perturbation effects as well as stable training of the GAN, as first proposed by [16]. We train separate GAN models for different datasets, each trained for 1.2M iterations, with 200k iterations in each of the first three stages on batches of 12, and 300k in the last two stages on batches of 8, that requires up to 1.5 d on an NVIDIA Tesla V100-SXM2-32GB. The Wasserstein GAN minimizes an approximation of the Earth Mover (EM) distance, that has been shown to manage issues with previous GANs such as mode collapse [2,3]. The discriminator D estimates the Wasserstein distance between the real and the generated distributions.

Similar to [6], for the NSynth dataset, we sometimes train conditionally on pitch with the goal of achieving independent control of pitch and timbre. To do that, a one-hot representation of musical pitch is appended to the latent vector. Unconditional GAN training (no learning of control parameters) was used for the BOReilly dataset or when combining the BOReilly and NSynth datasets into a single sound model.

For audio data representation, rather than the 2-channel IF used for GANSynth, we use a single channel, 2-dimensional log magnitude spectrum and the Phase Gradient Heap Integration (PGHI) method [25] for a non-iterative method to reconstruct the time signal. Marafioti et al. [19] found that the PGHI algorithm worked well on synthetic spectra produced by GANs. [13] showed that training the GANSynth architecture using the PGHI representation and inversion produces results equivalent to the IF representation for pitched sounds, and significantly better audio quality for wideband, non-pitched or fast changing signals such as pops, and chirps. Time-frequency representations of 16kHz sampled audio are computed using an FFT size of 512 with a hop size of 128 samples (i.e. 75% overlap between consecutive frames).

The RNN used in the SMF was originally developed in Wyse [28] for modeling NSynth data and is comprised of 3 gated recurrent unit (GRU) layers [5] with 256 hidden nodes each. A fully connected embedding layer takes the floating point audio and conditioning parameters to the GRU layer input. A softmax layer at the output produces a probability distribution across 256 values interpreted as mu-law encoded audio sample values predicting the next sample in time. RNNs

---

[2] https://animatedsound.com/datasets/.
[3] https://vimeo.com/dendriform.

are trained on the sound samples generated by the GAN latents sampled on a 21×21 grid, and conditioned on the parameters that index the grid. This stage was run on an NVIDIA 3090 on 256 sample length sequences in batches of 128 for 100K iterations.

3   Connecting the GAN and the RNN

The size of the GAN latent space (in our case, a fairly typical 128 dimensions) is too large to serve as a parametric interface for effective human control of musical performance. This motivates the dimension reduction accomplished by choosing points that define a subspace. There are various ways of "inverting" a GAN to find parameters corresponding to specific data space examples [29]. However, in practice we have found that generating a hundred or two random vectors does a reasonable job at generating sounds similar to much of the real data used for training. The designer auditions random samples and chooses a set which circumscribes the range of sounds the final synthesis model will be able to generate, as well as how they will be parametrically navigated.

After the choice of latent vectors/sounds is made, they are used as corners defining a subspace that is then sampled with a mesh pattern. Each low-dimensional mesh point indexes a point in the much higher-dimensional GAN latent space. The GAN is used to generate sounds for all points on the mesh. Then the pairing of each mesh point and the resulting GAN-generated sound can be used to train the RNN. Original and adapted grids generated in this way are available for auditioning online for the Trumpinet and BOReilly sets[4].

3.1   Parameter Linearization

GANs model the structure of the data space using an explicit distribution of latent vectors that allow the learned probability density function to be sampled. The space tends to be smooth in that nearby points in latent space yield nearby points in the output audio data space [10,15,18] giving rise to the GAN's remarkable ability to interpolate, or "morph" between data points. However, there is no guarantee that the perceptual space is linear with respect to the latent space. That is, a given delta in the latent parameter values can cause very different changes in the perception of the sound depending on the location in latent space. In practice, we have found that for latent values that correspond to sounds similar to those in the real dataset, parameter changes tend to have relatively small effects, where as at some points in the latent space between regions of real-data like sounds, there is a kind of boundary where small parameter changes result in large perceptual changes.

To address the issue of consistent interpolation which is central to sound model design, we introduce a Self Organizing Map (SOM) [17] that sits in the SMF system between the learned space of the GAN and the training of the RNN

---

[4] https://animatedsound.com/evomusart2022/#grids.

(Fig. 1). The latent vectors function as the SOM "weights" associated with each point on a 2D mesh, and the reduction of a measure of the perceptual difference between sound generated by neighboring latent vectors on the grid serves as the function driving the adaptation so that differences between sounds generated by neighboring mesh points become perceptually more uniformly distributed. The mesh point update equation is

$$g_{i,j} \mathrel{+}= \delta \sum_{m,n \in N} g_{m,n} \left(\sum_{p,q} |S_{p,q}^{i,j} - S_{p,q}^{m,n}|^2 \right)^{\frac{1}{2}} \tag{1}$$

where N is the 8-node neighborhood (horizontal, vertical, and diagonal) of $g_{i,j}$, δ is the step size, $S^{i,j}$ is the spectrogram generated by the GAN by the latent vector associated with mesh node i,j, and p,q indexes the time and frequency points of the spectrograms. The corners of the grid are always "pinned" to the initial latent vector chosen to define the sub-manifold, and for some experiments, we restrict movement of mesh points lying on the lines connecting corners to remain on those lines.

The adaptation of the latent vectors on the mesh is driven by the L2 distance between the 2D spectrogram images as a proxy for perceptual difference. Although audio perceptual distance is notoriously difficulty to quantify in general, sound corresponding to neighboring latent vectors are already organized by spectral proximity. We find that linearizing distances locally in this way yields significant improvements to the overall perceptual smoothness of the parameter space, and we validate this claim with user studies reported below.

We can visualize the mesh adaptation using the 2D grid space (Fig. 2). The contour plot represents the average difference in the spectrograms produced by one grid point and its eight neighbors. The effect of the adaptation can be seen by stretching the grid points back to their nominal index value locations which stretches the underlying space with it. In Fig. 2, the linearization of the perceptual space is seen in the regularization of the distance between contour lines on the contour plot and the reduction of the maximum difference.

4   Evaluation

As a system, we want to evaluate the capabilities compared to others that address the same or similar goals - the production of sound models that have minimal PRTs, can generate non-repetitive sounds for arbitrary lengths of time, and that can interpolate smoothly between parameter values. We also want to understand the kinds and quality of sound the models created by the system are capable of generating, particularly in terms of complexity.

4.1   Human Evaluation Adaptively Smoothed Latent Space

Our listening tests were designed to test for perceptual linearity between two points in the GAN's latent space by asking participants to listen to two sound

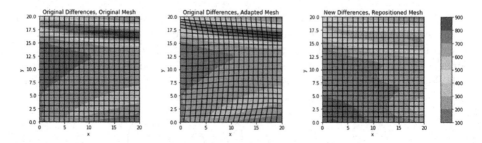

Fig. 2. The SOM adapting to reduce differences between mesh neighbors of the function value. The upper two mesh corners correspond to a clarinet and a trumpet sound playing the same pitch. The bottom two corners are complex BOReilly textures. A border-like structure of sudden change divides the two regions. The contour plot shows average spectrogram differences with it 8 neighbors at each grid location. (a) Initial mesh (b) adapted mesh (with edges pinned) over the original differences contour (c) the smoothed differences at their new mesh positions.

clips, one sampled from the adapted mesh space (pinned corners or pinned corners with constrained edges) and another sampled without this adaptation. The sound clips were created by first selecting two points in the GAN latent space, selecting 20 equidistant samples between those points and joining those samples to create one clip. The space between those two points was then adapted using our SOM technique and sampled again to create a second clip. These two clips formed one pair in a comparison trial with each sound lasting for 13–15 s. The mesh adaptation for the BOReilly sounds used pinned corners whereas for NSynth sounds used pinned corners with constrained edges. Our listening experiments were conducted on Amazon's Mechanical Turk (AMT) with user consent, are anonymized, and were approved by our university department's ethics review committee.

We recruited 40 participants on AMT and given that these participants may not be audio or sound experts, our experiment design used simple language and pairs of icons (see Table 1) to convey our intent and to gather meaningful responses from the test. The participants were required to listen to both sounds before answering the questions. No submissions from participants were rejected during these experiments. The participants were paid $0.10 per task which took less than 90 s on average.

We identified two types of non-linearity in sound interpolations. One type is when the interpolation takes a "detour" (e.g. passing through a flute sound during a transition from a clarinet to a trumpet, or passing through a pitch not between the pitch of the endpoint sounds) and another type when step sizes in the interpolation parameter results in the perception of irregular size steps in the quality of the sound. To probe for directness in transitions of sounds from one end point to the other, we asked participants to associate a "direct" icon or a "detour" icon with each pair of sounds. To test for irregular step sizes in the sampled GAN data space, the participants did the same with an "Even Steps" icon and a "Uneven Steps" icon. The mutually exclusive association of each pair of ions with the sounds could be made with one mouse click and drag[5]. Responses from 520 comparison trials for NSynth sounds and 840 comparison trials for BOReilly sounds were collected. The trials were loaded in a random sequence to AMT and its results are tabulated in Table 1.

Table 1. Human evaluation of sound navigation through the SOM-adapted space vs. the unadapted GAN grid (left). Mechanical Turk participants used the icons (right) to visually associate perceptual differences in the sounds in comparison trials. Icons represent the perception of a sound sequence as it transitions from its starting point to its end (Direct vs. Detour) as well as the perceptual measure of even or uneven jumps the sounds makes in its transition (Even vs. Uneven steps).

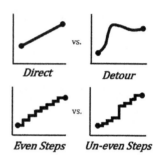

		Sound samples NSynth	BOReilly
Direct vs.	Mesh adapted	**57.50%**	**61.07%**
Detour	GAN Only	42.50%	38.92%
Even steps vs.	Mesh adapted	**59.42%**	**60.47%**
Uneven Steps	GAN only	40.58%	39.52%

4.2 Parameter Response Time

In this section, we demonstrate the ability of the SMF system to generate sound models that meet the playability requirements identified in the beginning of this paper. The RNN was trained using only same steady-state pitch parameters used for training the GAN on NSynth data, but RNN parameters can be arbitrarily manipulated during generation. Figure 3a shows a one-octave stepped arpeggio followed by a descending one-octave glide. We measure the PRT manually by verifying whether the wave period at a particular instance corresponds to the intended pitch at that instant. We find that the parameter response is immediate for both steps and glides as shown in Fig. 3.

---

[5] https://animatedsound.com/evomusart2022/ui/amt-instructions-template.html.

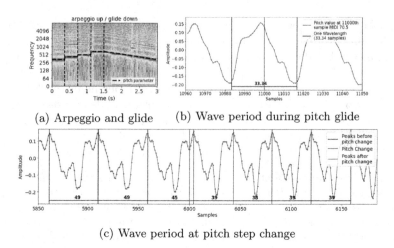

(a) Arpeggio and glide   (b) Wave period during pitch glide

(c) Wave period at pitch step change

Fig. 3. (a) Parameter changes and spectrogram of RNN output for (a) an arpeggio over an octave (midi number 64, 68, 71, 76) followed by a one octave glide. The PRT is more precisely quantified in (b) for a descending one-octave glide (MIDI note 76-64), the period of the waveform centered at the 11000 sample mark matches the gliding pitch parameter of MIDI note 70.5 (34.35 sample wavelength) exactly at that point, and (c) for pitch step where we identify peaks before and after the pitch change (green line) to show that the wave period changes immediately after the pitch steps from MIDI 64 (48.56 sample wavelength) to 68 (38.53 sample wavelength). (Color figure online)

4.3   Sound Quality Evaluation Based on Audio Classification

First we quantitatively test whether the pitch and timbre qualities of a GAN-generated audio are similar to RNN at the end of the multistage flow of the proposed SMF for the same parameter settings. GAN generated audio has been shown to be of high perceptual quality [6,21], and we hope to preserve the quality through the various stages.

Since the latent space of GAN consists of timbre of the two instrument classes as well as the timbres in-between the two classes, a class label cannot be assigned to every point in this latent space, as the in-between timbres cannot be labelled with a class. Therefore, the standard method of inception score computation [26] will not be applicable in this case.

For quantitative validation, we train an audio classification network [24] with the brass and reed instrument classes from NSynth dataset. This subset has 56–76 MIDI pitch values with velocity 127, with a total of 2,225 audio files, split into 80% training and 20% validation. The audio classification network consists of a ResNet model initialized with ImageNet pretrained weights. This scheme of training has achieved state-of-the-art audio classification performance when fine-tuned with standard audio classification datasets, as shown by [24]. We trained this network to classify the two instrument classes by fine-tuning it on our Nsynth subset data. The validation accuracy of this model is 100%.

In this experiment, we were interested in observing whether a set of audio files generated from a latent space of the GAN have the same distribution of logit values (values at the output layer before the class labels are assigned) in the audio classifier, as the set of audio files generated from the proposed SMF (i.e. GAN+RNN) system for the same parameter settings. Parameter settings, in this case, means the pitch and timbre indices from the GAN-generated latent space. We used 143 such pairs of audio files. The two logit values corresponding to the two audio classes (brass and reed) for each of these files, i.e. (SMF(brass),SMF(reed)) and (GAN(brass),GAN(reed)), are presented in Fig. 4a. The histogram of these logit values are shown in Fig. 4b. Qualitatively, we observe the distribution of logit 0 values of GAN and SMF audio files are similar, and the distribution of logit 1 values of the two types of audio files are similar. Moreover, 127 out of 143 pairs of audio files get classified into the same instrument class, i.e. 88.8% of the test pairs are classified into the same class. This analysis shows that the audio generated from the proposed SMF architecture are similar to that generated from the GAN.

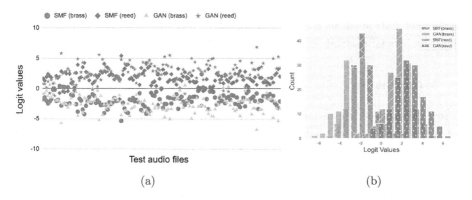

(a)   (b)

Fig. 4. Logit values from the penultimate output layer of the audio classifier for the two sets of 143 test audio files, one set from the GAN, and the other from the proposed SMF model (GAN+RNN). The two logit values are depicted as *(brass) and *(reed). (a) The raw logit values for all test audio files, and (b) the histogram of the logit values.

4.4   Continuous Interpolation of Pitch and Timbre

GANs are structurally unable to continuously interpolate parameters for audio because time is a dimension of the data representation. One-hot representations such as used for pitch in GANSynth produce audible artifacts at "in between" values. Wyse [28] showed that an RNN can interpolate between widely spaced conditioned pitch values. However, we have found the RNN is less capable of interpolating between timbres as can be seen in Fig. 5a. In contrast, the GAN can synthesize convincing timbres perceptually between training examples. When synthetic GAN data are used to train the RNN, the result is the best of both worlds - convincing in-between timbres that can be smoothly and continuously interpolated (Fig. 5b). A musical example illustrates the combined capabilities with fast and slow pitch changes including vibrato and a continuous morph between clarinet and trumpet over a rendering of the opening segment of George Gershwin's Rhapsody in Blue (Fig. 5c).

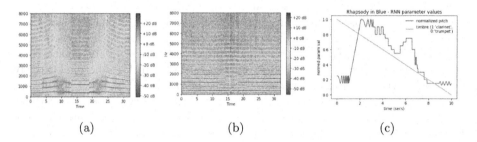

(a)   (b)   (c)

Fig. 5. Spectrograms of a steady-pitch trumpet-clarinet-trumpet glide with an RNN (a) trained at endpoints only, (b) trained with intermediate synthetic data from GAN. (c) Parameter sequence for a "reinterpreted" opening segment of George Gershwin's Rhapsody in Blue with glides, various note lengths, vibrato, and a continuous clarinet-to-trumpet instrument morph (audition online) (Audition at https://animatedsound. com/evomusart2022/#pitch-timbre) (Color figure online)

5   Conclusion

A few noteworthy limitations are left for future work. For example, by selecting a subspace of the GAN latent space, the SMF makes a trade-off between low dimensional control over a constrained sound space of the RNN and the hundreds of parameters and diversity of the GAN sound space. More control over that balance would benefit sound model design.

The linearization of the perceptual sound space with respect to parameters needs further exploration. Although the SOM (1) improved the perceived smoothness of transitions, they are still neither perceptually or objectively uniform. The neighborhood used to compute updates to the grid could be expanded, or paths between the anchor points could even depart from the 2D manifold in a search for smoother transitions similar to the way Esling et al. used sound descriptors for directing navigation through latent space.

Although the PGHI representation and inversion provides high quality resynthesis of non-pitched sounds, the current SMF is limited in the complexity of the temporal structure of audio textures it can capture. For example, previous synthesis models capable of learning to generate randomly spaced clicks conditioned on rate have needed lots of data to capture the temporal variability at any given rate parameter. However, GANs generate one fixed length sample for any given latent parameter vector. If the GAN is to provide the necessary variety of sound patterns for training a downstream model with this kind of complexity, we would have to identify a whole region of the GAN latent space to map to a single parameter value for training the RNN, not just a single point.

The innovations introduced at the system level for the SMF come from a) the use of the single channel and PGHI representation and reconstruction with the GANSynth architecture, b) the linearization of a slice of the latent space of the GAN using SOMs, and (c) the exploitation of the GAN parameter/sound pairing to train an RNN. The SMF contributes novel audio capabilities by combining immediate parameter response times, smooth interpolation capabilities of the GAN's conditioned and unconditioned parameters, "infinite" duration sound synthesis, and the ability to generate a wider variety of audio timbres more complex than pitched instrument sounds.

References

1. Antognini, J.M., Hoffman, M., Weiss, R.J.: Audio texture synthesis with random neural networks: improving diversity and quality. In: ICASSP 2019–2019 IEEE International Conference on Acoustics, Speech and Signal Processing (ICASSP), pp. 3587–3591. IEEE (2019)
2. Arjovsky, M., Bottou, L.: Towards principled methods for training generative adversarial networks. arXiv preprint arXiv:1701.04862 (2017)
3. Arjovsky, M., Chintala, S., Bottou, L.: Wasserstein generative adversarial networks. In: International Conference on Machine Learning, pp. 214–223. PMLR (2017)
4. Caracalla, H., Roebel, A.: Sound texture synthesis using RI spectrograms. In: ICASSP 2020–2020 IEEE International Conference on Acoustics, Speech and Signal Processing (ICASSP), pp. 416–420. IEEE (2020)
5. Cho, K., et al.: Learning phrase representations using RNN encoder-decoder for statistical machine translation. arXiv preprint arXiv:1406.1078 (2014)
6. Engel, J., Agrawal, K.K., Chen, S., Gulrajani, I., Donahue, C., Roberts, A.: Gansynth: adversarial neural audio synthesis. arXiv preprint arXiv:1902.08710 (2019)
7. Engel, J., et al.: Neural audio synthesis of musical notes with wavenet autoencoders. In: International Conference on Machine Learning, pp. 1068–1077. PMLR (2017)
8. Esling, P., Bitton, A., et al.: Generative timbre spaces: regularizing variational auto-encoders with perceptual metrics. arXiv preprint arXiv:1805.08501 (2018)
9. Gatys, L., Ecker, A.S., Bethge, M.: Texture synthesis using convolutional neural networks. In: Advances in Neural Information Processing Systems, pp. 262–270 (2015)
10. Goodfellow, I.: Nips 2016 tutorial: generative adversarial networks. arXiv preprint arXiv:1701.00160 (2016)
11. Griffin, D., Lim, J.: Signal estimation from modified shorttime Fourier transform. IEEE Trans. Audio Speech Lang. Process. **32**(2), 236–243 (1984)
12. Grinstein, E., Duong, N.Q., Ozerov, A., Pérez, P.: Audio style transfer. In: 2018 IEEE International Conference on Acoustics, Speech and Signal Processing (ICASSP), pp. 586–590. IEEE (2018)
13. Gupta, C., Kamath, P., Wyse, L.: Signal representations for synthesizing audio textures with generative adversarial networks. arXiv preprint arXiv:2103.07390 (2021)
14. Huzaifah bin Md Shahrin, M., Wyse, L.: Applying visual domain style transfer and texture synthesis techniques to audio: insights and challenges. Neural Comput. Appl. **32**(4), 1051–1065 (2019). https://doi.org/10.1007/s00521-019-04053-8
15. Jahanian, A., Chai, L., Isola, P.: On the "steerability" of generative adversarial networks. arXiv preprint arXiv:1907.07171 (2019)

16. Karras, T., Aila, T., Laine, S., Lehtinen, J.: Progressive growing of gans for improved quality, stability, and variation. arXiv preprint arXiv:1710.10196 (2017)
17. Kohonen, T.: Self-Organization and Associative Memory, 3rd edn. Springer, Heidelberg (1989). https://doi.org/10.1007/978-3-642-88163-3
18. Mao, W., Lou, B., Yuan, J.: Tunagan: interpretable gan for smart editing. arXiv preprint arXiv:1908.06163 (2019)
19. Marafioti, A., Perraudin, N., Holighaus, N., Majdak, P.: Adversarial generation of time-frequency features with application in audio synthesis. In: International Conference on Machine Learning, pp. 4352–4362. PMLR (2019)
20. Mirza, M., Osindero, S.: Conditional generative adversarial nets. arXiv preprint arXiv:1411.1784 (2014)
21. Nistal, J., Lattner, S., Richard, G.: Comparing representations for audio synthesis using generative adversarial networks. In: 2020 28th European Signal Processing Conference (EUSIPCO), pp. 161–165. IEEE (2021)
22. Nistal, J., Lattner, S., Richard, G.: Drumgan: synthesis of drum sounds with timbral feature conditioning using generative adversarial networks. arXiv preprint arXiv:2008.12073 (2020)
23. van den Oord, A., et al.: Wavenet: a generative model for raw audio. arXiv preprint arXiv:1609.03499 (2016)
24. Palanisamy, K., Singhania, D., Yao, A.: Rethinking CNN models for audio classification. arXiv preprint arXiv:2007.11154 (2020)
25. Průša, Z., Balazs, P., Søndergaard, P.L.: A noniterative method for reconstruction of phase from STFT magnitude. IEEE/ACM Trans. Audio Speech Lang. Process. **25**(5), 1154–1164 (2017)
26. Salimans, T., Goodfellow, I., Zaremba, W., Cheung, V., Radford, A., Chen, X.: Improved techniques for training gans. Adv. Neural Inf. Process. Syst. **29**, 2234–2242 (2016)
27. Ulyanov, D., Lebedev, V.: Audio texture synthesis and style transfer. https://dmitryulyanov.github.io/audio-texture-synthesis-and-style-transfer/ (2016). Accessed 10 July 2019
28. Wyse, L.: Real-valued parametric conditioning of an rnn for interactive sound synthesis. In: Proceedings of the 6th International Workshop on Musical Metacreation, ACM Conference on Computational Creativity, Salamanca (2018)
29. Xia, W., Zhang, Y., Yang, Y., Xue, J.H., Zhou, B., Yang, M.H.: Gan inversion: a survey. arXiv preprint arXiv:2101.05278 (2021)

Short Talks

An Application of Neural Embedding Models for Representing Artistic Periods

Rao Hamza Ali, Katie Rhodeghiero, Alexa Zuch, Saniya Syed,
and Erik Linstead[✉]

Machine Learning and Affiliated Technologies Lab, Fowler School of Engineering,
Chapman University, Orange, USA
{raali,rodeghiero,zuch,ssyed,linstead}@chapman.edu

Abstract. We showcase visualizations created for art periods of Dalí, van Gogh, and Picasso by leveraging deep neural embedding models like word2vec to represent color features. First, the embedding vectors are generated for every color used in artworks of these painters. Next, t-distributed Stochastic Neighbor Embedding (t-SNE) is applied to generate a two-dimensional visualizations of the color space. Colors used in close proximity on the canvas are observed as compact clusters in the visualizations. These visualizations are termed as fingerprints, as they uniquely depict each art period of a painter, by highlighting the color palette used in their works. The authors further provide commentary on the artists' art periods and how the fingerprints showcase their artistic evolution.

Keywords: Art periods · Neural embeddings · Word embeddings · t-SNE

1 Introduction

Art historians divide the flow of artworks through time and space into groupings called art periods, with the premise that artworks within an art period share significant artistic qualities. These qualities are based on a specific approach to the thematic or stylistic aspects of art, and by placing artworks in a particular period, historians define meaningful connections between the pieces. Influenced by art movements of the time and other significant events, artists have distinct art periods as well. An art movement is a collective name given to a series of art with a common style or philosophy, practiced by artists during a specific period of time [1]. Often an artist's works are divided into a combination of chronological and stylistic groups, each showcasing a unique style adopted by the painter which is easily identifiable through their paintings. We can use the art periods of Pablo Picasso as an example to highlight this key point. Picasso's work is divided into groups like Early and Late years; which signify chronological groupings, Blue and Rose Periods; which were influenced by personal experiences, and Cubist and Surrealist Periods; which focused on artworks with a unique art style [2]. Together these art periods highlight Picasso's versatility as a painter, but each

T. Martins et al. (Eds.): EvoMUSART 2022, LNCS 13221, pp. 325–340, 2022.
https://doi.org/10.1007/978-3-031-03789-4_21

one is influenced by different sources, not the art movement of the time. Similarly, Vincent van Gogh made contributions to Pointillism and the Neo and Post-Impressionist Movements but his artworks are often grouped into art periods based on his location when he painted a piece (Nuenen, Paris, Arles etc.) [9]. This implies that historians define art periods for an artist such that they transcend art movements and are closely tied to the personal life and philosophy of the artist.

As artworks continue to be digitized, it is becoming more accessible to analyze large sets of paintings altogether. Websites such as WikiArt [5], Artsy [3], The Art Story [6], and others, host high resolution digitized paintings of famous painters. They offer an avenue for the public to view artworks, especially those for which physical access may not be feasible. Abundance of online resources for these artworks allows analysts and those enthusiastic about machine learning approaches to art, to experiment and bring forward unique ideas in the generation, identification, and classification of paintings. However, almost all techniques applied are used to classify paintings between artists or art movements and not to distinguish paintings between art periods for an individual painter [21,23,26,35]. Deep neural networks have been trained to generate unique paintings and even implement transfer of stylistic features between artworks [13,14,24,27]. A new class of studies now uses not just the visual features of a painting for training a model, but also employs the use of the texture of the painting and the brush stroke patterns to make a classification decision, as shown in [7] and [36]. But perhaps distinguishing between art periods of an individual painter becomes a more challenging task as texture patterns can be similar across art periods for a painter and there are fewer paintings per group to train an accurate neural network on. Instead, in this paper we focus on how to represent each art period for a painter. We want to generate a fingerprint or a stamp that uniquely identifies the art periods. This generation process does not use the thematic or stylistic features in the artworks nor the texture patterns, which were used by the studies discussed earlier. As an alternative, we make use of the colors depicted in the paintings, and by analyzing what colors are painted close to each other on a canvas, across all paintings of an art period, we create a fingerprint that showcases the underlying palette of each period that is unique to an artist.

Our approach uses a deep neural word embedding model to analyze how different colors are used by an artist during a particular art period. Word embeddings are real-valued representations of words produced by semantic models [8]. The embeddings are learned in a way that a vector can be used to encode the definition of a word such that words with a similar meaning, over some corpus of text, have vectors that lie close to each other in the vector space. Representation of a word in this vector form also allows computation of distance with other words. This leads to the discovery over how words are used in some context and what the overall lexical map of the vocabulary is. Word embeddings can be generated via neural networks [41], probabilistic models [39], and dimensionality reduction techniques [31]. The inputs to these models are large collections of texts. Words are parsed from these collections and an embedding is generated for each one. To translate this approach for our study, we first generate collections of colors from the paintings, using a sliding window technique. This results in a set of linear arrays of colors that are present in some n × n space on a painting. A collection of these arrays, from all paintings in an art period, become the input to word2vec [29], a word embedding model. The vector space of the embeddings is high dimensional and cannot be visualized in its current form. We use t-Distributed Stochastic Neighbor Embedding (t-SNE) [28], a dimensionality reduction technique, to embed the high dimensional vectors in a two-dimensional space. This is done in a way that vectors close to each other in high dimensional space remain close in lower dimensions as well. Next, we generate a point for each vector in the two-dimensional space drawn with the color it represents. This results in a fingerprint for a set of paintings, showing how colors are used in relation to one another in an art period of a painter.

2 Data

We use the WikiArt website [5] as the source for the paintings. The website curates a large collection of paintings and groups them by art periods and painters. Using Python programming language [43] and the Selenium package [37], we extract the high resolution paintings and resize them to 516 × 516 pixels. This step normalizes each image to the same dimensions, making the next steps easier to generalize. Sketches were filtered out from the dataset to ensure that the color representation was equal across all artists. We store sets of paintings into separate collections determined by the art periods for each painter. The periods analyzed, in chronological order, are listed below, where N denotes the number of paintings used for each artist:

- Salvador Dalí (N=1,097)
  - Early Period
  - Transitional Period
  - Surrealist Period
  - Classical Period

- Vincent van Gogh (N=646)
  - Nuenen
  - Paris
  - Arles
  - Saint-Rémy
  - Auvers-sur-Oise

- Pablo Picasso (N=960)
  - Early Years
  - Blue Period
  - Rose Period
  - African Period
  - Cubist Period
  - Surrealist Period
  - Later Years

3 Methodology

3.1 word2vec

For each collection of paintings, we implement a word2vec model for them. A word2vec model uses a corpus of text entities or documents and is a two-layer neural network that processes words in the corpus and embeds them to a high dimensional vector space. While the model was first introduced to represent words in higher dimensions, the technique has been used to represent songs [19], code [42], genes [12], or graphs [16]. For our mechanism, we first generate 'documents' of colors for our corpus. We create 6×6 pixels wide sliding window with a stride of 3 pixels that goes across each image, starting from the top left position, to generate a list of colors of the 36 pixels under the filter at any given time. These lists of colors, in the form of their R, G, B values, become the documents for our corpus. To minimize the processing time, each color value is rounded to the nearest multiple of 3. That is, two colors with R, G, B values [0,0,0] and [0,1,1] are rounded to one color value [0,0,0]. After some experimentation, we observed that rounding the values did not affect the overall results but significantly reduced the time it takes the algorithm to generate the embeddings. Across each art period of a painter, we generate these color documents and pool them together in a single corpus. This becomes the input for the word2vec model. A word2vec algorithm utilizes either of two model architectures: continuous skip-gram or continuous bag-of-words (CBOW). In a skip-gram architecture, the model uses the current word to identify the context words surrounding it, weighing close context words heavier than those more distant [17]. The CBOW architecture involves using context words to identify the current word and a bag-of-words approach is used: the order of context words does not influence the prediction [45]. As we have generated our color documents by converting a 2D array of pixels into a one dimensional array, the positional information during the transformation is lost and the linear array no longer reflects the original position of colors, as they are depicted in the painting. To this point, we implement the algorithm using the CBOW model architecture.

We use the gensim implementation of the word2vec algorithm [33]. The implementation is widely used in research pertaining to generating word embeddings from a large corpus of texts [18,38], and allows selection of model architecture and a number of other hyperparameters. More specifically, the window size is kept to be 36, so that within a color array, each color is a potential neighbor to another color. The word2vec model outputs a vocabulary where each color is represented by a feature vector of size 100. The feature vector shapes the embedding of the color, in the context of its usage in a set of paintings. If an artist repeatedly uses the same set of colors in close proximity to each other, then the feature vectors of those colors will be close to each other as well. To determine how close two colors are in the vector space, we can compute a cosine distance between their feature vectors to determine the proximity.

3.2   t-SNE

The feature vectors are high dimensional and cannot directly be used to visualize the proximity of colors used in paintings by an artist. t-SNE is a statistical method that maps a high dimensional vector in a 2 or 3D space, for visualization. Based on Stochastic Neighbor Embedding [20], the method is a widely used dimensionality reduction technique which attempts to maintain the pairwise distance between data points in high dimension when translated to a lower dimensional space. Ideally, close neighbors in higher dimensions remain close in a lower dimension, and distant neighbors stay distant. t-SNE has demonstrated that it can capture local characteristics and reveal subtle structures in data visualization as well [15, 22, 25]. The main purpose of this method's implementation is to be able to visualize which sets of colors are in close proximity across all paintings of a single art period. We are aware that each artist will have used all colors available to them but we are more interested in how the colors are used, and their visualization using their feature vectors can get us closer to the answer. We use the sklearn's implementation of the t-SNE algorithm for a 2D space, which generates an array detailing the X and Y coordinate position of each color, by taking the color embeddings as input [10].

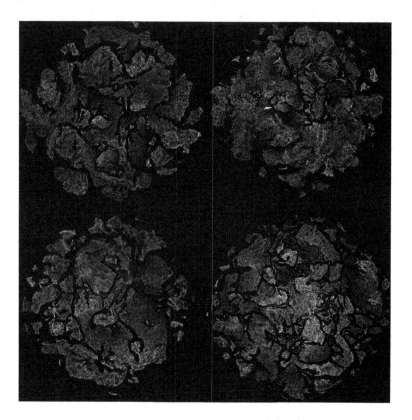

Fig. 1. t-SNE visualizations generated from art periods of Salvador Dalí, in chronological order: Early Period, Transitional Period, Surrealist Period, Classical Period. (shown left to right)

Next, we use the Processing programming language [32] to generate the visualization on a 3000 × 3000 sized canvas. The Processing framework gives us the freedom to control the spacing between each data point, for better visualization, and allows for generation of high resolution images. All parameters are kept the same except for the scale of the fingerprint, which is modified for some art periods to make theirs level in size with the others'.

4   Results

4.1   Salvador Dalí

We first present the fingerprints generated from the artworks of Salvador Dalí. Figure 1 shows the visualizations generated for the four art periods of Dalí in chronological order. We can observe that the fingerprints generated for each art period are not exactly alike. With the exception of his Classical Period, which used 369,252 unique colors (rounded to the nearest multiple of 3), we computed a color palette of around 250,000 colors, across all art periods. This average was observed for the other painters in the study as well. This means that the fingerprints are roughly using the same colors but the shape of the clusters, as evaluated by t-SNE, and the abundance of shades of one color or another, make each fingerprint unique. The embeddings generated for each art period make use of the positional information of each individual color. It is trivial that shades of one color will be compacted together in the high dimensional vector space, as they are most likely to be present together on a canvas. Beyond that however, the model also picks up on shades of different colors used closely on a set of paintings as well. This is why these fingerprints are not simply clusters of shades of each color but also include clusters of combinations of different colors, that were most likely used in proximity of each other, by the painter. These fingerprints will also help us visualize if painters used similar color combinations, as they went through different art periods.

Dalí's Early Period lasted around ten years and includes artworks he painted while he was still a teenager. Shades of yellow and green coincide with each other here, and across all art periods rather, to depict that he used shades of the two colors closely in his paintings. Figure 2 presents a few examples of this observation. Dalí had started to experiment with many different artistic styles, influenced by Impressionism, Cubism, Realism, and Dutch Baroque [30]. This led to his Transitional Period which only lasted a year and resulted in 32 paintings. This low number did impact our embedding and dimensionality reduction models, as we observe no discernible clusters for the fingerprint of this art period. We will further discuss this in a later section. This was also the year that Dalí experimented heavily to develop an artistic style of his own, leading to his Surrealist and Classical Periods.

Dalí is perhaps most renowned for his contributions to the Surrealism movement. His most recognized work, the Persistence of Memory, was painted during his Surrealist Period. The movement represented a reaction against rationalism and was characterized by unexpected juxtapositions in ordinary scenes that challenged a viewer's imagination [4]. There was no radical change observed in the color palette however, as seen from the fingerprint for that period. Dalí's

Fig. 2. Examples of interplay between yellow and green colors in Dalí's Early Period. (Color figure online)

Classical Period contains the most paintings for a period in our dataset. We generated the fingerprint using 635 paintings, from a corpus of over 18.5 million unique windows of colors. Brighter and more vivid colors are used in this art period compared to the previous three.

There are discernible clusters of colors and color combinations observed within Dalí's periods. These fingerprints highlight that he consistently utilized more cool colors than warm colors in his paintings. This can be observed as we discern more blue, purple, and green shades within his art as opposed to reds, oranges, and yellows. An interesting growth within his periods is the increasing use of green within his periods. While the color was present in his first two periods, we can see a heightened frequency at which he utilized different shades of green next to each other within his Surrealist and Classical periods. In addition, there's a steady increase in the brightness of colors he used. While he used many of the same colors throughout his painting career, it can be observed that the shades he utilized became more vivid during each period from Transitional to Surrealist to his Classical period. Dalí was artistically flexible across all periods but the way he used colors and their combinations in his paintings, did not see a major evolution.

4.2 Vincent van Gogh

Figure 3 shows the fingerprints generated for art periods of Vincent van Gogh. van Gogh's art periods are synonymous to his movements through Europe, as his work

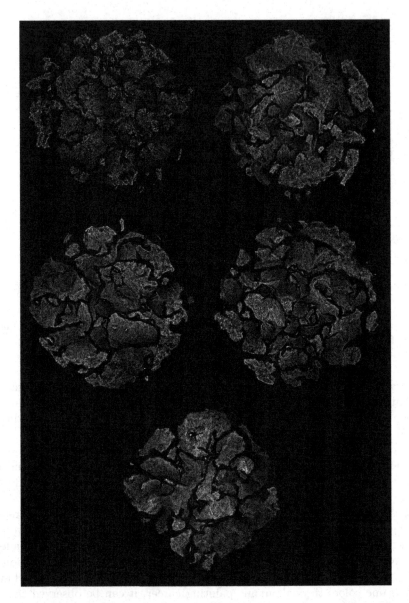

Fig. 3. t-SNE visualizations generated from art periods of Vincent van Gogh, in chronological order: Nuenen, Paris, Arles, Saint-Rémy, Auvers-sur-Oise. (shown left to right)

is heavily influenced by his surroundings and often depicts natural scenery. van Gogh stayed with his parents in Nuenen when he was still an emerging artist. During his two year stay, he completed numerous sketches, watercolor and oil paintings. It has been remarked that his palette consisted mainly of sombre tones, and showed no sign of the vivid colors he used in his later works [40]. This contrast is easily observed from the fingerprints as well. The one from van Gogh's Nuenen art period depicts earthy tones, and shades of brown are visible throughout the visualization. He continued to introduce more vibrant colors in his works after he moved to Paris. He painted portraits of friends, still life paintings, and views of the scenery. The true vibrancy of colors in his later works are not observed in the fingerprint of this period. Some bright colors and their shades do cover most of the visualization but the dull tones are still present. This is because he produced contrasting paintings during his time in Paris, as shown in Fig. 4. This period can be viewed as an important stage for van Gogh as he began to adopt a brighter color palette that is much recognized in his paintings.

Fig. 4. Contrast of color palettes used in van Gogh's works during his time in Paris.

These fingerprints illustrate van Gogh's affinity for bold colors that lasted throughout his life. All of his periods, except Nuenen, display varying arrangements of similar bright colors. His middle three periods of Paris, Arles, and Saint-Rémy highlight the development from slightly more subdued colors like cobalt and lavender to indigo and mustard, ultimately culminating in Auvers sur Oise with colors like lime, orchid, scarlet, and chartreuse. A surprising observation between the Saint-Rémy and Auvers sur Oise fingerprints is the decreased number of colors being observed and utilized. While Saint-Rémy displays many colors and many shades of certain colors like blue, purple, and red, Auvers-sur-Oise displays fewer shades, but overall brighter colors like the green, yellow, and red at the center of the fingerprint. All of his periods maintain similar color combinations with greens and blues, blues and purples, and reds and greens often appearing next to each other. Vincent van Gogh developed his signature use of colors early and carried it throughout his life.

Fig. 5. t-SNE visualizations generated from art periods of Pablo Picasso, in chronological order: Early Years, Blue Period, Rose Period, African Period, Cubist Period, Surrealist Period, Later Years. (shown left to right) (Color figure online)

4.3 Pablo Picasso

Pablo Picasso began painting at the age of thirteen and had a traditional, academic approach to his artworks during the early years. Though near the end of this art period, he did develop an interest in a more free-form art style [34]. The fingerprint for the period shows no unique color palette that Picasso adopted or any intricate color combinations he began his painting career with. The next two periods however, are distinctly renowned for the use of a unique color palette (Fig. 5). Paintings from the Blue Period are sombre in color and style, likely due to depression after a friend's suicide. The pieces are often monochrome with dark blue undertones, and while the fingerprint for this period shows other colors being used as well, a large area of the visualization is covered by blue and blue-green color combinations. In a contrast, during the Rose Period, Picasso used warmer shades in his paintings, depicting figures in his style. The fingerprint for this period shows large clusters of shades of red, orange, and pink, which Picasso used to represent more pleasant themes in his artworks. Examples of this contrast are shown in Fig. 6. The African Period shows a heavy influence from Oceanic and African art, though the warm colors used in the Rose Period were adopted as well. The African Period gave way to Picasso's Cubism, which is arguably his most famous art period. In this period, he depicted subjects broken down into fractured forms but there was no prominent color choices observed in its fingerprint. As Picasso moved into his Surrealist Period, he started using more vibrant colors, a shift from the previous periods, as can be observed from the fingerprint of this art period. The heavy use of bright shades of colors continued in his later years as well, where showed his versatility with different art styles.

Beginning with Picasso's Blue Period and tracking forward through his career, one can identify a gradual increase in the amount of green and yellow shades he utilized within his artworks. This ultimately culminates with his works from his Later Years displaying the greatest amount of greens and yellows. These all lie close together and gradually transition into the other colors. As we are only looking at the colors as they relate to the colors surrounding them, the model does not reflect frequency at which they occurred within the art and therefore we do not see an almost completely blue or red fingerprint. Picasso utilized the most shades of purple in his Surrealist Period, a color not largely seen in the fingerprint for his earlier or even later periods. Surprisingly, Dalí's Surrealist Period fingerprint also indicated an increased number of purple shades compared to earlier periods.

5 Discussion

The fingerprints generated for each art period show how color combinations were used by painters in their works. The colors are embedded in a high dimensional space and form clusters for colors that were more commonly painted together on a canvas. The t-SNE algorithm then attempts to showcase these clusters in a lower dimensional space and we use the clusters to make observations about

Fig. 6. Contrast between Picasso's Blue and Rose Periods. The Blue Period used a somber palette while the Rose Period used much warmer colors. (Color figure online)

color palette choices of each painter. The analysis does not use color frequency, which could further inform us regarding the numerical breakdown of color usage. This is a topic we wish to look into for a future project.

Wattenberg et al. [44] describe the effects of hyperparameters of the t-SNE algorithm on the visualizations it produces. They highlight that tuning hyperparameters can changes the vector positions in low dimensions. More precisely, they show experimentation with the perplexity parameter of the t-SNE model. This parameter is central to what structures t-SNE finds: either local or global, based on the number of neighbors estimated for a data point. In the original paper, a range between 5 and 50 was suggested by the authors for this parameter [28]. Watternberg et al. show different visualizations produced after changing the value of this parameter, for the same data set. Methods have also been proposed to automatically identify the optimal value of this parameter, through Bayesian optimization [11]. Given the sheer size of data points used for the embedding model, around 250,000 unique color values, we do not run into unexpected behaviors with our selection of the parameter value. After experimentation with different perplexity values, across different art periods, we generated all fingerprints with a perplexity value of 100. Distinct clusters were apparent in all visualizations and using the same value across all embeddings ensured that the results observed were at least not affected by this hyperparameter.

Wattenberg et al. further show that the size of clusters and the distances between them are not as meaningful as one would consider them to be. As t-SNE translates the distances between data points in higher dimensions to lower dimensions, it tries to scale those distances accordingly. As a result, dense clusters expand while sparse ones shrink. In our usage of the algorithm to generate the fingerprints, we comment instead on the combinations of colors in a cluster, or how much shades of a unique color fill the visual space. With a future study incorporating a frequency analysis, exact size of clusters can be determined as well. Finally, all fingerprints generated have clusters compacted in a small space. We identify the visually separable clusters and comment on their shape and color but refrain from discussing the gaps between clusters. Overall, the usage of t-SNE with a set perplexity value across all art periods, allows us to safely make observations about an artist's choice of a color palette, without falling into the traps of hyperparameter tuning effects.

Fig. 7. Fingerprint comparison of the earliest art periods of Dalí, van Gogh, and Picasso, respectively.

The fingerprints can be used to compare artists as well. Figure 7 shows a comparison of the earliest art periods of each of the three artists in our study. Looking at them side by side, van Gogh's dull palette becomes more apparent. While Dalí was experimenting with different art styles, using combinations of green and yellow effectively in his artworks, Picasso was working with a realist art style, in which shades of yellow and brown were used heavily to paint portraits. The fingerprints highlight these observations and further give the viewer an idea about other colors combinations the artists used when they were still developing their skills. The differences in forms and art styles are often compared between artists, as how the colors are used on a canvas presents more visual intrigue to the viewer. This study provides another avenue, to showcase the color palettes used by painters, and presents them visually, so that viewers can observe the striking similarities or differences between art periods and artists right away.

6   Conclusion

The main contribution of this paper is to showcase color palettes of art periods generated for three famous painters. Using word2vec models and the t-SNE algorithm, we first create vector representation of over 250,000 distinct colors, using collections of artworks from each art period, and then visualize them on a two-dimensional space. We term these visualizations as fingerprints, as they uniquely identify the art periods of each painter. We provide commentary on each art period and discuss how the fingerprints summarize the color choices the painters made.

References

1. Art movement definition: what is an art movement? https://www.eden-gallery.com/news/art-movement-definition. Accessed 23 Nov 2021
2. Art periods. https://www.pablo-ruiz-picasso.net/periods.php. Accessed 23 Nov 2021
3. Discover, buy, and sell fine art. https://www.artsy.net/. Accessed 23 Nov 2021
4. Surrealism. https://www.thedaliuniverse.com/en/salvador-dali/surrealism. Accessed 23 Nov 2021
5. Visual art encyclopedia. https://www.wikiart.org/. Accessed 23 Nov 2021
6. Visual art movements, artists, ideas, and definitions. https://www.theartstory.org/. Accessed 23 Nov 2021
7. Abry, P., Wendt, H., Jaffard, S.: When van Gogh meets Mandelbrot: multifractal classification of painting's texture. Signal Process. **93**(3), 554–572 (2013)
8. Bakarov, A.: A survey of word embeddings evaluation methods. arXiv preprint arXiv:1801.09536 (2018)
9. Brooks, D.: The paintings: a–z listings. http://www.vggallery.com/painting/mainaz.htm. Accessed 23 Nov 2021
10. Buitinck, L., et al.: API design for machine learning software: experiences from the Scikit-learn project. In: ECML PKDD Workshop: Languages for Data Mining and Machine Learning, pp. 108–122 (2013)
11. Cao, Y., Wang, L.: Automatic selection of t-SNE perplexity. arXiv preprint arXiv:1708.03229 (2017)
12. Du, J., Jia, P., Dai, Y., Tao, C., Zhao, Z., Zhi, D.: Gene2vec: distributed representation of genes based on co-expression. BMC Genom. **20**(1), 7–15 (2019)
13. Elgammal, A., Liu, B., Elhoseiny, M., Mazzone, M.: Can: creative adversarial networks, generating "art" by learning about styles and deviating from style norms. arXiv preprint arXiv:1706.07068 (2017)

14. Gatys, L.A., Ecker, A.S., Bethge, M.: Image style transfer using convolutional neural networks. In: Proceedings of the IEEE Conference on Computer Vision and Pattern Recognition, pp. 2414–2423 (2016)
15. Gisbrecht, A., Schulz, A., Hammer, B.: Parametric nonlinear dimensionality reduction using kernel t-SNE. Neurocomputing **147**, 71–82 (2015)
16. Grohe, M.: word2vec, node2vec, graph2vec, x2vec: Towards a theory of vector embeddings of structured data. In: Proceedings of the 39th ACM SIGMOD-SIGACT-SIGAI Symposium on Principles of Database Systems, pp. 1–16 (2020)
17. Guthrie, D., Allison, B., Liu, W., Guthrie, L., Wilks, Y.: A closer look at skip-gram modelling. In: LREC, vol. 6, pp. 1222–1225. Citeseer (2006)
18. Hamilton, W.L., Ying, R., Leskovec, J.: Inductive representation learning on large graphs. In: Proceedings of the 31st International Conference on Neural Information Processing Systems, pp. 1025–1035 (2017)
19. Herremans, D., Chuan, C.H.: Modeling musical context with word2vec. arXiv preprint arXiv:1706.09088 (2017)
20. Hinton, G., Roweis, S.T.: Stochastic neighbor embedding. In: NIPS, vol. 15, pp. 833–840. Citeseer (2002)
21. Kelek, M.O., Calik, N., Yildirim, T.: Painter classification over the novel art painting data set via the latest deep neural networks. Procedia Comput. Sci. **154**, 369–376 (2019)
22. Kobak, D., Berens, P.: The art of using t-SNE for single-cell transcriptomics. Nat. Commun. **10**(1), 1–14 (2019)
23. Levy, E., David, O.E., Netanyahu, N.S.: Genetic algorithms and deep learning for automatic painter classification. In: Proceedings of the 2014 Annual Conference on Genetic and Evolutionary Computation, pp. 1143–1150 (2014)
24. Li, M., Lv, J., Wang, J., Sang, Y.: An abstract painting generation method based on deep generative model. Neural Process. Lett. **52**(2), 949–960 (2020)
25. Li, W., Cerise, J.E., Yang, Y., Han, H.: Application of t-SNE to human genetic data. J. Bioinformat. Comput. Biol. **15**(04), 1750017 (2017)
26. Liu, S., Yang, J., Agaian, S.S., Yuan, C.: Novel features for art movement classification of portrait paintings. Image Vision Comput. **108**, 104121 (2021)
27. Luan, F., Paris, S., Shechtman, E., Bala, K.: Deep photo style transfer. In: Proceedings of the IEEE Conference on Computer Vision and Pattern Recognition, pp. 4990–4998 (2017)
28. Van der Maaten, L., Hinton, G.: Visualizing data using t-SNE. J. Mach. Learn. Res. **9**(11), 2579 2605 (2008)
29. Mikolov, T., Chen, K., Corrado, G., Dean, J.: Efficient estimation of word representations in vector space. arXiv preprint arXiv:1301.3781 (2013)
30. Mukkamala, K.: Salvador dali: a 20th century artistic genius, http://www.people.vcu.edu/~djbromle/modern-art/02/Salvador-Dali/index.htm. Accessed 23 Nov 2021
31. Raunak, V., Gupta, V., Metze, F.: Effective dimensionality reduction for word embeddings. In: Proceedings of the 4th Workshop on Representation Learning for NLP (RepL4NLP-2019), pp. 235–243 (2019)
32. Reas, C., Fry, B.: Processing: programming for the media arts. AI Soc. **20**(4), 526–538 (2006)
33. Řehůřek, R., Sojka, P.: Software framework for topic modelling with large corpora. In: Proceedings of the LREC 2010 Workshop on New Challenges for NLP Frameworks, ELRA, Valletta, Malta, May 2010, pp. 45–50 (2010). http://is.muni.cz/publication/884893/en

34. Richman-Abdou, K.: The evolution of picasso's painting style and what each artistic choice represents (Sep 2020). https://mymodernmet.com/pablo-picasso-periods/. Accessed 23 Nov 2021

35. Rodriguez, C.S., Lech, M., Pirogova, E.: Classification of style in fine-art paintings using transfer learning and weighted image patches. In: 2018 12th International Conference on Signal Processing and Communication Systems (ICSPCS), pp. 1–7. IEEE (2018)

36. Sablatnig, R., Kammerer, P., Zolda, E.: Hierarchical classification of paintings using face-and brush stroke models. In: Proceedings. Fourteenth International Conference on Pattern Recognition (Cat. No. 98EX170), vol. 1, pp. 172–174. IEEE (1998)

37. Salunke, S.S.: Selenium Webdriver in Python: Learn with Examples, 1st edn. CreateSpace Independent Publishing Platform, North Charleston (2014)

38. Sun, S., Luo, C., Chen, J.: A review of natural language processing techniques for opinion mining systems. Information fusion **36**, 10–25 (2017)

39. Tian, F., et al: A probabilistic model for learning multi-prototype word embeddings. In: Proceedings of COLING 2014, the 25th International Conference on Computational Linguistics: Technical Papers, pp. 151–160 (2014)

40. Tralbaut, M.E.: Vincent van Gogh. Viking Press (1969)

41. Trask, A., Gilmore, D., Russell, M.: Modeling order in neural word embeddings at scale. In: International Conference on Machine Learning, pp. 2266–2275. PMLR (2015)

42. Van Nguyen, T., Nguyen, A.T., Phan, H.D., Nguyen, T.D., Nguyen, T.N.: Combining word2vec with revised vector space model for better code retrieval. In: 2017 IEEE/ACM 39th International Conference on Software Engineering Companion (ICSE-C), pp. 183–185. IEEE (2017)

43. Van Rossum, G., Drake, Jr, F.L.: Python Reference Manual. Centrum voor Wiskunde en Informatica Amsterdam (1995)

44. Wattenberg, M., Viégas, F., Johnson, I.: How to use t-SNE effectively. Distill **1**(10), e2 (2016)

45. Zhang, Y., Jin, R., Zhou, Z.H.: Understanding bag-of-words model: a statistical framework. Int. J. Mach. Learn. Cybern. **1**(1–4), 43–52 (2010)

MusIAC: An Extensible Generative Framework for Music Infilling Applications with Multi-level Control

Rui Guo[1]([✉]) [iD], Ivor Simpson[2] [iD], Chris Kiefer[1] [iD], Thor Magnusson[1] [iD],
and Dorien Herremans[3] [iD]

[1] Department of Music, University of Sussex, Brighton, UK
r.guo@sussex.ac.uk
[2] Department of Informatics, University of Sussex, Brighton, UK
[3] Information Systems Technology and Design, Singapore University of Technology and Design, Singapore, Singapore

Abstract. We present a novel music generation framework for music infilling, with a user friendly interface. Infilling refers to the task of generating musical sections given the surrounding multi-track music. The proposed transformer-based framework is extensible for new control tokens as the added music control tokens such as tonal tension per bar and track polyphony level in this work. We explore the effects of including several musically meaningful control tokens, and evaluate the results using objective metrics related to pitch and rhythm. Our results demonstrate that adding additional control tokens helps to generate music with stronger stylistic similarities to the original music. It also provides the user with more control to change properties like the music texture and tonal tension in each bar compared to previous research which only provided control for track density. We present the model in a Google Colab notebook to enable interactive generation.

Keywords: Music generation · Music transformer · Music control · Controllable generation · Music representation · Infilling

1 Introduction

Music composition by artificial intelligence (AI) methods, especially using deep learning, has been an active topic of research in recent years [3,19]. In a recent survey of musical agents [30], twelve musical tasks such as accompaniment generation, melody/rhythm generation, continuation, arrangement, and style imitation are examined. In the deep learning era, all of these tasks have been explored to some extent.

When applying AI to music composition, however, an often ignored question is "why" one might wish computers to compose music. From the perspective

Supplementary Information The online version contains supplementary material available at https://doi.org/10.1007/978-3-031-03789-4_22.

T. Martins et al. (Eds.): EvoMUSART 2022, LNCS 13221, pp. 341–356, 2022.
https://doi.org/10.1007/978-3-031-03789-4_22

of the deep learning practitioner, the answer may be to explore the limits of AI models for creative tasks, and investigate whether they can generate music as human composers. On the other hand, musicians and composers may want to use AI as a source of inspiration, for instance, by rapidly offering several solutions. One such AI method is music infilling or inpainting [12,24]. It is used to extend pre-existent music materials, such as filling in the missing bars or tracks given the surrounding music information. It can write a new melody line given the existing bass and accompaniment track, or rewrite a few bars in the middle given the beginning and the end. Many reasonable solutions may exist that match the surrounding music progression and harmony. Without efficient track and bar music property conditions, however, the user has to generate the music repeatedly until it satisfies user's requirement.

Several research studies have used a transformer model [31] for symbolic music generation [9,12,15,17,18,27] and the results are promising. However, controlling the generation process is still limited in these approaches.

One common control for the music infilling system is track density [9,12], which is defined as the number of notes in a track divided by the total timesteps in that track. However, a sole density cannot easily change the accompaniment track from a monophonic style to a polyphonic style. A polyphony control can help to convert a monophonic track such as arpeggio to a more polyphonic texture such as a chord track or vice versa in a direct way, and that can be useful mostly for the accompaniment track. Another interesting control is the track occupation rate, which determines which ratio of a track is note occupied versus filled with rests. These track features may be useful as a composer may want to control the track texture.

Except for those track controls, a bar level tonal tension control [5,13] can help to create music with specific tension movements, e.g. from low to high, high to low or any tension shape. One use case is to change the tension of the beginning and ending of a piece so as to set certain moods.

To implement these controls, the respective track/bar properties are calculated and added to the input. We deliberately choose to use higher level human interpretable parameters as controls, including six features: key, bar tensile strain, bar cloud diameter, track density, track polyphony, and track occupation, and they are calculated from the input sequence directly. It may be useful to generate music according to the track/bar control parameter template fit to a particular scenario, such as high track note density, low track polyphony rate and high track occupation. As the model learns the relationship between these control tokens and the music, the controls can be changed to generate variations of the original music. In the experiments, we observe that an additional benefit of including more music properties in the input is that the generated music is more similar to the original music measured by pitch and rhythm related metrics.

In this paper, we propose an extensible framework for music generation by infilling reconstruction. Six musically meaningful control tokens are calculated and added to the original input. The effect of adding this conditioning information is examined in an experiment that uses seven objective metrics selected from the literature. Our simple model design makes it extensible so that we can easily include additional tokens in the future. The music infilling task, which involves reconstructing a missing segment of music, is used to validate our results by comparing the properties of original and generated examples. The results show that the model with added calculated music tokens to the input has more stylistic similarity to the original music. Google Colab notebook is shared for free exploration of this infilling system and gives a straightforward way to explore the effect of adding novel musically meaningful tokens to the input. The music generated by changing control tokens demonstrates the controllability of this method.

2 Related Work

Over the years, many different generative models have been developed for symbolic music generation [14,19]. Variational AutoEncoder(VAE) based models [11,24,29] usually generate short music pieces and explore different music features in the latent space. Generative Adversarial Network (GAN) based models [4] can generate longer music, but can be harder to train and may suffer mode collapse without careful parameter tuning [21]. Recursive Neural Networks [34], and more recently the powerful transformer based methods [17] can generate long music pieces but with less control explored so far compared to the VAE models.

Several improvements have been made since the transformer model was first used for music generation, related to both the input representation and the model structure. [18] uses "position" (timestep) and "duration" tokens to replace the "note on" and "note off" tokens [22]. This allows the model to learn to pair the "note on" and "note off" if they are far apart. [27] generates accompaniment given the melody track, and adds pitch, velocity, and duration embeddings in one timestep. [15] has a similar design and uses different output linear layers for different token types. The models by [9,12] generate music infillings similar to the task tackled in this research. Both models take the track note density as the control parameter, without providing any other track/bar level control features, we will explore adding the latter features in this research.

Some interactive interfaces have previously been designed specifically for the music infilling task. [2] and [20]'s interfaces are based on music chorale generation [16].

3 Proposed Model and Representation

The existing transformer-based methods offer few semantic controls for the generation process, or focus on continuous generation rather than infilling. Given the right input controls, music generation models may be driven and steered by relevant musical concepts and ideas. Our work is based on the following assumptions:

1. Including additional derived musical features can improve the performance of music infilling.
2. Using human interpretable music features allows the user to control the generated music.

Because the music infilling region is the model's prediction objective, it is natural to compare the generated music to the original. If the generated music has similar properties to the original infilled music region, then the model has performed well. Our model is versatile enough to allow multiple types of infilling. For instance, in pop music with multiple tracks, the infilling can work either by infilling a whole track or by infilling a bar across tracks, or both at the same time. Figure 1 shows an example of how we can formulate the infilling task. The input music has three tracks, the yellow block region masks the first track, and the blue block region masks the second bar. The aim of the model here is to reconstruct the masked music region given the surrounding information. Providing input with multiple tracks makes it possible to have the track properties separately, and the control for different tracks can be tested separately.

Fig. 1. An example of original music with two infilled regions. The yellow block masks the melody track, and the blue block masks the second bar. The notes of those two masked regions are replaced by a "mask" token in the model input. The target output of the model is to reconstruct the missing track/bar in the infilled region. (Color figure online)

3.1   Adding Control Features

We selected the following information to be added to the model input as controls from multiple levels. This is calculated from the MIDI data and provides high level musical concepts as conditions for the music generation.

1. Track level controls:
   - The track's note density rate: $number_{note}/timesteps_{total}$. This is calculated by dividing the number of notes in a track by the maximum time steps in that track.
   - The track's note polyphony rate: $timesteps_{polynote}/timesteps_{anynote}$. This is the number of timesteps with more than two notes divided by the total number of timesteps with any note.
   - The track's note occupation rate: $timesteps_{anynote}/timesteps_{total}$. This is the total number of timesteps with any note divided by the total number of time steps, including those with rests.

2. Bar level controls:
   - The tensile strain [13] of the notes in that bar: $\sum_{i=1}^{n}(note_{pos}[i] - key_{pos})/n$, which is the average of the difference from the note position to the key position. The note and key position are calculated based on the spiral array theory [5]. This is a tonal tension measure.
   - The cloud diameter [13] of the notes in that bar: $\max_{i\in[1..n-1],j\in[i+1..n]}(note_{pos}[i] - note_{pos}[j])$. This is another tonal tension measure, which only calculates the largest distance between notes in that bar. The calculation of the note position is also based on the spiral array theory.

Except for the above controls, the following information is also added to the model's input as auxiliary information. The key is calculated by [7,10]. The tempo, time signature, and track instrument number are extracted directly from the MIDI files.

- The key of the song, which can be one of 24 keys (major and minor).
- The tempo of the song, categorised into seven different bins.
- The time signature of the song, including 4/4, 3/4, 2/4, and 6/8.
- The track's instrument: The MIDI instrument number.

3.2   Data Representation

We use an adapted version of the "REMI" [18] token representation in this work. The "REMI" format includes position tokens to mark the position of the note inside a bar. The number of the position is related to the minimum duration of the note. We select the 16th note as the minimum note length, and a bar in 4/4 metre is thus divided into 16 different start positions. The position tokens range from "e_0" to "e_15", and the duration tokens range from "n_1" to "n_32". The maximum note length "n_32" represents two whole notes in the time signature of 4/4. The pitch tokens range from "p_21" to "p_108", representing A-1 to C7 respectively. There is a "bar" token to mark the start of a new bar. The velocity, tempo, and chord tokens proposed in [18] are discarded in the format used here. The dynamics of music is not the focus of this research, and by removing the velocity of each note, notes with the same duration can be grouped by using only one duration token after the pitch tokens. E.g. e_0, p_60, p_67, n_10 means note C3 and G3 have the same duration ($10 \times$ 16th note), which equals the summation of a half note (8 * 16th note) and an eighth note ($2 \times$ 16th note). Because the tonal tension information is included, the chord information is also removed.

To represent the "track" concept, a "track" token is added to the vocabulary list, similar to [27]. Up to three tracks are used in this work: "track_0" is the melody track, "track_1" is the bass track, and "track_2" is an accompaniment track. The track token is the first token of all the tokens in that track. More tracks can be added in the future if they are arranged in the same order, e.g. track_3 for drum and track_4 for a second melody.

Figure 2 shows a piece with three tracks. Before the calculated control information is added, the event list is: 4/4, t_3, i_0, i_32, i_48, bar, track_0, e_0, p_79, n_4, e_4, p_76, n_4, e_8, p_74, n_6, track_1, e_0, p_45, n_8, e_8, p_41, n_8, track_2, e_0, p_64, p_67, n_8, e_0, p_60, n_16, e_8, p_65, n_8, bar, track_0, e_0, p_69, n_4, e_4, p_71, n_4, e_8, p_72, nv6, track_1, e_0, p_43, n_8, e_8, p_48, n_8, track_2, e_0, p_59, p_65, p_67, n_8, e_8, p_60, p_64, n_8.

Fig. 2. Example of a musical segment in our dataset.

The control information that is included in our proposed framework is tensile strain (12 categories), cloud diameter (12 categories), track density/polyphony/occupation rate (each for 10 categories) as per the previous subsection. Because the calculation of the bar tonal tension is based on a determined key, the key of the song is also determined and added to the music input. After those calculated control tokens are added, the data representation for Fig. 2 becomes: 4/4, t_3, k_0, d_0, d_0, d_0, o_8, o_9, o_9, y_0, y_0, y_9, i_0, i_32, i_48, bar, s_2, a_1, track_0, e_0, p_79, n_4, e_4, p_76, n_4, e_8, p_74, n_6, track_1, e_0, p_45, n_8, e_8, p_41, n_8, track_2, e_0, p_64, p_67, n_8, e_0, p_60, n_16, e_8, p_65, n_8, bar, s_5, a_6, track_0, e_0, p_69, n_4, e_4, p_71, n_4, e_8, p_72, n_6, track_1, e_0, p_43, n_8, e_8, p_48, n_8, track_2, e_0, p_59, p_65, p_67, n_8, e_8, p_60, p_64, n_8. The tokens at the start of the event list are time signature, tempo, and key tokens. The track control tokens appear after the key token, followed by the instrument tokens. A "bar" token follows the instrument token, immediately followed by tension control. The "track" token is followed by the "position", "pitch" and "duration" tokens inside each track. The final vocabulary list is represented in Table 1.

3.3   Model Architecture

As the core task here is music infilling rather than forward generation, the model should ideally use bidirectional information. The transformer encoder-decoder model [31] which was originally developed for the seq-seq translation task, is adapted in this work. The infilling task in music can be likened to the corrupted token reconstruction task in natural language processing [8]. In our proposed

Table 1. The event vocabulary, including all calculated control tokens.

Token types	Tokens	Number
Position	e_0...e_15	16
Pitch	p_21...p_108	88
Duration	n_1...n_32	32
Structure tokens	bar, track_0, track_1, track_2	4
Time signature	4/4, 3/4, 2/4, 6/8	4
Tempo	t_0...t_6	7
Instrument	i_0...i_127	128
Key	k_0...k_23	24
Tensile strain	s_0...s_11	12
Cloud diameter	a_0...a_11	12
Density	d_0...d_9	10
Polyphony	y_0...y_9	10
Occupation	y_0...o_9	10
Model	mask, pad, eos	3
Total		360

framework, a transformer encoder-decoder is used to reconstruct the masked input in the encoder [28]. The bi-directional encoder makes each token in the encoder attend to other positions in the input, while the token in a one stack decoder language model can only attend to the tokens before the current token [26]. Our model has the same structure as the vanilla transformer [31] with two stages of training. Firstly, music grammar is learned in the pretraining stage and then specific tasks are learned in the finetuning stage. This process is similar to the work of [6,8,33].

During pretraining, we accustom the model to small masked sections: one "mask" token can replace up to three tokens. If the input x position from u to v is masked, and the $l = u - v$ is the masked token span length, the loss function is calculated as in Eq. (1):

$$L(\theta) = \log P(x^{u:v}|x^{\setminus u:v}; \theta), \quad 0 < u - v <= 3. \tag{1}$$

Up to 15% of the tokens in the input are randomly masked with a "mask" in pretraining. We only use one "mask" token to replace each span, which differs from other work [26] which uses a different mask token for each span masked. The lengths of the spans of the masked token are 3, 1, 2 and the frequency of the masked tokens with those span lengths is in the ratio of 2:1:1 in the training respectively.

After pretraining, the finetuning stage is used to train the model for the real application task with larger masked areas). The finetuning task includes three masking types corresponding to the application. For each song: 1. randomly select a bar, and mask all tracks in that bar. 2. randomly select a track, and mask all the bars in selected tracks. 3. randomly select bars, and randomly select tracks in that bar.

One "mask" token represents a track in a bar, and the decoder target is to reconstruct that masked bar track. Each "mask" in the encoder input is matched with a "mask" input in the decoder, and the decoder target output will end with an "eos" token. A "pad" token is also added to pad sequences of different lengths to match the batch size. Figure 3 shows masked encoder input and the decoder input and target output during pretraining/finetuning. During finetuning, if the first bar of Fig. 2 is infilled, the encoder input becomes: 4/4, t_3, k_0, d_0, d_0, d_0, o_8, o_9, o_9, y_0, y_0, y_9, i_0, i_32, i_48, bar, s_2, a_1, mask, mask, mask, bar, s_5, a_6, track_0, e_0, p_69, n_4, e_4, p_71, n_4, e_8, p_72, n_6, track_1, e_0, p_43, n_8, e_8, p_48, n_8, track_2, e_0, p_59, p_65, p_67, n_8, e_8, p_60, p_64, n_8. The decoder input is:mask,mask,mask, and the decoder target output is track_0, e_0, p_79, n_4, e_4, p_76, n_4, e_8, p_74, n_6, eos, track_1, e_0, p_45, n_8, e_8, p_41, n_8, eos, track_2, e_0, p_64, p_67, n_8, e_0, p_60, n_16, e_8, p_65, n_8, eos. We omitted the second bar's tokens to save page space.

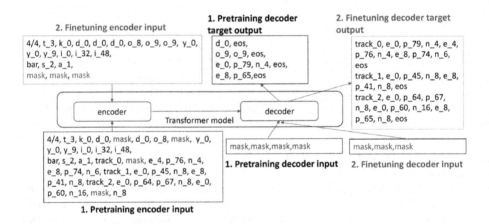

Fig. 3. The model encoder input, decoder input and decoder target output during pretraining and finetuning. The maximum masked span length is three for pretraining, and a "mask" token will replace a track in a bar during the finetuning stage.

4   Experimental Setup

We conducted an experiment to validate the musical quality of the output as well as the influence of the control features. Two models with the same vocabulary size were trained in the experiment: one with controls and one without. The model without control will not add the six calculated controls to the input.

4.1   Dataset

Any dataset used by our proposed model should have proper track/bar numbers. The maximum number of tracks in a song is limited to three, which includes mandatory melody and bass tracks, and an optional accompaniment track. The maximum bar length in a song is set to 16, which is enough for the infilling reconstruction and not too long for the model to compute.

To build our symbolic dataset, we filter the Lakh LMD-matched dataset [25] for songs that have both a melody and bass track, as well as an optional accompaniment track. After that, the key of the song and the tension metrics are calculated using [7,10]. A total of 32,352 songs remain after this step. To tackle the imbalance of the time signature in the remaining files, a subset with metre 2/4, 3/4 and 6/8 is pitch-shifted to the other 11 keys in the same mode. The same strategy is applied to a subset of songs with minor keys. A moving window size of 8 bars is used to create multiple dataset entries from a single song. All the calculated control features are added in this step.

4.2   Model Configuration and Training

One model is trained with all input and control tokens, the second models is trained without adding the control tokens. Both the encoder and decoder of the transformer have 4 layers, 8 heads, and the model dimension is 512. Both the models are trained for 10 epochs with 2 epochs of pretraining and the remaining 8 epochs for fine-tuning. The learning rate is 0.0001, and the training takes around 2 days per model on a Tesla V100 GPU. The training/validation/test data split ratio is 8:1:1.

4.3   Inference Strategy

Our token representation allows us to guide the model to only generate output that adheres to the representation's grammar. The grammar of the notes in a track in the regular expression format is (step pitch + duration)∗. In the inference stage, the tokens not in this grammar are removed by setting those notes' logit to -100, and then weighted sampling is applied to sample from the tokens. This makes sure that the output will not sample the incorrect tokens and the result always has a correct grammar.

5   Evaluation

To evaluate the generated music infillings generated by the model with and without controls, we select seven objective metrics based on pitch and rhythm similarity. We compare the difference of those features between the generated and the original music in the masked position. Then we check if our model can really control features of the generated music by changing track/bar controls through our developed Google Colab interface. Our experiment evaluates if the generated music follows the desired control features and is musically meaningful.

5.1   Objective Evaluation Using Selected Metrics

To compare the quality of the generated infilling by those two models, we selected five pitch-related metrics and two duration-related metrics inspired by [32]. The infilling generation task makes it meaningful to compare the metrics' difference between the generated infilling and the original music. A smaller difference means the generated infilling has more stylistic similarity to the original music. Note that there is not only one optimal way to infill music, and we assume the original one is the target here. In future work, this assumption may be tested by allowing for a human listening experiment to evaluate the generated infillings. Both the track and bar infilling are evaluated.

We selected 1,000 songs randomly from the testset and masked a random track/bar, to test each of the two models. The models then generate the infilling for the masked track/bar. Seven objective metrics are selected inspired by [32] including five pitch related metrics: 1) pitch number: the number of used pitches. 2) note number: the number of used notes. 3) pitch range: $pitch_{max} - pitch_{min}$. 4) chromagram histogram: the histogram of 12 pitch groups after categorising all the pitches 5) pitch interval histogram: the histogram of the pitch difference between two consecutive notes. Two duration features: 6) duration histogram. 7) onset interval histogram: the histogram of time between two consecutive notes. These seven features are calculated for the generated/original infilled track/bar. For the first three features we calculate the absolute difference between the feature for the generated and original music, normalised by the feature of the original music: $abs(feature_{gen} - feature_{ori})/feature_{ori}$ For the last four histogram features we calculate the sum of the square difference between the features of the generated and the original music, normalised by the sum of the square of the feature of the original music: $sum(square(feature_{gen} - feature_{ori}))/sum(square(feature_{ori}))$.

The mean and the standard deviation are calculated on those difference features and reported in Table 2. The left value in each cell is the result for the model without added control tokens, and the right value is the result for the model with added control tokens. All of the values, except the track pitch number standard deviation, show that the model with added control generates music more similar to the original music, especially in terms of melody, accompaniment track, and bar infilling. The added control work much like a template, and the generated music follows these conditions well.

5.2   The Interactive Interface and Controllability

A Google Colab notebook has been prepared for the exploration of this application.[1] The user can upload MIDI files or select MIDI files from the test dataset. Here "Imagine" from John Lennon is selected from the test dataset as an example.

After selecting/uploading the song, the user can choose to infill a track/bar without changing the control tokens, or change the track/bar controls first, and

---

[1] https://github.com/ruiguo-bio/MusIAC.

Table 2. The mean and standard deviation of the difference for the seven objective metrics between the generated and original music. The left value in each cell is the result from the model without added control tokens, and the right value is the result from the model with added control. The column header shows was was infilled: melody track, bass track, accompaniment track, or a random bar (all tracks in this bar).

Features	Melody		Bass		Accompaniment		Bar	
	Mean	std	Mean	std	Mean	std	Mean	std
Pitch number	0.45/0.39	0.57/0.46	0.55/0.52	0.76/0.78	0.57/0.41	0.69/0.52	0.41/0.33	0.79/0.58
Note number	0.82/0.29	2.71/0.85	0.63/0.29	1.25/0.71	0.97/0.41	2.41/0.73	0.42/0.32	0.90/0.71
Pitch range	0.59/0.49	0.93/0.74	0.62/0.58	0.92/0.87	0.80/0.55	1.05/0.76	0.55/0.38	2.55/1.54
Chroma hist	0.59/0.53	0.49/0.42	0.45/0.38	0.50/0.44	0.34/0.27	0.42/0.31	0.73/0.58	0.79/0.70
Pitch itv hist	0.44/0.39	0.46/0.40	0.50/0.45	0.55/0.53	1/0.84	0.75/0.63	0.66/0.60	0.77/0.75
Duration hist	0.55/0.42	0.61/0.46	0.77/0.61	0.77/0.68	1.03/0.74	0.93/0.78	0.52/0.45	0.64/0.61
Onset itv hist	0.45/0.35	0.55/0.41	0.74/0.61	0.71/0.70	0.86/0.69	0.85/0.77	0.44/0.38	0.63/0.58

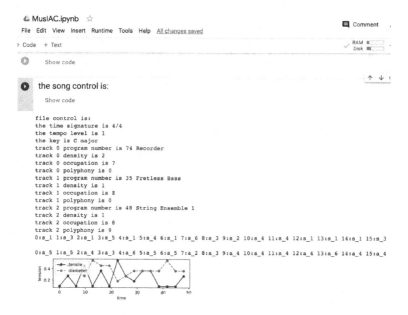

Fig. 4. The original music's control information including track/bar control and song key, tempo and time signature.

then generate the corresponding track/bar. The original control tokens of one section of "Imagine" are calculated and shown as in Fig. 4. The melody and accompaniment tracks have low note density, which means there are not many note onsets in that track. The accompaniment track is composed of mainly chord notes. The track/bar control can be changed by selecting the specific control type and value as shown in Fig. 5 (only a section is shown due to page limitations). To add more notes to those tracks, and make the accompaniment track less polyphonic, we first

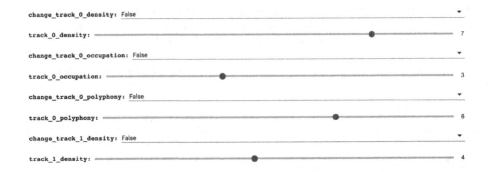

Fig. 5. The track/bar controls can be changed separately

Fig. 6. The first three bars of a section of "Imagine". The left figure is the original, and the right figure shows the infilled melody and accompaniment track with changed track density level from 1 to 5 and polyphony rate from 9 to 2. The original melody track has a low note density level of 1. The accompaniment track has low note density level 1 and high polyphony level 9. The infilled melody/accompaniment track match the selected controls, and the accompaniment is similar to Alberti bass, with more notes and less polyphony.

change the melody track density to level 8 from level 1. After the new melody track is generated, the accompaniment track is generated with density set to level 5 from level 1 and the polyphony level set to level 2 from level 9. The generated result is shown in the right figure in Fig. 6. The resulting music matches the desired control with a tolerance threshold of 1 (which means level 3 is accepted if the target level is 4 or 2). The resulting accompaniment track's texture is similar to Alberti bass, and both of the tracks have more notes added following the increase of the track density level control.

Based on the previous track's infilling result, the first bar's tensile strain is changed from level 1 to level 6 to increase the tension of the beginning. The infilled result is shown in Fig. 7. The first bar contains the subdominant of the F major chord, which is the second bar's chord. This new first bar, together with the following two bars gives the progression of IV/IV -> IV -> I, which is musically meaningful (from subdominant to tonic chord), and it also increases the tension of the first bar. The full 16 bars music/sheet of the original/generated music are in the supplement material.

Fig. 7. The first bar tonal tension is changed from 1 to 6. Here the "tensile strain" is changed, and the result shows that the first bar is the subdominant of the IV chord of C major. The second bar is subdominant and goes to I in the third bar. This result increases the tension but also progresses smoothly with the surrounding of the music.

The track/bar infilling operation can be repeated several times until the result is satisfactory. The generated MIDI/rendered wav file can be downloaded for further editing or imported in a digital audio workstation (DAW).

6   Conclusion

In this work, we propose an pretraining-finetuning transformer framework for the music infilling task with multiple levels of control, together with an intuitive interface. We selected track density, polyphony, and occupation level as track level controls to increase the user's controllability. This offers a greater steerability compared to existing systems with just density control [9,12]. We also added tensile strain and cloud diameter features per bar as controls for the tonality (tonal tension) of each bar. Control tokens work as a template on which the generated music can be conditioned. The generated result from the input with those added controls as conditions has a higher stylistic similarity to the original music, versus a model without controls.

To optimally demonstrate our proposed framework with a user-friendly interactive interface, we have made it available through Google Colab. In this interface, the user can modify the music while it is being generated.

In the future work, we will systematically check the controllability of each of the six control tokens and further evaluate the musicality with quantitative metrics. A listening test would also be useful to evaluate the musical quality, as there may be more good sounding possibilities than just the original music. We would also like to explore how to further increase the controllability of this model. Currently, our model learns to follow controls (i.e., features) that are already present or easy to calculate from our dataset. It is hard for the model to generate music with "unseen" musical features, i.e. hard to capture, implicit characteristics. In recent research, a transformer model was combined with a prior model to model the latent space [1]. If different music properties can be disentangled in the latent space [23], this will allow for direct manipulation of the generated music's properties even though these features were not explicit in the dataset.

Acknowledgement. This work is funded by Chinese scholarship Council and Singapore Ministry of Education Grant no. MOE2018-T2-2-161.

References

1. Akama, T.: A contextual latent space model: subsequence modulation in melodic sequence. In: Proceedings of the 22nd International Society for Music Information Retrieval Conference, pp. 27–34 (2021)
2. Bazin, T., Hadjeres, G.: NONOTO: a model-agnostic web interface for interactive music composition by inpainting. arXiv:1907.10380 (2019)
3. Briot, J.P., Hadjeres, G., Pachet, F.: Deep Learning Techniques for Music Generation. Springer, Heidelberg (2020). https://doi.org/10.1007/978-3-319-70163-9
4. Brunner, G., Wang, Y., Wattenhofer, R., Zhao, S.: Symbolic music genre transfer with CycleGAN. In: 2018 IEEE 30th International Conference on Tools with Artificial Intelligence (ICTAI), Volos, Greece, pp. 786–793 (2018)

5. Chew, E.: The spiral array: an algorithm for determining key boundaries. In: Anagnostopoulou, C., Ferrand, M., Smaill, A. (eds.) ICMAI 2002. LNCS (LNAI), vol. 2445, pp. 18–31. Springer, Heidelberg (2002). https://doi.org/10.1007/3-540-45722-4_4

6. Chou, Y.H., Chen, I., Chang, C.J., Ching, J., Yang, Y.H., et al.: MidiBERT-piano: large-scale pre-training for symbolic music understanding. arXiv:2107.05223 (2021)

7. Cuthbert, M.S., Ariza, C.: music21: a toolkit for computer-aided musicology and symbolic music data. In: Proceedings of the 11th International Society for Music Information Retrieval Conference, Utrecht, Netherlands, pp. 637–642 (2010)

8. Devlin, J., Chang, M.W., Lee, K., Toutanova, K.: BERT: pre-training of deep bidirectional transformers for language understanding. arXiv:1810.04805 (2021)

9. Ens, J., Pasquier, P.: MMM: exploring conditional multi-track music generation with the transformer. arXiv:2008.06048 (2020)

10. Guo, R., Herremans, D., Magnusson, T.: Midi miner - a Python library for tonal tension and track classification. arXiv:1910.02049 (2019)

11. Guo, R., Simpson, I., Magnusson, T., Kiefer, C., Herremans, D.: A variational autoencoder for music generation controlled by tonal tension. arXiv preprint arXiv:2010.06230 (2020)

12. Hadjeres, G., Crestel, L.: The piano inpainting application. arXiv:2107.05944 (2021)

13. Herremans, D., Chew, E.: Tension ribbons: quantifying and visualising tonal tension. In: 2nd International Conference on Technologies for Music Notation and Representation, Cambridge, UK, pp. 8–18 (2016)

14. Herremans, D., Chew, E.: MorpheuS: generating structured music with constrained patterns and tension. IEEE Trans. Affect. Comput. 10(4), 510–523 (2017)

15. Hsiao, W.Y., Liu, J.Y., Yeh, Y.C., Yang, Y.H.: Compound word transformer: learning to compose full-song music over dynamic directed hypergraphs. arXiv:2101.02402 (2021)

16. Huang, C.A., Cooijmans, T., Roberts, A., Courville, A.C., Eck, D.: Counterpoint by convolution. In: Proceedings of the 18th International Society for Music Information Retrieval Conference, Suzhou, China, pp. 211–218 (2017)

17. Huang, C.A., et al.: Music transformer: generating music with long-term structure. In: 7th International Conference on Learning Representations, New Orleans, USA (2019)

18. Huang, Y.S., Yang, Y.H.: Pop music transformer: beat-based modeling and generation of expressive pop piano compositions. In: Proceedings of the 28th ACM International Conference on Multimedia, Seattle, USA, pp. 1180–1188 (2020)

19. Ji, S., Luo, J., Yang, X.: A comprehensive survey on deep music generation: multi-level representations, algorithms, evaluations, and future directions. arXiv:2011.06801 (2020)

20. Louie, R., Coenen, A., Huang, C.Z., Terry, M., Cai, C.J.: Novice-AI music co-creation via AI-steering tools for deep generative models. In: Proceedings of the 2020 CHI Conference on Human Factors in Computing Systems, Honolulu, USA, pp. 1–13 (2020)

21. Muhamed, A., et al.: Transformer-GAN: symbolic music generation using a learned loss. In: 4th Workshop on Machine Learning for Creativity and Design at NeurIPS 2020 (2020)

22. Oore, S., Simon, I., Dieleman, S., Eck, D., Simonyan, K.: This time with feeling: learning expressive musical performance. Neural Comput. Appl. 32(4), 955–967 (2020)

23. Pati, A., Lerch, A.: Is disentanglement enough? On latent representations for controllable music generation. In: Proceedings of the 22nd International Society for Music Information Retrieval Conference, pp. 517–524 (2021)

24. Pati, A., Lerch, A., Hadjeres, G.: Learning to traverse latent spaces for musical score inpainting. In: Proceedings of the 20th International Society for Music Information Retrieval Conference, Delft, The Netherlands, pp. 343–351 (2019)

25. Raffel, C.: Learning-based methods for comparing sequences, with applications to audio-to-midi alignment and matching. Ph.D. thesis, Columbia University (2016)

26. Raffel, C., et al.: Exploring the limits of transfer learning with a unified text-to-text transformer. J. Mach. Learn. Res. **21**(140), 1–67 (2020)

27. Ren, Y., He, J., Tan, X., Qin, T., Zhao, Z., Liu, T.Y.: PopMAG: pop music accompaniment generation. In: Proceedings of the 28th ACM International Conference on Multimedia, Seattle, USA, pp. 1198–1206 (2020)

28. Song, K., Tan, X., Qin, T., Lu, J., Liu, T.: MASS: masked sequence to sequence pre-training for language generation. In: Proceedings of the 36th International Conference on Machine Learning, Long Beach, USA, vol. 97, pp. 5926–5936 (2019)

29. Tan, H.H., Herremans, D.: Music FaderNets: controllable music generation based on high-level features via low-level feature modelling. In: Proceedings of the 21st International Society for Music Information Retrieval Conference, Montréal, Canada, pp. 109–116 (2020)

30. Tatar, K., Pasquier, P.: Musical agents: a typology and state of the art towards musical metacreation. J. New Music Res. **48**, 105–56 (2019)

31. Vaswani, A., et al.: Attention is all you need. arXiv:1706.03762 (2017)

32. Yang, L.C., Lerch, A.: On the evaluation of generative models in music. Neural Comput. Appl. **32**(9), 4773–4784 (2020)

33. Zeng, M., Tan, X., Wang, R., Ju, Z., Qin, T., Liu, T.Y.: MusicBERT: symbolic music understanding with large-scale pre-training. arXiv:2106.05630 (2021)

34. Zixun, G., Makris, D., Herremans, D.: Hierarchical recurrent neural networks for conditional melody generation with long-term structure. In: 2021 International Joint Conference on Neural Networks (IJCNN), pp. 1–8. IEEE (2021)

A Study on Noise, Complexity, and Audio Aesthetics

Stefano Kalonaris[✉] [iD]

RIKEN Center for Advanced Intelligence Project, Tokyo, Japan
stefano.kalonaris@riken.jp

Abstract. Using computational processes to model aesthetic judgement is an important, if indispensable, endeavour when designing creative AI systems. In the music domain, studies have mostly concentrated on information-based approaches, albeit often offered as single-factor explanations, and developed in isolation from the ongoing debates taking place in other domains, particularly in cognitive science and philosophy of arts. In this paper, the notion of complexity is explored as a tool towards a cross-modal alternative to the methodological legacy rooted in isolated perceptual analyses of the aesthetic object. To this end, several metrics, some long-established in this field (*e.g.*, information dynamics), others derived/adapted from different domains (*e.g.*, processing fluency theory, soundscape ecology), or originally designed, are considered and compared. This set of metrics is applied to the aesthetic evaluation of *noise* music in an effort to generalise the discourse to musical expressions that further foreground the limitations of established practices and the exciting road ahead for computational music aesthetics.

Keywords: Computational aesthetics · Complexity · Japanoise

1 Introduction

Recent neuroscientific research points at the generality of the aesthetic appreciation process and confutes previously held beliefs that such process is merely linked to an object's aesthetic qualities, which can be measured by perceptual analyses. Aesthetic appreciation is, rather, about "assessing what value a stimulus has for the organism, in its current context, relative to previous experiences, its homeostatic state, and behavioral options" [32, p. 22]. Despite such evidence, it is still customary to endorse misleading assumptions, for example that aesthetic judgment is conditioned upon perceptual representation, or that there must be some objective mapping (a rule, a universal law) between perception and judgment. In other words, the belief that aesthetic judgment can be reduced to normative assessments of an art object's perceptual qualities. Among the disciplines that attempt a more holistic understanding of the aesthetic experience, *experimental aesthetics* argues for subject-based, inductive approaches derived from cognitive psychology or neuroscience. According to Leder's [17] revised cognitive model of information processing, for example, aesthetic judgement and

T. Martins et al. (Eds.): EvoMUSART 2022, LNCS 13221, pp. 357–368, 2022.
https://doi.org/10.1007/978-3-031-03789-4_23

aesthetic emotion are seen as output products of a recursive and complex network of connected stages in a continuous evaluation of an art work. Leder's model is an important step beyond single-factor explanations of the aesthetic experience, integrating perceptual, cognitive and affective processes. According to it, two connected and inter-dependent circuits are at work: an inner loop of *continuous affective evaluation*, comprising *automatic* and *deliberate* evaluation, and an outer loop which includes *social interaction discourse, context* and *pre-classification*. Computational aesthetics in the sound realm has so far explored almost exclusively the automatic evaluation sub-network of Leder's model, with particular focus on perceptual analyses (for a thorough review of what has been done to this end the reader is referred to [14]). The author acknowledges that, eventually, the integration of factors such as socio-cultural context, personality, domain knowledge/expertise, and memory integration, as posited in Leder's model, will be inevitable if one is to move beyond "doomed modernist attempts to define universal aesthetic measures" [9, p. 15]. Notwithstanding, this study takes a small, tentative step towards a more modular and cross-modal approach, whilst still being bound to the perceptual analyses sub-network scope. In particular, the author uses, adapts, revises and implements anew different metrics, with in mind to combine them into a sufficiently sensitive and descriptive audio aesthetic profile able to account for challenging musical expressions that have arisen from the 1970s onwards. Generally speaking, these are styles where the conceptual framework takes precedence over the perceptual, manifesting in radical aesthetic ruptures.

In this context, and lacking definitive descriptions and clear boundaries, the author's questions are: which aesthetic metrics can be useful? can one combine some of the known & tested metrics used for the evaluation of more conventional music with other, originally crafted ones, to better suit such musical expressions?

Before delving further into this endeavour, a brief definition of the musical domain of interest is due.

2   Conceptual over Perceptual

The music considered here is often as much about the audible as it is about the imagined, and it prompts a continuous shift of representation and of interpretation. In other words, it allows self enquiry, through processes of conceptual integration and meaning-making. Kramer [15] enumerates many characteristics (*e.g.*, fragmentations and discontinuities, multiple meanings and multiple temporalities, listener-determined meaning and structure, etc.), which can be problematic for established computational aesthetic judgement procedures, as it was shown in [14]. These procedures mostly focus on "the formal and perceptible qualities found in traditional and modernist examples of art" [20, p. 43] and music. The musical styles of interest, on the other hand, are akin to conceptual art, thus ontologically defying objective and quantitative accounts of one's experience of them.

In this wide horizon of musical expression, this study focuses on a particular sub-genre of *noise* music referred to as *Japanoise* in North America or simply as *Noise* in Japan.

2.1 Japanoise

The Japanese offshoot of noise music started developing in the early 1980s, splitting opinions of musicians and audience alike, and revealing "how discourses of musical globalization are continually reformed at the edge, through acts of sound-making, performance, and transcultural interpretations of popular media" [4]. Japanoise did not claim to be a genre. However, by circulation of tapes (reproducing of the experience of live gigs), eventually it became a more formalised phenomenon.

Described as "often unrelentingly harsh" [24, p. 7], it is said to tune into "the negative beauty of sublime experiences with sound" [24, p. 47]. Such notion of negative beauty, whilst not conforming to Kantian standards of balance, is arrived at through a redefined role of noise, repetition, stasis, and distortion. At the same time, through its expression of limit, excess, and endurance, Japanoise is paradoxically related with the Kantian notion of the sublime found in formless, boundless objects: it moves "beyond a hybridity of discrete forms becoming new discrete forms to an absence of form" [12, p. 138].

Japanoise' traits are such that "analytic listening – the separation of sections and understanding of music as articulate sound materials – is rendered problematic" [30, p. 282], as it uses sound to elicit a different aesthetic experience and to test the body's tolerance limits, whilst reclaiming autonomy within acoustic space in a horizon of national homogeneity and mono-cultural lattice [29].

To answer the questions posed in Sect. 1 with respect to Japanoise, this paper explores the notion of complexity, leaving more extensive studies for future endeavours.

3 Complexity

A general understanding/modeling of the music phenomenon *per se* can be based on different feature levels, and might distinguish between a general, auditory system's domain level (*e.g.*, intensity, duration, stream segregation, sensory dissonance, etc.), a syntactical and prosodic level (*e.g.*, contours, meter grouping, hierarchical structures, *Gestalt* grouping, etc.), and a music & culture-specific level (*e.g.*, harmonic and melodic systems and norms, etc.). Of these, and for this study, the author is exclusively concerned with the domain-general level, where sound complexity is thought to be paramount.

It is impossible to come up with a unified definition or description of complexity, as this notion holds as many different meanings as there are applications of it: algorithmic information theory, physical and/or dynamical systems, complex adaptive systems, mathematics, network theory, just to name a few. However, and insofar as this study is concerned, complexity is strongly linked to information theory, thus to the concept of entropy, as defined by Shannon [31].

3.1   Complexity and Computational Aesthetics

Such information-based viewpoint has served as the leading paradigm in computational accounts of the aesthetic experience. This lineage originated in Birkhoff's celebrated aesthetic measure [2] expressed as the ratio between order and complexity, and evolved through Bense's [1] and Mole's [21] Information Aesthetics, Stiny and Gips' Algorithmic Aesthetics [33], and Gell-Mann & Lloyds' Effective Complexity [7].

A quick word of caution is due here, in that complexity holds a fundamentally different value in noise music than it does in more conventional musical expressions and in information theory. Redundancy, for example, might be deliberately used as an aesthetic feature (*e.g.*, in minimalist or drone music). Interestingly, it has been posited [20] that *conceptual complexity* might be more relevant than perceptual complexities in the domain of conceptual art/music. Moreover, one must be aware that musical features used in the calculation of entropy or complexity must be chosen accordingly to the task at hand. For example, if said features are culture-specific (*e.g.*, tonal intervals, scale degrees, etc.), their utility for evaluating the types of organised sound of interest in this paper, some of which have been described as boring, formless and nonsense [26], will be limited, at best.

A description of the complexity-based aesthetic measures considered for this study follows.

4   Proposed Aesthetic Metrics

Drawing from Reber's *processing fluency* theory of aesthetic pleasure [27,28] developed in the visual art context, the notion of **Image Complexity**, hereinafter C_{img}, is borrowed and calculated with a given audio file's spectrogram as input. C_{img} simply measures the ratio between the original, uncompressed image and a compressed version of itself, using the ZIP/deflate compression algorithm. To account for axis/symmetry variance, the same metric is calculated for a 90 degree rotated spectrogram image, and the minimum of the two is taken as the final measure, as in [18].

Structural Complexity (C_{struct}) is defined in [8] as a measure of change of the feature space at different time scales. Here, the aggregation and distance functions (mean and Jensen-Shannon Divergence, respectively) used in their study are retained, but a fixed interval of 1 s and an overlap of 250 ms are used, given the short duration of the samples (see Sect. 5). The feature space for computing the distance metric comprises root mean square (rms), zero crossing rate, spectral centroid and spectral flatness. The features in [8] were not replicated since those are concerned with harmony, a property arguably lacking or not as salient in this study's musical domain of interest. This method needs further investigation and choices regarding suitable audio features warrant a more systematic and thorough study. However, it is presented as a proof of concept and as an opportunity for further development in this direction.

Spectral Complexity [16], hereinafter C_{spec}, is based on the number of peaks in the input spectrum. It is a salient notion in the field of soundscape ecology [25], which studies the relationship between humans, living organisms, and the environment, through sound, and by distinguishing the sonic horizon into three separate classes (*i.e.*, anthropophony, biophony, and geophony). In the author's implementation, the number of peaks (local extrema) is normalised so to have a consistent output range of $[0, 1]$ across all metrics.

Further inspiration from soundscape ecology is drawn, by employing the following three acoustic indices.

Spectral Entropy, hereinafter H_{spec}, is defined as the Shannon entropy of the normalised power spectral density (PSD) of the data [13], shown in Eq. 1. In this implementation, a Welch periodogram [36] was used for the computation of the PSD.

Temporal Entropy, H_{temp} from now on, is instead the Shannon entropy calculated with respect to the amplitude envelope $A(t)$ of a signal $x(t)$, obtained using the Hilbert transform as described in [34]. In practice, H_{temp} will tend towards 1 for noisy signals with many amplitude modulations and, conversely, towards 0 for a quiet signal.

$$H_{spec} = -\sum_{f=0}^{f_s/2} PSD(f) \log_2 PSD(f) \tag{1}$$

In this exploration of complexity-based measures for audio aesthetics, the *Information Rate* (IR) index, borrowed from Information Dynamics, was adopted. IR is the core of the *Audio Oracle* (AO) [5,6,35] algorithm, which has been employed in machine improvisation scenarios, and it is related to the notion of order in Birkhoff's aesthetic measure. In IR, Shannon's entropy H is substituted with a compression algorithm C which measures the number of bits required to represent the data with or without knowledge of the past. IR can thus be as expressed as in Eq. 2, with x being a given signal, x_n the current signal, and x_{past} the past signal.

$$IR(x_n, x_{past}) = C(x_n) - C(x_n|x_{past}) \tag{2}$$

IR has proven a valid alternative for the structural segmentation of audio, and for generating concatenative audio based on the predictions of the AO, but has not been formally used as a predictor/estimator of aesthetic value. To do that, the entropy of the IR series is measured, and referred to, unsurprisingly, as **Information Rate Entropy** (H_{ir}).

5   Experiment

"When it is admitted that experience is not just perceptual and conceptual, a common approach is to 'bracket' or exile the qualitative aspect, and concentrate attention on aspects that are reducible to scientific analysis [. . .]; the recalcitrant residua are then dubbed 'qualia' and thereafter largely ignored" [9, p. 5]

Interested in such qualitative residuals of experience, this section investigates whether the set of metrics defined in Sect. 4 can capture some of the intentionality, the deliberate obstinacy and intransigence at play in Japanoise; or, perhaps more mundanely, if they can offer a more subtle viewpoint when compared to other audio features normally used in music classification tasks (*e.g.*, chroma, pitch contours, beat & tempo estimation, etc.). To this end, it is worth noting the lack of audio datasets for this musical style, which is not surprising given how relatively niche it is. As it is always the case, real-world examples in audio format are normally problematic to use, due to copyright issues. In Japanoise's case, it is particularly difficult to circumvent this problem by means of "covers" or songs "in the style of", for obvious reasons. Therefore, and as a proof of concept, a small but ecologically valid dataset of Japanoise was used: a compilation of representative artists (*e.g.*, Aube, KK Null, Hijokaidan, etc.) of this music genre released by Steinklang Industries in 2008, and available for listening/purchase online.[1] There are 16 pieces in this collection, ranging from 2:31 to 7:40 min with an average duration of 5:07 min.

A proportional number of audio samples comprising air conditioning fans, funicular pulleys, sewing machines, and similar, were fetched from https://freesound.org, and three additional synthesised noise samples were added to this collection, for a total of 18 audio examples ranging from 1:57 to 7:51 min with a mean duration of 4:34 min. This set was collated so as to compare sounds that are vernacularly considered as noise, or "not music", to those which become sound objects of negative beauty, under specific conditions and sociopolitical definitions.

For each of these two collections, 100 random samples of 30 s were extracted, to match the dimensions of the GTZAN Genre Collection,[2] a notable dataset used in genre classification tasks which comprises 10 genres. Of these, two were used for further comparison: one was chosen as it can be considered a difficult listening experience for some, albeit commonly recognised as a legitimate exponent of musical expression, while the other was selected as it is referred to, for the common folk, as the epitome of "beautiful" music. These genres are *metal* and *classical*, respectively.

Table 1 shows the mean and standard deviation for each of the metrics proposed, for each set of sounds. Here, one notes that, with the exception of C_{struct}, there aren't systematic differences between noise-based collections (Japanoise and Soundscape) and the music collections. To investigate further, the approach used in [37] was followed and adapted (the original framework is meant for the evaluation of symbolic output of generative music systems).

---

[1] https://steinklangindustries.bandcamp.com/album/sk-in12-v-a-japanoise-of-death-ii-2008.

[2] http://marsyas.info/downloads/datasets.html.

Table 1. Basic description of the chosen metrics calculated for each sound collection. Row names use initials for each music collection (*e.g.*, J for Japanoise, etc.). Column names use abbreviations for Image Complexity (C_{img}), Spectral Complexity (C_{spec}), Structural Complexity (C_{struct}), Spectral Entropy (H_{spec}), Temporal Entropy (H_{temp}), and Information Rate Entropy (H_{ir}).

	C_{img}	C_{spec}	C_{struct}	H_{spec}	H_{temp}	H_{ir}
J	0.969 ± 0.001	0.193 ± 0.012	0.014 ± 0.012	0.584 ± 0.141	0.991 ± 0.003	0.920 ± 0.043
S	0.972 ± 0.001	0.199 ± 0.006	0.015 ± 0.014	0.526 ± 0.199	0.986 ± 0.008	0.927 ± 0.139
M	0.964 ± 0.001	0.195 ± 0.009	0.044 ± 0.092	0.643 ± 0.092	0.987 ± 0.003	0.930 ± 0.037
C	0.996 ± 0.001	0.194 ± 0.009	0.037 ± 0.014	0.571 ± 0.076	0.976 ± 0.008	0.931 ± 0.027

To compare the sound collections, a relative measure that generalises the result among features is expressed as the intra-set distances, and the difference of intra- and inter-set distances among pairwise collections. For each feature, a pairwise exhaustive cross-validation is carried out, whereby the Euclidean distance of one sample to each of the other samples is computed. Intra-set distances are computed with this procedure within one sound collection, whereas inter-set refers to the same procedure applied between two collections. The output, a histogram of distances for each feature, is smoothed via kernel density estimation to obtain a Probability Density Function (PDF). Figure 1 illustrates the results of this procedure for C_{struct} between the Japanoise and the classical set, whereas Fig. 2 shows the cross-correlation for the same metric but for all pairs of collections (with Japanoise as a reference).

Subsequently, basic descriptive statistics for these PDFs are calculated, for more insight: the mean can give an idea of the intra-set diversity and inter-set average similarity based on the different metrics, whereas the standard deviation provides an estimate of reliability of the mean value. Tables 2 and 3 aggregate this information for all intra- and inter-set cross-validation.

Finally, to calculate the difference between one collection's intra-set PDF and another collection's inter-set PDF, two further metrics are applied: the Kullback-Leibler Divergence (KLD) and Overlapping Area (OA) of two PDFs. Smaller KLDs and larger OAs will be indicators of similarity between the two collections, for the feature space of interest. Table 4 summarises the results in this study.

While a higher overall similarity between the Japanoise and the Soundscape collection is not particularly surprising, it is interesting to report that different measures highlighted/preferred other collections. Furthermore, the marginal differences between collections over the same feature and distance metric are not systematic.

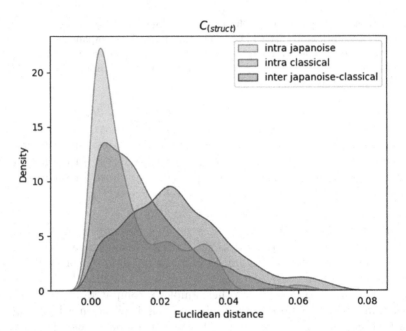

Fig. 1. Cross-validation for C_{struct}, shown for the pairwise comparison between Japanoise and the classical collection.

Table 2. Cross-validation results for the complexity-based features. Column IDs use abbreviations of the collections (*e.g.*, J for Japanoise, J/S for Japanoise/Soundscape, etc.)

	C_{img}	C_{spec}	C_{struct}
J: Intra-set	0.001 ± 0.001	0.013 ± 0.011	0.012 ± 0.012
S: Intra-set	0.001 ± 0.001	0.005 ± 0.006	0.015 ± 0.014
J/S: Inter-set	0.002 ± 0.001	0.01 ± 0.01	0.013 ± 0.013
M: Intra-set	0.001 ± 0.001	0.011 ± 0.008	0.022 ± 0.018
J/M: Inter-set	0.005 ± 0.001	0.012 ± 0.01	0.032 ± 0.021
C: Intra-set	0.005 ± 0.001	0.01 ± 0.007	0.015 ± 0.012
J/C: Inter-set	0.003 ± 0.001	0.012 ± 0.009	0.026 ± 0.015

6   Discussion

This study set out to investigate computational metrics for the evaluation of fringe, conceptual art music denoted as Japanoise, inspired by a modular approach proposed in the field of empirical aesthetics, and based on notions of complexity and entropy. This is but one strategy in dealing with automatic measures of aesthetic value, and it is arguable that a more balanced strategy in this domain

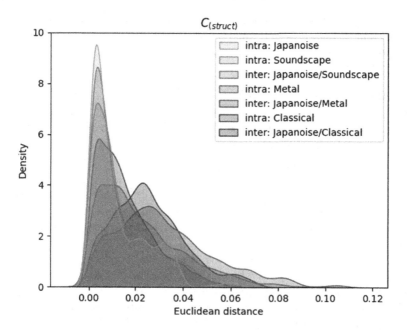

Fig. 2. Cross-validation for C_{struct}, shown for all pairwise comparisons.

Table 3. Cross-validation results for the entropy-based features. Column IDs use abbreviations of the collections (*e.g.*, M for Metal, etc.)

	H_{spec}	H_{temp}	H_{ir}
J: Intra-set	0.162 ± 0.116	0.003 ± 0.003	0.048 ± 0.037
S: Intra-set	0.226 ± 0.167	0.007 ± 0.008	0.107 ± 0.165
J/S: Inter-set	0.205 ± 0.142	0.006 ± 0.007	0.089 ± 0.115
M: Intra-set	0.102 ± 0.081	0.003 ± 0.003	0.039 ± 0.035
J/M: Inter-set	0.144 ± 0.104	0.005 ± 0.003	0.044 ± 0.036
C: Intra-set	0.087 ± 0.064	0.009 ± 0.007	0.031 ± 0.023
J/C: Inter-set	0.13 ± 0.093	0.015 ± 0.009	0.041 ± 0.032

must account for other methods, if one is to work towards integrated, modular frameworks, to this end.

For example, beyond the general auditory level of the music experience, Meyer [19] conjured up a synthesis of *Gestalt* theory and aesthetic pragmatism in order to explain the role of emotions in music. According to this viewpoint, musical enjoyment is proportional to the level of agreement or violation of perceptual musical expectation (which one acquires, allegedly, through statistical, probabilistic learning). Narmour [23] extended these concepts and formalised the into his Implication-Realization (I-R) model of melodic expectation. The I-R model has been applied in music both for generative tasks [3] and for musi-

Table 4. Kullback-Leibler Divergence (KLD) and Overlapping Area (OA) calculated between Japanoise's intra-set PDF and the other collections' inter-set PDF with respect to Japanoise.

	C_{img}		C_{spec}		C_{struct}		$H_i r$		H_{spec}		H_{temp}	
	KLD	OA	KLD	OA	KLD	OA	KLD	OA	KLD	OA	KLD	OA
J/S	**0.094**	**0.656**	0.141	0.683	**0.104**	**0.884**	0.088	0.754	0.037	**0.889**	**0.044**	**0.814**
J/M	2.259	0.083	**0.020**	**0.917**	0.109	0.746	**0.012**	**0.877**	0.016	0.815	0.264	0.585
J/C	0.249	0.406	0.041	0.905	0.151	0.668	0.036	0.851	**0.001**	0.778	0.173	0.708

cological analysis relating to melodic similarity [10]. While these ideas have been proven useful in a tonal context, they present issues when the *balance* between expectation and novelty is intentionally subverted for artistic reasons, as in the case of Japanoise.

In the limited scope of this study, the author tried to integrate different viewpoints and methodologies while still focusing on the general auditory level. A set of 6 complexity/entropy-based features was proposed and tested to assess whether it can offer a more nuanced view of conceptual and art music. While not able to verify this hypothesis, this study showed that, indeed, some of the strong boundaries resulting from using more tonal/music-oriented features were smoothed out. Perhaps it is the case that the aesthetic value of Japanoise, and other similarly extreme sonic expressions, is to be investigated primarily beyond the perceptual, auditory level. This links back to the other loops in Leder's information processing model of aesthetic appreciation, such as social interaction discourse and context [11,22]. At present, integrating automatic, computational metrics that can operate at these levels is still a matter of contention. In the awareness that much is left to be done, the author contends that there might be benefits in a multi-factor and cross-modal approach, such as the one undertaken here, and he endeavours to deepen insights through further experiments in this direction.

References

1. Bense, M.: Einfuhrung in die Informations Theoretische Asthetik (Introduction to Information-Theoretic Aesthetics). Rowohlt, Hamburg (1965)
2. Birkhoff, G.: Aesthetic Measure. Harvard University Press, Cambridge (1933)
3. Brown, A.R., Gifford, T., Davidson, R.: Techniques for generative melodies inspired by music cognition. Comput. Music J. **39**(1), 11–26 (2015)
4. Chronus Art Center: Japanoise and the Cultural Feedback of Global Media. https://bit.ly/2FheUfO. Accessed 02 Feb 2022
5. Dubnov, S., Assayag, G.: Music design with audio oracle using information rate. In: Proceedings of the 1st International Workshop on Musical Metacreation (MUME), Palo Alto (2012)
6. Dubnov, S., Assayag, G., Cont, A.: Audio oracle: a new algorithm for fast learning of audio structures. In: Proceedings of the International Computer Music Conference (ICMC), Copenhagen (2007)

7. Gell-Mann, M., Lloyd, S.: Information measures, effective complexity, and total information. Complexity **2**(1), 44–52 (1996). https://doi.org/10.1002/(sici)1099-0526(199609/10)2:1
8. Ginsel, P., Vatolkin, I., Rudolph, G.: Analysis of structural complexity features for music genre recognition. In: 2020 IEEE Congress on Evolutionary Computation (CEC), Glasgow, pp. 1–8 (2020). https://doi.org/10.1109/CEC48606.2020.9185540
9. Goguen, J.: Musical qualia, context, time, and emotion. J. Conscious. Stud. **11**(3–4), 117–147 (2004)
10. Grachten, M., Arcos, J.L.: Using the implication/realization model for measuring melodic similarity. In: Proceedings of the 16th European Conference on Artificial Intelligence (ECAI), Valencia, pp. 1023–1024. IOS Press (2004)
11. Grüner, S., Specker, E., Leder, H.: Effects of context and genuineness in the experience of art. Empir. Stud. Arts **37**(2), 138–152 (2019). https://doi.org/10.1177/0276237418822896
12. Hegarty, P.: Noise/Music: A History. Continuum, London and New York (2007)
13. Inouye, T., et al.: Quantification of EEG irregularity by use of the entropy of the power spectrum. Electroencephalogr. Clin. Neurophysiol. **79**(3), 204–210 (1991). https://doi.org/10.1016/0013-4694(91)90138-T
14. Kalonaris, S., Gifford, T., Brown, A.R.: Computational aesthetics and music: the ugly, the small and the boring. In: Proceedings of 7th International Workshop on Musical Metacreation (MUME), Charlotte (2019)
15. Kramer, J.D.: Postmodern concepts of musical time. Indiana Theory Rev. **17**(2), 21–61 (1996)
16. Laurier, C., et al.: Indexing music by mood: design and integration of an automatic content-based annotator. Multimedia Tools Appl. **48**(1), 161–184 (2010). https://doi.org/10.1007/s11042-009-0360-2
17. Leder, H., Nadal, M.: Ten years of a model of aesthetic appreciation and aesthetic judgments: the aesthetic episode - developments and challenges in empirical aesthetics. Br. J. Psychol. **105**(4), 443–64 (2014). https://doi.org/10.1111/bjop.12084
18. Mayer, S., Landwehr, J.R.: Quantifying visual aesthetics based on processing fluency theory: four algorithmic measures for antecedents of aesthetic preferences. Psychol. Aesthet. Creat. Arts **12**(4), 399–431 (2018). https://doi.org/10.1037/aca0000187
19. Meyer, L.: Emotion and Meaning in Music. University of Chicago Press, Chicago (1956)
20. Minissale, G.: Conceptual art: a blind spot for neuroaesthetics? Leonardo **45**(1), 43–48 (2012). https://doi.org/10.1162/LEON_a_00324
21. Moles, A.: Théorie de l'information et Perception Esthétique (Information Theory and Aesthetical Perception). Denoël, Paris (1973)
22. Mullennix, J.W., Kristo, G.M., Robinet, J.: Effects of preceding context on aesthetic preference. Empir. Stud. Arts **38**(2), 149–171 (2020). https://doi.org/10.1177/0276237418805687
23. Narmour, E.: The Analysis and Cognition of Basic Melodic Structures: The Implication-Realization Model. University of Chicago Press, Chicago (1990)
24. Novak, D.: Japanoise: Music at the Edge of Circulation. Duke University Press, Durham (2013)
25. Pijanowski, B., Farina, A., Gage, S., et al.: What is soundscape ecology? An introduction and overview of an emerging new science. Landsc. Ecol. **26**, 1213–1232 (2011). https://doi.org/10.1007/s10980-011-9600-8

26. Priest, E.: Boring Formless Nonsense. Experimental Music and the Aesthetics of Failure. Bloomsbury Academic, London (2013)
27. Reber, R.: Processing fluency, aesthetic pleasure, and culturally shared taste. In: Shimamura, A.P., Palmer, S.E. (eds.) Aesthetic Science: Connecting Minds, Brains, and Experience, pp. 223–249. Oxford University Press, New York (2012). https://doi.org/10.1093/acprof:oso/9780199732142.001.0001
28. Reber, R., Schwarz, N., Winkielman, P.: Processing fluency and aesthetic pleasure: is beauty in the perceiver's processing experience? Personal. Soc. Psychol. Rev. **8**(4), 364–382 (2004). https://doi.org/10.1207/s15327957pspr0804_3. pMID: 15582859
29. Roberts, S.: Make a joyous noise: the Pentecostal nature of American noise music. In: Goddard, M., Halligan, B., Spelman, N. (eds.) Resonances: Noise and Contemporary Music, pp. 107–120. Bloomsbury Publishing, New York (2013)
30. Sarpa, R.: Noise as material impact: new uses of sound in noise-related movements. In: Goddard, M., Halligan, B., Spelman, N. (eds.) Resonances: Noise and Contemporary Music, pp. 273–285. Bloomsbury Publishing, New York (2013)
31. Shannon, C.E.: A mathematical theory of communication. Bell Syst. Tech. J. **27**(3), 379–423 (1948). https://doi.org/10.1002/j.1538-7305.1948.tb01338.x
32. Skov, M.: Aesthetic appreciation: the view from neuroimaging. Empir. Stud. Arts **37**(2), 220–248 (2019). https://doi.org/10.1177/0276237419839257
33. Stiny, G., Gips, J., Salvadori, M.: Algorithmic Aesthetics: Computer Models for Criticism and Design in the Arts. Computer Models for Criticism and Design in the Arts. University of California Press, Berkeley (1978)
34. Sueur, J., Pavoine, S., Hamerlynck, O., Duvail, S.: Rapid acoustic survey for biodiversity appraisal. PLoS ONE **3**(12), e4065 (2008)
35. Surges, G.: Generative audio systems: musical applications of time-varying feedback networks and computational aesthetics. Ph.D. thesis, University of California, San Diego (2015)
36. Welch, P.: The use of fast Fourier transform for the estimation of power spectra: a method based on time averaging over short, modified periodograms. IEEE Trans. Audio Electroacoust. **15**(2), 70–73 (1967). https://doi.org/10.1109/TAU.1967.1161901
37. Yang, L.-C., Lerch, A.: On the evaluation of generative models in music. Neural Comput. Appl. **32**(9), 4773–4784 (2018). https://doi.org/10.1007/s00521-018-3849-7

Quality-Diversity for Aesthetic Evolution

Jon McCormack$^{(\boxtimes)}$ (ID) and Camilo Cruz Gambardella (ID)

SensiLab, Monash University, Melbourne, Australia
{Jon.McCormack,Camilo.CruzGambardella}@monash.edu
https://sensilab.monash.edu

Abstract. Many creative generative design spaces contain multiple regions with individuals of high aesthetic value. Yet traditional evolutionary computing methods typically focus on optimisation, searching for the fittest individual in a population. In this paper we apply quality-diversity search methods to explore a creative generative system (an agent-based line drawing model). We perform a random sampling of genotype space and use individual artist-assigned evaluations of aesthetic quality to formulate a computable fitness measure specific to the artist and this system. To compute diversity we use a convolutional neural network to discriminate features that are dimensionally reduced into two dimensions. We show that the quality-diversity search is able to find multiple phenotypes of high aesthetic value. These phenotypes show greater diversity and quality than those the artist was able to find using manual search methods.

Keywords: Quality diversity · Aesthetic measure · Generative art · Generative design · Evolutionary art · Fitness measure

1 Introduction

A long standing challenge in creative evolutionary applications has been to find suitable fitness measures [21], particularly when such measures need to consider 'subjective' elements, such as visual aesthetics and personal taste. While significant progress has been made in quantifying aesthetics and understanding human aesthetic judgement [13,15], evolutionary computing methods typically focus on optimisation: finding the fittest individual in a population. However, in many art and design applications there is no single, best design, rather a variety of possibilities that can be considered of interest. Moreover, complex generative systems can present a design space that is broad and unexplored, with many so-called 'Klondike spaces' [31,32] of creative gold that are hidden amongst the vast regions of the ordinary or uninteresting. Rather than a single optimum or best design, such systems may have *many* designs that the designer would consider worthwhile.

Typically the way around this problem would be to use human-in-the-loop methods, such as the Interactive Genetic Algorithm (IGA), which substitutes formalised fitness measures for human aesthetic judgement [4]. However the limitations of this approach are well known [37]: human evaluation creates a bottleneck; subjective comparison is only possible for a small number of individuals

T. Martins et al. (Eds.): EvoMUSART 2022, LNCS 13221, pp. 369–384, 2022.
https://doi.org/10.1007/978-3-031-03789-4_24

(i.e. <20); human users become fatigued after only a few generations; evolving to specific targets is often difficult or impossible; design space exploration without a goal is largely equivalent to a random walk. There have been many attempts to overcome these problems, e.g. distributed evolution with multiple users [36], but distributed techniques are obviously incompatible with individual designers or personal aesthetic preferences.

In this paper we present a method suited to the automated generation of diverse landscapes of creative alternatives, using the principles of *quality-diversity search* (QD-search, [34]). QD-search methods attempt to find a diverse range of high fitness individuals and have shown good success in a variety of domains [11], such as robotics [34,35,38] and the generation of content for video games [14]. For creative applications, the key challenge is in finding good, suitable, and independent measures of both quality and diversity. While our application focuses on a generative art system that produces line drawings suitable for physical plotting, the methodology presented here can apply to any visual art or design system. Our approach is based on the following assumptions:

- There is a creative system that can generate two-dimensional (2D) visual images (phenotypes) from some supplied parameters (genotypes).
- The format, quantity and order of the parameters is arbitrary.
- There is no restriction on the type or style of images produced, except that they can be represented as pixel-based 2D images.
- The system designer or artist is able to evaluate the aesthetic value or quality of the produced images (phenotypes).
- The creative aspects of the system are expressed by the images produced, i.e. there are no external factors or conditions that determine quality or difference in the produced phenotypes.

These are standard ways that an artist or designer would work with a generative system. While we restrict our study to 2D images, other formats, such as 3D forms could be easily accommodated by rendering the 3D form as a 2D image for evaluation (e.g. as in [26]).

To determine quality we first generate a random sample of phenotypes and ask the artist to evaluate their aesthetic quality manually, using this evaluation to derive a measure of quality specific to the artist and the system. Based on previous studies, which have suggested image metrics can serve as a good proxy for personal aesthetics [25], we analyse the aesthetically ranked phenotypes, computing various measures of complexity and image morphology, looking for high correlations between these measures and the artist-assigned measures of quality. This analysis allows us to formulate a computable measure of quality specific to the artist and the generative system.

Diversity can take a number of forms and hence, measures. As this study is focused on visual images, we consider diversity exclusively in the visual sense, i.e. identifying the range of visually distinct features that the system can generate. To measure this diversity computationally, we turn to neural networks trained to visually discriminate image features. Over the last few years Convolutional Neural Networks (CNNs) trained on very large image corpora have become highly successful at feature classification and object recognition – on par with human evaluation. Performing classification requires identifying the salient features of an image. For our system we used the ResNet-152 classifier, removing the last four layers of the network to expose a feature vector as the network's output. As this vector is large (2048 elements), we then employ dimension reduction methods to compute a final, 2-dimensional diversity measure.

Together, these computable measures of quality (aesthetic fitness) and diversity (visual features) allow us to generate a variety of forms that the artist should find interesting using QD search. Once found, these individuals can be further fine-tuned manually or accepted as successful products of the evolutionary generative system. Our results show that we were able to find a number of highly fit individuals that the artist had not been able to locate using other methods.

Before describing the system, experiments and method in detail, we provide a brief review and explanation of QD-Search and its application to visual creation.

2   Quality-Diversity Search

The use of evolutionary computing methods for design exploration has been gaining traction for the past 10 years. Lehman and Stanley [17] pioneered an approach that proposes a departure from fitness-driven optimisation, instead looking to find the 'best' pathway through the search space. Under this premise, they developed a series of experiments focusing on novelty and diversity [16], rather than on a fitness function that describes the expected performance of the populations being evolved, which enabled them to 'illuminate' areas of the search space that hadn't been revealed through optimisation-based approaches. Moreover, some of the solutions found in these previously unexplored areas of the search space proved to be as fit – if not fitter – than those found using traditional methods. This approach, they argue, is well suited for use in contexts in which either there is more than one optimal solution, or where objectives are not explicit (e.g. design and art).

Since the introduction of the novelty search principles in 2008 (see [17]), a wide range of methods that use them has been developed, incorporating different ways of measuring novelty, various combinations of diversity and fitness, and multiple underlying evolutionary algorithms to drive the search process [11]. For the work presented in this paper, we adopted an approach that combines optimisation and diversity (QD-search), as it bears resemblance to the way that human creative processes unfolds: generate a series of candidate solutions/objects/things, assess them under the light of what they are expected to be, but also in search of surprising elements, or as Alexander puts it, things that "display new physical order" [1, p. 1]. Select the 'best' ones – if there are any – and use them as starting point to repeat the process.

The MAP-Elites algorithm developed by [30] can be understood as a similar process. The goal is to evolve a landscape of diverse, highly fit individuals. To achieve this the algorithm requires a measure of fitness, as well as a way of classifying individuals into categories that account for their diversity. Interesting creative applications of this particular algorithm can be found in [7], where it is used in conjunction with generative adversarial networks (GANs) to evolve image style transfer blends, while trying to maintain the resemblance between the original image and the transformed one, as well as in the work developed by [14], where a constrained version of MAP-Elites is used to evolve bullet patterns of different levels of difficulty for video games.

3   Generative System

To test the suitability of QD-search in creative applications, we developed a generative art system using an agent-based line drawing model. Similar models have been effectively used in previous research, in addition to being recognised as artistically successful [2,3,22]. A series of mobile agents are released onto a virtual "canvas" and proceed to draw a trail over their fixed lifetimes. The drawing is complete when all the agents are exhausted. The cumulative paths are output as an svg file, to facilitate high quality plotting. We use a line drawing system as the intended output is physical drawings, plotted with various permanent ink markers on paper. An example svg image and plotted drawing is shown in Fig. 1.

The movement of each agent is determined by a series of summed noise functions, based on Perlin noise [33] and procedural fluid flow [5]. The system uses 17 different parameters (Table 1) to control the drawing, represented as normalised continuous real values in the range $[0 - 1]$. Parameters affect properties such as noise type (g_{17}) and frequency (g_6 & g_7), number of drawing agents (g_3), the pen type (g_{12} & g_{13}), horizontal, vertical or circular pathways (g_{14}, g_{15}, g_{16}), agent speed (g_2) and lifetime (g_3). Each normalised parameter, g_i is mapped to a parameter specific range, for example g_1 represents the width in pixels of the border from the edge of the canvas for agent placement and is mapped to the range $[0 - 400]$. The noise algorithm gene (g_{17}) maps to a set of five different discrete possibilities.

Together these gene parameters ($g_i, i = 1 .. 17$) form a complete genotype (G) which deterministically maps to a phenotype ($G \rightarrow P$) by simulating the agents moving over the canvas using the parameters specified in G. There is no randomness in the generation, so any individual genotype, G_k will always produce the same equivalent phenotype, P_k. Figure 2 shows some example phenotypes selected from a test set of randomly initialised genotypes. This test set was used to determine a computable fitness measure for the system, detailed next.

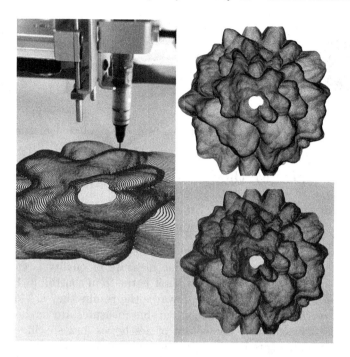

Fig. 1. A sample drawing. The software outputs an svg vector image (top right), which is then fed to a pen plotter that traces out the image onto paper (left). The final resultant drawing (bottom right) takes about 30 mins to plot.

Table 1. Genes used in the generative drawing system

Gene	Description	Gene	Description
g_1	Border width	g_{10}	Noise octaves
g_2	Agent speed	g_{11}	Noise falloff
g_3	Agent density	g_{12}	Agent/pen count
g_4	Noise strength	g_{13}	Agent/pen ratio
g_5	Noise displacement	g_{14}	Linear drawing style
g_6	Noise x-frequency	g_{15}	Circular drawing style
g_7	Noise y-frequency	g_{16}	Spiral drawing style
g_8	Noise z-scale	g_{17}	Noise algorithm
g_9	z-position		

Fig. 2. Five sample phenotypes selected from a pool of random genotypes.

4   Evolutionary Method

4.1   Fitness

Determining the aesthetic 'quality' of an artwork is complex [23], as there are multiple factors that will influence how it is perceived, interpreted and ultimately appreciated [15]. However, defining some measure of quality is crucial in the context of generative evolutionary art, as it is the 'rein control' [6,12] the artist needs to steer the generative process towards the results they are looking for.

Previous work has shown that computable measures are far better at capturing an individual artist's perception of aesthetics in a specific system over collective general perceptions of quality or aesthetic value [25]. Relatively simple measures, such as image complexity [19,20] or information content [29] have been used as fitness measures, for example. More complex systems, such as deep learning classifiers, have also demonstrated good success in capturing an individual artist's concept of aesthetic quality [27].

Human Fitness Evaluation. Building on our previous results [25], for this work we wanted to capture the artist's aesthetic preferences for the generative system in a formalised fitness measure. To do this we first generated a number of random phenotypes and asked the artist to evaluate their aesthetic quality using two different methods: direct numerical score and pairwise comparison ranking. The size of this dataset (257 images) was chosen as a compromise between getting a reasonable sampling of the design space and the overall fatigue and time required for the artist to perform both evaluation methods. The full dataset is available for download [24]. Using two different evaluation methods allowed us to compare the pros and cons of each method, along with providing an understanding of the consistency of subjective evaluation.

For the direct scoring method the artist looked at each drawing individually (presented in random order) and assigned each a real-valued numeric score from 0 (least appealing) to 5 (most appealing). For the pairwise comparison ranking process we used a browser-based application where pairs of images are displayed and compared by asking the user to answer the question "which one of these images do you like the most?". Comparing two images this way is the equivalent of a tournament (a battle for aesthetic superiority) where the possible outcome at each round (comparison) is one of 'win', 'loose' or 'draw'. Images were ranked using an implementation of the Glicko ranking system [9,10] based on their

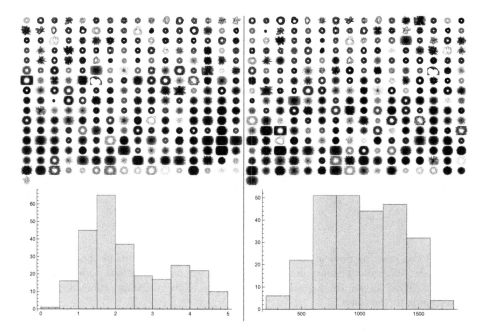

Fig. 3. Comparison of personal aesthetic evaluation of the same dataset using direct numeric score (left) and pairwise comparison (right). The images are shown in descending order from highest fitness at the top left. Histograms of the distribution are shown below the ordered images.

performance against other images. The ranking system gives each player (image) a score that becomes more accurate proportionate to the number of times it is part of a tournament outcome. The system also includes a rating deviation (RD) measure that represents the reliability of a player's rating. We performed sufficient comparisons to ensure that every image had an $RD < 250$, giving a high confidence in the ranking. The direct score ranking was performed after the pairwise comparison ranking. The results of these two methods of personal aesthetic ranking are shown in Fig. 3.

As the figure shows, there is some difference in the ordering, even though the same person was performing both rankings on the same dataset. This is likely due to a number of factors, including the close visual similarity of many of the random phenotypes (making differentiation difficult), fatigue (over 1000 comparisons were evaluated), and the imprecise nature of aesthetic judgment. Nonetheless, the two rankings have a Spearman rank correlation coefficient of $r = 0.74$ with a p-value $< 10^{-4}$, indicating a good consistency between the ranking methods.

To further understand the relationship between genotype space, phenotype space and aesthetic measure we generated two visualisations (Fig. 4). The visualisation on the left shows the genotype space dimensionally reduced from 17 dimensions to 2 dimensions using the t-SNE dimension reduction method [18],

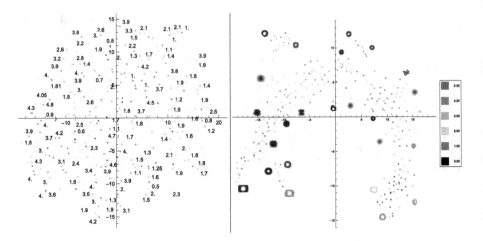

Fig. 4. Plots showing dimension reduced features (using the TSNE method) in geneo-type space (left) and phenotype space (right). Each point is colour coded based on aesthetic rating as per the legend. Selected points show the image (phenotype) that corresponds to the point.

with a perplexity of 15 and $\epsilon = 10$. Each point on the visualisation represents an individual genotype, and the point is coloured according to its aesthetic score as shown in the legend on the far right of the figure (the numerical rating is also shown next to each point in the diagram). As can be seen, the random sampling produces a uniformly distributed scattering of points and while there is a slight increase in higher fitness individuals in the lower left quadrant, there are no obvious regions of high aesthetic fitness. The visualisation on the right shows the same dataset, but this time in phenotype space. To compute the 2D position of each phenotype we again dimensionally reduced each image (rasterised to a resolution of 1024×768 pixels) using the t-SNE algorithm (perplexity $= 15$ and $\epsilon = 10$) and colour coded each phenotype based on its aesthetic score. In this visualisation some structure can be observed, with many high-fitness individuals located along the right-hand 'horseshoe' scattering of phenotypes, with a high concentration in the upper right quadrant. Notice also a smaller, isolated patch in the top upper-left quadrant. This visualisation shows that the phenotype space does have structure and that certain regions can be considered the 'sweet spots' or 'Klondike spaces', where high fitness individuals are more likely to be found. Additionally, the visualisation also shows that such regions are not unique, and there are multiple regions of high fitness and supporting the idea that there is no single best phenotype, just different regions of high quality, but visually distinct individuals.

Complexity and Morphological Measures. The same dataset of images were also evaluated using the image feature metrics described in [25]) and statistical measures of image intensity (mean, variance, centroid). The measures tested included image entropy and energy, morphological Euler number, algorithmic and structural complexity, fractal dimensional and fractal aesthetic measures (see [25] for details on each measure). These measures were calculated for each image and then compared to the artist-assigned rankings. The results of this comparison showed that the highest correlation was achieved by the skewness of an image's histogram (skew), and with the mean image intensity value (both with $r = 0.54$, p-value $< 10^{-3}$).

Based on these results, we selected mean pixel value (μ) as an approximation for fitness, since this measure demonstrated the equal highest correlation and is also computed efficiently. However, the obvious flaw in this measure is that the highest fitness individual is an all-white image, so we compensate by defining a 'hat' function with maximum fitness at the point $\mu = \gamma$:

$$F(I) = \begin{cases} (\gamma - \mu_{min})\mu(I) + \mu_{min} & \text{if } \mu_{min} \leq \mu(I) < \gamma \\ (\mu_{max} - \gamma)\mu(I) - \gamma & \text{if } \gamma \leq \mu(I) \leq \mu_{max} \\ 0 & \text{otherwise} \end{cases} \tag{1}$$

where $F(I)$ is the fitness of an image, I; $\mu(I)$ is the normalised mean intensity of I, μ_{min} and μ_{max} are points for minimum and maximum intensity boundaries for a non-zero fitness value (eliminating cases that are effectively all black or all white). For our system we use the values $\mu_{min} = 0.05$, $\mu_{max} = 0.95$ and $\gamma = 0.75$. Having devised a reasonable fitness measure, we then looked at how to measure diversity in a population of phenotypes using our system.

4.2   Diversity

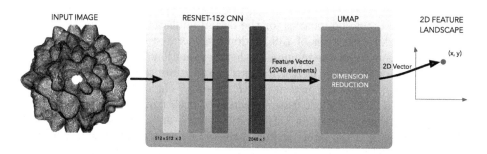

Fig. 5. Evaluating diversity: each image is fed into a CNN classifier (ResNet-152), with the last 4 layers removed, leaving a 2048 element feature vector as the network's output. This is then dimensionally reduced using a UMAP algorithm, giving a 2-dimensional feature space vector.

To map the system's design space – i.e. to visualise and understand the phenotypical differences between the drawings that it is capable of producing – we used a combination of a convolutional neural network (CNN, a modified version of ResNet152 trained on the ImageNet database of real images [8]) for feature extraction, and Uniform Manifold Approximation and Projection (UMAP) [28] for dimension reduction. Combining these methods we are able to classify generated images on a 2D plane, based on their visual characteristics (Fig. 5). This 2D space is then 'quantised' into a grid, where each cell represents a different visual class of object (Fig. 6).

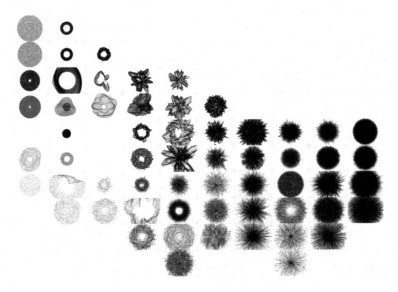

Fig. 6. Sample of the dataset used to train the UMAP model classified into a 10×10 grid.

In order to define boundaries for the design landscape, we trained the CNN + UMAP model with a set of 738 randomly generated images, which includes the 257 images used for the manual aesthetic evaluation. Images are fed into the CNN as vectors of shape $(w, h, \mathbf{c})$, where w and h are the width and height of the image in pixels and $\mathbf{c}$ represents the R, G and B channels of each image. The CNN returns a 2048 element feature vector for each image. This vector is then reduced to 2-dimensions using UMAP, which gives us a reasonable estimation of the boundaries of the latent search space of our generative system, which we use to perform the dimensional reduction of newly generated images.

4.3   MAP-Elites Implementation

Our implementation of quality-diversity search is based on MAP-Elites [30]. We use the measures of fitness and diversity introduced in Sect. 4.1 and Sect. 4.2 to evolve an elite population of drawings from our generative system.

The algorithm is initialised by creating an empty 2D *feature space,* quantised into a grid $s = (n \times n)$ cells. The total number of generations (e) and population size at each generation (λ) is defined.

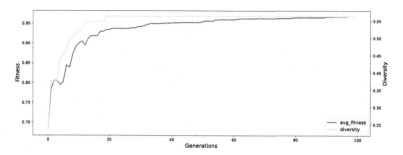

Fig. 7. Time series of evolutionary run showing mean population fitness (blue) and population diversity (yellow) (Color figure online)

At each generation, a random cell from the feature space is sampled. If the cell is empty, a population of randomly generated drawings is created. Otherwise, the drawing in the cell is used as a parent for the new generation, which is created using a simple mutation procedure, where we define mutation rate r – the probability of an allele (g_i) to be mutated – and mutation factor f – the maximum variation of a mutated allele.

Once a generation is created, we use *.png* versions of the svg drawings to perform pixel-based evaluation, which gives us the fitness of each drawing (Eq. 1), as well as their locations in the feature space. A drawing will be placed on the feature space grid if a) its corresponding cell is empty, or b) its fitness is higher than the one of the drawing occupying the cell. If a drawing is placed on the grid, it is also preserved in an archive.

The process repeats until the feature space grid has been updated for the desired number of generations.

5   Experiments and Results

Our experiments were devised to test the effectiveness of the proposed approach as support for creative discovery. The goal was to evolve a *landscape* of alternatives, where all the drawings produced by our generative system met a predefined quality standard based on the fitness function described in Sect. 4.1. The setup for these initial tests consisted of the following initial parameters: $s = (8 \times 8)$, $e = 100$, $\lambda = 25$, $r = 0.25$ and $f = 0.15$.

The trajectory of the evolutionary process can be observed in Fig. 7. Fitness is calculated as the mean fitness of all the drawings in the feature space. The ratio of cells in the grid that are populated is used as the population diversity measure. This trajectory shows how the feature space improves at different rates in both aspects. Diversity increases quickly, peaking at generation 60. Fitness, on the other hand, exhibits a slightly slower progression, where sudden increases in diversity produce slight setbacks that are overcome over a few generations.

Figure 8 shows the state of the feature space grid at significant stages of the evolutionary process. The image on the top left (a) shows the initial population placed on the feature space. Images b and c show the state of the feature space grid after increases in diversity, at generations 9 and 19. Finally, the image on the bottom right (d) shows the final elite population, at generation 99.

We ran the system several times and observed that the QD-search was consistently able to find a diverse range of high-fitness individuals. We compared these with forms the artist was able to find using an interactive version of the system that allows real-time manipulation of individual alleles in the genotype (Fig. 9). Some of the forms the QD-search was able to find were highly unusual, certainly not readily apparent from many hours of exploring using the interactive system. Figure 10 shows some examples of forms found using the QD-search method described in this paper, demonstrating the system is able to find high fitness individuals that are diverse in appearance.

6 Discussion

As our results demonstrate, QD-search provides an interesting way for artists and designers to explore the creative possibilities of a generative system. As shown in Fig. 6, the visual display of diversity can assist human artists in understanding

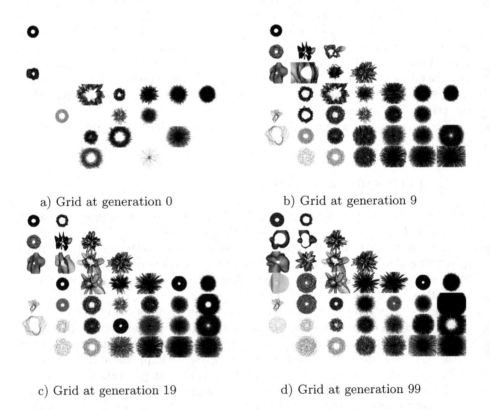

a) Grid at generation 0   b) Grid at generation 9

c) Grid at generation 19   d) Grid at generation 99

Fig. 8. Examples of the elite population at four significant steps in the evolutionary process

the visual possibilities that the system is capable of. Indeed, we had no idea the system could generate certain phenotypes that were found by QD-search, despite exploring the design space manually for several months.

While our results are promising, there are a number of limitations in the current study. Firstly, for fitness we used a simple function based on the mean intensity of the image, as this had the equal highest correlation with the artist assigned perception of aesthetic quality for this specific system. Clearly a more sophisticated fitness measure could give better nuances in high fitness individuals. Nonetheless, we were surprised at how well just using the function shown in Eq. 1 worked. However, such simple measures would be unlikely to generalise to other systems, so further work is needed to find high quality aesthetic fitness measures that work across different visual forms and styles.

Secondly, our results are limited to a single system and further research is needed to apply QD-search methods to a wider variety of creative systems. The fundamental challenge is in devising suitable computable measures of both quality and diversity that work for a specific generative system. However, the broad principles we have applied make this easy to test. Prior research has shown that while there exists reasonable computable proxies for specific aesthetic preferences [25], the specific measure varies between system and individual, requiring

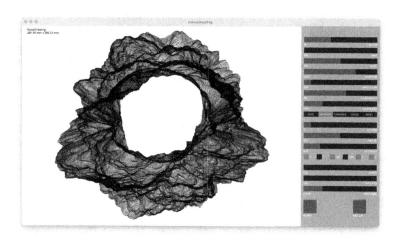

Fig. 9. Screen shot of the interactive version of the generative system, with controls for each allele of the genome on the right.

Fig. 10. Example high fitness phenotypes found using the QD-search system.

the kind of correlation evaluation we performed in Sect. 4.1. This requires significant human time, as the individual artist must manually rank or compare a sufficient number of random phenotypes to determine the best correlation with a variety of possible computable measures. Nonetheless, if the artist is willing to spend time to provide this information, the payoff can be significant. In our implementation QD-search is fully automated and doesn't require any further human evaluation once the initial fitness measure has been established.

7   Conclusion

We have demonstrated the use of QD-search methods in finding high fitness individuals in a generative art system. We began by generating a random sample of possible phenotypes and performing an artist-assigned measure of aesthetic quality on each. From this sample data we developed a fitness measure specific to the artist and the generative system, with good correlation between the computed measure and human-assigned scores. To compute a diversity measure we used a widely available CNN to provide a visual feature vector that was then dimensionally reduced from 2048 dimensions to two dimensions. Having both computable fitness and diversity measures allowed us to run a MAP-Elites QD-search and to find a series of diverse, high value individuals from the generative system.

While our results are currently limited to this single system, there are good reasons to believe that QD-search can be a valuable tool for artists and designers working with generative evolutionary systems. For future work we plan on testing the value of QD-search on more complex generative systems and on non-visual phenotypes such as sound synthesizers. The 2D layout of the QD-search also allows for interaction with the human designer, for example to clear certain cells and re-evolve the model for a specific diversity measure, or to click on an empty cell to direct the system to search for phenotypes with specific diversity measures.

References

1. Alexander, C.: Notes on the Synthesis of Form. Harvard University Press, Cambridge (1964)
2. Annunziato, M.: The nagual experiment. In: Soddu, C. (ed.) Proceedings of the First International Conference on Generative Art, Italy, pp. 241–250 (1998). http://www.generativeart.com/on/cic/ga98/book/16.pdf
3. Baker, E., Seltzer, M.I.: Evolving line drawings. In: Graphics Interface 1994, Banff, Canada, pp. 91–100, May 1994
4. Bentley, P.J.: Evolutionary Design by Computers. Morgan Kaufmann Publishers, San Francisco (1999)
5. Bridson, R., Houriham, J., Nordenstam, M.: Curl-noise for procedural fluid flow. ACM Trans. Graph. **26**(3), 46–47 (2007). https://doi.org/10.1145/1275808.1276435

6. Clynes, M.: Cybernetic implications of rein control in perceptual and conceptual organization. Ann. N. Y. Acad. Sci. **156**(2), 629–664 (1969). https://doi.org/10.1111/j.1749-6632.1969.tb14005.x

7. Colton, S.: Evolving neural style transfer blends. In: Romero, J., Martins, T., Rodríguez-Fernández, N. (eds.) EvoMUSART 2021. LNCS, vol. 12693, pp. 65–81. Springer, Cham (2021). https://doi.org/10.1007/978-3-030-72914-1_5

8. Deng, J., et al.: ImageNet: a large-scale hierarchical image database. In: IEEE Conference on Computer Vision and Pattern Recognition, CVPR 2009, pp. 248–255. IEEE (2009)

9. Glickman, M.E.: The glicko system. Boston University, **16**, 16–17 (1998)

10. Glickman, M.E.: Parameter estimation in large dynamic paired comparison experiments. J. R. Stat. Soc. Ser. C (Appl. Stat.) **48**(3), 377–394 (1999)

11. Gomes, J., Mariano, P., Christensen, A.L.: Devising effective novelty search algorithms: a comprehensive empirical study. In: Proceedings of the 2015 Annual Conference on Genetic and Evolutionary Computation, pp. 943–950 (2015)

12. Harvey, I.: Homeostasis and rein control: from daisyworld to active perception. In: Pollack, J.B., Bedau, M.A., Husbands, P., Ikegami, T., Watson, R.A. (eds.) Ninth International Conference on Artificial Life, pp. 309–314. MIT Press (2004)

13. Johnson, C.G., McCormack, J., Santos, I., Romero, J.: Understanding aesthetics and fitness measures in evolutionary art systems. Complexity, Article ID 3495962, 14 p. (2019). https://doi.org/10.1155/2019/3495962

14. Khalifa, A., Lee, S., Nealen, A., Togelius, J.: Talakat: bullet hell generation through constrained map-elites. In: Proceedings of the Genetic and Evolutionary Computation Conference, pp. 1047–1054 (2018)

15. Leder, H., Nadal, M.: Ten years of a model of aesthetic appreciation and aesthetic judgments: the aesthetic episode - developments and challenges in empirical aesthetics. Br. J. Psychol. **105**, 443–464 (2014)

16. Lehman, J., Stanley, K.O.: Abandoning objectives: evolution through the search for novelty alone. Evolut. Comput. **19**(2), 189–223 (2011)

17. Lehman, J., Stanley, K.O., et al.: Exploiting open-endedness to solve problems through the search for novelty. In: ALIFE, pp. 329–336. Citeseer (2008)

18. van der Maaten, L., Hinton, G.: Visualizing data using t-SNE. J. Mach. Learn. Res. **9**, 2579–2605 (2008)

19. Machado, P., Cardoso, A.: Computing aesthetics. In: de Oliveira, F.M. (ed.) SBIA 1998. LNCS (LNAI), vol. 1515, pp. 219–228. Springer, Heidelberg (1998). https://doi.org/10.1007/10692710_23

20. Machado, P., et al.: Computerized measures of visual complexity. Acta Psychologica **160**, 43–57 (2015). https://doi.org/10.1016/j.actpsy.2015.06.005

21. McCormack, J.: Open problems in evolutionary music and art. In: Rothlauf, F., et al. (eds.) EvoWorkshops 2005. LNCS, vol. 3449, pp. 428–436. Springer, Heidelberg (2005). https://doi.org/10.1007/978-3-540-32003-6_43

22. McCormack, J.: Enhancing creativity with niche construction. In: Fellerman, H., et al. (eds.) Artificial Life XII, pp. 525–532. MIT Press, Cambridge (2010)

23. McCormack, J.: Aesthetics, art, evolution. In: Machado, P., McDermott, J., Carballal, A. (eds.) EvoMUSART 2013. LNCS, vol. 7834, pp. 1–12. Springer, Heidelberg (2013). https://doi.org/10.1007/978-3-642-36955-1_1

24. McCormack, J.: Generative Line Drawings Dataset, February 2022. https://doi.org/10.26180/19119548.v1. https://bridges.monash.edu/articles/dataset/Generative_Line_Drawings_Dataset/19119548

25. McCormack, J., Cruz Gambardella, C., Lomas, A.: The enigma of complexity. In: Romero, J., Martins, T., Rodríguez-Fernández, N. (eds.) EvoMUSART 2021. LNCS, vol. 12693, pp. 203–217. Springer, Cham (2021). https://doi.org/10.1007/978-3-030-72914-1_14

26. McCormack, J., Lomas, A.: Deep learning of individual aesthetics. Neural Comput. Appl. **33**(1), 3–17 (2020). https://doi.org/10.1007/s00521-020-05376-7

27. McCormack, J., Lomas, A.: Understanding aesthetic evaluation using deep learning. In: Romero, J., Ekárt, A., Martins, T., Correia, J. (eds.) EvoMUSART 2020. LNCS, vol. 12103, pp. 118–133. Springer, Cham (2020). https://doi.org/10.1007/978-3-030-43859-3_9

28. McInnes, L., Healy, J., Melville, J.: UMAP: uniform manifold approximation and projection for dimension reduction. arXiv preprint arXiv:1802.03426 (2018)

29. Moles, A.A.: Information Theory and Esthetic Perception. University of Illinois Press, Urbana (1966)

30. Mouret, J.B., Clune, J.: Illuminating search spaces by mapping elites. arXiv preprint arXiv:1504.04909 (2015)

31. Perkins, D.N.: Creativity: beyond the Darwinian paradigm. In: Boden, M. (ed.) Dimensions of Creativity, chap. 5, pp. 119–142. MIT Press (1996)

32. Perkins, D.N.: The Eureka Effect: The Art and Logic of Breakthrough Thinking. W.W. Norton, New York (2001)

33. Perlin, K.: Improving noise. ACM Trans. Graph. (TOG) **21**(3), 681–682 (2002)

34. Pugh, J.K., Soros, L.B., Stanley, K.O.: Quality diversity: a new frontier for evolutionary computation. Front. Robot. AI **3**, 40 (2016). https://doi.org/10.3389/frobt.2016.00040. https://www.frontiersin.org/article/10.3389/frobt.2016.00040

35. Pugh, J.K., Soros, L.B., Szerlip, P.A., Stanley, K.O.: Confronting the challenge of quality diversity. In: Proceedings of the 2015 Annual Conference on Genetic and Evolutionary Computation, pp. 967–974 (2015)

36. Secretan, J., et al.: Picbreeder: a case study in collaborative evolutionary exploration of design space. Evolut. Comput. **19**(3), 373–403 (2011)

37. Takagi, H.: Interactive evolutionary computation: fusion of the capabilities of EC optimization and human evaluation. Proc. IEEE **89**, 1275–1296 (2001)

38. Tarapore, D., Clune, J., Cully, A., Mouret, J.B.: How do different encodings influence the performance of the MAP-Elites algorithm? In: Proceedings of the Genetic and Evolutionary Computation Conference 2016, pp. 173–180 (2016)

Classifying Biometric Data for Musical Interaction Within Virtual Reality

Chris Rhodes[1](✉) ⓘ, Richard Allmendinger[2] ⓘ, and Ricardo Climent[1] ⓘ

[1] NOVARS Research Centre, University of Manchester, Manchester, UK
{Chris.rhodes,Ricardo.climent}@manchester.ac.uk
[2] Alliance Manchester Business School (AMBS), University of Manchester, Manchester, UK
Richard.allmendinger@manchester.ac.uk

Abstract. Since 2015, commercial gestural interfaces have widened accessibility for researchers and artists to use novel Electromyographic (EMG) biometric data. EMG data measures musclar amplitude and allows us to enhance Human-Computer Interaction (HCI) through providing natural gestural interaction with digital media. Virtual Reality (VR) is an immersive technology capable of simulating the real world and abstractions of it. However, current commercial VR technology is not equipped to process and use biometric information. Using biometrics within VR allows for better gestural detailing and use of complex custom gestures, such as those found within instrumental music performance, compared to using optical sensors for gesture recognition in current commercial VR equipment. However, EMG data is complex and machine learning must be used to employ it. This study uses a Myo armband to classify four custom gestures in Wekinator and observe their prediction accuracies and representations (including or omitting signal onset) to compose music within VR. Results show that specific regression and classification models, according to gesture representation type, are the most accurate when classifying four music gestures for advanced music HCI in VR. We apply and record our results, showing that EMG biometrics are promising for future interactive music composition systems in VR.

Keywords: EMG · Interactive music · Machine learning · Music composition · Myo · Biometrics · Wekinator · VR · Virtual reality

1 Introduction

Interactive music is created when using a Gestural Interface (GI) (a wearable sensor or mobile device), or other sensory input devices, to map physiological behaviour with musical intention via Digital Signal Processing (DSP). Interactive music practice history is rich. One of the earliest examples of using gestural behaviours to compose music is the Theremin (1917) [14], followed by the analogue synthesizer (achieving market success in the 1970s) and later contemporary work using mobile wearable technologies, including those measuring biometrics,

T. Martins et al. (Eds.): EvoMUSART 2022, LNCS 13221, pp. 385–400, 2022.
https://doi.org/10.1007/978-3-031-03789-4_25

to manipulate sound [6,27]. Gestural information and biometrics are pursued within interactive music composition practice and history because it allows the human body to become a powerful instrument for musical expression, evident in contemporary music works [8,18].

Biometrics have been used in music composition and research since the 1960s, using Electroencephalography (EEG) to compose music [3]. Albeit a fruitful area of research, EEG datasets are not as mobile as other now commercially available biometric datasets such as EMG. Artists and researchers have been able to more easily access unique biometric datasets via the commercial release of the Myo armband GI in 2015 [17], which has widened accessibility for using such biometric information. The Myo provides both Inertial Measurement Unit (IMU) and EMG data (measuring muscle amplitude). EMG data is interesting to use in musical applications because it informs us of nuanced musical behaviours (i.e., during music performance). However, EMG data is highly complex and therefore Machine Learning (ML) must be used to deconstruct its complexity and render it usable. Wekinator is an open source ML software built on the Waikato Environment for Knowledge Analysis (WEKA) framework and offers several models of different types. It is popular amongst artists because of its accessibility regarding ML (using a Graphical User Interface (GUI) to train and run models). Wekinator has been used with biometric data in previous music gesture recognition research but seldom to compare ML models, identify optimal model choice and pair model choice within a performance context.

Recent technological advances and the improved affordability of VR equipment have allowed VR to be useful for education [7], military training operations [5] and music instrument performance [15]. Due to such promise, contemporary research has investigated the use of biometric EEG data, with a commercial Head Mounted Display (HMD) to create a Brain-Computer Interface (BCI) [1,16]. However, other forms of biometric data more significant for music practice can be used within VR to compose and perform music - namely, EMG. This is because the nuanced behaviour of arm muscles helps stimulate particular sounds and timbres in music performance. Biometric datasets are not considered when mapping gestural actions in current commercial VR equipment (i.e., the Oculus Quest (see Fig. 1b)). Since December 2019, optical sensors from the Oculus Quest HMD have been used to track user hands [12]. However, hand tracking via optical sensors is subject to environmental conditions found in music performance contexts, such as occlusion [4], and does not measure muscular information found in music performance. Considering such limitations, using EMG biometric information can make interactions within VR more sophisticated and better fitting of musical gesture and intention.

The Oculus Quest HMD is equipped with a Software Development Kit (SDK) which predicts three pre-defined gestures [20]. Whereas, the Myo SDK provides five pre-defined gestures [19]. Such a small set of pre-defined gestures for use with media systems/VR is limiting for musicians and researchers requiring bespoke gestures. Music literature using EMG data and ML seldom focuses on applying HCI to compose music within game engines. Popular avenues for using EMG data in current music practice are with physical music performers [10, 25]. Wider literature shows that using EMG data within game engines allows one to control gaming systems with natural control [28]. Therefore, combining the benefit of using EMG data with music performers and game engines (VR) is a logical step.

Performance gestures can be represented both dynamically and statically when using ML in music practice [23], which is problematic. This is because the gestural signal onset can be either omitted or included in the ML model training process and affect musical intention. Previous research has looked at the efficacy of ML models in Wekinator on two musical gestures used in piano practice [22] and has extended this investigation with further gestures, including model optimisation, plus the effect of including gestural signal onset on model accuracy/efficacy [23]. Our study is informed by this prior research. However, our paper provides a solution to the problem that using four unique music gestures (as detailed in Sect. 3.4), and nuanced gestural detailing (via EMG data and ML), to compose music within VR is not possible with commercial equipment despite VR being a powerful technology for music composition. When studying our gestures, it offers a solution to the issue that biometric data from the Myo can be processed differently by numerous ML models in Wekinator and that gesture representation type can affect model accuracy and mapping behaviour when using them with commercial VR equipment. The rest of this paper navigates a literature review (Sect. 2), our research method (Sect. 3), results (Sect. 4), applying the findings to music composition (Sect. 4.3) and conclusions (Sect. 5).

2   Literature Review

Using EMG data to develop complex interfaces has seen vast interest since commercial EMG sensors were available at consumer level in 2015. However, the data they provide is complex, so numerous studies have researched best methods of signal processing practice when working with EMG data. One study [2] analysed five time series feature extraction methods for EMG data, citing the Mean Absolute Value (MAV) method as optimal. The MAV is an amplitude estimate of EMG signals [2] and can be represented as follows, where X_k denotes kth model attribute input and N denotes attribute input sample size:

$$MAV = \frac{1}{N} \sum_{k=1}^{N} |X_k| \qquad (1)$$

Studies comparing ML models for gesture recognition in music, using biometric datasets, with Wekinator are sparse [23]. A study [9] compared two ML models when classifying four violin performance gestures (five including one non-musical gesture), using a Decision Tree (DT) J48 (via Wekinator) and a Hidden Markov Model (HMM), plus a Myo GI (using IMU and EMG data) to build an 'air violin'. The authors found that both models achieved high accuracies for prediction across all gestures, where the correctly classified instances percentage for the DT was 87.74% and the highest average accuracy for classifying a gesture was 99.3% for the HMM.

EMG information and ML is currently used within music instrumental research to study technique. A study [10] aimed to classify forearm gestures in the context of violin performance. The authors did this by analysing eight traditional violin bow strokes performed by five expert violinists and three students. A Myo sensor was used to record IMU and EMG information. Audio data was also captured. Regarding ML, multiple Deep Learning (DL) models were used, including a Convolutional Neural Network (CNN), a 3DMultiHeaded_CNN and a CNN_long short-term memory model. Recognition rates for all such models were >97%. Showing a promising comparison of ML models in violin performance for real-world use.

Another study [26] investigated user-designed gestures in a workshop setting, using two ML model types (static and dynamic) and a Myo GI with IMU and EMG data to realise designed gestures. In the work, workshop participants were asked to design a gesture and choose one of four ML models to represent those for music generation; one static model and three dynamic models. Three ML approaches were based on a Neural Network (NN) in Wekinator and one was based on a hierarchical HMM. The results from the study showed that a windowed regression technique (via a NN) was popular when representing gesture, albeit different user approaches to representing gesture via ML (static/dynamic model types) were noted. Thus, the study illustrates that gesture representation can be problematic when using ML with biometric data because of user subjectivity and the relationship between gesture type and artistic effect.

EMG information has been used in many fields using immersive gaming technologies such as VR. A medical research paper [21] used EMG and EEG biometrics to successfully investigate the use of VR to help with facial palsy rehabilitation. In this study, researchers worked with a participant with facial palsy with the aim of using VR to restore their facial features. The study found that most of the participant's facial features had been restored by using EMG and EEG information with a VR system (Oculus Rift) to aid rehabilitation.

A study [15] used a VR HMD (Oculus Rift CV1) and haptic feedback to allow performance with a 3D virtual 'air piano' in VR. User hands were tracked using an optical GI (Leap Motion) and a haptic feedback device was used to deliver tactile feedback of piano key presses within VR. 3 gestures were studied to play three piano pieces: one finger, two fingers from each hand and two fingers from a single hand. Sixteen participants were used and asked to play three pieces using the studied gestures. The user study of the work showed efficacy of using an optical GI and mid-air haptic feedback to play piano in VR.

3   Research Methodology

This section navigates technical hardware used (Sect. 3.1), technical software and processes used (Sect. 3.2), details regarding data processing and machine learning (Sect. 3.3) and gestures used (Sect. 3.4) in this study.

(a) Myo   (b) Oculus Quest HMD
armband

Fig. 1. Technical hardware used in this study.

3.1 Technical Hardware

The technical hardware used in this project are as follows:

Oculus Quest. The Oculus Quest is a standalone HMD (see Fig. 1b) equipped with four wide-angle tracking cameras for tracking user orientation and hands. It allows for six degrees of freedom [24]. The Oculus Quest is being used in this project as a second monitor (via Oculus Link software) rather than standalone. This detail is important to note because the Oculus Quest HMD cannot receive real-time data streams, over common communication protocols, within the Unreal Engine 4 (UE4) game engine. Therefore, using the Oculus Quest as a second monitor allows the transfer of real-time biometric data between UE4 and Max 8; allowing the player to use a greater level of gestural detail within VR (more on these gestures in Sect. 3.4). Hand tracking for the Oculus Quest replaces physical Oculus Touch controllers [20]. It allows the user to track their hands (via optical sensors around the Quest HMD) and represent their gestures more naturally within VR. Hand tracking is used in this study when using musical gestures within VR.

Myo Armband. The Myo armband (see Fig. 1a) is a GI which allows us to access two types of biometric information: 8-channels of 8-bit EMG data and orientation data via an IMU. The sensor transmits all data via Bluetooth and streams EMG data 200 Hz and IMU data 50 Hz [19]. It transmits data to a Bluetooth receiver within a space of <15 m. Biometric data is retrieved from the Myo SDK library developed by Thalmic Labs. The EMG data communicated by the Myo is unique to the sensor. This is because a GI offering EMG data is hard to obtain at consumer level. The Myo SDK contains three core elements to measure orientation via the IMU: gyroscope, acceleration and quaternions. The Myo contains 8 unique electrodes for observing EMG activity around the arm. At source, this EMG data has a floating point value range between -1 to 1. It is bipolar. We use two Myo armbands to measure EMG data on the left and right forearms in this project and at a fixed (referenced) point during model training and performance.

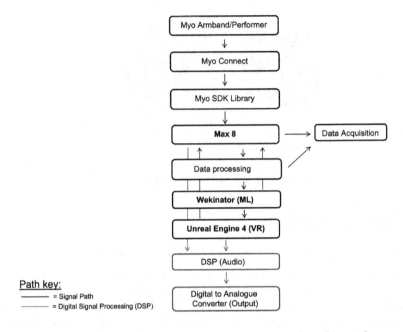

Fig. 2. Flow diagram of the software processes used in this study.

3.2 Technical Software and Processes

The technical software and processes used in this project are as follows (see Fig. 2 for a flowchart illustrating software processes):

Data Acquisition and Communication Protocols. A patch was created in Max 8 (a visual programming environment) to acquire biometric data from the Myo armband (via Myo SDK). Open Sound Control (OSC) and User Datagram Protocol (UDP) are used to transfer data from the Myo armband (acquired in Max 8) and send it to UE4 (a game engine software); and vice-versa.

Game Engine. UE4 is a game engine used to develop all game aesthetics via blueprint scripting (C++ object-oriented programming). Is it also used to develop for and host the Oculus Quest HMD. Procedural audio and 3D sound spatialisation/processing is also done within the engine.

Digital Signal Processing. All core DSP of audio signals is handled in Max 8. Some DSP is handled in UE4 for the purpose of local sound spatialisation. Classification model outputs are used in this project to compose music in real-time. This is done by mapping the model output to achieve convolution across several fixed media sound files in Max 8.

3.3 Data Processing and Machine Learning

Data Pre-processing and Post-processing. Max 8 is being used to pre-process EMG data received by the Myo by labelling all data parameters. Data parameters are then post-processed by scaling and mapping the data for DSP and ML. Data is scaled by applying an absolute value function to each EMG parameter (reducing its polarity) and then scaling it between 0–100, as described in another study [23]. However, this work builds on this method by using the minima and maxima recorded EMG inputs by the Myo user (first author) when performing our studied gestures (see Sect. 3.4) to affect the input scaling process, rather than using 0 and 1 as the minimum and maximum default input scaling values. We insert this step to help aid bespoke user EMG calibration. Following this, EMG data are post-processed through feature extraction, using the MAV; this is calculated via reducing the polarity of the raw EMG signal from the Myo through applying an absolute function and then calculating the respective mean of the signal (see Eq. 1). Giving an amplitude estimate of forearm muscles. The Myo is also calibrated before use via the Myo armband manager software.

Machine Learning. Wekinator handles all ML functionality in this project using EMG data solely from the two Myos used. In this work, we use two ML model types: continuous and classifiers. The gestures we study use both the left and right arms with a Myo armband on each arm. Therefore, we use two different instances of classifiers as the EMG data for both arms will be different according to sensor placement and other extraneous variables. The first classifier used for gesture 1 outputs 2 classes; class 1 is a resting gesture and class 2 is the performance of gesture 1 itself. The second classifier used for gestures 2–4 outputs 4 classes; class 1 is a resting gesture and classes 2–4 correspond to the specific gestures used in this study (see Sect. 3.4). Four continuous model instances are being used in this project, with a separate instance for each gesture (1–4). This is both because the EMG information for each gesture is very different/unique and because this model is used for the regression of a particular input (gesture), not the classification of different gestural states. The continuous model outputs a floating point value range between 0.0–1.0.

Wekinator provides the classifier models used in this work, namely: (i) kanearest Neighbour (k-NN), (ii) AdaBoost.M1 (ABM1), (iii) DT, (iv) Support Vector Machine (SVM), (v) Naive Bayes (NB) and (vi) Decision Stump (DS). The continuous models provided by Wekinator are: (i) Linear Regression (LR), (ii) Polynomial Regression (PR) and (iii) NN. Model evaluation metrics are taken from Wekinator's GUI, namely Cross Validation (CV) and Training Accuracy (TA), alike other studies in this area [13]. Models are trained using c.500 examples per class (10 ms per example), which was used as a baseline in other music performance gesture studies [23]. Model examples were recorded via manually pressing a start/end recording mechanism, as per the Wekinator GUI. See Table 1 for a summary of all available continuous and classifier ML models in Wekinator and their default values, as used in this work.

3.4 Performance Gestures Used

This research project uses four custom gestures for music composition within VR. They are inspired by musical interactions found during theremin performance and all use processed EMG biometric data as model inputs as described

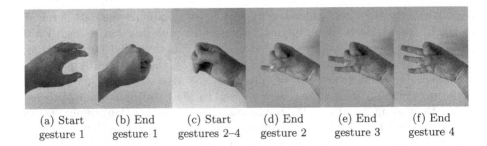

| (a) Start | (b) End | (c) Start | (d) End | (e) End | (f) End |
| gesture 1 | gesture 1 | gestures 2–4 | gesture 2 | gesture 3 | gesture 4 |

Fig. 3. Performance gestures used in this study.

in Sect. 3.3. The four gestures in this work use both continuous and classifier models, where they are paired to model type according to their aesthetic purpose. This project allows the user in VR to manipulate the velocity of three coloured spheres (green, red and blue) in randomised 3D space, which each have different timbres and sounds affixed to them, as a mechanic to compose interactive music. Increasing the velocity of each sphere is relative to gestural state and therefore model output. A continuous model is used to manipulate the velocity of each sphere (via gesture 1) because of its continuous dynamic output, where the minimum continuous model label does not move the sphere and the maximum label moves the sphere very quickly. We refer to this manipulation of each sphere's velocity as excitation. When each sphere becomes more excited, the sonic intensity of the sounds attributed to it (in Max 8) become more intense; achieved through the convolution of several fixed media sound files. Once each sphere is fully excited it flies towards a 3D musical atom and becomes part of a music sequencer, which the user can further manipulate sonically. Classifier models are used (via gestures 2–4) to select which sphere, and therefore sounds, to interact with and excite. They are ideal for this mechanic because they return discrete classification states. Performative information for each gesture is as follows:

Gesture 1. This gesture is performed by creating a fist gesture (i.e., squeezing) with the left hand, from a rested state (Fig. 3a) until a clenched fist gesture is actioned (see Fig. 3b). This gesture is inspired by its function to control amplitude in theremin performance [11].

Gesture 2. This gesture is performed by first placing the right hand in the resting position as seen in Fig. 3c, then extending the little finger forwards (as seen in Fig. 3d). This gesture is modelled on hand gestures widely accepted and used (namely the 'aerial fingering' technique) when playing the theremin [11].

Gesture 3. This gesture is performed by first placing the right hand in the resting position seen in Fig. 3c, then pointing the ring and little fingers forwards (as seen in Fig. 3e). It is also modelled on aerial fingering gestures seen when playing the theremin.

Table 1. Models used in Wekinator and their default values.

Type of model	Model name	Model parameters and default values	Model output range/type
Continuous (Soft limits[a])	NN	1 hidden layer with 1 node per layer	[0.0–1.0] (float)
	LR	No feature selection used with linear inputs. Colinear inputs are not removed	
	PR	No feature selection used. Polynomial exponent = 2. Colinear inputs are not removed	
Classifier	k-NN	No. of neighbours (k) = 1	[1–4] (integer)
	ABM1	Training rounds = 100. Base classifier = DT	
	DT	Model cannot be customised.	
	SVM	Polynomial kernel. Complexity constant = 1. Exponent = 2. Lower-order terms not used	
	NB	Model cannot be customised	
	DS	Model cannot be customised.	

[a]Where the maximum model output (0–1) can be surpassed.

Gesture 4. This gesture is performed by again first placing the right hand in the resting position seen in Fig. 3c and then pointing the middle, ring and little fingers forwards (see Fig. 3f). It is also modelled on aerial fingering gestures used in theremin performance.

Static vs Onset Gesture States. ML models can be trained by performing gestures in either static (omitting the onset of a gesture) or onset (including the onset of a gesture) states; as investigated in another study observing music performance gestures [23]. This research enquiry investigates how training models via four unique performance gestures can, in either gestural state, affect model accuracy and efficacy. We achieve this by either omitting or including gesture onset across all four performance gestures.

4   Results

This section will report all continuous (Sect. 4.1) and classifier model accuracies (Sect. 4.2) across gestures 1–4 (both static and onset gestural representations) and their application within interactive music composition in VR (Sect. 4.3).

4.1   Continuous Model Accuracies

Retrieved continuous model accuracies show that static performance versions of gestures indicate the highest accuracy levels, compared to the onset version of gestures (compare static and onset model CV and TA scores in Table 2, plus prediction behaviour during performance in Figs. 4 and 5). This is logical, as the static model training dataset contains lower variation than the onset model training dataset (for example, see Fig. 6). The NN model is the most accurate and stable (regarding mapping behaviour, as discussed later) of all the continuous models for both gesture types (static and onset) when performing gestures 1–4 (see Figs. 4 and 5). Both the LR and PR models perform similarly for gestures

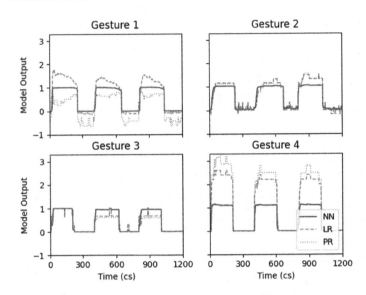

Fig. 4. Static continuous model output when performing gestures 1–4 over 12 s (1200cs).

1–4 (static models), albeit the PR model scores marginally lower for CV than the LR regarding the onset gesture 1 model. The weakest performing onset models are for gestures 2–3, which could be due to the similarity of muscle activation behaviours in the right arm and therefore datasets. However, it is interesting to note that the static models do not encounter this issue for gestures 2–3. We also see that both the LR and PR models are the weakest for gesture 1 across all static gesture models (albeit marginally).

The accuracy scores returned for gestures 1–4 in Table 2 seems to corroborate the mapping behaviours of continuous models (both onset and static) when performed after training. This is because the NN model appears the most stable, followed by the LR and then the PR. In terms of the contouring of model output (for both gesture types), the NN consistently provides the smoothest mapping. The LR provides the most linear and the PR is a hybrid of both the NN and LR. This is important to note as each individual continuous model output mapping has the potential to affect sonification mapping when composing interactive music. When observing the prediction behaviour differences between onset and static continuous models, we see that the NN onset model is faster to make a correct prediction than its static counterpart for gestures 2–4. However, the difference in prediction timing is marginal and the model output mapping is less smooth than the static model version. Regarding gesture 1, we see a very similar correct prediction speed for the NN model. This is likely because it is a less complex gesture than gestures 2–4.

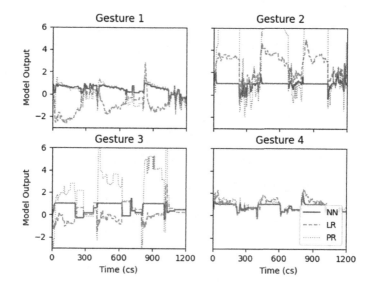

Fig. 5. Onset continuous model output when performing gestures 1–4 over 12 s (1200cs).

4.2 Classifier Model Accuracies

Accuracies retrieved from classifier models indicate that static classifier models are more accurate that onset models (see Table 3). This is because data variation is lower during static model training (see Fig. 6 for an example). All static classifier models perform very well except the DS. Interestingly, the DS model is the second poorest model for the gesture 1 onset classifier but the poorest for gestures 2–4. Interestingly, the most accurate onset classifier models for all gestures are the k-NN, ABM1 and DT models (see Table 3). The most accurate classifier models for gesture 1 (static and onset) are the k-NN, ABM1, DT and NB. However, the poorest are the SVM and then the DS. The most accurate classifier models for gestures 2–4 (static and onset) are the ABM1, then the k-NN and then the DT. The poorest performing is the DS (both gesture types).

When performing all gestures and testing model classification output (after training and in the same conditions), we see k-NN and SVM onset models are faster to make correct class predictions than static models for gesture 1, albeit with less accuracy than static models for gestures 2–4. DS onset models are also generally faster than static models to make correct predictions for gesture 1. However, the DS onset model is not very accurate regarding prediction speed or efficacy (including the static model) for gestures 2–4.

4.3 Application to Interactive Music Composition Within VR

Our classifier and continuous model results show specific machine learning algorithms are more efficient and reliable to use than others when predicting musical

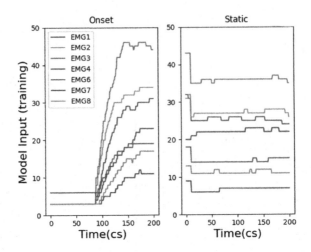

Fig. 6. Onset and static model output of gesture 1 being performed during model training.

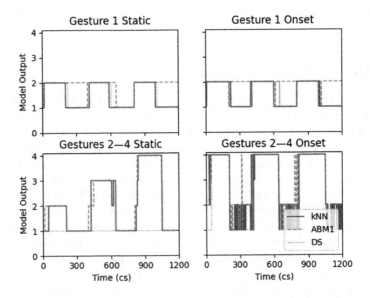

Fig. 7. Onset and static classifier model outputs of gestures 1–4 when being performed over 12 s (1200cs).

gestures for composition within VR (see Tables 2 and 3). This is important to note because interactive music relies on the real-time interaction with sound, often in a live environment (e.g., concert hall) or within interactive systems (VR). Therefore, using ML models to stimulate interactive music processes in VR can benefit from these findings when using the same studied gestures (Fig. 3).

Table 2. Accuracy of static and onset continuous models where 0 root mean squared error (RMSE) is optimal.

Gesture no.	Model	TA (S)[1]	TA (O)[2]	CV (S)	CV (O)	Class no.	No. class examples (S)	No. class examples (O)
1	NN	**0**	**0**	**0**	**0**	0.0	499	494
	LR	0.01	0.09	0.01	0.09	1.0	524	530
	PR	0.01	0.09	0.01	0.1			
2	NN	**0**	**0**	**0**	**0**	0.0	511	511
	LR	0	0.16	0	0.16	1.0	510	512
	PR	0	0.16	0	0.16			
3	NN	**0**	**0**	**0**	**0**	0.0	509	498
	LR	0	0.15	0	0.16	1.0	542	552
	PR	0	0.15	0	0.16			
4	NN	**0**	**0**	**0**	**0**	0.0	538	506
	LR	0	0.11	0	0.11	1.0	488	518
	PR	0	0.11	0	0.11			

[1] Static model   [2] Onset model

We observe that both gesture types studied in this work (onset and static) have different prediction speed characteristics, according to gesture (see Sects. 4.1 and 4.2). This means selecting a particular gesture type can allow a music practitioner to alter model predictive speed behaviour, according to how gestures are represented during model training. This is fundamental in performance situations when using ML systems to generate/perform interactive music, such as within VR systems. We also note that the disparate mapping behaviours of continuous model outputs (see Sect. 4.1) have the potential to create disparate musical mappings and thus inform model choice for musical intention, due to their contour, as noted in other research [23].

As seen in this study, continuous and classifier models are inherently different in their prediction behaviour type. This is because classifier models return fixed predictive states (labels/classes) and continuous models map data input in realtime. Therefore, both model types are useful in different musical contexts and interactive situations within VR. This is because a music practicioner may wish to either trigger Audiovisual (AV) events within VR (e.g., choose a sphere to excite) or control a real-time AV parameter (e.g., choose how *much* to excite a sphere). We combine and use the unique mechanics of both the classifier and continuous models together to form a unified gestural music instrument, when predicting our gestures in VR, where the models cannot drive the aesthetics of the piece in isolation (as seen with both hands in theremin performance).

We also see that using custom gestures via biometrics within VR is profound for interactive music and future musical expression within immersive digital environments. This is because custom gestures are more indicative of real

Table 3. Accuracy of static and onset classifier models where 100 (%) is optimal.

Gesture no.	Model	TA (S)	TA (O)	CV (S)	CV (O)	Class no.	No. class examples (S)	No. class examples (O)
1	k-NN	100	100	100	100			
	ABM1	100	100	100	100			
	DT	100	100	100	100	1	511	494
	SVM	100	90.76	100	90.76	2	500	534
	NB	100	100	100	100			
	DS	100	91.44	100	91.44			
2–4	k-NN	100	**99.95**	100	**99.85**			
	ABM1	100	**99.95**	100	**99.95**	1	513	508
	DT	100	**99.8**	100	**99.5**	2	488	499
	SVM	100	93.24	100	93.04	3	515	491
	NB	100	92.69	100	92.74	4	495	514
	DS	51.12	47.96	51.12	47.96			

world musical expression, which is not possible via interacting with digital worlds and a Digital Musical Instrument (DMI) within VR through analogue hardware equipment (i.e., Oculus Touch controllers). Custom gestures using EMG biometrics are also beneficial for future interactive music practice in VR because of limitations found when using optical sensors to track gesture.

When applying our results and models to interactive music practice within the VR space, it is clear that using custom gestures provides new levels of expression for interactive music. One can hear and see an example of using our gestures, their targeted models and study findings within an interactive music project for VR (created by the first author) via the following hyperlink: https://tinyurl.com/jpdubbfp. In light of our results, a NN model was used for gesture 1 and a k-NN for gestures 2–4.

5   Conclusions

We have observed that using custom music gestures, via EMG data, within VR provides a future immersive space with new methods for musical expression in composition. Our results show that: (i) particular continuous/classification ML algorithms (in Wekinator) are more efficient than others when predicting processed EMG datasets (ii) unique mapping behaviours can be found on continuous model output (according to gesture type (static and onset)) (iii) model accuracy is affected by gesture type (static and onset) and (iv) custom EMG gestures can be made via novel GIs and ML for use with commercial HMDs/VR and music practice, with high efficacy.

Future work will investigate the use of a multimodal capture system to track gestures which are more fluid in their states (i.e., switching between different gestures within a single class). In particular, we would like to investigate a possible threshold between a gesture considered more difficult (at data level) and an easier one. We will also investigate the generalisability of using our observed gestures with other participants/musicians, as the gestures observed in this study were trained and performed by the first author. The applications of this research have use outside of music, where using custom gestures for future gaming interaction in VR is particularly significant.

Acknowledgments. This project was supported by the Engineering and Physical Sciences Research Council with grant no. 2063473.

References

1. Andreev, A., Cattan, G., Congedo, M.: Engineering study on the use of Head-Mounted display for Brain-Computer Interface. arXiv:1906.12251 (2019)
2. Arief, Z., Sulistijono, I.A., Ardiansyah, R.A.: Comparison of five time series EMG features extractions using Myo Armband. In: 2015 International Electronics Symposium (IES), pp. 11–14 (2015)
3. Arslan, B., et al.: From biological signals to music. In: 2nd International Conference on Enactive Interfaces, p. 11 (2005)
4. Benalcázar, M.E., et al.: Real-time hand gesture recognition using the Myo armband and muscle activity detection. In: 2017 IEEE Second Ecuador Technical Chapters Meeting, pp. 1–6 (2017)
5. Bhagat, K.K., Liou, W.-K., Chang, C.-Y.: A cost-effective interactive 3D virtual reality system applied to military live firing training. Virtual Real. **20**(2), 127–140 (2016). https://doi.org/10.1007/s10055-016-0284-x
6. Bongers, B.: An interview with sensorband. Comput. Music J. **22**(1), 13–24 (1998)
7. Checa, D., Bustillo, A.: A review of immersive virtual reality serious games to enhance learning and training. Multimedia Tools Appl. (2), 5501–5527 (2019). https://doi.org/10.1007/s11042-019-08348-9
8. ComputerHistoryMuseum: Max Mathews Radio Baton Demonstration (2010). https://tinyurl.com/b78uznnt. Accessed 21 Nov 2021
9. Dalmazzo, D., Ramirez, R.: Air violin: a machine learning approach to fingering gesture recognition. In: Proceedings of the 1st ACM SIGCHI International Workshop on Multimodal Interaction for Education, pp. 63–66 (2017)
10. Dalmazzo, D., Waddell, G., Ramírez, R.: Applying deep learning techniques to estimate patterns of musical gesture. Front. Psychol. **11**, 3546 (2021)
11. Estrada, V.: Progressive Exercises for Theremin, vol. 1. Victor Estrada, 2nd edn. (2008)
12. Faulkner, C.: The Oculus Quest is getting controller-free hand tracking this week (2019). https://tinyurl.com/9t3u4ha4. Accessed 22 Oct 2021
13. Fiebrink, R., Cook, P.R., Trueman, D.: Human model evaluation in interactive supervised learning. In: Proceedings of the SIGCHI Conference on Human Factors in Computing Systems, pp. 147–156 (2011)
14. Hayward, P.: Danger! Retro-affectivity! The cultural career of the Theremin. Convergence **3**(4), 28–53 (1997)
15. Hwang, I., Son, H., Kim, J.R.: AirPiano: enhancing music playing experience in virtual reality with mid-air haptic feedback. In: 2017 IEEE World Haptics Conference, pp. 213–218 (2017)

16. Käthner, I., Kübler, A., Halder, S.: Rapid P300 brain-computer interface communication with a head-mounted display. Front. Neurosci. **9**, 207 (2015)
17. Martin, C.P., Jensenius, A.R., Torresen, J.: Composing an ensemble standstill work for Myo and Bela. In: Proceedings of the International Conference on New Interfaces for Musical Expression, pp. 196–197 (2018)
18. MusicSensorsEmotion: First Movement, "Biomuse Trio" (2010). https://tinyurl.com/ay4cyvcz. Accessed 21 Nov 2021
19. Nymoen, K., Haugen, M.R., Jensenius, A.R.: MuMyo-evaluating and exploring the MYO armband for musical interaction. In: Proceedings of the International Conference on New Interfaces for Musical Expression, pp. 215–218 (2015)
20. Oculus: Controllers and Hand Tracking (nd). https://tinyurl.com/4z8e9fc7. Accessed 02 Oct 2021
21. Qidwai, U., Ajimsha, M.S., Shakir, M.: The role of EEG and EMG combined virtual reality gaming system in facial palsy rehabilitation - a case report. J. Bodyw. Mov. Ther. **23**(2), 425–431 (2019)
22. Rhodes, C., Allmendinger, R., Climent, R.: New interfaces for classifying performance gestures in music. In: International Conference on Intelligent Data Engineering and Automated Learning, pp. 31–42 (2019)
23. Rhodes, C., Allmendinger, R., Climent, R.: New interfaces and approaches to machine learning when classifying gestures within music. Entropy **22**(12), 1384 (2020)
24. Robertson, A.: Oculus Quest Review: A Great Vision With a Frustrating Compromise (2019). https://tinyurl.com/4f2kw92n. Accessed 03 June 2021
25. Tanaka, A.: Sarah Nicolls performs Suspensions, by Atau Tanaka (2019). https://tinyurl.com/y5rrsj6v. Accessed 17 Jan 2021
26. Tanaka, A., Di Donato, B., Zbyszynski, M., Roks, G.: Designing gestures for continuous sonic interaction. In: Proceedings of the International Conference on New Interfaces for Musical Expression (2019)
27. Torre, G., Andersen, K., Baldé, F.: The hands: the making of a digital musical instrument. Comput. Music J. **40**(2), 22–34 (2016)
28. Zhang, X., Chen, X., Wang, W.h., Yang, J.h., Lantz, V., Wang, K.q.: Hand gesture recognition and virtual game control based on 3D accelerometer and EMG sensors. In: Proceedings of the 14th International Conference on Intelligent User Interfaces, pp. 401–406 (2009)

Generating Novel Furniture with Machine Learning

Nelson Vermeer[✉] and Andrew R. Brown

Interactive Media Lab, Griffith University, Brisbane, Australia
{nelson.vermeer,andrew.r.brown}@griffith.edu.au

Abstract. This paper introduces a machine learning tool for generating novel furniture designs. We employ a network graph to represent object structure and utilise two deep neural nets in combination to learn these network graphs, reproduce them, and generate variations on them. We apply the tool to the domain of furniture design and describe how the tool can create unique designs quickly and in large volume. This original generative approach allows a designer to efficiently consider novel design candidates. The option to train the system on multiple product types allows designers to explore designs that live between and outside the traditional concept of the domain object. We suggest that this workflow could be generalised for use beyond the domain of furniture design.

Keywords: Design language · Graph network · Deep neural nets · Generative design

1 Introduction

This paper explores the generation of novel object structures by employing the use of network graphs to describe objects and utilising them to train a generative artificial neural network (ANN) model with a representation of the objects' structure. The network model is used to generate object models similar to the training data from which a designer can develop new products.

Neural nets have been widely employed in the generation of new data, most notably generative adversarial networks (GANs) to generate realistic faces [1] or unique artworks [2]. This paper outlines an architecture that utilises two types of deep neural nets (DNN) in combination, a transformer and variational autoencoder, to achieve object structural representation using network graphs. This DNN architecture has been developed for use by a human designer as a tool for inspiration and co-creativity.

It has long been recognised that human intelligence, including creativity, can be augmented and supported by technologies. In this article we explore another example of this, the combined use of a graph-based design language and machine learning to generate novel designs. Understanding human capacity as involving external resources, especially computing ones, has been a topic of research in cybernetics that focused on coupled interactions between people and machines [3], and in human-computer interface design where technologies have been described as 'border' sources [4]. It has also

© The Author(s), under exclusive license to Springer Nature Switzerland AG 2022
T. Martins et al. (Eds.): EvoMUSART 2022, LNCS 13221, pp. 401–416, 2022.
https://doi.org/10.1007/978-3-031-03789-4_26

been explored in the appropriate balance of technical and critical aspects of practice [5] and in sociological research exploring distributed intelligence [6, 7] or what Pickering [8] refers to as a dance of agency between people and technologies. Much of this work finds its foundations in phenomenological and/or pragmatist philosophies of Whitehead [9], Dewey [10], Merleau-Ponty [11], Heidegger [12] and others. Recognising this tradition of co-creation with machines, this article outlines a technique for the generation of product design concepts by using machine learning to stimulate co-creative design thinking.

2 Background

Machine learning (ML) processes are increasingly being used in many creative disciplines, for example tracking consumer trends in fashion design [13] and in early-stage product design [14]. ML has also been utilised in areas of creative AI, and research and development of algorithmic design goes as far back as the 60s and 70s with Negroponte's and Frazer's work in computational architecture [15, 16].

In more recent years the combination of deep learning and design generation has been demonstrated in the field of architecture using GANs [17, 18, 19, 20]. AI has also been employed in product and industrial design across different phases of industrial design development by Fournier-Viger et al. [21]. It has been seen as a tool for creative inspiration for designers, for example in shape generation [22] and fashion generation [23].

Building on this history, this paper focuses on two areas. Firstly, the use of a multidisciplinary language (MDL) developed in the field of product design that can be used in different disciplines. Secondly, the utilization of neural nets to learn and generate new objects using the design language. We explore below some previous research in these domains.

2.1 A Graph-Based Design Language

Pattern languages have long been a feature of design practices. Perhaps most famously, the book "A Pattern Language" by Christopher Alexander, Sara Ishikawa and Murray Silverstein [24] was written to aid in architectural design and urban planning. It has subsequently been quite influential in software design. Such languages try to codify design structures at an abstract level such that they can be applied in various contexts.

The multi-disciplinary design language we developed uses network graphs to describe objects. In particular the graphs describe features as nodes and the relationships between them as edges. Network graphs have been used to describe many other structures including social networks [25], molecules [26], and roads between cities [27]. They have wide applications and are used in this paper to describe furniture structure. We build upon previous research in machine learning of network graphs in developing our generative design tool.

2.2 Deep Neural Nets (DNN)

Artificial Neural Networks (NN) are computing systems often used for machine learning which, in turn, is a subset of artificial intelligence (AI). Deep Neural Networks (DNN) that use multiple layers between input and output have been employed with great successes in many domains because of their ability to learn patterns [28] through exposure to many examples of the target data. DNN have previously been employed as design assistants, for example in choosing colours for design templates [29] and for converting drawings into HTML templates [30].

DNNs can be classified into three main categories—supervised, unsupervised [31] and reinforcement learning [32]—and a range of network architectures can be deployed, each with different capabilities. Supervised learning systems classify data or predict outcomes by being trained on labelled data, whereas unsupervised learning does not rely on labelled data to learn, rather the neural net learns features by clustering similar data together [33]. Reinforcement learning systems use "trial and error and delayed reward" to learn optimal action in an environment [34].

In this article we will focus on the use of two specific types of unsupervised DNNs, the transformer and the variational autoencoder, using them to learn patterns in network graph descriptions of product designs.

Network graphs and DNN are combined in graph convolutional neural nets (GCN), where the DNN is trained on graph data and models are used for prediction and/or classification [35]. Beyond the use of GCN to predict and classify, they can generate new data based on the training data. Notably, graph recurrent neural nets have been used to generate network graphs [36] and graph convolutional neural networks to generate molecular graphs [37].

3   The Architecture of a Generative Design Tool

In this section we will describe the approach taken to describe furniture objects as a network graph and to train DNNs on those graphs, producing models that can be stimulated to generate novel, yet recognisable, structures that can inspire new furniture designs.

3.1   Representing (Product) Structure as a Graph

Product designers deal with physical objects. The decomposition of a physical object enables a description of the fundamental structure of the object. What needs to be depicted in the graph representation are the fundamental parts of the object and how these are put together. Object elements and their relationships can be presented as a network graph as shown in Fig. 1 [38].

When it comes to graph representation in product design for our project, the overall objective is to describe furniture using a graph representation, then to convert that graph to a data format that a DNN can learn. After training, the neural net has an abstract model of the furniture and is able to generate a novel graph that will represent a new piece of furniture.

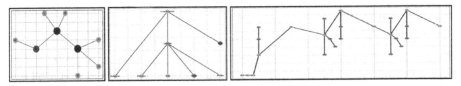

Fig. 1. Network graph representations of a) chemical structure [39], b) animal form [40] and c) musical organisation [41].

For our project we decomposed a set of furniture into structural elements and mapped the relationships between these elements, as shown in Fig. 2. These graphs can be used to describe and compare furniture, create a road map (a taxonomy) of furniture structure, and as training data for DNNs to learn those structures and then generate unique furniture.

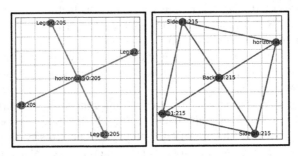

Fig. 2. Network graphs of a table and chair.

3.2 The Use of Deep Neural Nets

The DNNs that are of interest here are generative DNNs that learn by example and can produce data based on what they have learnt. Of use to creative practices, such as design, is the ability for the generative DNN to produce new data and not simply reproduce the learnt data. Generative DNNs have a stochastic nature to their architecture which means that the output will be unpredictably varied from the input.

There are two main types of DNN models that this paper is concerned with. Firstly, models that can accept and generate sequences and, secondly, models that can handle multidimensional data. Examples of sequential data are words in sentences and notes in music, and examples of multidimensional data are 2D images and 3D structures such as point clouds. The data from network graphs used to describe the furniture objects are 'flattened' into sequences. Given that the graphs can vary in size depending on the structural complexity of the object, a DNN system was required where variation in sequence size was permitted. Multi-dimensional data handling capabilities were required to enable the creative synthesis of designs from multiple starting points, for example a piece of furniture that combines elements of a table and a bookshelf. This two-step DNN approach was inspired by the idea that DNNs can learn and generate sequence data (a graph can be converted into sequence data) and as well as learning to generate data variation, however not necessarily in a single DNN model.

Two candidate DNNs for managing sequential data were considered, long short-term memory (LSTM) systems and transformers. After some experimentation we decided to use transformers because unlike LSTMs they avoid recursion and take in the sequence data as a whole due to the multi-headed attention mechanisms [42]. To manage the multi-dimensional aspects of the project, the use of Variational AutoEncoders (VAEs) and Generative Adversarial Networks (GANs) were considered. We selected VAEs because of the simpler architecture and training process [43]. Controlled sampling is also a simpler process. These DNNs are combined in an architecture shown in Fig. 3 where the Transformers are trained on the network graph data, once trained the model predicts an output for each training graph label. The transformer has been modified so that on each prediction it's latent space variable (LSV) is extracted and used to train the VAE. The trained VAE is sampled and the output is put back into the transformer for decoding into a novel graph.

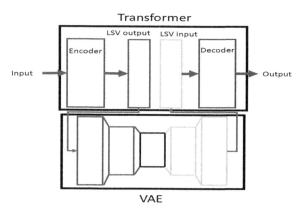

Fig. 3. The neural net architecture used for our generative design tool.

4   The Generation of Novel Graph Structures

In this section we outline our workflow and system architecture as summarised in Fig. 4.

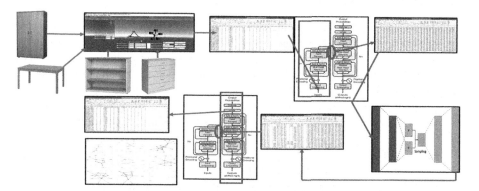

Fig. 4. The generative design tool architecture.

4.1 Object Analysis and Conversion to Graph

The first part of the process is to choose the domain objects to be represented. A standard set of labels is required for elements or features. This ensures that all objects in the domain can be constructed from these elements. The chosen set of objects are then converted into their graph representation based on the unique element set. The elements in an object will be represented as nodes in the graph and the relations between elements will be represented as edges between nodes.

Our chosen domain is furniture, and we selected the following set of objects:

- Chair
- Table
- Cupboard
- Shelf

The elements for the furniture were as follows:

- Back
- Sides
- Arms
- Legs
- Horizontal (seat or shelf)
- Drawer

A chair is defined by having, for example, four legs connected to a single horizontal (the seat) which is connected to a single back. This creates a star shaped graph with the horizontal in the centre as shown in Fig. 5.

The creation of the graph can be done manually, however using a tool to create the graph allows for a quicker and simpler process. We created tools for this purpose in Java as a Processing application and in C# as a Unity 3D application. The tools allow the user to draw graphs via mouse clicks and to save graphs as a CSV file for importing into Python neural network models.

4.2 Conversion of the Graphs to Training Data

The second step in the process is the conversion of the graphs into a form that can be used by the chosen DNN. The graph object (NetworkX object) is converted into sets of strings that represent the graphs as a concatenation of the adjacency list. An adjacency list is a way of representing a graph where each node is preceded with a list of adjacent (neighbouring) nodes. These nodes are connected to the node of interest via an edge.

The set of strings (adjacency lists) is further concatenated to a complete graph representation. Each graph is labelled by its furniture type. An example for a table object is as follows:

"Table": "horizontal@0, Leg@0-Leg@1-Leg@2-Leg@3/Leg@0, horizontal@0/Leg@1, horizontal@0/Leg@2, horizontal@0/Leg@3, horizontal@0".

This data is placed into a two-dimensional array for use in the next stage.

4.3 Training the DNN (Transformer) Model

The first DNN that is used is a transformer. The set of complete graph representations and their labels are used to train the transformer. After training, the transformer can predict a graph structure given an existing label as input. The process of training typically takes 600 epochs (loops) to achieve an accuracy of above 98%.

A transformer architecture includes an encoder and decoder with a layer that interfaces between the two. This layer creates a vector that holds what are known as the latent space variables. The LSVs define a graph representation (of any length) and are of a fixed size.

At the completion of training, the transformer is asked to predict a data output string (a graph representation) based on a given input (graph label), the labels used are the labels the transformer is trained on.

The latent space variables can be modified and put back into the decoder of the transformer, which will then output a new unique data set that resembles the training data format. We take advantage of this feature in the next stage of the process. Once trained, the LSVs are extracted and saved as a CSV file.

4.4 Using the Transformer's Latent Space Variables to Train a VAE

The LSVs can be used as training data (input and output) for a variational autoencoder (VAE). The VAE is employed because it can generate variations of the LSVs by generating data that morphs between features of two or more distinct data clusters. Sampling from the generated data allows us to select features across different parts of the latent space. In our experiments, typically 400 samples (LSV variations) are generated and then saved to a .CSV.

4.5 The Generation of Novel Graphs Using the transformer's Decoder

The output from the VAE can be used as an input to the decoder half of the trained transformer which will generate novel graph representations. Outputs may either resemble the original graphs or in-between representations of the original graph set. These generated in-between representations are new versions of the original graphs used for training.

4.6 Converting the Output String Representation to a Graph and Image

The novel graph representation will be in a similar format to the original training data strings. Each graph data component is converted back from a single string from the list which represents one graph. The Networkx library [44] is used to visualize the graph as images like those in Figs. 5, 6, 7, 8 and 9. The adjacency lists can be saved to a .CSV and reloaded in our Unity 3D tool to re-create a graph in 3D or to depict a 3D representation of the furniture.

4.7 Building the Machine Learning Architecture

All ANNs were programmed in Python using Jupyter Notebooks. The transformer was based on example code from the TensorFlow website [45] and modified to suit the inputs, output and extraction and inputting of the LSV. It also generated the final .CSV file that would be used by the object graph program to convert back into the 2D or 3D visual graph representation.

The VAE was also based on example code from the TensorFlow website [46] and modified to take in and generate the LSV. The LSVs data was maintained as .CSV files.

The tool is currently in prototype form and not yet integrated into a turnkey system. Currently, the workflow involves a transformer being trained on entire graphs with labels and it generates entire graphs. This process is computationally expensive and time consuming. For more efficiency as this process scales the graphs could be broken into node adjacency lists and processed in parallel. These could be converted into string representations and used as training data. This would speed up the process, however, it would require a new process of assembling the nodes and their adjacency lists that is yet to be defined.

5 Outcomes and Evaluation

When developing the generative design tool, tests were conducted with different numbers of input classes. Single classes, for example data representing only chairs, was used to validate the system to ensure that outputs matched inputs. The system was trained on multiple classes of furniture, at first two classes, then four, to verify that the system could generate designs that mixed features from these classes of objects in explainable ways. For example, input from three legged stools and four legged tables could result in the generation of a table with three legs.

Following these validation trials, we investigated the degree of novelty that was introduced in the generated output. The measure of novelty was the number (percentage) of unique outputs, an idea similar to what Richie calls the degree of a-typicality [47]. In keeping with the co-creative objective for our system, judgements about the value of the unique outputs is left to a human designer.

5.1 Generation of Novel Graphs

The graph outputs are based on the training data and so, by varying the diversity of input data, the designer/user can control the extent of novel graph output. Training on a narrow data set will result in output graphs with little to no variations. To allow for useful variation and novelty on the output graphs, training on graphs with overlapping elements and structural variation is important.

The next section discusses the use of table and shelf graph sets as training data. The graph representation of a table and a shelf is below in Fig. 5.

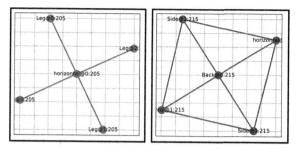

Fig. 5. Visualisation of graphs representing the table and shelf structures.

Generated graphs can be identical to the input data or they might introduce variations. Graphs are described as mutant or novel if there are additional edges and or additional nodes. For example, the graphs in Fig. 6 were generated by a model trained on both table and shelf data. They closely resemble the original table or shelf with minor changes. The variation is minor and only introduces (or reduces) elements that were in the original graph and so the novelty can be considered as "conservative".

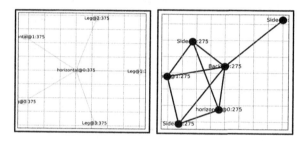

Fig. 6. Novel graphs that combine elements of a table and a shelf.

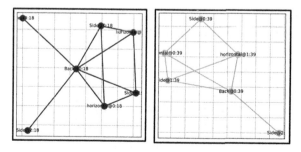

Fig. 7. Novel graphs that mix elements from several input classes.

The set of graphs shown in Fig. 7, can be considered to have "radical" novelty because they display more significant differences to the original graph (in this case both derived from a shelf structure). The resulting mutations are the result of cross sampling which produce designs that explore the possibility space beyond their own constituent parts.

A generated graph is considered a "hybrid" if it is a mutant with nodes of the same types that exist in *all* the original graphs in the training set. The graphs in Fig. 8 are samples of hybrids that start close to the table graph (top left) and move toward the shelf graph (bottom right). It can be observed that no new nodes (nodes that do not exist in the training graphs) are added in the generation process. This is what is expected from the system. This means that all graphs tend to maintain what [47] Ritchie (2007) refers to as 'typicality' to the class of furniture; they are valid buildable structures even if not practical.

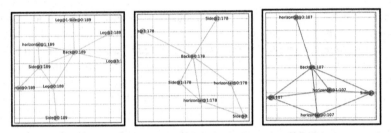

Fig. 8. Hybrid graphs that contain elements from all input types.

The next set of novel graphs are based on four training sets. To the table and shelf are added graphs for cupboards and drawers, as shown in Fig. 9. These have been chosen as there are sufficient differences between the graphs.

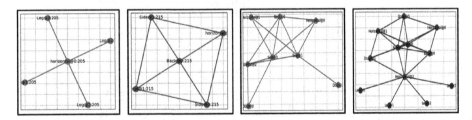

Fig. 9. Input graphs for a table, shelf, chest of drawers and cupboard.

A convenient way of representing the generated output from four sets of input is to sample evenly across the space between them and visualise as a 2D matrix with the input graphs at each corner. A sample of a 20 by 5 matrix of generated graphs based on the table, shelf, drawer and cupboard is shown in Fig. 10.

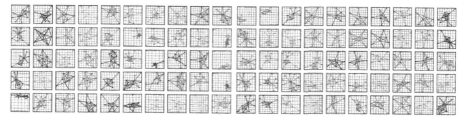

Fig. 10. A matrix of generated graphs.

As might be expected, the results from combining four training sets are more complex than combining two. The same types of novel graphs appear in the generated sets; conservative and radical mutants and hybrids. The additional complexity of these can be seen in the examples shown in Fig. 11.

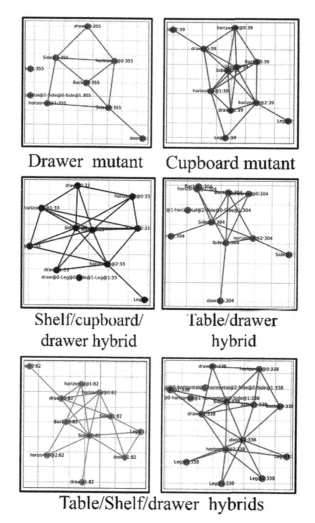

Drawer mutant   Cupboard mutant

Shelf/cupboard/   Table/drawer
drawer hybrid   hybrid

Table/Shelf/drawer hybrids

Fig. 11. Examples of novel graphs generated from training on four furniture types.

It is anticipated that this trend of reasonable novelty will be maintained even when using additional training sets. There will, of course, be additional time required for training as the data complexity increases.

5.2 Measuring the Extent of Novelty

When sets of graphs are generated by the system it is not often clear from the visual or tabulated output which graphs might be candidates for novel designs. The degree of unique novel output is a measure of the utility of the tool.

Programs were written to parse the generated data and identify those graphs that were identical to the input and to see how many unique mutations were in the set. The results for both the 2-input and 4-input cases are shown in Fig. 12. Novel graphs are those that differ from the input graphs, and unique graphs are distinct instances of novel graphs.

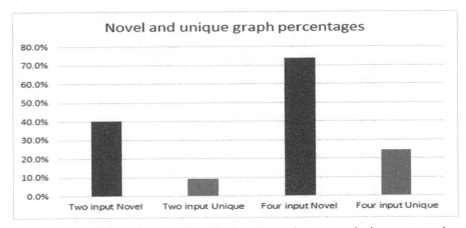

Fig. 12. The percentage of generated graphs that are not the same as the input or are unique mutations trained on two graphs, left, and trained on four graphs, right.

The more variety there is in the input the more likely it is that generated output is novel. In the 4-input case, around 75% of the output is a mutation (different from the input), the remainder are exact copies of the input graphs. Approximately 25% of the output are unique mutations, with the balance being duplicates of these. These unique mutations are the graphs of interest to the user. These are the ones that can be examined as potential for new design concepts.

5.3 Selecting and Refining Generated Designs

The current workflow can generate a large volume of graphs; in a sample of 20 by 20, 400 graphs are produced. The designer who is generating these graphs can inspect the set as a pdf file or as an adjacency list for each graph. Manually inspecting these outputs is a time consuming process and inefficient when a designer is only interested in graphs that are novel and unique.

Within the graph visualization section of the tool, each graph is compared against the original graph and against each unique mutation found thus far. If there is a match then the original graph is visualized with a counter indicating the number of unique graphs and the duplicates are ignored.

An example of a novel design created by the authors based on a mutant graph generated by the system is shown in Fig. 13. To model and render this design the designer identified the elements and connection and built a 3D model that adheres to the graph's constraints. This model is created in fusion 360, a 3D design software tool by Autodesk.

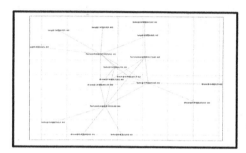  

Fig. 13. An example of a novel hybrid graph output from the tool and a designer's rendering of furniture based on that graph.

To assist in managing the volume of generated data, in future work the comparison of novelty could be more fine-grained, consisting of a spectrum novelty from conservative to radical. Further to the measurements of novelty, generated graphs could be assessed by aesthetic and/or practicality criteria to help further isolate useful candidates for designers to inspect.

6 Conclusion

This article describes a new method of generating unique furniture structures using machine learning. This has been achieved by providing a tool that can aid a designer by generating different design concepts in the form of graphs and applying a combination of two deep neural networks to generate variations of these graphs. We have described degrees of generated variation as either conservative, radical or hybrid to help distinguish them so as to assist filtering for review or elaboration by human designers. The generated graphs are a starting point that can inspire designers to create furniture that otherwise would not have come to fruition. The tool provides two main features, graphs that represent furniture design variations and graphs that live as hybrids between existing designs.

Our experiments thus far have focused on furniture design, however, due to the abstract nature of a graph representation the approach could be used to represent objects across different domains. This would facilitate the hybridisation of objects within a domain to provide a rich set of designs that are otherwise difficult and time consuming to create for a designer or design team. The tool is not built to replace the designer, but to extend and augment the designer and aid them in a co-creative process. This paper does not discuss the tools' viability for creativity support at this stage.

The outcome is successful within the limited range explored so far. There is still more to explore and improve in the workflow. We have shown that the process can generate novel graphs/furniture based on an original set. Our explorations used data sets based on four objects to train the DNNs. Generated output included a significant and useful selection of novel mutations of the input data. The final result was a new set of furniture design that maintained elements of the original furniture structure whilst also exhibiting unique structure.

Images presented in this paper can be viewed in high resolution at: https://anonym ous.4open.science/r/Generating-novel-furniture-with-machine-learning-link-5FB5.

References

1. Shen, Y., Luo, P., Yan, J., Wang, X., Tang, X.: FaceID-GAN: learning a symmetry three-player GAN for identity-preserving face synthesis. In: Proceedings of the IEEE Conference on Computer Vision and Pattern Recognition, Salt Lake City, pp. 821–830. IEEE (2018)
2. Mazzone, M., Elgammal, A.: Art, creativity, and the potential of artificial intelligence. In: Arts, p. 26. Multidisciplinary Digital Publishing Institute (2019)
3. Wiener, N.: Cybernetics: Control and Communication in the Animal and the Machine. Wiley, New York (1948)
4. Brown, J.S., Duguid, P.: Borderline issues: social and material aspects of design. Hum. Comput. Interact. Spec. Issue Context Des. **9**, 3–36 (1994)
5. Agre, P.E.: Computation and Human Experience. University of California, San Diego (1997)
6. Clancey, W.J.: Situated Cognition: Human knowledge and Computer Representations. Cambridge University Press, Cambridge (1997)
7. Clark, A., Chalmers, D.J.: The extended mind. Analysis **58**, 10–23 (1998)
8. Pickering, A.: The Mangle of Practice: Time, Agency and Practice. The University of Chicago Press, Chicago (1995)
9. Whitehead, A.N.: Process and Reality. The Free Press, New York (1929)
10. Dewey, J.: Art as Experience. Putnmans, New York (1934)
11. Merleau-Ponty, M.: Phenomenology of Perception. Routledge and Kegan Paul, London (1962)
12. Heidegger, M.: The Question Concerning Technology and Other Essays. Harper & Row, New York (1977)
13. Liang, Y., Lee, S.-H., Workman, J.E.: Implementation of artificial intelligence in fashion: are consumers ready? Cloth. Text. Res. J. **38**, 3–18 (2020)
14. Wisthoff, A., Ferrero, V., Huynh, T., DuPont, B.: Quantifying the impact of sustainable product design decisions in the early design phase through machine learning. In: International Design Engineering Technical Conferences and Computers and Information in Engineering Conference, p.V004T05A043. American Society of Mechanical Engineers (2016)
15. Negroponte N.: Toward a theory of architecture machines. J. Archit. Educ. **23**, 9–12 (1969)
16. Frazer J.: An Evolutionary Architecture, the Architectural Association, London (1995)
17. As, I., Pal, S., Basu, P.: Artificial intelligence in architecture: generating conceptual design via deep learning. Int. J. Archit. Comput. **16**, 306–327 (2018)

18. Newton, D.: Generative deep learning in architectural design. Technol. Archit. Des. **3**, 176–189 (2019)
19. Zheng, H., Yuan, P.F.: A generative architectural and urban design method through artificial neural networks. Build. Environ. **205**, 108178 (2021)
20. Wang, H., Huan, J.: AGAN: towards automated design of generative adversarial networks (2019)
21. Fournier-Viger, P.,Saqib, M.: Machine learning for intelligent industrial design
22. Sato, T., Hagiwara, M.: IDSET: interactive design system using evolutionary techniques. Comput. Aided Des. **33**, 367–377 (2001)
23. Sbai, O., Elhoseiny, M., Bordes, A., LeCun, Y., Couprie, C.: DesIGN: design inspiration from generative networks. In: Leal-Taixé, L., Roth, S. (eds.) ECCV 2018. LNCS, vol. 11131, pp. 37–44. Springer, Cham (2019). https://doi.org/10.1007/978-3-030-11015-4_5
24. Alexander, C., Ishikawa, S., Silverstein, M.: A Pattern Language. Oxford University Press, New York (1977)
25. Viégas, F.B.: dupuy, CSCW, vol. 4. pp. 6–10 (2004)
26. Sacha, M., et al.: Molecule edit graph attention network: modeling chemical reactions as sequences of graph edits. J. Chem. Inf. Model. **61**(7), 3273–3284 (2021)
27. Dupuy, G., Stransky, V.: Cities and highway networks in Europe. J. Transp. Geogr. (2), 107–121 (1996)
28. Looney, C.G.: Pattern Recognition Using Neural Networks: Theory and Algorithms for Engineers and Scientists. Oxford University Press (1997)
29. Colorful. (2019). https://colorful.co/. Accessed 26 Oct 2021
30. Robinson, A.: Sketch2code: generating a website from a paper mockup, dissertation, University of Bristol, Bristol (2018)
31. Delua, J.: Supervised vs. Unsupervised learning: What's the difference? (2021). https://www.ibm.com/cloud/blog/supervised-vs-unsupervised-learning
32. Kahn, G., Villaflor, A., Ding, B., Abbeel, P., Levine, S.: Self-supervised deep reinforcement learning with generalized computation graphs for robot navigation. In: 2018 IEEE International Conference on Robotics and Automation (ICRA), pp. 129–5136 (2018)
33. Sathya, R., Abraham, A.: Comparison of supervised and unsupervised learning algorithms for pattern classification. Int. J. Adv. Res. Artif. Intell. **2**, 34–38 (2013)
34. Sutton, R.S., Barto, A.G.: Reinforcement learning: an introduction (2018)
35. Kipf, T.N., Welling, M.: Variational graph auto-encoders. arXiv preprint arXiv:1611.07308 (2016)
36. You, J., Ying, R., Ren, X., Hamilton, W., Leskovec, J.: GraphRNN: generating realistic graphs with deep auto-regressive models. In: International Conference on Machine Learning, pp. 5708–5717. PMLR (2018)
37. Bresson, X., Laurent, T.: A two-step graph convolutional decoder for molecule generation. arXiv preprint arXiv:1906.03412 (2019)
38. Nayyar, R.: Representing graphs in data structures (2020). https://www.mygreatlearning.com/blog/representing-graphs-in-data-structures/.GreatLearningTeam
39. Akutsu, T., Nagamochi, H.: Comparison and enumeration of chemical graphs. Comput. Struct. Biotechnol. J. **5**(6) (2013)
40. Amesl, S.: Animal kingdom classification chart. https://www.exploringnature.org/db/view/Animal-Kingdom-Classification-Chart
41. Liu, X., Tse, C.K., Small, M.: Composing music with complex networks. In: Zhou, J. (eds.) Complex 2009. LNICST, vol. 5, pp. 2196–2205. Springer, Heidelberg (2009). https://doi.org/10.1007/978-3-642-02469-6_95
42. Vaswani, A., et al.: Attention is all you need. In: Advances in Neural Information Processing Systems, pp. 5998–6008 (2017)

43. Stewart, M.: GANs vs. Autoencoders: Comparison of deep generative models (2019). https://
towardsdatascience.com/gans-vs-autoencoders-comparison-of-deep-generative-models-985
cf15936ea. Towards Data Science

44. Networkx: Networkx network analysis in python. https://networkx.org/. Accessed 01 Oct
2021

45. Tensorflow: Transformer model for language understanding. https://www.tensorflow.org/text/
tutorials/transformer. Accessed 22 Oct 2021

46. Tensorflow: Convolutional variational autoencoder. https://www.tensorflow.org/tutorials/gen
erative/cvae. Accessed 10 June 2020

47. Ritchie, G.: Some empirical criteria for attributing creativity to a computer program. Minds
Mach. **17**, 67–99 (2007)

Correction to: SpeechTyper: From Speech to Typographic Composition

Jéssica Parente⬤, Tiago Martins⬤, João Bicker⬤,
and Penousal Machado⬤

Correction to:
Chapter "SpeechTyper: From Speech to Typographic
Composition" in: T. Martins et al. (Eds.): *Artificial Intelligence*
in Music, Sound, Art and Design, **LNCS 13221,**
https://doi.org/10.1007/978-3-031-03789-4_14

In an older version of this paper, there was an error in reference no. 18: the names of the cited paper were incorrectly published. This has been corrected.

The updated version of this chapter can be found at
https://doi.org/10.1007/978-3-031-03789-4_14

Author Index

Agirrezabal, Manex   84
Ali, Rao Hamza   325
Allmendinger, Richard   3, 385
Asonitis, Tasos   3

Banar, Berker   19
Becerra Saldana, Rafael Andres   259
Benatan, Matt   3
Bicker, João   212
Bisig, Daniel   36
Brouwer, Nielis   52
Brown, Andrew R.   401

Climent, Ricardo   3, 385
Colton, Simon   19
Concepción, Eugenio   68
Correia, João   162
Cruz Gambardella, Camilo   369

De Martin, Juan Carlos   243
Dijkzeul, Danny   52

Fernandez Fernandez, Javier   259

Galati, Francesco   243
Gambäck, Björn   195
Gerkens, Kevin   101
Gervás, Pablo   68
Grabe, Imke   84
Guckelsberger, Christian   292
Guo, Rui   341
Gupta, Chitralekha   308

Ha, David   275
Herremans, Dorien   179, 341
Hinrichs, Reemt   101

Javaheri Javid, Mohammad Ali   117

Kaliakatsos-Papakostas, Maximos   179
Kalonaris, Stefano   357
Kamath, Purnima   308
Kantosalo, Anna   292
Kiefer, Chris   341
Koppenhol, Levi   52
Krol, Stephen James   131

Lamiroy, Bart   148
Linstead, Erik   325
Llano, Maria Teresa   131
Lopes, Daniel   162

Machado, Penousal   162, 212
Magnusson, Thor   341
Makris, Dimos   179
Martins, Tiago   212
McAllister, Tyler   195
McCormack, Jon   131, 369
Méndez, Gonzalo   68

Nichele, Stefano   243
Novello, Alberto   228

Ostermann, Jörn   101

Parente, Jéssica   212
Pijning, Iris   52
Potier, Emmanuelle   148
Privato, Nicola   228

Rampado, Omar   228
Rhodeghiero, Katie   325
Rhodes, Chris   385
Riccio, Piera   243
Rico Garcia, Oneris Daniel   259

Salovaara, Antti   292
Simpson, Ivor   341
Syed, Saniya   325

Takala, Tapio   292
Tian, Yingtao   275

Uusitalo, Severi   292

van den Berg, Daan   52
Vermeer, Nelson   401

Witkowski, Olaf   259
Wyse, Lonce   308

Zhu, Jichen   84
Zixun, Guo   179
Zuch, Alexa   325
Zuluaga, Maria A.   243

Printed in the United States
by Baker & Taylor Publisher Services